A Secular Age beyo

This book traces the experiences of religion and secularity in eleven countries not primarily shaped by Western Christianity (Japan, China, Indonesia, India, Pakistan, Iran, Russia, Turkey, Israel, Egypt, and Morocco), and examines how the status of religion and the emergence of secularity have evolved in the course of the 20th century in these societies. All chapters do so in conversation with Charles Taylor's grand narrative of the North Atlantic World in his *A Secular Age* (2007). The case studies indicate that in all eleven cases, the state – building on colonial and imperial legacies – highly determines religious experience, by variably regulating religious belief, practice, property, education, and/or law. The book identifies the major critical junctures and path dependencies that have led to the different levels and modes of state regulation of religion and discusses the consequences of these for the possible emergence of something approaching Taylor's core condition of secularity – namely, the social acceptance of open religious unbelief and switching between religious affiliations (Secularity III).

Mirjam Künkler is a senior research fellow at the Swedish Collegium for Advanced Study (SCAS). Before joining SCAS, she taught Near Eastern Studies at Princeton University, where she also directed the Oxford-Princeton research cluster on "Traditional authority and transnational religious networks in contemporary Shi'i Islam" and co-directed the Luce Program on "Religion and International Affairs" for several years. Her publications include *Democracy and Islam in Indonesia* (co-edited with Alfred Stepan, 2013), and many articles, inter alia in *Comparative Studies in Society and History*, the *Asian Studies Review*, the *American Behavioral Scientist, Jahrbuch des Öffentlichen Rechts, British Journal of Middle Eastern Studies, Democratization, Party Politics*, and the *Journal of Law and Religion*.

John Madeley taught at the LSE for some three decades. Starting as a specialist in the government and politics of the Nordic countries, during the second half of his career he concentrated on researching and teaching the linkages between and contrasting patterns of religion and politics, especially across Europe's 50-plus countries. In addition to many journal articles and book chapters, he edited *Church and State in Contemporary Europe: The Chimera of Neutrality* (with Zsolt Enyedi;

2003), *Religion and Politics* (2003), and *Religion, Politics and Law in the European Union* (with Lucian Leustean; 2009).

Shylashri Shankar is the author of *Scaling Justice: India's Supreme Court, Anti-Terror Laws, and Social Rights* (2009), and co-author of *Battling Corruption* (2013). In the past she has been a Fellow at the Rockefeller Foundation's Bellagio Center in Italy and a co-convenor (together with Mirjam Künkler and Hanna Lerner) of a research group on constitutionalism and religion at the Center for Interdisciplinary Research (ZiF) in Bielefeld, Germany. She has published widely on law, religion, and development in India.

Cambridge Studies in Social Theory, Religion and Politics

Editors

David C. Leege, University of Notre Dame
Kenneth D. Wald, University of Florida, Gainesville
Richard L. Wood, University of New Mexico

The most enduring and illuminating bodies of late nineteenth-century social theory – by Marx, Weber, Durkheim, and others – emphasized the integration of religion, polity, and economy through time and place. Once a staple of classic social theory, however, religion gradually lost the interest of many social scientists during the twentieth century. The recent emergence of phenomena such as Solidarity in Poland, the dissolution of the Soviet empire, various South American, Southern African, and South Asian liberation movements, the Christian Right in the United States, and Al Qaeda have reawakened scholarly interest in religiously based political conflict. At the same time, fundamental questions are once again being asked about the role of religion in stable political regimes, public policies, and constitutional orders. The series *Cambridge Studies in Social Theory, Religion and Politics* will produce volumes that study religion and politics by drawing upon classic social theory and more recent social scientific research traditions. Books in the series offer theoretically grounded, comparative, empirical studies that raise "big" questions about a timely subject that has long engaged the best minds in social science.

Titles in the series

A Secular Age beyond the West: Religion, Law and the State in Asia, the Middle East and North Africa

Edited by

MIRJAM KÜNKLER
Swedish Collegium for Advanced Study

JOHN MADELEY
London School of Economics and Political Science

SHYLASHRI SHANKAR
Centre for Policy Research, New Delhi

CAMBRIDGE
UNIVERSITY PRESS

CAMBRIDGE
UNIVERSITY PRESS

University Printing House, Cambridge CB2 8BS, United Kingdom

One Liberty Plaza, 20th Floor, New York, NY 10006, USA

477 Williamstown Road, Port Melbourne, VIC 3207, Australia

314-321, 3rd Floor, Plot 3, Splendor Forum, Jasola District Centre, New Delhi - 110025, India

79 Anson Road, #06-04/06, Singapore 079906

Cambridge University Press is part of the University of Cambridge.

It furthers the University's mission by disseminating knowledge in the pursuit of
education, learning and research at the highest international levels of excellence.

www.cambridge.org
Information on this title: www.cambridge.org/9781108405614
DOI: 10.1017/9781108278195

© Cambridge University Press 2018

First published 2018
First paperback edition 2019

A catalogue record for this publication is available from the British Library

Library of Congress Cataloging in Publication data
NAMES: Künkler, Mirjam, 1977– editor.
TITLE: A secular age beyond the West / edited by Mirjam Kunkler, Princeton
University, John Madeley, London School of Economics and Political
Science, Shylashri Shankar, Centre for Policy Research, New Delhi.
DESCRIPTION: New York : Cambridge University Press, 2017.
IDENTIFIERS: LCCN 2017023931 | ISBN 9781108417716
SUBJECTS: LCSH: Secularism.
CLASSIFICATION: LCC BL2747.8 .S326 2017 | DDC 211/.609–dc23
LC record available at https://lccn.loc.gov/2017023931

ISBN 978-1-108-41771-6 Hardback
ISBN 978-1-108-40561-4 Paperback

Alfred C. Stepan (1936 to 2017): inspired teacher,
scholar, and friend

Contents

Tables and Figures

TABLES

FIGURES

xi

Contributors

Aslı Bâli is Professor of Law at UCLA School of Law, and Director of the UCLA Center for Near Eastern Studies. She is the co-editor of *Constitution Writing, Religion and Democracy* (Cambridge University Press, 2017) and author of numerous peer-reviewed and law review articles, including "The Perils of Judicial Independence: Constitutional Transition and the Turkish Example," in *The Virginia Journal of International Law* (2012); "Courts and Constitutional Transitions: Lessons from the Turkish case," in the *International Journal of Constitutional Law* (2013), and "Shifting into reverse: Turkish constitutionalism under the AKP," *Theory and Event* (2016).

Philip Gorski is Professor of Sociology, International Studies, and Religious Studies at Yale University. He received an AA from Deep Springs College, a BA from Harvard College, and a PhD from the University of California at Berkeley. His most recent book is *American Covenant: A History of Civil Religion from the Puritans to the Present* (2017).

Helen Hardacre is the Reischauer Institute Professor of Japanese Religions and Society at Harvard University. She earned her doctorate from the University of Chicago in 1980. She has done extended field study of contemporary Shinto, Buddhist religious organizations, and the religious life of Japan's Korean minority. She has also researched State Shinto and contemporary ritualizations of abortion in Japan. Before moving to Harvard in 1992, she taught at Princeton University (1980–1989) and Griffith University (Australia) (1990–1991). Her publications include

The Religion of Japan's Korean Minority (1984), *Lay Buddhism in Contemporary Japan: Reiyukai Kyodan* (1984), *Kurozumikyo and the New Religions of Japan* (1986), *Shinto and the State, 1868–1988* (1989), *Marketing the Menacing Fetus in Japan* (1997), and *Religion and Society in Nineteenth-Century Japan: A Study of the Southern Kanto Region, Using Late Edo and Early Meiji Gazetteers* (2002) and *Shinto: A History* (2016). Her ongoing research includes work concerning the issue of constitutional revision in Japan and its effect on religious groups.

Nader Hashemi is the Director of the Center for Middle East Studies and an Associate Professor of Middle East and Islamic Politics at the Josef Korbel School of International Studies at the University of Denver. He obtained his doctorate from the Department of Political Science at the University of Toronto and previously was an Andrew W. Mellon Postdoctoral Fellow at Northwestern University and a Visiting Assistant Professor at the UCLA Global Institute. He is the author of *Islam, Secularism and Liberal Democracy: Toward a Democratic Theory for Muslim Societies* (Oxford University Press, 2009) and co-editor of *The People Reloaded: The Green Movement and the Struggle for Iran's Future* (Melville House, 2011), *The Syria Dilemma* (MIT Press, 2013), and *Sectarianization: Mapping the New Politics of the Middle East* (Oxford University Press, 2017).

Christophe Jaffrelot is Senior Research Fellow at CERI-Sciences Po/CNRS in Paris. He teaches South Asian politics at Sciences Po and King's College. Among his most recent publications are *Religion, Caste and Politics in India* (2010) and *The Pakistan Paradox – Instability and Resilience* (2015) and as editor, *Pakistan: Nationalism Without a Nation?* (2002); *A History of Pakistan and its origins* (2004); *Hindu Nationalism. A Reader* (2007); with L. Gayer (eds), *Muslims of India's Cities. Trajectories of marginalization* (2012); and *Pakistan at the Crossroads – Domestic Dynamics and External Pressures* (2016).

Zhe Ji is Associate Professor of Chinese Studies at the Institut National des Langues et Civilisations Orientales in Paris. His main study areas are Buddhism and the relationship between state and religion. He has published numerous articles regarding Buddhism in contemporary China and co-founded the Centre d'Etudes Interdisciplinaires sur le Bouddhisme. His books include *Religion, Modernité et Temporalité: une sociologie du bouddhisme chan contemporain* (CNRS Editions, 2016) and *Making Saints in Modern China* (co-edited with David Ownby and Vincent

Goossaert, Oxford University Press, 2017). In 2014, he was nominated as Junior Member of the Institut Universitaire de France.

Gudrun Krämer is Professor of Islamic Studies at Freie Universität Berlin and director of the Berlin Graduate School Muslim Cultures and Societies. She has worked and published on modern Middle Eastern history and on Islam, democracy, and modernity. Her books include *Der Vordere Orient und Nordafrika ab 1500* (2016), *Hasan al-Banna* (2010), *A History of Palestine: From the Ottoman Conquest to the Founding of the State Israel* (2008), *The Jews in Modern Egypt* (1989), *Responsabilité, égalité, pluralism: Réflexions sur quelques notions-clés d'un ordre islamique moderne* (2000), and the edited volume (with Sabine Schmidtke) *Speaking for Islam: Religious Authorities in Muslim Societies* (2006). She is a member of the Berlin-Brandenburg Academy of Sciences and Humanities, the Tunisian Academy of Sciences (Bayt al-Hikma), and an Executive Editor of the *Encyclopaedia of Islam Three*. In 2010 she received the Gerda Henkel Prize.

Mirjam Künkler is a senior research fellow at the Swedish Collegium for Advanced Study (SCAS). Before joining SCAS, she taught Near Eastern Studies at Princeton University, where she also directed the Oxford-Princeton research cluster on "Traditional authority and transnational religious networks in contemporary Shi'i Islam" and co-directed the Luce Program on "Religion and International Affairs" for several years. Her books include *Democracy and Islam in Indonesia* (co-edited with Alfred Stepan, 2013; published in Arabic as *Al-Dimokratia va al-Islam fi Indonisia*, 2015); *Women's Juristic Authority in Shi'ite Islam* (with Devin Stewart, Edinburgh University Press, forthcoming 2018); as well as two volumes co-edited with Tine Stein: *Selected Writings by Ernst-Wolfgang Böckenförde*, 2017 (Vol. I) and 2018 (Vol. II). Künkler has guest-edited special issues and symposia for the journals *Party Politics* (March 2013), *Cambridge Journal of Law and Religion* (January 2013), *the American Behavioral Scientist* (July 2016), *Asian Studies Review* (December 2016), the *British Journal of Middle Eastern Studies* (January 2018), *Constellations* (June 2018) and the *German Law Journal* (May 2018).

Hanna Lerner is a senior lecturer of Political Science at Tel Aviv University. She is the author of *Making Constitutions in Deeply Divided Societies* (Cambridge University Press, 2011), co-editor of *Global Justice and International Labour Rights* (Cambridge University Press, 2016), and co-editor of *Constitution Writing, Religion and Democracy* (Cambridge University Press, 2017). Her research focuses on comparative constitution-making, Israeli constitutional politics, religion and democracy, global justice, and international labor.

John Madeley retired as Senior Lecturer in Government at the London School of Economics and Political Science in 2009, where he also served as the Dean of the Graduate School for three years. Starting as a specialist in the government and politics of the Nordic countries, during the second half of his career he concentrated on researching and teaching the linkages between and contrasting patterns of religion and politics, especially across Europe's 50-plus countries. In addition to many journal articles and book chapters, he edited *Church and State in Contemporary Europe: The Chimera of Neutrality* (with Zsolt Enyedi, 2003), *Religion and Politics* (2003), and *Religion, Law and Politics in the European Union* (with Lucian Leustean, 2010). Recent publications include "Constitutional Models and the protection of religious freedom" in S. Ferrari (ed.) *Routledge Handbook of Law and Religion* (2015) and "The curious case of religion in the Norwegian Constitution" in A. Bâli and H. Lerner (eds.) *Constitution Writing Religion and Democracy* (2017).

Shylashri Shankar is a senior fellow at the Centre for Policy Research in New Delhi. She has held academic positions at the University of Texas at Austin and the Center on Religion and Democracy, University of Virginia. In June 2011, she was a Bellagio Fellow at the Rockefeller Centre in Bellagio (Italy). She has a PhD in Political Science from Columbia University, an MSc from the London School of Economics and Political Science, an MA (Cantab) from the University of Cambridge, and a BA (Hons) from Delhi University. She is the author of *Scaling Justice: India's Supreme Court, Anti-Terror Laws and Social Rights* (2009) and co-author of *Battling Corruption* (2013). In the past she has been a Fellow at the Rockefeller Foundation's Bellagio Center in Italy and a co-convenor of a research group at the Center for Interdisciplinary Research (ZiF) in Bielefeld, Germany. She is currently working on a food biography of India (*Speaking Tiger*, 2017).

Charles Taylor is Professor em. of Philosophy at McGill University, Montreal. His most influential books are *Explanation of Behaviour* (1967), *Sources of the Self* (1989), and *A Secular Age* (2007). His newest book is *The Language Animal* (2016). He has been a recipient of numerous prizes and awards, among them the 2007 Templeton Prize, the 2008 Kyoto Prize in Arts and Philosophy, the 2015 John W. Kluge Prize for

Achievement in the Study of Humanity, and the 2016 Berggruen Prize for philosophy.

Jonathan Wyrtzen is an associate professor of Sociology, International Affairs, and History at Yale University. He received a BA and MA from the University of Texas at Austin and a PhD from Georgetown University. His research interests center on empire and colonialism, state formation and non-state forms of political organization, ethnicity and nationalism, and religion and socio-political activism in North Africa and the Middle East. His first book, *Making Morocco: Colonial Intervention and the Politics of Identity* (2015), examines the relationships among European imperial expansion, colonial policies of modernization and state formation, and the rise of Arabo-Islamic nationalism in Morocco. His current book project focuses on the making of the modern Middle East during the Long Great War (1911–31), examining the clash between colonial and local political projects set in motion during this period to replace the Ottoman Empire. His recent publications include "Colonial Legitimization-Legibility Linkages and the Politics of Identity in Algeria and Morocco" in the *European Journal of Sociology* (2017) and "Colonial War and the Production of Territorialized Space in North Africa" in *Political Power and Social Theory* (2017).

Preface

The inspiration for this book was born on a warm autumn day in the guesthouse of Boğaziçi University, in the early 2010s, where, overlooking the Bosphorus, many of the authors assembled, and other friends and colleagues gathered to discuss books that deeply stirred them and to which they wished to formulate a response. The group, made up mostly of sociologists and political scientists working on the nexus between politics, religion, and law, each an expert on a different country of the Middle East and Asia, soon settled on Charles Taylor's *A Secular Age*, a book that offers manifold entry points and intellectual foils to argue with and against, a book which with each reading takes on a new colour and evokes new imagery and insights. The path of working on this book together soon became an endpoint in itself, as the group grew closer and many of its members met again summer after summer in different constellations, working on new projects as this one came to completion, and with subsets of its members crafting new cooperations in research, publishing, and joint teaching. As editors we are deeply grateful for this gift of companionship, both with one another and the wider group of fellow-travelers, creating a net of interlocutors with whom it was a pleasure and honor to agree and disagree, to understand and to occasionally misunderstand. Thus, over time, these intellectual companions became companions also of the heart, and we hope the group will live on in its various manifestations for many years to come.

While producing this volume, numerous debts were incurred. We thank Marian Burchardt, Markus Dressler, Prasenjit Duara, Hadi Enayat, Aaron Glasserman, Matthias Koenig, Eric Lob, Roman Loimeier, David Martin, Tamir Moustafa, Eva Nisa, Saskia Schäfer, Benjamin Schonthal, Clemens

Six, Kristina Stoeckl, and Richard Wood for reading different drafts of the Introduction and/or Conclusion and for offering excellent comments. We further discussed various aspects of our comparative theses with Murat Akan, Said Arjomand, L. Carl Brown, José Casanova, Mark Farha, Şükrü Hanioğlu, Robert Hefner, Khaled Helmy, Amaney Jamal, Hans Joas, Franz-Xaver Kaufmann, Bill Kissane, André Laliberté, David Mednicoff, Pratap Bhanu Mehta, Matt Nelson, Detlef Pollack, Yüksel Sezgin, Tine Stein, Alfred Stepan, Narendra Subramanian, Bryan Turner, Björn Wittrock, Monika Wohlrab-Sahr, and Qasim Zaman, and benefited immensely from spirited conversations with them.

Princeton University's Center for the Study of Religion generously funded a retreat at the International Institute for the Sociology of Law (IISJ) in Oñati, Spain, where draft chapters were first presented. We thank the center and Robert Wuthnow for its support, and the IISJ for having offered an idyllic conference venue in one of the oldest universities on the Iberian peninsula. We thank Charles Taylor for having given us the opportunity to present some of our draft chapters at a conference he convened at the Institute for Human Sciences (IWM) in Vienna in June 2014. John Bowen, Craig Calhoun, Bernice Martin, David Martin, Michael Warner, and Charles Taylor generously offered comments and ideas that sharpened our ways of thinking about the relationship between Secularities I and III.

Finally, we thank Lew Bateman for supporting this project from the beginning and Sara Doskow for having seen it through. Anonymous readers and the series editors, Kenneth Wald, Richard Wood, and David Leege, asked compelling questions which forced us to re-think and re-draft. Helen Belgian-Cooper completed a superb job as copy-editor, and Velmurugan Inbasigamoni and Thomas Haynes were reliable contacts at the press for whose support and ideas we are deeply grateful.

The meaning of religion and non-religion and the sociocultural, economic and political consequences that flow from it remain at the core of intellectual quests both in the social sciences and humanities. We thank Charles Taylor for having nudged us into the conversation.

Mirjam Künkler, John Madeley, and Shylashri Shankar,
September 2015

I

Introduction

Mirjam Künkler and Shylashri Shankar

With his monumental study *A Secular Age*, Charles Taylor created a new highpoint in contemporary thought about historical processes of secularization and the relationship between the religious and the non-religious in Western modernity. As a comprehensive treatment of the nature and the philosophy of "the secular" in Latin Christendom, the book has since become a major reference point for students of religion in the public sphere. Sociologist of religion José Casanova goes so far as to describe it as "the best analytical, phenomenological and genealogical account that we have of our modern, secular condition" (Casanova 2010: 265).

In his magnum opus, Taylor offers a historically grounded account of the emergence of secularity as a contingent process in societies characterized by Western Latin (but explicitly not Eastern Orthodox) Christianity. This process is presented as "the fruit of new inventions, newly constructed self-understandings and related practices, and can't be explained in terms of perennial features of human life" (Taylor 2007: 22). Taylor identifies instead a series of departures from earlier religious life that have allowed older forms to be dissolved or destabilized in favor of new, diverse religious, spiritual, non- and anti-religious options around large questions of meaning of society, the cosmos, and the self.

A SECULAR AGE

Taylor's explicit focus on what he calls the "North Atlantic world" invites an exploration of secularity in other parts of the world. This is where our volume takes its starting point. Based on an international research cluster of country specialists interested in the nexus between politics and religion in countries of Asia, North Africa, and the Middle East, this volume comparatively investigates the place of religion and non-religion in countries outside the heartland of Latin Christendom. The case studies focus on the patterns of religion–state relations in the modern era, wherein each has created particular conditions of belief. Taylor identifies three notions of Secularity, of which he is most interested in the third. The first notion, Secularity I, is that of the classic differentiation theory (Casanova 1994): it emerges as political authority, law, science, education, and the economy are emancipated from the influence of religious norms and authority. Secularity II is the notion describing the decline of religious belief and practice, something some sociologists argued was the case in the Europe of the 1960s and which they predicted would be a universal trend. Today, European Secularity II, if religion really has been on the decline there at all, is regarded as the global exception rather than the rule (Berger 1999, Davie 2002).[1] But it is a third notion that particularly interests Taylor. Under Secularity III he understands a condition in which it is possible to not believe, and still aspire to live a fulfilled life; Secularity III emerges through "a move from a society where belief in God is unchallenged and indeed, unproblematic, to one in which it is understood to be one option among others, and frequently not the easiest to embrace" (Taylor 2007: 3). The shift to these new conditions of belief is reached by "a series of new departures," in which earlier forms of religious life are dissolved and new ones created. The way meaning is perceived has changed: What was once a human's "porous self" (going against God was not an option because life was lived in a social world peopled by spirits and fellow human beings) has been replaced by a "buffered self": a self aware of the possibility of disengagement. For non-believers, "the power to reach fullness is within [the human self]" (Taylor 2007: 8). This condition of Secularity III, according to Taylor, developed uniquely in the North Atlantic world, where it prevails today, and he leaves open the question of whether it could be, or has in the meantime been, realized in other parts of the world.[2]

---

[1] Berger points out that there really are two exceptions, one is geographical: Western Europe; but there is also a sociological exception: an international non-religious intelligentsia (2012: 2).

[2] Taylor in general acknowledges that there may be multiple secularities in the world today, but it is not clear which dimension of secularity (Secularity I, II, or III) he has in mind when he writes "secularity, like other features of 'modernity' . . . find rather different expression,

Secularity (in all three conceptions) in turn must be differentiated from secular*ization* and secular*ism*. Secularization denotes the historical process of the emancipation (of the state, law, science,...) from religious authority and norms. Secularism usually denotes the ideology that legitimizes the separation of religious and political authority, the expulsion of religious law from the legal system, and sometimes even the exclusion of religion from the public sphere. The concept "secularism" rarely makes an appearance in *A Secular Age*, although Taylor has written about it extensively elsewhere.[3] For social scientists, the relationship between Secularity I (a predominantly political and legal condition) and Secularity III (a predominantly cultural condition) is of greatest interest, as it calls for an exploration of the institutional dynamics behind the changes in the conditions of belief.[4] A discussion of Secularity I, in turn, cannot in most cases be isolated from a discussion of a particular state's policy of secularism, though as our chapters illustrate, the relationship between secularism and Secularity I is complex, and the two phenomena often intertwine in counterintuitive ways.

The intellectual stakes of exploring the meaning of religion and the secular outside the West are very high. Few scholars will dispute today the idea of multiple modernities (Eisenstadt 2000), and upon further probing many will also embrace the idea that secularity is not a condition unique to the West, but this is where the deep disagreements begin: can one talk of secularity in environments where the notion of religion may be largely incomparable to that born out of Latin Christendom (a monotheistic, exclusivist notion)? Can one talk of secularity in environments where religious identity is something not voluntarily acquired but imposed by state policies or social pressures? Can one talk of comparative secularity at all, when no state today can be characterized as entirely secular, in the

---

and develop under the pressure of different demands and aspirations in different civilizations" (2007: 21).

[3] In "The Meaning of Secularism" (2010), and "Why We Need a Radical Redefinition of Secularism" (2011), Taylor postulates a reconceptualization of the project of secularism: it should be thought of, he suggests, as the normatively desirable response of the democratic state to diversity; a response that aims at maximizing the republican values of liberty (here of religious belief and unbelief), equality (of religious and other worldviews), and fraternity (inclusion/participation of all voices, religious and non-religious, in determining public policy).

[4] Drawing on José Casanova (1994), Berger relates these two phenomena to one another by observing that "all institutions have correlates in consciousness." He views the emergence of a secular discourse, captured by Taylor's notion of the "immanent frame," as the correlate in consciousness to institutional differentiation (Secularity I). See Berger 2012: 315.

sense of enforcing a watertight wall of separation between religion and politics? And how well do conceptions of the secular and secularity travel if even when only applied to the West they are already so fiercely contested at their core?

The interplay between religious and political transformation has been a central theme in the social sciences and humanities, to a point where the sociology of religion was long regarded as the heart of the enterprise of sociological inquiry. As Philip Gorski points out in Chapter 2 of this volume, though the pedigree of secularization theory can be traced back for at least two centuries, its identifier is of more recent origin. Even Durkheim and Weber used the terms sécularisation/laïcisation and Säkularisierung, respectively, only in passing. It is only since the 1940s and 1950s that one can really speak of "secularization theory" as a dedicated research program in the social sciences. While the major premise – that "modernization" goes together with "secularization" – was widely accepted until the late 1970s, scholars disagreed over how to conceptualize secularization and what to regard as its proper indicators. For Bryan Wilson (1966), secularization denoted the institutional decline of religion, while David Martin saw it manifested in declining levels of membership in religious communities (Martin 1978), and Steve Bruce in declining levels and intensities of belief (Bruce 1992). Peter Berger argued in *The Sacred Canopy* (Berger 1967) that a defining feature of secularization was that the plausibility structures behind religious belief were seriously compromised, while Niklas Luhmann (1977) spoke of the "privatisation of religious decision-making." Scholars moreover disagreed over where these trends manifested themselves and whether one should regard them as universal or specific to particular geographies. Thomas Luckmann (1967) criticized that the diagnoses of declining levels and intensities of belief were premised on an impoverished notion of religion, and ignorant of the ways in which "invisible religion" continued to play an important role in modern society. David Martin (1978) cast doubt on the assumption of the universal character of religious decline and instead argued in favor of understanding differentiation as the one universal characteristic of secularization in the world. Despite these intense disagreements over what secularization meant precisely and how it manifested itself, secularization theory became the only theory, in the words of a major sociologist of religion "that was able to attain a truly paradigmatic status within the modern social sciences" (Casanova 1994: 17).

A cesura in the debate was José Casanova's 1994 book, in which the author took stock of how present empirical realities related to various aspects of secularization theory and in which he did the debate an enormous service by disentangling its various sub-theories. Casanova argued that the theory was only one-third defensible (1994: 17–20): while it was right about the functional and institutional differentiation of the religious from the political, legal, economic, scientific, and other spheres, it had, in his view, been proven wrong in its claims concerning the decline of religious belief and practice, and remained deeply questionable with respect to the inevitable privatization of religion. More recently, in particular in response to an intervention by Talal Asad, Casanova has distanced himself from the one sub-theory he earlier on sought to salvage and conceded that it is almost impossible to heuristically distinguish the privatization from the differentiation thesis.[5]

In the face of the continuing difficulties to analytically capture macrosocial dynamics in the relationship between religion and its outside (whether social, political, legal, or economic) in comparative and theoretically meaningful ways, newer research has turned to concentrate on examining boundary formation around the religious and the non-religious[6] and to revisit the question of path dependencies and critical junctures in Secularity I which were once David Martin's primary field of interest. In this volume, we take up these two re-directions: issues of boundary-formation and -activation receive particular attention in the individual chapters, while the conclusion aims to identify broader parallels and divergences in the path dependencies that emerge in subsets of the cases, although no claims are made to propose generalizable theories on paths of secularization (not least because the number of cases does not

---

[5] In addition, Casanova has become less certain regarding the normative justification of separation. "One could advance the proposition that of the two clauses of the First Amendment, 'free exercise' is the one that stands out as a normative democratic principle in itself, while the no-establishment principle is defensible only insofar as it might be a necessary means to free exercise and to equal rights. In other words, secularist principles per se may be defensible on some other ground, but not as intrinsically liberal democratic ones" (2006: 21). In that vein some scholars have called for a concentration on issues of religious freedom/free exercise rather than the expulsion of religion from public life when debating requirements for democratic religion–state relations. Taylor's plea for a re-conception of the concept of secularism can be seen in this light.

[6] Along these lines, a research group convened at the University of Leipzig under the banner of the Humanities Centre for Advanced Studies "Multiple Secularities - Beyond the West, Beyond Modernities" since 2016 investigates boundary-making between the religious and non-religious both in modern and pre-modern societies on a global scale.

permit such an endeavor, but also because as country specialists we are hesitant to engage in too crude abstractions).

In the following, we briefly introduce some of Taylor's main insights about the etiology and ontology of Secularity III, and how our contributors have responded to these. We then outline the case selection and theoretical angle taken in this volume and the special emphases emanating from this choice as compared to the narratives proposed in *A Secular Age*. We close by drawing attention to four issue areas around religion that have emerged as common themes across the eleven case studies of this volume, often in contrast or in variance with Taylor's account. We should note that these themes are necessarily synoptic, as we lay out a terrain of topics emerging from the comparative reflection that in our view would merit closer future examination.

THE "WHAT," "WHY," AND "HOW" OF SECULARITY III

The contributors to this volume take Taylor's work as their point of departure. *A Secular Age* has been praised for its achievement in fanning out the multiple fora, dilemmas, and processes of secularity, as opposed to positing a simple process of the retreat of religion in Western politics and society in the face of modern science twinned with economic and other changes (Taylor identifies the latter as "subtraction stories"). He argues that any satisfactory theory of secularization must be able to account for both religious belief and unbelief. In orthodox secularization theory, unbelief is tacitly assumed to be the most "natural" or "reasonable" default stance, because science and reason are assumed to stand on the side of secularity. Accordingly, the real task is to account for belief. In *A Secular Age*, however, Taylor turns the tables on the orthodox approach by arguing that it is unbelief, rather than belief, that is in need of explanation, since historically and across much of the contemporary world religious belief represents something close to a universal norm. What Taylor terms Secularity III is characterized by three phenomena: exclusive humanism (a humanism that does not appeal to transcendence), the availability of meaningful options between belief and unbelief (a belief in the self-sufficiency of human agency and a widening of the range of possible options [2007: 19]), and the availability of these meaningful options to a large majority of people (not just elites).

Taylor interprets the emergence of Secularity III by addressing three general questions:

i) What does secularity mean today in the North Atlantic world?
ii) Why did secularity arise and come to take the forms it did, and what consequences flow from that?
iii) How did secularity come to command the space it did?

The contributors to this volume address how much, if any, of Taylor's grand narrative can be found mirrored in the societies they study. They investigate whether the three dimensions of secularity that Taylor distinguishes enable interpretive accounts of the emergence of unbelief as a choice (Secularity III). They do so by tackling Taylor's "what," "why," and "how" questions in the context of a range of cases in countries that have been historically located beyond the ambit of Latin Christendom. In doing so, they find the importance of political factors in almost all cases to be key to understanding the distinctive patterns of secularization and the types of religion–state relations emerging from it. The resultant focus on the political and legal histories of the cases studied leads to a number of contrasts with Taylor's more phenomenological and genealogical treatment.

Taylor's answer to the "what" question in the context of Latin Christendom is the emergence of "exclusive humanism," a humanism that – unlike some earlier humanisms, such as the Christian humanism of Europe's renaissance – no longer felt the urgency, or even relevance, of appeals to transcendence. Anthropocentric shifts in the late seventeenth and eighteenth century create a "buffered self" which in turn opens the gate toward the possibility of an exclusive humanism: "the buffered identity, capable of disciplined control and benevolence, generated its own sense of dignity and power, its own inner satisfactions, and these could tilt in favor of exclusive humanism" (2007: 262). Though exclusive humanism heralds the birth of a secular age, religion does not wither away.[7] In his earlier work on the philosopher and psychologist William James, Taylor (2002) elaborates on his conception of what has happened to religion in the modern world. Drawing inspiration from Durkheim, he distinguishes between different Durkheimian forms of religion-society relations. "Paleo-Durkheimian" relations can be found in societies where religion is not yet differentiated; fundamentalist movements often champion this type of undifferentiated relations. Second, there are relations

---

[7] Talal Asad (2011) suggests that it is because Taylor is here working with an intuitive definition of religion in terms of *transcendent* – Christian – *beliefs* that he ignores the enchantments imposed on individual life by secular consumer culture as well as by modern science and technology.

where religiosity is transferred to a greater entity, such as ethnic entities (Mark Juergensmeyer's "ethnic religions"), or class or state entities (Robert Bellah's "civil religion"), which both are manifestations of "neo-Durkheimism." But it is the development of the post-Durkheimian age – one based on "expressive individualism" (Taylor 2002: 80) – that Taylor wants to draw attention to. Unlike James, and later Berger and Thomas Luckmann, Taylor does not regard the post-Durkheimian experience of faith as a process of necessary individualization. Even though "the spiritual as such is no longer intrinsically related to society" (Taylor 2002: 102), and though "the new framework has a strongly individualist component, this will not necessarily mean that the content will be individuating. Many people will find themselves joining extremely powerful religious communities, because that's where many people's sense of the spiritual will lead them" (Taylor 2002: 112). Although no longer intrinsically related to society, the spiritual can, and often does, then unfold in the framework of a community.

The "what" question is central to our comparative endeavor because the very concepts of religion and its cognates on which the term secularity is parasitic "do not denote anything fixed or essential beyond the meanings that they carry in particular social and cultural contexts" (Beckford 2003: 5). How much in comparative secularization processes should be seen as sui generis – that is, rooted in particular religious and cultural contexts? Several of the contributors highlight the emergence of a neo-Durkheimian age, one where religion is tied to ethnic or national identity, rather than the emergence of an "unbelieving ethos" in the societies they portray. Nearly all contributors point to a core set of twentieth-century state policies and watershed political experiences, including the emergence of nationalism and struggles for independence and democracy, that played a key role in bringing this condition about.

Taylor answers the "why" question for the case of the North Atlantic world with reference to processes of differentiation, which ultimately lead to a plurality of outlooks, religious and non-religious, creating a modern citizen imaginary that "sees us all as coming together to form [a] political entity, to which we all relate in the same way, as equal members" (Taylor 2007: 457). For Taylor, the essence of Secularity III is plurality, characterized by multiple and competing types of belief and unbelief, and the availability of these as meaningful options to a majority, and not just the elite. The emergence of exclusive humanism as a widely available option in the eighteenth century created a new situation of pluralism, a culture fractured between religion and areligion (2007: 21). The reactions not only to this humanism, but also to the matrix out of which it grew, multiplied the options in all directions. The consequence, for Taylor, of this pluralism and mutual fragilization "will often be a retreat of religion from the public square" (2007: 532).

Political secularism, he proposes, is best seen as a means of accommodating this pluralism (Taylor 2010). In Taylor's view, democratic societies should be organized not around a civil religion, as Jean-Jacques Rousseau thought necessary, but instead around a strong philosophy of civility, enshrining the norms of human rights, equality/nondiscrimination, and democracy (Taylor 2010: 32). For Taylor, when it comes to contemporary democracies, the qualifier "secularist" ought to refer primarily not to bulwarks against religion but to good faith attempts to secure liberty, equality and fraternity of all positions, religious and non-religious (Taylor 2010). But is such a trajectory the only one imaginable? What if, as Talal Asad (2011) asks, liberal democracy not only impairs the development of virtues necessary for dealing effectively with global crises, but also continually disrupts the conditions on which Taylor's Secularity III depends, namely legal and political protection of religious plurality and religious freedom? And what if, paradoxically, it is precisely the continual feeling of disruption, *of uncertainty*, that feeds both the power of liberal democracy and the promise of liberal reform?

In Taylor's account, century-long processes of gradual differentiation facilitate the emergence of a widening range of possible options of belief and unbelief, and, as such, Secularity III. These in turn nourish calls for the retreat of religion from public space: Secularity I. The cultural rise of Secularity III's "conditions of belief" precede and create the original historic possibility for Secularity I's institutional separation of religion and state in the West. The picture is rather different in most contributions to this volume. While differentiation played a large role in facilitating the emergence of a pluralism of outlooks, both religious and non-religious, it did so often as a consequence of sudden historical breaks, often disruptive and violent, such as the establishment of colonial administrations with all their consequent breaches in notions of authority, meaning, property rights, social organization, cosmology, etc. (Mamdani 1996). With independence, political elites often created polities in which positions of exclusive humanism or the option to not believe were hardly publicly available. The corollary to Taylor's narrative as regards the "why" question therefore lies in the central role of the state in shaping conditions of belief. Constitution-crafters and state makers usually tackled the challenge of plurality through institutional arrangements: some privileged one belief system (e.g. Shi'a Islam in Khomeini's Iran, Sunni Islam in Zia's

Pakistan, Orthodox and Conservative Judaism in Israel), others excluded religion from several aspects of public life (e.g. India's Representation of the People Act 1951 excluded religious rhetoric from election campaigns), or any aspect of public life altogether (e.g. *laiklik* in early republican Turkey and atheism in communist China and the USSR). As can be seen from this classification, exclusivist arrangements occurred in both democratic and authoritarian contexts. In the cases discussed in this volume, they were more the norm than the exception. The emergence of Secularity III or its survival after the inauguration of post-colonial polities was often put in jeopardy by such exclusivist institutional arrangements.

Taylor's answer to the "how" question (i.e. how Secularity III emerged) spans several histories, philosophies, and methodologies, and eschews the linear path often assumed in some cruder theories of secularization. Taylor's account is a multi-faceted, historically complex narrative that moves in a series of zig-zag trajectories, where the role of contingency in producing the outcome of Western Christianity's "Drive to Reform" is very important. The contributors share Taylor's eschewal of a crude linear explanation and instead draw on Taylor to recognize and explain the contingencies in their specific country-contexts. As de-colonization, war or revolution created fundamental breaks in nearly all cases presented here regarding how religion and the state relate, Taylor's grand narrative, stretching over several centuries, shrinks to a matter of decades in many of the cases, where the transitions of a porous to a buffered self, of meaning that is exogenous to one that is endogenous to the world, often took place within parts of just one, the twentieth, century. The contributors share Taylor's strong emphasis on historical contingency, but their cases underline more forcefully than Taylor does for his case of Latin Christendom the political construction of religion which is partly shaped by the encounter with the West and Western notions of religion, and its subsequent political institutionalization in the second half of the 20th century.

Three variations to Taylor's understanding of the trajectory of secularization in Latin Christendom stand out compared to the countries studied in this volume. First, in most case studies presented here, religion or patterns of practice and belief held in reference to more-than-human powers more often than not pervade the fabric of social life today, a fact also noted by Taylor as the contrast between the present-day North Atlantic and many other parts of the world. In the recent histories of these countries, the intensity of battles between belief systems led to partition in some (India and Pakistan in 1947), revolution in others (an ostensibly anti-religious revolution in Russia in 1917, and an ostensibly

TABLE 1.1 *Differences between Taylor's approach and the approach taken in this volume*

	Taylor	This volume
Goal	Phenomenological account of Secularity III	Causal account of Secularity I and its implications for Secularity III
Analytical Agenda	Not to explain genesis of secularity but to render secularity intelligible	To identify the critical junctures and path dependencies shaping Secularity I and their consequences for Secularity III
Mechanism	Differentiation creates conditions for the emergence of radical plurality and eventually, Secularity III, characterized by exclusive humanism, the availability of meaningful options between belief and unbelief, and the availability of these meaningful options to a large majority of people, not only elites	Regulation by the state, characterized by differential burdening, of religion strongly shapes conditions of belief, to the effect that the choice between religion and non-religion remains highly politically salient and religious belief does not become "one option among many." It is unbelief rather than belief that is in need of public justification

religious one in Iran in 1979), and coexistence in yet others (*pancasila* in post-1945 Indonesia). Second, the drive to reform internal to religious traditions has been highly impacted, in many ways limited, by political factors in the cases studied here. In some societies, elites have purposively harnessed religion to create a collective national identity; in others, religion was perceived as antithetical to modernization with the consequence that religious thought was marginalized from the public sphere and withdrawn from public deliberation. The link between authoritarian rule and its religious legitimation in Morocco, Iran, and Pakistan, for example, has meant that internal reform is viewed with suspicion (and indeed as undesirable) by most political elites as it invariably would bring the authoritarian nature of state-society relations into focus. The strong link between the majority religion and the state in Turkey, Iran, Israel, Pakistan, Morocco, and Russia has moreover reinforced cohesion inside both the majority and minority religions of these societies and stifled the public expression of the pluralism in beliefs and practices internal to these religious communities. Third, the encounter with the West has in most cases created certain path dependencies in terms of how religion is under-stood and regulated. Very often, post-colonial administrations continued to use the very institutional mechanisms which colonial or imperial adminis-trations had set up to regulate religious practice, religious law, religious space, and religious education. Conceptions of religion in colonial books of law carried over into the post-colonial period. Thus, what is evident from all country studies, whether democratic or not, is the impulse of the state to tame, suppress, co-opt, or mold religion in the name of "public order."

BEYOND THE WEST

The chapter case studies focus on China, Japan, Indonesia, India, Pakistan, Iran, Russia, Turkey, Egypt, Morocco, and Israel. In an attempt to transcend dichotomies of West and non-West, which often boil down to elaborations on Christian–Muslim or West–East contrasts, case studies have been selected that ensure diversity in several respects: First, the chapters discuss societies where various types of belief systems dominate. Rather than featuring only one or two Muslim cases, on the basis of which broad conclusions about the "Muslim world" are then formulated, the collection includes a diversity of several case studies from the Muslim world, both Arab and non-Arab, from the Middle East, South Asia, Southeast Asia, and North Africa, and with considerable intra-Islamic diversity where variously Sunni, Shi'a, and Sufi currents dominate. The volume also contains a chapter on Israel, which as the only predominantly Jewish country has received less attention in com-parative studies of secularity than it should. Furthermore, the collection includes a case of that significant part of Christianity which Taylor omits, that is Eastern/Orthodox Christianity, and as such, the country that has most influenced the development of religion in the twentieth century Orthodox Christian world: Russia. Finally, with discussions of societies whose majo-rities identify themselves as non-affiliated and/or Taoist/Confucian (China), Buddhist-Shinto (Japan), and Hindu (India), the volume includes cases with predominantly poly- and nontheistic cultures.[8]

---

[8] The absence of any treatment of Latin American and Sub-Saharan cases arises from the centrality there of various branches of Latin Christianity, principally Roman Catholicism and, increasingly, Pentecostalism, which has been the focus of David Martin's later work. No edited volume can include all potentially interesting cases, and ours is no exception; the Sub-Saharan Muslim-majority cases are a particular lacuna. We hope future comparative studies will place these cases into perspective with those of the Mashreq and the Maghreb and will more generally analyze how secularism comports with local religious cultures in Sub-Saharan Africa.

Second, the countries studied differ in their arrangements for the relationship between religion and law; Israel, India, and the Muslim states place a strong emphasis on religious law in some or all domains, while in China, Japan, and Russia, questions about the jurisdiction of religious law play little part in the secularization debate.

Third, the country cases vary in terms of political contestation and public participation: while some governments, such as in communist China and the Islamic Republic of Iran, are thoroughly authoritarian and largely shielded from public pressure and accountability, others are long-standing democracies, such as contemporary Japan and India, where questions of religious freedom and religious identity may determine electoral outcomes.

Thus, the cases brought together in this volume showcase diversity in three dimensions: religious makeup of the population, the status of religious law, and the nature of the political regime.

What becomes apparent when comparing the encounters between religion and state across a variety of cases is the importance of capturing the fact that the contact surface religions offer to their regulation by the state differs markedly from case to case in scope and nature. One can hardly deny that with every act of state interference into religious belief and practice, violence is done to religion, but the scope and intensity of such acts of violence may differ significantly. For example, in most Muslim societies, it was Islamic law that experienced profound interference by the twentieth-century state, while in Orthodox Russia, it was control over church property and appointments. In Confucian China, in turn, law and property issues were far less prevalent as points of contention between state and religious leaders by comparison with the issue of education. Accordingly, comparative accounts of Secularity III need to consider the differences in the contact surface between a given religious tradition and the state, and the conflicts that emerge from them. We aim to do so with reference to the concept of differential burdening.

Burdening Religion

The concept we have found to be most useful in our comparative endeavor is that of "differential burdening," a term adopted from US Supreme Court jurisprudence on free exercise, which captures the burden imposed through laws, regulations, court decisions, and practices by the state when regulating religion (e.g. Sherbert *v.*

Verner, 374 U.S. 398). This concept allows us to assess the extent to which a given religion (and religious beliefs) can(not) function freely, and also the space allowed for unbelief. Transposed to the sociology of religion, regulating a religion, and thereby privileging certain groups and dis-privileging others, is seen as burdening it (Finke). Privileging necessarily entails interfering with religious beliefs and practices, and thereby effectively endorsing some tenets and practices over others. Our case studies confirm the notion that state interference in religion can usefully be thought of as burdening the religious group concerned, even where the act is one of privileging: In a number of states discussed in this volume, the majority religion is ostensibly privileged by the state, in that state agencies finance places of religious worship, the salaries of religious dignitaries, and sometimes even the application of religious law. But this type of privileging also implies that formerly plural notions of religious law are reduced to one positive state-sanctioned law (e.g. inter alia, in Egypt, India, Indonesia, Iran, Israel, Morocco, and Pakistan), that religious dignitaries are trained in one state-sanctioned curriculum where formerly competing societal centers of learning offered a greater variety of curricula and interpretations (e.g. Turkey), and that places of worship follow state-sanctioned requirements (e.g. Buddhist temples in Japan). As the emerging modern state has increasingly interfered with religious life over the course of the twentieth century, all religions, including the majority religion, are being burdened. The extent to which they are depends in part on what can be called the "contact surface" they offer to their regulation by the state.

If we examine the processes of differentiation through the constitutional, legal, and bureaucratic apparatuses in our cases, pluralism is often contained by the state's intervention in religious affairs. The state draws boundaries in location and permeability by limiting and circumscribing the multiplicity of beliefs (and unbelief) that can exist in the public sphere.

The contributors discuss how state projects of secularism and the concomitant burdening of religion had an impact on the development of secularity in those societies. In some, the state project burdened religion as such by controlling most aspects of its exercise to such an extent that free exercise was prejudiced, as was pluralism. In others, the state, through laws and public policies, burdened the majority religion while conceding more autonomy to minority religions.

Responding to A Secular Age

The challenge for social scientists wishing to engage with Taylor's scholarship is that the explicit primary concerns of *A Secular Age* are not the institutional politics of religion and secularity, but what he calls "the conditions of belief, practice and doubt." Because of this, recent volumes that have used *A Secular Age* as a major reference point for debating secularity and secularization have generally centered on philosophical and methodological discussion (Warner et al. 2010, Calhoun et al. 2011) or, where they have broached important issues related to Secularity I, have remained broadly within similar geographical confines (e.g. Rosenfeld and Mancini 2015). Indeed, much of the recent relevant scholarship on politics and the secular continues to take the USA or other Western countries as the paradigm (exceptions are Burchardt et al. (2015) and Zemmin et al. (2016)).[9] In depth case studies on religion and politics in non-Western cases tend to present rich country-specific ethnographic data but usually make little attempt to place the cases examined in a common comparative analytical frame. Other comparative works, such as Katznelson and Stedman Jones (2010) and Bilgrami (2016), focus on questions of political philosophy and religious reform. While theirs are primarily contributions to comparative political theory and social thought, with Katznelson and Stedman Jones' (2010) especially to the literature on toleration, our book has an institutional focus that highlights the relationship between Secularities I and III, and mostly so with a narrower focus on the second part of the twentieth century. The chapters in this volume focus on the patterns and singularities of the role of religion in public life and the respective states' methods of addressing plurality and difference across a large geographical range, encompassing China, Japan, Indonesia, India, Pakistan, Iran, Russia, Turkey, Egypt, Morocco, and Israel. As elaborated below, a commitment to a shared analytical framework relying on Taylor's methodology of historically grounded analysis is combined with analytical tools emanating from the new institutionalist literature highlighted in Philip Gorski's contribution.

---

[9] The making of this volume has coincided with two others taking a similar starting point: Burchardt et al. (2015) and Zemmin et al. (2016). This manuscript was submitted to the press before their books were published and their lessons could not be taken into account; in the conclusion we do engage in depth however with the Wohlrab-Sahr and Burchardt theoretical framework which had been published earlier (2012).

PRINCIPAL THEMES OF THE VOLUME

The Legacies of Vision and Di-Vision

In considering the relevance of Taylor's analysis for understanding the presence or absence of Secularity III beyond the West, the collective focus of this volume lies on the relationship between the diverse "conditions of belief" (Secularity III) and the distinctive political and legal traditions with which they appear to be associated, including formal public institutions and spaces (Secularity I). This focus enables us to test the intuition that Taylor's work may underemphasize the significance of legal, political, and other factors in framing and influencing the conditions of belief that he foregrounds in his account. Each of the chapters makes a point of seeking to understand the role played by societal, economic, and political actors in channeling, curbing, and molding conditions of belief.

In the first chapter, Philip Gorski situates Taylor's main contribution to the secularization debate in his development of the notion of Secularity III. He identifies conceptual tools in the sociology of religion that can complement Taylor's by facilitating sociological rather than philosophical analysis. Drawing on Taylor, Niklas Luhmann, and Pierre Bourdieu, Gorski offers typologies to assist in the study of the relationships between Secularities I and III by distinguishing between various systems of Secularity I. For instance, his typologies help to point out why American secularism differs from Indian secularism, or how Turkish *laiklik* ought to be distinguished from French *laïcité* (compare also Künkler and Madeley 2014). Gorski further proposes a set of sensitizing concepts to help give causal accounts for the type of secular settlements to religious conflicts he observed. Drawing on Pierre Bourdieu's field theory, Gorski posits that one can also see secular settlements as the result of "classification struggles" over the dominant "principle of vision and di-vision" that governs relations between the religious and political fields: segmentary, functional, stratificatory, and center/periphery divisions. On the basis of the three Taylorian competing goods of liberty, equality, and fraternity (cp. Taylor's concept of secularism), and Bourdieu's classification struggles, Gorski then outlines four archetypal patterns of Secularity I: consociationalism, religious nationalism, radical secularism, and liberal secularism.

Drawing on Gorski's suggestion for the "translation" of Taylor's grand narrative into sociological theory by way of complementing the latter's analytical tools with those of other scholars, the subsequent chapters each present an account of particular secularization trends and processes outside the West. The combination of global scope and a commitment to a shared analytical framework relying on Taylor's methodology of historically grounded analysis, together with Gorski's conceptual addenda, constitutes the book's principal claim to fill a niche in the study of comparative secularization. In assessing how political and legal structures affect the conditions of religious belief and practice, the chapters highlight four major themes, which in our reading distinguish our case studies from Taylor's unit of analysis.

As we shall see, the overdetermining factor – in creating a major role for the state in formulating what religion is, and is not, and often intertwining it with loyalty to the nation – seems to be the experiences of colonialism and imperialism, and their legacies. Subsequent efforts by state elites and other actors to conceptualize and mark out the domains of the secular and the religious were shaped to a great extent by the encounter with the colonial powers and their religions, that is in most cases different forms of Christianity. The "imperial" encounter between Western powers and the rest of the world had a profound impact on virtually all traditions involved. During the half-millennium on which Taylor's narrative concentrates, the Latin Christian West successfully imposed elements of itself on the rest of the world by means of its great maritime empires, so spreading its influence even where its missionaries failed to convert those of other traditions to one or another form of Western Christianity. Many traditions were destroyed and supplanted, others weakened, and transformed in different ways, while yet others appeared to emerge paradoxically reinforced from the encounter – but none remained unaffected.

Notions of the "Secular" and the "Religious"

The first theme emerging from the case studies is a questioning of the applicability of notions of the secular and the religious in some of the societies under review. What is "secular" depends to a large extent on what is perceived as "religious," and vice versa (Duara 2008; van der Veer 2011). Zhe Ji highlights the fact that pluralism, where faith is but one position among many, is an old story in China, rather than a particularly modern condition of belief. Laypersons could believe in and practice the available teachings in a pluralistic way: there was no sense of a clear-cut and exclusive religious identity according to established criteria of orthodoxy. Religion was conceived not in terms of the object or content of belief, but rather by the manner in which beliefs and practices are systematically stimulated, justified, maintained, and transmitted. In fact, both religion and education were conceptualized in traditional China by the same term: *jiao*; with no explicit semantic distinction between them. Accordingly, Ji argues, to this day "education" retains a primacy in Chinese notions of the sacred.

In Japan as well as in China, translated trade treaties with Western (and Christian) imperial powers introduced a Western-influenced concept of religion into the local lexicon. Simultaneously, as Helen Hardacre points out, the Japanese government enacted draconian policies against Buddhism, resulting in the latter's loss of its former role in governance. The Buddhist authorities reacted with reform measures to conform the tradition to governmental notions of what religion proper ought to be, recasting the Buddhist belief system, and positioning it within the private sphere. It would be a mistake, suggests Hardacre, to imagine that the thinking of the ordinary, non-elite Japanese (other than Hidden Christians) was structured by a dichotomy between belief and unbelief. Ordinary people seem generally to have regarded the Buddhist clergy with respect, but the clergy was not called upon to demonstrate doctrinal orthodoxy and commitment as part of its temple affiliation. Not only was subscription to particular beliefs not axiomatic in Japan; belief or unbelief was not made a central issue. Instead, fulfilling the obligations of temple affiliation and showing deference to authority appear to have been key. Those in authority used Buddhism to regulate the populace, but for the most part did not regard it as binding on themselves. Thus, Hardacre shows, subordination of religion to the state meant that religious life could easily – though not inevitably – become formalistic, a matter of performance rather than an expression of personal conviction.

The lack of a clear dichotomy between belief and unbelief is also relevant to understanding the notion of "Hinduism" in India. Shylashri Shankar uses Taylor's concept of the "social imaginary" to highlight the interplay between three separate imaginaries of Hinduism – as a religion, a culture, and an ancient order – in the constitution and in subsequent interpretations by the apex court. These three partly competing and partly complementary imaginaries of Hinduism have generated a great deal of ambiguity about what constitutes "religion," "religious rhetoric," and "secularism" in contemporary India. In *A Secular Age*, Taylor differentiates between the social imaginary and social theory. While theory is often the possession of a small minority, the social imaginary is shared by large groups of people, if not the whole society. For Taylor, "imaginary" refers to the way ordinary people "imagine" their social surroundings, in images, stories, legends, etc. It is that common understanding which makes possible common practices (2007:171–172) and therefore belongs to the background understanding of the normal expectations people have toward one another. Shankar suggests that the imaginaries of Hinduism as a culture and as an ancient order are forms of lived experience which pertain to a person regardless of whether she or he is a believer or not. The immanent frame of the imaginary of someone like the Brahmin savant who views Hinduism as an ancient order or someone who talks about "Indian culture" would not include Taylor's trio of secularities but could fit into Taylor's notion of transcendence in Secularity III. This ambiguity has both complicated the state's efforts to manage the diversity of beliefs and aggravated the crisis of secularism in India. But by creating a "zone of ambiguity" for the state, it has prevented the state from being torn apart in the fierce battles between majority and minority religions and between co-religionists.

These considerations make it difficult in China, India, or Japan to draw the boundaries between the "religious" and the non-religious. Notably, all three have no dominant monotheistic tradition. In all the other cases included, whether shaped by Judaism, Orthodox Christianity, or Islam, conflict lines revolve more around the borders and gray areas of particular religions than around definitions of religion itself.

The "Secular" and the "Religious" According to Whom?

Related to the question of what constitutes religion and its absence is the question of who it is who draws the boundaries. Taylor observes, "secular societies are not just mankind minus the religion ... They produce not unillusioned individuals who see the facts of existence nakedly, but people constituted by a distinct set of ethical goods, temporal frameworks, and practical contexts" (Warner et al. 2010: 25). In the cases studied here, this set of ethical goods, temporal frameworks, and practical contexts is strongly conditioned by state policies – of what is recognized as religion and what is not, which ethical goods are stressed in public education and which ones are not, and how the state defines practices as public, thereby differentiating between private and public practices (by constructing and maintaining places of worship, establishing public religious holidays, etc.). As such, models of Secularity I are distinctively molded by political elites, the policies they devise, and the regulations they apply. Taylor's pointing to Secularity I as a project shaped by elites is a concern for several of the contributors. In Japan and Russia, state projects aimed at molding the secular citizen, while in Indonesia and Morocco the model citizen was a religious one. The cases of Turkey, Egypt, Israel, and India combine aspects of both, oscillating between more religious and more secular notions of citizenship. The case of Iran exhibits both models in subsequent fashion with the 1979 revolution representing the cesura between the two.

In Japan, Helen Hardacre suggests, it was in the Meiji Period (1868–1912) when secularity came to dominate public discourse. Recasting well-known aspects of modern Japanese history and religion in the light of Taylor's account, she shows that Japan may be seen as an early example of an elite-driven, westernizing, secularizing project undertaken in reaction against Western imperialism, preceding similar developments ("defensive developmentalism") in Turkey, Iran, India, Indonesia, and China. Challenging the view once dominant in Japan and elsewhere that secularity was a largely neutral by-product of modernization, her chapter reveals how debates among elites shaped the bureaucratic means through which the populace would be indoctrinated with secular morality.

For Russia, John Madeley discusses the paradoxically abortive attempt by Soviet elites to bring about the birth of secularity "as if by means of a virtual caesarian procedure." In January 1918, the revolutionary government issued a Decree on the Separation of the State from the Church and the Church from the School. The decree deprived the Russian Church of legal personality, thereby rendering it incapable of holding property in its own right.

In a way, the opposite project of an elite-driven formation of the religious and secular was at work in Indonesia. Mirjam Künkler shows how, in the post-independence period, state elites channeled their efforts toward creating not the secular but the "religious citizen" of Indonesia, the *manusia agama*. From the beginning of the constitutional era in 1945, the state was defined as a religious rather than a secular state, albeit without specifying a particular religion. To promote the religious citizen without specifying the religion was a way to transcend inter-religious divisions and to create a religious morality that was not uniquely Islamic, Hindu, or Christian. In contrast to the secular nation-building project of Japan, Indonesian nation-building involved the state promotion of a pan-religious ethos, the so-called *pancasila*, as well as the molding of the country's major mono- and polytheist religions in its light. The Ministry of Religion became the pivotal player in imposing these reforms. Religions that did not adapt were denied recognition, and their adherents lost the rights of full citizenship as a result. To profess one of the state-recognized religions was made a requirement for citizenship; non-religion, or Secularity III (where religion and non-religion are both viable options), was and is still today not a legal possibility in Indonesia.

The project of political elites forming a particular religious, rather than secularized, public sphere is also evident in Morocco's post-colonial history. Jonathan Wyrtzen discusses how the Moroccan monarchy, which claims the politico-religious title "Commander of the Faithful," has attempted to monopolize public religion since independence in 1956. Islam is recognized constitutionally as the official state religion, and the palace has reinforced the public presence of Islam, partly in order to pre-empt an Islamist challenge.

Israel, Turkey, Egypt, and India provide more mixed systems. Here, too, state elites took a leading role in delineating the public conception of religion, but state policies were not always aimed at reinforcing religious over secular notions of citizenship, or vice versa.

While the Israeli state formally recognizes thirteen non-Jewish religions, it grants official status to only one particular definition of Orthodox Judaism for purposes of conversion and marriage. The state thus continues to reject alternative religious (e.g. Reform and Conservative) or secular definitions of "who is a Jew." Moreover, within the territory of Israel, the state recognizes conversion into Orthodox Judaism only, while recognizing any type of conversion (e.g. Reform/Conservative) made abroad. As Hanna Lerner shows in her chapter, the problem is particularly acute for 300,000 immigrant Jews from the former Soviet Union. The Orthodox rabbinate, which enjoys exclusive authority in matters of Jewish marriage and divorce, does not recognize these immigrants as Jews, thereby denying them any chance of lawful marriage.

Kemal Atatürk went further than leaders in most other Muslim-majority states in monopolizing for the state the right to define religion and to privilege specific Islamic teachings over others. Unlike Iran, Indonesia, Egypt, Morocco, and Pakistan, whose courts continue to recognize Islamic law in some areas, Mustafa Kemal entirely eradicated religious law after the abolition of the caliphate in 1924 and erected a wholly secular legal system based on the French model. Religious education was prohibited for several years, as were religious political parties and organizations. After the 1950s, religion was gradually permitted to re-enter the public sphere, but only on state terms. Until today, the Presidency of Religious Affairs (*diyanet*) trains and certifies Islamic preachers and determines the content of sermons. Islam can be studied only in state schools, and all personnel of the mosques, including preachers, are civil servants. Alevism, which as much as 20 percent of the Turkish population may profess, remains unrecognized by the state and, as such, is discriminated against. Islam, as a state-defined religion, only includes Sunni Islam, though beyond the state's purview alternative forms of Islam continue to be practiced.

Egypt's history, too, exhibits an oscillation between religious and secular notions of citizenship and sometimes a combination of policies furthering both at the same time. Gudrun Krämer points out that Ottoman moder-nizer Muhammad Ali who introduced European legal codes without abol-ishing religious ones, sought to produce pious subjects, not secular ones. After independence, the state projected itself as the guardian of Egyptian identity, which would include the religions of the demographic majority and minority. Since the 1970s, the state elevated Islam to a source of law and promoted public professions of Islamic piety while at the same time invoking the concept of secularism to repress and control political Islam.

In India, some political elites worked to secularize the public sphere while others used religious motifs to "Hinduize" it. The colonial admin-istration used the Hindu, Muslim, and Christian elites to codify personal law regimes. These laws continued to operate after independence, but the scope of religious freedom was carved out mainly by the judiciary, and in a few instances by the democratically elected parliament (for Hindu perso-nal law) as well as civil society-religious group discussions (Christian personal law). The approach of Jawaharlal Nehru (the first Prime Minister of independent India), which incorporated a normative project of secularization into the constitution and removed religion from politics, would contain the hope of moving from Secularity I to III. But the Hindu nationalists, who rose to power in the 1990s, aimed to use religious motifs to win elections. The courts, as Shylashri Shankar points out, were drawn into these battles and through their judgments further muddled the notions of secularity and religion.

The Iranian case exhibits best the transition between both extremes. During the Pahlavi dynasty (1925–1979), the Iranian case resembled the Turkish and to some extent Russian cases, insofar as the clergy was deprived of its monopoly over education and jurisprudence. Institutions of Shiite Islam were pushed out of the public sphere and relegated to caring for the hereafter, without any remaining *necessity* of contact between the citizen and the clergy. Yet in contrast to the Russian case, the Pahlavi secularization policies were lost on the larger society; rigorous enforcement of secular policies legitimized the Shiite clergy and inspired a revival of religious practice. In 1979, social mobilization toppled the secularist monarchy and reversed the policies of differentiation by binding political and religious authority. What was once relegated to the private sphere was brought back into the public realm, specifically religious law, religious education, and religious authority. What remained the same, as Nader Hashemi shows, was that even after the 1979 revolution, state policy toward religion was driven by an elite that imposed its notions of "religious" and "secular" onto the populace.

Secularity, Religion, and Nationalism

The third theme is the link between secularity and nationalism in a state's conceptualization of the place of religion in public life. In Indonesia and India, the national project soon after independence became contrasted in the public imagination with the majority religion; nationalism therefore also stood for equality of the citizenry irrespective of religious identity – it served as an ideology to integrate a culturally and religiously diverse society. In other countries, such as Turkey, Iran, Egypt, and Morocco, the national project in the 1950s and 1960s became coterminous with the identification of the nation with the majority religion. In Israel and Pakistan, the link between the nation and religion was particularly strong as both consolidating states defined themselves against, and experienced wars with, neighbors of other religious backgrounds. In Japan, the link between religion and the nation was strong, too, although after 1945 it was no longer only the majority religion which was mobilized in favor of allegiance to the nation. From this comparative vantage point, India and Indonesia stand out for formulating decidedly inclusivist notions of the nation meant to embrace religious diversity. Some authors have pointed to the strong impression Indonesia's *pancasila* had on Nehru in this regard (Six 2017: 39).

In Indonesia, upon the country's independence in 1945, constitutional debates circled around the question of the proper place of Islam in the emerging state. Against calls for the introduction of Islamic law, opponents objected that the proclamation of an Islamic state would cause the Christian-majority islands in the East to secede. Over the years, the latter defined themselves as the "nationalists" and branded their opponents as "Islamists." Nationalism became linked to pancasila, the pan-religious ideology conceived by the country's first president, Sukarno. Although a rapprochement between Islamic elites and the state occurred during the last years of Suharto's presidency, the national project has to this day been defined as an inclusive project under which Muslims, Christians, Hindus, and Buddhists have equal rights.

In India as well, a major concern for the Constituent Assembly was how to douse the flames of post-Partition strife between Hindus and Muslims. The notion of a Hindu India was rejected by the framers and while the debates recognized the need to separate those aspects of religious dissentions that could demolish democratic stability, there was little agreement on how to achieve this objective. Some saw a secular state as the separation of state and church (religion would not be permitted in the public sphere). Others saw it as neutrality of the state toward religion, which could function in the public sphere. A third view maintained that while the state would treat all religions equally, the state had a duty to reform religious practices in line with principles of equality and justice (what Rajeev Bhargava [1998] refers to as "principled distance"). The constitution ultimately did not define the terms "Hindu," "religion," "secular," and "minorities," and left it to the courts and legislature to do so. Hindu nationalists continued to call for "Hindu India" over the decades, but others challenged this view and advocated a "secular" India.

In Turkey, religion, modernization, and the national project were closely interwoven early in the republic. With the end of the caliphate in 1924, Istanbul ceased to function as the center of a transnational Islam, and a new, national kind of Islam was conceived. This new Islam would complement rather than hinder Atatürk's modernization vision. As Aslı Bâli shows, far from conceiving nationalism as an anti-religious project, Kemal Atatürk spent the better part of his tenure developing a particular kind of state-sponsored Islam that could be put in the service of the national project.

In Iran, ideas of national self-definition and independence from the West nourished the 1979 revolution. Revolutionaries sought to regain the sovereignty they believed their nation had lost through the Shah's military and economic dependence on the United States and Britain in particular. In 1963, the Iranian government granted legal immunity to US citizens within the country, sparking a series of protests and demonstrations coordinated by the Shiite clergy through their tight religious and educational networks. Mosques became rallying places, and in 1979 they provided sanctuaries from the Shah's police and military. The Iranian case also points to the tension between nationalism and transnationalism in the Muslim world. Islam can be a potent force for national unification and mobilization, but its universalist message and global interconnectedness can also undermine nationalist movements. The post-revolutionary Iranian elite thus tried hard to portray the 1979 revolution not as an Iranian or Shiite revolution, but as an Islamic revolution representative of a more universal struggle which many Muslim societies at that time were fighting against despotism, dependency, and injustice. It is in this light that contemporary Iranian elites claim the 2011 uprisings in the Arab world are part of the same struggle against secular despotism that the 1979 Iranian revolution established.

In Morocco, Arabic-speaking elites struggling against colonialism defined the nation as Arab-Islamic. For these nationalists, policies of Arabization of the citizenry and the Islamization of the legal code were the chief instruments of nation-building. After independence, the Arabic triptych "Allah [God], al-Watan [the Nation], and al-Malik [the King]" was adopted in the constitution as the national motto. Over the past five decades of independence, the monarchy has defined Moroccan national identity, portraying itself as the embodiment of the united nation. Since 2001, King Mohamed VI has promoted pluralism and tolerance, diluting the Arab-Islamic character of national identity. The state now recognizes its own Arab and Berber heritages (in addition to secondary Saharan-Hassanic, African, Jewish, Andalusian, and Mediterranean influences). In terms of religion, this shift has involved a continued emphasis on Islam as a shared Moroccan identity, but also the promotion of tolerance and mutual understanding among faiths in Morocco.

Gudrun Krämer points out that the Egyptian resistance to Ottoman rule, and from 1882 on British colonialism, mobilized both secular and religious sentiments. The union between the crescent and the cross, and between Egyptian nationalism and religion remained supple and ambiguous in the inter-war period.

In the Israeli and the Pakistani contexts, religion became particularly strongly intertwined with nationalism, as the concept of the nation here hinges on the continuing centrality of Jewish and Muslim identity, respectively, for its citizens. In both states, symbols, metaphors, and the rhetoric of religion are often blended with national tropes meant to teach citizens that the survival of the nation's religion depends on the survival of the state. The political adversary is conceived also as a religious adversary. Disagreements about whether Judaism is an ethnic, national, or religious identity infuse the debates that Hanna Lerner analyzes in her chapter on Israel.

In the case of Pakistan, the *ulama* have reinvented themselves as the "custodians" of true Islam in light of the fact that the Sunni authorities of the Middle East have, so they argue, been corrupted by state elites, and Middle Eastern Islam has been "diluted" by politically driven reinterpretation projects. The survival of the religious tradition, so the argument goes, therefore requires the continued existence of Pakistan and the safe haven it grants to its scholars and religious leaders. Christophe Jaffrelot outlines how the intelligentsia defined religion as a collective identity in order to create a unified, modern citizenry. The shift from religious belief to religious identity – also emphasized in Nader Hashemi's chapter on Iran – is a variant of the secularization process that eventuated in an alternative form of secularity not captured in Taylor's conceptualization. Jaffrelot terms this "Secularity IV," a condition where religion has become a signifier for ethno-national identities. Secularity IV is epitomized by the "Pakistan movement," an ethno-religious nationalist movement fusing Islam with language identity. In Israel, similar arguments can be heard by Orthodox religious authorities who deem Judaism impossible without Jewish control over the principal religious sites.

In Japan, the relationship between Shinto and the sacralization of the emperor and the nation was particularly strong during the Meiji restauration, but even after 1945 religion was often put into the service of mobilizing imperial loyalties on behalf of modern nation-building. Village headmen and wealthy local gentry regularly sponsored lectures for the peasantry by Confucian teachers, popular Shinto preachers, and (late in the period) some of the leaders of the lay-centered new religious movements of the mid-nineteenth century. Authorities hoped to shore up allegiance to the social order by calling on preachers of all stripes to extol the conventional morality of filial piety, loyalty to the lord, modesty, frugality, and diligence.

Imperialism and Other Encounters with the West

The fourth common theme emanating from the case studies pertains to how the historical encounter between the West and other parts of Europe, Asia, the Middle East, and North Africa shaped the present struggles over modernity and the process of secularization. In all case studies, this encounter appears to be the single most important factor in structuring later public conceptions of religion and its desired role in the public.

South Asia's encounter with the West and its passage through colonialism resulted in an attempt to emulate Western science and rationalism, but only by a miniscule intellectual elite. In India, three elements are identified as central to the role played by Europeans in the construction of Hinduism as a religion: a Western Christian concept of religion, the idea that Indian religions formed one pan-Indian religion, and the needs of the colonial enterprise (Bloch et al. 2010: 7).

These moves to create a unified religion in India were closely linked to the legal codification of the colonial subject (Iqtidar 2011), and as Shankar shows, were retained after independence in the country's constitution and laws, thus significantly shaping the new social imaginaries of how religion and non-religion are experienced by India's diverse communities.

In the chapter on Morocco, Wyrtzen examines how the French imposition of a protectorate form of colonial rule from 1912 to 1956 established conditions for a specific form of "Moroccan secularity" through processes of pluralization and differentiation at the political, economic, and social levels that continued into the post-independence era. French rule introduced a special form of Secularity I, dividing between a modern bureaucratic and traditional state. Religion was used to legitimate the nominal maintenance of the spiritual and political sovereignty of the Sultan, but, at a practical level, Islam's public role was prescribed within the confines of the newly created ministry of religious affairs (*awqaf* or *habous*). The colonial state also partly reified pre-existing ethnic and religious classifications, and partly created these anew, by imposing separate judicial, educational, and administrative structures for Arabs, Berbers, and Jews. In the aftermath of constitutional reforms initiated in response to the Arab Spring protests in 2011, colonial legacies and Western exemplars have been relevant in ongoing debates about the outlines and boundaries of Moroccan secularity with regards to religious freedom, women's rights, ethno-pluralism, and the separation of powers between the monarchy and the parliament.

In Indonesia, the efforts by the post-independence governments to unify the various legal systems that had differentiated the colonial subject population based on ethnicity and religion were primarily driven by the desire to counter the colonial pluri-legal framework and instead provide "one law for all." Those favoring a law blind to religious identity were able to associate in the public imagination the advocates of Islamic law with a "colonial mindset," re-producing colonial divisions in the law instead of embracing an inclusive notion of the people irrespective of religious background. Institutionally, too, post-independence religion–state relations were shaped by imperial and colonial legacies: The bureaucratic basis laid during the Japanese occupation for the state regulation of religious affairs evolved into the key institution of managing religion after independence, the Ministry of Religious Affairs.

Japan's first encounter with secularity, argues Hardacre, was inseparable from mid-nineteenth-century Western imperialism. The Japanese were acutely aware of China's degradation and defeat in the Opium Wars, and they saw clearly that if they failed to strengthen Japan, Western powers would colonize the country.

In each of the case studies, the relationship between the process of secularization and that society's encounters with the West are embedded in and exemplified by the respective local debates about modernity.

CONCLUSION

In the *Devil's Dictionary*, the American satirist Ambrose Bierce describes religion as "a daughter of Hope and Fear, explaining to Ignorance the nature of the Unknowable" (2001: 266). The contributors to this volume have attempted to make the unknowable a little less inscrutable. What emerges from the analysis is the multiplicity of processes and the variations in Secularity I that make "secular regimes" or "secular states" – so often an underlying concept in the humanities and social sciences – problematic and reductionist terms. If anything, the case studies assembled here speak to "multiple secularities" or "varieties of the secular," thus continuing the nuancing of the term "secularization" used in Katznelson and Stedman Jones's volume (2010). While the social sciences have started to think of Secularity I as a continuum rather than some fixed quantity, determined by the level of regulation of religion by the state (Fox 2008), these case studies illustrate the need for additional heuristic dimensions able to capture the impact on religion of state policies. This effect differs markedly across different civilizational contexts, depending on the realms regulated by religious authorities prior to the emergence of the modern state. Accordingly, in Islam it is religious law that experiences profound interference by the twentieth-century state; in China's Confucian traditions, it is education. The importance of capturing this variation in "burdening" (how expansive is the contact surface of religion that can be affected by states policies?) in an account of Secularity I becomes apparent especially when comparing such encounters across various monotheistic and polytheistic, as well as non-theistic traditions.

What of the emergence of Secularity III that lies at the center of Taylor's story? In some states, such as Russia, the Taylorean trajectory has unfolded recognizably; in others, such as Pakistan or Iran, some elements are similar but the local conditions have given birth to yet other types of secularity that cannot be captured by either Secularity I, II, or III. While the answers to the question of why religion has in recent years persisted in challenging its exclusion from the public sphere appear to be country-specific, one of the most striking observations emerging from all chapters is that religion has in fact never been excluded from the public sphere, with the possible exception of Russia in the 1930s and China during the so-called Cultural Revolution; by contrast, all case studies testify to the manifold ways in which the modern state, far from marginalizing religion, put it into its service, often in order to legitimize national, developmental, and sometimes even economic goals. Counter-intuitively, this, as our contributors suggest, is the case even in Soviet Russia after 1943 and Atatürk's Turkey.

This latter insight challenges us to rethink how the struggle between religion and state is conditioned. Gorski reviews the line in political thought that conceives of secularization as a segmentary form of differentiation, in which "church" and "state" have identical structures and equal powers but separate jurisdictions. He notes that "from Augustine's 'two cities' through Marsilius' 'two swords' to Luther's 'two kingdoms', this was a common and recurring position in the history of Latin Christendom. The segmentary principle still has champions today, both amongst political liberals, advocating a strict 'separation of church and state', but also amongst religious sectarians, defending the autonomy of their communities" (Chapter 2: 44). The case studies of this volume point to the fallacy of this position, insofar as it conceives of "church"/organized religion and state as possibly equally strong competitors. In no country studied here do the institutional manifestations of religion and the state hold equal power. Indeed, it is unfeasible for organized religion to express demands vis-à-vis the state that could lead to a segmentary form of differentiation. The institutional means of the state, ranging from law to coercion, preclude a situation in which organized religion and state would have equal powers but separate jurisdictions. The stratificatory conflicts between principal actors in the religious and political fields have been won by the latter. Given this alternative account of Secularity I (regulation of religion by the state rather than mere differentiation), the conflicts to which the modern state, with its means of coercion and consent, is a party are not limited to conflicts concerning the proper relationship between the religious and non-religious fields, but also concern conflicts between and within religious communities. We return to this point in the concluding chapter. Accordingly, the case studies presented here suggest that the conditions of belief (Secularity III) need to be recognized not only as a product of internal reform within religions which must be their starting point, but also the enabling conditions of state policies, which necessarily produce and shape the conditions of belief – whether such policies stem from parliamentary decisions, executive decrees, or judicial rulings.

References

Asad, Talal. 2011. "Thinking about Religious Belief and Politics," in Robert Orsi (ed.) *Cambridge Companion to Religion Studies*. Cambridge: Cambridge University Press.

Beckford, James A. 2003. *Social Theory and Religion*. Cambridge: Cambridge University Press.

Berger, Peter L. 1967. *The Sacred Canopy: Elements of a Sociological Theory of Religion*, Garden City: Doubleday.

 1999. *The Desecularization of the World. Resurgent Religion and World Politics*. Washington DC: W.B. Eerdmans Pub. Co.

 2012. "Further Thoughts on Religion and Modernity," *Society* 49: 313–316.

Berger, Peter, Grace Davie, and Effie Fokas (eds.). 2008. *Religious America, Secular Europe: A Theme and Variations*. Aldershot: Ashgate.

Bhargava, Rajeev (ed.). 1998. *Secularism and its Critics*. Delhi: Oxford University Press.

Bierce, Ambrose. 2001. *The Enlarged Devil's Dictionary*, London: Penguin (first published 1906).

Bilgrami, Akeel. 2016. *Beyond the Secular West*. New York: Columbia University Press.

Bloch, Esther, Marianne Keppens, and Rajaram Hegde (eds.). 2011. *Rethinking Religion in India: The Colonial Construction of Hinduism*. London: Routledge.

Bourdieu, Pierre. 1984. *Distinction: A Social Critique of the Judgment of Taste*. London: Routledge.

Bruce, Steve. 2002. *God is Dead. Secularization in the West*. Oxford: Blackwell.

Burchardt, Marian, Monika Wohlrab-Sahr, and Matthias Middell (eds.). 2015. *Multiple Secularities Beyond the West. Religion and Modernity in the Global Age*. Berlin: De Gruyter.

Calhoun, Craig, Mark Juergensmeyer, and Jonathan VanAntwerpen (eds.). 2011. *Rethinking Secularism*. Oxford: Oxford University Press.

Casanova, José. 1994. *Public Religions in the Modern World*. Chicago: University of Chicago Press.

 2006. "Rethinking Secularization: A Global Comparative Perspective." *The Hedgehog Review* 12(3): 7–22.

 2010. "A Secular Age: Dawn or Twilight?" In Michael Warner (ed.) *Varieties of Secularism in A Secular Age*. Cambridge, MA: Harvard University Press, 265–281.

Davie, Grace. 2002. *Europe: The Exceptional Case: Parameters of Faith in the Modern World*. London: Darton Longman & Todd.

Duara, Prasenjit. 2008. "Religion and Citizenship Among Chinese." In Mayfair Mei-hui Yang (ed.), *Chinese Religiosities: Disjunctures of Modernity and Nation-State Formation*. Berkeley: University of California Press.

Eisenstadt, Shmuel N. 2000. "Multiple Modernities." *Daedalus* 129(1): 1–29.

Finke, Roger and Rodney Stark. 1993. "The Dynamics of Religious Economies." In Michele Dillon. (ed.), *Handbook of the Sociology of Religion*. Chicago: University of Chicago Press.

Fox, Jonathan. 2008. *A World Survey of Religion and the State*. Cambridge: Cambridge University Press.

Gordon, Peter E. 2008. "The Place of the Sacred in the Absence of God: Charles Taylor's A Secular Age." *Journal of the History of Ideas* 69(4): 647–673.

Iqtidar, Humeira. 2011. *Secularizing Islamists?: Jama'at-e-Islami and Jama'at-ud-Da'wa in Urban Pakistan*. Chicago: University of Chicago Press.

Katznelson, Ira and Gareth Stedman Jones (eds.). 2010. *Religion and the Political Imagination*. Cambridge: Cambridge University Press.

Künkler, Mirjam and John Madeley. 2014. "A Secular Age beyond the West: Forms of Differentiation in and around the Religious Field." In *Soft Power* 1(2): 41–62.

Luckmann, Thomas. 1967. *Die unsichtbare Religion*. Frankfurt am Main: Suhrkamp Verlag.

Luhmann, Niklas. 1977. *Die Funktion der Religion*. Frankfurt am Main: Suhrkamp Verlag.

Madsen, Richard. 2008. *Secularism, Religious Renaissance, and Social Conflict in Asia*. Martin Marty Center Web Forum.

Mamdani, Mahmood. 1996. *Citizen and Subject. Contemporary Africa and the Legacy of Late Colonialism*. Princeton: Princeton University Press.

Martin, David. 1978. *Toward a General Theory of Secularization* Oxford: Blackwell.

Rosenfeld, Michel and Susanna Mancini (eds.). 2016. *Constitutional Secularism in an Age of Religious Revival*. New York: Oxford University Press.

Six, Clemens. 2017. "Traces of a Transnational Mindset: Thinking Secularism for the Postcolonial Era" [ch. 1. of *Engaging the Believers: Secularism, Decolonisation, and the Cold War in South and Southeast Asia*.] Manuscript, 39–70.

Taylor, Charles. 2002. *Varieties of Religion Today. William James Revisited*. Cambridge: Harvard University Press.

2007. *A Secular Age*. Cambridge, MA: Harvard Belknap Press.

2010. "The Meaning of Secularism." *The Hedgehog Review* 12(3): 23–34.

2011. "Why we need a Radical Redefinition of Secularism" in Eduardo Mendieta and Jonathan VanAntwerpen (eds.), *The Power of Religion in the Public Sphere*. New York: Columbia University Press, 34–59.

2012. "Glaube und Vernunft. Ironie in der condition humana?" [Charles Taylor interviewed by Hans-Peter Krüger] *Deutsche Zeitschrift für Philosophie*, Akademie Verlag, 60:5, 763–784.

Turner, Bryan S. 2005. "Talcott Parsons's Sociology of Religion and the Expressive Revolution. The Problem of Western Individualism." *Journal of Classical Sociology* Vol. 5(3): 303–318.

2014. "Religion and contemporary sociological theories." *Current Sociology Review* Vol. 62(6): 771–788.

Van der Veer, Peter. 2011. "Smash Temples, Burn Books: Comparing Secularist Projects in India and China" in Craig Calhoun, Mark Juergensmeyer, and Jonathan VanAntwerpen (eds.), *Rethinking Secularism*. New York: Oxford University Press, 270–281.

Warner, Michael, Jonathan Van Antwerpen, and Craig Calhoun (eds.). 2010. *Varieties of Secularism in a Secular Age*. Cambridge, MA: Harvard University Press.

Weber, Max. 2008. *The Protestant Ethic and the Spirit of Capitalism with Other Writings on the Rise of the West*. Oxford: Oxford University Press.

Wilson, Bryan. 1966. *Religion in Secular Society*. London: C.A. Watts.

Wohlrab-Sahr, Monika and Marian Burchardt. 2012. "Multiple Secularities: Towards a Cultural Sociology of Secular Modernities." *Comparative Sociology* 11(8): 875–909.

Zemmin, Florian, Colin Jager, and Guido Vanheeswijck (eds.). 2016. *Working with a Secular Age. Interdisciplinary Perspectives on Charles Taylor's Master Narrative*. Berlin: De Gruyter.

2

Secularity I: Varieties and Dilemmas

Philip Gorski

"Modernity begets secularity." The conventional wisdom in the social sciences for most of the twentieth century (Wilson 1985), this simple premise has come under sustained attack over the last two decades, and from multiple directions. Noting the variability of religiosity across Western Europe, and its stubborn persistence and even resurgence most everywhere else, some sociologists of religion began to question confident predictions of religious decline (Berger 1999; Casanova 1994; Stark 1999b; Warner 1993). Others pointed to the vitality of religiously driven reform movements, sparking a lively debate amongst political theorists concerning the proper role of religious arguments in public life (Audi and Wolterstorff 1997; Benedict, Habermas, and Schuller 2006; Rosenblum 2000). Intellectual historians began to question the interpretive validity of the secularization story (Buckley 1987; Gillespie 2008; Gregory 2012; Turner 1985). Theologians chimed in as well (Milbank 2006; Placher 1996).

Since its initial publication, Charles Taylor's magnum opus, *A Secular Age*, has become a focal point for this far-flung debate, and rightly so (Taylor 2007). Ranging widely and confidently over multiple disciplines and literatures, Taylor has constructed a magisterial synthesis of these disparate disputes. More than that, he has fundamentally reframed the debate by arguing that the origins of Western secularity are to be found not in the growth of scientific knowledge, nor in the disruptions of modernization, but rather in changing "conditions of belief." The real upshot of Western secularity, he contends, is not that religious disbelief becomes the only option, but rather that it becomes a viable option, even an attractive one. For Taylor, then, the essence of secularity is plurality, characterized by competing versions of belief and disbelief, with a fully "immanent frame" of reference the "default option" for many. And secularism, he proposes, is best seen as a means of accommodating this pluralism (Maclure and Taylor 2011).

But useful as it may be for understanding the historical genesis of Western secularity qua cultural condition, Taylor's approach is less fruitful for explaining the global varieties of secularism cum institutional settlement. Or so I will argue in this chapter. Drawing on the systems theory of Niklas Luhmann, the field theory of Pierre Bourdieu, and recent work on historical institutionalism, I elaborate a fourfold typology of secular settlements and identify various sources of political instability and institutional change. I conclude on a normative note, juxtaposing four influential models of secularism with the three values which Taylor believes such systems should aim for: namely, religious freedom, civic equality, and political solidarity (Maclure and Taylor 2011).

THE SECULARIZATION PARADIGM: ORTHODOX AND NEO-ORTHODOX MODELS

There is no such thing as *the* theory of secularization. Rather, there is a *family* of theories, which share certain traits (Gorski 2000; Tschannen 1991, 1992; Yamane 1997). These traits include: 1) a stadial philosophy of history; 2) a propositional definition of religion; and 3) a positivist philosophy of science. In most narratives of secularization, Western history is divided into a succession of discrete stages, culminating in "modernity," and non-Western societies are located at various stages along the resulting continuum, though always behind the West. Stadial theories of historical development were first elaborated by leading thinkers of the Scottish Enlightenment, such as Adam Smith and Adam Ferguson, and subsequently influenced other important philosophies of history, including Comtean positivism and dialectical materialism. As for religion, secularization theories mostly treat it as a matter of "belief" or, in more philosophical terms, as a set of truth claims about cosmos, society, and self. On this account the purpose of religion is to tell us about the origins and operations of the natural, social, and inner worlds. Science, finally, is viewed as the authoritative arbiter of all manner of truth claims, as a method for testing and improving our understanding of these three worlds, and as a tool for increasing our ability to manipulate and master them. The pivotal moment in the orthodox narrative is typically the rise of experimental and empirical science in early modern Europe. The rise of science initiates the decline of religion. Reactionary forces may slow the decline, perhaps even reverse it for a time, but in the end, science and secularity will out. Such are the basic traits and the general story-line that have been passed down through successive generations of secularization theorists since the late eighteenth century.

While the family tree of secularization theory can be traced back for at least two centuries, the family name is of more recent origins. D'Holbach (1966) and Diderot (1819), for instance, never used the word "secularization." Even Durkheim and Weber did so only en passant (Gorski 2011). The term appears with increasing frequency during the 1920s and 1930s, but it is not until the 1940s and 1950s that one can really speak of "secularization theory" as a full-blown research program in the social sciences. Coinciding as it did with the professionalization of the social sciences and the closure of the theoretical canon in sociology (Smith 2003b; Vidich and Lyman 1985), secularization theory quickly bowdlerized all memory of its pre-sociological ancestors from the family history. Henceforth, textbook presentations of the orthodox theory would hold up Durkheim and Weber as the founding fathers – as, indeed, they still do (Norris and Inglehart 2004; Wilson 1985). This truncation of the family tree not only lends the theory greater academic legitimacy, but also strips away, or rather covers over, its underlying assumptions about metaphysics, history, and ethics.

As the tree grew, it sprouted various branches. All of the branches started from the same basic premise, namely, that "modernization" goes together with "secularization." But they diverged in how these two key terms related in reality. Some continued to emphasize science as the defining feature of the modern age (Wilson 1982). But others operated with an updated notion of "modernity" which highlighted the great transformations of the nineteenth and twentieth centuries: industrialization, urbanization, democratization, individualization, and so on (Acquaviva 1979). Likewise, some continued to emphasize declining belief as the defining feature of secularization (Bruce 1992). But others operated with a more multi-dimensional definition of religion that included membership in religious communities or participation in religious rituals (Martin 1978). Most also added a supra-individual and macro-social level of analysis as well. Some, such as Karel Dobbelaere, spoke of the "differentiation" of religious and non-religious "institutions" or "spheres" (Dobbelaere 1999). Others, such as Thomas Luckmann, spoke of the "privatization" of religion or its "evacuation" from public life (Luckmann 1967). Still others, such as Bryan Wilson, spoke of the "declining social significance" of religion in all areas of life (Wilson 1982). There was also an underlying and often unspoken disagreement as to whether secularization should be mourned or cheered, reflecting the split between religious and irreligious sociologists of religion. The former were more apt to see secularization in tragic terms, as Weber did, as a loss of "meaning" or cultural coherence (Berger 1969). The latter were more apt to see it in comic terms, as Comte did, as a process or liberation and enlightenment (Comte, Martineau, and Harrison 2000).

In the United States, secularization theory was doubly orphaned by the precipitous and simultaneous collapse of modernization theory and structural functionalism in the early 1970s. Despite the sudden loss of parental support, the orphan theory marched steadily and resolutely onward for another two decades, benefiting along the way from a policy of benign neglect on the part of the neo-Marxists and left Weberians who were busily conquering the fields of comparative politics and reviving the field of historical sociology, perhaps because they regarded religion as an epiphenomenon and historical relic unworthy of their attentions (Gorski 2005). Be that as it may, secularization theory became something like a "normal science," banished to the increasingly marginalized subfield of the sociology of religion. Its basic assumptions remained uncontested, leaving researchers to the task of empirical confirmation, conceptual elaboration, and operational refinements.

Beginning in the late 1970s, however, the orthodox account suddenly found itself confronted with a vexing series of "empirical anomalies" that it was ill-equipped to account for. Early warning signs included the Islamic Revolution in Iran, the Moral Majority in the United States, liberation theology in Latin America, and the Solidarity movement in Poland. Equally important, if less noticed at the time, at least in the West, were the emergence of global Pentecostalism, Sunni forms of Islamic fundamentalism, and the electoral gains of the Hindu right in India. The final wake-up call was, of course, the terrorist attack of September 11th.

The impact of historical events on social theory is often slow, but, by the late 1980s, intellectual shifts within the Western academy were breaking down longstanding resistance to the study of religion. One was the "cultural turn in the human sciences" or, more prosaically, the growing influence of cultural anthropology, especially in the neighboring fields of history and sociology, and the genesis of the new subfield of "cultural studies" (Bonnell, Hunt, and Biernacki 1999; Smith 2001). Another was the post-modern reaction against Enlightenment rationalism and the attack on positivist epistemologies and "master narratives" that accompanied it (Asad 1993; Caputo 2001; Lyotard 1984). Yet another was the multicultural and "subaltern" critique of Eurocentric universalism (Chakrabarty 2000) and attendant arguments for epistemological relativism (Collins 2000). By the turn of the millennium, the academic study of religion was not only respectable again; it was starting to become downright fashionable.

Orthodox secularization theory, meanwhile, now found itself under increasing attack from within sociology itself. In *Public Religions in the Modern World*, for instance, Jose Casanova argued that the theory was only one-third right: it was right about institutional differentiation of the religious and political spheres, but wrong in its claims concerning the privatization and decline of religious belief (Casanova 1994). Focusing more narrowly on predictions about religious decline, Rodney Stark and his various collaborators and disciples argued that "religious markets" obey the same laws as economic ones: where the markets are free and competitive, as in the United States, more kinds of religion will be produced and consumed; by contrast, where they are monopolistic and heavily regulated, as in the state churches of Western Europe, the quantity and variety of religious "products" will decline, with predictable effects on "consumption" (Finke and Stark 1988, 1992; Stark 1999a). In *The Secular Revolution*, Christian Smith and his collaborators focused on the dynamics of institutional differentiation (Smith 2003a). Far from being the inevitable result of impersonal processes of "rationalization," they argued, the evacuation of religious influences from many areas of social life, from the social sciences and social work to law and medicine, was actually the work of secularizing elites seeking to carve out arenas of expertise free of clerical control. Before the decade was out, one of the most prominent secularization theorists would publicly recant his earlier views (Berger 1999).

In Western Europe, however, the assault on secularization theory met with a chillier reception and eventually stimulated several counter-attacks. In his provocatively titled book, *God is Dead*, for instance, Steve Bruce argued that religion survives into modernity only when and where it finds "other work" to do, such as sustaining national identity, as in Ireland and Poland, or underwriting immigrant identity, as in the United States and amongst European Muslims (Bruce 2002). He conceded that the form of differentiation and the degree of disbelief varied across the West, but argued that these were just differences in pathways and pacing and that secularization would triumph in the end. Meanwhile, in their much discussed book,

Sacred and Secular: Religion and Politics Worldwide, Pippa Norris and Ronald Inglehart used data from the World Values Survey to revise and defend the orthodox account (Norris and Inglehart 2004). Situating themselves in the long line of materialist skeptics who trace religion to fear of the unknown, they argue that belief is a response to "existential insecurity." As science and social policy improve our understanding of, and mastery over, the world, they contend, religious belief falls away. If religious belief persists in the United States, this is due to a weak welfare state. And if religious belief appears to be on the rise outside the West, this is because of high birthrates among the devout. As social policies improve and demographics shift, secularization will triumph.

Critics of secularization theory have responded to such neo-orthodox accounts in various ways. Many have questioned whether there is one modernity exemplified by Western Europe. Some argue that there are "multiple modernities" and that non-Western modernities may leave more room for religion (Eisenstadt 2000; Hefner 1998; Sachsenmaier and Eisenstadt 2002). Others contend that the European outcome results from a series of historical contingencies, rather than from a set of structural necessities (McLeod 2000, 2007), and that Europe, rather than America, may prove to be the "exceptional case" (Davie 2002). Norris and Inglehart's analysis has been subjected to a more specific set of critiques concerning the validity of its measures of religiosity in non-Western contexts and the absence of direct measures of "existential security," its key independent variable (Gorski and Altınordu 2008). In the end, only time will fully settle these debates.

A SECULAR AGE: AIMS AND METHODS

Any theory of secularization must be able to account for both belief and unbelief. In the orthodox theory, unbelief is tacitly assumed to be the most "natural" or "reasonable" stance, because the orthodox theory claims that nature and reason are on its side. The real task, it is assumed, is to account for belief. At the individual level, this is typically done in terms of emotional states (fear) or cognitive backwardness (ignorance). This is Norris and Inglehart's argument (Norris and Inglehart 2004). At the social level, collective identity and communal solidarity are commonly invoked to explain belief. This is Bruce's approach (Bruce 2011). Once politics has become disentangled from religion, religion is stripped of its main function. In the orthodox and neo-orthodox accounts, then, secularization results when scientific rationality and institutional differentiation strip away the "artificial" supports for religious belief.

In *A Secular Age*, Charles Taylor turns the tables on the orthodox theory, by arguing that it is disbelief, rather than belief, that is really in need of explaining (Taylor 2007). Why? Because religious belief is the historical (and comparative) norm. As late as 1500, he contends, religious disbelief was still essentially unthinkable, and until fairly recently the vast majority of Westerners were religious believers. (It might be added that the vast majority of non-Westerners still are.) By "religious disbelief," it should be noted, Taylor does not mean religious disinterest. That can be found in every culture and any age, to one degree or another. Rather, he means "exclusive humanism," a fully atheistic worldview that rejects not only the notion of a personal God but belief in any sort of supra-natural order in favor of a purely "immanent" picture of the world. In short, Taylor tacitly changes the "dependent variable" of secularization theory from belief to disbelief.

Logically speaking, of course, the orthodox account is quite capable of providing a causal explanation for religious disbelief: in a word, science. But Taylor finds this account unconvincing for several reasons. Like Alvin Plantinga (Dennett and Plantinga 2011; Plantinga 2011), Taylor sees no prima facie conflict between science and religion.[1] Another is that Western science is itself the intellectual offspring of Western Christianity and was initially seen as reinforcing rather than undermining a theistic cosmology (Funkenstein 1986; Gaukroger 2006), as, for instance, in Newton's claim that celestial motion required divine supervision. Still another is that the orthodox account cannot explain how religion came to be viewed as a set of empirical propositions in the first place, how it made the journey from *mythos* to *logos* (Armstrong 2000).

Having rejected the master variable of the orthodox account, the rise of science, Taylor proposes an alternative: "conditions of belief." By this, he means "the whole context of understanding in which our moral, spiritual or religious experience takes place" (Taylor 2007: 3). These changes, he argues, concern not only our propositional understanding of the natural world, but also our pre-propositional pictures of the social world – what he calls our "social imaginary" – not to mention our understandings of "selfhood" (Taylor 1989), and, of course, the way in which these three

---

[1] He does not elaborate on this point, but it is not really a difficult one to defend, so long as one does not interpret the opening chapters of Genesis as a literal account of Creation, and does not interpret acts of divine Providence as violations of natural law.

worlds of nature, society, and the self are thought to be interrelated. For Taylor, then, the crucial question that must be addressed by secularization theory is this: what changes in the "conditions of belief" over the last five hundred years combined to make "exclusive humanism" seem like a plausible and even attractive option for many people?

Taylor's answer is nothing less than an intellectual history of Latin Christendom from late antiquity to the present day, recounted as a drama in three acts. The first act runs from the waning days of the Roman Empire to the end of the Middle Ages. During this era, Taylor argues, religious faith was sustained and reinforced by taken-for-granted assumptions about the natural, social, and psychic orders. In the second, temporally bounded by the Protestant Reformation and the French Revolution, these assumptions are attenuated and transformed. The natural world comes to be seen as an "immanent order" which obeys its own laws. The social world is now understood as a human construct that can be shaped for "mutual benefit." And the human person comes to be experienced as a "buffered self," characterized by external boundaries, "inner depths," and moral autonomy. As originally formulated, this world picture – what Taylor calls "the immanent frame" – did not exclude God. But neither did it logically require God. It could be reasonably interpreted as "open" or "closed" to divine transcendence. The third and concluding act in this drama is the "nova effect": the rapid pluralization of Western culture that follows the implosion of Latin Christendom during the early modern era. Unitarianism and spiritualism, Romanticism and utilitarianism, liberalism and ultramontanism, socialism and nihilism, humanism and anti-humanism, fundamentalism and syncretism, modernism and post-modernism – the range of available options increases exponentially from the nineteenth century onwards, first among the elites, and then among the popular classes as well. Today, the sheer range of "available options," religious and non-religious, is truly staggering. For Taylor, then, the defining characteristic of the secular age is not disbelief but pluralism – radical pluralism.

The aims of Taylor's book are not just diagnostic, however; they are apologetic as well, if not in a narrowly partisan way. To be sure, Taylor makes no secret of his Catholic faith, and he does seek to persuade the unbelieving reader that religious belief, or at least certain forms of belief, are a perfectly reasonable response to our shared secular condition. But he does not succumb to a Romantic nostalgia for cultural unity, nor does he wag his finger at non-believers. On the contrary, he insists that modern secularity has its positive sides, even for believers, and he acknowledges the attractions of the "closed" worldview of exclusive humanism, even for himself (Taylor and Heft 1999). For the reflecting person, then, the secular age is characterized not by the clarity of convictions, but by a "mutual fragilization" of all worldviews. Finally, with his notion of "the immanent frame," Taylor marks out a space of at least partially shared assumptions, where some sort of civil and rational dialogue should be possible within Western societies.

Taylor's method has provoked much befuddlement and criticism amongst historians and social scientists (Bubandt and Beek 2012; Warner, VanAntwerpen, and Calhoun 2010). Why does Taylor focus so much on the history of ideas, and so little on the history of power? Why doesn't he pay more attention to the varying trajectories of different societies? Why does he take a phenomenological approach to his subject, recounting, as it were, the successive forms and stages of Western "consciousness"? Taylor's choice of method is less surprising once one is clear about his primary aims. His central goal is not to *explain* the genesis of secularity to everyone; rather, he is aiming to render it *intelligible* to those of us who live in the West. He is not aiming to show that his is the best explanatory account of secularization that we have, but rather to show that various responses to secularization are reasonable. His aims, in short, are those of a historically and sociologically informed philosopher, not of a philosophically informed historian or social scientist. And since he is, finally, a philosopher, we social scientists have no right to demand anything more of him. What use, then, is his theory to us?

A SECULAR AGE II: LIMITATIONS AND ALTERNATIVES

In the first chapter of *A Secular Age*, Taylor distinguishes three dimensions or types of secularity: the evacuation of religion from "public spaces" (Secularity I); declining rates of religious belief and practice (Secularity II); and "conditions of belief" (Secularity III). As we have just seen, Taylor's main contribution to the secularization debate, and his principal interest in *A Secular Age*, is to develop the notion of "Secularity III." Further, as we have also seen, his principal aim in the book is not a causal explanation of Secularity III, but a phenomenological interpretation of it. Consequently, the book is of relatively limited value for social scientists and historians who are mainly interested in developing causal accounts of Secularity I or II, and for a number of reasons.

The first is analytical. Because Taylor is mostly interested in "conditions of belief," he spends relatively little time discussing the other two forms of secularity. Indeed, they serve mainly as heuristic foils for Secularity III. But however great its other failings, the orthodox paradigm does contain a rich trove of conceptual constructs and empirical operators. Like Taylor, most work operates with a basic distinction between the "social" and "individual" levels of secularization, roughly corresponding to Secularity I and II. But they go beyond Taylor in their efforts to distinguish various dimensions of secularization at the societal and individual levels of analysis. For instance, it is quite common, and also quite useful, to distinguish between "differentiation" and "privatization." As Casanova has ably shown, "separation of church and state" or, more broadly, the "autonomization of religious and social spheres," does not necessarily entail privatization. On the contrary, differentiation in this sense is a structural condition of possibility for "religious politics" of various kinds (Altınordu 2010), including para-church reform lobbies, church-based social movements, and confessionally based political parties. It is their "private" convictions that impel the members of such organizations to enter into the "public" sphere in the first place. And the fact that these organizations have no public role in supporting or legitimating the state allows them to adhere more closely to their religious principles and convictions (Toft, Philpott, and Shah 2011). The distinction between various dimensions of religiosity has also proven quite useful. Religious historians and social scientists have repeatedly demonstrated that various aspects of individual religiosity do not necessarily move in tandem with one another or vary regularly with one another from country to country or region to region. Religious belief, church membership, ritual participation, charitable giving – these and other measures are both analytically and empirically distinct from one another across time and space (Gorski and Altınordu 2008). This is not to imply that Taylor is unaware of these complexities and challenges – he clearly is – but rather to stress that they are not his main interest.

The second limitation of Taylor's approach is methodological. Because his aims are mostly interpretive and apologetic, he spends relatively little time on the social and political context of theological and philosophical debate. For example, there is little discussion of how national and monastic rivalries, and Imperial and Papal politics, influenced the outcome of the debate between "nominalists" and "realists" in the Middle Ages, or on how the loose-jointed institutional structure of the Holy Roman Empire may have contributed to the success of Luther's Reformation or shaped the state churches that were established in its wake, or on how electoral arithmetic and parliamentary coalitions impacted the variant systems of church–state relations that took shape across nineteenth century Europe. In short, Taylor has relatively little to say about how historical conjunctures, institutional constellations, and path dependencies led to divergent national trajectories in church/state relations – again, not because he is unaware of such variations, but because Secularity I is not his primary object of interest. The same might be said of his discussions of Secularity II. There is, in fact, enormous variation in the timing, shape, and degree of religious decline in the West (Gorski and Altınordu 2008; Höllinger 1996; McLeod 1996, 2007; McLeod and Ustorf 2003). In some parts of France and Germany, for example, signs of decline were already evident under the ancient regime. In other parts of Europe, including England and the Netherlands, rates of church attendance remained fairly stable until the late nineteenth century and did not drop significantly until the 1960s. In the United States, on the other hand, there is little evidence of decline even in the present day. Taylor is probably right about the changed conditions of belief in the secular age. Even the most devout evangelical in the United States is acutely aware that her Christian faith is just one "option"; indeed, she likely defines her faith largely as an individual or personal "choice." But this scarcely explains why only 2–3 percent of the Scandinavian population claims to attend church each week, while around 40 percent of Americans do (Chaves 2011; Putnam, Campbell, and Garrett 2010). In short, while *A Secular Age* has drawn renewed attention to the secularization debate, it is probably not the best starting point for scholars whose primary interest is in "Secularity II" or, as in the case of the present volume, in "Secularity I," to which I now turn my focus.

SECULARITY I: THEORETICAL CONCEPTS AND EXPLANATORY MECHANISMS

"Institutional differentiation and rationalization," "the autonomization of social spheres," "the evacuation of religion from public spaces": however useful such general concepts may be for capturing the secular trend toward Western secularity, they quickly prove too crude when we turn our attention to the varieties of Western – and non-Western – secularity in all of their ambiguity and complexity. What is needed is a more nuanced set of descriptive concepts and a richer stock of explanatory mechanisms. In this section, I highlight three potential sources of theoretical concepts: 1) the neo-functional differentiation theory of Niklas Luhmann; 2) Pierre Bourdieu's theory of "social fields"; and 3) the "historical institutionalism" advocated, for instance, by Peter Hall and Dietrich Rueschemeyer.

Differentiation was a core concept in social theory for much of the twentieth century. But it fell into ill repute within American sociology during the early 1970s, due to its association with Parsonsian functionalism.

However, it lived on in Continental Europe (Joas and Knöbl 2009), where it was eventually revived in the systems theory of the German sociologist, Niklas Luhmann. Luhmann distinguished four basic principles of social differentiation: "segmentation," "center/periphery," "stratification," and "functional" (Luhmann 1997).

Luhmann saw them as successive stages of social evolution.[2] But they can also be used as Weberian ideal types. One way they can be used is to describe the "internal differentiation" of a particular "religious system." Consider segmentation. "Religious pluralism" in modern societies often involves, inter alia, the co-existence of isomorphic but relatively disconnected religious communities. Differentiation between center and periphery is quite common as well. Here, one thinks of major cultic centers such as Jerusalem, Rome, Mecca, and so on. Stratification is evident wherever there is a clear distinction between religious masses and religious elites (e.g., monks, priests, scholars, gurus, adepts, etc.) Finally, contemporary religious organizations are often part of a religious system that is functionally differentiated from other sub-systems, such as the polity or the economy. Obviously, these principles are not at all exclusive of one another. A religious system can be differentiated in more than one way. Many contemporary religious systems exhibit all four types of internal differentiation.

Another way of using Luhmann's typology is to conceptualize religio-political differentiation – in Taylor's terms, types of Secularity I. For example, we might distinguish between consociational, imperial, confessional, and liberal forms of secularity.

1) *Consociational*: in this model, the religious system consists of segmentary communities which are all represented within the political system, either equally, in proportion to their numbers, or both, depending upon the context. The relationship of the political to the religious system is not defined in terms of the principle of

---

[2] Segmentation originates out of the clannic divisions between autochthonous groups of hunter-gatherers. Center and periphery are characteristic of the imperial systems that arise in the ancient world following the agrarian revolution. Stratification also emerges in ancient empires, but serves as the dominant principle of the ascriptive status systems of Medieval European societies, with their sharp divisions between nobles and commoners. Functional differentiation, finally, first emerges during the early modern era as the spheres of church, state, and society are increasingly premised on functional purposes and principles, rather than on particular groups or individuals. One need not accept Luhmann's account of social evolution, nor his anti-humanistic version of systems theory, in order to see the potential fruitfulness of these conceptualizations, which can easily be applied in a more ideal-typical fashion.

neutrality and/or non-interference, but rather of equality and/or even-handedness. The term "consociational" was originally coined to describe the system of social representation and power-sharing that obtained in a number of small European countries between the late-nineteenth and mid-twentieth centuries (e.g., the Netherlands, Belgium, Switzerland, and Austria) but was subsequently extended to a range of other "deeply divided societies" (Andeweg 2000; Lijphart 1969, 1996, 1998; Lustick 1979). In consociational democracies, society is divided into a number of isomorphic and autochthonous "pillars" (*zuilen*) or "camps" (*Lager*), each represented by a political movement or party. The relationship between the pillars is usually both cooperative and competitive: cooperative insofar as all of the "pillars" or "camps" were included in consultations about major policy decisions, but competitive insofar as spoils (e.g., funds, positions) are divided up according to electoral results. However, European consociational systems included non-religious pillars (i.e., socialist and liberal) as well as religious ones (i.e., Protestant and Catholic). Several non-Western countries (e.g., India and Malaysia) actually come much closer to the consociational ideal as defined here. And the Indonesian "pancasila" system approaches very near to the pure type (Sebastian 2004).

2) *Imperial.* In this model, which comes in several major and minor variants, the political center is firmly controlled by a relatively unified cultural elite. In the first major variant, the Constantinian, the elite is religious. Christian Rome is the paradigmatic example (MacMullen 1984; MacMullen 1997). In the second major variant, the Leninist, the elite is anti-religious. Communist Russia is the historical model, with Jacobin France an important harbinger (Froese 2008; Froese and Pfaff 2005; Vovelle 2002). In both variants, the elite uses the power of the state to proselytize for its worldview and persecute its enemies, with cultural uniformity being the long-term goal. In both variants, moreover, physical violence is frequently used not only against cultural opponents and material objects ("iconoclasm"). Because they typically generate fierce opposition and considerable instability that endangers political power, Constantinian and Leninist campaigns rarely last more than a generation. However, such hard-power campaigns may be followed by soft-power regimes that employ a mix of co-optation and coercion against opponents. The minor or soft-power variants might be called Mughal and Kemalist, respectively, the

references being to the Islamic rule of South India and the republican takeover in Turkey (Kuru 2009; Kuru and Stepan 2012). All four variants are joined together insofar as they regard their cultural opponents as fundamentally illegitimate.

3) *Confessional.* In this model, the missionary impulse of the imperial approach is renounced in favor of a spatial principle of religio-political differentiation. The religious and political systems are both dominated by one and the same religious community. Other religious communities are passively tolerated but not aggressively proselytized. The state does not attempt to conquer other states in the name of religion. Nor does it actively persecute members of other religions within its borders. Instead, religious difference is managed via a distinction between "public" and "private religion." The official religion of state monopolizes the "public." It enjoys exclusive access to public ritual, public office, public money, public space, and so on. Other religions are relegated to the "private sphere" of private homes, civil society, personal conscience, and so on. They are officially "tolerated." But they have a "second-class" status. Both the Ottoman "millet system" and the "Westphalian system" of post-Reformation Europe closely approach the confessional ideal (Barkey 2008; Kaplan 2002, 2007).

4) *Liberal Democratic.* In this model, all religions are regarded as equal, but all are relegated to the private sphere. The religious system consists of autonomous individuals who are free to join or leave individual religious communities and the religious system as a whole. But the political system is understood to be "secular" in the Western sense that it does not intervene in the religious system except to protect religious freedom and civic equality. France and the United States come closest to this model, though France arguably gives greater priority to civic equality and the United States to religious freedom. But most Western democracies are moving toward this system.

Each of these systems of Secularity I can be quite stable. Each, however, has certain distinctive vulnerabilities as well. For example, consociational systems can quickly collapse if the internal culture of the individual pillars dissolves or collapses (e.g., as in the Netherlands) or if one pillar is able and willing to assert its dominance over the others (e.g., Hindu nationalism in contemporary India). Imperial systems are highly vulnerable to elite corruption and economic stagnation. Confessional systems may be challenged by political alliances between heterodox religious groups and demographic decline of the orthodox religious community. Liberal Democratic regimes, finally, can devolve in a Kemalist or Mughal direction if an avowedly religious or anti-religious movement attempts to assert a privileged place within public life.

One advantage of the Luhmannian perspective is that it draws our attention to systemic vulnerabilities of this sort. One disadavantage is that it tends to occlude power dynamics, particularly elite conflicts within the religious system and boundary struggles between the religious and political sphere. By contrast, Pierre Bourdieu's "field theory" makes these dynamics more visible (Bourdieu and Wacquant 1992).

What is a social field (Martin 2003)? Objectively speaking, a social field is two-dimensional space of social positions. The vertical dimension is a status hierarchy. The horizontal dimension runs from orthodox to heterodox. In its objective moment, a social field is like a magnetic field, and individual actors in the field are like so many iron filings, arranged into characteristic patterns by magnetic forces. Subjectively speaking, a social field is more like a playing field, and social actors like so many players, competing with one another both individually and collectively, in accordance with some set of mutually understood rules. Many spheres of life are organized like this: educational systems, party systems, artistic communities, and so on.

Field theory differs from systems theory in two important respects. First, it views the external boundaries between fields, and also the internal divisions within them, as the result not of impersonal processes of mutation and evolution, as in Luhmann's approach, but rather of ongoing contestation and struggle (Bourdieu 1984, 1990). Second, it envisions such struggles not simply as struggles between system principles, but also as struggles between actors, both individual and collective, in contrast to Luhmann, who argues, somewhat paradoxically, that social actors are "outside" of social systems (i.e., in their "environments"). In short, field theory puts politics and power back in the system.

In thinking about the religious and political fields, it is useful to differentiate between three different scales or levels of contestation: 1) *Intra-communal* conflicts within religious communities, for example, between the religious elite (priests, monks, scholars, etc.) and their followers or clients, or between orthodox and heterodox groups or sects; 2) *Inter-communal* conflicts within the religious field as a whole, usually between different religious communities, concerning legal status, material resources, or physical space, and so on; and 3) *Interfield* conflicts involving alliances and rivalries between religious and political elites and their followers, focusing on public functions and policies, for example, control over schooling, social provision, family arrangements, etc.

Now, one very serious shortcoming of the systems approaches is that it focuses our attention mostly on one of these three types of conflict, namely interfield conflict, often to the exclusion of the other two. This is particularly true of studies of Secularity I in the Christian contexts, which are frequently framed as "church–state conflicts." More problematically still, the church–state framing is frequently extended to non-Christian contexts, where the religious field may be organized quite differently.

A field theoretic approach not only distinguishes these three types of conflict, it also implies that such conflicts are usually entangled with one another in sometimes consequential ways. Seen through this lens, "church–state conflict" becomes a game of three-dimensional chess, in which a move at one level is also a move at the other two, and pieces from one level may be deployed at another. Thus, a struggle between two monasteries may be entangled with a struggle between two rival sects, which may in turn be entangled with a struggle between two rival parties (Tambiah 1992). Complicating matters further, rival elites may also redeploy their followers as religious or political pawns.

Of course, they may not do so in a wholly arbitrary fashion. Like a chess board, a social field is a symbolic as well as physical space and is governed by certain written and unwritten rules. These rules determine what sorts of moves are allowed, and therefore also what types of combinations are possible. Religious elites are bound to certain religious teachings, ethical principles, and ritual duties, just as political elites may be bound to certain ideologies, policies, and symbols. These symbolic commitments place constraints on what sorts of strategic moves and combinations are possible and probable. Or, better, they determine the levels of symbolic work that will be required to put certain strategies into effect. For example, the historical animosities between Protestants and Catholics in the United States meant that a great deal of organizational and theological labor was required in order to cement the current alliance between conservative evangelicals and conservative Catholics. Meetings had to be held. Joint statements had to be written. Opposition to abortion and gay marriage were the glue that held the various pieces together. But that glue had to be found and applied.

Another important implication of Bourdieu's approach is that elite struggles often involve boundary struggles (Lamont and Fournier 1992;

Lamont and Molnar 2002). As with elite conflicts, it is useful to distinguish between inter-communal, intra-communal, and interfield boundary struggles. Inter-communal struggles typically involve the boundary between elites and masses and between orthodoxy and heterodoxy. For example, a Muslim engineer may claim religious authority based on his study of the Koran, but this claim will likely be disputed by many Muslim scholars. Likewise, a Turkish Alevi may claim to be an orthodox Muslim, but this claim will be challenged by most Sunnis and many Sufis. Intra-field boundary struggles may take various forms as well. Sometimes, they involve social boundaries. For example, a group of lower-caste Indians may claim civic or even ritual equality with upper-caste Hindus by converting to Buddhism or Islam. Other times, they involve physical boundaries. For example, Muslims might demand physical repartitioning of a Christian or Jewish holy site on the grounds that it is also a Muslim holy site, as has in fact happened on the Temple Mount in Jerusalem. Interfield struggles over the proper boundary between religion and politics may likewise be symbolic as well as physical. Thus, some American secularists demand that religious speech be banned from public debate on the grounds that it violates the principle of state neutrality. Meanwhile, some French republicans demand that headscarves be banned from public schools on the grounds that they threaten the principle of civic equality.

It is perhaps obvious, but nonetheless worth emphasizing, that elites sometimes exploit or even create boundary struggles for their own political purposes (Gorski 2013). For example, the provincial leader of an ethno-religious movement may pay a criminal gang to commit an incendiary act that will spark an ethnic riot in hopes that this will polarize the electorate along ethnic lines and drive his co-ethnics to the polls in an upcoming election. Indeed, there is considerable evidence that Hindu politicians sometimes do just this (Brass 2004, 2011). Their goal, however, is not just to win elections, but also to challenge the minority protections and reservations built into Indian secularism.

As I have argued elsewhere, we can distinguish two basic forms of boundary change between fields: changes in location and in permeability (Gorski 2013). We can further distinguish two forms of locational change: zero-sum and non-zero-sum. In zero-sum boundary changes, control over certain functions, institutions, and roles shifts from one field to another. The secularization of education is a paradigmatic example. In non-zero-sum boundary change, "wild" social space is incorporated into a social field. For example, a religious reform movement may impose greater uniformity over local customs governing marital practices. Changes in the permeability of boundaries also come in two sub-types. First, there are changes in the degree of permeability. For example, for much of American history, there was an unwritten rule forbidding clerical involvement in electoral politics. Even today, IRS rules forbid clergymen from making electoral recommendations from the pulpit. However, clergymen can and do run for high office in both parties (e.g., Jesse Jackson for the Democrats and Pat Robertson for the GOP). Second, there are changes in directionality. In the nineteenth century, members of the ministry often became presidents of universities. This is no longer the case, except at Evangelical colleges. Meanwhile, it is not unusual for a PhD in history to be appointed to a professorship at a divinity school. The boundary between the religious and scientific fields has remained permeable, but the directionality is now reversed.

Luhmannian systems theory provides some basic conceptual tools for distinguishing different types of Secularity I – what we might call "secular settlements." Likewise, Bourdieusian field theory helps us think about ongoing conflicts about status, authority, rules, and resources within a given system of secularity – what we might call "secularity struggles." But where do secular settlements come from, and why do they persist? Here, the insights of historical institutionalism provide a helpful resource (Mahoney and Thelen 2010; Pierson 2004). These insights are summarized in three concepts: "critical junctures," "path dependency," and "policy legacies." Historical institutionalists have shown again and again that fundamental renegotiations of social and economic policy are few and far between and typically occur during periods of acute political crisis, such as revolutions, wars, and depressions, whose severity is sufficient to break apart the existing "distributional coalitions" and challenge "institutional routines." And there is good reason to believe that this principle often obtains for secular settlements as well, though the crises in question may be of a different character in this case, arising out of increased levels of cultural pluralism or sharpened demands for civic inclusion. Historical institutionalists have also repeatedly shown that policy regimes, once established, often exhibit high levels of "path dependency" – that is, they are subject to incremental change, but only within narrow bounds. For example, a "corporatist" system of labor relations based on collective bargaining between "peak associations" may be "reformed" from time to time so as to incorporate newly powerful actors or purpose different macroeconomic goals, but barring a major crisis it is unlikely to evolve in the direction of a neoliberal policy regime of "free markets" and bureaucratic oversight. Once again, there are good reasons to expect that similar path dependencies will obtain with regards to secular settlements. Because they systematically advantage some actors over another, secular settlements are apt to create "distributional coalitions" that unite religious and political actors in favor of a particular policy regime. It is important to remember that such coalitions are held together not only by highly abstract principles, but also by very specific interests. Imagine the uproar that would follow if the American government suddenly offered uniform subsidies to religious schools and colleges, along with a set of detailed curricular requirements for in-school religious education; or if the French government suddenly withdrew such subsidies and requirements! The third and final insight that we may draw from historical institutionalism concerns "policy legacies." The stickiness of policies results not only from the veto power of distributional coalitions, but also from the internal routines of social organizations, such as government agencies and court systems, and from the division of labor between them. The routines and the loci of policy implementation often persist even when the goals and parameters of policy-making change. In some countries, such as the United States, India, and Israel, for instance, disputes about secularism have been mainly construed as issues of "religious freedom" and are typically processed through the courts (Jacobsohn 2003). Elsewhere, in Japan, Indonesia, and Malaysia, by contrast, they are treated more as issues of public order and addressed through central bureaucracies (Keyes, Kendall, and Hardacre 1994). And these routines have persisted across substantial changes in policy.

The foregoing conceptualizations do not lead directly to any "general laws" of secularism, nor even to any "empirical predictions" about specific cases, nor is that my aim here. My first aim has been to develop a theoretically grounded typology that enables us to distinguish various systems of secularism. The usual caveats apply: these ideal types will rarely be found in their pure forms in empirical reality; hybrid types are both possible and probable. My second aim has been to develop a set of sensitizing concepts that can help us to construct adequate causal accounts for the outcomes that we actually do observe – to help us understand why American secularism differs from Indian secularism, or why Turkish secularism differs from French secularism. Drawing on Pierre Bourdieu's field theory, I have argued that we should see secular settlements as the result of "classification struggles" over the dominant "principle of vision and division" that governs relations between the religious and political fields. This part of the account places the emphasis on actors and interests. Drawing on the work of historical institutional-ists, such as Peter Hall and Kathleen Thelen, I have argued that we should see secular settlements as "policy regimes" that crystallize during crucial conjunctures, evolve path dependently, and provide the raw

materials for new regimes. This part of my account highlights the importance of institutions and routines.

While this conceptual framework does not lead to "testable hypotheses,"
it does provide some theoretical orientation for the study of Secularity I. First,
it suggests that "founding moments" – particularly ones involving the writing
of constitutions and/or legal codes – are enormously important. Second, it
implies that systems of secularity are also systems of power that inevitably
privilege certain actors, certain communities, and certain types of religiosity
over others. Third, and finally, it urges us to look, not at "the separation of
religion and politics" *grosso modo* – for this has existed in some form at least
since late antiquity – but rather at the specific institutional form that this
differentiation takes and at the underlying principles that subtend them.

I now shift from an explanatory to a normative perspective.

CONCLUDING REFLECTIONS: THE SECULAR TRILEMMA

In his contribution to a dialogue on *The Power of Religion in the Public
Sphere*, Taylor argues that we must radically rethink the origins and aims of
secularism as a set of political principles and institutional arrangements
(Butler, Mendieta, and VanAntwerpen 2011). First, we must move beyond
the view – a myth in his opinion – that Western secularism arises in response
to the religious wars of the sixteenth and seventeenth centuries, as a means
of "taming" the violent propensies of religion by subordinating it to a
sovereign state (on this point, see also Cavanaugh 2009; Gorski and
Türkmen-Dervişoğlu 2012). Secularism, Taylor argues, arises, not so
much as a means of quelling religious unrest as of accommodating cultural
pluralism, initially of a confessional or denominational variety, to be sure,
but increasingly of an ethnic and cultural sort as well. Similarly, we must
move beyond the view that secularism is first and foremost an institutional
principle (e.g., "separation of church and state" or "the privatization of
religion"), or that it can be derived from a single principle (e.g., civic
equality or "public reason"). Instead, it is better to see it as a civic ideology
that seeks to balance different and potentially competing goods. In his
essay, Taylor enumerates three such goods: religious liberty, civic equality,
and political solidarity. Elsewhere, Taylor notes that there are potential
tradeoffs between these goods (Maclure and Taylor 2011). For example, if
a public official belonging to the majority faith affixes a religious emblem to
his uniform, members of minority faiths may worry that they will not be
granted equal treatment. Conversely, if a public official is banned from
wearing such a sign in a public space, such as a legislature, she may feel that

her religious freedom is being impinged upon. Finally, if a polygamous sect pressures an underage girl to marry a communal patriarch, and collects welfare benefits for her offspring even though she is working for the sect, principles of civic equality and political solidarity are clearly being violated.

What sorts of tradeoffs are involved in various models of Secularity I? Let us begin by enumerating four such models, all of which enjoy some currency in the modern world: consociationalism, religious nationalism, radical secularism, and liberal secularism. The dominant principle of religio-political differentiation in consociational systems is segmentary. Society is divided up into multiple and co-equal communities which are recognized and protected by the state and internally governed by their own leadership. Typically, each community possesses a wide complement of secondary institutions, ranging from schools and colleges to newspapers and television stations to social clubs and sports teams. How well does this version of secularism live up to each of Taylor's three principles? On the positive side of the ledger, it ensures: a high degree of collective equality between religious groups; a high degree of communal freedom within the religious group, as regards education, culture, and sociality; and a high degree of solidarity, not only within each group, but often between groups, at least across the national leaderships. On the negative side of the balance sheet, consociationalism often leads to: substantial restrictions on individual religious freedom (e.g., to convert or marry into another community or to practice or preach a heterodox version of one's own faith); to civic exclusion of unrecognized religions or worldviews; and high levels of internal hierarchy and stratification within religious communities.

Now consider a second system: religious nationalism. Like the imperial systems of old, it marries a "center/periphery" distinction with religio-political "stratification." The religious and political center is typically defined in terms of the demographically dominant faith group, and other groups relegated to the residual category of "other" or "foreign." Insofar as they try to defend themselves in democratic terms at all, religious nationalists argue that minority demands for religious accommodation or civic equality impose undue burdens on the numerical majority.[3] In fact,

---

[3] For example, students at a public school whose student body is overwhelmingly Christian should not be denied the right to pray in school just for the sake of a few atheists or Jews. Or, hard-working and well-educated Brahmins should not be denied a place in the civil service just for the sake of meeting a quota based on caste or religion.

however, religious nationalists most often couch their arguments in terms of ethnic precedence or cultural purity. Their most potent arguments, to put it plainly, are "we were here first" and "you are contaminating us." How do such systems stack up? The sharp division between in-group and out-group can have the effect of heightening solidarity and muting inequality within the in-group, of course, insofar as the salience of religious identity is increased and that of other divisions decreased. In other words, religious exclusion can be, and has been, a powerful tactic within larger strategies of nation-building, and not only within the West. But it exacts a very high price, first and foremost from religious minorities, who are subject to forms of exclusion ranging from stigmatiziation and harassment to banishment or genocide, but even from members of the religious majority, who must often subordinate their personal religious convictions to nationalistic political goals.

The third system is liberal individualism. Its structuring principle is a functional differentiation between religion and politics, in which the function of religion is salvation, however understood, and that of politics is protection, particularly of individual rights and private property. The advantage of this system is that it affords a high level of religious freedom and equality, both individual and collective, that is limited only by the "harm principle." Its disadvantage is that it leads to comparatively low levels of solidarity, especially within the political system, both because the rights principle is not balanced by corresponding duties, and because loyalty to the religious community often trumps devotion to the political community.

The fourth and final form of secularism that I wish to consider here is radical republicanism. Like liberal individualism, it presumes a functional separation of the religious and political spheres. But it does not really grant full parity to the two spheres. Rather, it tends to subordinate the religious sphere to the political sphere to a much greater degree, by drawing a very sharp line between public and private, excluding religion from the private sphere, and defining "private" in very narrow terms. French *laicite* and Turkish *laiklik* may be seen as different versions of this system. The selling point of this system is that it guarantees very high levels of political freedom, civic equality, and national solidarity. Its main costs are comparatively low levels of religious freedom, particularly insofar as public expression of religiosity is concerned, and hidden forms of civic inequality for religious citizens, who are required to check in their religion at the gate to the public square.

Thus, none of the extant systems of Secularity I maximize all three of Taylor's goods for all categories of citizens. All are therefore unstable to some degree. For example, the American system of liberal secularism is currently being challenged by religious nationalists intent on asserting – or, as they see it, *re*asserting – the Christian or Judeo-Christian character of the national project. The most radical versions of American religious nationalism – "dominion" or "Kingdom theology" – envision a return to the "godly law" of the Old Testament and the exclusion of non-believers and heterodox Christians from the polity. The Benelux system of consociationalism, meanwhile, has already collapsed due to ethno-nationalism in Belgium and liberal individualism in the Netherlands. The Turkish system of radical republicanism is also under serious challenge at the moment, both from liberal individualists desiring more personal freedom for themselves, and from religious parties desiring more civic equality for practicing Muslims. Whether these struggles will give rise to new and better forms of secularism, or merely to old and exclusionary versions of religious politics, remains to be seen.

References

Acquaviva, Sabino S. 1979. *The Decline of the Sacred in Industrial Society.* Oxford: B. Blackwell.

Altınordu, Ateş. 2010. "The Politicization of Religion: Political Catholicism and Political Islam in Comparative Perspective." *Politics & Society* 38: 517–551.

Andeweg, Rudy B. 2000. "Consociational Democracy." *Annual Review of Political Science* 3: 509–536.

Armstrong, Karen. 2000. *The Battle for God: Fundamentalism in Judaism, Christianity and Islam.* London: HarperCollins.

Asad, Talal. 1993. *Genealogies of Religion: Discipline and Reasons of Power in Christianity and Islam.* Baltimore: Johns Hopkins University Press.

Audi, Robert and Nicholas Wolterstorff. 1997. *Religion in the Public Square: The Place of Religious Convictions in Political Debate.* Lanham; London: Rowman & Littlefield.

Barkey, Karen. 2008. *Empire of Difference.* New York: Cambridge University Press.

Benedict, Jürgen Habermas and Florian Schuller. 2006. *Dialectics of Secularization: On Reason and Religion.* San Francisco: Ignatius Press.

Berger, Peter L. 1969. *The Sacred Canopy; Elements of a Sociological Theory of Religion.* Garden City: Doubleday.

1999. "Overview." In *The Desecularization of the World: Resurgent Religion and World Politics.* Washington, DC: Ethics and Public Policy Center/W.B. Eerdmans Pub. Co, 1–18.

Bonnell, Victoria E., Lynn Avery Hunt, and Richard Biernacki. 1999. *Beyond the Cultural Turn: New Directions in the Study of Society and Culture*. Berkeley: University of California Press.

Bourdieu, Pierre. 1984. *Distinction: A Social Critique of the Judgement of Taste*. London: Routledge & Kegan Paul.

    1990. *In Other Words: Essays Towards a Reflexive Sociology*. Cambridge: UK Polity Press.

Bourdieu, Pierre and Loïc J. D. Wacquant. 1992. *An Invitation to Reflexive Sociology*. Chicago: University of Chicago Press.

Brass, Paul R. 2004. "Development of an Institutionalised Riot System in Meerut City, 1961 to 1982." *Economic and Political Weekly*: 4839–4848.

    2011. *The Production of Hindu-Muslim Violence in Contemporary India*. Seattle: University of Washington Press.

Bruce, Steve. 1992. *Religion and Modernization: Sociologists and Historians Debate the Secularization Thesis*. Oxford; New York: Clarendon Press; Oxford University Press.

    2002. *God is Dead: Secularization in the West*. Oxford, UK; Malden, MA: Blackwell Publishers.

    2011. *Secularization: In Defence of an Unfashionable Theory*. Oxford; New York: Oxford University Press.

Bubandt, Nils and Martijn van Beek. 2012. *Varieties of Secularism in Asia: Anthropological Explorations of Religion, Politics and the Spiritual*. Abingdon; New York: Routledge.

Buckley, Michael J. 1987. *At the Origins of Modern Atheism*. New Haven: Yale University Press.

Butler, Judith, Eduardo Mendieta, and Jonathan VanAntwerpen. 2011. *The Power of Religion in the Public Sphere*. New York: Columbia University Press.

Caputo, John D. 2001. *On Religion*. London; New York: Routledge.

Casanova, José. 1994. *Public Religions in the Modern World*. Chicago: University of Chicago Press.

Cavanaugh, William T. 2009. *The Myth of Religious Violence: Secular Ideology and the Roots of Modern Conflict*. Oxford; New York: Oxford University Press.

Chakrabarty, Dipesh. 2000. *Provincializing Europe: Postcolonial Thought and Historical Difference*. Princeton: Princeton University Press.

Chaves, Mark. 2011. *American Religion: Contemporary Trends*. Princeton: Princeton University Press.

Collins, Patricia Hill. 2000. *Black Feminist Thought: Knowledge, Consciousness, and the Politics of Empowerment*. New York: Routledge.

Comte, Auguste, Harriet Martineau, and Frederic Harrison. 2000. "*The Positive Philosophy of Auguste Comte Volume 2*." Kitchener: Batoche.

Davie, Grace. 2002. *Europe – The Exceptional Case: Parameters of Faith in the Modern World*. Orbis Books.

Dennett, Daniel Clement and Alvin Plantinga. 2011. *Science and Religion: Are They Compatible?* New York: Oxford University Press.

Diderot, Denis. 1819. *Thoughts on Religion*. London: Darton, Longman & Todd.

Dobbelaere, Karel. 1999. "Towards an Integrated Perspective of the Processes Related to the Descriptive Concept of Secularization." *Sociology of Religion* 60: 229–247.

Eisenstadt, Shmuel Noah. 2000. "Multiple Modernities." *Daedalus* 129: 1–29.

Finke, R. and R. Stark. 1988. "Religious Economies and Sacred Canopies – Religious Mobilization in American Cities, 1906." *American Sociological Review* 53: 41–49.

Finke, Roger and Rodney Stark. 1992. *The Churching of America, 1776–1990: Winners and Losers in our Religious Economy*. New Brunswick: Rutgers University Press.

Froese, Paul. 2008. *The Plot to Kill God: Findings from the Soviet Experiment in Secularization*. Berkeley: University of California Press.

Froese, Paul and Steven Pfaff. 2005. "Explaining a Religious Anomaly: A Historical Analysis of Secularization in Eastern Germany." *Journal for the Scientific Study of Religion* 44: 397–422.

Funkenstein, Amos. 1986. *Theology and the Scientific Imagination from the Middle Ages to the Seventeenth Century*. Princeton: Princeton University Press.

Gaukroger, Stephen. 2006. *The Emergence of a Scientific Culture: Science and the Shaping of Modernity 1210–1685*. Oxford: Oxford University Press.

Gillespie, Michael Allen. 2008. *The Theological Origins of Modernity*. Chicago: University of Chicago Press.

Gorski, P. 2005. "The Return of the Repressed: Religion and the Political Unconscious of Historical Sociology." In *Remaking Modernity: Politics, History and Sociology*, edited by J. Adams, E. Clemens, and A. S. Orloff. Durham: Duke University Press, 161–188.

Gorski, Philip S. 2000. "Historicizing the Secularization Debate: Church, State, and Society in Late Medieval and Early Modern Europe, ca. 1300–1700." *American Sociological Review* 65: 138–167.

  2011. *The Protestant Ethic Revisited*. Philadelphia: Temple University Press.

  2013. "Bourdieusian Theory and Historical Analysis: Maps, Mechanisms and Methods." In *Bourdieu and Historical Analysis*, edited by P. S. Gorski. Durham: Duke University Press, 327–366.

Gorski, Philip S. and Ateş Altınordu. 2008. "After Secularization?" *Annual Review of Sociology* 34: 55–85.

Gorski, Philip S. and Gülay Türkmen-Dervişoğlu. 2012. "Religion, Nationalism, and International Security: Creation Myths and Social Mechanisms," in *Routledge Handbook of Religion and International Security*, edited by D. Hoover. London: Routledge.

Gregory, Brad S. 2012. *The Unintended Reformation: How a Religious Revolution Secularized Society*. Cambridge: Harvard University Press.

Hefner, Robert W. 1998. "Multiple Modernities: Christianity, Islam, and Hinduism in a Globalizing Age." *Annual Review of Anthropology* 27: 83–104.

D'Holbach, Paul Henri Thiry. 1966. *Systeme de la nature, ou Des lois du monde physique et du mondemoral*. Hildesheim: G. Olms.

Höllinger, Franz. 1996. *Volksreligion und Herrschaftskirche: die Wurzeln religiösen Verhaltens in westlichen Gesellschaften.* Opladen: Leske + Budrich.

Jacobsohn, Gary J. 2003. *The Wheel of Law: India's Secularism in Comparative Constitutional Context.* Princeton: Princeton University Press.

Joas, Hans and Wolfgang Knöbl. 2009. *Social Theory: Twenty Introductory Lectures.* Cambridge, UK; New York: Cambridge University Press.

Kaplan, Benjamin J. 2002. "Fictions of Privacy: House Chapels and the Spatial Accommodation of Religious Dissent in Early Modern Europe." *The American Historical Review* 107: 1031–1064.

2007. *Divided by Faith: Religious Conflict and the Practice of Toleration in Early Modern Europe.* Cambridge, Mass.: Belknap Press of Harvard University Press.

Keyes, Charles F., Laurel Kendall, and Helen Hardacre. 1994. *Asian Visions of Authority: Religion and the Modern States of East and Southeast Asia.* Honolulu: University of Hawaii Press.

Kuru, Ahmet T. 2009. *Secularism and State Policies Toward Religion: The United States, France, and Turkey.* Cambridge University Press.

Kuru, Ahmet T. and Alfred C Stepan. 2012. *Democracy, Islam, and Secularism in Turkey.* New York: Columbia University Press.

Lamont, Michèle and Marcel Fournier. 1992. *Cultivating Differences: Symbolic Boundaries and the Making of Inequality.* Chicago: University of Chicago Press.

Lamont, Michèle and Virag Molnar. 2002. "The Study of Boundaries in the Social Sciences." *Annual Review of Sociology* 28: 167–195.

Lijphart, Arend. 1969. "Consociational Democracy." *World Politics* 21: 207–225.

1996. "The Puzzle of Indian Democracy: A Consociational Interpretation." *American Political Science Review* 5(4): 258–268.

1998. "South African Democracy: Majoritarian or Consociational?" *Democratization* 5: 144–150.

Luckmann, Thomas. 1967. *The Invisible Religion: The Problem of Religion in Modern Society.* New York: Macmillan.

Luhmann, Niklas. 1997. *Die Gesellschaft der Gesellschaft.* Frankfurt am Main: Suhrkamp.

Lustick, Ian. 1979. "Stability in Deeply Divided Societies: Consociationalism Versus Control." *World Politics* 31: 325–344.

Lyotard, Jean François. 1984. *The Postmodern Condition: A Report on Knowledge.* Minneapolis: University of Minnesota Press.

Maclure, Jocelyn and Charles Taylor. 2011. *Secularism and Freedom of Conscience.* Cambridge, MA: Harvard University Press.

MacMullen, Ramsay. 1984. *Christianizing the Roman Empire (AD 100–400):* Yale University Press.

1997. *Christianity and Paganism in the Fourth to Eighth Centuries:* New Haven: Yale University Press.

Mahoney, James and Kathleen Ann Thelen. 2010. *Explaining Institutional Change: Ambiguity, Agency, and Power.* Cambridge; New York: Cambridge University Press.

Martin, David. 1978. *A General Theory of Secularization*. New York: Harper & Row.

Martin, John Levi. 2003. "What Is Field Theory?" *American Journal of Sociology* 109: 1–49.

McLeod, Hugh. 1996. *Religion and Society in England, 1850–1914*. New York: St. Martin's Press.

——— 2000. *Secularisation in Western Europe, 1848–1914*. New York: St. Martin's Press.

——— 2007. *The Religious Crisis of the 1960s*. Oxford; New York: Oxford University Press Inc.

McLeod, Hugh and Werner Ustorf. 2003. *The Decline of Christendom in Western Europe, 1750–2000*. Cambridge, UK; New York: Cambridge University Press.

Milbank, John. 2006. *Theology and Social Theory: Beyond Secular Reason*. Malden, MA: Blackwell Publishing.

Norris, Pippa and Ronald Inglehart. 2004. *Sacred and Secular: Religion and Politics Worldwide*. Cambridge, UK; New York: Cambridge University Press.

Pierson, Paul. 2004. *Politics in Time: History, Institutions, and Social Analysis*. Princeton; Oxford: Princeton University Press.

Placher, William C. 1996. *The Domestication of Transcendence: How Modern Thinking about God Went Wrong*. Louisville: Westminster John Knox Press.

Plantinga, Alvin. 2011. *Where the Conflict Really Lies: Science, Religion and Naturalism*. New York: Oxford University Press.

Putnam, Robert D., David E. Campbell, and Shaylyn Romney Garrett. 2010. *American Grace: How Religion Divides and Unites Us*. New York: Simon & Schuster.

Rosenblum, Nancy L. 2000. *Obligations of Citizenship and Demands of Faith: Religious Accommodation in Pluralist Democracies*. Princeton: Princeton University Press.

Sachsenmaier, Dominic and S. N. Eisenstadt. 2002. "*Reflections on Multiple Modernities European, Chinese, and other Interpretations*." Leiden; Boston: Brill.

Sebastian, Leonard C. 2004. "The Paradox of Indonesian Democracy." *Contemporary Southeast Asia* 26(2): 256–279.

Smith, Christian. 2003a. *The Secular Revolution: Power, Interests, and Conflict in the Secularization of American Public Life*. Berkeley: University of California Press.

——— 2003b. "Secularizing American Higher Education: The Case of Early American Sociology." In *The Secular Revolution*, edited by C. Smith. Berkeley: University of California Press, 97–195.

Smith, Philip. 2001. *Cultural Theory: An Introduction*. Malden: Blackwell.

Stark, R. 1999a. "Secularization, RIP." *Sociology of Religion* 60: 249–273.

Stark, Rodney. 1999b. "Secularization, R.I.P." *Sociology of Religion* 60: 249–273.

Tambiah, Stanley Jeyaraja. 1992. *Buddhism Betrayed?: Religion, Politics, and Violence in Sri Lanka*. Chicago: University of Chicago Press.

Taylor, Charles. 1989. *Sources of the Self: The Making of the Modern Identity*. Cambridge, MA: Harvard University Press.

    2007. *A Secular Age*. Cambridge, MA: Belknap Press of Harvard University Press.

Taylor, Charles and James Heft. 1999. "*A Catholic Modernity? Charles Taylor's Marianist Award Lecture, with Responses by William M. Shea, Rosemary Luling Haughton, George Marsden, Jean Bethke Elshtain*." New York: Oxford University Press.

Toft, Monica Duffy, Daniel Philpott, and Timothy Samuel Shah. 2011. *God's Century: Resurgent Religion and Global Politics*. New York: W.W. Norton & Co.

Tschannen, Olivier. 1991. "The Secularization Paradigm: A Systematization." *Journal for the Scientific Study of Religion* 30: 395–415.

    1992. *Les théories de la sécularisation*. Genève: Droz.

Turner, James. 1985. *Without God, Without Creed: The Origins of Unbelief in America*. Baltimore: Johns Hopkins University Press.

Vidich, Arthur J. and Stanford M. Lyman. 1985. *American Sociology: Worldly Rejections of Religion and their Directions*. New Haven: Yale University Press.

Vovelle, Michel. 2002. *La Révolution contre l'Eglise: de la Raison à l'être suprême*, vol. 130: Brussels: Editions Complexe.

Warner, Michael, Jonathan VanAntwerpen, and Craig J. Calhoun. 2010. *Varieties of Secularism in a Secular Age*. Cambridge, Mass.: Harvard University Press.

Warner, R. S. 1993. "Work in Progress Toward a New Paradigm for the Sociological Study of Religion in the United States." *American Journal of Sociology* 98: 1044–1093.

Wilson, Bryan R. 1982. *Religion in Sociological Perspective*. Oxford; New York: Oxford University Press.

    1985. "Secularization: The Inherited Model." In *The Sacred in a Secular Age*, edited by P. E. Hammond. Berkeley: University of California Press, 9–20.

Yamane, D. 1997. "Secularization on Trial: In Defense of a Neosecularization Paradigm." *Journal for the Scientific Study of Religion* 36: 109–122.

3

The Origins of Secular Public Space: Religion, Education, and Politics in Modern China

Zhe Ji

Concentrating on the emergence of secularity in *A Secular Age* as a contingent process in Latin Christendom did not stop Charles Taylor from recognizing that "secularization and secularity are phenomena which exist today well beyond the boundaries of this [the Latin Christian] world" (Taylor 2007: 21). At the same time, he insisted that, in line with his *cultural* approach to modernity (Taylor 2001), a possible global generalization on secularity could only be expected after studying the relative changes in various civilizational sites, since secularity should therein find different circumstances for its formation and expression. This chapter is an attempt to examine how the early Chinese experience of secularity could contribute to a better understanding of the global extension of secularism. It offers a brief analysis of the contexts, motives, processes, and consequences of the appropriation of Western ideas and institutions by Chinese political and cultural elites. Such analysis allows us to test the relevance of some insights that Taylor (2007) develops in his study of secularity in the Christian West to the Far East.

Taylor's concept of secularity is triplex (2007: 2–3; 20–21): secularity as the differentiation and rationalization of public spaces (Secularity I); secularity as the decline of religious belief and practice (Secularity II); and secularity as new conditions of belief (Secularity III), which in the West are characterized by the rise of exclusive humanism, that is the possibility of not believing in something divine. All three modes of secularity have analogues in the structuring of Chinese modernity. However, this chapter will focus on Secularity I and Secularity III, and how they relate to each other, as they both concern the external situation of religious changes. I argue that the pressure of international challenges and modernist narratives provided China with certain forms of religio-political differentiation, which relates to Secularity I as defined by Taylor, while at the same time stimulating the re-embedding of new forms of religiosity in public spaces. This process was multiple and complex and provoked unintended consequences. Moreover, what the first wave of Chinese secularization (during the late nineteenth century and the first half of the twentieth century) brought out was less a democratic arrangement of the competition of belief and disbelief (Taylor's Secularity III) than the renewal of power relations within the religious field and between the religious and non-religious fields (see Philip Gorski's theoretical analysis in Chapter 2 of this volume) in the context of building a nation-state.

In order to grasp the fundamental characteristics of the emergence and outcomes of secularity in modern China, one must take into account three basic issues around "religion" in the Chinese context, since what is "secular" in a society depends to a large extent on what is perceived as "religious," and vice versa (Duara 2008; van der Veer 2011). The first is the notion of "religion" in traditional China, which constitutes the conceptual preconditions of the expression of Chinese secularity. The second is the concrete institutional condition of the pre-modern lack of differentiation of the religious sphere on the one hand and (what in hindsight we consider) the non-religious spheres on the other. This is particularly crucial for a study of the separation of politics and religion, because the meaning of "separation" as a real socio-legal process is determined by how politics and religions have previously intersected and by the way in which they have preserved and legitimated themselves. The third and last issue revolves around the historical conjuncture of the religious field in the Bourdieusian sense at the moment of the genesis of secularity, which is essential to explain the varieties of modern "conditions of belief" in different countries.

Understanding the purpose and nature of education in imperial China is key to addressing these three issues. Education, or more precisely what was termed *jiao* (教, teaching or instruction) in China, was not only a function of religion or politics, but a way of constituting and thinking about religion and politics. *Jiao* was a meta-concept, signifying the sum of discourses and practices about the transmission of moral values for which education, religion, and politics were basic and concrete forms. In so far as secularity is a new institutional norm in public life, its formation in China means nothing less than the recomposition of *jiao*.

THE TRINITY OF RELIGION, EDUCATION, AND POLITICS
IN TRADITIONAL CHINA

Taylor defines "religion" in terms of "transcendence" (2007: 20), which involves belief in a good higher than human flourishing, in a higher power than secular authority, and a view of life as going beyond "this life." This definition is highly abstract. One can certainly find the concept of transcendence in Chinese religious traditions, for example in the Confucian notion of "Heaven" (*tian* 天), as Taylor has rightly claimed (see Taylor 2007: 50; 152). However, a closer observation of the "social imaginaries" of religion in China shows that Chinese literati did not conceive religion first and foremost in terms of the objects or contents of belief, but rather by the manner in which belief was systematically stimulated, justified, maintained, and transmitted. This is probably why "education/teaching" gained primacy in the Chinese notion of religion. In fact, both religion and education were conceptualized in traditional China by the same term: *jiao*; there is no explicit semantic distinction between them.

The fusion of religion and education in the Chinese language has been noted by James Legge (1815–1897), one of the first Western students of Chinese classics. In the introduction to his translation of collected Taoist texts published in 1891, he reminded readers that the so-called "Three Religions" – Confucianism, Taoism, and Buddhism – actually mean in Chinese "'the Three Teachings' of systems of instruction, leaving the subject-matter of each 'Teaching' to be learned by inquiry" (Legge 1891: 1). In fact, in premodern China there was no Confucianism, Taoism, or Buddhism, but rather the knowledge taught by Confucius and his successors, the perceptions and practices of the Tao, and the instructions given by Buddha.

Such a fusion is also true on the level of social organization in religious and educational domains. On the one hand, none of the Chinese religions had a Christian-style church. Rather, religious communities were organized in loosely structured "schools" (classified in a more detailed way into a series of categories of groupings), perpetuated above all by the continual teaching–learning practice between masters/teachers (*shi* 師) and disciples/students (*tu* 徒). Religious practices and their related rules, from collective rituals to individual meditation, often began with and aimed at "self-cultivation" by cultivating ties with some sacred knowledge, not dissimilar to Taylor's notion of transcendence emerging with Secularity III. Conceived as a kind of education, "religion" in traditional China was an implicit notion; in principle, any master who was capable of offering new teachings might create his own "religion." This is one of the reasons why pluralism, which is considered a new condition of belief in the Christian West, is rather an old story in China, where the "Three Teachings," diverse popular cults, and new religious movements emerged and coexisted side by side. Laypersons could believe in and practice the available religions/teachings in a pluralistic way: they did not have a clear-cut and exclusive religious identity in the Western sense.

On the other hand, both the content and the form of traditional education dealt with religion. Teaching emphasized religious concepts and manners, the mastery of which constituted a demarcation between the barbarian and the civilized, between the masses and the elites in China. Teachers (*shi* 師) as guarantors of moral order were endowed with a sacred status. Since the thirteenth century, the "teacher" has been venerated as one of "the five greatest things in the universe" together with Heaven, Earth, the emperor, and one's parents. Whether related to the teaching of classic texts or the transmission of practical knowledge in domains such as medicine, martial arts, and handcrafts, instruction was often organized around the worship of a holy figure – that is to say, a communal deity or a legendary master.

At the same time, ancient Chinese thinkers, especially Confucian ones, saw politics as a regime of education. Such a notion gave birth to a type of theocracy that justified the consecration of political power by means of educating people. *Liji* – the Confucian classic *The Book of Rites* – repeatedly expresses this idea, stating that a good government should follow the "instructions (*jiao*) of ancient kings" (*xianwang zhijiao* 先王之教) – that is to say, by rooting traditional cosmology and ethics in people's minds and behavior through the proper organization of sacrifices and rituals (*ji* 祭). In another ancient text regarded as a classic both by Confucianism and Taoism, *Yijing* or the *Book of Changes*, this political principle and its efficacy are summarized thus: "the sage-sovereigns establish their instruction (*jiao*) through cults so that all under heaven yield to them." Here, politics is nothing more than the socialization of individuals directed by the state through its regulation of religio-educative matters. In classical Chinese, this kind of governmental practice is called "*jiaohua*" (教化), or "transformation through education-religion." For this reason, *zheng* (政, politics) and *jiao* (教, education-religion) are so often employed together in classical Chinese that their combination has become one word – *zhengjiao* (政教) – which refers to regime or governmentality.

Peng Guangyu (or Pung Kwang Yu 彭光譽, 1844–?), the First Secretary of the Imperial Chinese Legation in Washington DC, expressed this notion perfectly in 1893, when he was invited to speak at the World Religious

Congress in Chicago as the representative of Confucianism: "In China *jiao* is *zheng* and *zheng* is *jiao*. Both *zheng* and *jiao* derive their authority from the Son of Heaven (*tianzi* 天子, emperor). Both instructions (*jiao*) by emperors and instructions by teachers are instructions through and for civility-ritual (*li* 禮)."[1]

In brief, the recipe for Chinese traditional governance consists in forging the political or power order, the moral-knowledge order, and the sacred-mystic order into a single and indivisible order. The pursuit of such an order conforms to the instruction of Dong Zhongshu (董仲舒, 179 BC–104 BC), the most important and successful promoter of Confucianism as the official ideology of the Chinese imperial state: *zheng*/politics is founded on *jiao*/instruction; *Liji* further pointed out that *jiao* is precisely founded on *ji*/sacrifice-ritual. In Taylor's terminology, this order can be described as being concerned with both transcendence and immanence.

It seems that this integral order of politics–education–religion held strong until the nineteenth century. However, from the mid-nineteenth century to the twentieth century, in the course of the genesis of a modern "politics" (*zhengzhi* 政治), the *jiao* as the key link between *zheng* and *ji* broke down. Over several decades, *jiao* divided progressively into "education" (*jiaoyu* 教育) and "religion" (*zongjiao* 宗教) in their modern senses. Such a rupture touched off a series of crucial changes in the relationships between belief, knowledge, and power. Finally, China transformed from a divine Empire into a secular Republican nation-state.[2]

"NEW LEARNING" AND THE BEGINNING OF CHINESE SECULARITY

This revolutionary mutation was one of the consequences of the expansion of the modern world order imposed by the West in the nineteenth century. The old, closed Chinese Empire under Manchu reign was in decline, while the West was at the climax of its first exploitative opening up of the world market through triumphant colonialism and imperialism. The results of the confrontation between China and modern European powers are well-known: a series of cultural shocks, commercial disputes, and diplomatic incidents led to the two Opium Wars in 1839–1860, in which China was humiliated.

---

[1] Peng (1896), cited by Chen Xiyuan (2002: 40–41). Here I translate this passage more literally than its English version of the time.

[2] The following parts of this chapter on the history of modern China are based on my Introduction for Ji (2011).

These defeats caused China to fall into a state of "anomie," which was seen above all as a crisis of education, first by the high officials for the "Foreign Affairs Movement" (*yangwu yundong* 洋務運動), who proposed to strengthen China against the West by adopting Western military technology, and then by "Reformers" (*weixin pai* 維新派), largely belonging to the middle and lower intellectual class, who campaigned for comprehensive social and legal reform. Education mattered to these groups because they felt that China lacked the technological abilities and administrative skills necessary to become a "rich and powerful" (*fuqiang* 富強) nation. Promoted by mandarins and men of letters such as Li Hongzhang (李鴻章, 1823–1901), Rong Hong (容閎, 1828–1912), Feng Guifen (馮桂芬, 1809–1874), Wang Tao (王韜, 1828–1897), and Zheng Guanying (鄭觀應, 1842–1921), education began to be modernized in the 1860s. The process was referred to as the "New Learning" (*xinxue* 新學) that would "save the country" (*jiuguo* 救國).

As the name suggests, the New Learning had new content. On the one hand, it entirely omitted the literary heritage, ethical principles, and ritual knowledge that constituted the core of the traditional official education and focused mainly on modern, Western-style scientific teachings about nature and the human world. Admittedly, the first educational reformers continued to aim to preserve traditional notions – an excellent illustration can be seen in the slogan "Chinese learning for fundamental principles and western learning for practical application" (*zhongti xiyong* 中體西用), proposed by Zhang Zhidong (張之洞, 1837–1909), a famous representative of the Foreign Affairs Movement. But precisely this acknowledgment of the applicability of Western learning in China was in itself new and showed that the need for a system of knowledge independent from the ancient moral code had been recognized. On the other hand, whether educational reformers were aware of it or not, the New Learning was far from neutral in its conception of values. It transmitted a vision of history as evolutionary and a conception of the world as an arena of competition, thereby constituting a demand for the transformation of China and its integration into the international order, which naturally gave moral impetus to the building of a nation-state.

The New Learning not only introduced a new political consciousness to Chinese society. In abolishing the Imperial Examination (*keju* 科舉), it also delivered a deathblow to institutional Confucianism (Gan 2003).

For more than a thousand years, Confucianism had embodied and given structure to the traditional unified order of religion, education, and politics in China. In this structure, Confucian officials and gentry fulfilled the multiple roles of scholar, ethical model, political leader, and expert in ritual; the Imperial Examination was the main mechanism to refill the ranks. Things began to change in 1862 after the Second Opium War, when the Chinese government created China's first modern school, or Tongwenguan (同文館). The new school aimed to train diplomatic staff by teaching foreign languages and subjects such as astronomy, mathematics, chemistry, medicine, mechanics, Western history and geography, and international law. Over the next forty years, more modern schools were established, and they coexisted with the Imperial Examination system. But inasmuch as the Examination continued to largely determine the distribution of political and moral privileges, these new schools struggled to attract social support and qualified pupils. The reformers therefore gradually replaced the Examination system with one based on the New Learning. By 1898, the process of the abolition of the Imperial Examination had begun, cloaked into successive programs of reform. In 1901, the traditional "academies" (*shuyuan* 書院), where candidates for the Imperial Examination were taught, were restructured into a three-tier system resembling Western schools. In 1902, the interpretation of Confucian Classics (the subject of the Examination) was replaced by questions related to a candidate's knowledge of history, politics, science, and technology. Two years later, the promulgation of *The School System of the Year Guimao* (*guimao xuezhi* 癸卯學制) marked the foundation of a modern Chinese education system. It was conceived by the mandarin Zhang Zhidong and based on the model of the Japanese education system introduced after the Meiji reform, outlined by Helen Hardacre in Chapter 5, this volume, on Japan. The design of the modern Chinese system of education provides an example of institutional dissemination par excellence, in that Chinese elites were strongly inspired by the Japanese reforms.

This new institution went further than just including the teaching of Western knowledge: it aimed to set up a unified school system throughout the whole country, providing compulsory education for all. In 1905, after repeated demands from several governors, the Emperor gave orders for the Imperial Examination to be abandoned.

The abolition of the Imperial Examination, which had existed since the early seventh century, drastically reduced the influence of Confucianism in the Chinese political and intellectual fields. From this moment on, a Confucianism deprived of the support of official education was reduced to being recycled under the heading of "philosophy" within the new system of disciplines, and its system of thought was re-expressed in westernized language (Thoraval 2002). It would never again be able to bring together scholars and religious experts under its banner.

In parallel, the nineteenth century Western conception of "religion" was progressively introduced into China, translated first into Japanese and then into Chinese using the Classical Chinese Buddhist term *zongjiao* (originally signifying Buddhist schools and teachings). *Zongjiao* assumed post-Enlightenment criteria for the legitimate form of religion. In contrast to the traditional Chinese concept of *jiao, zongjiao* was understood as a church-like institution distinct from society and politics (Goossaert 2008). Confucianism, deprived of its mechanism for the recruitment of specialized priests, was no longer considered by Chinese political and cultural elites as the perfect embodiment of an institutionalized religion. As a result, religious practices were passed on to popular cults and new religious movements, where they continued to subsist in a fragmented manner (Goossaert 2007).

In brief, the establishment of the New Learning and the abolition of the Imperial Examination undermined the foundations of Confucianism as a state religion and raised questions about its status as a "religion." These developments brought about a Chinese form of Secularity I, which in turn heralded a series of decisive events. In 1908, the Qing government promulgated the *Outline of the Imperial Constitution* (*Qinding xianfa dagang* 欽定憲法大綱) and *Nineteen Fundamental Principles* (*Zhongda xintiao shijiu tiao* 重大信條十九條), officially reducing the importance of Confucian ideology in the state. The Constitution was declared to be above the Emperor, and the state was no longer considered his private property. In 1910, after several years of debate, the *New Penal Code* of the Empire (*Daqing xin xinglü* 大清新刑律) was adopted, indicating at least formally that "law" had supplanted "civility-ritual" as the institutional basis for state intervention in the social order (Gan 2003: 243–264).

From its promulgation in 1912, the Constitution of the Republic of China adopted freedom of belief and the freedom from discrimination on the basis of religion (as well as ethnicity and class) as basic rights. Moreover, the Minister of Education, Cai Yuanpei (蔡元培, 1868–1940), published his program of general educational policy, *On the Orientation and Principles of the New Education*, which rejected certain educational principles of the imperial epoch, because "loyalty towards the Emperor [was] incompatible with the Republican regime, and … the primacy attributed to Confucianism was against the freedom of belief" (Cai 1984a: 136). The Minister ordered primary schools to stop reading the Confucian canon and told teacher-training schools to abandon such training. Although

"Confucianism's primacy" and the "reading of canons" subsequently made several brief comebacks at the regional level, the secularization of political and educational spaces became a norm in Republican Chinese society.

THE "BUILD SCHOOLS WITH TEMPLE PROPERTY" PROJECT AND THE RECOMPOSITION OF PUBLIC SPACE

The introduction of the New Learning not only severed the link between state religion and public education. It also gave rise to the "build schools with temple property" (*miaochan xingxue* 廟產興學) campaign, sending a shockwave through all traditional religions. A modern education system that could mobilize all citizens required a structured, nationwide network of schools, but national investment at the end of the Qing dynasty suffered from serious financial shortcomings. Faced with this challenge, Zhang Zhidong, in his famous 1898 *Exhortation to Study* (Zhang 1998), called for the requisition of 70 percent of the property and real estate of temples and monasteries to finance new schools. Implemented in the early twentieth century, the measure underwent two important phases of development in the 1920s and 1930s. This campaign to "build schools with temple property" inflicted an unprecedented setback on Buddhism, Taoism, and local cults. By transferring the considerable resources of the religious apparatus to political powers and to local lay cultural elites, the campaign destroyed the basis of Chinese popular religion (Goossaert 2006; Goossaert and Palmer 2011: 43–50).

It was not fortuitous that "temple property" was associated with the "building of schools." Superficially, "destroy temples to build schools" perhaps seemed a pragmatic measure, but fundamentally the reconfiguration of public space the program entailed was a requirement for erecting a modern nation-state. The temple property confiscated to build schools, whether it came from "improper cults" (*yinsi* 淫祀) excluded from imperial rituals or from Buddhist or Taoist monasteries, was generally neither "private" (*si* 私) property belonging to individuals or families, nor "official" (*guan* 官) property under government authority. Rather, it was "public" or "communal" (*gong* 公) property managed by the village, clan, or religious community. The expenses for the functioning of these temples and monasteries were met with the profits derived from collectively declared land and donations from followers. These religious apparatuses were the custodians of traditional morals, ethics, and knowledge. They organized day-to-day rituals and festivals and also occasionally took on commercial, medical, philanthropic, and even legal responsibilities.[3] In reality, they were the fabric of traditional public space and provided an elementary social network.

Early Chinese modernists thought it was harmful for public space to be controlled by a religious system. From this point of view, the "build schools with temple property" campaign was a project that seized control of public space under the framework of schools, which would rationalize the socialization process, thereby bonding local society and the modern nation-state. The "public" nature of temples and monasteries gave legitimacy to their requisition in that the New Learning movement had a public vocation. This was indeed the justification given by one of the campaign's principal architects, Zhang Zhidong. He maintained that requisitioning temple property for the development of education was not a repression of religions for purely budgetary reasons, nor was it linked to the power struggle between the different religious forces. Rather, it was for the "public" (*gong* 公) good (Zhang 1998: 9740).

The upheavals and consequences of this campaign influenced different religions to various degrees. Certain local cults were considered "superstitions" (*mixin* 迷信) and impediments to modernization. Coupled with the "anti-superstition" campaign, the "build schools with temple property" campaign had a sustained and severe impact on these cults (Goossaert 2003; Nedostup 2009). In contrast, Buddhism and Taoism, as established traditions, managed to elicit sympathy from the cultural and political elite and, thanks to their more powerful and structured capacity of mobilization, were able to survive these campaigns and even reconstitute themselves as modern-style movements of reaction against this modernization. They actively participated in the creation of schools (initially intended for monks and lay believers, and later for all) in order to legitimately retain control over their monastery property in the new political context. They later started trans-monastic, trans-lineage, and trans-regional associations in a bid to prevent the expropriation of their property by the secular government.

After the establishment of the Republic in 1912, these movements for the defense of monastic property became more organized and emerged as important actors in public life. Their strategies included public relations campaigns through private connections to highly placed officials as well as public protests backed by media coverage, publications, and recourse to

---

[3] On the public functions of Chinese religions and their temples, see Yang (1961, chapter 4); Goossaert (2000); Feuchtwang (2001); Katz (2009); Lagerwey (2010).

courts. Even if negotiation and protest did not always succeed, new concepts such as freedom of belief, nondiscrimination on the basis of religion, and rule of law defined the reorganization of religion. Institutional integration and political acumen became, for certain established religious groups, assets in the struggle to maintain a privileged position in the religious field. For example, confronted with repeated threats of requisition or illegal occupation of monastic property, Buddhism showed a remarkable capacity for national mobilization and political adaptation. This was one reason for the relative increase in Buddhism's influence on Chinese society in the first half of the twentieth century (Ji 2016).

CHRISTIAN SCHOOLS AND THE POLITICAL REGULATION OF RELIGION

Together with the abolition of the Imperial Examination, the "build schools with temple property" campaign not only separated education and religion in modern China, but also led to the emergence of new concepts and new mechanisms in public life and politics. These government acts changed the ground rules and the forms of organization in the religious field. Christian proselytism in China furthered this process.

In order to root themselves more firmly in Chinese society, and in contrast to their predecessors, nineteenth- and twentieth-century Western Christian missionaries expanded their focus from the Emperor and Manchu aristocracy to promoting popular education and charity. By 1860, Catholic and Protestant churches had founded about fifty schools, most of them elementary. Therefore, well before the emergence of New Learning, there already existed on Chinese territory a Western-style education distinct from traditional education. Admittedly, it was marginal for a long time, but the year 1860 marked a turning point. The defeat of the Qing in the Second Opium War concluded with the Treaty of Peking between the Qing government and Great Britain, France, and Russia. The Treaty authorized Western missionaries to purchase and rent land and to build churches in China. This opened the floodgates for the development of missionary activities and Christian education. The defeat also pushed Chinese reformists to carry out their project for the creation of modern schools, which would impart Western teachings. They drew inspiration from the practices and procedures of Christian schools and sought to attract their staff and pupils. This bolstered the legitimacy of the model of education represented by the Christian schools. By 1875, the number of Christian schools had reached 800, with more than

20,000 pupils in attendance. By 1900, there were more than 2,000 schools, with more than 40,000 pupils in total (Gu 1981: 226–228).

Due to the expansion of Christianity in China, the resulting territorial disputes, and the fear of Westernization among certain sections of the local elite, tussles broke out between the Chinese and foreign missionaries, and between believers and non-believers. These were referred to as "conflicts of religion" (*jiao'an* 教案) or "anti-Christian incidents" (Lü 1966; Zhang and Liu 1987). Since these conflicts involved foreigners, the imperial government was placed under considerable diplomatic pressure to resolve the issues.

In this context, the limits placed on Christianity (especially the Roman Catholic Church) by the French state at the beginning of the twentieth century – in particular the 1905 law of Separation of Church and State enacted – attracted considerable attention from the Chinese intellectual elite (Yang 2005). During 1904–1906, French *laïcité* became one of the most discussed subjects in Chinese journals. Liang Qichao (梁啟超, 1873–1929), a famous scholar and reformist at the time, even claimed in an article published in 1906 that the French law of 1905 "looks a small event, but actually it marks an end to world history" (quoted by Yang 2005: 18). For Liang, it was the sign that in Europe, political power had triumphed over religious power, resulting in the acceptance of the superiority of the secular state with regard to religion in public affairs. Liang and some other Chinese intellectuals at the time were encouraged by this turn of events because it provided a possible solution – the restriction of religious institutions, regulation of religion, and the separation of education and religion – to the "conflicts of religion."

Christianity became the foremost target of such attempts to restrict and regulate religious institutions. In 1906, the Qing government issued its first document regulating the running of Christian schools in order "to contain and restrict foreigners so that they do not interfere in politics-education of our country" (Yang 2007). Later, this anti-Christian/anti-Western dimension to the principle of the separation of education and religion was present in the "anti-religious campaign" and the "campaign for the recovery of educational rights (from Christianity)," as well as in the laws and government decrees promulgated in the 1920s on Christian schools.[4]

---

[4] On these campaigns and juridical constructions, see Bastide-Bruguière (2002); Yang and Guo (2010); Yang (2010).

After the 1920s, Christian schools were assimilated into the category of "private schools." In October 1926, the Republican government of Canton promulgated their *Regulations for Private Schools* (*Sili xuexiao guicheng* 私立學校規程), which made it obligatory for private schools to register with and accept control and supervision by the government. The *Regulations* also barred foreigners from occupying the position of Head Teacher. Mandatory religious disciplines, religious propaganda in the classroom, and compulsory attendance of religious ceremonies were forbidden.

During the twenty years following the 1927 establishment of unified Republican power by the Nationalist Party (Kuomintang 國民黨), these restrictions were further tightened to control the creation of new institutions and the content of teaching in such schools. Through these laws, the government educational authority could order the closure of private schools, including those created by foreigners and their churches, for reasons of "bad management" or "infringement of the regulations." Subjects in secondary education began to include "party thought" (*dangyi* 黨義) and "military training" (Zhou and Li 2008). However, these regulations did not slow the development of Christian schools, which continued to flourish during those years. Nevertheless they established a state monopoly of authority over education from a legal point of view, obliging religious institutions to tread a thin line between religious education and Chinese nationalism.

REARTICULATION OF RELIGION, EDUCATION, AND POLITICS

While the separation of religion and education and of religion and politics had been accepted as a founding principle of the modern state by Chinese political and cultural elites and had been reasserted several times by Republican legislation, those spheres can be seen less as opposite elements in a zero-sum game and more as complementary elements able to combine themselves in new forms.

First, while modern education encroached on the territory of religion and traditional education and tended to replace the latter, thereby forming a secular public space in which the state and private life met, this space also offered religion a new possibility to express itself in this transformed society. Since education was defined in the modern state as a major public concern, insofar as religion conformed to a fundamental social consensus, there was no reason to deny it access to the domain of education. Accordingly, as soon as modern educational space took shape, it became a new arena for religious competition.

This, effectively, was the course of events in China. At the beginning of the twentieth century, Chinese religions were strongly involved in secular education, and the promotion of education became a guaranteed method of gaining social recognition. In response to the challenge of the "build schools with temple property" campaign, Buddhism and Taoism not only took more care in the training of monks but also committed themselves in an organized way to the education of the population by creating numerous elementary schools (He 2005; Zuo 2008). According to the official statistics of 1930, out of the forty-three private schools existing in Peking, nineteen were founded by temples or monasteries (Wang 2006). Organizations associated with the popular cults and new movements such as the Red Swastika Society (*Hong wan zi hui* 紅卍字會) included in their program of charitable works aid to give poor people access to education. From its foundation in 1922 until the war against Japan broke out in 1937, the Red Swastika Society created one secondary school and eighty-four elementary schools across the country (Pu 2007). As for Christianity, although a foreign religion, it not only gained the confidence of the population by its actions with respect to elementary schooling, it also forged links with the Chinese cultural elite by its investment in higher education, thereby facilitating the integration of Christianity into Chinese society (Tan 1995; Leung and Ng 2007).

Thereafter, not only could religion, as a social force, gain access to the reorganized educative domain, but modern education gave new resources and momentum to religious change. For example, from the end of the nineteenth century to the first half of the twentieth century, Chinese lay Buddhists such as Yang Wenhui (楊文會, 1837–1911) and Ouyang Jian (歐陽漸, 1871–1943) were the first to introduce to Buddhism the school system and conception of the values of modern education, while placing greater emphasis on the academic aspects of Buddhism and the moral signification of intellectual virtue in Buddhist ethics. Consciously claiming the religious equality of lay believers and monks, they centered their practice on "Buddhology" (*foxue* 佛學), which enabled them to build up a group of lay Buddhists independent of the monastic institution (Ji 2009). Within the Buddhist clerical community, from the 1920s onwards, reformists influenced by the monk Taixu (太虛, 1890–1947) undertook the education of young monks in "institutes for Buddhist Studies" (*foxueyuan* 佛學院).[5] This reform cast off the limits imposed by the monastic

[5] On Buddhist institutes in the first half of the twentieth century, see Welch (1968). According to his statistics (Annex II), from 1912 to 1950, at least 71 Buddhist seminaries, training around 7,500 Buddhists, came into being in China.

framework and gave Buddhism a new institutional guarantee for its perpetuation.

In tandem, the modern state in China monopolized legitimate education and made strengthening political identity a fundamental objective of education. The nationalized model of education together with contemporary discourses on citizenship created a normative effect from which religious educational initiatives, including even the education of monks, were unable to extricate themselves. In 1915, the Beiyang (北洋) government promulgated the *Regulations for the Management of Temples and Monasteries* (*Guanli simiao tiaoli* 管理寺廟條例), which authorized them to found their own schools and encouraged them to impart religious and secular education. In 1920, Article 16 of the revised version of the *Regulations* stipulated that any meeting or conference of Buddhist or Taoist monks should restrict itself to three themes: first, "interpretation and promotion of religious doctrine"; second, "transformation and education of society"; third, "inspiration of patriotic thought."

The new *Regulations* of the National Government published in January 1929 retained this article, replacing "inspiration of patriotic thought" with "inspiration of revolutionary thought to save the country." Furthermore, Article 6 stipulated that schools, libraries, and other educational initiatives of temples and monasteries should necessarily include "party thought" – in other words, the ideology of the party in power, the Kuomintang – in their curriculum, literature, and discourse. As these *Regulations* gave local government a great deal of freedom to dispose of temple and monastery property, they were hotly disputed in Buddhist circles and had to be abrogated less than a year later.[6] However, their publication was in itself evidence of an attempt on the part of the Republican government to politicize religious education.

Of course, the incursion of politics into religious education was not always the consequence of direct state intervention. Indeed, as during the first half of the twentieth century, science, democracy, and nationalism constituted the paradigm of any discourse of legitimization; reformists from all sides attempted to integrate the existence and development of their own tradition in a modernist narrative, to formulate novel "immanent frames" (Taylor), and to reinvent themselves as a resource

---

[6] Cf. Chen (2008). Contested by Buddhists, these *Regulations* were replaced in December 1929 by a new concise version which no longer defined the actual content of education dispensed by religious institutions. This new version of the *Regulations* is still currently effective in Taiwan.

indispensable to the modernization of the political and moral orders of the new China. In this context, Confucians strove to find in their classics a Chinese basis for the rights of the individual and democracy (He 2001; Cheng 2007); Taoists interpreted the ancient practice of "interior alchemy" as a scientific method for strengthening the country (Liu 2009); and Buddhist reformists referred to some essential concepts of Republican politics, like "equality" and "revolution," for the promotion of their "Buddhism for the human realm" (*renjian fojiao* 人間佛教) (He 1998: chapter 3; Li 2002).

THE MODERN CRISES OF EDUCATION AND OF RELIGION

Despite this rearticulation of religion, education, and politics, the former two were also in inevitable tension with the latter. For Chinese people in the nineteenth and twentieth centuries, the nation, insofar as it represented their collective personality in relation to other nations, and particularly the West, constituted a necessary precondition for their entry into a globalizing world. The state was seen as the representative of the nation and, in view of the global expansion of imperialism and colonialism, as the fundamental guarantor of the perpetuation of China. Owing to the paramount importance of nationalist politics, education, and religion – which were also mechanisms for the production of meaning – found themselves facing a crisis of growing relativization of their autonomy and sacredness.

In the first half of the twentieth century, those actors in the educational and religious fields actively participating in the building of the nation-state were aware of this crisis to varying degrees and reacted in different ways. The "educational independence" (*jiaoyu duli* 教育獨立) current of thought, which appeared at the same time as the "save the country through education" (*jiaoyu jiuguo* 教育救國) movement and whose main exponents were Cai Yuanpei, Hu Shi (胡適, 1891–1962), and Fu Sinian (傅斯年, 1896–1950), revealed the delicate relationship between education and politics.[7]

The "independence" here referred to the independence of education from politics. This call for independence was not only a reflection of the divergence between a liberal vision and a nationalist vision of education (education for the perfection of personality versus education for forming the national citizen), but concerned the different conceptions of the respective roles of education, politics, and religion in the rebuilding of moral order. For

---

[7] For a history of the "educative independence" thought, see Jiang (2008).

example, in 1912, Cai Yuanpei made a distinction between two types of education: one "subordinate to politics" and the other "beyond political order." He stated that politics was limited to the "phenomenal world," that it pursued welfare in the present, whereas the fundamental aim of education, like religion, was to go beyond politics to achieve understanding of the "noumenal world." But education, as opposed to religion, which, he suggested, rejects the earthly world, would establish this-worldly experience as the modality of apprehending the noumenal world. For this reason, he proposed to supplement the three types of education (military-citizenship, utilitarian-practical, and moral-civic) linked to the political orders by an aesthetic education and a "worldview" education, which went beyond the boundaries of politics (Cai 1984a: 130–137). Basing himself on the secularization theories of the time, he also suggested replacing religion, which was declining, with aesthetic education (Cai 1984b: 30–34).

Religious movements were not without reservations about the primacy attributed to state building. On this level, even the monk Taixu, who with his Buddhism for the human realm is considered to be the closest among his contemporaries to the Nationalist regime, never renounced his universalist stance and the moral supremacy of religion. Taixu and his disciples maintained that Buddhist cosmology constituted a value-based foundation for a genuine democratic state. They were opposed to radical nationalism and had watered down the xenophobic content of nationalism with the Buddhist concept of "non-self" (*wuwo* 無我), turning it into a non-violent and non-substantive concept (Gong 2003). Liang Shuming (梁漱溟, 1893–1988), the "last Confucian" (Alitte 1986), felt that the way forward for China was not to build up a powerful state but to form a set of "new rites and customs" (*xinlixu* 新禮俗) on which to reconstruct Chinese society. In the 1930s, based on this vision, he tried to promote "popular education" (*pingmin jiaoyu* 平民教育) and "rural construction" (*xiangcun jianshe* 鄉村建設). Liang Shuming's idea was a cultural particularism; because it was founded on the conviction that the renaissance of China depended on an indigenous morality-based society, it took on a nationalist aspect. However, the important point is that this cultural nationalism did not submit moral order to the state and did not entrust politics to take on the responsibility of social reconstruction. Therefore, for Liang Shuming, the relationship between politics and education in a nation-state was inverted: education was not a means to an end for politics, but the end in itself.

It is regrettable that all these initiatives in the educational and religious domains were abandoned and condemned to have only an ephemeral or partial influence. Since the 1930s, the Japanese invasion further strengthened the national consciousness of the Chinese people; nevertheless, wars seriously disrupted the process of state building in China: the promised constitutional reform stagnated; the pressing task to "save the country" marginalized the projects of building a civil society. After the victory of the anti-Japanese war in 1945, China became a frontline in the global confrontation between the Soviet Union and the United States. In 1949, the victory of the Chinese Communist Party (CCP) over the Kuomintang signalled the decisive victory of the Soviet Union in East Asia as well as the dawning of a new era in China. Government policies during the first years of CCP rule could be summarized as the "étatization of society," as they were designed to establish the totalitarian power of the state by destroying the autonomy of any social force (Ji 2008a). In the religious field, only Buddhism, Taoism, Protestantism, Catholicism, and Islam were recognized as legal. Each set up an official national-level, monopoly association or Church whose top positions were occupied by pro-CCP religious figures or even members of the CCP. Non-official religious associations were all wiped out. On the one hand, the state attempted to keep religion under its absolute control by this statist institutionalization; on the other hand, it advocated atheist or anti-religious views so as to deprive all religions of political legitimacy. Taoist and Buddhist activities were denounced as "feudal superstitions" (*fengjian mixin* 封建迷信) and Protestantism and Catholicism were labelled the tools of foreign imperialists. New religious movements were considered the weapons of anti-revolutionaries and repressed harshly. Within a short period, hundreds of thousands of monks and nuns were regrouped, coerced to study the official ideology and participate in manual labor. Millions of religious believers were forced to register with the government and were put under surveillance. In the domain of education, schools set up by religious organisms were confiscated or closed down. Even private schools run by non-religious organisms were abolished. The educational system was reorganized according to the Soviet model, and teachers had to go through several rounds of "thought reform" (*sixiang gaizao* 思想改造, brainwashing). In 1957, after the Anti-rightist Campaign to punish and eliminate intellectuals discontented with the communist rule, the public sphere based upon the freedom of association and expression disappeared completely from China. During the Cultural Revolution (1966–1976), the destructive secularization policy of the CCP reached its most radical phase: even official Churches and associations were forbidden to organize activities; monasteries, temples, and other religious sites were closed, confiscated, or destroyed; religious books were burned; and clerics were forced to resume secular life. Meanwhile, the youth were mobilized to participate in "class struggles." Primary and secondary education was cut down from 12 years to 9 years, and most universities were closed.

It was a miserable time under the shining colors of continual revolution. The communist state successfully penetrated the whole social fabric, from associations, local communities, and families, to personal and private life. It no longer made sense to talk about the distinction between the public and the private in face of an omnipresent state. In this context, the state eliminated all religions in order to establish itself as the single sacred authority and reformed education to continuously reproduce its ideological slaves. During Mao Zedong's twenty-seven-year rule, tens of millions of people died of political persecution or famine caused by political errors, and hundreds of millions of people lost their basic human liberty.

This deplorable situation began to change after the death of Mao in 1976. Since the 1980s, religious activities began to resume. However, it was only after the mid-1990s that religions began to flourish due to the presence of several favorable conditions – the development of the economy, the intensification of the social and cultural exchanges on both domestic and international levels, the relative liberation of the private sphere, and the limited restoration of the public sphere. However, state control of religions is still tight. One can even say that the fundamental system set up in the 1950s has remained in place over the recent three decades: the state still controls the official monopoly on Churches and associations, restrains the development of popular cults and new religious movements, and maintains its authority in distinguishing between religion, superstition, and sect. Even though there is a scope for negotiations and collaborations between certain religious groups and the post-Mao authoritarian state when religions are "useful" in a limited realm, ranging from tourism to nationalism, the state can repress any religious group considered to endanger its "stability" (Koesel 2014; Laliberté 2015; Ji 2015). Education is now open to private investment due to its commercialization, but in principle religious organizations are forbidden to enter this market.

In order to evade the constraints imposed by the state and ideological conflicts with the officially atheist CCP, many religious movements and phenomena have taken a non-religious form in contemporary China. For example, until the repression of the Falun Gong following its protest before the central government in 1999, many *qigong* (气功) movements, despite their religious features, were very popular in China and presented themselves as self-therapy skills or "somatic science" (Palmer 2007). Today many popular cults, originally considered superstitions, have been re-established in the name of protecting cultural heritage and local folk culture. They are even supported sometimes by local governments in order to promote tourism. In such a context, the phenomena related to "traditional culture" (*chuantong wenhua* 傳統文化) are worth noting. This category binds together religion and education and, under this banner, comprises transversal projects of social reconstruction, placing its hope of a moral revitalization in the study of classic canons, traditionalist aesthetic tastes, ritual practices, and family ethics (Ji 2008b; Dutournier and Ji 2009; Billioud and Thoraval 2015).

The most remarkable example of this process was the "children's classics reading movement," initiated in the middle of the 1990s by the Taiwanese Wang Caigui (王財貴), which later spread throughout mainland China. This movement not only led to the re-emergence of teaching in the style of "family schools" (*sishu* 私塾) outside of the official system, thereby paving the way for Confucianism to recapture society, but also cast doubt on the need for the state monopoly on education (Dutournier 2011). This movement, together with certain other phenomena linked to the renaissance of "traditional culture," has been the subject of heated debates on cultural conservatism and nationalism, as well as on the relationship between China and the West. This phenomenon demonstrates yet again that, where religion, education, and politics are concerned, the questions of how to deploy and limit these three axes, of what dimension and specific signification to attribute to them, and, above all, of how to interweave them, will continue to be pivotal in the reconstruction of the public in China, even in the twenty-first century.

CONCLUSIONS

By means of a cursory historical retrospective, this chapter has tried to show how historical conjuncture, cultural tradition, and the strategies adopted by social groups determined together the beginning and development of a secularity in modern China. Faced with the impact of Western forces, Chinese political and cultural elites had to renew state ideology and government practices, paving the way for the emergence of modern education imbued with secular rationality and nationalism. The education reforms from the 1860s to 1905s broke the trinity of politics–education–religion and set off an institutional and functional differentiation, thereby becoming the first motor of the secularization of public space. This recomposition of religion, education, and politics was far from a steady, balanced process. Its impact varied from religion to religion according to their relations with the political authorities, their relative position in the religious field, and their capacity to adapt to new circumstances. If politics, education, and religion had re-intersected one another around the redefined public good, they were at the same time competing for primacy in the building of the moral order.

If we study the relationship between religion and politics and the modern evolution of the religious field in China in light of Gorski's theoretical framework developed from the theories of Luhmann and Bourdieu, modern Chinese secularity presents two models of differentiation: stratificatory and center–periphery. Even though the Republican period (1912–1949) witnessed the separation of politics and religion, these two spheres were never of equal status. Religion was consistently subordinated to nation-state building, the major goal of modernization. This constitutes the foundation of a system in which "politics leads, religion follows" (*zhengzhu jiaocong* 政主教從), a system that is still in effect today in China and seen by some scholars as distinctively Chinese (Zhuo 2008). On the other hand, even though it had never been completely colonized by the West, China accepted the superiority of the West in modernization. Hence, even though Christianity never dominated China, both the Nationalist and the Communist governments took it as the only standard religious model for reforming China's traditional religions, and both regarded secularism as the only reasonable principle for structuring the relationship between politics and religion. This is actually the reflection of the center–periphery relationship between the West and China in the relationship between politics and religion in China. The structure of "politics leads, religion follows" and the acceptance of the Western category of religion – these two factors have also transformed the configuration of the Chinese religious field. Chinese religious traditions, movements, and groups are divided into a set of dichotomies: the religious and the non-religious (e.g. Confucianism), religion and superstition (e.g. some popular cults), religion and sects or heresies (from reactionary secret societies to Falun Gong), each endowed with its political legitimacy or illegitimacy.

Last but not least, it should be pointed out that one cannot, starting from the standpoint of cultural particularism, interpret Chinese secularization as an incommensurable experience. Nothing strange, if some motifs in this story – such as the anti-superstition campaign, reform discourses, and nation-building projects – seem similar to what we can find during the formation of secularity both in the West and in other non-Western countries. In fact, modernity, of which secularity is an essential feature, has become a global issue. Western modernities and non-Western modernities involve deeply interrelated stories, even if they cannot be unified in a single history. From this point of view, Taylor's monumental study of Western secularity lays a foundation and offers a fruitful point of departure even for the study of non-Western secularities. For the same reason, the study of non-Western secularities is not only necessary for a better self-understanding of the modern changes of the non-West, but also potentially helpful for a better understanding of the modern West. In this context, the Chinese case reminds us that education is a crucial issue of secularity, since, in the final analysis, a question raised by secularity is above all about how a person should be politically educated, and how politics should be morally organized under modern conditions.

Bibliography

Alitte, Guy S. 1986. *The last Confucian: Liang Shu-ming and the Chinese Dilemma of Modernity*. Berkeley: University of California Press.

Bastid-Bruguière, Marianne. 2002. "La campagne antireligieuse de 1922," in Vincent Gossaert (ed.), *L'anticléricalisme en Chine (Extrême-Orient, Extrême-Occident 24)*. Saint-Denis: Presses Universitaires de Vincennes, no. 24, 77–93.

Billioud, Sébastien and Joël Thoraval. 2015. *The Sage and the People: The Confucian Revival in China*. Oxford: Oxford University Press.

Cai, Yuanpei 蔡元培. 1984a. "Duiyu xinjiaoyu zhi yijian" 對於新教育之意見, in Gao, Pingshu 高平叔 (comp.), *Cai Yuanpei quanji* 蔡元培全集, Beijing, Zhonghua shuju, vol. 2, 130–137.

———1984b. "Yi meiyu dai zongjiao shuo" 以美育代宗教說, in Gao, Pingshu 高平叔 (comp.), *Cai Yuanpei quanji* 蔡元培全集, Beijing, Zhonghua shuju, vol. 3: 30–34.

Chen, Jinlong 陳金龍. 2008. "Minguo *Simiao guanli tiaoli* de banbu yu feizhi" 民國《寺廟管理條例》的頒布與廢止, *Fayin* 法音, no. 4: 54–59.

Chen, Xiyuan 陳熙遠. 2002. "'Zongjiao': yige Zhongguo jindai wenhuashi shang de guanjianci," "宗教"——一個中國近代文化史上的關鍵詞, *Xin shixue* 新史學, tome 13, no. 4: 37–66.

Cheng, Anne. 2007. "Des germes de démocratie dans la tradition confucéenne?," in Mireille Delmas-Marty and Pierre-Étienne Will (eds.), *La Chine et la démocratie*. Paris: Fayard, 83–107.

Duara, Prasenjit. 2008. "Religion and Citizenship in China and the Diaspora," in Mayfair Mei-hui Yang (ed.), *Chinese Religiosities: Afflictions of Modernity and State Formation*. Berkeley: University of California Press, 43–64.

Dutournier, Guillaume. 2011. "Les 'écoles familiales' en Chine et à Taiwan: triple regard sur un traditionalisme éducatif," in Ji, Zhe (ed.), *Religion, éducation et politique en Chine moderne (Extrême-Orient Extrême-Occident 33)*. Saint-Denis: Presses universitaires de Vincennes, 171–208.

Dutournier, Guillaume and Ji, Zhe. 2009. "Expérimentation sociale et 'confucianisme populaire': le cas du Centre d'éducation culturelle de Lujiang," *Perspectives chinoises*, 4: 71–86.

Feuchtwang, Stephan. 2001. *Popular Religion in China. The Imperial Metaphor*, Surrey: Curzon.

Gan, Chunsong 干春松. 2003. *Zhiduhua rujia jiqi jieti* 制度化儒家及其解體, Beijing, Zhongguo renmin daxue chubanshe.

Gong, Jun 龔雋. 2003. "Tiaoshi yu fankang: yi jindai dongya fojiao chuantong yu zhengzhi guanxi zhong de liangge anli wei zhongxin" 調適與反抗——以近代東亞佛教傳統與政治關系中的兩個案例為中心, *Renjian fojiao, xinhuo xiangchuan: di si jie Yinshun daoshi sixiang zhi lilun yu shijian xueshu yantaohui lunwen ji* 人間佛教, 薪火相傳——第四屆印順導師思想之理論與實踐學術研討會論文集, Taoyuan: Hongshi foxueyuan, text online: www.awker.com/hongshi/special/arts/4art9.htm

Goossaert, Vincent. 2000. *Dans les temples de la Chine. Rites populaires et religion savante*. Paris: Albin Michel.

——— 2003. "Le destin de la religion chinoise au XXᵉ siècle," *Social Compass*, 50 (4): 429–440.

——— 2006. "1898: The Beginning of the End for Chinese Religion?," *The Journal of Asian Studies*, 65 (2): 307–336.

——— 2007. "Les mutations de la religion confucianiste (1898–1937)," in Flora Blanchon and Ran-Ri Park-Barjot (dir.), *Le Nouvel Âge de Confucius. Modern Confucianism in China and South Korea*. Paris: PUPS: 163–172.

——— 2008. "Republican Church Engineering: The National Religious Associations in 1912 China," in Mayfair Mei-hui Yang (ed.), *Chinese Religiosities: Afflictions of Modernity and State Formation*. Berkeley: University of California Press, 209–232.

Goossaert, Vincent and David Palmer. 2011. *The Religious Question in Modern China*. Chicago and London: University of Chicago Press.

Gu, Changsheng 顧長聲. 1981. *Chuanjiaoshi yu jindai Zhongguo* 傳教士與近代中國, Shanghai, Shanghai renmin chubanshe.

He, Jianming 何建明. 1998. *Fofa guannian de jindai tiaoshi* 佛法觀念的近代調適, Guangzhou, Guangdong renmin chubanshe.

He, Jinlin 賀金林. 2005. "Qingmo seng jiaoyu hui yu siyuan xingxue de xingqi" 清末僧教育會與寺院興學的興起, *Anhui shixue* 安徽史學, no. 6: 28–34.

He, Xinquan 何信權. 2001. *Ruxue yu xiandai minzhu* 儒學與現代民主, Beijing, Zhongguo shehui kexue chubanshe.

Ji, Zhe 汲喆. 2008a. "Secularization as Religious Restructuring: Statist Institutionalization of Chinese Buddhism and Its Paradoxes," in Mayfair Mei-hui Yang (ed.), *Chinese Religiosities: Afflictions of Modernity and State Formation*. Berkeley: University of California Press, 233–260.

——— 2008b. "Eduquer par la musique. De l'Initiation des enfants à la musique classique' à la 'culture de soi' confucéenne des étudiants," *Perspectives chinoises*, no. 3: 118–129.

——— 2009. "Jushi fojiao yu xiandai jiaoyu" 居士佛教與現代教育, *Beijing daxue jiaoyu pinglun* 北京大學教育評論, 7(3): 39–62.

(ed.). 2011. *Religion, éducation et politique en Chine moderne (Extrême-Orient Extrême-Occident 33)*. Saint-Denis: Presses universitaires de Vincennes.

2015. "Secularization without Secularism: The Political-Religious Configuration of Post-89 China," in Tam Ngo and Justine Quijada (eds.), *Atheist Secularism and its Discontents. A Comparative Study of Religion and Communism in Eurasia*. Basingstoke: Palgrave Macmillan, 92–111.

2016. "Buddhist Institutional Innovations," in Vincent Goossaert, Jan Kiely, and John Lagerwey (eds.), *Modern Chinese Religion II: 1850–2015*. Leiden: Brill, 731–766.

Jiang, Chaohui 姜朝暉. 2008. *Minguo shiqi jiaoyu duli sichao yanjiu* 民國時期教育獨立思潮研究, Beijing, Zhongguo shehui kexue chubanshe.

Katz, R. Paul. 2009. *Divine Justice: Religion and the Development of Chinese Legal Culture*. London/New York: Routledge/Taylor and Francis Group.

Koesel, Karrie J. 2014. *Religion and Authoritarianism: Cooperation, Conflict, and the Consequences*. Cambridge: Cambridge University Press.

Lagerwey, John. 2010. *China: A Religious State*. Hong Kong: Hong Kong University Press.

Laliberté, André. 2015. "The Politicization of Religion by the CCP: A Selective Retrieval," *Asiatische studien/Etudes asiatiques*, vol. 69, no. 1: 185–211.

Legge, James (ed. and trans.). 1891. *The Textes of Tâoism* (Sacred Books of the East series, vol. 39). Oxford.

Leung, Philip, Yuen Sang, and Peter Tze Ming Ng (eds.). 2007. *Christian Responses to Asian Challenges: A Glocalization View on Christian Higher Education in East Asia*. Hong Kong: Centre for the Study of Religion and Chinese Society, Chung Chi College, CUHK.

Li, Xiangping 李向平. 2002. "Ershi shiji Zhongguo fojiao de 'geming zouxiang': jianlun 'renjian fojiao' sichao de xiandaixing wenti," 二十世紀中國佛教的 "革命走向" —— 兼論 "人間佛教" 思潮的現代性問題, *Shijie zongjiao yanjiu* 世界宗教研究, no. 3: 42–56.

Liu, Xun. 2009. *Daoist Modern: Innovation, Lay Practice and the Community of Inner Alchemy in Republican Shanghai*. Cambridge: Harvard University Asian Center/HUP.

Lü, Shiqiang 呂實強. 1966. *Zhongguo guanshen fanjiao de yuanyin 1860–1874* 中國官紳反教的原因1860–1874, Taipei, Zhongyang yanjiuyuan jindaishi yanjiusuo.

Nedostup, Rebecca. 2009. *Superstitious Regimes: Religion and the Politics of Chinese Modernity*. Cambridge and London: Harvard University Asia Center.

Palmer, David A. 2007, *Qigong fever: Body, Science and Utopia in China*. New York: Columbia University Press.

Pu, Wenqi 濮文起. 2007. "Minguo shiqi de shijie hong wan zi hui" 民國時期的世界紅卍字會, *Guizhou daxue xuebao (shehui kexue ban)* 貴州大學學報(社會科學版), no. 2: 89–96.

Tan, Shuangquan 譚雙泉. 1995. *Jiaohui daxue zai jindai Zhongguo* 教會大學在近現代中國, Changsha: Hunan jiaoyu chubanshe.

Taylor, Charles. 2001. "Two Theories of Modernity," in Gaonkar Parameshwar (ed.), *Alternative Modernities*. Durham: Duke University Press: 172–196.

2007. *A Secular Age*. Cambridge, MA: The Belknap Press of Harvard University Press.

Thoraval, Joël. 2002. "Expérience confucéenne et discours philosophique. Réflexions sur quelques apories du néo-confucianisme contemporain," *Perspectives chinoises*, 71: 64–83.

van der Veer, Peter. 2011. "Smash Temples, Burn Books: Comparing Secularist Projects in India and China," in Craig Calhoun, Mark Juergensmeyer, and Jonathan Van Antwerpen (eds.), *Rethinking Secularism*. New York: Oxford University Press, 270–281.

Wang, Wei 王煒. 2006. "Minguo shiqi beijing miaochan xingxue fengchao: yi Tieshan si weili" 民國時期北京廟產興學風潮——以鐵山寺為例, *Beijing shehui kexue* 北京社會科學, no. 4: 61–66.

Welch, Holmes. 1968. *The Buddhist Revival in China*. Cambridge, MA: Harvard University Press.

Yang, C. K. 1961. *Religion in Chinese Society. A Study of Contemporary Social Functions of Religion and Some of Their Historical Factors*, Berkeley and Los Angeles: University of California Press.

Yang, Sixin 楊思信. 2005. "'Jiaoyu he zongjiao fenli' sixiang shuru jiqi dui Zhongguo jiaoyu de yingxiang" "教育和宗教分離"思想輸入及其對中國教育的影響, *Jiaoyushi yanjiu* 教育史研究, no. 4: 16–21.

2007. "Shilun wanqing minchu zhengfu jiaohui xuexiao zhengce de yanbian" 試論晚清民初政府教會學校政策的演變, *Liaocheng daxue xuebao* 聊城大學學報, no. 6: 92–97.

2010. "Minguo zhengfu jiaohui xuexiao guanli zhengce yanbian shulun" 民國政府教會學校管理政策演變述論, *Shijie zongjiao yanjiu* 世界宗教研究, no. 5: 118–128.

Yang, Sixin 楊思信 and Guo, Shulan 郭淑蘭. 2010. *Jiaoyu yu guoquan: 1920 niandai Zhongguo shouhui jiaoyuquan yundong yanjiu* 教育與國權: 1920年代中國收回教育權運動研究, Beijing, Guangming ribao chubanshe.

Zhang, Li 張力 and Liu, Jiantang 劉鑒唐. 1987. *Zhongguo jiao'an shi* 中國教案史, Chengdu, Sichuan sheng shehui kexue yuan chubanshe.

Zhang, Zhidong 張之洞. 1998. "Quanxue pian" 勸學篇, in Yuan Shuyi 苑書義, Sun Huafeng 孫華峰 and Li Bingxin 李秉新 (comp.), *Zhang Zhidong quanji* 張之洞全集, Shijiazhuang, Hebei renmin chubanshe, vol. 12: 9703–9770.

Zhou, Nan 周楠 and Li, Yongfang 李永芳. 2008, "Minguo shiqi sili gaodeng xuexiao shulun" 民國時期私立高等學校述論, *Anhui daxue xuebao (zhexue shehui kexue ban)* 安徽大學學報(哲學社會科學版), 32(3): 114–119.

Zhuo, Xinping 卓新平. 2008, *Quanqiuhua de zongjiqo yu dangdai Zhonghuo* 全球化的宗教與當代中國, Beijing, Shehui kexue wenxian chubanshe.

Zuo, Songtao 左松濤. 2008, "Jindai Zhongguo fojiao xingxue zhi yuanqi" 近代中國佛教興學之緣起, *Fayin* 法音, no. 2: 34–38.

4

The Formation of Secularism in Japan

Helen Hardacre

INTRODUCTION

This chapter represents an attempt to understand the early history of secularism in Japan in the light of Charles Taylor's *A Secular Age*. Following a skeletal reprise of those elements of Taylor's work that seem most relevant, it attempts to recast well-known aspects of modern Japanese history and religion in the light of Taylor's account. The chapter closes with an assessment of the attempt to extend Taylor's characterization of secularism to Japan.

The Secularizing Discourse of the Early Meiji Period in Taylorian Perspective

Taylor's complex portrayal of the secular contains many strands of evidence and argument at different levels, ranging from individual "dilemmas" and "cross-pressures" and the transformations of elite thought to broad social change. Among these, the perspective that seems most closely to match the changes through which Japan became a secular society is Taylor's presentation of secularism as a project of elites.[1] He develops this characterization in stages, beginning with his discussion of "the

The author benefited greatly from many stimulating discussions with the members of *Religion 1097: Secularism Beyond the West* (Harvard University, 2011): Gregory Clines, Adam Lyons, Michael Lesley, Seth Robinson, Claire Tyree, Alyssa Yamamoto, Seiji Hoshino, and Hideaki Kurita; and also with Albert Craig and Jason Josephson.
[1] This perspective on secularism is one of several stances seen in current scholarship; for a study laying out the options with extensive references, see Gorski and Atlnordu (2008: 55–85, especially p. 74).

disciplinary society" (Taylor 2007: chapter 2). By around 1800, he writes, European elites came to regard a "civilized" country as one that curtailed disorder (which they identified with sin) by restricting carnival and other aspects of popular religion, confining the insane, and, in a more positive mode, educating the masses in rationality, self-discipline, and self-control. These elite interventions depended on a prior assumption of the malleability of human nature and on elites' confidence that they could mold the masses in imitation of civilizing ideals. Taylor asserts that elites absorbed buttressing ideas from Deism: namely, that "human flourishing" is the highest purpose of Divine Providence; that reason is sufficient to discern the order of existence; a denial of miracles; and the idea that the universe operates according to impersonal rules (Taylor 2007: 222–224). Temporal frames of reference changed, so that the image emerged of societies evolving through stages, based on ideas of the Scottish Enlightenment. Naturally, European society was characterized as "civilized," while the rest of the world occupied less developed stages (Taylor 2007: 289–292). At an individual level, these changes brought elites an "ethic of freedom," "disengaged reason," and a "sense of invulnerability" (Taylor 2007: 300). Taylor holds that secularization originated in the changed conditions of belief that characterize this disciplined, rational order (Taylor 2007: 295). He emphasizes repeatedly that this complex process cannot be reduced to a "subtraction theory," according to which in modernity humanity attains to rationality by shedding religious beliefs (see for example pp. 22–29, passim; 157, 169, 245, 253, 270, 294, 530–531, 573–579).

The idea of secularism as an elite project emerges even more sharply in the works of Talal Asad (2003: 205–256) and his interpreters. For example, summarizing Asad's work, Partha Chatterjee's (2006: 60) characterization accurately expresses what unfolded in Japan:

In all countries and in every historical period, secularization has been a coercive process in which the legal powers of the state, the disciplinary powers of family and school, and the persuasive powers of government and media have been used to produce the secular citizen who agrees to keep religion in the private domain.

Japan's first encounter with secularism was inseparable from mid-nineteenth century Western imperialism. The Japanese were acutely aware of China's degradation and defeat in the Opium Wars, and they saw clearly that if they failed to strengthen Japan, Western powers would colonize it. Determination to prevent colonization was a powerful force in the Meiji Restoration of 1868, a revolution that overthrew the Tokugawa shogunate and brought to power a small group of oligarchs from Western Japan. The new government struggled to fortify and modernize the country within restrictive, unequal treaties.

Western powers pressured Japan to Westernize in order to be considered "civilized," making this transformation a condition for revision of trade treaties that disadvantaged Japan through extraterritoriality provisions, onerous tariffs, and other diplomatic humiliations. National pride was stung by clichés about the savagery of "Orientals," deployed to justify shielding foreigners from the Japanese legal system. The tariffs burdened the new government and prevented it from protecting nascent Japanese industries. Nothing less than Japan's independence was at stake. In an effort to escape this semi-colonial subjugation, Japan complied as fast as possible with Western demands for reform, ushering in a massive campaign of Westernization. Educating the people and creating a modern military were the first orders of business. The Ministry of Education was established in 1871, inaugurating a program of compulsory education following American and French models. Conscription was instituted in 1873. In that same year a debate arose in the government over a plan to invade Korea. While the proponents were eventually defeated, it was widely assumed that Japan should acquire colonies of its own, along the lines of the Western empires.

As Japan entered treaty relations with Western powers, it was necessary to find a Japanese term for "religion."[2] The word eventually appropriated was *shūkyō*, meaning, literally the "teachings" (*kyō*) of a "sect" (*shū*). This word had been used previously in technical Buddhist writings, but it was not part of the vernacular. Several pre-modern terms expressed the idea of faith or designated groups practicing different styles of worship, but pre-Meiji Japan did not conceive of religion as a general phenomenon, of which there are local variants such as Buddhism, Judaism, Christianity, etc.[3] *Shūkyō* pointed toward a propositional definition of religion. It did not immediately become part of the vernacular following its use in treaties, but such early Westernizers as Fukuzawa Yukichi and members of the Meiroku Society used it (Norihisa 1979: 13–17).

---

[2] Japan's treaty partners sought freedom for Christian missionaries to proselytize in Japan, and such provisions had to be translated into Japanese.

[3] The shift to the perspective of "world religions" had yet to emerge; see Masuzawa Tomoko (2005).

Japanese Secular Thought

By the mid-1870s, a vigorous debate on "civilization and enlightenment" (*bunmei kaika*) in the new Japan was underway, producing a discourse of secularism. Promotion of secular thought under Western influence and pressure is an aspect of Japan's experience that has no parallel in Western history (obviously) or in Taylor's narrative. Partha Chatterjee's (2006: 62) remarks on the circumstances governing the appearance of secularism in Asia are highly instructive:

[S]ecularization is necessarily a normative project formulated and directed by a small elite minority. The historical challenge before this elite is to steer the project by using the coercive legal powers of the state as well as the processes of reform of religious doctrine and practice – all within a global context where power must be legitimized by a large measure of popular consent. This is a task that is unprecedented in Western history.

We will examine the thought of Fukuzawa Yukichi (1834–1901), widely regarded as "*the* central figure in Japanese thought during the second half of the nineteenth century," the person more responsible than any other for providing the "intellectual impetus" for Japan's modernization.[4] Fukuzawa was well read in the Scottish Enlightenment thinkers, and had thoroughly absorbed their stadial theory of civilization (Craig 2009: 11–32). Fukuzawa's goal as a writer, journalist, translator of Western texts, exponent of Western ways, and later as educator and founder of Japan's first private university, was "to create in Japan a civilized nation as well equipped in the arts of war and peace as those of the Western world" (Craig 1992: 214).

Fukuzawa and the rest of the intellectual elite of the early Meiji period (1868–1912) began life as members of the samurai class at the end of the preceding Tokugawa period (1600–1868). They were educated in the Confucian classics and trained to remain aloof from "superstition." Because of a national policy requiring everyone to be a parishioner of a Buddhist temple, elites supported Buddhist ancestral rites, and were buried or cremated by Buddhist ceremony. They did not usually, however, admire Buddhism. Their Confucian teachers regarded Buddhism as otherworldly and its clergy as corrupt. Elites criticized Buddhism as irrational and overly concerned with the afterlife. Those in authority regarded

---

[4] These characterizations are widely accepted among historians of Japan, expressed here by Fukuzawa's biographer Albert Craig (1992, 2009). Fukuzawa's *An Outline of Civilization* (1875, Bunmeiron no gairyaku) is believed to have sold several tens of thousands of copies. Meanwhile, his *Conditions in the West* (Seiyō jijō), first series 1866, is said to have sold more than 250,000 copies.

Buddhism as they regarded religion generally: useful for regulating the populace, but unsuitable as a philosophy for themselves.[5] Thus, in the transition to the Meiji period, elites did not pass through anything analogous to Taylor's turn to Deism. Their Confucian background was sufficient to provide a humanist, mostly atheist, this-worldly mindset.

The early Meiji elite had educated themselves in Western languages, history, philosophy, and culture, often including intense study of Dutch and then English when they were young men before the Restoration, and later through periods of foreign travel and study. They regarded education as essential to maintaining Japan's independence from predatory Western imperialism. Many of them entered the new government[6] and encouraged Westernization of society. In 1871, the government commanded all men to cut off their topknots, making Western haircuts the norm. All male civil servants were to wear Western attire, and students soon adopted Western-style uniforms. Women's fashions shifted to Western style more slowly, beginning with parasols, shawls, and other accessories. The Rokumeikan, or Deer Cry Pavilion, a hall in central Tokyo adjacent to the imperial palace, became an emblematic site for these sartorial reforms. Prominent members of Japanese government and elite society met with Westerners at the Rokumeikan to display their mastery of English and such Western conventions as ballroom dancing and public mixing of the sexes. The aristocracy adopted Western formal dress for the Rokumeikan balls, which were frequently pictured in woodblock prints. These changes in dress, deportment, and styles of social interaction undoubtedly produced many stresses that Taylor (Taylor 2007: chapters 16–18) might describe as "dilemmas" and "cross-pressures." Cartoonists had great fun parodying the elite as it enacted Western ways.[7] The great divide between the modernizing elite and the mass of the rural peasantry; the ironies of life among an elite that knew more about Western thought and society than about Japan's own intellectual history; the mixture of hubris, arrogance,

---

[5] Nevertheless, Fukuzawa insisted on continuing the tradition of periodic Buddhist memorial rites for parents and friends as an important obligation even after the Restoration, and he claimed that he refused to associate with people who neglected this duty; see Koizumi Takashi (2011). An older, English-language essay by Koizumi (1994) contains much of the same material.

[6] Fukuzawa, however, remained aloof from government.

[7] Kawanabe Kyōsai (1831–1889), a woodblock-print artist and painter, turned caricaturist in the Meiji period. He parodied the pretensions of the Westernizing elite by portraying them as pipe-smoking monsters in top hats or as monster school teachers drilling monster pupils on the alphabet.

and vanity among the bureaucracy – all these elements provided rich subjects for Japanese writers.[8]

A perennial optimist, Fukuzawa believed that Japan could become a rational, ethical society based on science, the spirit of independence, and education. He did not regard religion as essential to Western civilization or to Japan's attainment of civilization, yet he wrote more than eighty essays on religion (Craig 2009: 103; Koizumi 1994: 109).[9] In one piece particularly notable for its utilitarian pragmatism, he wrote that Japan should conform to Western ways in religion and permit the practice of Christianity, if only to escape being ostracized by Western nations.[10] He was not, however, an advocate of Christianity; he compared the medieval Japanese Buddhist saint Shinran (1173–1262) favorably to Luther, noting that while Shinran had preached universal salvation, rejected killing, and inspired his sect to massive growth, Luther was responsible for a century of bloody religious wars (Craig 2009: 109). Despite admiring Shinran, however, Fukuzawa tended to disparage Japanese popular religious life and to regard it as based on ignorance: "[A lack of rational thinking] gave rise to [the Japanese people's belief] that demons and gods exist. They named the causes of calamities 'evil gods' ... and of nature's blessings, 'good gods' ... In Japan, the myriad gods of Shinto... were just such beings" (Craig 2009: 122). For Fukuzawa and other Meiji elites, loyalty to

---

[8] See, for example, Nagai Kafū's short story concerning a young newly appointed prefectual governor and his wife that involves their overwhelming joy in attending a Rokumeikan ball, called "Shinnin chiji." The story emphasizes the pathos of the characters' ambition and vanity and ends with their deaths from tuberculosis; See Nagai Kafū, Shinnin chiji, in *Kafū zenshū*. 29 vols. Tokyo: Iwanami shoten, vol. 2: 173–224.

[9] Fukuzawa's attitude to Christianity in particular and religion in general was contradictory and evolved over his lifetime. As a young man, he expressed the loathing of Christianity that was typical of the elite at the end of the Tokugawa period. According to Koizumi Takashi, however, in lessons he set for his sons in 1871, he wrote that God (which he transliterated as *goddo*) determines the events of life, and that God must be obeyed (Koizumi, 2011: 7–8). In other contexts, such as his *An Encouragement of Learning* (1872–1876, *Gakumon no susume*) he referred to "Heaven," as in this famous passage that begins the work: "It is said that heaven does not create one man above or below another man. This means that when men are born from heaven they are all equal." [David A. Dilworth, translator, with Umeyo Hirano, Sophia University Press, 1969: 1.] In his translation of Western texts, Fukuzawa sometimes used "Heaven" as a translation for "God." Fukuzawa had a number of friends and acquaintances among Christian missionaries, and after his son Ichitarō expressed the desire to be baptized in 1884, Fukuzawa's attitude toward Christianity softened considerably, and he retracted his former opposition to the propagation of Christianity in Japan.

[10] Shūkyō mo mata seiyōfū ni shitagawazaru o ezu (1883). *Fukuzawa Yukichi Zenshū* vol. 9: 529–536.

the nation was the highest value. Loyalty meant a commitment to Japan becoming a rich country with a strong military (*fukoku kyōhei*). Fukuzawa worried, however, that without some transcendent authority to inspire loyalty, the nation's resolve might falter: "It is extremely difficult to maintain morality without religion. The great scholars of the West constantly struggle with this problem. Yet ... in Japan ... our samurai have been able to maintain a high personal morality while ignoring religion ... One reason ... is that they were aided by Confucianism" (quoted in Craig 1992: 409). While Confucianism might have performed this useful function in the past, however, Fukuzawa regarded it as outmoded and inappropriate to modern Japan. As a provisional measure to sustain morality, he recommended that the government nurture indigenous piety. As the masses grew more rational, he believed, they would be able to slough off religion and superstition and cultivate themselves in loyalty, like the elite.[11] He imagined Japan's ideal transformation as a "subtraction story," in which religion would be supplanted by philosophy, but the problem of secular morality's ultimate source remained unresolved.

Fukuzawa's publications emerged alongside debates on religion in the journal of the Meiroku Society, a group of intellectuals to which he belonged.[12] The Meiroku Society was founded by Mori Arinori in 1873 to promote civilization and enlightenment. It published forty-three issues of its journal over the years 1874 to 1875, for a public exchange of views on a wide range of issues facing the new Japan.[13] The Society distinguished between individual belief and outward practice, regarding private conviction as the essence of religion. Ultimately, they rejected the idea of a state religion for Japan (Maxey 2014: 143–144). Like secularizing European elites before them, Meiroku Society members were supremely confident of their ability to mold society to adopt their vision. Regarding the relation of religion to the state, Mori wrote, "I feel that religious

---

[11] Fukuzawa Yukichi. 1958–1971. Tokkyō no setsu (1883). In *Fukuzawa Yukichi Zenshū* vol. 9: 294, quoted in Craig (1992: 411).

[12] Fukuzawa operated a newspaper called *Jiji shinpō*. He often developed his ideas through serialized editorials and then published a collection of them separately. His views became well known among the educated class and within the government.

[13] A comprehensive survey of the thought of early Meiji Japanese secularists would have to include Inoue Kowashi, a highly influential bureaucrat and one of the drafters of the Meiji constitution of 1889. I hope to address his position in a separate essay at a later date. The Meiroku Society's journal submissions regarding religion have been surveyed by Trent Maxey (2014) and Jason Josephson (2012) in much greater detail than will be possible in the present chapter.

matters should be left to the individual preference of the people since the government's responsibility is only to protect human life and property" (Braisted et.al. 1976: 78). Nishi Amane, who wrote several essays on religion for the Society's journal, took the position that since the state cannot compel the people to believe in any particular creed, it should stay out of the question of belief entirely:

[T]he government offices for supervising religions should be allowed no more control over religion than is necessary to prevent religious disturbances. We need not bother to question whether people believe in foxes, badgers, Buddhas, or angels. The fate of the various religions is entirely their responsibility, not ours. We are interested only in preventing injury by religion to temporal rule, protecting this principle strictly, and punishing those who transgress it. Nor is the state concerned with whether a certain religion is right or wrong. (Braisted et al. 1976: 59–60)

At the time, the government was in the midst of the Great Promulgation Campaign (1870–1884, Taikyō senpu undō), in which it relied on a group of nativist scholars and Shinto activists to compose and propagate a national creed loosely based on Shinto. The Campaign failed miserably and exposed the government to widespread ridicule for the fabricated nature of the creed and the incompetence of the people recruited to preach it.[14] Fukuzawa wrote in 1875, "Shinto has not yet established a body of doctrine ... Shinto has always been the puppet of Buddhism ... It is only an insignificant movement trying to make headway by taking advantage of the imperial house at a time of political change."[15] The views of Fukuzawa and the Meiroku Society members can be understood as a critique of the government's heavy-handed efforts to indoctrinate the people in what amounted to a state doctrine.[16] The failure of the Campaign ultimately turned the government toward acceptance of limited religious freedom,

---

[14] A small number of nativist (*kokugaku*) figures, mainly from the faction of Hirata Atsutane, held office in the early Meiji government. Bureaucrats composed an official creed loosely based on Shinto, and authorized Shinto priests to create a network of preachers to spread it to the populace. Because the creed had no basis in popular religious life, however, and because it was composed of platitudes about obeying authority and revering the emperor (who previously had played no role in popular religious life), the people found it incomprehensible and its priests ludicrous.

[15] Fukuzawa Yukichi, *Bunmeiron no gairyaku*, 18th edn. (Tokyo: Iwanami Shoten, 1983): 195. This passage is also discussed and translated in part in Muraoka Tsunetsugu (1964: 210).

[16] On the Great Promulgation Campaign, see Hardacre (1986). Fukuzawa and others no doubt recalled and hoped to avoid repetition of the foreign relations disaster that occurred following the 1868 roundup of some 3,000 "hidden Christians" who had emerged when Catholic missionaries had returned to Japan. Their exile, harsh treatment,

which was the position of Fukuzawa and the Meiroku Society. That ideal was included in the 1889 Meiji constitution's 28th article: "Japanese subjects shall, within limits not prejudicial to peace and order, and not antagonistic to their duties as subjects, enjoy freedom of religious belief."[17]

Meiji Buddhist Reform Movements

In a recent work, Taylor (2011: 35) characterizes the kind of religion that is acceptable to secularizing elites: "A good, or proper, religion is a set of beliefs in God or some other transcendent power, which entails an acceptable, or, in some versions, a 'rational' morality. It is devoid of any elements that do not contribute to this morality and thus of 'superstition.' Chatterjee (2006: 60) summarizes how such a religion could emerge: "Sometimes this has been done by putting external and forcible constraints on the public political presence of religion ... More compatible with liberal political values, however, and in many ways the more successful process has been the secularization resulting from an internal reform of religion itself."

As we shall see, early Meiji persecution of Buddhism stimulated reform movements that greatly transformed Buddhist intellectuals' conceptions of the essence of Buddhism, turning it into a set of individual beliefs from which "superstitious" elements had been eliminated. The new Meiji government withdrew the patronage that Buddhism had formerly enjoyed through two moves: an 1868 edict calling for "separation of the Buddhas from the Kami" (Kami are the supernaturals of Shinto), and laws legalizing clerical marriage and meat eating (1872).[18] The separation edict was

and the death of 600 of them had been regarded among Western diplomats and in the foreign press as spectacular evidence of Japan's barbarity.

[17] The Constitution of the Empire of Japan, 1889; www.ndl.go.jp/constitution/e/etc/co2.h tml, accessed November 27, 2011. The constitution and the Imperial Rescript on Education (1890) were central to the efforts of elites to mold the populace into loyal subjects of the empire, but spatial limitations make it impossible to discuss them more fully in this chapter.

[18] During the Tokugawa period (1600–1868), the shogunate patronized Buddhism in many ways. It required the entire populace to affiliate with a Buddhist temple. Virtually no exceptions were made. Once a family became a parishioner of a temple, the affiliation was maintained over future generations, regardless of the personal beliefs of any of the living members, even including the priests of Shinto. The shogunate enforced these regulations through a religious court presided over by Magistrates of Temples and Shrines. Their verdicts constituted cumulative precedents. These courts adjudicated a wide range of matters: disputes of all kinds involving temples and shrines; the behavior of priests, the duties of lay parishioners to maintain the temple in good repair and guarantee the priest's

widely understood to encourage the extermination of Buddhism. Temples were ransacked. Kami images and symbols were taken out of temples, Buddhist images and personnel were removed from shrines, and thousands of priests were forced to laicize. The former requirement that everyone be a temple parishioner was allowed to lapse. Temple and shrine lands were seized and many temples razed or their buildings converted to secular purposes (Grapard 1984). This edict, which represented the adoption of the most virulent anti-Buddhist views of "hard-line Shinto and Nativist scholars," resulted in the destruction of as many as 125,400 temples, or 63 percent of the total (Jaffe 2001: 58).[19] The edict drastically undercut Buddhism's economic base and undermined society's respect for it. Likewise, the government's abandonment of its role as enforcer of sectarian law, signaled by the edict allowing priests to marry and eat meat, plunged Buddhist denominations into debate over clerical marriage.[20] Both of these policies stimulated reformist attempts to restore Buddhism's honor, its authority among the people, and the government's trust. The result brought Buddhism into line with secularists' ideas of the proper sort of religion for modern Japan.

Inoue Enryo (1858–1919), an influential Meiji-period Buddhist reformer, writer, and educator, dedicated his career to ridding Buddhism of "superstition." His aim was to reform Buddhism from within and thus to transform it into a respected adjunct of government. He especially wanted to extirpate belief in demonic spirits. To that end, he composed an encyclopedic study of popular beliefs in monsters (*yōkai*) and became known as

---

livelihood, temple ownership of land and the division of its produce between the temple and its tenant-cultivators, and a host of other matters. The relation between Buddhism and the state in the early modern period was very advantageous to Buddhism. Buddhist temples had considerable autonomy in the way they dealt with peasants residing on temple land. The shogunate reiterated its regulations for each Buddhist sect and confirmed each temple's landholding with each new shogun's accession and also frequently made gifts of land to significant temples. The assumption was that the temple would draw its material support from the produce of that land, received as taxes from peasant cultivators. The state's underwriting and enforcement of internal sectarian hierarchies and rules confirmed that the relevant institutional arrangements bore the imprimatur of the state and gave the sects great power over their clergy. The sects acquired great wealth in many cases, and many temples were rich enough to act as moneylenders. Buddhism acquired a captive audience of parishioners to support it materially and to be indoctrinated in its teachings.

[19] This figure obscures significant regional differences, so that while some areas strove to wipe out Buddhism, others, where there was less anti-Buddhist or pro-Shinto sentiment, showed a reduction of temples by one-quarter to one-third; see Hardacre (2002: 153ff).

[20] The major exception was the Jōdo Shinshū denomination, whose priests had married since the medieval period.

"Dr. Monster" (*yōkai hakase*). He inveighed against popular beliefs in possession by animal spirits such as foxes and badgers; beliefs in astrology, the power of curses, and divination; and belief in *tengu* (winged spirits, combining bird and human characteristics, that represented evil mountain ascetics reborn in monstrous form). Inoue also sought to purge Buddhism of cosmological elements that were not confirmed by science, such as the notion that the universe centers on the cosmic mountain Sumeru. Inoue further asserted that true Buddhism is entirely in accord with science, and was prepared to jettison as "superstition" anything that did not meet scientific standards. He ended up describing Buddhism as a set of private, individual beliefs shorn of superstition, thus aligning Buddhism with the secularists' ideal. Later, Buddhist reformers of the 1890s continued Inoue's anti-superstition campaign as the central element of their agenda (Josephson 2006).

Early Meiji Buddhism struggled to reconcile its world-denying aspect with the national goal of Japan becoming a rich country with a strong military. Reformers tried to rebuild Buddhism in line with the new government, by "modernizing" themselves through foreign study, and by encouraging the religion to take on new social roles (Yoshida 1992: 2–6). Shimaji Mokurai (1838–1911) was one of the most talented young Buddhist clerics to be sent abroad for study. European travel led him to advocate religious freedom, separation of religion from state, and the concept of human rights. He regarded human rights as an important index of the level of a society's development. Like Inoue Enryo, he tried to reconcile Buddhism with science. He also attempted to ally Buddhism with Western ideas of truth in an effort to harmonize Buddhism with Western philosophy (Ikeda 1976). Ōuchi Seiran (1845–1918), a Buddhist layman active from the Restoration to the 1890s, argued for a trans-sectarian lay Buddhism. He argued that the state should stay out of the realm of religion, and also that Buddhism could be a powerful means of enlightening the people. Both men wrote prolifically and founded a number of Buddhist societies and journals. Both held that Buddhism should engage in social welfare work, a position that we can regard as resisting the assertion that religion should be entirely absent from the public domain.[21] Buddhist reform campaigns clearly illustrate the way in which elites' secularizing agendas stimulated the creation of new religious

---

[21] Commenting on Meiji Buddhist charity, Winston Davis (1989: 330–332) sees it as a way for Buddhism to ingratiate itself with the government; the interpretation offered here does not necessarily conflict with Davis' view.

forms conforming to those agendas. Secularism and religion thus may be regarded as mutually constituted phenomena in Meiji Japan.

The Anti-Superstition Campaign in Education

The public schools were the single most important agency in spreading a secular outlook among the people. Mori Arinori (1847–1889), founder of the Meiroku Society, served as Japan's first Minister of Education from 1885 to 1889. His administration put in place anti-superstition measures that persisted through the first decade of the twentieth century. A drive to eradicate popular belief in *tengu* was central to the effort. *Tengu* were believed to cause illness through spirit possession, and people traditionally employed healers to perform cures through exorcisms. The Ministry of Education tried to stamp out these "superstitions" through textbooks on Morality, a compulsory subject introduced to the public schools from 1880.[22] To develop Morality pedagogy, the government convened a blue-ribbon committee that included Inoue Enryo.[23] Anti-superstition lessons were incorporated into Morality textbooks, under such titles as *Meishin ni ochiru na* (Don't fall into superstition!) and *Meishin o sakeyō* (Avoid superstition!). One example from these lessons was the story of an old woman who consulted a physician only after several unsuccessful attempts to have shamans and faith healers cure her of trachoma. By the time she got to a "real" doctor (one trained in Western medicine), it was too late, and she became blind. She deeply regretted that she had "fallen into superstition" (Figal 1999: 93–96).

Secularism and State Shinto

In the same timeframe as Buddhist reforms and the educational system's anti-superstition measures, Japanese nationalism, also a defensive reaction against Western imperialism, burgeoned into an ideological, semi-religious phenomenon of its own: State Shinto.[24] State Shinto became an important element of Meiji secularism in the sense of its use by the government and the media to suppress heterodox religions of the period

---

[22] The earliest Morality textbooks were compiled by Motoda Eifu (1818–1891), an influential Confucian advisor to the government, who had also contributed to the drafting of the Imperial Rescript on Education (1890).

[23] Inoue later devoted an entire volume to *tengu*, called *Tenguron* (1903).

[24] For an overview of recent scholarship on State Shinto, see Okuyama (2011). For an historical study of State Shinto, see Hardacre (1989).

and to mold imperial subjects. According to Thomas Dubois (2005: 119), this phenomenon in Japan was mirrored in "the attempts ... of the states of postcolonial Asia to replicate sacred and transcendent principles of national unity":

These attempts occasionally used religion overtly, as in state cults or religious monarchies, but more frequently involved the pseudo-sacralization of the state. This was most spectacularly pursued through the equation of the national body with cultic figures, such as the Japanese Meiji Emperor, Mao Zedong, or Sukarno, who were themselves the embodiment of transcendent struggles for national wealth and power, Marxist destiny, and anti-imperialist territorial integrity, respectively. In each case the new state created and held fast to a sacred ideology that was meant to galvanize citizens by inspiring them with visions of the national past, present, and future. As it had in Europe, the national essence became the soul of public life, while other beliefs, particularly those defined as "religious," were often cordoned off to an optional and private realm. (Dubois 2005: 119)

In effect, State Shinto solved the puzzle that had so perturbed Fukuzawa as he worried how morality could be upheld without a transcendent religious authority. The answer emerged in a cult of the nation and the monarch, transcending the privatized sphere of religion, its observances made obligatory for imperial subjects, whatever their personal religious beliefs. The glorified "national structure" or "national polity" (*kokutai*) and the imperial house ultimately emerged as morality's transcendent source.

At the time of the Restoration's 1868 edict to "separate Buddhas from Kami," however, Shinto did not exist as a freestanding, independent religious tradition. During most of its history, it had been cocooned within Buddhism, and during the early modern period many shrines were either administered by Buddhist clergy or simply managed informally by the peasantry. Except for a handful that had become pilgrimage sites, shrines were predominantly local institutions lacking horizontal networks. There was no theology uniting the whole or even a significant portion of them. Thus, shrine priests, never so well educated as Buddhist clerics, were not prepared to function on a national stage in 1868, as the failure of the Great Promulgation Campaign had amply demonstrated.

In response to this reality, the bureaucracy took charge. All shrines and their priests came under national management; they were incorporated into a uniform ranking system and ordered to perform an annual calendar of ritual coordinated with the emperor's palace rites. All shrines were designated public facilities for the performance of state ritual. They were explicitly *not* to be regarded as religious. This bureaucratic fiction could never be truly reconciled, however, with traditional shrine devotions, private ceremonies, and local festivals that were overwhelmingly religious in character and to which the people were deeply attached.

In order to refocus shrines on the nation, the government constructed new shrines to honor deified emperors and historical imperial loyalists, to provide a symbolic bulwark against foreign influence in the port cities, and to commemorate the war dead.[25] As mainland Japanese moved into Okinawa and Hokkaidō, they established shrines there that were also incorporated into the national system. By 1945, some 1640 shrines had been established in the colonies throughout the Japanese empire. During the early Meiji period, shrines were administered alongside temples, but as of 1900 the shrines were given their own Shrine Bureau within the Home Ministry.

Seen in the light of Taylor's account of secularization, shrines were transformed to serve as official sites for obligatory expressions of loyalty to the nation, while religion was relegated to the private sphere. Only within the private sphere did people enjoy freedom of religion. Buddhist priests were forbidden to stand for election, and Shinto priests were forbidden to preach – elements pointing toward a prohibition on religious expression in the public realm by these clerics. Yet while the public sphere was shaped by these exclusions, overall this is not a story of "subtraction" but of centrally orchestrated creation, addition, sculpting, and molding of a ritual order explicitly placed outside the sphere of religion, to glorify the nation and its transcendent source of morality, the emperor. Not only that, State Shinto was also an integral part of secularizing efforts to eradicate heterodox religions.

Modern Media Police the Boundaries of Religion

In 1894, the newly established newspaper *Yorozuchōhō* built its circulation through sustained exposés of the new religion Renmonkyō (literally, "Church of the Lotus Gate") and its founder, Shimamura Mitsu (1831–1904), accusing her and her followers of sexual and financial misconduct, besmirching Shinto's image, and leading the people into superstition. *Yorozuchōhō* was a Tokyo daily tabloid, and had gained

[25] Some of the state-created new shrines included satellites of the Ise Shrines (Yokohama Kōtai Jingū, facing the major harbor for foreign ships, and other shrines called Daijingū or Kōtai Jingū); shrines for imperial loyalists (e.g., Minatogawa Jinja 1872); shrines for the war dead (Yasukuni Shrine, whose predecessor was established in 1869, and the Nation-Protecting Shrines that served as Yasukuni's provincial satellites); shrines dedicated to an emperor (Meiji Jingū, Kashihara Jingū, Heian Jingū); and overseas shrines.

popularity exposing the scandals of upper-class society.[26] Shimamura's biographical details have not been determined with certainty, but it seems that she began healing in Kokura in the late 1870s and moved to Tokyo in 1882. When a cholera epidemic struck that year, she began to distribute "holy water," which she claimed could cure cholera.[27]

From the late 1870s through 1895, there were annual outbreaks of cholera, dysentery, typhoid fever, smallpox, and diphtheria. Major cholera outbreaks with death tolls of more than 10,000 occurred in Japan in 1879, 1882, 1885, 1886, 1890, and 1895 (coinciding with Renmonkyō's major growth). Over 70 percent of those infected died, meaning that contracting the disease was a virtual death sentence. Moreover, there was no cure at the time. A medical system had been established in Japan in 1874, while a public health system was established in 1879, but the only effective measure to slow cholera's spread was by quarantining the victims. To be quarantined was to be given up for dead, so people were understandably reluctant to comply with quarantine orders. Perhaps in response, public health enforcement was shifted to the police as of 1893. Since medical science had so little to offer, perhaps it is not surprising that people would have flocked to Renmonkyō for holy water, a treatment that was arguably not much less effective than the measures that government could provide.

In 1882, the government introduced a distinction between shrine Shinto and the sectarian varieties of Shinto, implicitly limiting the sphere of recognized religious groups outside of the shrines, Buddhism, or Christianity to organizations belonging to one of thirteen Shinto sects. Numerous religious associations formed from healing cults or a founder's revelations affiliated with Taiseikyō, one of the recognized Shinto sects, as a means of acquiring recognition and protection from police investigations. Taiseikyō's criteria for accepting such affiliations were loose and flexible, even accepting groups with no real claim to Shinto identity.[28] In

---

[26] The *Yorozuchōhō* was founded in 1982 by Kuroiwa Ruikō (1862–1920). The paper itself was a tabloid, issued daily in Tokyo, which specialized in revealing scandals in upper-class society, as well as serializing the publisher's many mystery novels. The Christian reformer Uchimura Kanzō was briefly on its staff, but left in 1899, calling the paper's staff a group of "social outsiders" (*fugūsha*), implying that they focused on scandal because of a sense of their own inferiority; see Ariyama (1979).

[27] For comprehensive accounts of Renmonkyō and its suppression, see Takeda (1991).

[28] Taiseikyō was founded by Hirayama Seisai (1815–1890), who before the Meiji Restoration had been a shogunal official involved in foreign relations (he was among those who met Commodore Perry and also received Dutch and Russian emissaries). Later he was made head priest of the Hikawa Shrine, where Emperor Meiji had promulgated

1883, Shimamura affiliated her group with Taiseikyō, evidently hoping that the merger would provide protection from further police scrutiny, although Renmonkyō's doctrines were derived from Buddhism. The group marked that year as the date of its official founding.

Renmonkyō grew to 900,000 members, and at such a fast pace that by 1884 it was able to erect buildings in Kokura and Tokyo that occupied a whole city block – a massive and unusual display of wealth for a newly established religion of the time. The number of branch churches rose rapidly in Japan, with overseas branches in Hong Kong and Shanghai. The group's phenomenal growth was also evident in Shimamura's meteoric rise in the ranks of Taiseikyō, reaching its top ranking of Grand Master (*daikyōsei*) by 1890. Renmonkyō's stunning growth, wealth, and promotion of holy water gave it a "public" character at odds with secularists' beliefs about religion's rightful confinement to the private realm.

But after sustained attack in 1894 by *Yorozuchōhō* and other newspapers, membership dropped sharply. The papers criticized the use of holy water, claiming that Renmonkyō's meetings were places of assignation and sexual impropriety, that Shimamura herself (over sixty by now, which meant that she was a very old woman for Japan of that time) was sexually immoral, and also that she led the female members into immorality, even forcing them to have abortions. This gendered dynamic in *Yorozuchōhō*'s attack displayed palpable misogyny. Other religious groups used holy water or equally "superstitious" elements in curing, however, so this factor did not set Renmonkyō apart definitively. One of *Yorozuchōhō*'s most telling criticisms was the charge that Renmonkyō sullied the purity of Shinto. The gist was as follows: Renmonkyō falsely calls itself "Shinto." To allow it to exist in any form "is to allow the spiritual basis of Shinto to be destroyed, to damage the dignity of the imperial ancestors, and to despoil the entirety of the imperial dignity and the prestige of our national polity" (Takeda 1991: 42). For this reason, "this evil religion should be denied the name of Shinto," and the authorities should disband it immediately:

Shinto is the Way enshrining the spirit of Japan's imperial ancestors; our people do not revere Shinto because it is a religion, but because it is the Way, which deifies the

---

the Charter Oath announcing the formation of the Meiji government and its founding principles. Founded in 1879, Taiseikyō venerated the emperor and perpetuated the teachings and pantheon of the Great Promulgation Campaign. Practice centered on recitation of the *misogi harai* prayer, a major prayer in the Shinto tradition. The group acted as an umbrella for various groups, such as Renmonkyō and Misogikyō, which were otherwise unaffiliated with recognized religious organizations. See Kamata (2002).

imperial house and reveres the national polity. As a result, for Shinto to be injured is for the national polity and the imperial house to be injured, and for the noble spirits to be defiled. (Takeda 1991: 42)

Having no independent media of its own, Renmonkyō was unable to respond effectively, and could only get its point of view to the public through the filter of the very newspapers that were dedicated to its destruction.

Comparing *Yorozuchōhō*'s coverage of Renmonkyō with that in other papers, we find that while *Yorozuchōhō* carried ninety-four articles about the group from late March through late April 1894, the older, established newspapers did not find Renmonkyō nearly so newsworthy.[29] For example, during the period of the *Yorozuchōhō* exposé, the *Asahi shinbun* carried six articles, while the *Yomiuri shinbun* carried three, excluding rebuttals that Renmonkyō itself placed with both papers in a futile effort to counter the charges against it.[30]

Even after the 1882 division between shrine and sect Shinto, the existence of miscellaneous religious associations outside the sphere of State Shinto had been more or less tolerated, provided for under the mechanism of affiliation with a recognized Shinto sect. But *Yorozuchōhō* argued that the bureaucrats administering religious affairs were not doing enough to uphold Shinto. Arousing prurient interest through lurid suggestion, the paper's sustained coverage focused public attention on the paper's demand that the religion be disbanded, eventually goading Taiseikyō, the police, and the Bureau of Temples and Shrines to act against Renmonkyō. Taiseikyō stripped Shimamura of her Grand Master ranking, and the Bureau repeatedly required Shimamura and other leaders to appear for questioning. The public health officers within the police determined that Renmonkyō's "holy water" was unfit for human consumption and ordered that its distribution cease (April 28, 1894).[31] While this order did not officially disband the religion, its numbers dropped precipitously and made it impossible to carry on.

The incident quickly escalated to a "witch hunt," determined to rid society of an evil in an era of repeated epidemics. Renmonkyō was an easy target; having grown to a massive size overnight, it had not yet had time to develop a doctrine of significant philosophical depth. Its growth was

[29] The full text of each article in the *Yorozuchōhō* series is available in Takeda (1989; 1991). The 1991 article contains the final two days of coverage, the longest by far.
[30] These figures are based on a survey of the digital archives of both newspapers.
[31] Takeda (1991: 49–51).

mainly dependent upon its reputation for cholera-curing holy water, and without that, Renmonkyō may not have had much to offer. Japan's newly established medical and public health systems undoubtedly regarded holy water both as a harmful superstition and a challenge to their authority. When police prohibited holy water distribution, Renmonkyō was bound to lose members, no matter what the newspapers said about it. It is difficult, however, to estimate the likelihood that the police would have acted without *Yorozuchōhō*'s reporting.

The media emerged at the end of the nineteenth century as a new, non-government agent seeking to narrow the sphere of tolerated religions and to suppress religious associations of which it disapproved by fomenting widespread public disapproval. The Renmonkyō incident is integrally related to secularism, because *Yorozuchōhō*'s coverage worked to convince readers that only "approved" forms of religion should be allowed, and that society is endangered if a heterodox religion shows rapid growth, conspicuous wealth, or women in public roles. In spite of bureaucratic rhetoric to the effect that Shinto is not a religion, *Yorozuchōhō* proceeded as if it were a state religion whose honor and purity were polluted by Renmonkyō's very existence. This incident was a precursor for a similar persecution of another female-headed religion, Tenrikyō, in 1896.[32] The incident probably encouraged the leaders of yet another rapidly expanding, female-founded new religious movement of the early twentieth century, Ōmoto, to purchase their own nationally circulating newspaper, so that in the event of a media attack like *Yorozuchōhō*'s they would have a way to tell their side of the story.[33] Renmonkyō's inability to respond effectively to media attack for want of its own mouthpiece illustrates vividly the way in which the public sphere in a secular state can appear to be a level playing field for all voices, but operate in fact to exclude and suppress religions that refuse to confine themselves to the private realm (Asad 2003: 182–186). The Renmonkyō incident inaugurated an antagonistic relation between religion and media in Japan that arguably persists to the present day.

---

[32] Tenrikyō was founded in 1838 by Nakayama Miki (1798–1887) as a healing cult, later developing a comprehensive teaching and religious practice based on worship of a universal deity she called "God the Parent." Miki denied that her teaching was "Shinto," but her successors forged a link in order to escape persecution. After 1945, Tenrikyō repudiated the idea that it derived from Shinto.

[33] While Ōmoto operated a national newspaper successfully, that was not sufficient to save it from persecution. It was brutally suppressed in 1921 and again in 1935. See Hardacre (1998).

CONCLUSION

Viewed in the light of Charles Taylor's account of secularism, Japan may be seen as an early example of an elite Westernizing, secularizing project undertaken in defensive reaction against Western imperialism, preceding similar developments in Turkey, India, Indonesia, and China. Earlier scholarship viewed secularism as a passive, neutral by-product of modernization, but examining secularism as an elite project allows us to understand it as an historical phenomenon with actors who debate the social roles of religion and create bureaucratic mechanisms for the production of a secular populace. We see more clearly how elite debates informed the bureaucracy that created the institutional means for indoctrinating the populace with elite ideals. We obtain a new understanding of Buddhist reform movements as acting in tandem with the bureaucracy to "privatize" Buddhism, in line with secularists' conception of religion as properly belonging to the private sphere, along with an element of resistance in the call for Buddhist social welfare measures. We have seen how secularism in Japan is integrally related to nationalism and its sacralization of the state and the monarch. This understanding allows us to develop a perspective on State Shinto as providing an analog to a state religion, precisely and paradoxically because of the fiction that it was *not* a religion. We can see how the media acted to depress society's tolerance for heterodox religions, ostensibly to uphold Shinto's honor, thereby stimulating the government to suppress forms of religion that did not conform to the secular order. Beyond these discrete results, however, we can see that Japan's secularizing project brought social institutions into line with it, forced religion to respond to it, and allowed the media to create a profitable role for itself in policing religion. Taylor's work thus reveals unexpected connections among the actors and institutions that transformed Japan into a secular society and that brought Japanese religions into conformity with a secular ideal.

Bibliography

Ariyama Teruo. 1979. "Risōdan kenkyū 1." *Momoyama Gakuin Daigaku shakaigaku ronshū* 13(1): 37–64.

Asad, Talal. 2003. *Formations of the Secular*. Stanford: Stanford University Press.

Braisted, William Reynolds. Assisted by Adachi Yasushi and Kokuchi Yūji. 1976. *Meiroku zasshi, Journal of the Japanese Enlightenment*. Cambridge, Massachusetts: Harvard University Press.

Chatterjee, Partha. 2006. "Fasting for Bin Laden: The Politics of Secularization in Contemporary India." In *Powers of the Secular Modern: Talal Asad and His Interlocutors*. Edited by David Scott and Charles Hirschkind. Stanford: Stanford University Press, 57–74.

Constitution of the Empire of Japan. 1889. www.ndl.go.jp/constitution/e/etc/c02.html.

Craig, Albert. 1992. *The Autobiography of Fukuzawa Yukichi*, revised translation by Eiichi Kiyooka, with a Preface and Afterword by Albert Craig. Lanham, New York, and London: Madison Books.

2009. *Civilization and Enlightenment: The Early Thought of Fukuzawa Yukichi* Cambridge, Massachusetts and London: Harvard University Press.

Davis, Winston. 1989. Buddhism and the Modernization of Japan. *History of Religions* 28(4): 304–339.

Dubois, Thomas David. 2005. "Hegemony, Imperialism, and the Construction of Religion in East and Southeast Asia." *History and Theory* Vol. 44, No. 4: 119.

Figal, Gerald. 1999. *Civilization and Monsters: Spirits of Modernity in Meiji Japan*. Durham and London: Duke University Press.

Fukuzawa Yukichi. 1983. *Bunmeiron no gairyaku* 18th edn. Tokyo: Iwanami shoten.

1958–1971. *Fukuzawa Yukichi Zenshū*. 22 vols. Tokyo: Iwanami shoten.

1969. *An Encouragement of Learning*. David A. Dilworth, translator, with Umeyo Hirano, Tokyo: Sophia University Press.

Gorski, Philip S. and Ates Atlnordu. 2008. "After Secularization?" *Annual Review of Sociology* 34: 55–85.

Grapard, Allan. 1984. "Japan's Ignored Cultural Revolution: The Separation of Shintō and Buddhist Divinities in Meiji and a Case Study: Tōnomine." *History of Religions* 23: 240–265.

Hardacre, Helen. 1986. "Creating Shintō: The Great Promulgation Campaign and the New Religions." *Journal of Japanese Studies* 12/1: 29–63.

1989. *Shinto and the State, 1868–1988*. Princeton: Princeton University Press.

1998. Asano Wasaburō and Japanese Spiritualism in Early Twentieth-Century Japan. In *Japan's Conflicting Modernities, Issues in Culture and Democracy, 1900–1930*. Edited by Sharon A. Minichiello. Honolulu: University of Hawaii Press, 133–153.

2002. *Religion and Society in Nineteenth-Century Japan: A Study of the Southern Kantō Region, Using Late Edo and Early Meiji Gazeteers*. Michigan Monograph Series in Japanese Studies Number 41. Ann Arbor: University of Michigan Press.

Ikeda Eishun. 1976. *Meiji no shin bukkyō undō*. Tokyo: Yoshikawa Kōbunkan.

Jaffe, Richard. 2001. *Neither Monk Nor Layman: Clerical Marriage in Modern Japanese Buddhism*. Princeton and Oxford: Princeton University Press.

Josephson, Jason. 2006. "When Buddhism Became a 'Religion': Religion and Superstition in the Writings of Inoue Enryo." *Japanese Journal of Religious Studies* 33(1): 143–168.

2012. *The Invention of Religion in Japan*. Chicago: University of Chicago Press.

Kamata Tōji. 2002. *Hirayama Seisai to Meiji no Shintō*. Tokyo: Shunbunsha.

Koizumi Takashi. 2011. "Fukuzawa Yukichi to shūkyō." *Igirsu tetsugaku* 34: 5–18.

1994. "Fukuzawa Yukichi and Religion." *Asian Philosophy* 4(2): 109–124.

Masuzawa, Tomoko. 2005. *The Invention of World Religions, Or, How European Universalism Was Preserved in the Language of Pluralism.* Chicago and New York: University of Chicago Press.

Maxey, Trent. 2014. *The "Greatest Problem": Religion and State Formation in Meiji Japan.* Cambridge, Massachusetts: Harvard University Press.

Muraoka Tsunetsugu, *Studies in Shinto Thought*, translated by Delmer Brown and James Araki. Tokyo: Ministry of Education, 1964.

Nagai Kafū. 1962–1974. *Kafū zenshū.* 29 vols. Tokyo: Iwanami shoten.

Okuyama Michiaki. 2011. "'State Shinto' in Recent Japanese Scholarship." *Monumenta Nipponica* vol. 66, no. 1: 123–145.

Suzuki Norihisa. 1979. *Meiji shūkyō shisō no kenkyū.* Tokyo: Tokyo Daigaku shuppankai.

Takeda Dōshō. 1991 "The Fall of Renmonkyō and Its Place in the History of Meiji Period Religions." In *New Religions. Contemporary Papers on Japanese Religions.* Edited by Inoue Nobutaka. Translated by Norman Havens. Institute for Japanese Culture and Classics. Kokugakuin University: Tokyo, 25–57.

1989. "Yorozuchōhō ni yoru Renmonkyō kōgeki kyanpēn." *Nihon bunka kenkyūjo kiyō* 63: 67–176.

1991. "Yorozuchōhō ni yoru Renmonkyō kōgeki kyanpēn-2." *Shintō shūkyō* 144: 74–96.

Taylor, Charles. 2007. *A Secular Age.* Cambridge, MA: Belknap Press of Harvard University Press.

2011. "Western Secularism." In *Rethinking Secularism*, edited by Craig Calhoun, Mark Jurgensmeyer, and Jonathan VanAntwerpen. Oxford: Oxford University Press, 35.

Yoshida Kyūichi. 1992. *Nihon kindai bukkyōshi kenkyū.* Tokyo: Kawashima shoten.

5

Law, Legitimacy, and Equality: The Bureaucratization of Religion and Conditions of Belief in Indonesia

Mirjam Künkler

INTRODUCTION

A secular age, which Charles Taylor suggests has emerged in what he refers to as the "North Atlantic World," is one in which religious belief is no longer the default position to live a fulfilled life. Compared to the *Age of Belief*, which characterizes medieval Christendom, conceptions of the natural, subjective, and social world have changed. During the *Age of Belief*, the natural world was viewed as a cosmos and as the creation of God; the self was understood as a "porous self" open to be acted upon by transcendental powers; and the social world was defined by hierarchical relations, structured by the prospect of salvation. In the *Secular Age* that exists today in the North Atlantic World, according to Taylor, the views of all these three spheres have been disenchanted. The view of nature is one of a mechanistic universe, the self is "buffered" against the influence of transcendental powers, and the social world is viewed as one to which all have equal and direct access: identity is categorical, not relational. Time is imagined no longer as teleological, as leading to a particular goal, but instead as open in its purpose. The disenchantment in these conceptions of the natural, the subjective, and the social world have opened new possibilities for experiencing fulfillment, and hence religious belief is no longer viewed as necessary to live a fulfilled life. An *immanent frame* has emerged, in which for many exclusive humanism has taken the place of religious belief.

Does this picture also apply to present-day Indonesia? Is religion but one option among many and "frequently not the easiest to embrace"? Is the self "buffered" against the influence of transcendental powers, and the social world viewed as one to which all have equal and direct access? Is there an immanent frame for a present-day Indonesian citizen in the same way that Taylor argues is the case for a present-day Canadian?

If secularity involves the move from a society where belief in God is in principle unchallenged to one where it is one option among others, post-independence Indonesia (1945–) is not secular. If modern secularity is a field of increasingly "multiform contestation," Indonesian society is not a secular society. It is unsecular by law, in that Indonesian citizenship is tied to religious identity. It is impossible to register as an atheist, agnostic, or adherent of one of the non-recognized religions. One can also hardly speak of multiform contestation, in that religions hardly compete with one another. Conversion rates are very low and proselytization prohibited. Yet secularity in the sense of a social imaginary, an appreciation for the differentiation between religious and political authority, and the acknowledgment of religious plurality (a consequence of Taylor's Secularity I) surely exist. With that simultaneity of a state-induced impossibility of Taylor's Secularity III and a socially embedded understanding of Secularity I, Indonesia presents a special case. Like Senegal and, until recently Turkey, it is a Muslim-majority state in the process of translating democracy into its own institutional legacies and of crafting its own brand of democratic religion–state relations. Unlike Turkey and Senegal, it is a case where, although religious and political authority is separated, citizenship is tied to religion.[1] This implies that one's declared religious affiliation determines the type of religious education and personal law one is subject to. Moreover, religions are in some ways highly regulated by the state. As I will argue, in an effort to subordinate all social and civic life in the two post-independence authoritarian regimes (1959–1965, and 1966–1998) to the twin goals of political order and economic growth, state bureaucrats sought to "modernize" religion and thereby highly bureaucratized it. Indonesia is therefore a classic case of a "marker state,"[2] a state marking its citizens in religious terms.

---

[1] Senegal, Turkey, and Indonesia, together with Albania and Mali, represent the five countries in the Muslim world that underwent democratization processes and were coded, in the three indices on regime type considered most authoritative in the discipline of Political Science (Polity IV, Freedom House, BTI), as democracies between 2000 and 2011. See, for instance, Mirjam Künkler 2012.

[2] Taylor introduced the notion of being "religiously marked" in the 2013 Unseld Lecture on "Religion and Secularism in Modern Democracies," given at the University of Tübingen, June 4, 2013. http://forum-humanum.org/mediathek/sprecher-einzelansicht/sprecher/prof-dr-charles-taylor/.

What are the conditions of belief in such a state, where public religion is highly determined by political and legal regulations, because the category of what religion is is itself to a high degree a product of bureaucratic decision-making?

BUREAUCRATIZATION: THE RESPONSE OF A "PAN-RELIGIOUS" INDONESIAN STATE TO QUESTIONS OF RELIGION AND RELIGIOUS IDENTITY

Indonesia is a multi-religious, multi-cultural, and pluri-legal state. Its 88 percent Muslim majority is internally highly heterogeneous and bound together more by the overall label than by agreement in matters of faith and notions of religious law. Its religious minorities, that is Christians (9 percent), Hindus (1.7 percent), Buddhists (0.07 percent), and Confucians (0.05), are also internally highly heterogeneous.

After independence in 1945, Indonesian leaders faced questions similar to those state founders in India and elsewhere encountered: what kind of state should Indonesia become, and should the state be based on a core ethos? In addition to Islam and Christianity, ancient traditions of Buddhism, Hinduism, and Confucianism, as well as several hundred indigenous belief systems, existed across the archipelago. In the process of state- and nation-building, the founding elite decided that in order to overcome existing schisms and attain national unity, they had to fundamentally reform the fragmented colonial legal system which, they believed, was unfit for a unitary modern nation-state.

Before independence in 1945, the country's judicial system had been separated into colonial, customary (*adat*), and Islamic legal systems. Customary legal systems existed side by side in those areas ruled indirectly, with nineteen different jurisdictions based on cultural and linguistic particularity (Künkler 2017). Against the background of the great plurality in culture, religion, and legal traditions, the founders recognized that in order to preserve the territorial unity of the new state, they had to accommodate cultural particularity and allow at least some degree of religious and legal diversity. Thus, the motto of Indonesia became "*Bhinneka Tunggal Ika*," or "Unity in Diversity." Of particular concern to the founders was the question of what role religion, especially Islam, was to play in independent Indonesia: on the one hand, after centuries of colonial rule, here was a chance to create a state where Islam would be the primary source of law. On the other, cultural norms that created and conserved great diversity across the archipelago would make a shared and uniform understanding of Islam and Islamic law difficult. Moreover, the proclamation of an Islamic State (*Negara Islam*) could provoke non-Muslim islands in the East of the archipelago to secede. Over June and July 1945, a drafting committee appointed by the Japanese occupying power debated intensively the nature of the future state (Kusuma and Elson 2011; Künkler 2017). Nationalist leader Sukarno had proposed five principles as the guiding ideas for the constitution's preamble. The "pancasila" (panca – five; sila – principles) – notably Sanskrit rather than bahasa Indonesia or Arabic – committed Indonesians to (1) "the belief in the one and only God," (2) a "just and civilized humanity," (3) the unity of the country, (4) democracy "guided by the inner wisdom of unanimity arising out of deliberations among representatives," and (5) social justice. While Sukarno and what later came to be called the nationalist bloc favored leaving references to religion relatively neutral,[3] others demanded that a commitment to follow Islamic law be inserted into the draft. Yet others took the position that Islamic law should only be made binding for Muslims. This last position, the so-called Jakarta Charter, was the position agreed upon after intense debate and the repeated threat of a breakdown of the proceedings. It was agreed on, like all provisions, on the basis of consensus rather than majority vote. Yet, when independence was prematurely declared on August 15, after the Indonesians realized that Japan had surrendered to the Allied powers in the aftermath of Hiroshima and Nagasaki, the Jakarta Charter was missing. A special committee had undertaken last-minute changes to the final constitutional draft on the morning of August 15 and omitted the Jakarta Charter from the document. Some Arabic terms were replaced by terms in bahasa Indonesia. The Arabic word for "preamble," mukaddimah, was replaced by the Indonesian pembukaan; in paragraph 6 the provision that the president of Indonesia be Muslim was deleted; and in one formula which suggested that Indonesian independence had been achieved by the grace of Allah, the

---

[3] Sukarno first presented the pancasila on June 1, 1945 in his speech later designated "the birth of pancasila." Sukarno's thinking exposed distinct parallels with Islamist thought – however intentional and possibly instrumental this may have been. He explicitly drew parallels between the fourth principle and Islamic concepts of musyawarah (deliberation), and mufakat (consensual unanimous decision-making arising out of such consultation). In contrast to Islamists, however, Sukarno believed strongly in a separation of religion and state, not only for the sake of national unity, but also, notably, for the sake of religion, drawing on the experience that state interference in religious matters under Dutch rule had significantly compromised religious leaders.

word "Allah" was replaced by "Tuhan yang Maha Kuasa," bahasa Indonesia for "Almighty God."[4]

Confronted with these consequential changes in the preamble and the constitution, Islamic groups temporarily withdrew their support from the national government. Only the appearance of the Allied Powers in September 1945 and the subsequent attempt by the Netherlands to re-occupy the country swayed some to renew their loyalty to Jakarta, while others declared independent Islamic states. Reluctantly, regional elites who had hoped for the establishment of an Islamic state complied with the new constitution, fully expecting that, within a year or two, countrywide elections for a constituent assembly would take place and a new constitution would be drafted that replaced the pancasila state by an Islamic state.[5]

Amid the war of independence against the Dutch in 1945–1949, the elections originally planned for January 1946, however, were not held until 1955. Even once the constituent assembly was elected in 1955, and between 1956 and 1957 deliberated over a new constitution, the two-thirds majority that was needed for turning Indonesia into an Islamic state could not be reached. The assembly's inability to reach a consensus on the future nature of the state caused Sukarno to declare martial law in March 1957. Months later, he reinstated the 1945 constitution and re-affirmed pancasila without the Jakarta Charter – that is, without the duty for Muslims to abide by Islamic law. The unitary, non-Islamic, but pan-religious formula that had been adopted in 1945 henceforth became the most characteristic feature of the country's post-independence political system.

THE POLICY OF AGAMASASI: TURNING RELIGION INTO THE BUILDING BLOCK OF INDONESIAN NATIONAL IDENTITY

Pancasila proved very useful in providing a pan-religious national ethos to a pluralistic society, and could have been a window of opportunity for

---

[4] For the complicated back-and-forth on the question of religion and Islamic law between different factions in the constitutional drafting bodies in 1945, see Anshari (1976) and Kusuma and Elson (2011).

[5] Indeed, the first national elections were originally planned for January 1946. It is interesting to note that the provision of the 1949 Hague Agreement between the Netherlands and Indonesia, which would have transformed Indonesia into a federal state, opened up the increased possibility of the revival of the Jakarta Charter, because it necessitated a new constitution and because it would have allowed for the implementation of Islamic law in the Muslim-majority federal units while not in others. The fact that this possibility was opened up by the disdained Dutch allowed the advocates of pancasila to portray Islamist voices as "anti-nationalists" who bought into the "Dutch" trap that would split up the country.

positive and negative religious freedom to become an integral part of Indonesia's basic rights catalogue. However, the principle was soon undermined by the post-independence state's policy of requiring religions to be recognized as such by the state. With this approach, the Indonesian policy toward religion closely resembled that of Meiji Japan, where Shintoism was elevated to a pan-religious national ethos, and religious communities were compelled to fit government-defined categories to avert being shut down (De Bary et al. 2006: 118–121; Hardacre 1989). Being an adherent of a state-recognized religion (*agama*) became a requirement for citizenship. Those Indonesians who did not profess an *agama* were referred to as "*orang yang belum beragama*" – people who do not yet (!) have a religion – "implying that they would need to adopt an *agama* if they were to become full participants" in the new state (Chalmers 2006: 125). Official identification cards listed the person's religious affiliation, and Indonesians who wanted to enter the military or public service needed to prove that they were a member of a state-recognized *agama*. In the political and legal usage, *agama* or a state-recognized religion was distinguished from *kepercayaan*: non-theistic belief systems (Aragon 2000: 15, 33, 325; Chalmers 2006: 125; Schrauwers 2000: 57).

The Indonesian government followed the Japanese model and entrusted the task of delineating what a religion is to the bureaucracy. The elevation after the country's independence of the Japanese-founded Office of Religious Affairs into a full ministry was originally viewed as a concession to organized Islam in exchange for Islamic groups' political support of the central government. As such, the Ministry of Religious Affairs (MORA) was distrusted by the more secular-minded members of the Sukarno administration. However, it soon evolved into one of the largest ministries, and increasingly proved useful for putting organized Islam into the service of consolidating the power of the central administration. Thus, the ministry in fact came to play an important role in the nation-building process (Emmerson 1978; Lev 1972: 49–56).

While the MORA channeled funds into private religious schools and subsidies to hospitals run by the country's large Islamic organizations, the ministry also increasingly came to "manage" religion. In 1952, it passed a regulation (No.9 of 1952, Article VI) which required that for a community to be recognized as having an *agama*, it had to profess an internationally recognized monotheistic creed with a holy scripture, embrace the idea of prophethood, and adhere to universal ethical teachings (i.e., not exclusively belonging to a particular race, tribe, or ethnicity) (Atkinson 1987;

McDaniel 2010: 96; Ramstedt 2004b: 9).[6] At that time, all other faiths that did not fit the strict ministerial definition were referred to as *aliran kepercayaan*, or "currents of belief." The 1952 regulation explicitly rejected non-theistic belief systems, including Hinduism, Buddhism, Confucianism, and other indigenous religions, and referred to them as "dogmatic opinions that belonged to tribes which were still backward" (Ramstedt 2004b: 9).

The MORA initially recognized three religions: Islam, Protestantism, and Catholicism. If adherents of *kepercayaan* (currents of belief) wanted to become full members of a "progressive nation," they had to homogenize and rationalize their belief systems along monotheistic lines. The adherence to belief systems that not only hampered the progress of the nation but also openly clashed with pancasila was incompatible with full membership in the political community (Ramstedt 2004b: 9). In 1958 Hinduism and in 1965 Buddhism and Confucianism were recognized, after they each had undergone a state-induced process of "internal reform" along monotheistic lines (Howell 1982: 511–517). This internal reform required the revivification and "reinvention" of ancient traditions, rituals, narratives, and texts as well as the prioritization of certain elements over others in order to locate an omnipotent, omniscient, and omnipresent supreme deity, a holy scripture, and a prophet.[7]

The experience of Balinese Hinduism is particularly illustrative in this regard. In order to meet the criteria put forth by the MORA, Hindu intellectuals rebuilt the entire Hindu belief system following a monotheistic model. In order to emphasize the "oneness of God," Brahman was promoted to the "supreme god" and given an Indonesian name, while other gods were turned into his "angels" and "saints." The Vedas were declared the equivalent of the Qur'an and the Bible, and the Vedic sages (*rishis*) became "prophets." Collections of mantras were transformed into

---

[6] Because of the opposition from Balinese Hindus, the 1952 definition of agama was later repealed, and replaced by another definition in 1961 which included as necessary elements a prophet, a holy scripture, the absolute lordship of Tuhan Yang Maha Esa (god), and a system of law (Intan 2006: 45; Mulder 1978: 4).

[7] Confucianism (to which today 0.7 percent of Indonesians adhere) was removed from the list of recognized religions in a 1978 ministerial directive (Minister of Home Affairs Directive No. 477/74054/BA.01.2/4683/95 of November 18, 1978) against the backdrop of anti-Chinese policies during Suharto's New Order that also prohibited the celebration of Chinese New Year and other Chinese festivities (Abalahin 2005; Heriyanto Yang 2005). Confucianism was only re-recognized as a religion when the ministerial directive was lifted in 2001.

three-times-a-day prayer (Tri Sandhya), approximating the form of
Islamic *salat* (McDaniel 2010: 96–97; Ramstedt 2004b: 11–12).

In Suharto's New Order (1966–1998), the activities and political role of
the MORA grew steadily. The ministry was placed under direct supervision
of the President, who not only appointed his close allies to it but also
singlehandedly oversaw the formulation and implementation of its policies,
as the regime deemed the strict control of the ministry essential for fighting
against its so-called enemies within and without, particularly "communist
and the Chinese instigators" (Surbakti 1991: 127–137, 366). Under the
New Order, anyone who did not profess a recognized religion risked being
identified as an atheist and by association a communist (O'Shaughnessy
2009: 169). More than half a million fell victim to the anti-communist
pogroms that characterized the early years of Suharto's ascent (1965/1966).
Many of those who originally adhered to the so-called *aliran kepercayaan*
were forced by the government to either relinquish their "backward" faiths
or to transform them into a recognized *agama*. Between 1966 and 1980,
mass conversions to Islam and Christianity, and to a lesser extent Buddhism
and Hinduism, took place especially among adherents of indigenous belief
systems (Ginting 2004: 226; Hefner 2004: 105; Ramstedt 2004a: 196;
2004b: 17). As Schiller (1996) demonstrates in the case of the Ngaju
indigenous religious community, Indonesian bureaucrats were inclined to
interpret indigenous practices as varieties of Hinduism and Buddhism and
register their adherents as members of these traditions in order to attain
religious and cultural homogeneity and create the ideal Indonesian citizen:
the "manusia pancasila" – the Pancasila man/woman (O'Shaughnessy
2009: 169; Ramstedt 2004b: 17). By doing so, authorities were not only
converting people from an *aliran kepercayaan* to a recognized religion
(*agama*), but also inducted them into Indonesian citizenship (Freston
2001: 81).

Thus, following in the footsteps of the colonial administrations, the
post-independence bureaucracy undertook far-reaching processes of
homogenizing the country's various religions, as these were redefined
and remodeled to fit state-defined categories mostly informed by monotheism, and citizens were forced to transform their religious practices to
fit these "reformed" religions. Indeed, one can argue that public policies
towards religion during the New Order (1966–1998) exhibited parallels
with the policies and practices Taylor outlines in the context of the "rage
to order" (2007: 63). Indigenous belief systems were slowly erased from
public life as their adherents were forced to officially identify with the
state-recognized religions. Over time this led to a deeper public

consciousness of what constitutes 'proper religion', which religious practices were 'pure', and which ones 'syncretistic' and therefore less desirable. Carnevalesque forms of religious ritual and distinctly local (for example: Javanese) ways of celebration were increasingly viewed with suspicion. This 'religious disciplinization,' which features prominantly also in Taylor's narrative (Taylor 2007: 77ff), gave rise to increased calls for the formal adoption of Islamic law in the family courts and for the promotion of legal aspects of Islam at the expense of more ritualistic and mystical approaches to religious experience.

RELIGION AND RELIGIOUS LAW IN INDONESIAN COURTS

Similar to state leaders in other post-colonial regimes, from Bourguiba in Tunisia to Nehru in India, at the time of independence Indonesian leaders were keen to put an end to the multiplicity of legal systems and unite the nation under one law (Salim 2008: 75). *Adat*, or customary law, particularly targeted due to its "feudal, imperialist and anti-republican connotations" was gradually phased out and replaced by positive law (Lev 2000: 33–70; Ramstedt 2004b: 8). By the time the central state had prevailed over all separatist struggles in 1969, the last customary courts were replaced by state courts. Islamic law, however, was more difficult to abolish. The state, fighting the war of independence, simultaneously fought secessionist movements across the islands that advocated the establishment of local Islamic states.

Being marginalized since the dissolution of the Constitutional Assembly and the 1959 establishment of Sukarno's "Guided Democracy" (a coalition of nationalists, communists, and socialists), Islamic groups had assisted Suharto's military takeover in 1966 and participated prominently in the anti-communist pogroms of 1965/66. Since the Muslim modernist party Masyumi had been banned by Sukarno in 1960, Islamist and Islamic leaders hoped for the revival of political Islam in Suharto's New Order and were thus bitterly disappointed when Suharto upheld the ban of Masyumi, and in 1973 went so far as to "simplify" the party system by forcing remaining Islamic parties to merge into one of two regime-sanctioned opposition parties.

In compensation, Suharto gave in to two Islamist demands. He set up the Indonesian Ulama Council (MUI) in 1975 that gave representation to leading modernist thinkers and scholars, and issued *fatwas* on urgent legal questions, including dietary issues. Secondly, Suharto and the military also watered down the draft Marriage Law that was eventually passed

in 1974. Initially, the law was envisioned to make marriage exclusively a
state matter by stipulating that "a marriage is valid if it is performed
before an official marriage registrar" (Cammack, Young, and Heaton
2008: 301). As such, it was still in line with the post-independence project
of legal unification that envisioned the replacement of all particularist law
by one uniform and countrywide civil code (Butt 2008: 269). But in
exchange for forcing Islamic leaders to accept the regime's exclusion of
political Islam, Suharto and the MORA made a profound concession on
the Marriage Law. In the final draft that was passed, the law permitted an
exception for Muslims: while all marriages of the non-Muslim population
needed to be certified in civil registries, the law left an opening for Muslim
marriages to be certified by Islamic courts. As such, the law recognized
Islamic courts and signified a clear departure from earlier legal reform
projects that foresaw the phasing out of religious courts and the unification of the legal system.

The law also permitted two different legal standards on marriage. It did
so by distinguishing between marriages that were "valid" and marriages
that were "legal." Marriages that fulfilled the known standards of an
Islamic marriage contract were "valid," whereas to be "legal" from a
civil law point of view, marriages had to fulfill the standards specified in
the Marriage Law. For instance, the 1974 law prohibited polygyny for
civil servants. For ordinary citizens, polygyny was made more difficult as
it required the written consent of the first wife accompanied with proof
that she was unable to perform her duty as a wife. It also required proof
on the part of the husband that he had the material means to support
more than one wife and their offspring. The 1974 law also required only
the consent of the marrying parties, whereas the Islamic courts could
continue to demand the consent of the woman's legal guardian, and disregard the minimum marriage age set in civil law at 18 for the woman and
21 for the man.

As Islamic family law (aside from the 1974 Marriage Law) remained
uncodified and rulings in the Islamic courts could differ significantly
from one court to another, the MORA tried to make inroads in the
early 1990s to effect some standardization in the application of law. In
1991, it issued a Compilation of Islamic Law (Kompilasi Hukum Islam
or KHI), decreed per presidential instruction Nr. 1, that was to give
direction as to the most authoritative opinions and regulations that
religious judges (*hakim agama*) ought to invoke. Obviously, the compilation was not a code for *hakim*s to follow, but it narrowed the range of
interpretations available, and quickly replaced citations of the Islamic

books previously used (classical books of *Shafi'i fiqh*). This was especially important as the Religious Judicature Act of 1989 withdrew the existing possibility for civil registries to overrule *hakim agama* decisions, so that the Islamic courts now became full courts of first instance (Federspiel 1998). Though the New Order had still not been able to make Islamic family law entirely a state issue, the court reform as well as the introduction of the KHI presented important steps toward the bureaucratization of Islamic law and the unification of Islamic jurisprudence across the archipelago (Mawardi 1998; Nurlaelawati 2010). Indeed, "religious court judges began to see themselves as part of the wide state bureaucracy and law enforcement apparatus, rather than upholders of Islamic law" (Butt 2008: 274).

The family matters of the other four recognized religions continued to be dealt with in the civil courts. Although the 1974 Marriage Law did not explicitly prohibit inter-religious marriages, it is often interpreted to preclude unions between adherents of different religions, because marriage is defined as a contract carried out according to the religion of both parties (O'Shaughnessy 2009: 170). Once again in a step to appease Islamic constituencies in exchange for political support, Suharto solidified the government's anti-inter-religious marriage stance in 1983 with a decree that de-authorized civil registries to register mixed marriages where one partner was a Muslim. The 1991 KHI went one step further and in Article 40-c explicitly prohibited Muslim men from marrying non-Muslim women – directly contradicting the dominant Shafi'i position on the matter (Mawardi 1998: 61). The reason was of pragmatic nature: the offspring of couples with a non-Muslim mother tended to adopt the mother's rather than the father's religion, and thereby contributed to the growth of non-Muslim religions in Indonesia.

THE UNSECULAR POLITICS OF DEMOCRACY

After prolonged demonstrations in the capital and the occupation of the parliamentary building by student movements, President Suharto was forced to resign and hand over power to his vice-president Habibie in May 1998. The first free elections since 1955 were held in June 1999, and the chairmen of Indonesia's two largest Islamic organizations were elected to important political positions. Abdurrahman Wahid, chairman of the Nahdlatul Ulama, was elected president; Amien Rais, chairman of the Muhammadiyah, became speaker of parliament. The newly elected legislature (MPR) soon set out to amend the 1945 constitution in a manner reflective of the desired democratization of the political system. In four rounds, major amendments were drafted, debated and passed between 1999 and 2002. The MPR accepted the outcome of a referendum in East Timor (which had been occupied and declared a province in 1976) in favour of independence, which thereby was released from association with Indonesia, and able to establish itself as a new state in 1999. The resolution that had ordered the indoctrination of Pancasila as a national ideology was revoked. Individual rights were significantly strengthened, both in the constitution and through the creation of new institutions that would further promote and aim to guard the rule of law.

The amended constitution reaffirmed in Article 28E the right of Indonesians to worship in accordance with their religions; and to express an opinion and attitude in accordance with their conscience. But although Article 28I recognizes the right to freedom of thought and conscience, negative religious freedom, i.e. the freedom to be agnostic, was (as before) not adopted in the constitutional amendments. Moreover, most of the rights enshrined in Article 28 are subject to Article 28J(2), which permits their limitation by legislation if directed at "protecting the rights and freedoms of others and [in] accord with moral considerations, religious values, security and public order in a democratic society".

On the one hand then, positive religious freedom and freedom of conscience were affirmed, together with numerous others that now make up a broad catalogue of individual rights in the amended constitution. At the same time, the possibility was created for legislation to limit these rights. Individual rights, including religious freedom (which to begin with only exists as a right to religion, but not freedom from religion), can be restricted if deemed to be contrary to "moral considerations" or "public order". Indeed, legislation and high court jurisprudence in the post-reformasi period on issues such as blasphemy, polygamy and inter-faith marriage have limited individual rights enshrined in Article 28, and justified doing so with reference to public order (Butt 2010; Crouch 2012; Pausacker 2012).

A second development, which has particularly affected inter-faith and intra-Islamic relations, is the increased prominence of the Indonesian Ulama Council (MUI). Although not formally endowed with any political authority, the council regularly issues fatwas and opinions on matters of public interest. Since the council is widely considered authoritative, few politicians today dare to take a stance openly in opposition to MUI's take on a given matter. Over the years, the council has issued provocative fatwas against the Ahmadiyya, against interfaith marriage, and against 'secularism, pluralism, and liberalism'. It has declared the Ahmadiyya non-Muslims and therefore not part of Indonesia's recognized religious groups. As such, those openly professing to be Ahmadiyya have been compelled to convert to a recognized faith, usually Sunni Shafiʿi Islam. Local branches of the MUI have also declared Shiites as infidel, and fueled intra-Islamic tensions by portraying Shiʿi aspects of fiqh and ritual in derogatory ways. In 2016, the MUI played a most dishonorable role when, together with other groups, it accused the highly popular non-Muslim governor of Jakarta, called Ahok, of blasphemy, effectively ending his political career. Ahok had criticized politicians who, in his view, instrumentalised a Qur'anic reference in order to discourage Muslims from voting non-Muslims into office. Following a campaign inspired by MUI's accusation, Ahok lost re-election and was controversially jailed for insulting Islam.

Beside the national level, the local level too has experienced important changes that affect conditions of belief. As part of the democratization process, the country started in 2001 to significantly decentralize governmental functions down to the units of municipalities and districts (of which today more than 500 exist, in 34 provinces). Development and public expenditure came under the purview of these sub-provincial "regencies" of Indonesia rather than the center or the provinces. Until 2012, in more than 60 percent of the country's districts, regulations were passed that signaled an Islamizing agenda (Parsons and Mietzner 2009, Pisani and Buehler 2016). Such regulations cluster around South Sulawesi, West Java, and West Sumatra and range from banning alcohol, to enforcing dress codes and curfew laws (e.g. for women who shall not walk outside without a male guardian after sundown), to compelling couples to recite the Qur'an at their wedding. For instance, a 2009 regulation in Tasikmalaya (West Java) specified that all Muslims must fight against corruption, fornication, prostitution, gambling, and consuming alcohol. It also pronounced as illegal: abortion, using pornography, charging interest, "practicing traditional healing if it leads people towards polytheism (*syirik*)," or spreading heterodox sects.[8] Officials (men and women) were ordered to wear Islamic dress on Fridays, and schools were told to ensure that all pupils could recite the Qur'an. In yet other regions, the so-called *shariʿa*-based bylaws have had a decisively local flavor. In Bulukumba in South Sulawasi, public signs were issued in

---

[8] Surat Ederan Bupati Cianjur No 451/2717/ASSDA.1.

Arabic script, arguably to play up regional specificity as an act of defiance against the culturally homogenizing policies of Jakarta. Some of these bylaws clearly violate the rights granted in Article 28 of the constitution, yet review mechanisms are weakly institutionalized and, as just noted, public order considerations may be applied to justify limitations on rights.

One may, as John Bowen (2013) does, see the *shari'a*-based bylaws as new signs of provincial or regional distinctiveness and authenticity. In his account, demands for *shari'a* are deeply situated in the history of the fight for independence against the Dutch, the ensuing struggles for autonomy against Jakarta, and debates about the relative role of religion in the country's law and politics. In the post-1998 era of reform and decentralization, *shari'a* signifies the resurgence of local capacities to define and exploit ideas of authenticity, autonomy, and morality – ideas which have strong political, cultural, and often religious dimensions. Whether Bowen is right in seeing the bylaws as part of a larger process of redefining and re-legitimizing the country's institutions, or whether one should, as other observers do, consider the religious bylaws as a sign of Indonesia captured by a nation-wide religious frenzy in the aftermath of democratization and the state's withdrawal from over-regulating society, democratization has profoundly altered conditions of belief. There is yet no debate about, and indeed very little awareness of, the violence done unto all religions, Islam included, in the 1950–1980s due to the provisions of the MORA. There is also still very little questioning of whether tying citizenship to religion is compatible with democracy and in particular with the freedom of religion guaranteed in the constitution.

CONCLUSIONS

Through bureaucratization, religion in post-independence Indonesia was not only made "manageable" but also put into the service of government policy. Alternative sources of meaning and beliefs were subjugated; those belief systems not recognized were effectively suppressed (e.g. Kejawen, Judaism, Shiism) and alternative sources of meaning within recognized religions undermined and marginalized. The type of functional conflicts regarding the relation of religious truth to other sources of truth that Gorski charts following Luhmann (see chapter 2) were made impossible through state policy that withdrew the availability of a non-religious identity. The state bureaucracy was also involved in ascertaining and defining religion, notably in requiring of Hinduism and Buddhism to fulfill certain criteria of monotheism. The state thereby became a party in the conflicts *within* religious communities that Gorski outlines. It did so in all four dimensions (segmentary, center/periphery, stratificatory, functional conflicts). Religious practices were redefined and "purified"; creeds were "rationalized" and standardized by the state, often to make them "modernist," "rationalist," "humanist," and "tolerant." *Agamasasi* was particularly aimed to fight against communism, "to extirpate indigenous religions that do not easily support development, to meld and smooth over differences among Indonesian religions, to neutralize any influence that religious sects have to take issue with national platforms [and] to support the dissociation of religious and ethnic identities" (Aragon 2000: 312, Schrauwers 2000: 92). Agamasasi was instrumental in reducing ethno-religious heterogeneity and promoting a singular monotheistic image of religion.

Creating the political and legal conditions for the emergence of Secularity III (exclusive humanism, the possibility of non-religion) in post-independence Indonesia has been subordinated to national culture, a national ethos that celebrates managed diversity. Indeed, the strong urge to nationalize is prevalent beyond the politics of managing diversity – one may also look at the attempts of the KHI to nationalize Islamic law, to mold it into an Indonesian brand sensitive to regional cultural specificities, something specifically Indonesian and thus separate from Arab or South Asian Islamic legal traditions. God is not one choice among several; Indonesian citizens have the choice between different paths toward God. Secularity II in the sense of a diminution of religious beliefs and practices is discouraged by the state, and state policies since 1945 have actively promoted religion and religiosity, within state-sanctioned frames. Nevertheless, the separation of religious and political authority (a part of Secularity I) has been a building block of the Indonesian state since 1945 and represents an overall societal consensus. Even though Islamist populist movements campaign in favor of the expansion of the jurisdiction of Islamic law, they generally do not propose that the highest offices of political authority ought to be reserved for religious dignitaries. The Indonesian state, both under authoritarian and democratic governments, has actively cultivated a social imaginary where one does not live in an "immanent frame," in "cosmic, social and moral orders which can be fully explained on their own terms," but instead within a national frame that is expression of and works toward (1) the belief in God, (2) a just and civilized humanity, (3) national unity, (4) democracy guided by the inner wisdom of unanimity arising out of deliberations among representatives, and (5) social justice (the five pancasila principles).

Throughout the downfall of the New Order regime and transition to democracy, the *pancasila-* and *agamasasi-*based nation-building project has been, to a great extent, successful at projecting a unified national identity and creating and preserving relatively peaceful inter-island and interfaith relations. Even the spirals of anti-Chinese and later Christian–Muslim violence that flared up during the Indonesian transition to democracy in 1998 – but died down again after 2002 – have not been able to undermine the overall belief that Indonesia is a multi-religious and multi-cultural society that lives from its diversity. In the post-1998 rounds of constitutional reform, those voices advocating a re-communalization of the legal system remained in the minority and the pancasila character of the national constitution was eventually retained and affirmed. As far as the state-recognized religions are concerned, Azra notes that "by and large, religious diversity and peaceful coexistence among the followers of different religions in Indonesia remain intact and prospects for religious pluralism ... are quite bright" (Azra 2008: 119). The picture is different if one takes into account prospects for intra-Islamic tolerance. Particularly Shiites and Ahmadiyyah have suffered severe persecution in recent years and those intellectuals, especially writers and artists, who openly challenged Islamic orthodoxies, are under threat (Schäfer 2015).

Taylor suggests that rather than pursuing policies of secularism that understand the latter in the sense of a strict separation, contemporary secular regimes should be thought of as such only if they attempt to maximize three goods: equality (between religions, as well as between religion and non-religion), liberty (of religious belief and practice, as well as of the choice not to believe and practice), and fraternity (inclusion of all voices in "the ongoing process of determining what the society is about (its political identity)") (Taylor 2010: 23). Taylor's approach aims to refute that secularism can be thought of in terms of timeless principles; instead, he suggests it must be recognized as requiring ongoing renegotiation in society. His notion of secularism is therefore not one of strict separation of religion and state, but one that balances between the three goals and, in doing so, remains responsive to the changing needs of society. Indonesia's post-independence religion–state relations can be viewed in light of Taylor's three goals. Until the country's democratization in 1998, the goals of hearing all voices (fraternity) and ensuring free choice (liberty) were largely made subservient to the goal of equality (treating all recognized religions as largely equal). Fraternity was violated when the MORA imposed a monotheistic notion of religion on poly- and non-theistic faiths, and thereby promoted internal elite-driven reforms of Hinduism and Buddhism that fulfilled bureaucratic requirements. The principle of liberty was violated when MORA made state recognition of religion (*agama*) a requirement for citizenship, thereby de facto banning the profession of alternative faiths, including Judaism, Shi'i Islam, heterodox Sunni variants of Islam, and other local belief systems. The absence of the freedom not to profess a religion (negative freedom of religion), as well as the continuing requirement for recognized religions to abide by state-sanctioned definitions are hard, if not impossible, to reconcile with the post-1998 promises of democracy. In the medium-term, constitutional jurisprudence will need to address these deficits.

Yet for Taylor, fraternity also implies maintaining "relations of harmony and comity between the supporters of different religions and *Weltanschauungen.*" How can these relations of harmony and comity be created? The role of the democratic state is limited in this regard. It can set the ordering frame for such relations, by guarding the rule of law, and prosecuting violations of it, in particular acts of intolerance towards others and persecution on the basis of religion. But it cannot force its citizens to appreciate each other for their difference: It cannot impose on its citizens the private belief that expressions of persuasions other than their own, be they religious, political, cultural, or philosophical, are intrinsically valuable (Böckenförde 1967). Because of its liberal commitments, the democratic state cannot, unlike its authoritarian counterpart, impose cohesion and relations of harmony and comity from above. Instead, these must be created in civil society: It is civil society that needs to work toward nourishing the ties that bind communities together and citizens to one another, and that transform potentially divisive experiences of difference into a conscious affirmation of pluralism. Given the role some religious leaders, notably of the Indonesian Ulama Council (MUI), have played in inciting inter-religious conflict and intra-Islamic intolerance in Indonesia, it is unclear that religion will be a helpful resource in this endeavor.

Bibliography

Abalahin, A. J. 2005. "A Sixth Religion? Confucianism and the Negotiation of Indonesian Chinese Identity under the Pancasila State." In A. C. Willford and K. M. George (Eds.), *Spirited Politics: Religion and Public Life in Contemporary Southeast Asia.* Ithaca: Cornell University Press, 119–142.

Anshari, Saifuddin. 1976. *The Jakarta Charter of June 1945: A History of the Gentleman's Agreement between the Islamic and the Secular Nationalists in*

Modern Indonesia. M.A. thesis, Institute of Islamic Studies, McGill University.

Aragon, L. V. 2000. *Fields of the Lord: Animism, Christian Minorities, and State Development in Indonesia*. Honolulu: University of Hawai'i Press.

Atkinson, J. M. 1987. "Religions in Dialogue: The Construction of an Indonesian Minority Religion." In R. S. Kipp and S. Rodgers (Eds.), *Indonesian Religions in Transition*. Tucson: University of Arizona Press, 171–186.

Benda, H. J. 1958. *The Crescent and the Rising Sun; Indonesian Islam under the Japanese Occupation, 1942–1945*. The Hague: W. van Hoeve.

    1958. "Christiaan Snouck Hurgronje and the Foundations of Dutch Islamic Policy In Indonesia." *The Journal of Modern History*, Vol. 30, No. 4 (Dec., 1958): 338–347.

Bowen, J. 2013. "Contours of Shari'a in Indonesia." In M. Künkler and A. C. Stepan (Eds.), *Indonesia, Islam And Democracy*. New York: Columbia University Press, 149–167.

Böckenförde, Ernst-Wolfgang. 1991. "The Rise of the State as a Process of Secularisation." In *State, Society and Liberty. Studies in Political Theory and Constitutional Law*. Oxford: Berg, 26–46. Newly translated in Ernst-Wolfgang Böckenförde. *Religion, Law and Democracy. Selected Writings*. Oxford: Oxford University Press, 2018.

Butt, Simon. 2008. "Polygamy and Mixed Marriage in Indonesia: Islam and Marriage Law in the Courts." In T. Lindsey, ed. *Indonesia: Law and Society*. Singapore: ISEAS, 266–287.

    2010. "Islam, the State and the Constitutional Court in Indonesia." *Pacific Rim Law & Policy Journal*, 19(2): 279–301.

Cammack, M., Young, L. A., and Heaton, T. 2008. "Indonesia's Marriage Law." In T. Lindsey (Ed.), *Indonesia: Law and Society*. Singapore: ISEAS, 288–312.

Casanova, J. 2006. "Rethinking Secularism: A Global Comparative Perspective." *The Hedgehog Review*, 8 (1–2), 7–22.

Chalmers, Ian. 2006. *Indonesia: An Introduction to Contemporary Traditions*. Oxford: Oxford University Press.

Crouch, M. A. 2012. "Law and Religion in Indonesia: The Constitutional Court and the Blasphemy Law." *Asian Journal of Comparative Law*, 7(1): 1–46.

De Bary, William Theodore, Carol Gluck, Arthur E. Tiedemann, W. J. J. Boot, and William M. Bodiford. 2006. *Sources of Japanese Tradition. Part II (1868–2000)* (2nd edn.). New York: Columbia University Press.

Feith, Herbert. 1962. *The Decline of Constitutional Democracy in Indonesia*. Ithaca: Cornell University Press.

Emmerson, D. K. 1978. "The Bureaucracy in Political Context: Weakness in Strength." In K. D. Jackson and L. W. Pye (Eds.), *Political Power and Communications in Indonesia*. Berkeley: University of California Press, 82–136.

Federspiel, H. M. 1998. "Islamic Values, Law, and Expectations in Contemporary Indonesia." *Islamic Law and Society*, 5(1): 90–117.

Freston, P. 2001. *Evangelicals and Politics in Asia, Africa, and Latin America*. Cambridge, UK: Cambridge University Press.

Ginting, Juara T. 2004. "The Position of Hinduism in Karo Society (North Sumatra)." In M. Ramstedt (Ed.), *Hinduism in Modern Indonesia: A Minority Religion Between Local, National, and Global Interests.* London: RoutledgeCurzon, 226–241.

Hardacre, Helen. 1989. *Shinto and the State, 1868–1988.* Princeton: Princeton University Press.

Hefner, R. W. 2004. "Hindu Reform in an Islamizing Java: Pluralism and Peril." In M. Ramstedt (Ed.), *Hinduism in Modern Indonesia: A Minority Religion Between Local, National, and Global Interests.* London; New York: RoutledgeCurzon, 93–108.

Heriyanto Yang, Y. 2005. "The History and Legal Position of Confucianism in Postindependence Indonesia." *Marburg Journal of Religion, 10(1):* 1–8.

Howell, Julia D. 1982. "Indonesia: Searching for Consensus." In C. Caldarola (Ed.), *Religions and Societies, Asia and the Middle East.* Berlin; New York: Mouton, 497–548.

Intan, Benyamin Fleming. 2006. *"Public Religion" and the Pancasila-based State of Indonesia: An Ethical and Sociological Analysis.* New York: Peter Lang.

Joas, Hans. 2009. "Die säkulare Option. Ihr Aufstieg und ihre Folgen." *Deutsche Zeitschrift für Philosophie*, Akademie Verlag, 57(2): 293–300.

Koenig, Matthias. Jenseits des Säkularisierungsparadigmas? Eine Auseinandersetzung mit Charles Taylor. *Kölner Zeitschrift für Soziologie und Sozialpsychologie*, (2011), Vol. 63: 649–673.

Kusuma, A. B. and Elson, R. E. (2011). "A Note on the Sources for the 1945: Constitutional Debates in Indonesia." *Bijdragen tot de Taal-, Land- en Volkenkunde,* 167(2/3): 196–209.

Künkler, Mirjam. 2008. "Zum Verhältnis Staat-Religion und der Rolle islamischer Intellektueller in der indonesischen Reformasi" in Stephanie Garling and Simon W. Fuchs (eds.), *Religion in Diktatur und Demokratie – Zur Bedeutung von religiösen Werten, Praktiken und Institutionen in politischen Transformationsprozessen.* Wuppertal: Villigster Profile, 84–102.

Künkler, Mirjam. 2012. "Religion-State Relations and Democracy in Egypt and Tunisia: Models from the Democratizing Muslim World – and their Limits." *Swiss Political Science Review*, 18: 114–119.

2017. Constitutionalism, Islamic Law, and Religious Freedom in post-independence Indonesia" in Asli Bali and Hanna Lerner (eds.) *Constitution Writing, Religion and Democracy*, Cambridge University Press, 179–206.

2016. Künkler, Mirjam and Yüksel Sezgin, "The Unification of Law and the Post-colonial State. Limits of State Monism in India and Indonesia," *American Behavioral Scientist*, 60(8), July 2016, 987–1012.

Lev, Daniel. 1972. *Islamic Courts in Indonesia; A Study in the Political Bases of Legal Institutions.* Berkeley: University of California Press.

2000. *Legal Evolution and Political Authority in Indonesia: Selected Essays.* The Hague: Kluwer Law International.

Mawardi, Ahmad Imam. 1998. *Socio-Political Bacground of the Enactment of Kompilasi Hukum Islam Di Indonesia.* M.A., Institute of Islamic Studies, McGill University, Montreal.

McDaniel, June. 2010. "Agama Hindu Dharma Indonesia as a New Religious Movement: Hinduism Recreated in the Image of Islam." *Nova Religio: The Journal of Alternative and Emergent Religions*, 14(1): 93–111.

Mulder, N. 1978. *Mysticism and Everyday Life in Contemporary Java: Cultural Persistence and Change*. Singapore: Singapore University Press.

Nasution, Harun. 1989. *Refleksi Pembaharuan Pemikiran Islam: 70 Tahun*. Jakarta: Lembaga Studi Agama dan Filsafat.

Natsir, Mohammad. 1973. *Capita Selecta*. Jakarta: Bulan Bintang.

Nurlaelawati, Euis 2010. *Modernization, Tradition and Identity: The Kompilasi Hukum Islam and Legal Practice in the Indonesian Religious Courts*. Amsterdam: University of Amsterdam Press.

O'Shaughnessy, Kate. 2009. *Gender, State and Social Power in Contemporary Indonesia: Divorce and Marriage Law*. London; New York: Routledge.

Parsons, Nicholas and Marcus Mietzner 2009. "Sharia By-Laws in Indonesia. A Legal and Political Analysis." *Australian Journal of Asian Law*, 11(12): 190–217.

Pausacker, H. 2012. "Playboy, the Islamic Defenders' Front and the Law: Enforcing Islamic Norms in Post-Soeharto Indonesia?" *Australian Journal of Asian Law*, 13(1): 1–20.

Pisani, Elizabeth and Michael Buehler. 2016. Why do Indonesian politicians promote *shari'a* laws? An analytic framework for Muslim-majority democracies. *Third World Quarterly*, Vol. 38 (3), 734–752.

Ramstedt, M. 2004a. "The Hinduization of Local Traditions in South Sulawesi." In M. Ramstedt (Ed.), *Hinduism in Modern Indonesia: A Minority Religion Between Local, National, and Global Interests*. London: RoutledgeCurzon, 184–225.

— 2004b. "Introduction: Negotiating Identities. Indonesian 'Hindus' Between Local, National, and Global Interests." In M. Ramstedt (Ed.), *Hinduism in Modern Indonesia: A Minority Religion Between Local, National, and Global Interests*. London; New York: RoutledgeCurzon, 1–34.

Salim, Askar. 2008. *Challenging the Secular State: The Islamization of Law in Modern Indonesia*. Honolulu: University of Hawaii Press.

Schäfer, Saskia 2015. Renegotiating Indonesian secularism through debates on Ahmadiyya and Shia, *Philosophy and Social Criticism*, 1–12.

Schiller, A. 1996. "An 'Old' Religion in 'New Order' Indonesia: Notes on Ethnicity and Religious Affiliation." *Sociology of Religion*, 57(4): 409–417.

Schrauwers, Albert. 2000. *Colonial "Reformation" in the Highlands of Central Sulawesi, Indonesia, 1892–1995*. Toronto: University of Toronto Press.

Soekarno, *Under the Banner of Revolution (Dibawah Bendera Revolusi)*.

Sukarno. 2006 "Pancasila membuktikan dapat mempersatukan bangsa Indonesia." In Floriberta Aning (Ed.), *Filsafat Pancasila menurut Bung Karno*. Yogyakarta: Media Pressindo.

Surbakti, R. A. 1991. *Interrelation Between Religious and Political Power under New Order Indonesia*. PhD thesis, Northern Illinois University, DeKalb.

Taylor, Charles. 1998. "Modes of Secularism." In Rajeev Bhargava (ed.) *Secularism and its Critics*. New Delhi: Oxford University Press.

2007. *A Secular Age*. Cambridge, MA: Harvard Belknap Press.

2010. "The Meaning of Secularism," *The Hedgehog Review*, Fall, 23–34.

2012. "How to Define Secularism." In Alfred Stepan and Charles Taylor (eds.) *Boundaries of Toleration*. New York: Columbia University Press, 59–78.

Yamin, Mohammed (ed.). 1959. *Naskah Persiapan Undang-Undang Dasar 1945*. Volume I. Jakarta: Yayasan Prapanca.

6

Secularity and Hinduism's Imaginaries in India

Shylashri Shankar

INTRODUCTION

The continuing relevance of religious beliefs and politicized religion in countries like India, where economic liberalization has marched alongside muscular nationalism (or, in Charles Taylor's words, confessionally defined nationalism), requires us to revisit the claim that secularization – the process of the emergence of an "unbelieving ethos" and/or the decline/privatization of religion – occurs with modernization.[1] Since the 1990s, the Bharatiya Janata Party (BJP) and its battlecry of Hindutva – a literal meaning is "Hindu-ness" – has been an increasingly forceful contender in India's political arena, having led a coalition government at the center in 1996 and from 1998 to 2004, and a majority government since 2014. The Indian Supreme Court's judgments in three recent cases illuminate the problems politicized religion creates for secularism in the Indian context.

In 1996, two cases (henceforth *Hindutva* case) were heard together by the Supreme Court of India on whether the use of the term "Hindutva" in election speeches by the winning candidates was illegal because it pertained to religion and therefore contravened a law that forbade the use of

Senior Fellow, Centre for Policy Research, New Delhi. I am grateful to Pratap Bhanu Mehta, the participants of the workshop at IISJ in Onati (Spain) and to Subhadra Banda for research assistance. Parts of this chapter were published in *Soft Power*, Vol. 1, Iss. 2, Jul.–Dec., 2014.
[1] The claim about the privatization of religion in orthodox secularization theory has been challenged by Casanova (1994) and others who argue that the theory is only one third right – it was right about the institutional differentiation of religious and political spheres, but not about the decline of religious beliefs. See Philip Gorski, Chapter 2 in this volume, for a discussion of these debates.

religious rhetoric in election speeches.[2] The two politicians (Prabhoo and Joshi) argued that the concept of Hindutva was cultural and nationalistic rather than religious; their opponents said the concept pertained to Hindu religion. Citing the difficulty of defining a Hindu, the then Chief Justice of India, J.S. Verma concluded that the term "Hindutva" and "Hinduism" could not be equated with narrow fundamentalist religious bigotry.

"The word "Hindutva" is used and understood as a synonym of "Indianisation," that is the development of uniform culture by obliterating the differences between all the cultures coexisting in the country". (para 40, *Praboo v Kunte*; see fn note 3). The answer to whether the use of the word "Hindutva" in an election speech is religious or not depends on the context, said the judgment. The mere word itself ought not to be narrowly construed as a religious term "unless the context of a speech indicates a contrary meaning or use." In the abstract, said the Court, "these terms are indicative more of a way of life of the Indian people and are not confined merely to describe persons practicing the Hindu religion as a faith."[3] In the case of *Prabhoo*, the court ruled that the speeches amounted to corrupt practices under the Act, while in *Joshi*, it did not. In the *Joshi* case, the court equated Hinduism – which it saw as "Indianization" or culture – with Hindutva, which was deemed to be nonreligious nationalist rhetoric.

"Hindutva" with "Hinduism," but this one did so and likened both with "a way of life." The judgment was criticized by several scholars for giving legitimacy to Hindu nationalist ideology, with the upshot being Hindutva = Hinduism = way of life and not a religion = Indianization = development of a uniform culture, even if the judges themselves may not have meant to say so (Nauriya 1996). Not surprisingly, the Hindu right viewed the ruling as giving judicial imprimatur to "Hindutva" as an ideology that expressed nationalism and Indianness rather than a religion, and legitimizing its use in politics.[4]

What made the Hindutva judgment even more ironic is that in a previous judgment (*Bommai v. Union of India*), the Supreme Court recognized the

---

[2] *Dr. Ramesh Yeshwant Prabhoo v. Prabhakar K. Kunte* AIR (1996) SC 1113; *Manohar Joshi v. Nitin Bhaurao Patil* (1996) 1 SCC 169. The Constituent Assembly's decision that religion would be delinked from politics was codified in Section 123(3) of the Representation of People Act (1951), which forbade the use of religious rhetoric in election campaigns.

[3] *Prabhoo v. Kunte*:161: para 43.

[4] Asserting that Hindutva was synonymous with nationalism and "Bharateeyatva," BJP party leader Vajpayee argued in a public meeting that the concept did not merit further debate as the Supreme Court had defined it in totality in its judgment (*Times of India*, June 7, 1996).

potential of "Hindutva" as a divisive religious mobilizing concept.[5] In
Bommai, the Court reviewed the constitutionality of the dismissal of BJP-
led state (sub-regional) governments for participating in unsecular activities. The dismissal came in the wake of riots between Hindus and Muslims
in these states following the destruction of an ancient mosque in northern
India. The Court ruled that a state government pursuing an unsecular
policy was acting contrary to the constitutional mandate and could be
dismissed under Article 356. "Unsecular" activities included a political
party's ideological plank (in this case BJP's Hindutva) in elections that
had the effect of eroding the secular philosophy of the Constitution:

> If a political party espousing a particular religion comes to power, that religion
> tends to become, in practice, the official religion. All other religions come to
> acquire a secondary status, at any rate, a less favorable position … under our
> Constitution, no party or organization can simultaneously be a political and a
> religious party. It has to be either. (*Bommai v. Union of India*: 236)

The judgments resulted in a paradox: The BJP was implicitly granted
recognition as a political party (*Hindutva* judgment) and condemned as a
religious party (*Bommai* judgment), though the court in *Bommai* maintained
that no party could be a religious *and* a political party. How do we understand
these inconsistencies in the court's interpretations? Should we attribute it to
the whims of individual justices? But of the three justices in the Prabhoo and
Joshi cases, one (J. S. Verma) had also ruled in the Bommai case.

Scholars have explained these contradictory rulings under the broad
rubric of a "crisis of secularism," caused variously by constitutional ambiguities, colonial rule, social justice concerns of a liberal democratic state, and
the disjuncture between an elite-driven normative project and the demands
imposed by requirements of democratic consent (Needham and Sunder
Rajan 2006). For instance, when the Constituent Assembly decided that
India would not be a Hindu state, it did not specify what it meant for the
country to be a secular one. The term "secularism" itself was not incorporated until the 42nd Amendment in 1976. Other inconsistencies are that the
Constitution exhorts the state to treat all religions with equal respect
and simultaneously charges it to reform unequal religious practices

---

[5] *Bommai* v. *Union of India*, 1994 SC 1918. In *Bommai*, seven justices agreed that "secularism" was a basic feature of the Constitution. Only two, including Justice Verma (who later
decided the *Hindutva* case) refrained from expressing an opinion on the definition of
"secularism." For the seven Justices, the meaning of secularism ranged from seeing the role
of the state as one of passive neutral religious tolerance to an active protection of all
religions. A majority ruling is not obvious in *Bommai*, since there was no order of the
entire court; the nine judges expressed themselves through six opinions.

(particularly in Hinduism), and correct historical wrongs perpetrated on the lowest castes (of Hindus) and other groups through affirmative action in government jobs and political constituencies.[6] Another set of contradictions is highlighted by Chatterjee (2004): religious law First, the state seeks to separate religion and politics, but at the same time involves itself in the regulation, funding, and administration of religious institutions. Second, despite legally demarcating minority religious communities and giving them the right to follow personal law and to administer educational institutions, there is no procedure for determining who would represent these minorities in their dealings with the state. So, reform efforts in the minority communities are blocked by fears that it would result in a loss of identity, while, on the other hand, the secular state is seen as being biased toward the minorities and compromised by its legal protection of allegedly backward practices of these communities. Chatterjee advocates a process of obtaining democratic consent for reforms from within each legally constituted minority community.

A more recent explanation for the contradictory judgments can be drawn from Charles Taylor. In *A Secular Age*, Taylor argues that for purposes of understanding the struggle, rivalry, or debate between religion and unbelief in Latin Christendom, we have to understand religion as combining three dimensions of transcendence.

It is our relation to a transcendent God which has been displaced at the centre of social life (Secularity I); it is faith in this God whose decline is tracked in these theories (Secularity II), and the third dimension is the emergence of new conditions of belief ... the sense that there is some good higher than, beyond human flourishing. (Secularity III) (Taylor 2007: 20)

Secularity thus has three meanings for Taylor: i) As a public space emptied of God;[7] ii) As a falling off of religion/religious practice; iii) As a move from a society where belief in God is unchallenged and unproblematic to one in which it is understood to be one option among others and frequently not the easiest to embrace. He argues that Secularity III is

---

[6] About 80 percent of Indians are Hindus (2011 Census) and occupy a caste within a top-down hierarchy of Brahmin (priest), Kshatriya (warrior/King), Vaishya (trader), and Sudra (farming/lowest castes). The caste system not only determines the individual's social status on the basis of the group to which he is born, but also differentiates and assigns occupational and economic roles (especially in rural areas). See Louis Dumont's classic *Homo Hierarchicus* (1981) for a treatise on the organizing principles of the caste system and its implications.

[7] "The norms and principles we follow, the deliberations we engage in, generally don't refer us to God or to any religious beliefs: the considerations we act on are internal to the 'rationality' of each sphere" (Taylor 2007: 2).

characterised by the rise of exclusive humanism (a belief in the this-worldly aspect of human agency without the help of a god) along with the availability to a majority of citizens, a diverse set of options that include belief and unbelief. It is important to note that for Taylor, religion does not wither away or become privatized in Secularity III.

Taylor is careful to limit his explanation to the Latin Christian world because while "it is very hard to demonstrate that an 'unbelieving ethos' could not have arisen in any other religion, nevertheless, it seems to me to be overwhelmingly plausible" (Taylor 2009: 267).[8] The plausibility, for Taylor, derives from the absence of enabling conditions, which produced Secularity III in the modern West. The contradictory rulings by India's apex court would be partly explained by the high religiosity of the Indian milieux. He writes:

> An age or society would then be secular or not, in virtue of the conditions of experience of and search for the spiritual. Obviously, where it stood in this dimension would have a lot to do with how secular it was in the second sense, which turns on levels of belief and practice, but there is no simple correlation between the two, as the case of the US shows. As for the first sense, which concerns public space, this may be uncorrelated with both the others (as might be argued for the case of India). But I will maintain that in fact, in the Western case, the shift to public secularity has been part of what helped to bring on a secular age in my third sense. In this meaning, as against sense 2, at least many milieux in the United States are secularized, and I would argue that the United States as a whole is. Clear contrast cases today would be the majority of Muslim societies, or the milieux in which the vast majority of Indians live ... here are big differences between these societies in what it is to believe, stemming in part from the fact that belief is an option, and in some sense an embattled option in the Christian (or "post-Christian") society, and not (or not yet) in the Muslim ones. (Taylor 2007: 3–4)

But is Taylor right to lump all the non-Christian societies into a single category? Taylor's and the other explanations do not highlight a more fundamental contradiction, namely how "Hinduism" is imagined by India's Constitution. As we shall see, India epitomizes a society where the notions of "religion," "belief," and "disbelief" are less unambiguous than in Taylor's Latin Christendom, where a belief system (Hinduism) was given the epithet of "religion" by the colonial power and by some Indian nationalists. This definition was retained after independence in the country's constitution and

---

[8] Taylor's approach is less useful for explaining the global varieties of secularism (see Gorski, Chapter 2, this volume) or the myriad institutional settlements between the state and religious communities and politics or for explaining the consequences of the interaction between ideas, institutions, and political regimes for religious persecution and intergroup toleration (Katznelson and Stedman-Jones 2010).

laws along with other competing and pre-existing notions of what the belief system constituted, including a notion of Hinduism as "not religion" and of the state governing a public space emptied of God. To explain the contradictions in the judiciary's interpretations of Hindutva and Hinduism and in the Indian state's management of religious diversity, the article draws on a concept used by Charles Taylor, namely "social imaginaries" – the kind of collective understanding a group has to have in order to make sense of their practices.[9] I argue that the contradictions stem from the inability of the Constitution to reconcile three different imaginaries of Hinduism – as a religion, as an ancient order, and the notion of Indianness as a culture. But these contradictions, while stoking discord, have also provided a buffer zone from which the state can achieve some sort of equi-distance (in Rajeev Bhargava's terms; see Bhargava 2015), principled or otherwise, from such conflicts.

In the next sections, I discuss three stylized imaginaries of Hinduism as a religion, ancient order, and Indianness as a culture and show how these weave through the Constituent Assembly debates on the role of the new state vis-à-vis religion, and problematize how Hinduism is tackled in the political and legal arenas.

SOCIAL IMAGINARIES OF HINDUISM

"I speak of 'imaginary' (i) because I'm talking about the way ordinary people 'imagine' their social surroundings," while "(ii) theory is often the possession of a small minority, ... what is interesting in the social imaginary is that it is shared by large groups of people, if not the whole society" (Taylor 2007: 171–172).

If one adopts Taylor's distinction between "theory" and "social imaginary," then the only way to assess a social imaginary would be to collect accounts of lived experiences of millions of Indians. It is also highly probable that these ethnographies will reveal the presence of not one but multiple social imaginaries, overlapping and jousting with each other. These imaginaries would include, among others, the state's social imaginary constructed by a constitution and interpreted by the courts, religious

---

[9] I agree with Taylor's view of secularism not as an institutional principle of separation or accommodation of religion, but as a civic ideology that seeks to balance "different and potentially competing goods" through some sort of principled equi-distance (in Rajeev Bhargava's terms). The "principled" aspect is more problematic because empirical evidence suggests that the state's attitude is governed more by what Pratap Bhanu Mehta (2007) calls a modus vivendi. Also see Akeel Bilgrami's (2014) critique of some parts of Taylor's view of secularism.

leaders' social imaginary disseminated through preaching and lectures
and practices adopted by the followers, the lived experiences of different
types of ordinary people, and the imaginaries of political leaders displayed
through their election manifestoes and speeches and subscribed to by
those who vote for them.[10] Taylor's own approach to experiencing the
world and in recounting the transformation of social imaginaries, as Jon
Butler (2010) points out, stresses ideas and theory more than experience
and ordinary people. It is unclear who constitutes the "we" in a social
imaginary in *A Secular Age* that "so seldom inquires about the social
imaginaries of ordinary people ... as opposed to the social imaginaries
described and created by prominent thinkers" (Butler 2010: 198).

It may be useful to drop the theory–social imaginary dichotomy and refer
to the lived experiences of three stylized slices of experiences that have
created overlapping and competing imaginaries of "Hinduism" in India.

Hinduism is a Religion

Sindhu is the term used by ancient Greeks and Persians to refer to peoples
(not religions) beyond the river Indus.[11] European travelers and missionaries
regarded Indian traditions as heathen or pagan, and called it "gentooism,"
"the religion of the Hindus," and then "Hindooism"/"Hinduism" by the end
of the eighteenth century. Can Hinduism be called a religion? Sociologist
Emile Durkheim defined religion as a unified system of beliefs and practices
having to do with the sacred, that is to say the beliefs and practices which are
bound up in a moral community called the Church. Anthropologist Clifford
Geertz (1993) viewed religion as a system of symbols which acts to establish
powerful, pervasive, and long-lasting moods and motivations in men by
formulating conceptions of a general order of existence and clothing these
conceptions with such an aura of factuality that the moods and motivations
seem uniquely realistic. These definitions imply that a 'religion' has to possess
a set of characteristics.

Three elements are identified as central to the role played by Europeans in
the construction of Hinduism as a religion: a Western Christian concept of
religion, the idea that Indian religions formed one pan-Indian religion, and the
needs of the colonial enterprise. Different religious phenomena came to be
seen as parts of one religion, Hinduism, and the core was drawn from

---

[10] As weak proxies for ethnographic work, I refer to colonial geographers, travelers, and
other accounts of the "Hindoo," and to the biography of a Brahmin savant.

[11] This section's analysis draws from Bloch et al. (2010).

Brahmanism, with its texts and priests (see Dalmia and von Stietencron 1995). These moves to create a unified religion in India were closely linked to the legal codification of the colonial subject (Vishwanathan 2008).

The characterization of Hinduism as a religion thus has to be understood within the frame of debates on British colonialism's role in India. Whether colonialism is seen as a project of cultural control and the conquest of India as the conquest of knowledge (Cohn 1996), or of oriental empericism (Ludden 1993), these narratives agree that colonialism developed an understanding of caste that allowed it to dismantle a previous power structure and make it into a "hollow crown" (Dirks 1987), while a Western Christian concept of religion resulted in the postulation of one religion, Hinduism, which unified the diversity of doctrines, texts, practices, and gods that existed in on the subcontinent (Keppens and Bloch 2010).

Simultaneously, Nineteenth-century Indian intellectuals who resisted the proselytization by Christian missionaries also engaged in constructing a Hindu religion, a modern Hinduism that would be respectable in the eyes of the world and would provide the basis for a morality of actions in the secular world. Revivalist movements like Arya Samaj discovered in Hinduism a monotheistic God, a Book, and congregational worship (Van der Veer 2002). These reform movements led by and consisting mostly of intellectuals, Brahmins, and elites transformed Indian traditions into a unified religion, and are held to be precursors of the Hindu nationalists today (Thapar 1989). These perspectives emphasize the deliberate construction of Hinduism as a religion.

While the constructivist view holds a dominant position, its critics argue that non-Muslim Indians shared a common identity in pre-colonial India, and therefore such identity was coterminous with religious identity (Lorenzen 1999).[12] Other shortcomings of the constructivists include ambiguity about the nature of the process of construction, lack of clarity on whether Brahmanism really exists or existed in India, and, if it did exist, the absence of answers on why non-Brahmins accepted Brahmanism as their religion, and the absence of a clear relationship between the motives for the construction and the fact of the construction of Hinduism (Keppens and Bloch 2010).

Adherents of this imaginary and who espouse liberal values would argue that the religio-political differentiation as envisaged by the

---

[12] In response to the question of what makes this identity into religious identity, Lorenzen (1999: 28) replies that religions are associated with a particular emotion or emotional experience that corresponds to Rudolph Otto's *mysterium tremendum et fascinans* (a unique point of origin/a personal experience of the sacred).

constitution in India mirrors Gorski's segmentary model, wherein religious groups are recognized and protected by the state and internally governed by their own leadership. But their critics would say that the state interferes in the internal governance of these groups (particularly in Hinduism) and that the model is in reality stratificatory, whereby the state enjoys a higher position vis-à-vis religion. But these models only apply to this imaginary of Hinduism, which is the one that Taylor refers to, and it also informs the *Bommai* judgment discussed earlier, where BJP's use of Hindutva was classified as religious rhetoric. If this were the only imaginary, then Taylor would be right to say that public secularity (I) has not been achieved in India, and that belief is not yet an option (among many) in India (as it is, in his view, in the Christian North Atlantic). However, this is not the only imaginary present in India. Let us now turn to a Hinduism that bears no relation to religion.

Hinduism is an Ancient Order

In *The Last Brahmin*, Rani Siva Sankara Sarma (2007) writes about the views held by his Brahmin savant-father whom he calls "the last Brahmin." The book, which portrays the lived experience of a scholar of the Vedas, gives us a glimpse of a different imaginary. This "last Brahmin" declares from his deathbed at the age of 80 that neither of his sons is eligible to perform his funeral rites because one (the narrator) is a non-believer, and the other (the narrator's older brother) is a "Hindu convert" because he espouses Hindu nationalism. The father declares that Brahmins are a people free of – or outside – religion; there is no place for the term "Hindu" or "religion" in the canonical Vedic tradition for the followers of the ancient order.

Attempting to understand his father's distinction between Brahmin and Hindu, the narrator asks whether the followers of the ancient order recognized the word "Hinduism." The father replies:

On the banks of the sacred and serene Krishna river, at a convention of Pandits [scholars], the propriety and impropriety of the term "Hindu" came up for discussion. Then the noble and venerable savant [an illustrious scholar] … stated through illustrations that the terms Hinduism and Hindu were used first by foreigners, that these words are not related to Bharatiya [Indic] culture. However, grammarians concur that even phonic improprieties have verbal existences. Therefore, when something is absent in the discourse but prevalent in popular usage, the learned must remain indifferent towards such phonic improprieties. When followers of the ancient order who practice varna dharma [caste system] are called Hindus, one should accept this with similar indifference. (Sarma 2007: 61)

Here, the view of Hinduism as an ancient order is based not on religion, but on varna (a classificatory system), which does not allow for entry or exit from the Order. "Whether you belong to Christianity or Islam, or Buddhism or Hinduism, as per the ancient order you can only be an Untouchable. This is so because the ancient and everlasting norm has no relation with religion" (Sarma 2007: 60). Therefore, in this view, there is no connection between temples and the Brahmins of the ancient order, nor is there any sympathy for Hindu nationalist ideology, which would be dismissed as proxy Christianity and antagonistic to the aims of the ancient order. Nor would the state would have a role in reframing or changing the classificatory system.

Adherents of this imaginary would say that Taylor's Secularity I and II have no place in their Hinduism since they do not practice religious beliefs, and hence the existence or non-existence of God in public space is moot. They would also say that they are engaged in a search for a fullness that is unrelated to the notion of a God, and that fullness could be akin to Taylor's exclusive humanism.[13] While adherents of this imaginary do not form the majority, its presence in the way Hinduism is imagined in the Constitution does give this view more weight as a meaningful choice available to some.

Hinduism is an Imaginary Entity/Indianness as a Culture

The appropriateness of viewing Hinduism as a religion, and of Brahmanism as its basis, is challenged by scholars (Balagangadhara 1994, Staal 1989) who argue that "religion" is better thought of as a model of "explanation" that applies only to the Jewish, Christian, and Islamic worlds. This position echoes the views of travelers and scholars from previous centuries who expressed their inability to understand indigenous practices in India through the lens of religion. Balagangadhara takes five characteristics of religion – a scripture, a standard world view where claims are made on the origin on the world, an authority to settle conflicts, excommunication, and an organization to transmit – and shows how Hinduism does not possess these. The scriptures

---

[13] This view resonates with the argument made by Rajeev Bhargava about "early Vedic religion" in India meeting the requirements that characterize Taylor's exclusive humanism: the belief that there is no other world but this, and that no human flourishing exists except in this world. Early Vedic religion would also meet Taylor's third criterion: that human flourishing is achieved by human agency without the help of God. "The correct performance of ritual independent of gods achieves everything desired in this world" (Bhargava 2015: 114).

and texts present multiple stories of the origin of the world; a Rig Veda hymn says that, in the ultimate analysis, who created the world does not matter all that much.

There was neither non-existence nor existence then; there was neither the realm of space nor the sky which is beyond. What stirred? Where? In whose protection? Was there water bottomlessly deep? Who really knows? Who will here proclaim it? Whence was it produced? Whence is this creation? The gods came afterwards, with the creation of the universe. Who then knows whence it has arisen? Whence this creation has arisen – perhaps it formed itself, or perhaps it did not – the one who looks down on it, in the highest heave, only he knows – or perhaps he does not know.[14]

Balagangadhara argues that on other counts too – no central concept of God, no sole prophet or founder, no authoritative scripture – Hinduism does not qualify as religion.[15] So, what is Hinduism? His reply is that it is not possible to formulate the question "If Hinduism is not a religion, what else is it?" Neither does he replace "Hinduism" with the term "culture." Instead, he claims, Hinduism, the phenomenon constructed by the West, is an experiential entity only to the West and not to those in India. In this sense, Hinduism is not a part of the Indian culture. It has no existence outside of the Western experience of India (Balagangadhara 2011). Notions of "secular," "secularization," and "religion" belong to the language of Western Christianity, says Balagangadhara, and those Indian intellectuals and reformers who adopt these terms to discuss Hinduism are "theologians in a secular guise." Instead, Balagangadhara prefers to interrogate the subject of an "Indian culture," a culture without "religion" in the Christian sense.[16]

---

[14] *The Poetry of Creation* – Rig Veda Book 10 Hymn 129 (10.129): 358.
[15] This view does not into consideration the fact that two centuries of a constructed Hindu religion ought to be infused in some fashion in the social imaginary of different groups of modern Hindu Indians. As Will Sweetman (2003) points out, Balagangadhara makes the mistake of treating Christianity as the prototype of "religion," when all one can say is Hinduism is not a religion like Christianity but one cannot say that Hinduism is not a religion (2003).
[16] The idiom of culture was used by V.D. Savarkar, the future president of the Hindu Mahasabha and ideologue of the present-day Hindu nationalists, in his 1922 book *Hindutva: Who is a Hindu?* But he uses it differently from Balagangadhara; Savarkar combines territory (the land of the Indus) with Hindu culture and Hindu people to argue for a reinterpretation of the word Hindu. As Jaffrelot (1996: 32) points out, this view emphasizes the racial and ethnic substance of the Hindu nation. "In sum, Sarvakar's notion of Hindutva rests on cultural criteria rather than on a racial theory and is accordingly in tune with the Brahaminical world view but at the same time it represents an ethnic nationalism which borrows much from western theories." However, the Brahminical world view is, as we see from the debates in *The Last Brahmin*, is not one but multiple, and so is the use of culture.

Such an imaginary would explain the Hindutva judgment discussed at the beginning of the chapter, where the Supreme Court equated Hinduism with "Indian culture" and "a way of life."

Let us now examine the interplay between these three imaginaries in the Constituent Assembly's debates on conversion.

INDIA'S CONSTITUTIONAL IMAGINARY

The "We, the people … " that constitutions often begin with, implies that the document contains a social (constitutional) imaginary of "the people" of a country. As mentioned earlier, a major concern for the 207-member Constituent Assembly (CA) was how to douse the flames of religious strife between Hindus and Muslims resulting from the Partition of the country into India and Pakistan. It is important to understand what the CA members, many of whom hailed from ordinary backgrounds, thought of the Indian state's relationship with Hinduism. When the principle of separation of state and religion was proposed, it generated a lot of opposition.[17] While the debates recognized the implicit need to separate those aspects of religious dissention that could demolish democratic stability, there was little agreement on how to achieve this objective. Some saw a secular state as the separation of state and church (religion was not permitted in the public sphere). Others saw it as neutrality of the state toward religion, which could continue to function in the public sphere. A third view maintained that while the state would treat all religions equally, the state had a duty to reform religious practices in line with principles of equality and justice.

The texture of the debates in the CA reveals that the members utilized all three imaginaries to argue their case. Those who saw Hinduism as a

---

[17] Partha Chatterjee argues that the nature of the majority religion (way of life rather than belief) meant that the constitutional debates on secularism were primarily political, not theological. The debate was on what constituted a proper sphere for religion and disbelief, but the implied consensus was that the state would control large domains. This, he argues, was a function of the way the nationalist movement appropriated control over the outer and inner domains; the emergent nationalist imagination divided society into two domains: the outer material public domain (public institutions and civil society), namely the social space where creative borrowing from the West could take place; and the inner domain (tradition and a distinct cultural identity, including religion and family life), where the nationalists situated the sovereignty of the nation. There is an additional dimension to the political debates, which Chatterjee does not address. The texture of the debates reveals the tension between those who saw Hinduism as a way of life or as an ancient order, and those who treated it as a religion akin to other world religions. Both wanted to influence the social imaginary of independent India, and both sets of views, more or less, succeeded.

way of life/an ancient order and Indianness as a culture found themselves on the same side and pitted against those who treated Hinduism as a religion. The overlapping and often contradictory pulls of the three imaginaries left their mark on the Indian constitution's conception of the new state's relationship with religion. If Hinduism was treated as a religion, how could the state conform to neutrality and separation of state and religion, and still reform unjust social practices within the Hindu caste system? If Hinduism was an ancient order based on the caste hierarchy, how could the state undertake social justice for the lowest castes? And if Hinduism was part of an Indian culture, how could the state bar it from political discourse? The constitution incorporated all three types of imaginaries, which sometimes coexisted and sometimes collided, and in doing so produced a resilient buffer zone between the state and religion. The CA debate on proselytization and conversion illustrates the point.

Most conversions in independent India occur among scheduled castes and tribes (SC/ST) who want to improve their low social standing by converting to religions – Buddhism, Islam, and Christianity – that promise "equality." Conversion presupposes a prior element of propagation. The question of whether the Indian state ought to allow a fundamental right to propagate provoked heated discussions in the Constituent Assembly on December 3, 1948. The clause discussed was "the right freely to profess, practice and propagate religion."

One view was that the state ought not to permit the right to propagate. Two delegates from opposite ends of the spectrum converged on this conclusion. Tajamul Husain, a Muslim who espoused the classic liberal approach of seeing religion as a private affair between man and his God, said: "If you start propagating religion in this country, you will become nuisance to others . . . I submit, Sir, that this is a secular State and a secular state should not have anything to do with religion."[18] He suggested a substitute phrase – "practice religion privately." A Hindu delegate, Loknath Misra, said that secularism itself was a "slippery phrase" and "a device to bypass the ancient culture of the land."[19] He recommended either banning all religions or choosing Hinduism as the state religion. By allowing propagation, said Misra, the Constitution was paving the way for the complete annihilation of Hindu culture, the Hindu way of life and

---

[18] Constituent Assembly Debates (henceforth, CA Debates), December 3, 1948: 817.
[19] CA Debates, December 6, 1948: 823. Jawaharlal Nehru (later India's first Prime Minister) objected to Misra's reading of his position, but the chair (Vice President) vetoed Nehru and said that Misra represented a particular point of view that needed to be heard.

manners.[20] His reasoning was that it was not really possible to separate religion from "the ancient culture."

Those favoring a right to propagate argued their case either on the grounds of a quid pro quo for minorities, or on the assumption of benign and reasoned attempts at conversion or as an integral part of the right to freedom of expression. Lakshmi Kant Maitra, a Hindu, wanted the state to allow propagation because he said that minorities, such as Christians, had given up their claims to reserved seats (affirmative action) in the state legislatures in exchange for a right to propagate. Hence, the majority community "should allow this privilege to the minority community and have it for themselves as well."[21] These debates highlight an ambiguity – how to create a level playing field between proselytizing religions and something (Hinduism) that was seen as a religion and as an ancient culture which one entered by birth and exited by death; the CA was unable to resolve it. The right to propagate (subject to some restrictions) was included in the fundamental right to religious freedom.

The CA members used all three imaginaries to construct the new state's relationship with religion, and, by doing so, peppered the Constitution with many contradictions. Ultimately, the Constitution did not define the terms "Hindu," "religion," "secular," and "minorities," leaving it to the courts and legislative amendments to do so. In the next section, we shall see how these contradictions produced by the three imaginaries arose to bedevil the judiciary's interpretations of Hinduism and, consequently, Hinduism's relationship with a secular state. Each sub-section discusses a clash between two imaginaries.

THE JUDICIARY'S INTERPRETATION OF HINDUISM

Hinduism as a Religion and as a Culture

The Hindu Marriage Act, 1955, defines a Hindu as one who is not a Muslim, Parsi, Christian, or Jew. The sect would be "Hindu" if the individuals were "Hindus," said a Constitution Bench of the Court in *Sastri Yagnapurushdasji* v. *Bhudardas Vaishya*, a case that concerned the identification of an institution as a "Hindu institution."[22] The judges rejected the notion of Hinduism as a religion, and preferred to see it as a culture. Referring to the territorial, not the creedal significance of the term, the

---

[20] CA Debates: 824.   [21] CA Debates, December 6, 1948: 833.
[22] *Sastri Yagnapurushdasji* v. *Muldas Bhudardas Vaishya* 1966 3 SCR 242.

judges said that the usual tests applied to a recognized religion or religious creed would turn out to be inadequate in dealing with Hindu religion.

When we think of the Hindu religion, we find it difficult, if not impossible, to define Hindu religion or even adequately describe it. Unlike other religions in the world, the Hindu religion does not claim any one prophet; it does not worship any one God; it does not subscribe to any one dogma; it does not believe in any one philosophic concept; it does not follow any one set of religious rites or performances; in fact, it does not appear to satisfy the narrow traditional features of any religion or creed. It may broadly be described as a way of life and nothing more. (*Sastri Yagnapurushdasji* v. *Vaishya*)

By 1976, the court seemed to have thrown in the towel: "It is a matter of common knowledge that Hinduism embraces within itself so many diverse forms of beliefs, faiths, practices and worship that it is difficult to define the term 'Hindu' with precision."[23] The legal definition of Hinduism, as legal scholar Marc Galanter (1984: 395) points out, is neither a measure of religious belief nor a description of social behavior as much as a civil status describing everyone subjected to the application of "Hindu law" in the areas reserved for personal law.

Hinduism as a Religion and as an Ancient Order

In a judgment on whether "Jains" could be classified as a "minority," the apex court failed to reconcile the imaginaries of Hinduism as a religion and as an ancient order. The rationale underpinning the dismissal of the appeal to notify the "Jain" community as a minority highlights the ambiguities introduced by two imaginaries of Hinduism.[24] The court said:

The word "Hindu" conveys the image of diverse groups of communities living in India. If you search for a person by name Hindu, he is unidentifiable. He can be identified only on the basis of his caste as upper caste Brahmin, Kshatriya or Vaish or of lower caste described in ancient India as Shudras. Those who fall in the Hindu class of "Shudras" are now included in the Constitution in the category of Scheduled Castes with special privileges and treatment for their upliftment. This was found necessary to bring them at par with upper castes in Hindu society.

Hinduism, the court said, could be called a general religion and common faith of India, whereas Jainism was a special religion formed on the basis of quintessence of Hindu religion. "Their only difference from Hindus is that Jains do not believe in any creator like God but worship only the perfect

---

[23] *CWT* v. *R Sridharan* (1976) 4 SCC 489.
[24] *Bal Patil and Anr.* v. *Union of India and Ors* (2005) 6 SCC 690.

human-being whom they called Tirathankar." Therefore, Jains could not be a minority, since a minority "signifies an identifiable group of people or community who were seen as deserving protection from likely deprivation of their religious, cultural and educational rights by other communities who happen to be in majority and likely to gain political power in a democratic form of Government based on election." The judgment's rationale was that the caste basis of Hindu society meant that no section or distinct group of people could claim to be in majority. "All are minorities amongst Hindus. Many of them claim such status because of their small number and expect protection from the State on the ground that they are backward."

These muddled interpretations replicated themselves in cases dealing with conversions from Hinduism and the retention of affirmative action benefits by such converts. In pursuance of its mandate to deliver social justice to historically discriminated groups, the Constitution provides affirmative action in political constituencies, government jobs, and educational institutions to scheduled castes and scheduled tribes. Could those who retained their affiliations to their old communities after converting to another religion (e.g. Christianity) retain their constitutional privileges to affirmative action? The court said yes in the case of scheduled tribe converts to other religions, but was more equivocal about scheduled caste converts.[25] In a case concerning a scheduled caste convert's rights, the Supreme Court said that a caste "is more a social combination than a religious group." This position highlights the conflict between two imaginaries of Hindusim – as an ancient order and as a religion. It said that renunciation of Hinduism and adoption of another religious faith did not mean that a person ceased to be a member of the caste in which he was born.

A caste may consist not only of persons professing Hindu religion but also persons professing some other religion as well, conversion from Hinduism to that other religion may not involve loss of caste, because even persons professing such other religion can be members of the caste [i.e. caste as an ancient classificatory system]. This might happen where caste is based on economic or occupational characteristics and not on religious identity or the cohesion of the caste as a social group is so strong that conversion into another religion does not operate to snap the bond between the convert and the social group. This is indeed not an infrequent phenomenon in South India where, in some of the castes, even after conversion to Christianity, a person is regarded as continuing to belong to the caste. (*Arumugam* v. *Rajagopal*)[26]

[25] *State of Kerala and Anr* v. *Chandramohanan* (2004) 3 SCC 429.
[26] AIR 1976 SC 939: 946. A similar position prevailed more recently in *Kodikunnil Suresh and J. Monian* v. *N.S. Saji Kumar* (2011) 6 SCC 430.

Religion, Hinduism, and Hindutva

The interplay between the three imaginaries of Hinduism in the legal structure makes the inconsistencies between the court's rulings in the *Hindutva* cases and the *Bommai* judgment more comprehensible. Neither the Constitution nor the Representation of Peoples Act (1951) defines "religion." The judges in the *Hindutva* case reviewed previous rulings on what constituted a "matter of religion," who decided it, and, to a lesser extent, what constituted a reasonable restriction based on "public order, morality and health." They found a mixed bag. Initially, the courts had allowed religious denominations to decide what constituted a matter of religion,[27] but made a distinction between the right to manage affairs in matters of religion (a fundamental right of the religious denomination) and the administration of property (a secular function), subject to state supervision. Later, the court gave itself the right to determine what could or could not be seen as a religious practice, and whether a particular rite was regarded as essential by the tenets of a particular religion.[28] Social justice concerns for the scheduled castes and tribes compelled the court to curtail the freedom of denominational authorities in "matters of religion." For instance, the court upheld the Madras Temple Entry Authorization Act (1948), which allowed hitherto excluded castes, such as scheduled castes, to enter a Hindu temple.[29] Non-essential activities that could be controlled by the state came to include appointment of priests and state legislation on administration of religious institutions.[30] The ambiguities introduced by the three imaginaries on Hinduism the judiciary to expand the state's influence over issues allowed that were initially interpreted as religious ones.[31]

---

[27] *Hanif Quareshi* v. *State of Bihar*, 1958 SC 731, *Ratilal* v. *State of Bombay*, 1954, SCR 1055.

[28] *Sardar Syedna Taher Saifuddin Saheb* v. *The State of Bombay*, AIR 1962 SC 853. Judgments variously deprived Khadims of the Durgah Committee of Ajmer (a Sufi sect) many of their traditional rights, said some practices were integral to Hindu faith, whereas praying in the mosque was not integral to Muslim faith.

[29] *Venkataramana Devaru* v. *the State of Mysore*, AIR 1958 SC 255.

[30] *Commissioner, Hindu Religious Endowments* v. *Lakshmindra Thirtha Swamiar* (1954), SCR 1005.

[31] A similar approach prevailed in the treatment of non-Hindu religions. The court informed Muslims that, on the basis of the court's reading of the texts and the advice of a Hindu pundit, "cow sacrifice" was not an essential practice of the Muslim faith. In the case of Muslim institutions, the Supreme Court has maintained in almost all cases that regulation of a waqf (Islamic charitable trust) by the state is reasonable. *Bashiruddin Ashraf* v. *State*

HINDUISM AND A SECULAR AGE

We can comprehend the troubles faced by the Indian state in managing conflicting pluralisms only if we parse out the competing imaginaries of Hinduism. The presence of these three stylized imaginaries puts India too within a variant of Secularity III because the multiple pluralisms consist of belief, unbelief, and non-belief.

The Indian case also complicates the notion of social imaginaries used by Taylor in *A Secular Age*. Concepts of religion/secular, church/state, natural/supernatural could be seen as binaries that originate within Christian theology; they do not completely explain or make sense in the non-Christian world. Taylor, perhaps, would not disagree with this statement. In Warner et al. (2010: 301), Taylor admits that he "has neglected the way in which Western understandings of religion were informed through the pre-colonial and the colonial encounters with other parts of the world."

Other scholars have analyzed the internal complexity of Hinduism as "thick and thin religions" (Sudipta Kaviraj), and as "religion and faith" (Ashis Nandy). Let us examine Kaviraj's (2010) analysis because parts of it resonate with the distinction between Hinduism as an ancient order/way of life/culture, and Hinduism as a religion. Kaviraj makes a distinction between thick religion – its internal contents are a vast catalogue of beliefs about large and small things and all of them are crucial to the practice of that particular faith – and thin religion. For Kaviraj, the religion of Hindu nationalists is thin because it is entirely indifferent to the sectarian practices of everyday worship:

[I]ndeed its primary purpose is to make them redundant ... There is a certain paradox in the way it orders the world: it uses a broad and inclusive movement for all Hindus and groups linked to Hinduism by their origin; but the entire purpose is to harden and inflame the boundary between this expansive Hinduism and other selected adversaries, particularly Muslims.

---

of Bihar. Courts have often held that a person born a Muslim remained a Muslim until he openly renounced the Islamic faith; the mere adoption of some non-Islamic forms of worship or customs was not considered tantamount to such a renunciation. This affected Muslim communities of Indian converts such as the Khojas, the Bohras, and the Kutchi Memons, who retained their non-Muslim traditions relating to such matters as inheritance and succession, while adhering to Muslim law in other matters. See the High Court of Kerala's *Shihabuddin Imbichi Koya Thangal* v. *K.P. Ahammad Koya* judgment from 1970. For example, *Fidahusein* v. *Mongbibai* (1936); *The Controller of Estate Duty, Mysore, Bangalore* v. *Haji Abdul Sattar Sait* (1972).

Kaviraj, the irony is that the primary purpose of this inclusion is exclusion of other communities "from a sense of participating in a historically common and interactive religious culture" (Kaviraj 2010: 348). For Kaviraj, an inverse relationship exists between the thickness of religious beliefs and the size of religious communities. In India, it is thin religion that is pervasive, political (not ethical), intolerant (not accommodating), and has the goal of amassing mundane power (not indifferent to power). "It is misleading to hold that in India either religion is becoming stronger, or the secularization thesis is disconfirmed" (Kaviraj 2010: 350). He concludes that the story of Indian modernity, particularly of Hindu religion, shows a process in which "a thin Hindu identity seeks to overcome segmentation and produce a collective agency to menace minorities and demand a homogenizing and intolerant version of nationalism" (Kaviraj 2010: 354). While Kaviraj's analysis explains the nature of "Hindu" in Hindu nationalism, it subsumes the notion of Hinduism as an ancient order within the category of religion.

But the 'ancient order' imaginary plays an important role in creating the ambiguities in the state's attitude to Hinduism. A dialogue between a Hindu official and a spiritual leader clarifies the notion of Hinduism as an ancient order:

The ruler's race, religion, character, are not important to me. All I need is that in this country government must provide facilities for a practitioner of the ancient order to lead his life comfortably. Similarly for Mohammadans, Parsees. In matters of faith, tolerance and non-alignment are meaningless. In matters of faith there must be total equality ... For a genuine practitioner of the ancient dharma, his faith is the same as his mode of living. In his life it is woven into every context. For him there are no separable categories such as social matters and matters of faith. (Sarma 2007: 191–192)

Perhaps this faith articulated by the *Last Brahmin* is the same as the faith alluded to by Ashis Nandy, but different in form and content to the one explicated in Kaviraj's "thick religion." Sarma, the narrator of *The Last Brahmin*, analyses Hinduism in modern India as the cultural consequence of colonialism, and as a disguised form of Christian monotheism. Within this Hinduism is subsumed Nandy's Hinduism as an ideology, Kaviraj's thin religion, and perhaps parts of Kaviraj's thick religion. So what are we left with in Hinduism as an ancient order as outlined by Sarma?[32] It is a social imaginary pertaining to Brahmins, that too a particular type of Brahmin – a scholar of the Vedas. It offers us access to a distinct indigenous

[32] Parts of Sarma's view resonate with that of "Vedic religion" explicated by Bhargava (2015).

perspective informed by Sanskrit cultural heritage and literary tradition.[33] Though espoused by a minority, it ought not to be dismissed since it has influenced apex court judges who tend to be upper caste and Hindus.

CONCLUSION

The ambiguity introduced by the multiple imaginaries of Hinduism has both weakened and strengthened Indian democracy and secularism. The tussle between the "secular" Indian and the "Hindutva" Indian has intensified in recent years in the public, political, and legal arenas. The use of Hindutva does not map as neatly onto Hinduism as a religion in the way that Islamists in Egypt, Indonesia, and Turkey are identified with the institution of Sharia laws. Though the BJP's successful 2014 election campaign was primarily about promising "development" and ending corruption, its subsequent behavior in variously justifying, legitimizing, or maintaining a deafening silence on the violence unleashed by its supporters on members of the Muslim minority and lower caste, has generated concerns about the erosion of pluralism in the country. For instance, a government panel headed by a retired apex court judge found that the BJP and the members of a regional party were complicit in riots against Muslims in a north Indian state in 2013. In other instances, mobs with Hindu nationalist elements lynched members of the minority community over the issue of eating and storing beef, while the Prime Minister remained silent on the murder. The murders of two scholars who advocated rationalist points of view, and the more recent arrest of a student (from a lower caste Hindu background) on grounds of sedition have triggered debates on who has the right to define the attributes of a "good and loyal Indian" citizen.

Taylor speaks of "belief and unbelief, not as rival theories," but as "the different kinds of lived experience involved in understanding your life in one way or the other, on what it's like to live as a believer or an unbeliever" (Taylor 2007: 5). The imaginaries of Hinduism as an ancient order and Indianness as a culture are forms of lived experience which pertain to a third category – one who is neither a believer nor an unbeliever. The existence of this category has simultaneously problematized the state's efforts to manage diversity and increased concerns among scholars and

---

[33] As the translator points out, the book is written in the voice of the disinherited and non-believing son of the Veda pandit who is the last Brahmin within *The Last Brahmin*.

others about a crisis of secularism in India, but has also created a buffer or a zone of ambiguity for the state and prevented it from being torn apart by the fierce battles between majority and minority religions, and between co-religionists.

While Taylor's concept of social imaginaries helps us understand the production of these ambiguities, the trajectory of secularities expounded in *A Secular Age* are less relevant to the Indian context. Taylor's notion of moral order is more useful here. Taylor (2004), in *Modern Social Imaginaries*, explains the notion of a moral order as carrying a definition not only of what is right, but of the context in which it makes sense to strive for and hope to realize the right (at least partially). One type of moral order, he says, is based on the idea of the Law of a people, which has governed this people and which, in a sense, defines it as a people. The other type of moral order is organized around hierarchy in society that expresses and corresponds to a hierarchy in the cosmos. For instance, the king is in his kingdom as the lion among animals, the eagle among birds, and so on. Any deviation from the order would be met with a violent backlash.

In the Indian case, the imaginaries support different types of moral orders that conflict with each other and with the state's goals. The jostling for dominance by the different imaginaries has acted as a check on the perpetual dominance by one imaginary. For instance, with the election of the NDA coalition led by the Hindu nationalist BJP in 1996, concerns bloomed about the dominance of Hindu nationalism, but by the time the UPA-led coalition took over in the first decade of the twenty-first century, the specter of muscular Hindu nationalism was less threatening. Today, the ascendance of the Narendra Modi-led BJP government since 2014 has renewed the fears about the exclusion and even victimization of non-Hindus on the one hand, and, on the other hand, also produced the hope that a focus on economic revival would inhibit the exclusionary elements of Hindutva. Taylor's statement about India being a country that has not yet emptied its public space of religion is correct. About 90 percent of adult Indians surveyed in a Gallup poll in 2009 said that religion was an important part of their daily lives, but it is unclear which imaginary of Hinduism they are referring to.[34]

What can the state do to tackle the ambiguities? Taylor (2011), in *The Power of Religion in the Public Sphere*, argues that the point of state neutrality is to avoid favoring or disfavoring not just religious positions, but any basic position, religious or nonreligious. Institutional formulae,

---

[34] www.gallup.com/poll/142727/religiosity-highest-world-poorest-nations.aspx#2

such as the separation of church and state, are at best shorthand heuristics. Instead, constructing a democratic life together may depend more on being able to engage in shared positive pursuits, such as exploring ways to work for common goals like liberty, equality, etc. As Craig Calhoun says in his conclusion in the same book, this suggests that we should not understand the public sphere entirely in terms of argumentation about the truth value of propositions, but as a realm of creativity and social imaginaries in which citizens give shared form to their lives together, a realm of exploration, experiment, and partial agreements. Scholars such as Jurgen Habermas, Charles Taylor, and Judith Butler, among others have converged on the point that excluding religion from the public sphere would undermine the solidarity and creativity they seek for citizens. Compared to the past, the recent diminishing relevance of caste and religion in winning elections in India is an indicator that the multiple imaginaries associated with Hinduism may have allowed religion to remain in the public sphere without necessarily undermining, in a definitive way, the solidarity and creativity available to citizens. While alarmists might say that such a situation will not continue under the present Hindu nationalist regime, a more optimistic view might be correct in saying that the debates in present-day India are part of a vibrant pluralism that will continue to ebb and flow in the longer term.

Bibliography

Balagangadhara, S.N. 1994. *The Heathen in his Blindness: Asia, the West and the Dynamic of Religion*. Lieden: Brill.

2003. *Mapping Hinduism: "Hinduism" and the Study of Indian Religions, 1600–1776*. Halle: Franckesche Stiftungen.

2011, March 5. "Ontological and epistemological commitments of 'Hinduism'." www.google.co.in/search?client=safari&rls=en&q=ontological-and-epistemological-commitments-of-hinduism&ie=UTF-8&oe=UTF-8&gfe_rd=cr&ei=W9z1WNXWFOXx8Af_7JvoAg

Bhargava, Rajeev. 2015. "We (in India) Have Always Been Post-Secular," in Michael Rectenwald et al. *Global Secularisms in a Post-Secular Age*. Berlin: De Gruyter.

Bilgrami, Akeel. 2014. *Secularism, Identity and Enchantment*. Cambridge (Boston): Harvard University Press.

Bloch, E., M. Keppens, and R. Hegde. 2010. *Rethinking Religion in India: The colonial construction of Hinduism*. London: Routledge.

Butler, Jon. 2010. "Disquieted History in *A Secular Age*," in M. Warner, J. Van Antwerpen, and C. Calhoun. *Varieties of Secularism in a Secular Age*. Cambridge, MA: Harvard University Press, 193–216.

Chatterjee, Partha. 2004. *The Politics of the Governed: Reflections on Popular Politics in Most of the World*. New York: Columbia University Press.

Cohn, Bernard. 1996. *Colonialism and its Forms of Knowledge: The British in India*. Princeton: Princeton University Press.

Dalmia, V. and H. von Stietencron. 1995. *Representing Hinduism: The Construction of Religious Traditions and National Identity*. Delhi: Sage.

Dirks, Nicholas. 1987. *The Hollow Crown*. Cambridge: Cambridge University Press.

Dumont, Louis. 1981. *Homo Hierarchicus*. Chicago: University of Chicago Press.

Galanter, Marc. 1984. *Competing Equalities: Law and the Backward Classes in India*. Berkeley: University of California Press.

Geertz, Clifford. 1993. "Religion as a Cultural System," in Clifford Geertz, *The Interpretation of Cultures: Selected Essays*. Fontana Press, 87–125.

Jaffrelot, Christophe. 1996. *The Hindu Nationalist Movement and Indian Politics*. New Delhi: Penguin.

Kaviraj, S. 2010. "On Thick and Thin Religion: Some Critical Reflections on Secularization Theory," in I. Katznelson and G. Stedman-Jones. *Religion and the Political Imagination*. Cambridge: Cambridge University Press: 336–355.

Bloch, Ester, and Marianne Keppens. 2010. "Introduction," in *Colonial Construction of Hinduism*. Edited by Bloch Ester, Marianne Keppens, and Rajaram Hegde. New York: Routledge.

Lorenzen, D.N. 1999. "Who Invented Hinduism?" *Comparative Studies in Society and History*, 41: 630–659.

Ludden, David. 1993. "Orientalist Empiricism and Transformations of Colonial Knowledge." In *Orientalism and The Post-Colonial Predicament*. Edited by C.A. Breckenridge and Peter Van der Veer. Philadelphia: University of Pennsylvania Press, 250–278.

Mehta, Pratap Bhanu. 2007. "India's Unlikely Democracy: The Rise of Judicial Sovereignty," *Journal of Democracy*, Vol. 18(2), 70–83.

Nauriya, Anil. 1996. "The Hindutva Judgments: A Warning Signal." *Economic and Political Weekly*, 31 (1) January 6, 10–13.

Needham, A.D. and R. Sunder Rajan. 2006. *The Crisis of Secularism in India*. Chicago: University of Chicago Press.

Sarma, R.S.S. 2007. *The Last Brahmin*. trans. D. Venkat Rao, New Delhi: Permanent Black.

Staal, Fritz. 1989. *Rules Without Meaning: Ritual, Mantra, and the Human Sciences*. New York: Peter Lang.

Sweetman, Will. 2003 "Hinduism" and the "History of Religion." *Method and Theory in Study of Religion*, 15: 329–353.

Taylor, Charles. 2004. *Modern Social Imaginaries*. Durham: Duke University Press.

2007. *A Secular Age*. Cambridge, MA: Belknap Press of Harvard University Press.

2010. "Afterword: Apologia pro Libro suo," in M. Warner et al. (eds.), *Varieties of Secularism in a Secular Age*, 300–310.

2011. "Why We Need a Radical Redefinition of Secularism," in E. Mendieta and J. Van Antwerpen, *The Power of Religion in the Public Sphere*. New York: Columbia University Press, 34–59.

Thapar, Romila. 1989. "Imagined Religious Communities? Ancient History and the Modern Search for a Hindu Identity," in *Modern Asian Studies*, (23): 209–231.

Van der Veer, Peter. 2002. "Religion in South Asia," *Annual Review of Anthropology*, (31): 173–187.

Vishwanathan, Gauri. 2008. "Colonialism and the Construction of Hinduism," in G. Flood (ed.), *The Blackwell Companion to Hinduism*. Hoboken: John Wiley and Sons: 23–44.

7

Secularity without Secularism in Pakistan: The Politics of Islam from Sir Syed to Zia

Christophe Jaffrelot

INTRODUCTION

The trajectory of secularization described by Charles Taylor in *A Secular Age* in respect of the West is largely unknown elsewhere, especially among the societies of the South. According to Taylor, this Western trajectory relies on three notions of secularity that are complementary but not mutually exclusive: the first (Secularity I) refers to the evacuation of religion from the public sphere; the second (Secularity II) designates the decline of religious beliefs and practices; and the third (Secularity III), which is key to Taylor's innovative analysis, refers to changes in the "conditions of belief" whereby religion becomes one choice among many. Secularity III is over-determined by the parameter of intellectual pluralism and, in empirical terms, by the extent of behavioral diversity regarding gender relations, education, etc. It refers to the "conditions of belief" that shape "social imaginaries" – and are shaped by them as well.

In Taylor's narrative, during the ancien régime – whose reference point Taylor situates in the Europe of 1500 – the world was enchanted, so much so that it was not possible to think of it in non-religious terms. The first secularization occurred during "the Age of Mobilization," which resulted in the creation of nation-states and the birth of industrial capitalism in the nineteenth century. The key feature of this age lay in the growth of "an unheard of pluralism of outlooks, religious and non- and anti-religious, in which the number of possible positions seems to be increasing without end"

This book chapter draws from a working paper whose anonymous referees I want to thank for their insightful comments ("Secularization without secularism in Pakistan", *Research in question*, n° 41 (2012), http://www.sciencespo.fr/ceri/sites/sciencespo.fr.ceri/files/qdr41.pdf).

(Taylor 2007: 437). The emergence of multiple secularities, and particularly Taylor's notion of Secularity III – that finds expression in a "disenchantment of the world" – was fostered by an urbanization process that disrupted old local communities, (Taylor 2007: 440), although city-life is not held to be incompatible with religious belief per se. But the Age of Mobilization was not an age of triumphant individualism, it was a time when "people are persuaded, pushed, dragooned, or bullied into new forms of society, church, association" (Taylor 2007: 445). This was a time of collective ideologies emphasizing the importance of class and nations. For Taylor, the age of individualism comes later, from the 1960s onwards, and arises in what he calls the "Age of Authenticity." This period can even be defined as the time of "'expressive' individualism," a phase – still continuing today – where individuals are not only self-centered for egotistic, hedonist and consumerist reasons, but are also allergic to any form of collectivity. This overall secularization process, in Taylor's account, is not linear: pockets of the Age of Mobilization display some resilience. During it, new forms of belief develop, especially through subjective spirituality (Taylor 2007: 508). Thus, Securalities I, II, and III are elements of the secularization process which can develop side by side and reinforce each other. In this chapter, I argue, proceeding from the case of Pakistan, that there may be others.

While the world is rather disenchanted in the urbanized West, where individualism and capitalism have fostered the completion of this process, it is still enchanted in the rural South and even in large sections of towns and cities where traditional mindsets and social structures display a remarkable resilience – and sustain old conditions of belief. In South Asia, the kind of secularization that Taylor associates with the Age of Mobilization is not preponderant in villages, where social institutions which shape key "conditions of belief," such as castes, kin, and tribes, are still dominant. Things are different in cities, where alternative modernities are in the making and prepare the ground for alternative forms of secularity. In South Asia, like in most of the other regions of the world, the encounter with the West resulted in an attempt at emulating the scientific mind that had crystallized in Europe. But this new rationalism remained limited to a minuscule intellectual elite, the "intelligentsia," and this group, instead of confining its original creed to the private sphere, to a large extent reinvested its sense of religion in its definition of collective identity. This shift from religious belief to religious identity, which Nader Hashemi's chapter on Iran (Chapter 9) also emphasizes, is a variant of the secularization process or an alternative form of secularity that Taylor has not paid attention to. This – what I shall call "Secularity IV" – is ideology driven.

This chapter, then, concentrates on Secularity IV as an elaboration of a category one can find in Taylor's work, but not in *A Secular Age*. It pays less attention to Secularity II and Secularity III, relying instead on a more top-down approach through an analysis of the politics and public policy initiated by state leaders. This is partly intentional and partly due to the fact that an ethnographic, empirical approach of the first decades of Pakistan's history is beyond this author's capacities. I draw on Charles Taylor's work in order to highlight a disconnect between the historical process of secularization and the political project of secularism, and to argue that if secularism can develop without secularization, some forms of secularization can also develop without resulting in secularism. While India is a case in point, Pakistan shows in its way that alternative forms of secularization are compatible with political trajectories ignorant of secularism.[1]

In *A Secular Age*, Charles Taylor almost ignores the question of secularism, but he pays a great deal of attention to it in an article titled "The meaning of secularism," where he defines this "-ism" as the art of accommodating a plurality of religious and non-religious ways of life (Taylor 2010). He considers that a secular polity needs to fulfill three criteria – it must respect the free exercise of religion: "there must be equality between people of different faiths" and "all spiritual families must be heard" (Taylor 2010: 23). In contrast to French *laïcité*, Taylor does not define secularism by the exclusion of religion from the public realm; instead, he draws inspiration from South Asian scholars who have theorized the practices of their region. Rajeev Bhargava, whose work on India is abundantly cited by Taylor, points out that "secularism is compatible with the view that the complete secularization of society is neither possible nor desirable" (Bhargava 1998: 489). Elaborating on this idea, Bhargava defines secularism by two features:

(a) secularism is fully compatible with, indeed even dictates, a defense of differentiated citizenship and the rights of religious groups, and

(b) the secularity of the state does not necessitate strict intervention, non-interference or equidistance but rather any or all of these, as the case may be. In short the secular state need not be equidistant

---

[1] As Philip Gorski writes: "For Taylor, the essence of secularity is plurality, characterized by competing versions of belief and disbelief. And secularism, he proposes, is best seen as a way of accommodating this pluralism. But useful as it may be for understanding the historical genesis of Western secularity qua cultural tradition, Taylor's approach is less fruitful for explaining the global varieties of secularism cum institutional settlement." Gorski, Chapter 2 (this volume), p. 34.

from all religious communities and may interfere in one religion more than in another. All this goes to show that a critique of Indian secularism on the ground that it acknowledges group rights or it fails to be neutral will not wash. (Bhargava 1998: 520)

In the above quotation, Bhargava draws from "b)" the notion of "principled distance" that needs to guide the secular state. But the "a)" is more important for our purposes here because it introduces a qualitative difference between secularization and secularism: it implies not only that secularism can develop without secularization, but that it can flourish more easily in a non-secularized society where religious diversity will sustain secularism.

In the first section, I argue that this alternative trajectory of secularization is illustrated by the development of Muslim separatism in South Asia during the British Raj, when Syed Ahmed Khan (1817–1898), Mohammed Iqbal (1877–1938), and then Mohammad Ali Jinnah (1876–1948), the father of Pakistan, invented a new form of identity politics based on a territorialized and communitarian version of Islam. In fact, as South Asian scholar Ashis Nandy points out, religion became part of an ethno-religious nationalist ideology. He identifies four kinds of relations between politics and religion: first, where the leader is religious in public and private (Mahatma Gandhi); second, where the leader is not religious in either spheres (Nehru); third, where the leader is religious in private, but not in public (Indira Gandhi); and finally, where the leader is non-religious in private, but religious in public (V.D. Savarkar, the father of Hindu nationalism, and Mohammad Ali Jinnah, the Founder of Pakistan). The first section focuses especially on the fourth category, where religion is instrumentalized as an ideology and a political device for mobilizing supporters (Nandy 1990). For Nandy, "The goal of those holding such an instrumental view of religion has always been to homogenize their co-believers into proper formations and, for that reason to eliminate those parts of religion that smack of folkways and threaten to legitimize diversity, interfaith dialogue and theological polycentrism" (Nandy 1990: 77). Hence, the key distinction of Nandy between "religion-as-ideology" and "religion-as-faith." Religion-as-ideology is a variant of secularity that is not necessarily at odds with his definition of secularism since his notion of secularism, at least during the Age of Mobilization, does not rely so much on the decline of belief as on the accommodation of religious and non-religious beliefs, which the ideology of Pakistan did not preclude. Indeed, in 1947 the new state claimed to make room for all kinds of religious and non-religious affiliations.

But this attempt at promoting secularism, which will be examined in the second section, was incomplete and ephemeral because of the shallowness of Pakistan's Secularity I. From the 1970s onwards, as will be seen in the third section, Pakistan implemented policies of Islamization. While this policy was implemented at the expense of Secularity I – the differentiation of the religious and the political domain – it was intended to assert the autonomy of the public sphere vis-à-vis the religious leaders. There is, therefore, a certain continuity between the policy that Ayub Khan implemented on behalf of secularism and the one Zia-ul-Haq pursued on behalf of Islam. They both transformed the conditions of beliefs at the expense of traditional forms of Islam.

SECULARITY IV: RELIGION AS IDEOLOGY – A NEO-DURKHEIMIAN CATEGORY?

Islam as a Political Identity: From the Aligarh Movement to the "Two-Nation Theory"

Drawing her theoretical inspiration from Luhmann, Magrit Pernau (2003) convincingly argues that the Muslim middle class that developed during the British Raj initiated a rather classic secularization process that relates squarely to Taylor's Secularity II (decline in religious belief and practice) and the theories of the author who Pernau cites: Niklas Luhmann. For Luhmann (1995), this process is primarily due to the differentiation of social functions which results in the transformation of religion as a sub-system among others, along with the political sphere, the economic sphere, inter alia. Indeed, the colonization of India deprived the former Muslim rulers of political power, without making India a "dar ul harb" (literally, a House of War) since the British did not prohibit the call to prayer, the observation of Ramadan, or the preaching of Islam. The ulama (religious scholars or literati) continued to monopolize knowledge, but only in the religious field, since the new, modern state recruited its administration from a different milieu – that of modern educated members of the native-born intelligentsia. This differentiation deepened when political leaders emerged from this group and adopted a modernist perspective that was distinctively different from that of the ulama, even though they claimed to speak on behalf of Islam. As Pernau suggests, they were preparing the ground for a form of "secularization without secularism" that had remained rather marginal in Europe.[2] This

---

[2] Referring to the Khilafat movement, Pernau (2003) highlights that the discourse of the Muslim politicians in the defense of Islam was saturated with religiosity, something Muslim politicians in quest of popular legitimacy were bound to be accustomed to. But

alternative secularization route was taken in the second half of the nineteenth century, when it appeared that the initial stage of secularization à la Luhmann made many trajectories possible.

After the 1857 Revolt, which was largely attributed to Muslims by the British, the repression that affected the Muslim minority convinced some of its leaders that a new emphasis on education was needed to cope with the critical situation. Two alternatives took shape in the 1860s–1870s, which two cities came to symbolize: Aligarh and Deoband, both located near Delhi. The Deobandis believed in religious education, but they decided to promote their understanding of the Muslim traditions by using modern, British techniques (Metcalf 1982). The Aligarhians did not only want to modernize the education techniques, but also the content of what was taught. This move, which was initiated by Syed Ahmed Khan (1817–1898), resulted in the first significant attempt at secularizing Islam in South Asia.

Sir Syed – as he came to be known after the British granted him this title – was a modernist. Drawing his inspiration from European scholars, he assumed that their scientific mindset and Islam were fully compatible – and aspired to demonstrate it.[3] He created the Scientific Society in 1864 and, after a trip to England, the Anglo-Mahommedan College (1875) of Aligarh that was designed along the Oxford–Cambridge model (Lelyveld 1978).

The Muslims of India as a Political Community

The secularization impact of Sir Syed, however, did not fully follow the Western pattern. It was not associated with the disenchantment process. In fact, Sir Syed initiated an alternative form of secularization by reinterpreting Islam in terms of identity politics. Descending from the Moghul aristocracy but educated in English – he worked for years as an employee of the East India Company – Sir Syed epitomized the new intelligentsia of late nineteenth century British India. Nostalgic for the heyday of the Empire, he had realized that to save the Islamic civilization and community of India, Muslims had to undergo a reform process. But this process

she pertinently concludes that "The absence of an ideology of secularism, however, is no indication whether or not secularization did take place" (ibid., p. 38).

[3] Syed Ahmed Khan (1967) argued that Islam "is a rational religion which can march hand in hand with the growth of knowledge. Any fear to the contrary betrays lack of faith in the truth of Islam." See also Troll (1978).

did not imply that Islam as a culture and "a way of life" (to use one of the favorite definitions of Hinduism by the proponents of Hindutva ideology) had to be neglected.

The action of Sir Syed took a political turn when, by means of the Local Self-Government Act, the government started to democratize local bodies in 1882. Sir Syed immediately realized that the law of numbers would affect the Muslim minority (about 20 percent of the total population), at a time when it was already losing ground to a rising Hindu English-educated intelligentsia (who also benefited from the recognition of Hindi as an official language in 1899 in the United Provinces, the crucible of the Moghul Empire where Aligarh was located; Brass 1974). For Sir Syed, democratization was the perfect recipe for a civil war without arms:

The object of civil war is to determine in whose hands the rule of the country shall rest. The object of the promoters of the National Congress [which asked for more devolution of power from the British] is that the Government of India should be English in name only, and that the internal rule of the country should be entirely in their own hands. (cited in Robinson 1974: 119)

Sir Syed viewed the relations between Hindus and Muslims in political terms:

I consider [that] the experiment which the Indian National Congress wishes to make is fraught with danger and suffering for all the nationalities of India, especially Muslims. The Muslims are a minority but a highly united minority. At least traditionally they are prone to take the sword in hand when the majority oppresses them. If this happens, it will bring about disasters greater than the ones which came in the wake of the happenings of 1857. (cited in Mahmood and Zafar 1968: 53–54)

The Muslim League was created mainly by Aligarhians in 1906, when the British announced their intention to democratize the provincial legislative councils. Its first demand concerned the establishment of a separate electorate for the Muslims. This measure aimed at guaranteeing some representation in the assemblies to the Muslim minority. By granting it, the British fostered the constitution of this group into a political community. From the 1909 elections onwards, the Muslims of British India formed an electoral college of their own.

The leader of the Muslim League, Mohammed Ali Jinnah, gave this community the attributes of a nation in the framework of his "two-nation theory" when he claimed that Hindus and Muslims belonged to "two different civilizations" and could not, therefore, share the same destiny[4] – hence the claim not only for a separate electorate, but for a separate nation-state: Pakistan.

The Territorialization of Indian Islam

The politicization of the Muslims' identity in India took a new turn with their transformation, according to some of their leading ideologues, into a territorialized nation. Such an evolution ran contrary to the natural inclination of many traditional leaders of the community who adhered to pan-Islamism. The strength of this sentiment was evident from the sympathy many Indian Muslims showed toward their brothers who – in Egypt or in Tunisia, for example – were suffering from European colonialism (Hasan 1985). Pan-Islamism found expression in a militant way during the Khilafat movement (1919–1921) (Minault 1982). Sir Syed was probably the first to promote a territorialized variant of Islam in India, largely as a result of the Hindi–Urdu controversy. This dispute arose when Hindi-speaking leaders from the Hindu community objected to the use of Urdu in the administration of the United Provinces and Bihar. These areas coincided, by and large, with the stronghold of the Aligarh movement since the educational institutions created by Sir Syed recruited most of their students, teachers, and staff members from the United Provinces. Representing the Urdu-speaking Muslims of North India, Sir Syed developed a "communal" identity which largely overshadowed the universal dimension of the Ummah (Shaikh 1989). He emphasized the Muslims' territorial sense of belonging to India by equating this sentiment to the Hindus' own feelings in a very audacious way when he dared to claim that both groups were immigrants (something the nationalist Hindus – who pretend to be the sons of the soil – were strongly to reject): "Just as the high caste Hindus came and settled down in this land once, forgot where their earlier home was and considered India to be their own country, the Muslims also did exactly the same thing – they also left their climes hundreds of years ago and they also regard this land of India as their very own."[5]

While Muslim separatism took shape in the United Provinces among Urdu speakers, the Muslim League could not claim this area because Hindus represented about 85 percent of the population. Muhammad Iqbal, a poet turned politician who was president of the Muslim League in 1930 and 1932, was the first Indian Muslim to ask for a separate land

---

[4] See Jinnah's speech as President of the Muslim League during the Lahore session of March 1940 (cited in Syed Sharifuddin Pirzada (1970: 337–338)).

[5] Cited in V.P. Varma (1980: 430).

for the Muslims of India. In his 1930 speech as leader of the Muslim League, he said: "I would like to see the Punjab, North-West Frontier Province, Sind and Baluchistan amalgamated into a single state. Self-government within the British Empire, or without the British Empire, the formation of a consolidated Northwest Indian Muslim state appears to me to be the final destiny of the Muslims, at least of Northwest India."[6] In fact, it was Iqbal, not Jinnah, who was the real founder of the two-nation theory that sees Hindus and Muslims not as two religious communities but as two nations with specific interests and cultural features. With Iqbal, religion becomes an ideology. For him, nationalism and Islam had to be equivalent – hence his demand of a separate state for the Muslims of India:

> In Muslim majority countries Islam accommodates nationalism for there Islam and nationalism are practically identical; but in Muslim minority countries (if the community has majority in a viable territory) it is justified in seeking self-determination as a distinct cultural unit. ... Patriotism in the sense of love for one's country and even readiness to die for its honour is a part of the Muslim's faith. (Tariq 1973: 136)

Known as Muffakir-e-Pakistan ("The Inceptor of Pakistan"), Iqbal wrote to Jinnah in 1937: "A separate federation of Muslim Provinces ... is the only course by which we can secure a peaceful India and save Muslims from the domination of non-Muslims. Why should not the Muslims of North-West India and Bengal be considered as nations entitled to self-determination just as other nations in India and outside India are?"[7]

This form of nationalism runs parallel to those of some of Iqbal's Hindu contemporaries. The father of the Hindutva school of thought, V.D. Savarkar, emphasized similarly secular elements of the majority community of India: its racial unity, its language (Hindi), and its territory (Jaffrelot 1996, chapter 1). There is one significant difference, however: for Savarkar, the territory of the Hindus had a sacred quality since it was the place where the gods had lived, as told by the epics and as evident from the pilgrimage routes (Jaffrelot 2004). In the case of the North Indian Muslims, their nation could not even claim that its territory was sacred. Its definition of "muslimness" was more profane.

Ultimately, Jinnah resigned himself to claim the provinces where Muslims were in a majority – Punjab, North-West Frontier Province, Baluchistan, Sind, and Bengal – even though the Muslim leaders of these regions did not consider Islam as a structural feature of their political

---

[6] www.allamaiqbal.com/person/biography/biotxtread.html
[7] www.allamaiqbal.com/person/biography/biotxtread.html

identity until the 1940s. The 1940 Lahore resolution, which is considered as the charter of the movement for Pakistan, thus read:

> Resolved that it is the considered view of this session of the All-India Muslim League that no constitutional plan would be workable in this country or acceptable to the Muslims unless it is designed on the following basic principles, viz., that geographically contiguous units are demarcated into regions which should be so constituted, with such territorial readjustments as may be necessary, that the areas which the Muslims are numerically in a majority, as in the North-Western and eastern zones of India should be grouped to constitute Independent States in which the constituent units shall be autonomous and sovereign. (Pandey 1979: 154)

SECULARIZATION AS ETHNICIZATION

From Sir Syed to Jinnah, Islam lost some of its ritual quality to become the identity marker of a nation in the making. This process exemplifies the transition toward the Age of Mobilization described by Taylor – all the more so as the key figures of the Pakistan movement were not religious persons (Jalal 1985).[8] In fact, the main architects of this transformation were elites of the community who were threatened by Hindu majorities in the United Provinces as well as the Bombay Presidency, Jinnah's province. These proponents of Muslim separatism opposed traditionalists who remained attached to rituals. Iqbal said: "Islam is not a religion in the ancient sense of the word. It is an attitude – an attitude, that is to say, of freedom and even of defiance of the universe. It is really a protest against the entire outlook of the ancient world. Briefly, it is the discovery of man" (Iqbal 1961: 153). More specifically, he considered that the Muslims of India had ethnic characteristics in common – and not only Islam as a religion. He argued "Muslims of India can have no objection to purely territorial electorates if provinces are so demarcated as to secure comparatively homogeneous communities possessing linguistic, racial, cultural and religious unity" (Razzaqi 1979: 65–66). This ethnicization process culminated in the addition of another key component of nationalism: a territory. The movement for Pakistan offers an excellent illustration of Gellner's (1964: 168) theory of nationalism: it is a case of ethno-religious nationalism.[9]

---

[8] Ayesha Jalal, in her masterpiece (1985), argues that Jinnah did not adhere to even the most basic requirements of Islam.

[9] Gellner as a theoretician of nationalism sounds much more to the point than Gellner as a specialist of Islam, the capacity in which he wrote: "no secularisation has taken place in the world of Islam: (...) the hold of Islam over its believers is as strong, and in some ways

Ethnicization was a route toward secularization. It delineated an identity-building process reifying the religious symbols: by contesting "religion-as-faith," "religion-as-ideology" valorized the cultural manifestations of Islam at the expense of spirituality. Muslims of India not only paid more attention to their territory and the language they spoke there, but also transformed some practices and sacred references in identity symbols (the Qur'an, the Tazyas, etc.).

This route toward secularization seems to illustrate a process that Charles Taylor analyses in his book on William James. In his language, it belongs to the "neo-Durkheimian" moment. In the Durkheimian phase there is no differentiation between the religious and the profane. Therefore, in the Christian world, "the social sacred is defined and served by the church" and "the spiritual dimension of existence is quite unhooked from the political" (Taylor 2003: 74–75); in the neo-Durkheimian era, "confessional allegiances have come to be woven into the sense of identity of certain ethnic, national, class, or regional group" (Taylor 2003: 77). Taylor points out that in this context "the senses of belonging to group and confession are fused, and the moral issues of the group's history tend to be coded in religious categories." For Taylor, as a result of this process "a potential decline in belief and practice is retarded or fails to occur" (Taylor 2003: 78). This conclusion can reflect a certain mental confusion. The "belief" in question is not purely religious any more, especially in the case of societies which valorize their sacred symbols in order to fight the domination of groups claiming some cultural superiority – a very common scenario, as Taylor points out. As he says, in the neo-Durkheimian moment, "the religious language is the one in which people find it meaningful to code their strong moral and political experience, either of oppression or of successful state-building around certain moral principles" (Taylor 2003: 79). The Pakistan movement, on the contrary, shows that this alchemy results in a transformation of religion into a "religion-as-ideology" which is part of the secularization process. In the case of oppression, religion becomes the language of a nationalistic ressentiment; in the case of state-building, it becomes part of the official rituals, sometimes as an official creed (which means that the old rituals do not have the same signification any more). In both cases, this kind of secularity – "Secularity IV" – is another route toward secularization.

---

stronger now than it was a 100 years ago. Somehow or other Islam is secularisation-resistant" (Gellner, "Islam and Marxism: Some Comparisons," *International Affairs*, 67 (1), 1–6).

What could this secularization mean for secularism in Pakistan? On the one hand, secularization prepared the ground for secularism inasmuch as it differentiated the religious from the political and created the plurality of mindsets that Taylor presents as a key feature of the Age of Mobilization. On the other hand, Islam being the official raison d'être of the new state, how could it make room for other religions – as in any secular regime – and for the diverse sects within Islam?

STATE-LED SECULARIZATION AND THE SHORTLIVED QUEST FOR SECULARISM (1947–1971)

Sir Syed prepared the ground for the secular repertoire, not only because he looked at Islam as a set of cultural features associated with a particular community rather than as a doctrine based on rituals and beliefs, but also because he wanted to promote the coexistence of ethno-religious groups. In 1883, he declared:

> my Hindu brethren and my Muslim co-religionists breathe the same air, drink the water of the sacred Ganga and the Jamuna, eat the products of the earth which God has given to this country, live and die together ... I say with conviction that if we were to disregard for a moment our conception of Godhead, then in all matters of everyday life the Hindus and Muslims really belong to one nation (qaum)[10] ... and the progress of the country is possible only if we have a union of hearts, mutual sympathy and love.[11]

Jinnah echoed this speech of Sir Syed in his famous declaration of August 11, 1947, three days before the official foundation day of Pakistan:

> You may belong to any religion or caste or creed that has nothing to do with the business of the state. ... We are starting with this fundamental principle that we are all citizens and equal citizens of one state ... Now I think we should keep that in front of us as our ideal and you will find that in [the] course of time, Hindus would cease to be Hindus and Muslims would cease to be Muslims, not in the religious sense, because that is the personal faith of each individual, but the political sense as citizens of the state. (Burki 1999:26)

How far could this secular perspective be implemented after independence, given not only the Islamic identity on which the Pakistan movement

---

[10] Elsewhere, Syed Ahmed Khan emphasized that Hindus and Muslims have mixed blood to give birth to a racial and cultural synthesis: "the blood of both have changed, the colour of both have become similar ... we mixed with each other so much that we produced a new language – Urdu, which was neither our language, nor theirs" (Muhammad 1972:160).

[11] Cited in V.P. Varma (1980: 430). Traditionalists could not share this analysis because they could not "disregard for a moment [their] conception of Godhead."

had been built, but also the resilience of traditionalist and fundamentalist schools of thought in South Asian Islam?

Three Schools of Thought

Sir Syed and Jinnah were not the only proponents of Islam in the public sphere before and after 1947. Other schools of thought – which may be called "traditionalist," "fundamentalist," or "Islamist" – also articulated a Muslim ideology.

While the Aligarh movement and the Muslim League had prepared the ground for a secular Pakistan, two other kinds of movement had been actively supporting alternative political projects. This plurality illustrates that Pakistan had entered the "secular age" in its own way. The traditionalists, mostly ulama, had rallied around Islamic colleges (including Deoband) before forming the Jamiyat-i-Ulama-i-Hind (JUH) in 1919, in the framework of the Khilafat movement (Hasan 1985). They had mobilized to defend the status of the Caliph of the Ottoman Empire because they believed in the ummah. As custodians of Islam, they did not believe in its territorialization, but were more concerned with the preservation of the Sharia. The ulama were less interested in the creation of a Muslim nation (*qaum*) than in the protection of a Muslim community (*millat*). Therefore, many JUH leaders, including Maulana Azad, joined the Congress Party and came to be known as the "Muslim nationalists." They were confident that Gandhi and Nehru would establish a secular regime where religions would coexist in a multicultural framework respectful of personal laws. Many ulama, however, did not share their optimism and feared that the Hindu nationalist movement would affect Congress rule. In 1946, they rallied around the Muslim League during the election campaign in Punjab, on behalf of "Islam in danger" because independence was approaching. In 1947, ulama migrated to Pakistan in large numbers.

The Islamists followed a parallel course. In 1941, the Islamic reform thinker Maududi (1976) had created the Jama'at-e-Islami (JI), a fundamentalist party arguing for an Islamic state. He had published a book theorizing political Islam in 1939. For him, like for Azad, Islam could not be territorialized, and the very idea of a Muslim homeland was a contradiction in terms. Yet, he migrated to Pakistan in 1947.[12]

While the Muslim Nationalists remained in India, many ulama and Islamists migrated to Pakistan and contested the Muslim League's

---

[12] On Maududi and the Jama'at-e-Islami, see Seyyed Vali Reza Nasr (1994 and 1996).

political project immediately after Partition through three organizations. While the Islamists supported the JI, the traditionalists rallied around two organizations: the Jamiyat-e Ulema Islam (JUI), a Deobandi movement which had been created in 1945 and whose headquarters were transferred to Karachi with Shabbir Ahmad Usmani as its leader, and the Jamiyat-e Ulema-e Pakistan (JUP), a Barelwi movement that was formed in 1948.[13]

Neither Secularism, nor Theocracy: The 1956 Constitution

The making of the Pakistani Constitution was a very delicate exercise because of the lack of any substantial consensus regarding the role of Islam in the new state[14] – a development similar to the one highlighted by Hanna Lerner in this volume about Israel (Chapter 9), whose Constituent Assembly was eventually unable to adopt a Constitution. On the one hand, the Muslim League leaders were in favor of a secular regime. On the other hand, traditionalists and Islamists demanded an Islamic state.

After the demise of Jinnah, Prime Minister Liaquat Ali Khan became the key Muslim League figure. On March 12, 1949, he had an Objectives Resolution adopted by the Constituent Assembly that reflected his sense of compromise:

"1. Sovereignty belongs to Allah alone but He has delegated it to the State of Pakistan through its people for being exercised within the limits prescribed by Him as a sacred trust.

2. The State shall exercise its powers and authority through the chosen representatives of the people.

3. The principles of democracy, freedom, equality, tolerance and social justice, as enunciated by Islam, shall be fully observed.

4. Muslims shall be enabled to order their lives in the individual and collective spheres in accordance with the teaching of Islam as set out in the holy Qur'an and Sunnah.

5. Adequate provision shall be made for the minorities to freely profess and practice their religions and develop their cultures.

6. Pakistan shall be a federation.

---

[13] The Barelwis form a community of Sunnis following the Hanafi school of jurisprudence, which was initiated in a town of North India, Bareilly (hence their name) by Ahmed Raza Khan (1856–1921).

[14] The "consensus" issue is at the heart of Farzana Shaikh (2009).

7. Fundamental rights shall be guaranteed.
8. The Judiciary shall be independent."[15]

Unsurprisingly, the more convoluted articles of this blueprint of the Constitution are those regarding the role of religion. A specialist of the relations between religion and politics in the early years of Pakistan, Leonard Binder, ironically concluded: "Thus is God sovereign, the people sovereign, parliament sovereign, and the state sovereign in Pakistan. It would indeed be a narrow-minded person who was not satisfied with such a compromise" (Binder 1963: 149). To build on this compromise was very complicated. The President of the traditionalist JUI, Maulana Shabbir Ahmad Usmani, who had supported the Muslim League before Partition and was a League member in the Constituent Assembly, was to make Liaquat Ali Khan's task difficult. As the most highly placed alim who had broken the monopoly of the Congress among the ulama, he had direct access to the prime minister. But he had different ideas and was under pressure from Maududi who met him in April 1948. He wanted "to set up a truly Islamic state" where the clerics would play an official role and asked for the formation of "a committee consisting of eminent ulama and thinkers . . . to prepare a draft . . . and present it to the Assembly" (Binder 1963: 140–141).

The main bone of contention had to do with the shari'a: "The ulama desired to enshrine the principle of the supremacy of the shari'a, while the politicians, or most of them, found this principle acceptable so long as it was not clearly defined" (Binder 1963: 144); the Muslim League leaders could not go against Islam, but they wanted to keep its role vague. In mid-April 1949, the 25 men of the Basic Principles Committee in charge of drafting the Constitution decided "to set up a board of experts consisting of reputed Scholars well versed in Ta'limat-i-Islamia to advise on matters arising out of the Objectives Resolution" (Binder 1963: 156).[16] This committee drew its inspiration from the medieval Islamic theory of the caliphate to emphasize the need to select heads of the state endowed with spiritual qualities. For its members, he had to be a Muslim de jure.

In reaction, the Muslim League leaders gave up the secular views of Jinnah that had become untenable – after all, if Pakistan had been created to give the Muslims of the Raj a homeland, its chief had to be a good Muslim. However, they tried "to relegate Islam to the sphere of policy rather than

---

[15] "Objective resolution is passed," www.storyofpakistan.com
[16] Among those who took part in the committee were Maulana Saiyid Suleiman Nadvi, the successor of Shibli at the helm of the Nadwat-al-ulama who came from Lucknow in spite of his age, and Mufti Muhammad Shafi, the right hand man of Usmani.

law" (Binder 1963: 184) – hence Liaquat Ali Khan's emphasis on the Islamic notion of social justice and the development of his concept of "Islamic socialism."

While the rulers of Pakistan tried to accommodate the more militant advocates of an Islamic state in the Assembly, they did not compromise on core issues. The Ahmadiyas are a case in point. Ahmadiyas (or, as they are also known in South Asia, Qadianis) are the followers of Mirza Ghulam Ahmad, a nineteenth-century Punjabi Muslim from the district of Qadian who claimed that he was a reincarnation of Muhammad as well as Jesus Christ and Krishna. He rejected the notion of Jihad for a more quietist, but intensely proselytizing modus operandi (Friedmann 1989). Ahmadiyas have been attacked by other Muslims since the late nineteenth century because of their "heterodox" character. After the creation of Pakistan, the fight intensified further. The objective of the first campaign in the Punjab in 1949 was to declare the Ahmadiyas as non-Muslims. The second one, in 1953 was more violent and rallied Maududi around this cause. The government arrested several Islamist leaders, including Maududi, and justified this with reference to the "necessary unity" of all the Muslims and the "freedom of religion." More importantly, the ruling elite seized this opportunity to exclude the religious leaders from the drafting committee of the Constitution.

Eventually, the 1956 Constitution specified that the President of Pakistan could only be a Muslim (art. 32), that "No Law would be passed against the teachings of Qur'an and Sunnah and the existing laws would be made Islamic in character" (art. 18), that steps would "be taken to enable the Muslims of Pakistan individually and collectively to order their lives in accordance with the Holy Qur'an and Sunnah," and that the teaching of the Qur'an would be made compulsory for all Muslims. The Hindu members of the Constituent Assembly had unsuccessfully objected to the provision that the head of state had to be Muslim. Still, at least art. 18 recognized "Freedom to profess, practice and propagate any religion and the right to establish, maintain and manage religious institutions."

The Islamic Republic of Pakistan, as evident from its official name, was not a secular country since non-Muslims did not enjoy the same rights as Muslims; at least one right was denied to them: to see one of them in the position of head of state. But it was not a theocracy either since non-Muslims were allowed to live their religion fully, and the shari'a was not the only law. This compromise was institutionalized by General Ayub Khan after his coup in 1958.

Ayub Khan or Secularization Through Statism: Bringing Power Relations Back into the Picture

Pirs and 'Ulama: The Political Influence of Religious Leaders

In contrast to the ulama (religious scholars), the more rural Pirs draw their inspiration and their prestige from mysticism.[17] Their disciples consider them saints and often donate land and money. A Pir's influence over his disciple (or murid) is especially strong in rural Pakistan; but he must have "'ma'rifa (gnosis) and be able to bestow blessings (barakah)" (Malik 1998: 57). Pirs have been, and still sometimes are, political figures. Land is the most effective source of their influence – especially under an elective (more or less democratic) regime when the vote of the masses mattered. Pirs guarantee the local villagers' participation in the barakah. This is "tied to absolute obedience (itâ'ath) and the giving of oneself in favour of the pîr" (Malik 1998: 58). Politicians from the Muslim League and other secular and religious parties have used the local influence of Pirs to win seats (evident from their key role in the 1946 elections in Punjab) (Gilmartin 1979). But others, such as Ayub Khan, feared that the Pirs and their mystic orders would become rival centers of power.

The "Statization" of Islam

One year after Khan's coup, Javed Iqbal, the son of the poet-philosopher Muhammad Iqbal (1873–1938), published a book, *Ideology of Pakistan*, demanding the abolition of shrines and the curbing of the influence of the Pirs and ulama on behalf of modernist views (Javed Iqbal, 1959). Ayub Khan's fight against the influence of the clerics was unleashed on behalf of these enlightenment-driven values, but his aim is better understood in terms of power relations.

He tried first to reduce the financial autonomy of all the Waqf. These Islamic endowments consisted of donated estates, buildings, shrines, etc., which could not be transferred and were, therefore, inalienable. The waqfs gave additional influence to Pirs and Ulema through financial autonomy to

---

[17] On what she calls "pirism," see A. Schimmel, *Mystical dimensions of Islam*, Chapel Hill, N. C., 1975, p. 22. A Pir may, for instance, be a descendent of a saint and act as a custodian of the tomb/shrine, or claim the Prophet as an ancestor, or head a madrasah (Qur'an school). On the Pirs in South Asia, see Adrian C. Mayer, "Pir and Murshid," *Middle Eastern Studies*, 3/1967, 160–169, and two chapters of the same edited volume: David Gilmartin, "Shrine, succession, and sources of moral authority," in Barbara Metcalf (ed.), Moral conduct and authority, Berkeley, California University Press, 1984, 221–240 and Richard Eaton, "The political and religious authority of the shrine of Baba Farid." In ibid., 333–356.

develop networks of Qur'anic schools. Claiming that Pirs were ignorant or even corrupt and had mismanaged the Waqf properties, Ayub Khan tried to reduce their power by promulgating the West Pakistan Waqf Property Ordinance (1961), by which all the profitable Waqf properties were transferred to the state.

While the Pirs were the primary targets of the Waqf Ordinance, Ayub Khan's education policy aimed at the ulama. The Awaqf Department designed a curriculum for training the ulama, and an "Ulama Akademi" was even established in 1970. The two-year course was intended "to 'enrich' the classical theological syllabus with modern subjects" (Malik 1998: 67). While many Qur'anic schools had been nationalized through the West Pakistan Waqf Property Ordinance, Ayub Khan wanted also to reform their curricula in the name of modernity. In 1961, a committee for the revision of the curricula was formed. Interestingly, among the eleven members of the Committee, only three had a madrasah background (Malik 1998: 155 note 30). The committee recommended the inclusion of new subjects such as Euclidean mathematics, at the expense of traditional subjects which were explicitly regarded as unimportant or even archaic. While Urdu was to remain the medium of instruction in primary schools, it had to be replaced by English or Arabic afterwards. Religious education would include "instruction in the Qur'an, Hadith, and other traditional subjects, as well as issues of national importance and the propagation of an Islamic nation or even of an Islamic community (*ummah*). This meant the transformation of Islam from a theological concept to an ideological one" (Malik 1998: 128). Indeed, Ayub Khan pursued the alternative secularization route that Sir Syed and Jinnah had initiated by promoting Islam as culture in an ethno-religious nationalistic perspective at the expense of Islam as a belief system.

To translate this modernist outlook into a new Constitution was not easy. Ayub Khan wanted "to renege on the concessions made to the men of religion in 1956" in the new Constitution he promulgated in 1962 (Gaborieau 2004: 244). He ensured that the adjective "Islamic" disappeared from the official name of the country, but the subsequent uproar led to the restoration of this key word in 1963. The new Constitution also created an Advisory Council of Islamic Ideology "to make recommendations to the Central Government and the Provincial Governments as to means of enabling and encouraging the Muslims of Pakistan to order their lives in all respects in accordance with the principles and concepts of Islam (art. 204 (a))." The Council, however, retained a pluralist perspective from two points of view. First, it was supposed to represent the various Muslim schools of thought: though plurality (one of Taylor's key words) was restricted to the majority religion (by definition in the case of a Muslim council), at least the existence of intra-Islamic plurality was recognized[18]. Second, two judges of the Supreme Court or of one of the state High Courts had to be part of the Council whose Chairman – the only full timer – had to be a Supreme Court judge. In any case, the President of the Republic exerted the final authority over the council. As Ayub Khan (1967: 194) made clear in his autobiography, "There was obviously no place for a supra-body of religious experts exercising a power of veto over the Legislature and the Judiciary."

The Ayub Khan era added one dimension to the secularization route that Pakistan had taken in 1947 and only marginally amended in 1956: a statist attempt at "colonizing" Islam, to use Malik's word. With Jinnah, Islam was supposed to endow the nation-state formed by the Muslims of the British Raj with an identity; with Ayub Khan, the nation-state started to discipline Islam in order not only to instrumentalize it, but to neutralize potential rivals among the religious leaders. The nationalization and reform of traditional institutions in a top-down perspective tended not only to make them more secular (see the curricula of the Qur'an schools) but also to marginalize their leaders. This form of secularization, here, is the by-product of power relations. Secularism benefited from this changing role of the state. Not only was religion confined to some aspects of the public sphere, a certain amount of religious diversity continued to be recognized, at least among Muslims – including the Ahmadiya minority.

Legitimation Politics and Islamization Policies (1972–1988): Secularity I Held in Check

While the clerics (or traditionalists) and the Islamists were held in check in the 1950s and 1960s, Islam could not be downplayed in the polity of Pakistan. Certainly, the architects of the country had promoted a politico-cultural version of Islam, but this repertoire structured the national identity of the country in such a way that it was impossible for the modernists to fully marginalize the religious dimension of Islam. Not only were traditionalists and Islamists acting as pressure groups, but secular politicians were prepared

---

[18] This recognition met the expectations of the different schools of thought of Islam which, in reaction to the interference of the state in religious affairs – including education – were organizing themselves: as early as 1955, the Ahl-e Hadith people, well known for their sense of organization, had created the Markaz-e Jam'iyyat Ahl-e Hadith; in 1959, all the three other schools of thought followed: the Deobandis founded the Wafaq al-Madaris al'Arabiyyah; the Barelwis, the Tanzim al-Madaris al'Arabiyyah; and the Shias, the Majlis-e Nazarate shi'ah Madaris-e Arabiyyah.

to resort to Islam in the public sphere for legitimizing their rise to power or their rule. This is the turn the Pakistani trajectory took in the 1970s and 1980s, first during the democratization phase under Bhutto and, second, during the military regime of his successor, Zia. Both leaders remained in the logic of the secularization perspective that the founding fathers of Pakistan had in some respects initiated: Bhutto instrumentalized Islam as an ethno-nationalist identity marker in order to mobilize "his" people against India; Zia, in spite of his greater proximity to the traditionalists, pursued the state-oriented centralization strategy that Ayub Khan had implemented against the Pirs and the ulama on behalf of a very different politics of Islamization.

The 1971 Trauma and Z.A. Bhutto's Islamic Agenda

The 1971 war recreated the conditions of the existential fear that the Muslims had felt in the last decades of the Raj. It was a trauma in more than one way. First, the defeat in East Pakistan against the separatists supported by the Indian army, was perceived in Pakistan as yet another loss against India. Second, this defeat resulted in the separation of East from West Pakistan. Third, the birth of Bangladesh – and the development of a separatist movement in East Pakistan in the first place – exposed the shallowness of the "Pakistani ideology": Islam had not succeeded in transcending ethno-linguistic (sub-) identities.

Inheriting the disaster of 1971, Bhutto reacted the same way Jinnah had in the 1940s when he argued that Hindus were posing a threat to Muslims: by building on their Islamic identity in order to foster a sense of unity and self-esteem.[19] He did it as a populist who mixed religion and politics, especially at the time of general elections. In 1969 the motto of his party, the Pakistan People's Party, was "Islam is our faith. Democracy is our polity. Socialism is our economy."[20] But Bhutto indulged in Islamization politics also under pressure from fundamentalist groups such as the Jama'at-e-Islami.

The 1973 Constitution, which was more respectful of parliamentarianism and federalism, was also more Islamic than its predecessor. The government had a timeline of nine years to evolve shari'a norms for the country. The "Advisory Council for Islamic Ideology" was "rechristened" the "Council of Islamic Ideology," with new functions in this regard.

---

[19] The importance of Islam as a national ideology in Bhutto's politics is well illustrated by four lectures he gave on this creed from 1948 to 1976: Z.A. Bhutto, Thoughts on some aspects of Islam (www.scribd.com/doc/28835156/Zulfikar-Ali-Bhutto-s-Thoughts-on-Islam).

[20] Z.A. Bhutto, Pakistan and the alliances, Lahore, Pakistan People's Party, 1969.

Interim reports were to be produced each year and a final one was due after seven years, which was to be discussed in parliament and respective laws enacted within two years.[21] Art. 2, for the first time, recognized Islam as "the State Religion of Pakistan." Freedom of speech and expression were restricted "in the interest of the glory of Islam" (art. 19). Elaborating on previous similar provisions, art. 31 read:

(1) "Steps shall be taken to enable the Muslims of Pakistan, individually and collectively, to order their lives in accordance with the fundamental principles and basic concepts of Islam and to provide facilities whereby they may be enabled to understand the meaning of life according to the Holy Qur'an and Sunnah.

(2) The State shall endeavor, as respects the Muslims of Pakistan

(a) to make the teaching of the Holy Qur'an and Islamiat compulsory, to encourage and facilitate the learning of Arabic language and to secure correct and exact printing and publishing of the Holy Qur'an;

(b) to promote unity and the observance of the Islamic moral standards; and

(c) to secure the proper organization of Zakat, (usher) (see below), auqaf and mosques."

More importantly, art. 260 defined for the first time who was a Muslim, and who was not. Non-Muslims included Christians, Hindus, Sikhs, Buddhists, Parsis, and Ahmadiyas.[22] In addition to this provision, to make the men of religion and the fundamentalists even happier, Bhutto approved of the second amendment to the Constitution in September 1974, which declared the Ahmadiya a "non-Muslim sect."[23] This decision, by precluding the equal recognition of different schools of thought within Islam, sealed the fate of secularism as defined by Taylor.

Bhutto was trying to use religion as a political repertoire on the domestic as well as the international scene. Internationally, he hosted the second meeting of the Organization of the Islamic Conference in 1974 in Lahore, where he promoted the notion of the "Islamic bomb" that Pakistan's nuclear program was likely to produce. Domestically, he propagated the notion of "Islamic socialism" (musawat-e Muhammadi – Mohammedan

[21] As Jamal Malik points out, "Bearing this in mind, the Islamization under Zia was only the consequent policy laid down by the Constitution of 1973" (ibid., p. 50).

[22] www.pakistani.org/pakistan/constitution/part12.ch5.html

[23] www.pakistani.org/pakistan/constitution/amendments/2amendment.html

equality – in Urdu) in the late 1960s and then, in the late 1970s, he tried to woo the Jama'at-e-Islami (JI) by proclaiming that "the law of the country was now sharia law" (Gaborieau 2004: 245). In the same vein, drinking, gambling, and nightclubs were banned and Sunday was replaced by Friday as the weekly holiday.

By declaring the Ahmadiya non-Muslims and claiming that the status of the shari'a could be upgraded, Bhutto "open(ed) the floodgates of funda-mentalism" (Gaborieau 2004: 245), or at least betrayed the secular creden-tials of his predecessors. However, he pursued one of their objectives: the subjugation of alternative religious centers of power by the state. In 1971, he brought all the foundations resulting from the nationalization of Waqf properties under the authority not of state governments, but of the Central Government. In the domain of education, Bhutto's government had the higher diplomas of the Qur'an schools (din madaris) recognized by the University Grant Commission (UGC). An equivalence committee of the UGC was also established. Following its recommendations, the Ministry of Education recognized certain certificates of Qur'an schools as equivalent to BA degrees so that the graduates of the religious schools could play "an effective role in the field of Education" (Malik 1998: 129).

Bhutto's era prepared the ground for Zia's Islamization policy which – still more paradoxically – reinforced the statist dimension of seculariza-tion à la Ayub Khan.

Zia's Islamization Politics

While Zia's Islamization policy could be partly attributed to his personal inclinations – he was a practicing Muslim from the Punjabi conservative lower middle class whose family had been forced to migrate by Partition, and who had close links with the JI – like Bhutto he used Islam as a key element of his legitimation strategy. After deposing Bhutto (and later execut-ing him) in a military coup in 1977, Zia needed to boost his legitimacy. This is evident from his relationship with the Council of Islamic Ideology (CII), which was asked to evaluate in July 1979 whether "the prevailing system of election (was) un-Islamic" (Malik 1998: 40). The CII submitted a report responding in the negative, but this was rejected by Zia who appointed a new committee. Its members first came to the conclusion that a "parliamen-tary system of government, which was in accordance with Islam, would be more appropriate for Pakistan" (Malik 1998: 41). But later, in 1983, the CII considered that "in the light of the Qur'an and Sunnah, elections on the basis of political parties are not valid" (Malik 1998: 41). Zia greatly benefited from this "handsome gift from the CII members" (Malik 1998) in his fight against his opponents from the PPP and other groups. The (anti-secular) recognition of the CII in a new role could, here again, be best explained in terms of power relations. And the CII wanted to go further. It returned to the proposal of the Ta'limat-e Islamiyyah Board of 1951 which discarded both the parliamentary and the presidential systems. Zia did not expect the Council to go that far – neither did he want it to do so. This is the irony of his Islamization policy, which was replete with contradictions: to instrumentalize Islam was not an easy task, especially when the head of the state pursued a state-oriented agenda that was intended to submit religion to political authority; and eventually Zia, who expressed his "utter disappointment regarding the ulama" (Malik 1998: 47), had to hold them in check.

However, if the difference with Bhutto's regime was more one of degree than nature, Zia's Islamization policy marked a qualitative shift away from "Islam as identity" since it resulted in a partial transformation of the legal, educational, and fiscal systems and, more importantly, made a significant impact on the "conditions of belief" that fostered sectarianism.

THE JUDICIAL REFORMS   Zia's judicial reform established an additional, Islamic legal system, parallel to the civil and the martial ones. In each regular court shari'a benches made of three qazis (Islamic judges) were introduced, whose main mission was to "examine and decide the question whether or not any law or provision of law is repugnant to the injunction of Islam."[24] In that case, the incriminated law became void, although one could make an appeal to the newly created Appellate Bench of the Supreme Court. The shari'a benches were reserved to lawyers who were also ulama. But Zia became fearful of the shari'a benches which had the potential to become sources for alternative power centers. He disbanded them a year after their creation and established a Federal Shari'a Court whose members were requested to take a loyalty oath to the president.

Zia used the Federal Shari'a Court to continue the nationalization process of Islam that Ayub Khan had initiated. In reaction to the Waqf Property Act, religious organizations had been formed and had approached the courts, including the Supreme Court. The CII decided to intervene too, especially to

---

[24] Cited in Weiss (1987: 11). In fact, the Court fulfilled additional, smaller tasks. In 1985, for instance, it was asked to examine a circular of the Awaqf Department prohibiting the saying by its employees of "durud (request for mercy upon the Prophet and praise) or salam, which was regarded as shirk by puritans. The matter ended in a case before the Federal Shariat Court in 1985, but could not be solved for good reasons. The circular was withdrawn" (J. Malik, ibid., p. 59).

contest the way some Waqf properties were submitted to land reform. It condemned the Awaqf Department more than once because, according to its members "the confiscation of the Waqf by one or more persons or by the State was in contradiction to shari'a and ought to be revoked" (Malik 1998: 65). Zia's government referred the issue to the Federal Shari'a Court, which examined all kinds of Waqf Ordinances. It considered, eventually, that nationalization of this kind of property was not against the shari'a. The state was all the more willing to fight against the Waqf holders as it promoted a rigorous, Salafi brand of Islam that was opposed to the cult of saints and the Pirs, generally speaking. In the 1977 elections, Pirs had again played a major role (Ewing 1983).

The main feature of judicial reform, which was known as the Nizam-e-Islam (Islamic rule) program, lay in the enforcement of hudud punishments. Islamic provisions in the penal code provided for new punishments for three types of crime: theft (*saraka*), fornication and adultery (*zina*), and the consumption of alcohol or drugs (*al-sharab*). The most common punishment was lashing, whose practical implementation was explained in the surprisingly detailed Execution of the Punishment of Whipping Ordinance (1979). But more severe punishments were envisaged for the most serious crimes: the amputation of the right hand for theft and stoning to death for zina offenses, for instance (Carroll 1982).

THE EDUCATIONAL REFORMS   In the educational domain, some reforms were a result of judicial reforms; a shari'a faculty was set up in the Quaid-e-Azam University in 1979 to train Islamic lawyers. But Zia paid personal attention to the larger question of the Qur'an schools. As early as September 1978, he commissioned a report on the Qur'an schools of the Sargodha division that he used as a prototype for assessing their situation nationally. This survey, which took place during the following year, resulted in recommendations regarding the addition of modern subjects such as science and technology in the curriculum. Interestingly, the chairman of the National Committee for Qur'an schools that was in charge of the survey, A. W. J. Halepota, had already been involved in the drafting of the 1961 report. Even though Zia was in favor of Islamization while Ayub Khan wanted to promote secularization, the former followed in the footsteps of the latter for one obvious reason: his statist orientation.

The Halepota report recommended not only the inclusion of modern subjects, but also more uniformity between Qur'an schools which were, therefore, bound to lose some of their autonomy. Networks of Qur'an schools, including major Deobandi institutions, resisted Zia's policy for this very reason. But the government, which toyed with the idea of establishing a National Institute for Qur'an schools, was adamant. It achieved some of its objectives by pursuing the policy that Bhutto had initiated of recognizing religious degrees. Zia paid personal attention to this matter and eventually the degrees of Qur'an schools were recognized as equivalents to the BA and MA qualifications of the UGC,[25] provided they reformed themselves and fulfilled accreditation criteria. The Tanzim of the Barelwis, for instance, adopted a new curriculum. Qur'an schools also agreed to play this game because Zia's policy provided for the allocation to some of the *zakat* money to them – which would remain free in spite of the cost of their modernization. But for that, they had to register under the Societies Act (1860). Obviously, Zia was trying to establish a new network of clients whose patron was the state and its leaders. As Jamal Malik points out, everybody was supposed to benefit from this policy:

The President sought the acceptance of his leadership by the Ulama and thus an "Islamic" legitimation of his rule. For the bureaucracy and the colonial sector, formalization of the [Qur'an schools] served as a means to bring them under control and thus to neutralize them politically. The Ulama, in contrast, aimed at finally escaping their "backwardness" and achieving social recognition without giving up their tradition. (Malik 1998: 172)

In fact, I would argue that the ulama profited from this policy more than anybody else – and certainly more than the state bureaucracy which, in fact, somewhat lost control of the Qur'an schools whose growth accelerated dramatically.[26] This loss of control was partly due to the inability of the state to micro-manage the schools: even though they had to be registered, checking their curriculum was virtually impossible.[27] It was also partly due to the fact that the Qur'an schools received some of their funds from foreign sources, including Saudi Arabia. Poor parents who valued religious education were even more prepared to send their children to Qur'an schools now that these free of charge schools also offered modern subjects.[28]

---

[25] In 1982, diplomas of Qur'an schools (*Din Madaris*) were recognized as equivalent to the Master degrees in Islamiyat (Muslim civilization) and Arabic.

[26] To my mind, its assumption that things would turn otherwise can be attributed to the superiority complex of the modern elite, which not only underestimated the traditional one, but also despised it.

[27] One cannot rule out that the administration was sometimes sympathetic to traditionalist Qur'an schools and sometimes not incorruptible.

[28] The Qur'an schools could be free of charge when the teachers and the building maintenance were paid by the state or/and foreign money.

TABLE 7.1 *Numbers of students and teachers of Qur'an schools in different years and provinces*

Province	1960		1971		1979		1983	
	S*	T**	S	T	S	T	S	T
West Pakistan	44,407	1,846	45,238	3,186	99,041	5,005	259,827	7,394
Punjab	24,842	1,053	29,096	2,063	80,879	2,992	124,670	3,549
Sindh	6,218	401	5,431	453	8,344	1,245	37,949	1,080
NWFP	7,897	312	8,423	515	7,749	673	78,439	2,217
Baluchistan	519	46	1,207	95	1,814	95	8,083	280
Azad Kashmir	n.a.	n.a.	n.a.	n.a.	n.a.	n.a.	1,644	41
Northern Areas	763	23	1,083	60	n.a.	n.a.	4,384	125
Islamabad	n.a.	n.a.	n.a.	n.a.	n.a.	n.a.	4,638	133

*S = Students, ** T = Teachers
Source: J. Malik, op. cit., p. 178

While the number of Qur'an school students remained almost the same in West Pakistan in the 1960s, it increased by 119 percent between 1971 and 1979 and jumped by 160 percent in only 4 years, from 1979 to 1983. The growth was particularly dramatic in Sindh, with 53.6 percent and 354 percent, respectively. But the largest numbers of Qur'an schools were located in the NWFP (−8 and +91 percent, respectively) where the Zia government supported the development of the schools in the context of the Afghanistan war, in order to channel Afghan refugees and to train militants likely to resist the Soviets. Punjab, which represented 48 percent of the total in 1983, shows a more steady growth in the 1970s and early 1980s, with 56 and 54 percent, respectively.

According to Jamal Malik, between 1978 and 1985, the Deobandi Madaris (schools) produced the largest number of Maulanas: 3,530 (52.6 percent of the total), against 3,179 between 1960 and 1977; then came the Barelwi Madaris with 3,093, against 464 (over a shorter period, though: 1974–1977); and finally the Ahl-i-Hadith, with 1,276. If we add the 299 graduates from Shia seminaries, the Qur'an schools granted their degree to as many students in 1984–1985 as in the 17 pre-Zia years, from 1960 to 1977: 3,601 against 3,643 (Malik 1998: 228). This expansion of the Qur'an schools was fostered by the support they received from abroad. The Sunni and the Shia institutions were helped by Saudi Arabia and Iran, respectively, who, after Khomeini's revolution fought a proxy war for the leadership of the Muslim world. Riyad supported especially the Ahl-e-Hadith, who in some cases even employed very well-paid Saudi teachers (Malik 1998: 229). The influence of Iran was especially noticeable in the Gilgit area, where teachers were also better paid and students given a more substantial allowance than in other Shia schools (Malik 1998: 261).

By 1988, when Zia left the scene, the number of Qur'an schools had increased by 12,000.[29] The growing importance of these schools was probably the most significant dimension of Zia's Islamization policy,

---

[29] Ian Talbot, *Pakistan: A Modern History*, London: Hurst, 1999, p. 279. Other, anonymous experts give different figures: between 1979 and 1988, 1,151 new Din Madaris would have been registered according to International Crisis Group. (ICG, Pakistan: madrassas, extremism and the military, ICG Asia Report, n° 36 [July 29, 2002], p. 9.) But Vali Nasr, assuming that the number of unregistered Din Madaris was much higher, estimates that there were 25,000 institutions of that kind at the turn of the twenty-first century (S.V.R. Nasr, "Islam, the state and the rise of sectarian militancy in Pakistan," op. cit., p. 90).

which meant both the disbursement of additional funds and the opening up to Saudi money.

FISCAL REFORMS   In the short term, however, the fiscal dimension of this policy made a stronger impact. The payment of the alms tax, the *zakat*, as well as its agricultural counterpart, the *ushr*, used to be a private obligation for Muslims in Pakistan. They generally represented 2.5 percent of annual savings and acted as a tax on wealth. One of the provisions of the 1973 Constitution already requested the government to levy it. But no move had been made by Bhutto in that direction. In 1979, Zia decided to transform this duty into a legal obligation. The Zakat and 'Usher Ordinance was issued in 1980. The *zakat* component took effect in 1981, whereas the *ushr* one was postponed repeatedly until 1983.

The *zakat* administration that was already in place was refurbished in order to be more effective in the collection and distribution processes that Malik summarizes as follows: "On the first day of the fasting month of Ramadan, the Zakat Deducting Agencies (banks, post-offices etc) by means of deduction at source withdraw 2.5 percent from all saving accounts above a certain exemption limit (fixed at Rs. 1,000 in the first year of *zakat* deduction, 1980). They transfer the *zakat* thus collected to the Central Zakat Fund (CZF). This fund is fed also with proceeds from 'voluntary zakat' and 'donations' and from funds of other institutions. Following certain criteria, the *zakat* is then distributed among the Provincial Zakat Funds (PZFs) and the National Zakat Foundation (NZF). Following prescribed quota, the PZFs turn over funds to the Local Zakat Funds (LZFs) to other institutions, to the needy (mustahqin) and to the National Zakat Foundation" (Malik 1998:95).

While the *ushr* has been distributed in the locality where it was collected, the distribution process of the *zakat* shows a whole bureaucratic pyramid in action. Indeed, the Islamization policy, here again, simply deepened the influence of the state apparatus over religious institutions, a process initiated by Ayub Khan. That was evident from the Tehsil/Taluka/Subdivisional and Local Committees (Removal of Chairman and Members) Rule (1981) which allowed the removal of the chairman of a *zakat* local committee by the bureaucracy. In 1981, *Al Zakat*, an influential national monthly publication – Provincial Zakat Administrations published their own *Al Zakat* journal every three months – took pride in the fact that 250,000 people were engaged in the *zakat* administration (Malik 1998:96).

Zia's "Islamization" policy, in fact, promoted sectarianism. Indeed, as soon as his project regarding the *zakat* and *ushr* was made public, Shia leaders objected that according to Shia jurisprudence, these monies could only be given by individuals according to their conscience.[30] In reaction to the promulgation of the law, the Shia orchestrated a mammoth demonstration in Islamabad (Mayer 1987). As a result, on April 27, 1981, the Ministry of Finance issued a Notification allowing Shias to claim an exemption from the payment of this tax. However, the controversy exacerbated a new line of cleavage between Shias and Sunnis.[31] First, those who did not pay the *zakat* and the *ushr* seemed to be second-class Muslim citizens. Second, and more importantly, the episode led Shias to create new organizations based on Shia khums, which contributed to further Shia–Sunni differentiation and in the medium term fostered a phenomenon known as "sectarianism" in Pakistan.

To sum up, Zia promoted Islam in an unprecedented way in Pakistani politics, but for complex reasons and with unintended consequences. An orthodox Muslim, Zia embarked on an Islamization policy also for political reasons since this repertoire provided him with legitimacy – something which, as a putschist, he lacked. That was evident from the drafting of the question he asked in the 1984 referendum:

Do the people of Pakistan endorse the process initiated by General Muhammad Zia-ul-Haq, the President of Pakistan, for bringing the laws of Pakistan in conformity with the injunctions of Islam as laid down in the Holy Quran and Sunnah of the Holy Prophet (PBUH) and for the preservation of the Islamic ideology of Pakistan, for the continuation and consolidation of that process, and for the smooth and orderly transfer of power to the elected representatives of the people? (Rizvi, 2003: 276)

Of the voters, 98.5 percent said "Yes." How could anyone have said "No" to Islam?

But Zia did not want the religious leaders – whom he despised – to gain too much influence. Therefore, he pursued the statist agenda that Ayub Khan had initiated in order to cut them down to size. Islam continued to be defined in terms of collective identity at the expense of its religious content. While there is, therefore, a certain continuity between the two

---

[30] For the Shias, the non-Sayyids (Sayyids being descendants of the Prophet) are not supposed to give Zakat (but Khums) to the Sayyids (Khums represent one fifth of the annual savings of a non-Sayyid, half of which should be given to the Imam or his representative).

[31] All the more so, as to fill the relevant CZ-50 form "within three months preceding the Valuation date" was not an easy task. In 1982, whereas they thought they had won the case, many Shias discovered that the tax had been levied on their assets because they had not filed the right form on time.

generals, Zia's Islamization policy made a difference vis-à-vis secularism. While minorities had been protected in the 1950s and 1960s, they were the first collateral victims – including the Shias – of what amounted to a policy of "Sunnization." The revision of the Blasphemy Law inherited from the British was a case in point. The Pakistan Penal Code (PPC) and the Criminal Procedure Code (CPC) were amended in 1980, 1982, and 1986 in such a way that, eventually, blaspheming the Qur'an and the Prophet were punishable, respectively, by life imprisonment and by life imprisonment or death.[32] Muslims were the primary victims of these new regulations, but minorities felt targeted too. Indeed, they were affected by new forms of segregation: separate electorates were introduced for the Hindus, Sikhs, Baha'is, Jews, and Kalash, who till then voted with other Pakistanis and protested against this technique of marginalization.

CONCLUSION

The case of Pakistan throws some interesting light on Taylor's approach to secularization and secularism. First, it shows that in addition to the three forms of secularity he has theorized, there may be a fourth one – "religion-as-ideology," to use Ashis Nandy's words – that only partly corresponds to his "neo-Durkheimian" category since he considers that it is not part of a secularization process. This "Secularity IV" is best epitomized by the Pakistan movement, an ethno-religious nationalism where Islam plays a major role as an identity marker associated with language. Pakistan offers here a good illustration of the bifurcation between Islam as culture vis-à-vis Islam as religion that Olivier Roy has recently highlighted (Roy 2010). Sir Syed, Mohammad Iqbal, and Jinnah achieved such a transformation by promoting a territorialized and a politicized definition of Islam.

Taylor's definition of secularism is useful for understanding an aspect of the Pakistan movement: its promotion of Islam did not preclude the future of secularism as defined by Taylor as an "ism" based on respect for diversity. After 1947, from Jinnah to Ayub Khan, the rulers of the new state tried to observe a measure of secularism by protecting the rights of

---

[32] Art. 295 B of the PPC said: "Whoever will fully defiles, damages or desecrates a copy of the Holy Quran or of an extract therefrom or uses it in any derogatory manner or for any unlawful purpose shall be punishable for imprisonment for life. and art. 295 C said: Whoever by words, either spoken or written or by visible representation, or by any imputation, innuendo, or insinuation, directly or indirectly, defiles the sacred name of the Holy Prophet Mohammed (PBUH) shall be punished with death, or imprisonment for life, and shall also be liable to fine."

the minorities while they pursued a state-driven secularization agenda by fighting religious leaders (Pirs and ulama). But their successors retained only the latter dimension. Bhutto's and Zia's Islamization policies, paradoxically, affected religious leaders in the sense that they standardized religion and transformed the state into a centralized manager of Islam. Their approach was power-oriented: as political leaders who were keen to curb the influence of religious leaders, they resorted to state power and instrumentalized Islam to acquire additional sources of legitimacy. There was a strong element of continuity there since the leaders of the 1970s and 1980s, be they civilian or military, were as eager as their predecessors of the 1950s and 1960s to use the state machinery. In fact, some of the initial institutions continued to play the same standardization role – even after the substance of the policies had changed.

However, the state could not fully control the Islamic institutions – including the Qur'an schools – which it promoted. And, in fact, Zia's Islamization policy prepared the ground for the growth not only of sectarianism, but also of Islamism in the country.

References

Bhargava, R. 1998. "What is secularism for?" In R. Bhargava (ed.). *Secularism and its Critics*. Delhi: Oxford University Press, 486–522.

Binder, L. 1963. *Religion and Politics in Pakistan*. Berkeley: University of California Press.

Brass, Paul. 1974. *Language, Religion and Politics in North India*. Cambridge: Cambridge University Press.

Burki, Shahid Javed. 1999. *Pakistan: Fifty Years of Nationhood*. Boulder: Westview Press.

Carroll, Lucy. 1982. "Nizam-i-Islam: Processes and Conflicts in Pakistan's Programme of Islamization, with Special Reference to the Position of Women." *Journal of Commonwealth and Comparative Politics*. 20(1): 57–95.

Ewing, Katherine. 1983. "The Politics of Sufism. Redefining the Saints of Pakistan." *Journal of Asian Studies*, XLII (2), February: 251–268.

Friedmann, Yohann. 1989. *Prophecy Continuous: Aspects of Ahmadi Religious Thought and its Medieval Background*. Berkeley: University of California Press.

Gellner, Ernest. 1964. *Thought and Change*. London: Weidenfeld and Nicholson.

Gilmartin, David. 1979. "Religious Leadership and the Pakistan Movement in the Punjab." *Modern Asian Studies*. 13 (3): 485–517.

Gaborieau, Marc. 2004. "Islam and Politics." In C. Jaffrelot (ed.), *A History of Pakistan and its Origins*. London: Anthem Press, 237–251.

Hasan, Mushirul. 1985. "The Khilafat Movement: A Reappraisal," in Mushirul Hasan *Communal and Pan-Islamic Trends in Colonial India*. Delhi: Manohar.

Iqbal, Javed. 1959. *The Ideology of Pakistan*. Karachi: Sang-e-Meel Publications.

Iqbal, Muhammad. 1961. *Stray Reflections : The Private Notebook of Muhammad Iqbal* [Also includes: "Stray Thoughts"]. Lahore: Iqbal Academy Pakistan: www.iqbalcyberlibrary.net/pdf/844.pdf

Jaffrelot, C. 1996. *Hindu Nationalism and Indian Politics*. New York: Columbia University Press.

    2004. "From Indian Territory to Hindu Bhoomi: The Ethnicization of Nation-State Mapping in India." In John Zavos, Andrew Wyatt, and Vernon Hewitt (eds.). *The Politics of Cultural Mobilization in India*. New York: Oxford University Press, 197–215.

Jalal, A. 1985. *The Sole Spokesman: Jinnah, the Muslim League and the Demand for Pakistan*. Cambridge: Cambridge University Press.

Lelyveld, David. 1978. *Aligarh's First Generation: Muslim Solidarity in British India*. Princeton: Princeton University Press.

Luhmann, Niklas. 1995. *Social Systems*. Stanford: Stanford University Press.

Mahmood, Safdar and Javaid Zafar. 1968. *Founders of Pakistan*. Lahore: Publishers United.

Malik, Jamal. 1998. *Colonization of Islam: Dissolution of traditional institutions in Pakistan*. Delhi: Manohar.

Maududi, Abu al-A'la al-. 1976. "Political Theory of Islam." In Khurshid Ahmad (ed.). *Islam: Its Meaning and Message*. London: Islamic Council of Europe.

Metcalf, Barbara. 1982. *Islamic Revival in British India: Deoband, 1860–1900*. Princeton: Princeton University Press.

Minault, Gail. 1982. *The Khilafat movement: Religious Symbolism and Political Mobilization in India*. New York: Columbia University Press.

Muhammad, Shan. 1972. *Writings and Speeches of Sayyid Ahmad Khan*. Bombay: Nachiketa Publications.

Nandy, A. 1990. "The Politics of Secularism and the Recovery of Religious Tolerance." In Veena Das (ed.). *Mirrors of Violence: Communities, Riots and Survivors in South Asia*. New Delhi: Oxford University Press, 69–93.

Pandey, B.N. 1979. "The Demand for Pakistan." In B.N. Pandey, ed. *The Indian Nationalist Movement, 1885–1947. Select Documents*. London: Macmillan Press.

Pernau, M. 2003. "Middle Class and Secularization: the Muslims of Delhi in the Nineteenth Century." In Imtiaz Ahmed and Helmut Reifeld (eds.). *Middle Class Values in India and Western Europe*. New Delhi: Social Science Press. 21–41.

Pirzada, Syed Sharifuddin. 1970. *Foundations of Pakistan – All India Muslim League Documents: 1906–1947*. Karachi: National Publishing House.

Khan, Syed Ahmad. 1967. "Islam and Science." In K. Satchidananda Murty *Readings in Indian History, Politics and Philosophy*. London: George Allen and Unwin Ltd.

Mayer, Ann Elizabeth. 1987. "Islamization and Taxation in Pakistan." In A. Weiss *Islamic Reassertion in Pakistan. The Application of Islamic Laws in a Modern State*. Lahore: Vanguard, 59–78.

Nasr, Seyyed Vali Reza. 1994. *The Vanguard of Islamic Revolution: The Jama'at-i Islami of Pakistan*. London: IB Tauris.

1996. *Mawdudi and the Making of Islamic revivalism*. New York: Oxford University Press.

Razzaqi, Shahid Hussain. 1979. *Discourses of Iqbal*. Lahore: Sh. Ghulam Ali & Son.

Rizvi, Hasan-Askar. 2003. *Military, State and Society in Pakistan*. Lahore: Sang-e-Meel Publications.

Robinson, Francis. 1974. *Separatism among Indian Muslims*. Cambridge: Cambridge University Press.

Roy, O. 2010. *Holy Ignorance: When Religion and Culture Part Ways*. London: Hurst.

Shaikh, Farzana. 1989. *Community and Consensus in Islam: Muslim Representation in Colonial India, 1860–1947*. Cambridge: Cambridge University Press.

2009. *Making Sense of Pakistan*. London: Hurst.

Tariq, A.R. 1973. *Statements and Speeches of Iqbal*. Lahore: Sh. Ghulam Ali.

Taylor, Charles. 2010. "The Meaning of Secularism." *The Hedgehog Review*. 12(3): 23–34.

2003. *Varieties of Religion Today. William James Revisited*. Cambridge (Mass.): Harvard University Press.

Troll, Christian. 1978. *Sayyid Ahmed Khan: Reinterpretation of Muslim Theology* Delhi: Vikas.

Varma, V.P. 1980. *Modern Indian Political Thought*. Agra: Lakshmi Narain Agarwal.

Weiss, Anita. 1987. "The Historical Debate on Islam and the State in South Asia." In A. Weiss (ed.). *Islamic Reassertion in Pakistan: The Application of Islamic Laws in a Modern State*. Lahore: Vanguard, 1–20.

8

Charles Taylor's *A Secular Age* and Secularization from Below in Iran

Nader Hashemi

INTRODUCTION

Recent scholarship in the social sciences on secularism has sought to define the concept and its manifestation in three dimensions.[1] Charles Taylor's magnum opus, *A Secular Age*, sticks to this three-fold characterization by describing the decline of religion in public spaces as "Secularity I," the decline of belief and practice as "Secularity II," and the changing conditions of belief over the *longue durée* as "Secularity III."[2] It is this last dimension of Secularity III where Taylor parts company from other scholars who have written on the topic.

A Secular Age is primarily a book about the history of ideas. Taylor seeks a deep understanding of the historical evolution and trajectory of secularity in the West by writing a comprehensive intellectual history of the subject. This strikes me as one of the most useful and versatile ways of grappling with the topic for two reasons: 1) because it grounds the debate on secularity with historical depth; and 2) because of its cross-cultural potential in terms of understanding the "multiple histories" of secularity on a global level, particularly in the non-Western world.[3]

In this chapter, I focus on Taylor's notion of Secularity III and the changing social conditions of belief in the context of Iran's modern experience, focusing primarily on the twentieth century. The emphasis will be on the institutional and political arrangements that have affected the process of secularization and the debate on secularism in Iran in the lead up to the 1979 Revolution and its aftermath. I argue and provide

---

[1] Keddie (2003b), 14–30, and (1997), 21–40; Casanova (2006), 7–22.
[2] Taylor (2007), 1–22. [3] Hashemi (2010), 325–338.

evidence for a de facto secularization process within the Islamic Republic that is a direct result of the failure of clerical rule in Iran. This is particularly evident among intellectuals, Iranian youth, and the urban middle class. The final part of this chapter will comment on the applicability of Taylor's thesis both to Iran and to the broader Muslim world, noting key similarities and differences between the history of secularity in the West and the modern Muslim Middle East.

IRAN AND SECULARIZATION: PRELIMINARY REMARKS

Over the last twenty years, Iran has experienced an intense intellectual debate on secularism.[4] This has been a direct result of Iran's post-revolutionary experience with political Islam in power and with the perceived failure of the 1979 Revolution in terms of what it promised and what it actually delivered. A broad consensus exists today within Iran, principally among the political opposition, that in the aftermath of a democratic transition the principle of political secularity must form the bedrock of any future democratic constitution. All of Iran's leading intellectuals, human rights activists, student leaders, and political figures – from Abdolkarim Soroush and Akbar Ganji to Shirin Ebadi and Mohsen Kadivar – agree on this point. For example, in the official charter of Iran's oppositional Green Movement, political secularism is stipulated as an important political principle.[5] This intellectual transformation among former Islamist supporters of the 1979 Revolution has been described by Asef Bayat as the emergence of "post-Islamism," which includes as one of its key features the idea of a soft form of political secularity which is needed to sustain a functioning democracy.[6]

At the level of society, contrary to the popular perception of Iran in the West, a process of secularization is discernible, especially among the middle class and youth segments of society. A February 2004 poll showed that 45 percent of Iranians had negative feelings toward religion, and a government report found that 75 percent of the public and 86 percent of school children "do not say their daily prayers."[7] In the same year Iran's Ministry of Religious Affairs revealed that only 3 percent of Iranians attend Friday prayers, compared to about 50 percent that did so before

---

[4] Soroush et al. (2002); Hajjarian (2001); Alavitabar (2004), 80–83. For a good overview and summary of this topic in English, see Kamrava (2008) and Rajaee (2007).

[5] "The Green Movement Charter," Hashemi and Postel (2011), 338.

[6] Bayat (2007) and (2013), 35–70.   [7] Peterson (2010), 122.

the revolution, and that up to half of Tehran's population reportedly did not fast during the month of Ramadan in 2011.[8]

Iran is a very modern society with high rates of urbanization (about 70 percent), low fertility rates (about 1.7 percent), and literacy levels of about 94 percent for men, 88 percent for women, and 99 percent among the youth.[9] While these statistics suggest secularizing trends, data from the World Values Survey confirms that a process of decline of religious belief and practice (Secularity II) is underway in Iran, in contrast to other Muslim-majority societies. When judged in terms of mosque attendance, the importance of raising children with Islamic values, and the rise of individualism, Iran ranks at the top of these secularizing trends in comparison to Pakistan, Egypt, Saudi Arabia, Turkey, Indonesia, Morocco, Jordan, and Iraq.[10] How does one begin to explain and interpret these trends?

According to my reading, the key institutional variable that has affected the process and debate on the secular before the 1979 Revolution as well as in today's Iran has been the authoritarian state's policies. Since 1925, it has attempted to ideologically impose on society a particular worldview and lifestyle, with little input or negotiation with society, while repressing opposition movements and censoring dissident views. The enveloping context of political authoritarianism in which this process has occurred has informed opposition to the state and generated a social reaction and backlash among segments of society. This contributed to the desecularization of politics and society before the Iranian Revolution and its converse, albeit gradually, after the toppling of the Pahlavi monarchy.

In one sense, Iran has almost come full circle. The 1979 Revolution was predicated on a rejection of the secular nationalism of the Pahlavi regime and its authoritarian, modernizing, pro-Western policies. Thirty-seven years later, secularism has returned to Iran, but with a critical difference. Prior to 1979, state-imposed secularism alienated segments of society, whereas today the impetus for secularism has emerged from within civil society, buttressed by intellectual and moral arguments that have sunk

---

[8] Esposito (2010), 107 and Mostaghim (2011). Also see Khosrokhavar (2007), 453–463. One indication of this secularizing trend is the high levels of secularity among Iranian expatriate populations in the West, most of who are middle class. I'm unaware of any academic study on the topic, but it can be observed that when given free choice, Iranians abroad opt for a lifestyle that is secular and with little difference in the level of religiosity between them and the host communities in which they live in.

[9] UNESCO Institute for Statistics, "Adult and Youth: National, Regional and Global Trends, 1985–2015 (June 2013)," www.uis.unesco.org/Education/Documents/literacy-statistics-trends-1985–2015.pdf.

[10] Moadell (2009), 126–136.

deep roots within Iran's political culture. This desire for a secular age and its manifestation both at the political and sociological level challenges a clerical oligarchy that dominates the state and which has criminalized any open and free public discussion of the secular. In the sections that follow I provide some historical background to these developments.

THE POST-COLONIAL STATE AND THE DEMISE OF SECULARISM: LESSONS FROM IRAN

The modern state of Iran is inseparable from the emergence of the Pahlavi monarchy in 1925. Reza Khan (1878–1944), a commander of the imperial guard and Minister of War, consolidated power amid the chaos of tribal insurrections, Soviet and British penetration, economic decay, and the corrupt rule of the decrepit Qajar dynasty.[11] Proclaiming himself the new king of Iran, he ruled autocratically while launching a massive modernization and secularization program that is comparable, though not identical to, the policies of Mustafa Kemal Atatürk in neighboring Turkey. The infrastructure of a centralized and modern state, with new roads, railways, a modern education system, a bureaucracy, a banking system, and a conscript-army, began to take shape.[12] The transformative effects of these policies were felt throughout Iranian society, but especially by the Shiite clergy whose powers and privileges were significantly curtailed in the area of law and education. Commenting on the diminution of the role of religion in public affairs, Karen Armstrong observes that "Shah Reza Pahlavi would ... not only equal but even surpass Atatürk's ruthless secularization."[13] Gavin Hambly disagrees, and notes that in "his dealings with the ulama [clergy], Riza Shah, contrary to what is often asserted, was quite circumspect, and there is no evidence that he ever considered launching an assault upon Islam such as Atatürk mounted in Turkey. He preferred to ignore rather than confront the ulama [clergy]."[14] The truth lies somewhere in between these two observations.

Reza Pahlavi was forced to abdicate in 1941 by the Allied Powers due to his pro-German sympathies. He was replaced by his 21-year-old son, Mohammad Reza Pahlavi (1919–1980), who continued his father's modernizing and secularizing policies, gradually at first but with more intensity and determination as he consolidated power. The key developments that

---

[11] Abrahamian (2008), 63–96.   [12] Ansari (2003), 40–74.   [13] Armstrong (2000), 198.
[14] Hambly (1991), 232–233. On Reza Pahlavi's 1934 visit to Turkey, see Marashi (2003), 99–119. Also see Bayart (1994), 282–299 and Akhavi (1980), 28–59.

significantly affected the perception of secularism in Iran were to unfold after the 1953 coup d'etat. The coup restored Mohammad Reza to the throne after he fled the country during a period of democratization led by the charismatic liberal-democratic Prime Minister, Mohammad Mossadeq. At the time, the nationalization of the British-controlled Iranian oil industry coupled with fears of a Communist takeover resulted in a joint CIA-MI6 coup that restored the young Pahlavi king to power and returned Iran to the orbit of pro-Western allies in the Middle East.[15]

It is important to clarify that the ruling ideology of the new Pahlavi order was not as dogmatically secular and overtly hostile toward religion as the Kemalist project in Turkey. Rather, the ideological orientation of the regime was based on a unique form of monarchical nationalism that viewed the nation as inseparable from the Pahlavi monarchy and the kingdoms that had preceded it. In the official pronouncements of the state, Iran's Islamic identity was downplayed and its pre-Islamic identity elevated, specifically in terms of a glorification of ancient Persian empires, kings, and dynasties.[16]

The character of the new regime that emerged in the aftermath of the 1953 coup was similar to other post-colonial regimes in the Muslim world in terms of its political authoritarianism, its commitment to modernization, and its secular development goals. According to one Iran scholar "as a generalization, it can be said that the phrase, '*L'état, c'est moi*', accurately describes how the country [of Iran] was managed" during this period.[17] All independent political forces, from the communist left to the religious right were crushed and a powerful centralized state quickly established its hegemony over society.

The pattern of state–society relations that unfolded in Iran in the ensuing decades was to have enormous consequences in terms of the desecularization of politics and the rise of a religious-based opposition. This pattern was reproduced in other Muslim societies in the post–World War II era: an autocratic modernizing state, often with critical external support, suffocated secular civil society, thus forcing oppositional activity into the mosque, inadvertently contributing to the rise of political Islam.[18]

---

[15] For background, see Katouzian (1999), 95–112 and (2004), 1–26.

[16] In his interpretation and recollection of Iranian history, the Shah's references to Islam were always laudable and very respectful. He writes that in Iran we also "developed the Shiah branch of the Moslem faith, in which I *fervently believe*" (emphasis added). For his references to Islam, see Shah Pahlavi (1961), 21, 23–24.

[17] Hambly (1991), 267.

[18] Mirsepassi (2000), 65–95, provides an excellent overview of this development in Iran from which I draw upon. Also see Moaddel (2002), 46–55.

A set of top-down, forced modernization, secularization, and Westernization policies by the state within a short span of time generated widespread social and psychological alienation and dislocation. Rapid urbanization and changing cultural and socio-economic relationships, combined with increasing corruption, economic mismanagement, rising poverty, and income inequality, undermined the legitimacy of the ruling regime. These developments reflected badly on secularism given that the ruling ideology of many post-colonial regimes in the Muslim world (Iran included) were openly secular-nationalist.[19]

Despotism, dictatorship, and human rights abuses, for a generation of Muslims growing up in the post-colonial era, thus came to be associated with the political project of secularism. Muslim political activists who experienced oppression at the hands of secular national governments concluded that secularism is an ideology of repression.[20] This observation applies not only to Iran but also to Tunisia, Algeria, Egypt, Syria, Iraq, Yemen, Turkey, and many other Muslim-majority countries in the latter half of the twentieth century.

This point seems to be under-appreciated by some scholars who write on the topic of Middle Eastern and Islamic politics. John Waterbury, for example, demonstrates sympathy for the policies of the Mubarak regime in dealing with its domestic opposition. In a widely cited essay on the prospects for political liberalization in the Middle East, he argued: "it is not at all self-evident that repression will fail. Here too Mubarak has been exemplary."[21] Waterbury's overall discussion of democracy in the Middle East suffers from a clear secular and modernization theory bias where he mistakenly assumes that the question of religion's normative relationship with government has been democratically negotiated in Egypt and thus any public manifestation of religious identity in the public sphere is an abnormality and a threat to political development. In short, the Islamists are the problem and the secularists are their potential victims who face "immense risks." The point that seems lost on Waterbury is that the secularists within Muslim societies are often allied with the repressive apparatus of the authoritarian state, thus delegitimizing them (and the perception of secularism) in the eyes of the more religious segments of the population. This pattern has been repeated in the aftermath of the Egyptian military coup of July 3, 2013.[22]

---

[19] Kian-Thiébaut (1998), 211–226; Keddie (2003a), 132–169. Also see Nasr (1998), 32–37.
[20] I am indebted to Richard Bulliet for drawing my attention to this point.
[21] Waterbury (1994), 41.
[22] Abou El Fadl (2013), http://www.abc.net.au/religion/articles/2013/07/11/3800817.htm.

Echoing Aslı Bâli's contribution to this volume (Chapter 10), Nilüfer Göle argues that in the context of Turkey, contrary to the Western experience with secularism, in the Middle East secularism "is not neutral and power-free."[23] The authoritarianism of the colonial and post-colonial state along with its secularizing policies has made it an active and biased participant in the modern political history of Muslim societies. It has accumulated a track record, a list of failed policies, and also a list of victims. Far from being neutral and democratic, the secular post-colonial state in Muslim societies and the elites that support it have generally bolstered authoritarianism rather than political liberty.

"This fact explains why, contrary to common belief, the westernized elites in the Middle East are very often not the most democratic," observes Göle.[24] In contrast to the West, therefore, where secularism has historically been a force for political and religious pluralism and democratization, in Muslim societies, secularism's legacy has been nearly the exact opposite.

Karen Armstrong succinctly captures this key interpretive point when she writes that in "the West, secularization has been experienced as liberating; it had even, in its early stages, been regarded as a new and better way of being religious." But in Muslims societies "secularization was experienced as a violent and coercive assault. When later fundamentalists claimed that secularization meant the destruction of Islam, they would often point to the example of Atatürk."[25]

The concept of secularism, therefore, has become highly politicized in Muslim societies, first due to the modern encounter between Europe and the Middle East in the form of colonialism and imperialism, and subsequently due to the behavior and failure of post-colonial regimes whose reigning ethos has been decidedly secular. Summarizing these developments, Vali Nasr has observed:

Secularism in the Muslim world never overcame its colonial origins and never lost its association with the postcolonial state's continuous struggle to dominate society. Its fortunes became tied to those of the state: the more the state's ideology came into question, and the more its actions alienated social forces, the more secularism was rejected in favor of indigenous worldviews and social institutions – which were for the most part tied to Islam. As such, the decline of secularism was a reflection of the decline of the postcolonial state in the Muslim world.[26]

---

[23] Göle (1996), 20.   [24] Ibid.   [25] Armstrong (2000), 192.
[26] Vali Nasr, "Secularism: Lessons from the Muslim World," 69.

Until 1979, Iran's story with respect to secularism broadly fits into the above narrative, which it shared with many other Muslim societies. With the seizure of the state by Ayatollah Khomeini and his disciples, Iran was to move in a different direction. Religion had achieved political power. An ideological state emerged that sought to de-secularize Iran and undo the policies of the Pahlavi regime. The new Islamist-controlled state developed an identity deeply shaped by Iran's negative experience with Western imperial intervention in the Middle East over the past 200 years and specifically with US policy toward Iran after 1953. While the popular base of support for the new Islamist regime was qualitatively different from that of the Pahlavi regime, in that is had extensive grass roots support, political authoritarianism continued to dominate the landscape of the Islamic Republic.

In the first decade after Khomeini's death in 1989, a reform movement arose, and with it a new intellectual paradigm that gradually developed an indigenous form of Islamic-friendly political secularism. This transformation was significant because it was organically rooted in Iranian civil society and it developed a following among former supporters of Ayatollah Khomeini, most of who have come to reject the idea of a clerical-dominated "Islamic state."[27]

THE SECULARIZATION OF NORMS IN IRAN AND THE RISE OF A REFORM MOVEMENT

One measure of the rise of political secularism in Iran is the frequent conservative attacks on those who believe in the secularization of Iran's political system. In the lead up to the 2013 presidential election, for example, the all-powerful head of Iran's judiciary, Sadegh Larijani, stated that all "individuals and political groups ... related to the Reformist era who sought secularism as a replacement for Qur'anic and Islamic teachings must note that that era has ended and that they can no longer emerge, because the Iranian nation does not accept the ideas of this group." He added that all "those who believe in secular thought and seek to replace Western democracy for Qur'anic understanding must know that ... the country's political situation is not conducive for their managerial activities" and they can play no role in Iranian political life.[28]

---

[27] Asef Bayat's thesis on post-Islamism, (1994), explains this development. Also see Ghobadzadeh (2015).
[28] "Warning from the Head of the Judiciary about the Rise of Seditionists," *BBC Persian* (2013).

The Commander of the Islamic Revolutionary Guard Corps, General Rahim Safavi, has similarly warned of a subversive plot where "the enemy is trying to topple the system through using the idea of the separation of state and religion as a weapon."[29] After a series of pro-democracy protests in November 2002, echoing the above remarks, Iran's powerful former President, Hashemi Rafsanjani, delivered a speech to members of the fundamentalist *Basij* militia before they were sent into the streets to intimidate pro-democracy protesters. He stated: "Satan is using his cavalry and infantry to exploit the current situation because he thinks our people are backing him which is absolutely wrong." Criticizing the notion of a separation of religion and state, Rafsanjani added: "They [the pro-democracy protesters] thought that in an Islamic country the priest will do the priest's job and Caesar will do Caesar's job [b]ut that will never happen."[30]

Similarly, the speaker of the newly elected hardliner-controlled parliament, Gholam Ali Haddad Adel, in a lecture at the main mosque at Tehran University warned of the growing threat of secularism in Iran. In his lecture, he referred to certain groups who in the guise of promoting democracy were really trying to "weaken [our] religious government and promote secularism in society by promoting this unwelcome idea in our universities."[31] These frequent calls for combating secularism would not have been issued had there not been a significant domestic pressure calling for the de facto separation of religion and state.[32]

This attack on secularism has deeper roots that can be tracked back to the writing of Ayatollah Khomeini. In his famous lectures on "Islamic Government," delivered while in exile in Iraq in 1970, he observed:

---

[29] "IRCG Commander warns of 'crawling' subversive move," *Islamic Republic News Agency* (IRNA) (2001).

[30] "'Be on guard for Satan's cavalry' Rafsanjani to Basij," *Agence France Presse*, November 25, 2002. In an April 1995 visit to India, then President Hashemi-Rafsanjani had a decidedly different take on the value of political secularism. He stated: "Secularism is the best way of running the affairs of the country with so many religious and ethnic diversities" (Jawed Naqvi, "Iran seeks Kashmir role, warns of U.S. Involvement," *Reuters*, April 19, 1995).

[31] "Parliamentary Speaker: Secularists are Trying to Separate the Seminaries from the Universities," *Shargh* (Tehran), November 15, 2004.

[32] For more criticism of secularism by Iranian hard-liners, see Ayatollah Emami Kashani's Friday Prayer Sermon at Tehran University, December 10, 2004, where he criticized the West for trying to promote "Islamic secularism" in the Muslim world. "Ayatollah Emami Kashani: The Arrogant (powers of the West) are Trying to Promote Irreligion and Immorality Among Iranian Youth," *Keyhan* (Tehran), December 11, 2004.

This slogan of the separation of religion and politics and the demand that Islamic scholars not intervene in social and political affairs has been formulated and propagated by the imperialists; it is only the irreligious who repeat them. Were religion and politics separate in the time of the Prophet ... Did there exist, on one side, a group of clerics, and opposite it, a group of politicians and leaders? ... These slogans and claims have been advanced by the imperialists and their political agents in order to prevent religion from ordering the affairs of this world and shaping Muslim society, and at the same time to create a rift between the scholars of Islam, on the one hand, and the masses and those struggling for freedom and independence, on the other.[33]

Khomeini's successor, Ali Khamenei, has repeatedly echoed these sentiments during his tenure as the Supreme Leader of the Islamic Republic of Iran (1989–). In an address to the members of the Assembly of Experts, for example, he affirmed that "colonialist powers have always advocated a separation of religion from politics," adding that under the former regime of the Shah "Iran experienced the secular form of government which brought wide-scale ethical corruption." In this speech, he referred to secularism as a form of Satanism. "Differences in views are acceptable in the framework of the Islamic system [but] we should be vigilant towards the satanic methods of some, who intend to weaken the presence of religion and propagate the separation of religion and politics under the cover of expressing their political views." He concluded by noting that the "Iranian nation has established a religious-oriented government which, thank God, has brought enormous social, political and administrative blessings so that the Iranian nation will never substitute the religious administration with a secular one."[34]

Documenting the emergence of a movement for political secularism in Iran is a difficult endeavor, partly because any explicit public demand for the separation of religion and politics is a punishable offense.[35] It is not a coincidence, therefore, that one of the most important political documents calling for secularism, written by the dissident investigative journalist

[33] Khomeini (1981), 38. Khomeini makes the same point, linking the separation of religion and politics to an imperialist plot to weaken the Muslim world. See his lecture on February 19, 1978 in Najaf, "In Commemoration of the First Martyrs of the Revolution," in Khomeini (1981): 219.

[34] "Meeting between Members of the Assembly of Experts and the Leader of the Revolution," September 10, 2002, http://farsi.khamenei.ir/news-content?id=18754.

[35] For example, Mohsen Kadivar, a dissident liberal cleric, was arrested in February 1999 and jailed for allegedly misleading public opinion, insulting Ayatollah Khomeini, and advocating the separation of religion from politics. Around the same time the Iranian sociologist Hossein Ghazian was arrested when his polling institute conducted a survey that revealing high levels secularization in segments of Iranian society.

Akbar Ganji, came from behind the walls of Tehran's Evin prison.[36] In private conversations with foreign journalists, many of the leading theoreticians and activists in the reform movement, according to Afshin Molavi, whisper the words "secular democracy," while in public they use the more acceptable and ambiguous term "Islamic democracy." Molavi observes that many reformists now view "the mingling of religion and politics with suspicion, and while [they] ... won't say so out loud, [they] ... have [effectively] morphed into secular democrats."[37]

IRANIAN STUDENT GROUPS AND SECULARISM

Since the 2009 Green Movement protests, Iranian student groups have been severely repressed. This is because they form the backbone of the pro-democracy struggle in Iran, and they have been one of the most vocal segments of civil society calling for a secularization of the political system. They are a significant group given that approximately two-thirds of Iran's population is under the age of thirty, and they are highly educated. The evidence of secularizing trends from this group can be found in many places. Students at Avicenna University in Hamedan, for example, held a mock referendum in May 2003 to ascertain which political constitution they favored most. There were three choices on the ballot: 1) the first draft of the existing constitution of the Islamic Republic of Iran, which envisioned a liberal-democratic political system; 2) the 1979 clerical-dominated constitution that was ratified in a national referendum; and 3) the 1989 revised version of the clerical-dominated constitution of 1979 that entrenched clerical supremacy.

The referendum results were almost unanimous: 91.84 percent of the voters chose the first option – the original, liberal-democratic and *secular* constitution that was drafted by the provisional government of Mehdi Bazargan.[38]

Further evidence of the secularization of political norms could be observed in the lead up to the parliamentary election in February 2004, when the leading Iranian student organization, *Daftar-e Tahkim-e*

---

[36] Ganji ([unpublished] 2002).   [37] Molavi (2003).

[38] "Symbolic Referendum at Avicenna University takes place," *Iranian Students News Agency* (ISNA), May 17, 2003. A mock ballot was posted on the Amir Kabir University website, May 14, 2003. A 2003 opinion poll at Tehran Medical University revealed similar results, where 80 percent of those polled supported radical changes to the Iranian constitution ("Analysis: Iran voting, a legitimacy test?," *United Press International*, November 20, 2003).

Vahdat ("Office for Strengthening Unity") announced a general boycott. The slow pace of the reform process and the steady de-democratization of Iranian politics were cited as reasons. Abdullah Momeni, one of the student leaders, observed that the biggest challenge facing Iranian politics in 2004 was the question of secularism. While not explicitly using the "s" word, he cited as an example the Guardian Council's rejection of a parliamentary bill to join an international convention for women's rights as resulting from an overdependence on religious principles. He stated: "As long as this contradiction between earthly beliefs and religious beliefs is not resolved, the parliament will not regain its stature and in the next parliament, religious principles will have priority over earthly matters."[39] Students would boycott the forthcoming elections, he stated, until this question was resolved.

A few months earlier, in the midst of a general crackdown on internal dissent, twenty-eight Iranian student groups from different universities sent an open protest letter to United Nations Secretary General Kofi Annan. The letter was titled: "Mr. Secretary General: Bring Justice to this Injustice!"[40] After decrying the existence of "political apartheid" in Iran and expressing their frustrations with the slow pace of political change, the letter went on to list various articles from the UN Declaration of Human Rights (UDHR), followed by a detailed accounting of how these rights are being violated in Iran today. One paragraph read:

Article 5 of the UDHR states: "No one shall be subjected to torture or to cruel, inhuman or degrading treatment or punishment." Yet, in Iran, many political activists, students, and even ordinary people are subjected to torture, and to other forms of cruel, inhuman, and degrading treatment and punishment. For example, prisoners and those in custody are often tortured at length physically and mentally, degraded, beaten, flogged, deprived of sleep while sitting or standing, and subjected to fake execution acts.[41]

In terms of the question of secularism, this document does not mention the term *explicitly*, but it does call for "the separation of private and public spheres," which the students claim is "severely abridged in today's Iran." The separation of the public and private sphere is a critical

---

[39] "Office for Fostering Unity: The Student Movement Will not Take Part in the Elections," *Farhang-e Ashti* (Tehran), December 9, 2003.

[40] Open Letter to Kofi Annan, "Mr. Secretary General: Bring Justice to this Injustice!," July 6, 2003. It originally appeared on the Amir Kabir University website. See "Formerly Pro-Government Student Organization Calls for Separation of Religion from the State," *Radio Farda*, July 8, 2003.

[41] Ibid.

requirement for the emergence of a liberal-democratic polity.[42] The inclusion of this demand by Iranian students in a document that explicitly calls for democracy and respect for universal standards of human rights reveals the growing secular and liberal-democratic orientation of Iranian youth.[43]

Bahman Kalbasi, twenty-six (at the time of writing), was a pro-democracy student leader, formerly with the Islamic Student's Association at Esfahan University. After the student uprising in July 1999, he was imprisoned for his activism and subsequently expelled from the university, prompting him to immigrate to Canada to resume his studies. In an interview I conducted with him I asked him how students of his generation understood the concept of secularism.

"The separation of the clergy from the state, the clergy out of power, or anti-clericalism," was his first comment on the topic, which he claimed was representative of the mainstream of Iranian students that he knew.[44] He qualified his answer by adding: "not that the clergy should not be elected to office but that they should not have special [constitutionally guaranteed] rights to be in power because they are clergymen."[45]

Reflecting on the theme of secularism in Iran, Kalbasi stated: "later for myself, when I studied it, I wanted [secularism] to be implemented to its fullest capacity." When I asked him to elaborate, he added: "my hope is that politicians would leave all their religious beliefs at the door of the parliament even though I know this might not be possible." He went on to express sympathy for the French government's version of secularism, with particular reference to the complete neutrality of public schools from all ostentatious displays of religious symbolism.

When asked if there was any internal debate among students in Iran over the value of secularism he responded with a firm "no," except for an extreme minority of rightwing students. "The only debate among students," he said, "is on the different strategies to best reach this goal [of political secularism], not on its desirability."[46]

---

[42] Benhabib (1992), 89–120.
[43] Reformists and Conservative politicians on both sides of Iranian political divide have been discussing the value of separating the private from the public sphere. See "God Hasn't Died in this Society Yet: A Conversation with Alireza Alavitabar," *Middle East Report*, no. 212 (Fall 1999), 30 and comments by Amir Mohebian, editor of the conservative newspaper *Resalat* in Karl Virk, "The Appearance of Change in Iran," *Washington Post*, January 15, 2004.
[44] Interview, January 5, 2005.   [45] Ibid.   [46] Ibid.

THE GROWING CLERICAL DEMAND FOR "SECULARISM"

One of the most significant yet unrecognized developments inside Iran today is the increasing secularization of political ideas among important segments of the clergy. This transformation bodes well for Iran's long-term political development because it undermines the ideological basis and legitimacy of the ruling oligarchy which justifies its rule in the name of Islam. This development also serves to realign an important political constituency – which looks to religious clerics for leadership – away from an authoritarian conception of state–society relations and toward a political model that is more democratic, liberal, and functionally secular. The case of Ayatollah Hossein Ali Montazeri (1922–2009) is a perfect illustration of the steady secularization of religious thought in Iran today.

Ayatollah Montazeri was one of the leading senior Shia theologians in the Islamic world. Born into a poor family in 1922 in Najafabad, he rose through the ranks of the religious seminaries to the senior position of a grand ayatollah primarily due to his exceptional erudition and broad following as a source of religious authority. His reputation was enhanced due to his opposition to the Pahlavi monarchy, for which he served time in jail, where he was tortured. For all of these reasons he was designated as the official successor to Ayatollah Khomeini in 1985.

It was soon after this time, in the midst of increasing internal repression and a wave of political executions, that Ayatollah Montazeri began his criticism of the post-revolutionary order. As a result, he was soon removed as Khomeini's heir apparent and all formal ties with the ruling regime were severed. Montazeri retired to his home in the clerical city of Qom to resume his teaching and study as well as to reflect upon the relationship between religion and politics in Iran.[47]

Ayatollah Montazeri significantly gradually revised his ideas on the relationship between religion and government prior to his death when he endorsed a quasi-secularization of the Iranian political system. In doing so, he was openly challenging the moral basis of legitimate political authority of the Islamic Republic. In 2003, he gave two revealing interviews to the European press, which one can cite as evidence of his support for a functionally secular, yet religious-friendly, political system in Iran.

In November 2003, the German paper *Welt am Sonntag* (Hamburg) asked him:

---

[47] Ali Montazeri ([unpublished], 2000).

[Question:] Six years ago you criticized the rule of Ali Khamenehi. Now that your house arrest is over, have you changed your mind on this topic?

[Answer:] A political system should not and cannot be based on the rule of one individual. We need a collective system where the people are the most important element.

[Question:] Are you suggesting that the rule of the supreme clerical authority, *Velayat-e faqih*, should be eliminated, in other words, the absolute rule of the clergy, and as a result are you questioning the leadership of Ali Khamenehi, the leader of revolution?

[Answer]: Exactly. The absolute rule of the clergy is wrong. An ayatollah's *only* responsibility is responding to theological questions. Economic, political and other issues should be the preserve of the experts in these fields. They should make the decisions about these issues, not the clergy.[48]

More important, however, was Ayatollah Montazeri's interview with *El Pais* (Madrid), a few months earlier. In response to the reporter's queries about his views on the relationship between religion and politics, Montazeri clearly stated he was against any type of religious dictatorship and that "if the presence of religion in government leads to a dictatorship, I am against such a presence." He then added a comment which should be quoted in full:

If such a presence [of religion in politics] results in what we are grappling with now in Iran, then I am strongly against the mixing of religion and state. If such coexistence means interference by Ali Khamenei in all affairs of the country, and lives of the people, then I state categorically that I am fundamentally against any type of religious government, and advocate the separation of church and state.[49]

---

[48] Emphasis added. Wrase (2003). Translated from Persian from Iranian reformist website www.emrooz.ws, November 11, 2003.

[49] Higueras (2003). I thank Sara Pelizer for help with this translation. Also see Montazeri's warning to the Iraqi people that they should learn from Iran's mistake and prevent clerics from direct control over public affairs. "Ayatollah Montazeri: Iraq should learn from Iran's experience," BBC Persian Service, January 20, 2005: www.bbc.co.uk/persian/iran/story/2005/01/050120_si-montazeri-iraq.shtml. During the 2005 Iranian presidential election campaign Montazeri gave another interview which can be read as a de facto call for the separation of religion and state. He argued in favor of limiting the power of the Supreme Leader to "religious matters" while increasing the power and independence of the country's president. See Holmes and Moody (2005). To be clear, Montazeri never came to reject the role of clerics in politics or Khomeini's theory of *velayat-e faqih*. His ideas on this topic underwent a democratic transformation that sought to preserve the

Ayatollah Montazeri's influence, as a leading Shia theologian, has been extensive, not only on matters of religion but also on politics. Reformist politicians routinely sought his endorsement for their oppositional political views and journalists and religious intellectuals credited him with inspiring them to pursue a path of political dissent.[50] When pro-democracy protests unfolded after the stolen 2009 presidential election, Montazeri openly supported the protesters. His defiant support for democracy earned him the designation as the "moral conscience of the Green Movement" and it was during this time that he issued an important *fatwa* arguing that the Islamic Republic lacked moral, political, and religious legitimacy.[51]

The mid-ranking cleric, human rights activist, and religious scholar Mohsen Kadivar is Montazeri's most prominent student. In a series of influential books in the late 1990s, he provided an exhaustive critique of Khomeini's doctrine of *velayat-e faqih* (guardianship of the Islamic jurist) that garnered him publicity and eventually landed him in jail. Relying exclusively on Shi'i sources, Kadivar launched a solid theological and scholarly refutation of the ruling ethos of conservative clergy in Iran while simultaneously remaining within the bounds of Shi'i jurisprudence. Kadivar's basic argument in his book, *Theses on the State in Shi'i Jurisprudence*, was that Khomeini's thesis on the guardianship of the Islamic jurist was simply one thesis among many that Shi'a theologians have expounded over the years, ranging from a religious justification of monarchy to democracy. Therefore, Khomeini's thesis on the guardianship of the Islamic jurist can in no way be considered *the* definitive or authoritative political model for the Shi'a school of jurisprudence.[52]

In his subsequent and more controversial book, *Theocratic Government*, Kadivar painstakingly investigates and refutes Khomeini's doctrine of government by divine mandate (*velayat-e faqih*) by arguing that Khomeini's religio-political thesis, upon investigation, does not stand up to critical scrutiny even from within the paradigm of Shi'a Islamic religious and political thought. Kadivar has since gone on to develop his views on the

---

leadership role of clerics in politics but subject more democratic safeguards. See his *Didgah-ha: Payam-ha va nazariat-e montasher-ye fagih aliqadr Ayatullah al-ozma Montarzeri*, volume 1 (Qum: 2003) available at: https://amontazeri.com/book. For a brief survey see von Schwerin (2015), 183–194.

[50] See the comments by Emadeddin Baghi and Mohsen Kadivar on Ayatollah Montazeri in Barker (2004).

[51] Sadri and Sadri (2011), 151–164.

[52] Kadivar discusses nine different theories on government that Shi'a theologians have produced over the years. Kadivar (1997), 58, 80, 97, 108, 112, 127, 141, 154, 175.

relationship between religion and liberal democracy in Iran in new and creative ways. He has written that:

the *velayat-e faqih* [rule of the Islamic jurist] in the political sphere, be it appointive or elective, absolute or conditional, is not supported by valid religious proof. Islam has basically not offered a fixed and specific model for the political management of society. The *velayat-e faqih*, being an autocratic rule of God based on the divine rights of the jurists, is incompatible with democracy. Democracy, being based on principles such as popular sovereignty and participation, the rule of law and human rights, is evidently incompatible with clerical rule, and the *velayat-e faqih* is simply a type of religious dictatorship. The illusion of compatibility of the *velayat-e faqih* with democracy is due to the lack of familiarity with the jurisprudential terminology, on the one hand, and the theory of democracy, on the other. The fundamental incompatibility between democracy and the *velayat-e faqih* is not an obstacle to the democratic management of an Islamic society. The majority of its Muslim citizens can have a democratic government while remaining committed to their Islamic faith and ethical values. Islam as a religion can be integrated with democracy as the method of modern political life.[53]

Mohsen Kadivar has since emerged as a leading clerical proponent of liberal democracy in Iran today. In his recent writings he has gone onto to develop a quasi-secular theory that reconciles the relationship between religion and democracy that is rooted in the principle of equality of all citizens before the law, regardless of religion, gender, or ethnicity.[54] In a 2012 lecture on the topic, he argued quite forcefully that the secularization of the Islamic Republic of Iran is now "unstoppable."[55]

In brief, Mohsen Kadivar's religious scholarship is impeccable and his public pronouncements on contemporary social and political issues are taken seriously by friend and foe alike. The potency of his critique is due to his use of Shi'a jurisprudence to undermine the ruling (hard-line) Islamic jurists who demand a monopoly on religious interpretation when it comes to the relationship between religion and politics. Kadivar's books are widely read and seriously debated within the seminaries of the Shi'i Islamic world. No serious student of Shi'a Islam interested in the relationship between religion and government could afford to ignore what one

---

[53] Kadivar (2002). Available on line at www.kadivar.com/Htm/English/Papers/Velayat-e%20Faghih.htm and partially reprinted as Mohsen Kadivar, "God and His Guardians," *Index on Censorship* 33 (October 2004), 64–71.

[54] For Kadivar's views on the tension between Islam and human rights, see his interview "Human Rights and Religious Intellectualism," *Aftab*, no.27 (August 2003), 54–59.

[55] Kadivar (2012). For a summary see Poucher Harbin (2012), http://today.duke.edu/2012/04/kadivartalk.

scholar has aptly called Mohsen Kadivar's "sacred defense of secularism."[56]

Other Iranian clerics who have theorized on the topic of Islam and secularism include Mohammad Mojtahed-Shabestari, Mostafa Mohaqqeq-Damad, Hassan Yusefi-Eshkevari, Mohsen Saidzadeh, Ayatollah Yusef Sane'i, Ayatollah Abdolkarim Musavi-Ardabili, Ayatollah Mohammad Ali Gerami, Ayatollah Mehdi Haeri-Yazdi, and Ayatollah Seyed Hussain Mousavi Tabrizi. Although not as influential in religious stature as Ayatollah Montazeri, their piercing criticism of the post-revolutionary status quo, with a special emphasis on the relationship between democracy, human rights, and religion, suggests the emergence of a clerical attempt to reconcile a soft form of secularism with the demands of democracy while remaining within an Iranian Muslim political and cultural milieu. While this is a very important development in terms of the long-term prospects for liberal democracy in Iran, clerics are not the only group in society that has been pushing for a de facto secularization of the political system. Dissident journalists, women's rights activists, and workers have offered similar critiques.

The empirical evidence listed in the above pages is only a small sample of a growing indigenous movement of what I call "Muslim secularism" in contemporary Iran. A comprehensive chronicling of this trend would have to also include the proliferation of open letters by former supporters of Ayatollah Khomeini who in the past thirty-seven years have become disillusioned with the political status quo in the Islamic Republic and now, to varying degrees, support a de facto secularization and the full democratization of the political order.[57] Similarly, one would also have to list the growing sociological and anthropological evidence of the transformations of religious practice and behavior among a broad cross-section of Iranian society that can be interpreted as proof of the secularization of norms and values.[58]

All things considered, as Iran's Islamic Revolution reached its twentieth anniversary, a political trend in support of the idea of a separation of religion and state was already clearly visible. According to Ebrahim Yazdi, a former protégé of Khomeini and opposition leader: "[T]wo decades of

---

[56] Sadri (2003), 185–189. Also see Matsunaga (2007), 317–329.
[57] The open letters I am referring too are by Mohammad Nourizad, Mohsen Sazegara, Ghassem Sholeh-Sadi, Ayatollah Jalaledin Taheri, Ezzatollah Sahabi, and the numerous open letters by reformist parliamentarians and intellectuals in the spring and summer of 2003 to the Supreme Leader, Ali Khamenei. They have only increased in quantity with the passage of time.
[58] Kazemipur and Rezaei (2003), 347–361.

government in the name of religion has actually created a very indigenous movement toward secularism."[59] Fariborz Raisdana, a reformist activist and political commentator added: "Twenty-five years ago, you would never find Muslim students in favour of [a] separation of church and state. Today, many people support that."[60]

One of the positive aspects about the movement for secularism in the Islamic Republic of Iran is that it is entirely an indigenous one. There is a home-grown theory of secularism that has developed based on Iran's own experience with religious government and which has sunk deep roots in Iranian political culture. Abdolkarim Soroush is the most famous theoretician of Islamic secularism in Iran but there are many others, some of whose views have already been discussed.[61] A consequence of this is that attempts to dismiss "secularism" as a foreign conspiracy or alien concept ring hollow in the ears of many Iranians who have been on the receiving end of Islamist rule and who understandably blame, in part, the non-secularity of their political system for many of their socio-political ills. This realization could only have come about after first welcoming the fusion of religion and government, then experiencing it for several decades, and finally drawing the appropriate political lessons from the experience. In other words, it is has been the actual "lived experience" of religious rule that has shown it to be an impediment to political development. Thus, the lived reality of religion in power has been profoundly illuminating for a generation of Iranians (especially young people) and has produced valuable lessons on the merits of secularism as a moral value and political necessity.

Secondly, the development of secularism in Iran is directly connected to the ideological transformation of important political constituencies. The members of the urban lower middle class are known for their deep religiosity and politicization. Many of Ayatollah Khomeini's most devout followers hailed from this stratum of society. It is interesting to note that many of the leaders of the reform movement who are firm supporters of political secularism today also come from this sector of society. A social profile of the following people would confirm this: Akbar Ganji, Hamid Reza Jalaeipour, Mashallah Shamsolvaezin, Emadodeen Baghi, Alireza Alavitabar, Said Hajjarian, Abbas Abdi, and many of the student leaders in the *Daftar-e Takhim-e Vahdat*, just to name a few. To the extent that this ideological transformation is representative of broader support for political secularism in Iran, it is highly significant for Iran's future democratic prospects in that

---

[59] Siddiqui (2002).   [60] Slackman (2002).   [61] Matin-Asgari (1997), 95–115.

it suggests the embracing of secular politics from sections of society that previously opposed the separation of religion and government.

Finally, in terms of a broader discussion on the theoretical and practical relationship between religion, secularism, and democracy, there are parallels here which students of European and American political history should recognize. As Frank Lambert notes in *The Founding Fathers and the Place of Religion in America*,[62] James Madison and Thomas Jefferson's decision to create a "wall of separation" in the US constitution between church and state emerged against the backdrop of an America that served as a safe haven for persecuted religious sects and dissenters fleeing the wars of religion in Europe.

In other words, the actual "lived experience" of mixing of religion and politics in Christendom produced a series of lessons that the founding fathers of American democracy took to heart in the creation of a democratic society.[63] Jefferson and James Madison did not insert this amendment into the constitution as the result of a sudden epiphany. Nor were they relying on a certain Christian proclivity for secularism which scholars such as Bernard Lewis, Ernest Gellner, and Samuel Huntington suggest are at the root of the difference between the West and the Muslim world in terms of religion–state relations.[64] Much more relevant was the actual "lived experience" of the mixing of religion and politics in Europe. Certain inferences were drawn from this experience for the new American republic in terms of the normative role of religion in government. A similar process and pattern of democratic learning has been underway in post-revolutionary Iran.

CRITICAL REFLECTIONS ON TAYLOR AND IRAN

In his authoritative chapter in this volume, Philip Gorski (Chapter 2) provides a succinct overview of the scholarly debate on secularity with specific reference to Charles Taylor's *A Secular Age*. He carefully discusses the analytical and methodological strengths and weaknesses of Taylor's contribution to the topic while noting that "Taylor has relatively little to say about how historical conjunctures, institutional constellations and path dependencies led to divergent national trajectories in church/state relations, not because he is unaware of such variations, but because

---

[62] Lambert (2003).   [63] Feldman (2002), 346–428 and Witte (2005), 21–69.
[64] Lewis (2003), 96–116; Gellner (1996), 15–29; Huntington (1996), 56–78, 207–218.

Secularity I is not his primary object of interest. The same might be said of his discussions of Secularity II."[65]

As an alternative approach, Gorski suggests that the theoretical concepts associated with "historical institutionalism" advocated by the Cambridge School around Peter Hall provides a more suitable entry point for those interested in the comparative study of secularism. He lists the concepts of "critical junctures," "path dependency," and "policy legacies" as important reference points for developing "a set of sensitizing concepts that can help us construct adequate accounts for the outcomes" that explain why American secularism is different than Indian secularism or why Turkish secularism is different than the French version.[66] All of this suggests, according to Gorski, that "Taylor's approach needs to be complemented by other approaches to be fruitful for explaining the global varieties of secularism cum institutional settlement." These recommendations apply perfectly to the case of Iran and its modern experience with secularism.

Taylor is not to be faulted for this, as he clearly states in his introduction that *A Secular Age* is not a study of secularity on a global scale; rather, his main concern is with Secularity III, with a regional focus on "the West, or the North Atlantic world ... with the civilization whose principal roots lie in what used to be called 'Latin Christendom'." Even in this context he acknowledges severe limitations in that "there are many regional and national paths to secularity within the North Atlantic world, and I haven't been able to do justice to all of them." While acknowledging the need to study the global varieties of secularity, he suggests that this is best approached by first studying secularity in its "different civilizational sites before we rush to global generalization."[67]

A comprehensive scholarly study of secularity in the context of Islamic civilization has yet to be written. If one anyone were to pursue this project, Gorski's insights and recommendations would be worth paying close attention to. Doing so would help delineate the specific "founding moments," "critical junctures," "path dependencies," and "policy legacies" that have shaped the origins and the various trajectories of secularity within Muslim societies while simultaneously pointing out how the nature of the subject and its political manifestations has been qualitatively different from the Western experience.[68]

---

[65] Philip Gorski, "'Secularity I': Varieties and Dilemmas," in this volume.   [66] Ibid.
[67] Taylor (2007), 21.   [68] Hashemi (2012) and (2009).

Given that Taylor's primary concern in *A Secular Age* is explicating how an exclusive (non-religious) humanist option became an attractive choice for many in the West, this begs the question: will such an option ever be available to the people of Iran? Answering this question demands an entire book unto itself. But drawing upon Taylor's work and what I have already written, I offer the following preliminary remarks.

The processes of secularization and desecularization in Iran are intimately tied to the activities of the modern state. With its capacity to project power with the help of modern technology, the state has been able to monitor, control, and it impose its will on society, particularly in the formal realms of social and political life. This applies both to the state-imposed secularism of the Pahlavis (until 1979) and its converse, state-imposed religiosity under the clerics (since 1979).

Opportunities for Iranians to engage in an open, uncensored, and unrestricted public debate on religion itself, or the theme of secularity, or the normative relationship between religion and politics, have been few and far between. Over the course of the past century, the rare moments when this opportunity existed roughly coincide with the Constitutional Revolution (1906–1911), the Mossadeq years (1941–1953), the first year after the 1979 Revolution, and the first term of Mohammad Khatami's reformist presidency (1997–2001). It is not a coincidence that these moments overlap precisely with political openings for democracy, when the prospects for a transition from authoritarianism seemed to be on the horizon. Herein lies an answer to the question about the possibility of humanist option for Iranians.

Unless and until Iranians are free from state coercion, the humanist option will not exist. Legal safeguards to protect freedom of speech and inquiry, not in an absolute or an ideal sense, but in a meaningful way, must first exist and this can only happen after democracy has been consolidated. It is not a coincidence, for example, that the period over which Taylor traces the emergence of secularity – from approximately 1500, when religious disbelief was unthinkable, until today, when it is a living option for many – coincides with the long and turbulent history of democratization in the West.

The second point of comparison between the West and the Muslim world is one of timing. The West has been grappling with the question of religion's role in politics and society for a longer period of time than have Muslim societies. It is only in the late nineteenth century that we begin to see a serious engagement with this topic among Muslim intellectuals. The speeches and writings of Jamal ad-Din Al-Afghani, Muhammad Abdu, and Rashid Rida stand out as important early engagements with this theme. Their arguments were to shape the contours of modern Islamic political thought for successive generations of Muslims. It is significant to point out, however, that this initial Muslim engagement with modernity takes place in the context of the colonial and imperial encounter with Europe, where the struggle for self-determination from foreign control took precedence over the debate on the normative relationship between religion and state. This has dramatically shaped the political and moral context in which debates on modernization and secularism have taken place in the Middle East.

The third point is that the modernization process in the Muslim world has been qualitatively different in many respects from that of the West. Unlike in Europe, where it was largely an indigenous process, Muslim societies experienced modernization as a direct result of the colonial and imperial encounter with Europe. Instead of innovation based on an engagement with civil society, the modern Muslim experience was largely one of imitation in an attempt by post-colonial elites to catch up to the West by accelerating the modernization process.

In other words, most political change since the era of formal independence has been forced top-down on Muslim societies in an authoritarian fashion. It has not occurred via a bottom-up indigenous process of social evolution and gradual transformation buttressed by intellectual and moral arguments that had organic roots. In 1935, for example, Reza Pahlavi ordered his troops to go into the streets of Tehran to forcibly remove – at the point of a bayonet – the veil from the heads of Iranian women.[69] Two generations later, in the same authoritarian manner, Ayatollah Khomeini and his Islamic revolutionaries imposed a mandatory dress code on Iranian women with even more determination and rigor. The rise of an Islamist opposition in Iran, therefore, can be viewed as a counter-reaction to draconian secularist policies that were imposed by the Western-backed monarchical dictatorship. The cycle of authoritarian repression continues.

The final critical difference between Iran and the West, one of enormous consequence for the process of secularization, has been the direct intervention by external powers into the Middle East. The modern Iranian experience embodies this state of affairs. There is a long and sordid history of foreign – Russian, British, and later American – intervention in thwarting Iran's internal development, the most dramatic form being the 1953

[69] Chehabi (1993), 209–229.

Anglo-American coup that toppled the government of the liberal nationalist Mohammad Mossadeq. This put an end to a process of democratization that was in place during the previous decade and marked an abrupt, forceful end to the era of democratic secularism that had dominated Iranian politics for the previous half century.

As I have argued above, a consequence of this event was the emergence of an Islamist movement that gradually became a chief vehicle for political opposition culminating in their seizure of the state in 1979. How different might Iran be today had its natural course of political development not been thwarted by intervention from abroad? Would Iran be a democracy today and might the secular humanist option – rooted in Iran's own internal tradition of "Persian literary humanism" – be a viable choice for Iranians?[70]

References

"Analysis: Iran voting, a legitimacy test?," *United Press International*, November 20, 2003.

"Ayatollah Emami Kashani: The Arrogant (powers of the West) are Trying to Promote Irreligion and Immorality Among Iranian Youth," *Keyhan* (Tehran), December 11, 2004.

"Ayatollah Montazeri: Iraq should learn from Iran's experience," BBC Persian Service, January 20, 2005, www.bbc.co.uk/persian/iran/story/2005/01/0501 20_si-montazeri-iraq.shtml.

"'Be on guard for Satan's cavalry' Rafsanjani to Basij," *Agence France Presse*, November 25, 2002.

"Formerly Pro-Government Student Organization Calls for Separation of Religion from the State," *Radio Farda*, July 8, 2003.

"God Hasn't Died in this Society Yet: A Conversation with Alireza Alavitabar," *Middle East Report*, no. 212 (Fall 1999), 30

"IRCG Commander warns of 'crawling' subversive move," *Islamic Republic News Agency* (IRNA), July 17, 2001.

"Meeting between Members of the Assembly of Experts and the Leader of the Revolution," September 10, 2002, http://farsi.khamenei.ir/news-content? id=18754.

"Office for Fostering Unity: The Student Movement Will not Take Part in the Elections," *Farhang-e Ashti* (Tehran), December 9, 2003.

"Parliamentary Speaker: Secularists are Trying to Separate the Seminaries from the Universities," *Shargh* (Tehran), November 15, 2004.

"Symbolic Referendum at Avicenna University takes place," *Iranian Students News Agency* (ISNA), May 17, 2003.

---

[70] Dabashi (2012). See also de Bellaigue (2013).

"Warning from the Head of the Judiciary about the Rise of Seditionists," *BBC Persian*, July 24, 2013.

Abou El Fadl, Khaled. 2013. "The Collapse of Legitimacy: How Egypt's Secular Intelligentsia Betrayed the Revolution," *Religion and Ethics*, July 11, www.abc.net.au/religion/articles/2013/07/11/3800817.htm.

Abrahamian, Ervand. 2008. *A History of Modern Iran*. Cambridge: Cambridge University Press, 63–96.

Akbar Ganji. 2002. "Manifesto on Republicanism" (unpublished).

Akhavi, Shahrough. 1980. *Religion and Politics in Contemporary Iran*. Albany: State University of New York Press, 28–59.

Alavitabar, Alireza. 2004. "Sekularism va democracy" ("Secularism and Democracy)," *Aftab* 33: 80–83.

Ali, Montazeri and Ayatollah Hossein. 2003. *Didgah-ha: Payam-ha va nazariat-e montasher-ye fagih aliqadr Ayatullah al-ozma Montarzeri*, volume 1 (Qum); available at: https://amontazeri.com/book

2000. *Bakshi az Khaterat-e Ayatollah Montazeri* ("A Portion of the Memoir of Ayatollah Montazeri"). Qom, unpublished.

Ansari, Ali. 2003. *Modern Iran Since 1921: The Pahlavis and After*. London: Pearson Education Limited, 40–74.

Armstrong, Karen. 2000. *The Battle for God*. New York: Alfred Knopf.

Barker, Kim. 2004. "Iran loses faith in clerics: Change elusive in rigid society," *Chicago Tribune*, May 2.

Bayart, Jean-Francois. 1994. "Republican Trajectories in Iran and Turkey: A Tocquevillian Reading." In Ghassan Salamé (ed.), *Democracy with Democrats?: The Renewal of Politics in the Muslim World*. London: I.B. Tauris, 282–299.

Bayat, Asef. 2007. *Making Islam Democratic: Social Movements and the Post-Islamist Turn*. Stanford: Stanford University Press.

2011. "The Green Movement Charter." In Nader Hashemi and Danny Postel (eds.), *The People Reloaded: The Green Movement and the Struggle for Iran's Future*. New York: Melville House, 338.

2013. *Post-Islamism: The Changing Faces of Political Islam*. New York: Oxford University Press.

Benhabib, Seyla. 1992. *Situating the Self: Gender, Community and Postmodernism in Contemporary Ethics*. New York: Routledge.

Casanova, Jose. 2006. "Rethinking Secularism: A Global Comparative Perspective," *The Hedgehog Review* (Spring & Summer): 7–22.

Chehabi, Houchang. 1993. "Staging the Emperor's New Clothes: Dress Codes and Nation-Building under Reza Shah," *Iranian Studies* 26 (Fall): 209–229.

Dabashi, Hamid. 2012. *The World of Persian Literary Humanism*. Cambridge, MA: Harvard University Press.

de Bellaigue, Christopher. 2013. *Patriot of Persia: Muhammad Mossadegh and a Tragic Anglo-American Coup*. New York: Harper Perennial.

Esposito, John. 2010. *The Future of Islam*. New York: Oxford University Press.

Feldman, Noah. 2002. "The Intellectual Origins of the Establishment Clause," *New York University Law Review* 77, No. 346: 346–428.

Gellner, Ernest. 1996. *Conditions of Liberty: Civil Society and its Rivals.* New York: Penguin.

Ghobadzadeh, Naser. 2015. *Religious Secularity: A Theological Challenge to the Islamic State.* New York: Oxford University Press, 2015.

Göle, Nilüfer, "Authoritarian Secularism and Islamist Politics: The Case of Turkey." In Augustus Richard Norton (ed.), *Civil Society in the Middle East,* Volume 1. Leiden: E.J. Brill, 20.

Hajjarian, Saeed. 2001. *Az shahed-e qodsi ta shahed-e bazari: 'Orfi-shodan-e din dar Sepehr-e siyasat* (From the Sacred Witness to the Profane Witness: The Secularization of Religion in the Sphere of Politics) (Tehran: Tarh-e No).

Hambly, Gavin. 1991. "The Pahlavi Autocracy: Riza Shah, 1921–1941." In Peter Avery, Gavin Hambly, and Charles Melville (eds.), *The Cambridge History of Iran: From Nadir Shah to the Islamic Republic,* Volume 7. Cambridge: Cambridge University Press, 232–233.

Hashemi, Nader. 2009. "Secularism." In John Esposito (ed.), *The Oxford Encyclopaedia of the Islamic World,* revised edition. New York: Oxford University Press.

   2010. "The Multiple Histories of Secularism: Muslim Societies in Comparative Perspective," *Journal of Philosophy and Social Criticism,* vol. 36, nos 3–4:325–338.

   2012. *Islam, Secularism and Liberal Democracy: Toward a Democratic Theory for Muslim Societies.* New York: Oxford University Press.

Higueras, Georgina. 2003. "Entrevista: Gran Ayatolá Montazeri: Estoy en contra de la dictadura de la religion en Irán (Interview: Grand Ayatollah Montazeri: I am against the religious dictatorship in Iran)," *El Pais* (Madrid), September 22.

Holmes, Paul and Barry Moody. 2005. "Interview: Dissident Cleric Rails Against Iran's System," *Reuters,* May 20.

Huntington, Samuel. 1996. *The Clash of Civilizations and the Remarking of World Order.* New York: Simon and Schuster.

Kadivar, Mohsen. 2012. "Evolution of the Relationship of Islam and the State in Post-Revolutionary Iran," lecture at Duke University, April 18.

   2004. "God and His Guardians," *Index on Censorship* 33 (October), 64–71.

Kadivar, Mohsen. 2003. "Human Rights and Religious Intellectualism," *Aftab* no.27 (August), 54–59.

Kadivar, Mohsen. 2002. "The Velayat-e-Faqih and Democracy," Paper delivered at the 36th Annual Meeting of the Middle East Studies Association (MESA) in Washington DC, November 24. Available on line at www.kadivar.com/Htm/English/Papers/Velayat-e%20Faghih.htm

   1997. *Nazariyaha-ye dawlat far fiqh-e Shi'a (Theses on the State in Shi'i Jurisprudence).* Tehran: Nashr-e Ney.

Kamrava, Mehran. 2008. *Iran's Intellectual Revolution.* Cambridge: Cambridge University Press.

Katouzian, Homa. 2004. "Mosaddeq's Government in Iranian History: Arbitrary Rule, Democracy, and the 1953 Coup." In Malcolm Bryne and Mark Gasiorowski (eds.), *Mohammad Mosaddeq and the 1953 Coup in Iran.* Syracuse: Syracuse University Press, 1–26.

1999. *Musaddiq and the Struggle for Power in Iran*. New York: I.B. Tauris.

Kazemipur, Abdolmohammad and Ali Rezaei. 2003. "Religious Life Under Theocracy: The Case of Iran," *Journal for the Scientific Study of Religion* 42 (September), 347–361.

Keddie, Nikki. 1997. "Secularism and the State: Towards Clarity and Global Comparison," *New Left Review* 226 (November–December): 21–40

2003a. *Modern Iran: Roots and Results of Revolution*. New Haven: Yale University Press.

2003b. "Secularism and its Discontents," *Daedalus* (Summer): 14–30.

Khomeini, Ayatollah Ruhollah. 1981. "Islamic Government." In *Islam and Revolution: Writings and Declarations of Imam Khomeini*, translated and annotated by Hamid Algar. Berkeley: Mizan Press.

Khosrokhavar, Farhad. 2007. "The New Religiosity in Iran," *Social Compass* 54 (September 2007): 453–463.

Kian-Thiébaut, Azadeh. 1998. *Secularization of Iran: A Doomed Failure? The New Middle Class and the Making of Modern Iran*. Paris: Peeters.

Lambert, Frank. 2003. *The Founding Fathers and the Place of Religion in America*. Princeton: Princeton University Press.

Lewis, Bernard. 2003. *What Went Wrong?: The Clash Between Islam and Modernity in the Middle East*. New York: Harper Collins.

Marashi, Afshin. 2003. "Performing the Nation: The Shah's Official State Visit to Kemalist Turkey, June to July 1934." In Stephanie Cronin (ed.), *The Making of Modern Iran: State and Society under Riza Shah, 1921–1941*. London: Routledge/Curzon, 99–119.

Matin-Asgari, Afshin. 1997. "Abdolkarim Soroush and the Secularization of Islamic Thought in Iran," *Iranian Studies* 30 (Winter/Spring): 95–115.

Matsunaga, Yasuyuki. 2007. "Mohsen Kadivar: An Advocate of Postrevivalist Islam in Iran," *British Journal of Middle Eastern Studies* 34 (December): 317–329.

Mirsepassi, Ali. 2000. *Intellectual Discourse and the Politics of Modernization: Negotiating Modernity in Iran*. Cambridge: Cambridge University Press.

Moaddel, Mansoor. 2002. *Jordanian Exceptionalism: A Comparative Analysis of State-Religion Relationships in Egypt, Iran, Jordan, and Syria*. New York: Palgrave, 46–55.

2009. "The Iranian Revolution and its Nemesis: The Rise of Liberal Values among Iranians," *Comparative Studies of South Asia, Africa and the Middle East* 29: 126–136.

Molavi, Afshin. 2003. "Letter From Iran," *The Nation*, October 13.

Mostaghim, Ramin. 2011. "Many Iranians didn't fast for Ramadan, police chief says," *Los Angeles Times*, October 31.

Naqvi, Jawed. 1995. "Iran seeks Kashmir role, warns of U.S. Involvement," *Reuters*, April 19.

Nasr, Vali. 1998. "Religion and Global Affairs: Secular States and Religious Oppositions," *SAIS Review* 18 (Summer–Fall): 32–37.

Nasr, Vali. 2003. "Secularism: Lessons from the Muslim World," *Daedalus* 132, no. 3 (Summer): 310–314.

Open Letter to Kofi Annan. 2003. "Mr. Secretary General: Bring Justice to this Injustice!" July 6.

Peterson, Scott. 2010. *Let the Swords Encircle Me: Iran – A Journey Behind the Headlines.* New York: Simon and Schuster.

Poucher Harbin, Julie. 2012. "Kadivar: Secularization of the Islamic Republic of Iran Unstoppable," *Duke Today*, April 18, http://today.duke.edu/2012/04/kadivartalk.

Rajaee, Farhang. 2007. *Islamism and Modernism: The Changing Discourse in Iran.* Austin: University of Texas Press.

Sadri, Ahmad and Mahmoud Sadri. 2011. "Delegitimizing the Islamic Republic of Iran with a Fatwa: The Significance of Ayatollah Montazeri's Post-election Legal Ruling of July 2009." In Nader Hashemi and Danny Postel (eds.), *The People Reloaded: The Green Movement and the Struggle for Iran's Future.* New York: Melville House, 151–164.

Sadri, Mahmoud. 2003. "Sacral Defense of Secularism: Dissident Political Theology in Iran." In Negean Nabavi (ed.), *Intellectual Trends in Twentieth-Century Iran: A Critical Survey.* Gainesville: University Press of Florida, 185–189.

Shah Pahlavi and Mohammed Reza. 1961. *Mission for my Country.* New York: Hutchinson, 21, 23–24.

Siddiqui, Haroon. 2002. "Democracy and Islam: Will the Twain Meet?" *Toronto Star*, February 3.

Slackman, Michael. 2002. "Frustrated by Deadlock, Iranians Seek New Voice," *Los Angeles Times*, July 26.

2002. *Sonnat va Sekularism: Goftar-hayi az Abdolkarim Soroush, Mohammad Mojtahed Shabestari, Mostafa Malekian, Mohsen Kadivar* (Tradition and Secularism: Essays by Abdolkarim Soroush, Mohammad Mojtahed Shabestari, Mostafa Malekian and Mohsen Kadivar). Tehran: Serat.

Taylor, Charles. 2007. *A Secular Age.* Cambridge: Harvard University Press.

UNESCO Institute for Statistics. 2013. "Adult and Youth: National, Regional and Global Trends, 1985–2015 (June)," www.uis.unesco.org/Education/Documents/literacy-statistics-trends-1985–2015.pdf.

Virk, Karl. 2004. "The Appearance of Change in Iran," *Washington Post*, January 15.

von Schwerin, Ulrich. 2015. *The Dissident Mullah: Ayatollah Montazeri and the Struggle for Reform in Revolutionary Iran.* New York: I.B. Tauris.

Waterbury, John. 1994. "Democracy Without Democrats?: The Potential for Political Liberalization in the Middle East." In Ghassan Salamé (ed.), *Democracy Without Democrats: The Renewal of Politics in the Muslim World.* New York: I.B. Tauris.

Witte, Jr., John. 2005. *Religion and the American Constitutional Experiment*, 2nd edition. Boulder: Westview Press.

Wrase, Michael. 2003. "Ein Ayatollah ist nur für religiöse Fragen zuständig (An Ayatollah is only responsible for religious questions)," *Welt am Sonntag* (Hamburg), November 9, 2003; www.emrooz.ws, November 11.

9

The Politics of Jewish Secularization in Israel

Hanna Lerner

INTRODUCTION

In *A Secular Age*, Charles Taylor tells the story of secularization in Latin Christendom in the North-Atlantic West. Taylor draws in particular from the history and culture of three countries – Britain, France, and the United States – "with occasional glances elsewhere" (Taylor 2007: 424). His account traces the emergence of new conditions of belief, which ended the era of what he terms "naïve" religious faith (Taylor 2007: 19). Taylor, as a Christian believer, explores the transition from "a condition in 1500 in which it was hard not to believe in God, to our present situation just after 2000, where this has become quite easy for many" (Taylor 2007: 427, 437). To what extent is the conceptual framework that Taylor presented in his magnificent book, *A Secular Age*, relevant to understanding current debates over secularism and secularity in the State of Israel, which was established as the state for the Jewish people? Do Israeli Jews live in a secular age similar to the one described by Taylor? What are the meanings of "secular," "secularity," "religious," and "religion" in the contemporary Israeli context? What is the relationship between Taylor's story of the emergence of secularity in the North-Atlantic West and the story of the emergence of Jewish secularity in that world, which led to the creation of the State of Israel as a political manifestation of a Jewish identity? Answering these questions, with all their ramifications, is a project that could require book as long as Taylor's monumental volume.[1] One important component in such a comparison between

[1] For an excellent overview of the manifold aspects of Jewish secularization in the past two and a half centuries, see the five volumes edited by Yirmiahu Yovel and David Shaham (2007).

the stories of Christian and Jewish secularization lies in the disparities between the two religious traditions. Taylor himself acknowledges that concepts such as "secular" or "religious" must be investigated against the background of their particular genealogy in their appropriate religious context. Thus, while the common term "Judeo-Christian" suggests many links and similarities between the two religious traditions, in many respects the two diverge. For example, one of the central differences between Judaism and Christianity is reflected in the tight link between religious and ethnic identities that characterize Jewish tradition, while such a link does not exist in the Christian context. As Judith Butler (2011: 72) puts it, "it makes a different kind of sense to refer to a secular Jew than to a secular Catholic." Such a comprehensive investigation into the emergence of secular Judaism in the West goes beyond the scope of this chapter. Instead, the chapter aims at highlighting two central differences between Taylor's story of secularity in the Christian North-Atlantic West and the story of Jewish secularization which began at the end of eighteenth century in Europe and continues to stir contemporary Israeli politics.

Firstly, while Taylor's story focuses on the dominant religion shared by the majority of the population, Jewish secularization in Europe is the story of minority groups living in predominantly Christian societies. Taylor pays little attention to non-Christian perspectives in his account, yet the interaction between the Jewish ghetto and the Christian majority within which it existed is a crucial part of the Jewish story. The extent to which Jewish communities in Europe were merely influenced by the societal, political, and cultural transformation of the Christian majority or took an active part in advancing them, is a question left for historians and sociologists to debate. Similarly, the point regarding Taylor's internal perspective on the Christian-dominated Western culture is neutral and inconsequential with regard to whether he *should* have addressed the relations between the Christian majority and the minority religions within these societies, or whether the existing non-Christian communities within and outside the West had any significant influence on the evolution of secularization that he describes.[2] My main point is that, while Taylor's story hardly acknowledges the existence of other religions within his Western Christian story of secularization, the story of Jewish secularization not only cannot ignore the religious "other" among which Jews lived as a minority community, but that the transformations that occurred within the hegemonic "other" are usually perceived as the initiating factor, the starting point, of the story.

---

[2] For a critical view, see Shakman Hurd (2008) and Asad (2003).

Some of the transformations in the European Jewish collectivity which resulted from this interaction will be traced in broad brushstrokes in the first part of the chapter. This part will also demonstrate how the schism between competing ideational reactions to the processes of modernization and secularization described by Taylor, which divided nineteenth century European Jewish collectivity between those who continued to hold a transcendental self-understating (i.e. religious or Orthodox Jews) and those who adopted a modernist, immanent self-understanding (i.e. secular Jews), continues to inflame conflicts over Jewish identity in twenty-first-century Israeli politics.

The second difference focuses on the relationship between Taylor's three types of secularity, defined by him as Secularity I, referring to the retreat of religion from the public sphere, Secularity II, which denotes the decline of religious beliefs and practices, and Secularity III, which describes a situation where belief in God has become only one option among many. While in Taylor's account of the "post-Durkheimian" Western Secular Age these three types of secularity are overlapping, in the Israeli context, the struggle over the role of religion in the public sphere (Secularity I) has continued ever since the foundation of the state as a sovereign state for the Jewish people.

The tight link between religious and ethnic components of Jewish identity underpins this perpetual conflict. The ongoing conflict in Israel over its definition as "Jewish and democratic" relates to the two most significant divisions within Israeli society: the rifts between the Jewish majority and the Palestinian minority, and the rift within the Jewish majority population, between those who hold a secular-liberal view and those who advocate for a religious-Orthodox understanding of Judaism and for greater establishment of religion. The second part of the chapter focuses on the latter, intra-Jewish conflict over the regulation of religion in the modern state. It exemplifies the way in which the perpetual conflict in Israel over the partial establishment of Orthodox Judaism – especially in the area of marriage and divorce for Jews – reflects a more intricate relationship between Secularities 1, 2, and 3, compared with Taylor's story of secularization in the West.

JEWISH SECULARIZATION IN EUROPE AND THE EMERGENCE OF THE ZIONIST MOVEMENT

Taylor describes a process of secularization that occurred in countries where Christianity was the dominant religion and "naïve" religious faith was by and large a Christian faith. As he acknowledges, "our societies in the West will forever remain historically informed by Christianity" (Taylor

2007: 514). By contrast, the story of Jewish secularization, which began about two and a half centuries ago in Europe, is a story of minority groups living in predominantly Christian societies. Thus, accounts of Jewish secularization tend to describe the secularization process in terms of reactions to the Western Christian-majority processes of secularization and modernization, which affected the Jewish traditional world. Since the end of the eighteenth century, European modernization "has infiltrated into the Jewish street and its surrounding" (Yovel 2007a), and transformed it in various – and contradictory – ways.[3] European Enlightenment and secularization forced Jews to change their own perception of themselves as well as how they were perceived by the non-Jewish communities (Avineri 1981: 7). Some adopted a cosmopolitan perspective alienated from all Jewish religious traditionalism, while various segments among the Jewish collectivity reacted in defensive self-isolation by promoting a rigid religious orthodoxy (Samet 1988). Others developed elements of Jewish nationalist ideology which were later combined into Zionism.

The most profound effect of what Charles Taylor terms "the Age of Mobilization" and the formation of European nation-states on the diasporic Jewish collectivity was the extension of civic rights of citizenship to the Jews and other previously discriminated communities (Shimoni 1995: 12).[4] Influenced by the liberal ideas of the Enlightenment, legal emancipation for the Jews was progressively and gradually promoted across the West, beginning in the 1780s with the legislation of Austro-Hungarian emperor Joseph II. In 1789 Jews were granted full citizenship in the United States of America, and in 1791 in revolutionary France. By the 1870s, despite heated public controversy and clericalist and reactionary objections, the legal emancipation of Jews in western and central Europe was completed. After centuries in which Jews in Europe lived in largely autonomous corporative communities and maintained distinct ethnic-religious identities, civic emancipation facilitated their increasing integration into the social structure of the European states. As a result, the traditional roles played by Jewish shared community institutions were transformed, with the authority of Jewish communal leadership becoming less comprehensive (Shimoni 1995: 12). Most critically, the extension of civic rights increasingly exposed Jews to the educational as well as linguistic, cultural, and intellectual homogenizing influences of the evolving European states.

---

[3] For comprehensive accounts of this transformation see: Katz (1998, 1987) and Frankel and Zipperstain (1992).

[4] Also see Israel Bartal (1994) and Avineri (1981).

These influences stimulated an inner Jewish intellectual effervescence that came to be known as *Haskala*, a Jewish version of the Enlightenment (*Aufklärung* in German). Emanating mainly from Berlin at the turn of the eighteenth century, its main ideological underpinning was the claim that Judaism was inherently compatible with universal human reason, and thus "secular knowledge" should be applied to Jewish cultural heritage (Shimoni 1995: 14). The seminal formulation of this integrationist ideology was expressed in the writings of Moshe Mendelssohn (1729–1786), who viewed Jewish tradition in purely liturgical terms, while advocating absolute loyalty of Jews to the state(s) in which they resided.

The *Haskala* created ambivalence among the Jewish intelligentsia. On the one hand, the ideology of *Haskala* went hand in hand with Reform Judaism, which began developing in the nineteenth century mainly in Germany, Austria-Hungary, and the United States, and which eliminated prayers and practices that included "national" elements, such as the use of Hebrew language or expressions of longing for Zion and the belief that messianic redemption from exile would bring about return to an independent existence in Zion (Meyer 1988). In contrast to this view, which perceived Judaism as religion, others emphasized its cultural/national aspects, expressed most vividly through the evolution of the Hebrew language for purposes of both religious service and literature. The emergence of Hebrew newspapers, such as *Hamelitz, Hamagid*, and *Kol Hamevaser*, in the second half of the nineteenth century contributed to the replacement of Yiddish as an everyday Jewish language.[5] There were great regional differences in the intellectual evolvement of Haskala, between Eastern European and western or central European *maskilim* (Frankel and Zipperstein 1992). Yet overall, the normative common denominator shared by all *maskilim* was that the preferential option for the Jews everywhere was the attainment of civic rights and their integration into the host society of the state in which they were domiciled (Shimoni 1995: 25–33). In 1862, the first nationalist exposition of a secular character by a Jew, calling for the return to Jewish independence in Zion, was published in Germany by Moshe Hess. Yet his book, entitled *Rome and Jerusalem*, went either largely unnoticed or was ridiculed by the Jewish intelligentsia (Shimoni 1995: 19).

This attitude toward a nationalist Jewish ideology dramatically altered in the following decades, when many supporters of Jewish *Haskala* who believed in the prospects of liberal emancipation and integration into the

---

[5] On the renewal of the Hebrew language, see: Yovel and Shaham (2007) Vol. 2, 234–328.

host state and society became disillusioned. The turnabout began already in the 1870s and continued in the 1880s with the growth of loosely interrelated groups and associations known as *Hovevei Zion* (Lovers of Zion). It escalated in the wake of the 1880s pogroms in Russia, which led to the emigration of nearly three million Jews from Russia between the years 1882 and 1894, mostly to North or South America and Australia. Less than 1 percent of those immigrants arrived in Palestine (Klier and Lambroza 1992). Large parts of the Jewish intelligentsia were surprised by widespread condonation of the pogroms by the Russian government, as well as by progressive revolutionaries in Russia (Shimoni 1995: 31). The disillusionment experienced by a segment of the Jewish intelligentsia was, according to historians and social scientists, the crucially formative factor in the emergence of the Eretz-Israel-oriented nationalist ideology later known as Zionism (Shimoni 1995: 46; Avineri 1981: 3–13). In 1882, Leo (Yehuda Leib) Pinsker published in Berlin a booklet titled *Autoemancipation: An Appeal to his compatriots by a Russian Jew* (in German: *Autoemancipation: Mahnruf an seine Stammesgenossen von einem russischen Juden*), which became "for the ideology of Zionism what Marx and Engels' *Communist Manifesto* was for that of socialism" (Shimoni 1995: 33). In this pamphlet, Pinsker argued that the option of integration into the Christian majority societies was impossible to realize in reality and offered a diagnosis of the Jewish problem, according to which the ultimate defect lay in the Jews' condition of national home-lessness (Shimoni 1995: 33). Fourteen years later, in 1896, the Jewish secularized Viennese journalist, Theodor Herzl, published his book *The Jewish State*, in which he proposed the organized exodus of Jews to an autonomous territory of their own, not necessarily Palestine.[6] In the following year, Herzl and other educated liberal Jews who previously advocated Jewish integration into their host societies convened the inaugural congress of the Zionist Organization in Basel, Switzerland.

The emergence of the Zionist movement was thus a result of the advancement of European secularization, but also by itself was a basis for the evolution of Jewish secularism. Alongside cultural changes within the Jewish communities, Zionist ideology reflected the emergence of new forms of Jewish politics, seeking to disconnect it from the anticipation for the coming of the Messiah, from rabbinical authorities and from norms embedded in the divine and transcendent, and to base it on earthly reality

---

[6] Historians debate to what extent the Dreyfus Affair had influenced Herzl's views regarding the future of Jews in Europe. See, for example, Cohn (1970).

and the actual powers that operate within it.[7] Indeed, most ultra-Orthodox Jews rejected Zionism for its generally atheist approach and because the Zionist principle of self-emancipation violated religious doctrine, according to which only God could redeem the Jewish people and return them to the land of Israel. Yet Zionism did not reject completely the religious component in Jewish identity. Religious leaders played a significant role in the emergence of the Zionist ideology from its very inception.

While many traditionalist rabbis adopted during the nineteenth century an integrationist ideology, similarly to religious reformers to whom they objected,[8] various rabbis and religiously observant Jews advocated the idea of resettling Eretz-Israel and supported the groups and associations of *Hibat Zion* (Lovers of Israel). Such reaffirmation of the attachment to Zion developed by and large as a defensive reaction to Reform Judaism which spread particularly in Central and Western Europe, and which rejected the notions of return to Zion and restoration of the Temple ritual as essential ingredients of the messianic vision (Shimoni: 42). Rabbis such as Yehiel Michel Pines, for example, who were receptive to Enlightenment influences yet deplored Reform Judaism embraced a religious-ethnicist definition of Jewish identity and aligned themselves with advocates of a resettlement program in Eretz-Israel, and afterwards with the Zionist organization (Shimoni: 43; Salmon and Kutscher 1988).

Thus, since the early days of the Zionist movement, it included various secular and religious components. Secularists and traditionalists within the Zionist organization held competing perspectives regarding the definition of Jewish identity and the purpose of the resettlement program, and the relationship between them was a perennial source of dissonance that remains unresolved to this day. Leading members of the Zionist organization included intellectuals such as Ehad Ha'am (1856–1927), who defined himself as agnosti, and considered the goal of Zionism as creating a shared identity for the Jewish people based on common culture, rather than religion, as well as religious leaders such as Yitzchak Yaacov Reines (1839–1915), the founder of *Mizrachi* (a Zionist religious movement) for whom the political-territorial aspect of Jewish identity was a supplemental component to traditional national-religious definition of Jewish identity.

---

[7] Yovel 2007a, "Introduction," XXIV. See also Chowers 2012.
[8] These Rabbis were part of a Jewish neo-orthodoxy which reformulated traditionalism in a way that was compatible with integration into the local European society. For example, Samson Rafael Hirsch from Germany (Shimoni: 50).

Some observers have emphasized that the confluence of secular and religious tributaries within the Zionist movement was not only a source of perpetual conflict, but also a significant factor behind its success. In the words of historian Gideon Shimoni, while all other popularly based new political movements that emerged in modern Jewish life – such as the Socialist Jewish Bund, founded in 1897, and the Orthodox association, Agudat Israel, founded in 1912 – appealed only to segments of Jewry, by class or by mode of identity on the religious-secular divide,

Zionist ideology alone drew upon the mythic force of the Jewish *ethnie* as a whole, looking Janus-faced, backward to the ethnic past, which was inseparable from religion, as well as forward to a modernized ethnic future in the shape of a nation in its own state. In dialectical terms, it purported to form a synthesis out of the thesis of traditionalism and the antithesis of enlightened modernism. (Shimoni 1995: 45)

The establishment of the State of Israel is usually perceived not only as a direct consequence of Jewish secularization, but also as a source of renewed thriving and flourishing of this process. This was achieved through the revival of Hebrew as an everyday language rather than a language of prayer (the Orthodox language in Israel is still Yiddish), and other forms of secular Jewish culture, art (theater, literature, music, etc), secular ideology, and modern ways of life. Yet, as the next sections will demonstrate, Israeli independence did not mitigate the internal controversies on the definitions of Jewish identity. The inherent ambiguity regarding the essence of Israel as a state for the Jewish people continues to underpin Israeli politics up to the present time.

FOUNDATION OF THE STATE OF ISRAEL

The establishment of the State of Israel indicated a major difference between the story of Christian secularization in the West and that of Jewish secularization, with regard to the role of institutions and the political struggle over religious regulations. In Taylor's story of secularization, the link between religious and political identity (i.e. between confession and a people/nation) was one of the central characteristics of what he terms the Age of Mobilization (between 1800 and 1960), which preceded the current Age of Authenticity (post-1960s). In the Age of Mobilization, belief was sustained by a "neo-Durkheimian" identification of believers with the state (Taylor 2007: 455). The neo-Durkheimian ideal-type meant that "religious belonging was central to political identity" (Taylor 2007: 455). This link between religion and political identity had given way in the post-1960s Age of Authenticity to "a post-Durkheimian" world that is the current Secular Age, which means that "our relation to the spiritual is being more and more unhooked from our relation to our political societies ... a thoroughly post-Durkheimian society would be one in which our religious belonging would be unconnected to our national identity" (Taylor 2007: 516). In the Western Secular Age, Secularity III (when religious belief is only one position among many) goes hand in hand with Secularity II (decline of religious belief and practices), and is conditioned on Secularity 1 (differentiation of religion in the public sphere). As Taylor writes, "we live in a world of what John Rawls has described as 'overlapping consensus'" (2007: 532).

Taylor by no means suggests that the post-Durkheimian Secular Age is universally shared by all countries in the world. As he acknowledges, it is limited to "twenty-first-century North Atlantic societies not riven by ethnic-confessional differences (i.e. we're NOT talking about Northern Ireland)."[9] Israel is outside the West not only geographically but also in terms of its secularity story. As the rest of the chapter will illustrate, in the case of Israeli secularization, the relationship between Secularities. 1, II, and III is much more complex, and the tight link between the three, as described by Taylor, is difficult to find. While large parts of Israeli society have developed many characteristics included in what Taylor defines as Secularity III (modernization, spiritualization, etc) and Secularity II (decline of religious belief and practices),[10] the conflict over the influence of religion on state institutions and the public sphere is far from over. The intricate relationship between the cultural, ethnic, national, and religious components of Jewish identity continues to hinder the completion of an Israeli process of secularization in the sense of Taylor's Secularity 1, and perpetuates the conflict over the role of religion in the public sphere. As within the Zionist movement, religious

---

[9] Taylor 2007: 515. Parenthesis and emphasis in the original.
[10] Ongoing polls show decline in attachment of Israeli Jews to Jewish tradition and religion between 1991 and 1999, but increase in this attachment between 1999 and 2009. The changing trend may be explained by the mass immigration from the former Soviet Union during the 1990s and the assimilation of Russian immigrants into Israeli society, and their adoption of Jewish practices and traditions during the first decade of the twenty-first century. The trend also reflects the growth of Orthodox and Ultra-Orthodox populations in Israeli society in recent years. In 2009, 43 percent of the respondents defined themselves as "secular not anti-religious," and 3 percent as "secular, anti-religious." 32 percent defined themselves as "traditional," 15 percent as "Orthodox," and 7 percent as "Ultra-Orthodox." To the question "to what extent to you observe tradition?" 16 percent replied "not at all," 44 percent relied "to some extent," 26 percent "to a great extent," and 14 percent "meticulously" (see Arian and Keissar-Sugarmen 2012).

authorities and religious law continue to play an important role in Israeli politics and even monopolize some state institutions (e.g., the regulation of marriage and divorce). In that sense, while some sections in Israeli society aspire to advance into the Age of Authenticity, the large majority of Israeli society remains locked in the dynamics of the Age of Mobilization, during which the state was born.

The foundation of a sovereign state for the Jewish people in 1948 did not end the conflict between religious and secular tributaries which characterized the Zionist movement from its inception. Rather, it transformed the ideological debate into a political conflict over the regulation of religion in the modern state. The Israeli Declaration of Independence explicitly defined Israel as "a Jewish state in Eretz-Israel" which would be open for Jewish immigration and for the ingathering of the exiles. At the same time, it stated that the State of Israel "will ensure complete equality of social and political rights to all its inhabitants irrespective of religion, race or sex; will guarantee freedom of religion, conscience, language education and culture; it will safeguard the Holy Places of all religions; and will be faithful to the principles of the Charter of the United Nations."[11] In 1992, the character of Israel was formally defined as "Jewish and Democratic,"[12] which marked the continuing debate over the exact meaning of this definition and whether the "Jewishness" of the state should be interpreted in strictly religious or rather more cultural or national terms.

Viewed from the internal perspective of the Jewish majority population in Israel, the "religion and state" debate in Israel is usually perceived in terms of "synagogue and state," characterized by deep division between secular and non-Orthodox Jews on the one side, and Orthodox and ultra-Orthodox Jews on the other. In addition, however, the existence of a large Palestinian minority within Israeli territory created another, intra-religious, dimension to the conflict over the Jewish nature of the state and emphasized the dual ethnic-religious character of Jewish identity. Indeed, although the non-Jewish population of Israel has, since independence, been approximately 20 percent of the population, non-Jews were consistently excluded from Israeli nationhood (Kimerling 1994; Smooha

---

[11] The Declaration of the Establishment of the State of Israel: www.knesset.gov.il/docs/eng/megilat_eng.htm

[12] Basic Law: Human Dignity and Liberty and Basic Law: Freedom of Occupation. For full text of the two basic laws see: www.knesset.gov.il/description/eng/eng_mimshal_yesod1.htm

1997). While the inter-ethnic rift within Israeli society is inseparable from the intra-Jewish debate over the definition of Israel as "Jewish and democratic,"[13] the rest of the chapter will focus on the latter, aiming to illustrate the way in which, in contrast to Taylor's story on the emergence of the Secular Age in the West, in Israel, the conflict over Jewish secularization still revolves around questions of religious regulations and political institutions. I will focus, most particularly, on one of the most heated areas of dispute in the conflict of religious establishment in Israel, namely on the regulations governing Jewish marriage and divorce.

THE RELIGIOUS-SECULAR CONFLICT IN ISRAEL: MARRIAGE AND DIVORCE LAW

The conflict between secular and religious definitions of the Jewish state was one of the reasons for the decision, a year and a half after independence, to refrain from drafting a formal constitution.[14] Despite an overwhelming secular majority in the Knesset (Israeli parliament),[15] the political leadership at the time preferred not to make controversial constitutional decisions regarding the role of religious law and institutions. Instead of enacting a formal constitution, the Knesset decided in June 1950 that the constitution would be enacted in a gradual manner through a series of individual Basic Laws that would eventually be assembled into a formal constitutional document.

In the absence of a written constitution, the relationship between religion and state in Israel evolved through a set of consociational arrangements that included parliamentary legislation, judicial precedents, and public conventions. These arrangements, known as "the religious status quo," effectively determine the non-separation between religion and state in certain areas, such as observance of the Sabbath, observance of *kashruth* (dietary laws) in government institutions, exemption of Orthodox students from military service, autonomy of state-funded religious educational institutions, and exclusive jurisdiction of Jewish Orthodox authorities in matters of personal law. While in many respects Israeli legal and constitutional system represent the state's commitment to liberal values such as equality,

---

[13] For a revealing analysis of the interplay between the Arab-Jewish tension and the religious-secular conflict in Israel, see Karayanni (2007).

[14] For description of the debates, including alternative explanations for the decision to refrain from drafting see: Hanna Lerner (2011: chapter 3).

[15] In the first Knesset, only 16 out of 120 members represented religious parties.

liberty, and pluralism, its partial establishment of religion demonstrates the state's commitment to an Orthodox vision of Judaism. This is particularly the case with the regulation of marriage and divorce.

At independence in 1948, Israeli Knesset decided to preserve the Ottoman *Millet* system and recognized the legal autonomy of all religious traditions in the area of personal law. Religious monopolies over marriage and divorce were maintained with respect to eleven recognized religions in Israel.[16] The application of the *Millet* system after independence differed from the way it operated under British Mandate in that under British rule, Rabbinical Courts could apply Jewish law in personal status issues only to those who were officially registered as members of the Jewish religious community. By contrast, the State of Israel ceased to maintain such official registration of communal membership. Consequentially, thousands of Jews who immigrated to Israel after 1948 were unable to marry or divorce.[17] Five years after independence, the Knesset was thus required to resolve this "regulative vacuum"[18] and debated whether personal law for Jews in Israel should be entrusted to the Orthodox Rabbinical authorities or regulated by civil marriage laws.

During the debates, some secular members of the Knesset criticized the Orthodox rabbis, who do not recognize gender equality, as followers of "medieval traditions."[19] By contrast, the religious parties claimed that a unified system of marriage and divorce according to Halachic rule was essential for preserving unity among the Jewish people. Otherwise, they argued, religious Jews will not be able to marry descendents of those married outside of religion. Eventually, the Knesset enacted the *Jurisdiction of Rabbinical Tribunals (Marriage and Divorce) Law*, which established that "matters of marriage and divorce of Jews in Israel, being nationals or residents of the state, shall be under the sole jurisdiction of the rabbinical tribunals" (section 1) and that "marriage and divorce of Jews shall be held in accordance with religious law" (section 2). The Rabbinical Courts have concurrent jurisdiction with the civil family courts in claims for maintenance and additional claims related to divorce (section 4).

---

[16] The *Millet* system was maintained under the British Mandate with some modifications. Based on the Palestine Order in Council 1922, Paragraph 83 in: Drayton, *Laws of Palestine*, vol. iii, 2587.

[17] Israel's first Minister of Justice, Pinchas Rozen, claimed that this issue was problematic not only for the religious Jewish population but also for the secular Jews, since no civil regulations of marriage and divorce existed. *Government Meeting Minutes*, August 25, 1953, 5.

[18] Verhaftig, *Knesset Records* 5, 1408–1409.

[19] Ada Maymon, *Coalition Board Meeting Minutes*. August 17, 1953.

Similar arrangements exist with respect to all other fourteen recognized religions in Israel (Rubinstein 1967; Layish 2006).

The reasons for the 1953 legislation, which became a critical juncture in the evolution of religion–state relations in Israel, are subject to historiographic debate. Some researchers analyze the decision in the context of the coalitional agreement between Mapai, the leading party, and the religious parties, which underpinned the consociational arrangements of the "religious status quo" (Cohen and Susser 2000; Friedman 2005; Don-Yehiya 1999; Harris 2002). Alternatively, other scholars analyze the 1953 legislation in the context of the national conflict over the state's identity and the political leadership's attempt to exclude non-Jews from Israeli nationhood (Shapira 1996; Shafir and Peled 2002; Triger 2005; Sezgin 2013). According to this approach, the religious monopoly on marriage and divorce was designed to promote the homogenization of Jewish identity on the one hand while differentiating non-Jewish identities on the other. A third approach suggests that the political actors at the time did not view this legislation as a turning point in the development of religion–state relations in Israel and did not intend it to remain rigid for the next generations, but rather as a required temporary compromise, for coalitional reasons, at that fragile state-building period (Lerner 2014). Consequently, when, during a government meeting, one of the ministers criticized the bill as lacking an arrangement for civil marriage, Prime Minister Ben Gurion replied: "one should propose a civil marriage bill," suggesting that he did not believe that Rabbinical jurisdiction would prove to be immutable.[20] This approach is supported by later expressions of regret voiced by Ben Gurion and other Mapai leaders for decisions they made in the early years of the state, in light of the entrenched religious institutional arrangements, particularly in the area of marriage and divorce.[21] Moreover, conviction that religious traditions would gradually change and adopt modern democratic values was explicitly expressed during the Knesset debate on the 1953 Rabbinical Jurisdiction law as one of the justifications for the enactment of the legislation which was recognized (even by those who voted for the law) as inegalitarian and illiberal.[22] However, contrary to these hopes, the religious regulation of marriage and divorce is often criticized for its violation of individual rights of hundreds of thousands of Israeli citizens, particularly of women. The

---

[20] Government Meeting Minutes, April 17, 1953.
[21] Ben Gurion, for example, is cited in Rubinstein (1972), Strum (1995).
[22] Knesset Records, August 26, 1953, p. 2559.

religious marriage and divorce institutions in Israel have proved to be very difficult to change.

PERPETUAL CONFLICT OVER CIVIL MARRIAGE

For more than six decades, the status of personal law in Israel continues to stand at the heart of the political, legal, and public conflict between secular and Orthodox perspectives of religious establishment in Israel. It is often argued that the Orthodox monopoly on marriage and divorce infringes on basic liberties and violates the individual rights of hundreds of thousands of Israeli citizens (Shiffman 2001). Women, in particular, are discriminated against by the patriarchal religious legal system, since Jewish law gives men the power to deny their wives divorce (Halperin-Kedar 2004: 227–62; Raday et al. 1995; Swirksi and Safir 1991). According to Jewish law, divorce cannot be imposed by court ruling but requires the husband's explicit consent. While men who refuse divorce may be sanctioned and even imprisoned, over the years an estimated 100,000 women in Israel have been either denied a divorce or have had to comply with conditions set by their husband in order to get divorced.[23] Israel's Equal Rights for Women Law (1951) explicitly specifies that the law does not pertain to matters of marriage and divorce. Israel even included two reservations in the same domain when signing the UN Convention on the Elimination of All Forms of Discrimination against Women in 1991.[24] Furthermore, the status quo regarding personal law determines that formal state recognition is denied in case of the marriage conducted by non-Orthodox religious rabbis (such as Reform and Conservative Jews), or in the case of interfaith couples, and people who are defined by the rabbinical authorities as "barred from marriage" (*psuley chitun*) for various reasons.[25] Among those that cannot marry in Israel are an estimated 300,000 immigrants from the former Soviet Union, who are not considered Jews by the Halacha, yet are not associated with any other religion (Shiffman 2001).

---

[23] Orit Lotan, *"Mesoravot Get" (Denied of Divorce) in Israel*. Report Presented to the Knesset Committee on the Status of Women (2005).

[24] See www.un.org/womenwatch/daw/cedaw/reservations-country.htm (last accessed: May 1, 2017).

[25] For example, the Rabbinical court does not recognize the marriage of children born to women who did not obtain a religious divorce from their previous marriage before having a child with another man or a marriage between a man from a priestly family (Cohen) and a divorced women.

Over the years, the Israeli legal system developed several alternatives to circumvent some of the limitations set by formal religious marriage, such as the institution of "common-law couples" (*yeduim betzibur*). Israeli law does not include a clear definition of "common-law marriage," but over the years a series of laws and court decisions recognized equal rights to "common-law couples" in issues such as inheritance, pension and taxation, custody of children, and adoption (Halperin-Keddari 2001; Lifschitz 2006). Additionally, many Israelis travel abroad to marry in civil ceremonies that are recognized by the state on their return.[26] The Supreme Court even ordered the state to register same sex couples that married in other countries as married.[27] The most recent legislative development occurred in March 2010, when the Knesset passed the *Spousal Covenant for Persons Having No Religious Affiliation Act*.[28] The bill was initiated by the *Israel Beitenu* party, a right-wing party mostly supported by former immigrants from the Soviet Union, in order to resolve the problem of the estimated 300,000 former immigrants who cannot marry in Israel since they are defined by the state as "lacking a religion." However, in contrast to the initial intention, the final version of the legislation did not provide a comprehensive option of civil marriage. The limited bill allows couples who are *both* considered as not members of any religion to formally register as couples, and to have equal legal rights and obligations as a married couple. The new bill maintained the authority to decide who is considered not Jewish in the hands of the Orthodox Rabbinical authority. Moreover, it did not allow for interfaith marriage and did not apply if only one partner had no religion. Between 2010-2016 only 120 couples have registered under the "Spousal Covenant" Act.[29]

While mitigating some of the effects of basic rights violations caused by religious law, these alternative arrangements have not resolved all the difficulties that have resulted from Orthodox rabbinate's monopoly on personal law in Israel.[30] For example, Rabbinical Courts continue to

---

[26] In 1963 the Supreme Court ruled that the state should register couples that married in a civil ceremony abroad as married. HJC 143/62 *Funk-Schlezinger v. Ministry of Internal Affairs*.

[27] HCJ 3045/05 *Yossi Ben-Ari and others v. Director of Population Administration, Ministry of Interior*.

[28] For English translation of the Act: www.justice.gov.il/MOJHeb/LiskaMispatit/RasamHazugiut

[29] Hiddush, "Spousal Covenant: 120 Couples in Six Years", *Hiddush News*, 11 December 2016 (in Hebrew).

[30] For criticism of the Supreme Court as an agent of political maintenance rather than an agent of sociopolitical change see, for example, Barzilai (1998); Hofnung (1997).

wield sole jurisdiction over marriage dissolution even in cases in which the divorcing couple was married in a civil procedure abroad.[31] Moreover, the separation between religious and secular courts has entailed an inherent clash of authority within the Israeli judicial system. More than once, the Rabbinical Court has refused to accept an authoritative ruling of the Supreme Court.[32]

Despite wide public protest, the exclusive jurisdiction of Rabbinical Courts over matters of marriage and divorce has not been altered by either parliamentary legislation, judicial intervention, or constitutional enactment. While minor reforms have been introduced to minimize the religious control over marriage and divorce,[33] frequent parliamentary efforts to introduce civil marriage have consistently failed due to the persistent objection of the religious parties. The weakening of the Knesset as an effective body for introducing institutional change in religion–state relations is evident in the reluctance of the Knesset to amend the regulations pertaining to marriage and divorce. The Knesset's decreasing effectiveness in addressing contentious issues in religion–state relations is commonly explained by the growing parliamentary influence of the religious parties following the 1977 elections. The victory of the Likud party over the hitherto dominant Labor party signaled the transformation of the Israeli political system from a dominant party system to one of two similarly sized competing blocks. Under the new conditions, Knesset representatives of religious parties largely determined the composition of the coalition governments.

In face of the increasing influence of religious parties in the legislature, liberal-secular activists turned to the Supreme Court in their attempt to promote their agenda. Since the 1980s, the struggle between the religious and secular camps has increasingly moved from the legislature to the judiciary, and the Israeli Supreme Court showed its willingness to challenge the religious authorities (Mautner 1993). While the "status quo" was recognized as a political principle for accommodating the religious-secular divide, it was never anchored as a legal imperative by Court rulings. Indeed, over the years, the Israeli Court has attempted to alter the religious status quo arrangements

---

[31] HCJ 2232/03, *Roe* v. *Tel Aviv Rabbinical Court* (2006).

[32] One of the most famous examples for such a clash was around the case of *Bavli* v. *the Grant Rabbinical Court* (1994). See Scolnicov (2006).

[33] For example, in 2008 the Knesset amended the 1973 Spouses' Property Relations Act so that marital assets registered in the name of one party could be divided before an actual divorce was granted.

in its rulings, particularly when these arrangements conflicted with basic human rights stated in Israel's Declaration of Independence or in the Basic Law: Freedom of Occupation and Basic Law: Human Dignity and Liberty (Corinaldi 2003).[34]

However, Israeli legal and political scholars are intensely divided over the question of whether the Israeli Supreme Court has been truly "activist" in its judicial approach over the years (Hofnung 1996; Barzilai 1998; Gavison 1998). Studies have demonstrated that although the Court favored the liberal-secular worldview in most rulings, its effect on the religious status quo, in general, and on the personal law arrangements, in particular, has been limited in scope (Liviatan 2009; Wood 2008).

Hope for secular reform of the existing religious status quo arrangements was renewed in 2003 when the Knesset's Constitution, Law, and Justice Committee attempted to draft a constitutional proposal for the State of Israel. This was the most comprehensive attempt to write a constitution and to address the most controversial issues that had divided Israeli society since independence. Many in the liberal camp supported this endeavor, as in their view this was an opportunity to reform inegalitarian religious status quo arrangements. However, the Committee's report of 2006 did not achieve acceptable compromise formulations for controversial religion–state issues. Rather, in the view of the Committee's chief legal advisor, law professor Ruth Gavison (2006), "if the Constitutional Committee had any substantial achievement," it was in the way it "exposed the opposing positions regarding the most fundamental constitutional questions." Thus, although the Knesset's Constitution, Law and Justice Committee acknowledged that the existing marriage and divorce laws in Israel must be changed,[35] the constitutional proposal it drafted not only refrained from introducing a genuine secular reform that would end what is perceived to be the infringement of basic rights in the area of personal law, it even suggested imposing constraints on the Supreme Court that would cause it to refrain from intervening in matters of religious arrangements in the domain of personal law (Lerner 2009).

---

[34] For example, the 1989 and 1994 Supreme Court decisions against municipal refusal to appoint women or non-Orthodox Jews to their local religious councils. HJC 699/89 *Anat Hofman* v. *Jerusalem City Council* 48(1); HJC 4733/94 *Yehudit Naot* v. *Haifa City Council* 59(5). For more on the developments in the "status quo" arrangements in both court rulings and legislation, see Corinaldi (2003).

[35] The report stated that "it is inconceivable that people who cannot marry by religious law cannot marry in Israel at all" ("Constitution in Broad Consent: Report" 2006).

CONCLUDING REMARKS

The story of Israeli secularization is far from over. This chapter has mainly focused on inner Jewish debates which continue to reflect an inherent and historical disagreement among Jews regarding the definition of Jewish identity and the role of religion in their public or communal life. This conflict characterized the Zionist movement from its very inception and persists to divide Jewish society in Israel today.

The relationship between Jewish secularization and Zionism is a topic widely debated by historians and social scientists (Porat 2013; Fischer 2015; Dorfman 2015). In recent years, a growing number of scholars have aimed at challenging the linear perception of the genesis of Zionism as a project of national self-determination resulting from Jewish liberation from religious traditionalism.[36] Similarly, the impact of Israeli independence on the process of Jewish secularization and on the relationship between Jewish religion and secularity has been critically debated by scholars. The controversy, infused by competing political, sociological, and ideological approaches, particularly escalated after the 1967 war and the emergence of *Gush Emunim* as a radical-religious Zionist ideological movement advocating Jewish resettlement of greater Eretz-Israel (Shafir and Peled 2002). The impact of *Gush Emunim* on Israeli policies in the West Bank in the post-1967 decades adds new dimensions to the debate on Jewish secularity and religiosity in contemporary Israel. Does this radical movement represent a reaction to secular or even religious Zionism, or a continuation of the Zionist ideology? To what extent are Israeli government policies in the West Bank the result of circumstantial developments? Or do they rather reflect a continuing territorial resettlement policy rooted in a religious resettlement ideology and Zionist practice crystallized in the nineteenth century? These and many other questions deserve much broader discussion. Similarly, the relations between Jewish self-perceptions and the prolonged Israeli–Palestinian conflict require greater attention than this chapter could have offered.

Bibliography

Arian, Asher and Ayala Keissar-Sugarmen. 2012. *A Portrait of Israeli Jews: Beliefs, Observance and Values of Israeli Jews 2009*. Jerusalem: The Guttman Center for Surveys of the Israeli Democracy Institute.

---

[36] For an excellent overview of the various positions in this debate, see Yehuda Goodman and Shlomo Fisher (2004).

Asad, Talal. 2003. *Formations of the Secular: Christianity, Islam, Modernity.* Stanford: Stanford University Press.

Avineri, Shlomo. 1981. *The Making of Modern Zionism: The Intellectual Origins of the Jewish State.* London: Weidenfeld and Nicolson.

Bartal, Israel. 1994. "Reactions to modernity in Eastern Europe: Enlightenment, Orthodoxy and Nationality." In Shmuel Almog, Jehuda Reinharz, and Anita Shapira, *Zionism and Religion.* Zlman Shazar Center for Jewish History, 21–32.

Barzilai, Gad. 1998. "Courts as Hegemonic Institutions: The Israeli Supreme Court in a Comparative Perspective." *Israel Affairs* 5:2–3, 15–33.

1998. "Judicial Hegemony, Party Polarization and Social Change." *Politica: An Israeli Journal for Political Science and International Relations* 2.

Ben Porat, Guy. 2013. *Between State and Synagogue: The Secularization of Contemporary Israel.* Cambridge: Cambridge University Press.

Butler, Judith. 2011. "Is Judaism Zionism?" In Eduardo Mendieta and Jonathan Van Antwerpen, *The Power of Religion in the Public Sphere.* New York: Columbia University Press.

Cohen, Asher and Bernard Susser. 2000. *Israel and the Politics of Jewish Identity: The Secular-Religious Impasse.* Baltimore: The Johns Hopkins University Press.

Cohn, Henry J. 1970. "Theodor Herzl's Conversion to Zionism." *Jewish Social Studies* 32(2): 101–110.

Constitution, Law and Justice Committee. 2006. Constitution in Broad Consent: Report of the Constitution, Law and Justice Committee Regarding Proposals for the Constitution of the State of Israel. In Hebrew. Available at: http://main.knesset.gov.il/Activity/Constitution.

Corinaldi, Michael. 2003. "Freedom of Religion in Israel: What Changed in the 'Status Quo'?" *Sha'arey Mishpat* 3(2).

Chowers, Eyal. 2012. *The Political Philosophy of Zionism: Trading Jewish Words of an Hebraic Land.* Cambridge and New York: Cambridge University Press.

Dorfman, Avihay. 2015. *Freedom of Religion and Freedom from Religion: A Democratic Perspective.* Jerusalem: The Israel Democracy Institute (Hebrew).

Don-Yehiya, Eliezer. 1999. *Religion and Political Accommodation in Israel.* Jerusalem: Floersheimer Institute for Policy Studies.

Fischer, Yochi. 2015. *Secularization and Secularism: Interdisciplinary Perspectives.* Jerusalem: Van Leer Institute and Hakibbutz Hameuchad (Hebrew).

Frankel, Jonathan and Steven J. Zipperstain. 1992. *Assimilation and Community: The Jews in Nineteenth Century Europe.* Cambridge: Cambridge University Press.

Friedman, Menachem. 2005. "These are the Chronicles of the Status-Quo: Religion and State in Israel." In Uri Dromi (ed.). *Brethren Dwelling Together. Orthodoxy and Non-Orthodoxy in Israel: Positions, Propositions and Accords.* Jerusalem: Israel Democracy Institute (Hebrew).

Gavison, Ruth. 1998. *The Constitutional Revolution: A Reality or a Self Fulfilling Prophecy?* Jerusalem: Israel Democracy Institute.

2006. "Lessons from the Constitutional Process in the 16th Knesset." In Constitution in Broad Consent: Report, 2006.

Goodman, Yehuda and Shlomo Fisher. 2004. "Understanding Secularity and Religiosity in Israel: The Secularization Thesis and Conceptual Alternatives."

In Yossi Yona and Yehuda Goodman, eds. *Maelstrom of Identities: A Critical Look at religion and Secularity in Israel*. Jerusalem: Van Leer Institute and Hakibbutz Hameuchad Publishing, 346–390 (Hebrew).

Halperin-Kedar, Ruth. 2004. *Women in Israel: A State of Their Own*. Philadelphia: University of Pennsylvania Press.

2001. "Towards Concluding Civil Family Law – Israel Style," *Bar Ilan Legal Studies* 17 (Hebrew).

Harris, Ron. 2002. "Absent Minded Misses and Historical Opportunities: Jewish Law, Israeli Law and the Establishment of the State of Israel." In Mordechai Bar-On and Zvi Zameret (eds.), *On Both Sides of the Bridge: Religion and State in the Early Years of Israel*. Jerusalem: Yad Ben Zvi, 21–55 (Hebrew).

Hofnung, Menachem. 1997. "Authority, Power and Separation of Powers: Israeli Judicial Review in Comparative Perspective," *Mishpatim* 28 (in Hebrew).

1996. "The Unintended Consequences of Unplanned Constitutional Reform: Constitutional Politics in Israel." *American Journal of Comparative Law* no. 44.

Karayanni, Michael. 2007. "The 'Other' Religion and State Conflict in Israel: On the Nature of Religious Accommodations for the Palestinian-Arab Minority." In W. Brugger and M. Karayanni (eds.), *Religion in the Public Sphere: A Comparative Analysis of German*, Israeli, American and International Law. Berlin: Springer.

Katz, Jacob. 1998. *Out of the Ghetto: The Social Background of Jewish Emancipation, 1770–1870*. Syracuse: Syracuse University Press.

1987. (ed.). *Towards Modernity: The European Jewish Model*. New York: Transactions.

Kimerling, Baruch. 1994. "Religion, Nationality and Democracy in Israel," *Zemanim* 50 (in Hebrew).

1997. "History Here, Now." In Yechiam Waitz (ed.), *From Vision to Revision: A Hundred Years of Historiography in Zionism*. Jerusalem: The Zalman Shazar Center (Hebrew).

Klier, John Doyle and Shlomo Lambroza (eds.) 1992. *Pogroms: Anti-Jewish Violence in Modern Russian History*. Cambridge: Cambridge University Press.

Layish, Aharon. 2006. *Women and Islamic Law in a Non Muslim State: A Study Based on Sharia Courts in Israel*. New Brunswick: Transaction Publishers.

Lerner, Hanna. 2009. "Entrenching the Status Quo: Religion and State in Israel's Constitutional Proposals." *Constellations* 16: 3, 443–61.

2011. *Making Constitution in Deeply Divided Societies*. Cambridge: Cambridge University Press.

2014. "Critical Junctures, Religion and Personal Law Regulations in India and Israel." *Law and Social Inquiry* 39(2): 287–415.

Lifschitz, Shachar. 2006. "Spousal Registration – Preliminary Design." In A. Barak and D. Friedman (eds.), *Book In Memory of Prof. Shava*. Tel Aviv: Ramot-Tel Aviv University Press (Hebrew).

Liviatan, Ofrit. 2009. "Judicial Activism and Religion-Based Tensions: The Case of India and Israel," *Arizona Journal of International and Comparative Law* 26(3): 583–621.

Mautner, Menachem. 1993. "The Decline of Formalism and the Rise of Values in Israeli Law." *Iyunei Mishpat* 13 no. 3.

Meyer, Michael A. 1988. *Response to Modernity: A History of the Reform Movement in Judaism*. London: Oxford University Press.

Raday, Frances, Carmel Shalev, and Michal Liban-Kooby (eds.). 1995. *Women's Status in Israeli Society and Law*. Jerusalem: Shocken.

Rubinstein, Amnon. 1967. "Law and Religion in Israel." *Israel Law Review* 2, 384–399.

   1972. "Right to Marriage." *Israel Yearbook on Human Rights* 3, p. 250, n. 40.

Shakman Hurd, Elizabeth. 2008. "Books in Review: A Secular Age, by Charles Taylor." *Political Theory* 36: 3.

Salmon, Yosef and Carol Kutscher. 1988. "Yehiel Michael Pines: From the Vision of Zionism to the Reality." *Modern Judaism* 8(1): 65–82.

Samet, Moshe. 1988. "The Beginning of Jewish Orthodoxy." *Modern Judaism* 8(3): 249–270.

Scolnicov, Anat. 2006. "Religious Law, Religious Courts and Human Rights within Israeli Constitutional Structure." *International Journal of Constitutional Law* 4(4).

Sezgin, Yüksel. 2013. *Human Rights under State-Enforced Family Law in Israel, Egypt and India*. Cambridge: Cambridge University Press.

Shafir, Gershon and Yoav Peled. 2002. *Being Israeli: The Dynamics of Multiple Citizenship*. Cambridge: Cambridge University Press.

Shapira, Yonathan. 1996. *Politicians as a Hegemonic Class: The Case of Israel*. Tel Aviv: Sifriat Poalim (Hebrew).

Shiffman, Pinhas. 2001. *Civil or Sacred: Civil Marriage and Divorce Alternatives in Israel*. Jerusalem: The Association for Civil Rights in Israel.

Shimoni, Gideon. 1995. *The Zionist Ideology*. Brandeis University Press.

Smooha, Sammy. 1997. "Ethnic Democracy: Israel as an Archetype." *Israel Studies* 2:2.

Strum, Philippa. 1995. "The Road Not Taken: Constitutional Non-Decision Making in 1948–1950 and Its Impact on Civil Liberties in the Israeli Political Culture." In Ilan S. Troen and Noah Lucas (eds.), *Israel: The First Decade of Independence*. Albany: State University of New York Press, 83–104.

Swirski, Barbara and M. P. Safir. 1991. *Calling the Equality Bluff: Woman in Israel*. New York: Pergamon Press.

Triger, Tzvi. 2005. "Remembrance of Laws Past: Israel's Adoption of Religious Marriage and Divorce Law as a Means for Reviving the Jewish People's Lost Manliness." In Hannah Naveh and Orna Ben-Naftali (eds.), *Trials of Love*. Tel Aviv: Tel Aviv University Press (Hebrew).

Wood, Patricia J. 2008. *Judicial Power and National Politics: Courts and Gender in the Religious-Secular Conflict in Israel*. Albany: State University of New York Press.

Yovel, Y. 2007. "Introduction: Modernization and Secularization in the Jewish Culture." In Yirmiahu Yovel and David Shaham, *New Jewish Time: Jewish Culture in a Secular Age – An Encyclopedic View*. Jerusalem: Keter, Vol. 1, XV.

Yovel, Yirmiahu and David Shaham. 2007. *New Jewish Time: Jewish Culture in a Secular Age – An Encyclopedic View*. Jerusalem: Keter.

10

A Kemalist Secular Age? Cultural Politics
and Radical Republicanism in Turkey

Aslı Bâli

INTRODUCTION

In *A Secular Age*, Charles Taylor provides an alternative narrative of
secularity as it emerged in Western Christianity.[1] In response to the
extensive commentary engendered by the book, Taylor has acknowledged that his conception of the project "neglected the way in which
Western understandings of religion were informed through the precolo-
nial and then the colonial encounter with other parts of the world."[2] This
chapter considers one side of the mutually constitutive process alluded to
by this concession. Taylor's acknowledgment of the significance of non-
Western encounters is largely concerned with colonial relations. Turkey
is a particularly interesting case because it was *never colonized* and yet
the Ottoman Empire and later the Turkish Republic were thoroughly
marked by mutually constitutive encounters between the Middle East and
the West.[3]

The transplantation of Western conceptions of secularity outside of
the West is, in some ways, the obverse of the story Taylor traces.

Professor of Law, UCLA School of Law. I owe thanks to Murat Akan, Sujit Choudhry,
Kabita Datla, Bernard Haykel, Mirjam Künkler, Hanna Lerner, Karuna Mantena, Soli Özel,
Intisar Rabb, Joan W. Scott, Shylashri Shankar, and Seana Shiffrin; and participants at the
Workshop on Comparative Processes of Secularization at the Oñati Institute and the NYU
Law Constitutional Transitions Colloquium for their helpful comments on earlier drafts.
This draft was originally completed in 2014 with only minor subsequent edits to reflect later
developments.
[1] Taylor (2007).   [2] Taylor (2010), at 301.
[3] Nilüfer Göle has shown that anxieties about Islam are central to contemporary debates
about secularity in the West. Göle (2010), 243–264.

Perceptions of Western secularity and modernity helped shape the idiosyncratic social imaginaries, to use Taylor's term, of reformers in the late Ottoman and early republican periods.[4] The result was a partial assimilation of select aspects of the "Western" project,[5] producing, in turn, some of the antinomies that now characterize the attendant, institutionalized (and evolving) form of "secularism" – *laiklik* – in Turkey.[6] The analysis offered herein begins with the origins of the Republican project of secularization and proceeds through an examination of two critical cotemporary debates – on the use of headscarf[7] and on the scope and content of religious education[8] – that are central to battles over the character of secularism in Turkey's development as a "Westernized" Muslim-majority country.[9] Turkish reformers understood secularization as a necessary element of Westernization, yet the result was a secularization process that not only departs from, but in some ways reverses the processes Taylor describes in the West. Whereas for Taylor secularity is a means of accommodating pluralism, in the Turkish case it is an instrument of homogenization, as exemplified by the state's deployment of education and gender to fashion a new citizenry.[10] In what follows, I will employ Taylor's categories of Secularity I and Secularity III to illustrate the relationship between his

---

[4] For a discussion of late Ottoman reformers, see Hanioğlu (1997): 133–158. For a discussion of the beliefs underlying Kemalist reforms, see Mardin (1981).

[5] On the centrality of Westernization to the Turkish project of modernizing the state, see Berkes (1978); see also Ahmed (1993).

[6] The Turkish conception of secularism borrows heavily from Western models, though it has been indigenized and departs from any of the key models discussed by Taylor. *Laiklik*, the Turkish word for secularism, derives from the French word *laïcité*. While the Turkish model resembles the French disestablishmentarian and anti-clerical approach, the Turkish state involved itself in the production of official religious doctrine to an extent not seen in France. Turkish *laiklik* has even less in common with Anglo-American conceptions, as neither the strict separation of religion from the state nor the neutrality of the state with respect to religions is compatible with the Turkish state's emphasis on controlling religion on the one hand and the role of religion as a constitutive element of the ethno-national identity of modern "Turks" on the other.

[7] The centrality of struggles concerning the headscarf to debates about secularism transcend the Turkish context. See, for example, Mernissi (1987), Göle (1997b), Zuhur (1992), and Scott (2009).

[8] For a study of recent Turkish debates on religious education, see Pak (2004).

[9] For a discussion of the role of public education curricula in Westernization and secularization projects, see Dinç (2012).

[10] The approach I adopt here in viewing secularization as intrinsic to a homogenization project distinguishes this study of the Turkish constitutional headscarf cases from the earlier literature.

analysis and approaches to secularization embodied by Turkish state policy.[11]

The relationship between religious and state authority established at the founding of the republic complicates any expectation of a supposedly strict separation. Despite disestablishing clerical authority and adopting some Western precedents,[12] Turkey did not embrace institutional differentiation.[13] The Turkish case represents a challenge to the conventional wisdom that institutional differentiation (or Taylor's Secularity I) is a prevalent characteristic present in those states that assert their "secular" character. I will examine ways in which the Turkish Republic sought to achieve a form of secularization that, borrowing Taylor's terminology, was more focused on "altering the conditions of belief" for the underlying population (Secularity III) than on achieving institutional differentiation between the political and religious spheres.[14] Indeed, by retaining the late Ottoman bureaucratic structure of placing the regulation of religion under state supervision, the Turkish Republic ensured that religion would be subsumed under the state rather than separated from it. Yet, this was not so much in tension with Western secularity as a continuation of earlier reform efforts based on influential Western models of religious disestablishment through direct state intervention and later controls.[15]

---

[11] Taylor's typology of secularity set forth in *A Secular Age* includes three categories. I do not take up a discussion of Secularity II, decline in religiosity, as this dimension is largely absent in the Turkish case.

[12] Berkes (1978).

[13] The state regulates religion to such a degree that Diyanet is effectively the highest authority in Turkey on *sunni* Islam. Rather than institutional separation (Secularity I), the state simultaneously subsumed religion and sought to evacuate religious dogma from the public realm. These competing constitutional commitments – subsuming religious authority under the state *and* insisting on the non-religious character of the state – introduce an inherent tension in the Turkish conception of secularism that, viewed from outside, borders on incoherence.

[14] Altering the conditions of belief was an element of the secularization project driven by a commitment to positivist rationality, yet secularizing reforms were not designed to accommodate the possibility of unbelief (which is essential to Taylor's Secularity III). Rather, the goal was to induce a new understanding of religion that better suited the reformers concept of modernity.

[15] On the influence of Enlightenment ideas and Jacobin politics on Turkish reformist thinkers, see Bozdoğan (2001) (especially chapter 2), Kadıoğlu (1996), and Bozdoğan and Kasaba, eds. (1997) (see especially Kasaba, chapter 2, "Kemalist Certainties and Modern Ambiguities").

SECULARITY AND MODERNITY IN TURKISH REPUBLICAN HISTORY

The period of state-led modernization (with roots in late Ottoman reforms) set in motion the particular Turkish trajectory of secularity and the attendant reconstruction of the role of Islam and religious identity in the republic.[16] The Turkish state was heavily invested in controlling and managing Islam from the outset.[17] Instead of separating the political from the religious, the state subsumed religion and sought to alter its cultural significance as well as its substantive doctrine. This was accomplished by state-driven reforms in religious education and in the cultural manifestations of religious practice.

The republican secularization project pursued several at times conflicting objectives, none of which sought institutional separation between religion and the state. Rather, the state sought to bring religious institutions (and the endowments associated with them) under its control while producing a state-sanctioned Islam that would coexist with and even support the secularization process. The Turkish population was to identify with and share a homogenized and privatized sunni-Hanafi identity – with its mosques, religious endowments, clerics, and even weekly sermons prescribed by the state – as a source of national solidarity, but religion would be afforded no other place in the public, political life of the republic.

The transformative reforms undertaken by the republic at its founding produced an enduring cultural politics. Contemporary debates about the significance of the headscarf or the content of religious education can only be understood when situated in the context of earlier battles to define the relationship of religion and state. The next section historicizes the relationship between the categories of "Islam," "secular," and "modern" in Turkey in order to situate the current renegotiation of state–religion relations and its relationship to Taylor's typology of secularization.[18]

---

[16] This brief summary draws on extensive scholarship on this period, notably Hanioğlu (1993), Şerif Mardin (1992), and Hakan Yavuz (2007).

[17] For a detailed discussion of the reforms at the founding of the Republic in 1923 see Mardin (2006), chapter 12: 233–236.

[18] In invoking the terms "modernity," "Islam," and "secularity," I do not mean to suggest that they have singular meaning. The idea of "modernity" is highly contested. See, e.g., Eisenstadt, ed. (2002). The same is true of the plurality of traditions, institutions, beliefs, practices, cultures, and doctrines connoted by the term "Islam." See, e.g., al-Azmeh (1993). And, by the same token, competing conceptions of secularity attendant to these understandings of Islam, too, are plural. See, e.g., Jakobsen and Pellegrini, eds. (2008).

Islam and State-led Modernization

Turkish modernization fashioned self-consciously on the West is in some ways exceptional for not being colonial or postcolonial. Rather, it was a process initiated by the Ottoman Empire's elite that reached its apex under single-party rule during the modern republic's state formation period (1923–1938).[19] The Ottoman reforms had been concerned with centralizing and strengthening the state rather than liberalizing or democratizing the political order. The priority given to state institutions in the modernization effort was largely preserved in the transition from Ottoman to republican Turkey.[20] The most important change in the modernization strategy from the Ottoman to the republican period was the elimination of one set of actors from the governing military and bureaucratic elite: the *ulema*.[21] Notwithstanding the elimination of the religious intellectual elite and bureaucracy, however, the republic was also heir to the ambivalent and not necessarily hostile relationship of late Ottoman state authority to Islam.

The founding ideology – Kemalism – combined European enlightenment premises with a strong emphasis on scientistic rationalism and legacies of romantic nationalism.[22] The citizenry of the republic was expected to internalize its precepts as a new national ethos, displacing (if not replacing) an exclusively religious moral universe with a new public moral order organized around other commitments.[23] In describing the founding view of Kemalism, one scholar characterized it as being founded

---

[19] For a discussion of the late Ottoman conception of modernization through European models, see Deringil (1998).

[20] For a detailed discussion of this transition, see Zürcher (2004).

[21] On the significance of this change, see Bein (2011). Bein offers a history of *ulema* scholars' attempts in the late nineteenth and early twentieth centuries to engage with the new Westernizing concepts while resisting the most far-reaching reforms. In the end, the failure of the *ulema* intellectuals to prevent their own institutional abolition resulted from decisions to seek pragmatic engagement with the state by legitimizing secularist projects.

[22] The six principles of "Kemalism" – named after the founding statesman of the republic, Mustafa Kemal Atatürk – are nationalism, republicanism, statism, populism, revolutionarism, and secularism. For a detailed discussion of Kemalism, see Ahmed (1993). Despite these principles, Kemalism has remained a relatively indeterminate ideology. At a minimum, however, it is associated with a strong commitment to some conception of secularism, through what that means has varied over the decades.

[23] Education was designed "to be a 'school for national values' producing a citizenry of ethnic and civic 'Turks' through a chauvinistic form of Kemalist nationalism." Parla and Davison (2004), at 121, 248. Religion was also deployed to give ethnic content to this identity – ethnic Turks belonged to the Hanafi school of the Sunni denomination – though as a civic matter Turks were to be secular: Ergil (2013).

on two pillars: laicism and a unified national curriculum. These pillars, in turn, would ensure that "the people will be beholden to neither *shari'a* nor any ideology in making policy choices in their temporal affairs."[24] The national curriculum of unified public education would provide the public with a foundational training in humanism, rationalism, and the precepts of Kemalism that would enable them to constitute a republican citizenry competent to take deliberative decisions consistent with contemporary (read: Western) standards.

Following the dismemberment of the Ottoman Empire in part under pressure from minority nationalisms, the consolidation of the rump territory of the empire around a single national and cultural project was deemed central to state formation. Accordingly, the early republican state-building project centered on three intertwined projects: Turkification, secularization, and Westernization.[25] The production of a homogenous ethno-national identity to consolidate the loyalties of the population built into the concept of "Turkishness" a secularized *sunni* (Hanafi) identity.[26] Thus, state-building and its goal of modernization required first the production of a homogenous nation of *sunni* Turks to sustain the state and then the secularization of that identity to conform to the requirements of modernization.[27]

In a sense, the Turkish project required an intertwining of what Taylor treats as separate dimensions of secularity: institutional differentiation and the transformation of conditions of belief. The latter was to be accomplished top-down through state-driven reforms that were not designed to accommodate a diversity of moral commitments, but rather to alter the moral universe of the citizenry by redefining the mores of the public sphere. The former, institutional differentiation, was partially accomplished by insisting on the non-religious character of the state.[28]

---

[24] "Atatürk devrimlerinin iki temel taşı, Layisizm ve Eğitim Birliğidir. Millet bütün dünya işlerinde ne şeriat ne de herhangi bir ideolojinin baskısında olmayarak, yalnız günün şartları içinde kendisi için en yararlıyı düşünerek karar verir: Öz Atatürkçülük budur" Atay (2006).

[25] I have written about this elsewhere in some detail. See Bâli (2012).

[26] On the centrality of Sunni-Hanafi identity to the definition of "Turkishness" adopted by the state, see Ali Çarkoğlu and Barry Rubin, eds. (2006). The mobilization of Islamic identity served different purposes at different times, from fostering unity in the war of independence to recruiting religiously observant constituencies to support state policies in later republican periods.

[27] Modernization was conflated with the cultural markers of the West, and particularly of France. See Göle (1997a); see also Parla and Davison (2004), at 1–15.

[28] Here there is a differentiation between the religious and secular spheres, though they are both present in the institutions of the "secular" state, which engages in ferocious regulation of religion.

However, religion was also shaped by the state through its control of mosques, the clergy, and religious education. Indeed, the intertwining of disestablishmentarianism with the social engineering project of the state yielded a form of secularization that eschewed institutional differentiation between political and religious authority in order to produce a new moral temporal universe, hostile to diversity but committed to secularity.

In the early stages of state formation, the republican elite undertook the rapid disestablishment of religious authority, abolishing the caliphate, the office of Şeyh ül-Islam, and the shari'a courts, while outlawing religious orders.[29] The *ulema* were replaced with a much narrower civil service of prayer leaders and preachers under state control through the Directorate of Religious Affairs (or *Diyanet*).[30] The sheer scale and speed with which these reforms were undertaken – and the resulting transformation of the social landscape of the republic – sets this period apart as a critical juncture in the production of a Turkish secularization process.[31] Islam was removed from the constitutional order in 1928, and by 1937 the principle of secularism was incorporated by constitutional amendment. The secularizing reforms were complemented by other cultural measures, such as replacing the Arabic alphabet, purging Arabic and Persian vocabulary from the language, banning Islamic dress-codes, changing the calendar and public holidays, and replacing religious ritual in public life with a new set of secular civic rites associated with nationalist republicanism.[32] All of these measures were complemented by the abolition of religious education and the unification of all instruction under a single secular national curriculum through newly instated state-controlled public education.

The most visible signifier of Kemalist transformation was the role of women in the founding generation, who were to adopt "modern," Western dress-codes, uncover their hair, attain literacy and educational

---

[29] Ahmed (1993), Hakan Yavuz (2003), and Shankland (1999).

[30] On the creation and history of Diyanet, see Başbakanlık Diyanet Işleri Bakanlığı: https://diyanet.gov.tr/tr/kategori/kurulus-ve-tarihce/28.

[31] The idea of a critical juncture is borrowed from historical institutionalists who argue that the contingent emergence of a new space of opportunity may yield a set of political compromises or outcomes – a policy regime – that develops in a path dependent fashion. Understanding the events preceding the founding of the republic as a rupture that produced a critical juncture helps explain why the particular political settlement of the 1920s and 1930s produced a durable and institutionalized regime invoked by all subsequent debates on secularity in the Turkish context. This framing is informed by Philip S. Gorski's contribution to this volume (Chapter 2).

[32] On this cultural transformation, see Tapper, ed. (1991).

equality, and enter the workforce. This public makeover of Turkish women was the tip of the iceberg, with the more thorough-going transformation below the water line accomplished through educational reform. Public education accorded a "modern" role to religion in the new nation-state, a role that was privatized and secularized on what the reformers viewed as a European reformation model. Indeed, the instrumentalization and reconceptualization of religion as part of the state-building process was deemed a prerequisite for placing Turkey in the company of Western states. This goal, memorably defined as the need to attain the level of *çağdaş medeniyet* (contemporary civilization),[33] located the production of a new "Islam" at the center of the Turkish state's modernization process. The Ministry of Education worked in tandem with Diyanet to produce the curriculum necessary for a new Islam that would sustain the commitments of the founders.[34]

Given the founders' view that the demise of the Ottoman Empire was a consequence of its heterogeneity, their emphasis on homogenizing the population and organizing it around a universalized conception of national identity subsuming religious identity is not surprising. Yet, the internal contradictions of a secularizing project emphasizing the production of an official "private" version of religious identity is in clear tension with Taylor's account of secularity. If Taylor understands the emergence of secularity as a necessary democratic response to diversity, the Turkish case is an example of state elites harnessing secularity to very different ends. Indeed, in the Turkish case secularity serves as an instrument of the republican drive for homogenization to tame rather than accommodate diversity.

The state's twin projects of homogenization and secularization intersected in educational reforms. Reforms to education began first with the "scientific *medrese* code" adopted by the Turkish Grand National Assembly in May 1921, which was offered until 1924, when all *medreses* were closed and the new Law of Educational Unification was adopted.[35]

---

[33] For a discussion of this concept (in Turkish), see *Atatürkcü Düşünce* (1992).

[34] In describing the goals of the reformers, one author notes that "the primary task for the Kemalists was to convince the people to believe in the merits of a secular society through a new system of national education" Pak (2004).

[35] On the Law of Unification and subsequent education reforms, see Süleyman Bozdemir "Atatürk Döneminde Eğitimdeki Gelişmeler," [Developments in Education during Ataturk's Period], Çukurova University Working Paper Series 2009, http://turkoloji.c u.edu.tr/ATATURK/arastirmalar/suleyman_bozdemir_ataturk_donemi_egitim_gelis meler.pdf.

The Law of Unification placed all educational institutions under the authority of the Ministry of Education, abolishing both public religious education and training offered by private religious orders in favor of a single curriculum of centralized education. Diyanet was established and tasked with producing an official interpretation of an "enlightened" Islam, in contrast to the alleged reactionary orthodoxy of Ottoman Islam.[36] This new Islam would provide the content for limited, state-sanctioned religious training. The imams of the nation remained a body of civil servants trained in state schools before serving in state-controlled mosques. Religious curricula were limited to the university level, and a new set of Imam-Hatip (prayer leader-preacher) schools were tasked with offering a four-year tertiary education at twenty-nine locations in the country.[37] During this same period, beginning in 1927, courses on religion were removed from the primary and secondary school unified national curriculum.[38]

If the production of a new state-sanctioned "modern" *sunni-Hanafi* Islam was a central plank of the founding vanguards' project to forge a new nation, its most visible symbol was the abolition of a gender-segregated public sphere. The construction and display of new gender identities were important instruments for forging the image of the republic. New fashions for women, a new role for them in public life, and employment were all rapidly introduced and immediately publicized, yielding a form of top-down state feminism as another facet of modernization.[39] The symbolic significance, for instance, of the many mixed gender state functions – galas and ballroom dances – with women dressed in the latest European fashions photographed surrounding Atatürk was not lost on the state elites.[40] The liberation of the modern republican woman from the stranglehold of tradition, culture, and religion and the embrace of the state's modernist project was nowhere better exemplified than in women's public unveiled presence on the streets of Turkey's Western cities.

The twin pedagogical projects of curricular reform and the transformation of gendered public spheres were expected to produce a secularized

---

[36] The collection of public speeches given by Atatürk in this period has numerous examples of references to the "true," "enlightened," and "rationalist" Islam in contrast to retrograde orthodoxies of earlier periods. See generally *Atatürk'ün Söylev ve Demeçleri* (1989).

[37] For a history of the development and evolution of Imam-Hatip Schools, see Çakmak 2009: 825–846.

[38] For a discussion of the removal of religion courses from the national curriculum, see Tank (2005), Ayhan (1999), and Berkez (1964).

[39] White (2003).   [40] Özyürek (2006) (see especially ch. 3).

population for the secularizing state. The early period of republican state-building reforms was presided over by the single-party authoritarian rule of the Republican People's Party (CHP). The CHP was comprised of political cadres drawn from the traditional elites of Istanbul and Ankara, a socially cohesive group that shared a clear ideological commitment. With the end of the CHP's single-party rule following World War II, a center-right political party, the DP, emerged claiming to represent the Anatolian periphery against the long-governing secular bureaucratic intelligentsia of the Western cities.[41] The DP came to power in 1950 and remained in power until a military coup in 1960. Though it shared a commitment to the basic Kemalist model of modernization through secularization, the DP was adept at employing religious discourse and the language of traditional culture to distinguish itself from the republican state elite.

When the DP was ousted, the coup leaders believed that changes to the political order were necessary to stave off the dangers they associated with the excesses of the party. The antidote to the danger of populist authoritarianism was the introduction of limited forms of political liberalization, particularly through a new constitution. This new constitution eventually witnessed the formation in 1969 of the first pro-Islamic political party of the republic, the National Order Party.[42] The creation of a political framework that might accommodate a religiously oriented party was in part a function of the employment of religion by the military elite. For instance, the emphasis placed by the military regime of 1960–1961 on the consistency between modernization and enlightened Islam led to a period during the 1960s in which the state rapidly expanded religious training programs to produce "enlightened" men of religion.[43] The disfavored Imam-Hatip schools of the earlier period flourished and grew to be a parallel vocational educational system that fully bifurcated secondary education in Turkey. Later, as left-right polarization took hold of Turkey in the 1970s, Islam was

---

[41] On the rise of the DP and its efforts to distinguish itself from the CHP, see Yavuz (2003).

[42] The NOP (or *Milli Nizam Partisi*) was dissolved following the 1971 military intervention. It was reformed as the National Salvation Party (or *Milli Selamet Partisi*) in 1972, and was a partner in three coalition governments in the 1970s. The NSP was dissolved together with all other political parties following the 1980 military coup. It was reconstituted as the Welfare Party (*Refah*) in 1981. After the closure of Refah by the Turkish Constitutional Court (TCC) in 1998, it regrouped as the Virtue Party (*Fazilet*). When Fazilet, too, was closed by the TCC, the movement splintered and formed two separate parties: the conservative Felicity (*Saadet*) Party and the reformist Adalet ve Kalkınma (Justice and Development) Party, which is currently the governing party in Turkey, known by its acronym as the AKP.

[43] Yavuz (2003).

once again seen as instrumentally useful to military elites as a central plank in the anticommunist platform of the state.

The growing importance of anticommunism to state elites and center-right actors in Turkey led to a marked increase in the political salience of Islam to the state in the 1970s.[44] The channeling of discontent through religious platforms, encouraged by the state, in turn, contributed to the conditions of possibility for the later formation of numerous political parties with Islamist leanings, notably the Welfare Party (*Refah*) following the 1980 military coup. The role assigned to Islam in countering political fragmentation was substantially enhanced, but the contradiction in the deployment of religion by the secular state as a unifying and stabilizing force in Turkish society soon gave way to political crisis.

Islam and State-led Liberalization

If the state-led modernization period involved the production of a new "enlightened" Islam manifest in the unified national curriculum and the "emancipation" of women from gender segregation and headscarves, the state-led liberalization period was marked by tolerance for more populist forms of religiosity. This tolerance was partly a result of the displacement of traditional state elites by a bureaucracy increasingly drawn from the Anatolian hinterlands, but is more readily explained as part of a state legitimation strategy following the military coup of 1980. The post-1980 military-regime period and the subsequent years of civilian rule under ANAP (*Anavatan Partisi*, or Motherland Party) from 1983 to 1991 ushered in a period of adaptation and integration in state policies toward Islam. Among the notable changes in this period were the relaxing of repressive state policies toward heterodox Islam (especially *Sufi* orders and the Alevi community), the imposition of mandatory religious instruction in the national curriculum under the 1982 Constitution, and the permissive environment created for unofficial and private religious educational networks and private sector Islamist enterprise.[45] While social forces and private actors had a role in these developments, the flourishing of a new

---

[44] Ibid.
[45] For a discussion of the permissive environment for religion following the 1980 military coup, see Mardin (2006).

Islamist sector was also a consequence of changes in the policies of the Turkish state.[46]

Chief among the changes of the 1980s was a decision by the military leadership of the coup period to introduce a form of state-led Islamization from above.[47] The term Turkish-Islamic Synthesis (*Türk-Islam Sentezi*) was borrowed from an intellectual nationalist movement – Aydınlar Ocağı – as the ideal vehicle for the state's new orientation toward Islam. Synthesizing conservative elements of Turkish nationalism with Islam, a new state-led religious approach to education was developed in the hopes of countering the processes of social and political fragmentation that preceded the polarization and political violence of the 1970s. The state's growing investment in more aggressively disseminating its own brand of *laik* Islam through mandated religion courses in public education set the stage for a new terrain of cultural contestation. While in clear tension with any conception of secularity-as-institutional-differentiation (Secularity I), this project was continuous with the earliest state efforts at transforming conditions of belief to suit their broader policy objectives.[48]

By turning to a homogenizing and nationalist model of Islam, the military elites felt they might popularize a "moderate" form of Islam to contain the influence of non-Turkish Islamist modes of thinking following the Iranian revolution and the resurgence of political Islam in the Arab world. Further, the relaxation of repressive secularism offered the possibility of a new moral (religious) underpinning for the market-oriented social order they were then introducing under international pressure. In this vein, the military-regime-era president, Kenan Evren, harnessed the language of Islam to defend the massive economic restructuring program the government had undertaken.[49] As economic reforms took hold, newly emergent middle classes in Turkey's heretofore neglected periphery began

---

[46] The rise of a conservative middle class in Turkey after 1980 coincided with the emergence of Islamist movements across the Middle East. In the Turkish case, religious resurgence was mediated through the formative (and counterintuitive) role played by state institutions in the reinvigoration of Islamist politics in post-1980 Turkey.

[47] For the most thorough discussion (in Turkish) of this development, see Copeaux (1998).

[48] Taylor's Secularity III views secularity as a transformation of conditions of belief to accommodate the possibility of unbelief. While the Turkish conception of secularity is invested in transforming the conditions of belief, it is in the service of producing a modern and privatized religious identity rather than tolerating unbelief. In this sense, Taylor's category enables us to see the stark contrast between the Western trajectory and Turkish secularization processes.

[49] Copeaux (1998). For a critical history of the economic liberalization policies, see Odekon (2005).

to assert their own claims on the state – from within by joining and advancing through the civil service, and from outside as a provincial private sector articulating its own demands.[50] With the earlier emphasis on top-down state-planning restrictions on the private sector lifted, the Anatolian provinces, which saw little investment under state-planning, became the locus of the small to mid-size private enterprise that now flourished.[51] The impact of economic liberalization was the emergence of newly empowered religious populations moving from the periphery to the center of the country's seat of power.

These emerging actors asserted both economic and cultural influence. As a consequence, a new form of cultural politics developed in Turkey's Western cities, with large populations challenging the givens of the earlier cultural revolution in education and gender norms. The reopening of the debates of the founding over the proper relationship between the state and religion that ensued was wrenching. Religious populations demanded a voice in state policy going forward and began searching for a political platform that reflected their interests and cultural values. Subtle shifts occurred under the technocratic government appointed by the coup leaders, with Turgut Özal as prime minister, which laid the groundwork for the introduction of religious claims in the public sphere. With the pre-1980 political elite excluded from civilian governance until 1987, a lower echelon of civil service cadres now competed for elected office and transformed the cultural identity of the Turkish parliament. These new politicians drawn from the emerging bourgeoisie of Anatolia were more religious in their private lives, traditional in their cultural tastes, and conservative in their political preferences than the social echelons from which MPs had traditionally been drawn. When political restrictions were lifted in 1987, Necmettin Erbakan, the leader of an Islamist-oriented political movement, re-entered politics, formed the new Refah party, and quickly drew support and electoral success.[52]

---

[50] Cizre-Sakallıoğlu (2000): 481–508.
[51] For a discussion of the emergence of this Anatolian bourgeoisie and its association with a new pro-market, pro-Islam sector, see "Islamic Calvinists: Change and Conservatism in Central Anatolia" (European Stabilization Initiative, 2005), www.esiweb.org/pdf/esi_do cument_id_69.pdf.
[52] Erbakan led the National Outlook (*Milli Görüş*) movement. For a discussion of Erbakan's role in the rise and demise of the Refah party, see Yavuz (2003) (especially chapters 9 and 10). Refah's greatest electoral success was in the 1995 general elections, where they gained the largest share of seats in parliament: 158 of 550. Turkish Parliament Archives, "1995 Yılı Genel Seçimlerinde Partilerin Aldıkları Oylar ve Oranları" (1995

Unfortunately for Erbakan, military elites proved willing to go to extraordinary lengths to maintain the equilibrium in state–religion relations put in place after the coup. The rise of Refah and its efforts to bring a religiously inflected political platform into government resulted in a military call to order, a stark reminder that Kemalist elites still set the boundaries of permissible political action. Refah's proximate mistake was a bid to introduce a bill in parliament to lift a de facto headscarf ban at universities.[53] The result was significant military pressure on the coalition civilian government led by Refah, which eventually collapsed in June 1997.[54] The unseating of Refah was followed by the eventual closure of the ousted party by the Turkish Constitutional Court in 1998 for violating the constitutional precept of secularism. Among the core issues cited by the military in its confrontational stance toward Refah was the increasing visibility of headscarved women in the country's Western cities and especially on urban university campuses.[55]

NEGOTIATING LAIKLIK IN MODERN TURKEY

The origins of current controversies over defining the *laik* state lie, unsurprisingly, in the recourse made by the state to Islam in its production of Turkey's local variant of secularity. As at the founding, the exclusion of religion from the public, political sphere was combined with the selective accommodation and incorporation of religion whenever state elites deemed it expedient after the 1980 military coup. The flourishing of official Imam-Hatip schools that offered a public curriculum of religious training, a newfound tolerance for private Quranic schools, and a host of other policies suggested a new era of public tolerance for religious expression after 1980. As more religious and conservative sectors of the country benefited from policies of economic liberalization, religiously observant men and women began to appear more frequently in the commercial centers, university campuses, and public spaces of the provincial cities and even the western cities of the country. While the increased presence of religiously observant

General Election Party Votes and Vote Shares), www.tbmm.gov.tr/develop/owa/secim ler.secimdeki_partiler?p_secim_yili=1995.

[53] On the attempted headscarf bill of 1996, see Kavakçı (2010), at 64–71.

[54] These events were famously dubbed a "post-modern coup" Çandar (1997).

[55] There were also political and economic dimensions to the conflict between Refah and the military. For instance, Erbakan sought (unsuccessfully) to relax controls on fundraising for Islamic endowments and to make civil service positions more open to religious constituencies. On this broader context, see Gülalp (1999).

men might go unmarked, the increased visibility of headscarved women in the country's urban centers became a source of intensifying friction.

Tensions over the public expression of religion gave rise to new debates on the prerequisites for the production of secular citizens through public education. Following the 1997 intervention against Refah, the military issued eighteen recommendations that it required the civilian government to adopt.[56] These included the shuttering of private religious courses and the expansion of the unified national curriculum from a duration of 5 to 8 years, effectively abolishing Imam-Hatip middle schools and restricting the introduction of vocational religious training to the high school level. The perceived relationship between religious secondary school training and an increase in headscarved women on university campuses also led the state to introduce new policies designed to limit access to universities for Imam-Hatip graduates. The demographic shifts and political struggles that led to the re-emergence of debates over the symbolic role of women and the nature of state-controlled religious education spilled into legal debates about the constitution of the republic and the relationship between state and religion. In the following sections, I consider first the headscarf debates of the post-coup era, and then the ongoing debates over the structure and role of Imam-Hatip schools and religious education more generally.

The Headscarf Debates

The place where the presence of headscarved women was most galling to Kemalist state elites was university campuses.[57] The idea that educated women would resist the secularizing pressures of the Turkish state's pedagogy was a particular affront. In one of its rulings on the question of headscarves on university campuses, the Council of State (*Danıştay*) made this objection explicit:

[G]irls with insufficient education were wearing headscarves under the influence of the environment and traditions without having any particular thought in mind. However, the girls who have sufficient education not to surrender to the public pressure and traditions are known to cover their heads while opposing the secular republican principles ... For these people, the headscarf, beyond an innocent

---

[56] Hakan Yavuz (2000), especially 37–42.
[57] For the definitive introduction to the headscarf debates in Turkey, see Elver (2012). The similarity to the French debates on schoolgirls wearing headscarves is striking: Scott (2009).

habit, is a symbol of a world ideology that is antithetical to women's liberation and our republic's main principles.[58]

The clear message of the *Danıştay* decision was that women who would wear headscarves on university campuses were doing so with the deliberate intention of undermining the republican principle of secularism and not as an "innocent" expression of religious identity based on their traditionalism or lack of education. Whereas headscarved women in provincial and rural areas of Turkey might represent a form of benign traditionalism, women who chose to wear headscarves despite being educated and exposed to urban Kemalist culture represented a malign threat to the redemptive mission of the state. The appearance of headscarved women in large numbers at universities challenged the Kemalist premise that education would ineluctably sustain the secularization of the public sphere central to the state's preferred model of modernization.

Beginning with the transition from military rule to civilian government in 1983, the headscarf controversy produced two camps. The newly elected ANAP government under prime minister Özal sought to lift a ban on headscarves in universities, but state elites resisted. In 1984, the Higher Education Council (known by its Turkish acronym, YÖK) modified its headscarf ban, under pressure from ANAP, allowing certain forms of "modern" headscarves (which covered the hair but not the neck and shoulders) to be worn on campuses.[59] Still, throughout the 1980s university administrators took it upon themselves at regular intervals to bar girls in headscarves from entering their campuses, supported by a series of rulings by the *Danıştay* in defense of such bans. The perverse effect of these policies was to bar women from attending university in the name of the state's mission to "liberate" women from the strictures of religion. In light of the absence of any injunction against the attire or personal appearance of religiously observant men, the irony of these policies was redoubled. Yet, the banning of headscarved women from campuses had no clear legal grounding apart from decrees issued by YÖK. As a result, ANAP, the majority party in parliament, tried to create a legal basis to block the

---

[58] Council of State Decision No. 1984/330 (*Danıştay kararı*, E. 1983/207, K. 1984/330). Translation available in Kavakçı (2010) at 55–56, n. 72.

[59] The irony of re-describing what had previously been deemed the *traditional* Anatolian headscarf of the 1920s as more "modern" is striking. Because this headscarf is worn loosely and may partially reveal hair it is deemed more compatible with modern Turkey than a stricter headscarf. Thus, the more recent practice of stricter covering (sometimes referred to as *türban*) that emerged among religious Turks who moved to the country's urban centers due to economic dislocation is treated not as "modern" but as retrograde.

headscarf ban by passing Law No. 3511 in 1988 to allow female university students to enter university dressed in accordance with their religious convictions.[60] The Turkish Constitutional Court (TCC) found the law unconstitutional within a year.

In its reasoning, the Court defended a version of secularism that required *exclusion* of religious expression from the public sphere, noting the centrality of secularization to the state's core identity and projects. According to the Court, secularism:

> sped up the [Turkish] march toward civilization. In fact, secularism cannot be narrowed down to the separation of religion and state affairs. It is a milieu of civilization, freedom and modernity, whose dimensions are broader and whose scope is larger. It is Turkey's philosophy of modernization, its method of living humanly. It is the ideal of humanity … The dominant and effective power in the state is reason and science, not religious rules and injunctions.[61]

Thus, secularity is defined by the Court as a set of substantive commitments rather than mere separation of religion from the state. The pedagogical role of the state is to produce a civilized citizenry committed to a public ideology of modernization. This project did require a differentiated moral universe, one that involved, at a minimum, distinct public and private moral commitments of its citizens. Yet it bears repeating that this transformation in conditions of belief does not accommodate diversity, but rather imposes a state-driven homogenization, requiring public fealty to the univocal ideology of the state while simultaneously conferring a state-defined private religious identity.[62]

---

[60] The bill was vetoed by the former head of the military junta, Kenan Evren, now serving as the civilian president. The popular and parliamentary outrage expressed over President Evren's veto led him to claim that he opposed the wording of the bill rather than the lifting of the ban. A revised bill was then passed by parliament and sent to President Evren for a second time. Though he signed the second bill into law, he immediately brought a challenge to the law before the TCC.

[61] TCC decision, E. 1989/1, K. 1989/12, March 7, 1989, *AMKD* (Constitutional Court Reports), No. 25, 133–65. Translation available in Özbudun and Gençkaya (2009) at 147.

[62] In this sense, while the state surely understood the process of secularization as one that altered the conditions of belief for the underlying population, the project in no way corresponds to Taylor's meaning of Secularity III. The Kemalist project was far less concerned with accommodating pluralism in moral and religious belief than it was with transforming the social role of religion. Though Kemalism is often viewed as "atheistic" by religiously observant Muslims – and many early republican theorists are rumored to have been atheists – the secularization project of the state sought to instrumentalize religion rather than to undermine religious belief or accommodate unbelief.

The Court's reasoning did not bring to a close the headscarf debate, but it was a watershed moment in the constitutional debate. Numerous subsequent efforts to lift the headscarf ban through legislative and constitutional reform foundered.[63] Despite enormous societal pressure to lift the ban – with some surveys reporting that over 60 percent of all Turkish women wear some version of head covering, and consistent surveys showing that over 70 percent of Turks supported lifting the ban at universities – the issue was abandoned for a decade after Refah's fall.[64]

The AKP was formed in 2002 as the most recent iteration of successor parties to Refah. Competing almost immediately after its formation in the general elections of 2002, the AKP garnered the plurality of the vote and formed a government under the eventual premiership of Recep Tayyip Erdoğan, the former mayor of Istanbul.[65] The party did not tackle the issue of the headscarf in its first term, but after returning to power with a larger share of parliamentary seats following a general election in 2007, the party addressed the issue headlong with an attempted constitutional amendment.[66] Though the proposed amendments garnered enough votes to win parliamentary passage through the ordinary mechanisms for the amending of the Turkish constitution, the opposition CHP brought a constitutional challenge. The CHP alleged that the amendments violated the unamendable constitutional precept of secularism. In a separate case before the TCC, the state prosecutor initiated proceedings for the closure of the AKP on the grounds that it served as a focal point for anti-secular activities by virtue of proposing the amendments. In the end, in a controversial decision the TCC annulled the amendments based on their alleged incompatibility with secularism. While the party narrowly escaped constitutional closure, the Court also censured the AKP and issued a clear warning that further activity in this vein would likely result in closure. The AKP, fresh from winning the largest share of the vote in a general election and holding both the premiership and

---

[63] See Kavakçı (2010) at 59; Özbudun and Gençkaya (2009), at 106–109.

[64] For reports on such survey data, see for example, Öğret (2010), Çarkoğlu and Toprak (2006).

[65] On the AKP's formation and rise to power – as well as Erdoğan's struggle to serve as premier despite a law excluding him from public office following an earlier imprisonment for allegedly anti-secular activities – see Hakan Yavuz (2009); see also Hale and Özbudun (2010).

[66] The AKP called early elections in 2007 as a referendum on its policies following a confrontation with the military over the party's efforts to select Abdullah Gül, a prominent member of the AKP, as president. Ömer Taşpınar, "The Old Turk's Revolt: When Radical Secularism Endangers Democracy," *Foreign Affairs* (November/December 2007).

the presidency of the republic, was not immune to threats of constitutional closure for contesting the cultural politics of secularity.[67] Years later, once the AKP consolidated its control of critical state institutions, including YÖK and the higher appellate courts, the headscarf ban was eventually lifted with a whimper in late 2010 through a change in regulatory interpretation of rules governing campuses rather than legislative or constitutional reform. Two years after that, a "democratization package" of legislative reforms also witnessed the lifting of the ban on headscarves in government buildings and for civil servants.[68]

The long battle for inclusion ended through the AKP's electoral victories and correlated demographic changes in the civil service that makes up the state. Yet, to the elite accustomed to governing Turkey, the headscarf continues to symbolize the intolerable threat of backsliding on the redemptive mission to secularize and modernize the nation.[69] Moreover, the increased presence of headscarved women on university campuses is also related to anxieties about the formal pedagogy of the state as the increasing availability of officially sanctioned secondary schools offering religious training is identified as a mechanism for promoting public forms of religiosity. Accordingly, the proliferation of headscarves on university campuses has been accompanied by renewed contestation over the secularizing pedagogical role of the state in the realm of vocational religious training.

Religious Education Debates and the Imam-Hatip Schools

The founding of the republic witnessed the near abolition of all forms of religious education. By the 1940s, a serious shortage in religiously trained personnel and the introduction of multi-party elections ushered in a softening of the policies restricting religious education. Over the years from the 1950s to 1980s the definition of secondary education would expand and contract, with Imam-Hatip schools sometimes offering education beginning from the sixth grade and at other times being restricted to only the final four years of high school education. Meanwhile, from the

---

[67] For a detailed discussion of the constitutional battle and an analysis of the Court's reasoning, see Bâli (2012).

[68] On the lifting of the headscarf ban on campuses, see Head (2010). On the legislative reforms that ended the headscarf ban in government buildings, see Arsu and Bilefsky (2013).

[69] The Social Science Research Council's blog on secularism had notable contributions to the debate in 2008. See, e.g., Kadıoğlu (2008), Göle (2008), and Benhabib (2008).

1950s to the 1970s elective religion courses expanded in the public education curriculum, migrating from primary school to being offered in every grade beginning in the fourth year of primary school and continuing through the end of secondary school.[70]

The 1980 military coup added momentum to the expansion of religious training. The coup-era government oversaw the opening of thirty-five additional Imam-Hatip schools from 1980 to 1983, and these schools were now operating from middle school forward. Further, the 1982 constitution specified that religion courses offered in the fourth and fifth years of primary school would be compulsory, together with an additional mandatory two hours of religious curriculum each week in middle school and one hour each week in high school.[71] The military was convinced, as the founding era statesmen had been, that religion would enable them to fashion a more docile and unified citizenry, in this case healing the political cleavages that had produced clashes between the right-wing and left-wing parties throughout the 1970s.

Return to civilian government under Özal ushered in a further expansion of the Imam-Hatip educational sector, with 90 new schools opened between 1984 and 1989. The subsequent decade of coalition governments witnessed ebbs and flows in the religious educational sector, but by the time of the soft military coup of February 28, 1997, the number of Imam-Hatip schools had ballooned to 600 schools, with more than 200,000 students.[72]

Education reform proved to be an important goal of the military's next intervention in civilian politics in 1997. As with the headscarf controversy, the military viewed the Imam-Hatip schools as a cultural battleground for vouchsafing the achievements of Kemalism. The eighteen measures imposed by the military intervention of 1997 occasioned a restructuring of the religious educational sector. First, the expansion of the unified continuous national curriculum through the eighth grade forced Imam-Hatip middle schools to close and restricted vocational religious instruction to four-year

---

[70] On the introduction and expansion of elective religion courses under the unified national curriculum, see Simsek and Yildirim (2004), chapter 7.

[71] The 1982 military-coup-era constitution, still in effect in Turkey as of 2013, imposed mandatory religion courses through Article 24, which provides that "instruction in religious culture and moral education shall be compulsory in the curricula of primary and secondary schools." On the post-coup introduction of compulsory religion courses, see Kaplan (2006).

[72] The numbers of Imam-Hatip schools and students in 1997 are provided in Pak (2004), at 334.

secondary school training. Second, a new coefficient was assigned to vocational school graduates when they took the national university entrance examination, leaving them at a systematic disadvantage compared to graduates of ordinary secondary schools. Finally, Imam-Hatip school graduates were also excluded for the first time from employment in several state bodies, including the police force and the military.[73] The result of the combined measures was an immediate decline in Imam-Hatip enrollments, driving the number of Imam-Hatip students down from 200,000 in 1997 to 64,000 by 2002.[74] The coefficient rule led to occasional stories of successful students being forced to travel abroad for university education, reinforcing the message that Imam-Hatip students' access to Turkish university education was restricted.[75] The 1997 restructuring created three enduring debates: the exam coefficient for vocational school graduates, the number of years of training that the schools might offer, and the content of the mandatory religious curriculum in the non-vocational schools. Each of these issues has resurfaced as a source of controversy as the AKP sought to relax rules governing religious training while continuing to exclude heterodox Islam from the content of the religious curriculum.

Since the AKP first came into office, it has engaged in a process of reforming the state from within, particularly on the question of the regulation of religion. Much like earlier state elites, the AKP has deployed education as a means of shaping the Turkish citizenry and redefining the Turkish variants of Secularity I and Secularity III, this time to better reflect the preferences of religious constituencies. This has been accomplished in part through the appointment of new civil servants to the lower cadres of the state bureaucracy drawn from a broader swathe of Turkish society than has previously been the case.[76] By virtue of holding office and presiding over a period of relative political stability in Turkey (from 2002 to 2013), the AKP put in place a sympathetic cadre of civil servants that subtly shifted the

---

[73] Bacık and Aras (2002), at 392.   [74] Ibid.

[75] "OSS dorduncusu imam hatip'ten," *Genç Dergisi*, July 1, 2007, http://gencdergisi.com/5092-oss-dorduncusu-imam-hatipten.html.

[76] The civil service has become friendlier to Imam-Hatip graduates and more hostile to restrictions placed on their access to higher education under the AKP. Even the composition of the Board of Education, long a bastion of Kemalist control over the national curriculum, has shifted in the direction of including Imam-Hatip graduates. See, e.g., "YÖK'e imam hatipli üye" [An Imam-Hatip Graduate Joins YOK], *Radikal*, March 2, 2009, www.radikal.com.tr/turkiye/yoke_imam_hatipli_uye-924127.

positions adopted by key state institutions. For instance, the identity of the bureaucratic cadres in Diyanet witnessed substantial turnover in this period.[77] As a result, the Ministry of Education, YÖK, and Diyanet have become the terrain for pitched battles between AKP constituencies and those that oppose the AKP on Kemalist or secularist grounds.[78]

In an oft-cited speech, Prime Minister Erdoğan articulated his government's goal of producing a generation of "religious youth" through the introduction of educational reforms.[79] Those comments, together with the content of the proposed reforms – with the effect of expanding optional religious training to eight years and strengthening religious offerings at non-religious public schools – gave rise to new fears of Islamization of the state. Countervailing liberalizing initiatives – such as reforms to the mandatory religious curriculum to include information about heterodox Muslim sects, like the minority Alevi community's beliefs and practices[80] – have been eclipsed by the controversy over the expansion of religious vocational training.

The AKP initiative that met with the greatest resistance in the area of religious education was the indirect expansion of Imam-Hatip education. The military-imposed education reform measures of 1997 had introduced a requirement of an eight-year unified and continuous national education, abolishing vocational middle schools and limiting religious training to

---

[77] Fatma Tütüncü documents the introduction of female preachers wearing headscarves as civil servants in Diyanet by the AKP since 2004. She also discusses a variety of other changes at Diyanet under AKP leadership. See Tütüncü (2010).

[78] The battles over the Turkish state's relationship to religious education since the 1970s reflect what Gorski has termed a functional conflict between the religious and political fields, based on his reading of Bourdieu and Luhmann.

[79] Fulya Ozerkan, "Turkey PM Recep Tayyip Erdogan sparks furor by saying he wants to 'raise a religious youth,'" *Reuters*, February 9, 2009. http://news.nationalpost.com/2012/02/09/turkey-pm-recep-tayyip-erdogan-sparks-furor-by-saying-he-wants-to-raise-a-religious-youth/

[80] Alevi families sued multiple Turkish governments in domestic courts and before the European Court of Human Rights for requiring their children to attend mandatory religion courses depicting *sunni-Hanafi* orthodoxy as the only legitimate form of Islam. Following the European Court's decision in *Hasan/Eylem Zengin* v. *Turkey*, Turkish courts agreed to exempt Alevi students from religion courses unless the curriculum was reformed. Under new reforms in the 2011–2012 academic year, 130 pages on Alevism, Shi'ism, and Sufism were added to the textbooks used for the compulsory religion courses. See Tosun (2011) and Yıldırım (2011). Diyanet, which had not recognized non-Sunni communities like the Alevi, issued a "clarification" in July 2012 that it embraced all Islamic beliefs, though Alevi house of worship – the *cemevi* – continued to be denied the state-funding afforded to mosques. "Diyanet'ten Alevilik Açıklaması," *Haber Türk*, July 31, 2012 [Diyanet offers clarification on Alevis].

high school. Under the AKP's "4+4+4" education reform bill, introduced in February 2012, the unified continuous national education was reduced to four years of primary education while the number of compulsory years of education were increased from eight to twelve. While the initiative was defended by the government as a mechanism for keeping students in education through the end of secondary school – to improve their mathematical competence and achievement on aptitude tests – it was widely understood as a mechanism to allow children to pursue intensive religious education at a younger age.[81] Immediately preceding this initiative, the government had succeeded in getting YÖK to equalize the university examination coefficient attached to all secondary school graduates, whether secular or vocational-religious.[82] The combination of these two initiatives removed the principal 1997 restrictions on Imam-Hatip education.[83]

Public concerns about this new educational initiative centered on two issues. The first was the fear that the Imam-Hatip sector would expand dramatically and even eclipse secular public education in middle and high school due to private contributions that gave such schools an enhanced budget.[84] A second set of concerns related to the implementation of expanded compulsory education in a resource-scarce environment. Due to the scarcity of places available in existing public secondary schools, families faced with compulsory education requirements were given the option of correspondence schools. Many worried that under the pretext of expanding compulsory education through twelve years, the government was actually encouraging traditional families to take their daughters out of school after four years of primary education by opting for correspondence education from home. The Ministry of

---

[81] See, e.g., Finkel (2012); and "4+4+4 ve dindar nesil eleştirisi," *CNN Türk*, October 17, 2012 ("4+4+4 and the religious generation critique"), www.cnnturk.com/video/guncel/2012/10/17/4.4.4.ve.dindar.nesil.elestirisi/49652.643590/index.html.

[82] Such an initiative had previously been attempted and veoted by then-president Ahmet Sezer in 2004. Sezer then argued that to equalize the coefficient would be to encourage an increase in the ranks of Imam-doctors, Imam-policemen, and Imam-lawyers, and that those who wished to pursue secular professions in higher education should not opt for vocational religious-training in secondary school. "Sezer YÖK yasasını veto etti," *Hürriyet*, May 28, 2004 ("Sezer vetos YÖK bill").

[83] Indeed, by expanding secondary education from 7 to 8 years (with the reduction of primary education from 5 to 4 years), the 4+4+4 initiative expands the Imam-Hatip curriculum beyond all precedents.

[84] The private funding of Imam-Hatip schools by religious foundations has been a significant source of controversy. See, e.g., Cameron-Moore (2012) (noting that "privately funded by foundations these [Imam-Hatip] schools often have better facilities than state counterparts").

Education eventually declared that correspondence education would only be permitted for the last four years of compulsory education, that is the high school years.[85]

Whether the AKP is seeking to fully Islamize Turkish society remains an open question as the Imam-Hatip sector has witnessed dramatic growth since the introduction of the 2012 reforms.[86] What is indisputable, however, is that Kemalists and their pro-Islamic counterparts regard religious dress and religious education to be the terrain of their competition to define or redefine the relationship between religion and state. In the process, debates over the headscarf and Imam-Hatip schools have also occasioned a return to the debates of the founding over the definition and precepts of *laiklik*. As originally conceived, the constitutional principle of secularism and the Kemalist deployment of secularization policies were designed to be homogenizing, rather than accommodating a democratic diversity of beliefs. The cyclical recurrence of debates over the relationship between state and religion may, however, have had a pluralizing effect, even if unintended.

CONCLUSION: THE CONTEMPORARY ISLAM-MODERNITY BINARY

The relationship between Islam and modernity is at the heart of the idiosyncratic "narrative of secularity" characterizing the Turkish case. Battles over the national curriculum and the values it instills have erupted cyclically for generations. At the same time, a reversal of the ban on headscarves in public institutions is deemed by stalwart Kemalists as a reversal of the achievements of the Turkish state with respect to secularization *and* backsliding away from the accomplishments of Turkish "modernity." The specificities of the modernizationist ideology that emerged out of the late Ottoman experience entailed a particular conception of Turkish identity, which has since placed the state on a collision course with its own religiously observant society. Modernity was endowed with specific connotations dependent on the production of a public culture best exemplified by "enlightened" secular curricula in schools and the production of emancipated "modern" Turkish women. From the founding, the state's role as a

---

[85] Babacan (2012).
[86] For an argument that Kemalist elites and AKP counter-elites offer competing conceptions of secularism, see Kuru (2007).

political agent that disestablished *medreses* and unveiled the Turkish woman was central to Kemalist modernization.

Symbolically, the banned headscarf is a synecdoche for the state's preferred ideology while the content of education is at the heart of its reproduction. The modern, Western-dressed woman of the center symbolized the new Turkey, while the provincial or rural woman wearing her traditional headscarf marked the periphery where the state's modernizing reforms had not (yet) penetrated. Despite efforts to describe headscarved women as representing a retrograde form of anti-secular fundamentalism, however, their presence in the malls, cafes, restaurants, and university campuses of Turkey's westernized cities represents a thoroughly modern vision of entitlement to express private religious identities. Headscarved women are no longer consigned to the provinces as rural laborers of agrarian Turkey, but constitute educated and politically active forces to be reckoned with in the modern bastions of official secularism. The resistance of headscarved women to policies of exclusion from universities and public sector positions was not an attempt to reclaim "traditional" identities, but rather an assertion of a new and non-traditional role for women from a broader cross-section of Turkish society.[87] The empowerment of Muslim women – as opposed to their alleged subjugation by religion or tradition – has transformed the headscarf into a symbolic challenge to the state's gendered model of secular emancipation.

Similarly, the emergence of an educated religious elite that has seized the reins of power – including a three-time prime minister and later president who is an Imam-Hatip graduate – represents an unexpected challenge to the pedagogical state. Suddenly, the content of the state's pedagogical role is being determined by the very cultural periphery the state had once sought to evacuate or at least exclude. Moreover, a political class has emerged that is willing to use the national curriculum as part of their project to produce a religious youth where the state once committed its educational resources to the production of a Kemalist citizenry.

While ominous to many secular Turks, these developments also represent a break from earlier path-dependent cultural crises in Turkish politics. The presence of alternative paradigms of modernity and enlightenment that reflect the empowerment of previously marginalized religious constituencies may, in the best case scenario, endow the Turkish public sphere with the characteristics of pluralized conditions of belief (in

---

[87] In this respect, lifting the headscarf ban may be less about equality between women and men than about equality between women of different social classes.

the place of Kemalist orthodoxy) more akin to Charles Taylor's vision of a tolerant secularity accommodating of democratic diversity.

As Şeyla Benhabib has argued, democratic iterative processes in which debates over the boundaries of state–society relations recur and yield renegotiation may generate new meanings that help transcend original obstacles to democratic accommodation. In particular, Benhabib has argued that "through such iterative acts a democratic people which considers itself bound by certain guiding norms and principles reappropriates and reinterprets these, thus showing itself to be not only the *subject* but the *author of the laws*."[88] Whether Turkey under the AKP remains democratic is currently very much in doubt. Still, one way to characterize the debates that have erupted under AKP rule over the place for religion in the state is to view them as the renegotiation of a founding bargain that excluded the Turkish periphery from the original modernizing commitments of the state. The Turkish Republic is now being challenged to develop a model of modernity that is inclusive of a heterogeneous Turkish society, comprising both religiously observant and secular social groups. The national institutions that were designed to produce a homogenous public of modern, Western, secular Turks must now grapple with a more complex process of identity formation. In the best case, the incorporation of a religious public will occasion an adaptation of secularity to become a means of *accommodating* rather than suppressing diversity. In the worst case, newly empowered religious publics will use their control of the levers of state power to enact equally repressive measures, this time in the name of an Islamizing project. The dialectic between Turkish secularity and Islam will continue in either case, whether through a new politics of accommodation or through new battles over repression.

The transformations overseen by the AKP represent not necessarily the undoing, but potentially the culmination of the Kemalist project, which is now confronted with robust and local alternative models of its own founding project of modernization. Where Charles Taylor's narrative of secularity emphasized a transition occasioned by the implosion of Latin Christendom and the "rapid pluralization of Western culture," the Turkish case represents a clear contrast. In Turkey, the implosion of a religiously tolerant imperial model under the Ottomans (under the fragmenting pressures of nationalisms in a heterogeneous empire) yielded a homogenizing nationalism that subsumed rather than separated religion. The emergence of pro-Islamic political actors in Turkey that embrace

---

[88] Benhabib (2007), at 454.

aspects of the republic's basic framework – modernization and popular sovereignty – and offer reinterpretations of the core tenet of secularity has transformed the state's trajectory. Although the AKP has shown a pronounced tendency to over-reach in reversing some of the tenets of Kemalist secularization, there have also been those within the party, and certainly among its constituency, who have called for a more tolerant and pluralist approach.[89] Contestation over the definition of secularism and the identity of the Turkish Republic is now witnessing a role reversal in which the erstwhile excluded periphery now controls the center. This shift has set the stage for a new chapter in the uneasy tension between Islam and modernity in the Turkish context. Should this shift occasion a renegotiation that is more accommodating of religion while retaining some elements of secularity, then perhaps the century-long Turkish republican experiment may yet yield a Kemalist secular age.

References

"4+4+4 ve dindar nesil eleştirisi," *CNN Türk*, October 17, 2012 ("4+4+4 and the religious generation critique"), www.cnnturk.com/video/guncel/2012/10/17/4.4.4.ve.dindar.nesil.elestirisi/49652.643590/index.html.

"Diyanet'ten Alevilik Açıklaması," *Haber Türk*, July 31, 2012 [Diyanet offers clarification on Alevis].

"Islamic Calvinists: Change and Conservatism in Central Anatolia" (European Stabilization Initiative, 2005), www.esiweb.org/pdf/esi_document_id_69.pdf.

"OSS dorduncusu imam hatipten," *Haber 5*, July 13, 2007, http://gencdergisi.co m/5092-oss-dorduncusu-imam-hatipten.html.

"Sezer YÖK yasasını veto etti," *Hürriyet*, May 28, 2004 ("Sezer vetos YÖK bill").

"Turkish Politics: The anti-capitalist Muslims," *The Economist*, July 18, 2013.

"YÖK'e imam hatipli üye" [An Imam-Hatip Graduate Joins YÖK], *Radikal*, March 2, 2009, www.radikal.com.tr/turkiye/yoke_imam_hatipli_uye-924127.

Ahmad, Feroz. 1993. *The Making of Modern Turkey*. London and New York: Routledge.

[89] The excesses of Prime Minister Erdoğan made international headlines during the summer of 2013. Peterson (2013) and Arango (2013). Some argued that these excesses paved the way for a newly politicized generation of Turks to embrace more liberal values; de Bellaigue (2013). But where Erdoğan was criticized for his authoritarian style and excessive reach into the private lives of Turkish citizens, Abdullah Gül was praised for reflecting the moderate face of the party; Idiz (2013). And other more pluralist forces from within the AKP's own constituency were also cited for showing solidarity with secularist protesters. "Turkish Politics: The anti-capitalist Muslims," *The Economist*, July 18, 2013; and Taştekin (2013).

al-Azmeh, Aziz. 1993. *Islams and Modernities*. London and New York: Verso.

Arango, Tim. 2013. "Turkish Liberals Turn Their Backs on Erdogan," *New York Times*, June 19.

Arsu, Sebnem, and Dan Bilefsky. 2013. "Turkey Lifts Longtime Ban on Head Scarves in State Offices," *New York Times*, October 8.

Atatürk'ün Söylev ve Demeçleri (Atatürk Kültür, Dil ve Tarih Yüksek Kurumu Atatürk Araştırma Merkezi, 1989).

Atatürkcü Düşünce. 1992. Ankara: Türk Tarih Kurumu Press.

Atay, Falih Rıfkı. 2006. Atatürkçülük Nedir? Istanbul: Pozitif Publishing.

Ayhan, Halis. 1999. *Türkiye'de Din Eğitimi: 1920-1998*. Istanbul: Marmara University Faculty of Religion Foundation.

Babacan, Nuray. 2012. "Açık eğitim üçüncü 4 yıla çekiliyor," [Correspondence education limited to third 4-years], *Hürriyet*, February 28.

Bacık, Gökhan, and Bülent Aras. 2002. "Exile: A Keyword in Understanding Turkish Politics." *The Muslim World* 92: 387–406.

Bâli, Aslı. 2012. "The Perils of Judicial Independence: Constitutional Transition and the Turkish Example." *Virginia Journal of International Law* 52(2) (Winter): 235–320.

Başbakanlık Diyanet Işleri Bakanlığı, T.C. "Diyanetin Kuruluş ve Tarihi Gelişimi" [The Founding and History of Diyanet]: https://diyanet.gov.tr/tr/kategori/k urulus-ve-tarihce/28.

Bein, Amit. 2011. *Ottoman Ulema, Turkish Republic: Agents of Change and Guardians of Tradition*. Bloomington: Stanford University Press.

Benhabib, Şeyla. 2007. "Democratic Exclusions and Democratic Iterations." *European Journal of Political Theory* 6: 445–462.

2008. "What is that on your head? Turkey's new legislation concerning the 'headscarf'," *Dialogues on Civilization*, March 5.

Berkes, Niyazi. 1978. *Türkiye'de Çağdaşlaşma* [Modernization in Turkey]. Istanbul: Doğu-Batı Yayınları.

1964. *The Development of Secularism in Turkey*. Montreal: McGill University Press.

Bozdemir, Süleyman. 2009. "Atatürk Döneminde Eğitimdeki Gelişmeler" [Developments in Education during Ataturk's Period], Çukurova University Working Paper Series 2009, http://turkoloji.cu.edu.tr/ATATURK/arastirma lar/suleyman_bozdemir_ataturk_donemi_egitim_gelismeler.pdf.

Bozdoğan, Sibel. 2001. *Modernism and Nation Building: Turkish Architectural Culture in the Early Republic*. Washington: University of Washington Press.

Bozdoğan, Sibel, and Resat Kasaba (eds.). 1997. *Rethinking Modernity and National Identity in Turkey*. Seattle and London: University of Washington Press.

Çakmak, Diren. 2009. "Pro-Islamic Public Education in Turkey: The Imam-Hatip Schools." *Middle East Studies* 45(5): 825–846.

Cameron-Moore, Simon. 2012. "Turkish School Reforms Raise Debate on Islamism," *Reuters*, March 20.

Çandar, Cengiz. 1997. "Post-modern Darbe," *Sabah*, June 27.

Çarkoğlu, Ali, and Barry Rubin (eds.). 2006. *Religion and Politics in Turkey*. New York: Routledge.

Çarkoğlu, Ali, and Binnaz Toprak. 2006. *Religion, Society and Politics in Changing Turkey*. TESEV (Turkish Economic and Social Studies Foundation).

Cizre-Sakallıoğlu, Ümit. "Politics, Society and Financial Liberalization: Turkey in the 1990s." *Development and Change* Vol. 31(2) (March 2000): 481–508.

Copeaux, Etienne. 1998. *Türk Tarih Tezinden Türk-Islam Sentezine (From the Turkish History Thesis to the Turkish-Islamic Synthesis)*. Amkara: Tarih Vakfı Yurt Yayınları.

de Bellaigue, Christophe. 2013. "Turkey's Hidden Revolution: How Prime Minister Erdogan Accidentally Fostered a Generation of Turkish liberals," *Slate*, August 26.

Deringil, Selim. 1998. *The Well-Protected Domains: Ideology and the Legitimation of Power in the Ottoman Empire 1876–1909*. London: IB Tauris, 1998.

Dinç, Sait. 2012. "Atatürkçülük Düşünce Sistemine Göre Laiklik Ilkesi," [The Secularism Principle in Ataturk-ist Thought], Çukurova University Working Paper Series.

Eisenstadt, Shmuel Noah (ed.). 2002. *Multiple Modernities*. New Brunswick: Transaction Publishers.

Elver, Hilal. 2012. *The Headscarf Controversy: Secularism and Freedom of Religion*. New York and Oxford: Oxford University Press.

Ergil, Doğu. 2013. *Turkey's Turkish Identity Question*. Institut de Relations Internationales at Stratégiques.

Finkel, Andrew. 2012. "What's 4+4+4?," *New York Times*, March 23.

Göle, Nilüfer. 2008. "A Headscarf Affair, A Women's Affair?," *Immanent Frame*, February 21.

1997a. "Secularism and Islamism in Turkey: The Making of Elites and Counter-elites." *Middle East Journal* 51(1).

1997b. *The Forbidden Modern*. Michigan: University of Michigan Press.

2010. "The Civilizational, Spatial and Sexual Powers of the Secular." In Michael Warner, Jonathan Van Antwerpen, and Craig Calhoun (eds.), *Varieties of Secularism In A Secular Age*. Cambridge, MA: Harvard University Press.

Gülalp, Haldun. 1999. "Political Islam in Turkey: The Rise and Fall of the Refah Party." *The Muslim World* 89(1): 22–41.

Hakan Yavuz, M. 2003. *Islamic Political Identity in Turkey*. New York: Oxford University Press.

2009. *Secularism and Muslim Democracy in Turkey*. New York: Cambridge University Press.

2000. "Cleansing Islam from the Public Sphere," *Journal of International Affairs* 54(1)(Fall): 21–42.

Hale, William, and Ergun Özbudun. 2010. *Islamism, Democracy and Liberalism in Turkey: The Case of the AKP*. New York: Routledge.

Hanioğlu, M.S. "Garbcılar: Their Attitudes Toward Religion and Their Impact on the Official Ideology of the Turkish Republic," *Studia Islamica* No. 86 (August 1997): 133–158.

Hanioğlu, Şükrü. 2008. *A Brief History of the Late Ottoman Empire*. Princeton: Princeton University Press.

Idiz, Semih. 2013. "Abdullah Gul Steps Up During Turkish Crisis," *Al-Monitor*, June 7.

Jakobsen, Janet R., and Ann Pellegrini (eds.) 2008. *Secularisms*. Durham: Duke University Press.

Kadıoğlu, Ayşe. 2008. "The Headscarf and Citizenship in Turkey." *Immanent Frame*, April 23.

1996. "The Paradox of Turkish Nationalism and the Construction of Official Identity." *Middle Eastern Studies* 32(2) (April).

Kaplan, Sam. 2006. *The Pedagogical State: Education and the Politics of National Culture in Post-1980 Turkey*. Stanford: Stanford University Press.

Kavakçı, Merve. 2010. *Headscarf Politics in Turkey: A Postcolonial Reading*. New York: Palgrave.

Kuru, Ahmet. 2007. "Passive and Assertive Secularism: Historical Conditions, Ideological Struggles and State Polices Toward Religion." *World Politics* 59(4): 568–594.

Mardin, Şerif. 1992. *Türkiye'de Din ve Laiklik* [Religion and Secularism in Turkey]. Istanbul: Iletişim Yayınları.

Mardin, Şerif. 1981. "Religion and Secularism in Turkey." In Ergun Özbudun and Ali Kazancigil, *Atatürk: Founder of a Modern State*. Hamden: Archon, 191–219.

Mardin, Şerif. 2006. *Religion, Society and Modernity in Turkey*. Syracuse: Syracuse University Press.

Mernissi, Fatima. 1987. *Beyond the Veil*. Bloomington and Indianapolis: Indiana University Press.

Odekon, Mehmet. 2005. *The Costs of Economic Liberalization in Turkey*. Bethlehem: Lehigh University Press.

Öğret, Özgür. 2010. "Uncovering a Real Headscarf Debate in Turkey," *Hürriyet*, October 20.

Özbudun, Ergun, and Ömer Faruk Gençkaya. 2009. *Democratization and the Politics of Constitution-Making in Turkey*. Budapest: CEU Press.

Ozerkan, Fulya. 2009. "Turkey PM Recep Tayyip Erdogan Sparks Furor by Saying he wants to 'Raise a Religious Youth,'" *Reuters*, February 9: http://news.nationalpost.com/2012/02/09/turkey-pm-recep-tayyip-erdogan-spark s-furor-by-saying-he-wants-to-raise-a-religious-youth/

Özyürek, Esra. 2006. *Nostalgia for the Modern: State Secularism and Everyday Politics in Turkey*. Durham: Duke University Press.

Pak, Soon-Young. 2004. "Cultural Politics and Vocational Education: The Case of Turkey." *Comparative Education* 40(3): 321–341.

Parla, Taha, and Andrew Davison. 2004. *Corporatist Ideology in Kemalist Turkey: Progress or Order?* Syracuse: Syracuse University Press.

Peterson, Scott. 2013. "Turkey's Protests Reveal Conflicting Visions of Society," *Christian Science Monitor*, June 6.

Scott, Joan W. 2009. *The Politics of the Veil*. Princeton and Oxford: Princeton University Press.

Shankland, David. 1999. *Islam and Society in Turkey*. Huntingdon: The Eothen Press.

Simsek, Hasan, and Ali Yildirim. 2010. "Turkey: Innovation and Tradition." In Iris C. Rotberg (ed.), *Balancing Change and Tradition in Global Education Reform*, 2nd edn. Lanham: Rowman & Littlefield, 149–180.

Tank, Pınar. 2005. "Political Islam in Turkey: A State Controlled Secularity." *Turkish Studies* 6(1): 3–19.

Tapper, Richard (ed.). 1991. *Islam in Modern Turkey: Religion, Politics and Literature in a Secular State*. London and New York: IB Tauris.

Taşpınar, Ömer. 2007. "The Old Turk's Revolt: When Radical Secularism Endangers Democracy," *Foreign Affairs* (November/December).

Taştekin, Fehim. 2013. "Turkey's Gezi Park Protesters Regroup for Ramadan," *Al-Monitor*, July 14.

Taylor, Charles. 2010. "Afterword: Apologia pro Libro suo.," In Michael Warner, Jonathan VanAntwerpen, and Craig Calhoun (eds.), *Varieties of Secularism In A Secular Age*. Cambridge, MA: Harvard University Press.

Taylor, Charles. 2007. *A Secular Age*. Cambridge, MA: Harvard University Press.

Tosun, Ayşe. 2011. "Alevilik, din dersi kitaplarına giriyor," *Zaman*, April 1.

Turkish Parliament Archives. 1995. "1995 Yılı Genel Seçimlerinde Partilerin Aldıkları Oylar ve Oranları" (1995 General Election Party Votes and Vote Shares), https://www.tbmm.gov.tr/develop/owa/secimler.secimdeki_parti ler?p_secim_yili=1995.

Tütüncü, Fatma. 2010. "The Women Preachers of the Secular State." *Middle Eastern Studies* 46(4): 595–614.

White, Jenny B. 2003. "State Feminism, Modernization and the Turkish Republican Woman." *NWSA Journal* 15(3): 145–159.

Yıldırım, Mine. 2011. "Turkey: Changes in School Religious Education Fail to Resolve Fundamental Problems," *Forum 18 News*, August 23.

Zuhur, Sherifa. 1992. *Revealing Reveiling: Islamist Gender Ideology in Contemporary Egypt*. Albany: SUNY Press.

Zürcher, Eric. 2004. *Turkey: A Modern History*. London and New York: IB Tauris.

11

Enigmatic Variations: Russia and the Three Secularities

John Madeley

Charles Taylor's "judgment of secularity" attaches most particularly to the North Atlantic world (or the modern West) as compared to and contrasted with "almost all other contemporary societies" and "the rest of human history, Atlantic or otherwise" (Taylor 2007: 1). The boundary condition, which defines the geographical limits of this "one particular civilization, that of the modern West," he identifies as coinciding with the heritage of Latin Christendom in contradistinction to Islam, Hinduism, and other great civilizational cultures, including that of Eastern Orthodox Christianity. So far as Europe is concerned, the East–West line this suggests differs from that of the so-called Iron Curtain identified by Churchill in 1946 as running "from Stettin in the Baltic to Trieste in the Adriatic" – it runs instead somewhat to the East, raggedly tracing a more or less distinct line from near Kirkenes, the closest significant town to the border between Lutheran Norway and Orthodox Russia in the far north, down to Dubrovnik, close to the border on the Adriatic between historically Roman Catholic Croatia and historically Orthodox Montenegro. Although there have been many cultural, economic, political, and military cross-overs between the worlds of Latin Christianity and Eastern Orthodoxy, the direct implication of Taylor's thesis is that in general to the west of it, within Latin Christendom, a distinctive set of developments occurred over the last half-millennium which ushered in the Secular Age of the contemporary West.

This chapter concentrates on the case of Russia, the largest of the historically Orthodox countries excluded from Taylor's analysis, and attempts to

The author is grateful for helpful comments and suggestions to Edwin Bacon, David Martin, Marat Shterin, Kristina Stoeckl, and Steven White.

illuminate what implications his thesis has for the conditions of religious belief in the predominantly Orthodox parts of Eastern Europe – Western Europe's extensive "other half." In addition to its size and historical importance, the Russian case has a particular interest and significance because of its distinctive political, religious, and cultural traditions and a rich heritage of literary, theological, and philosophical reflection which can be compared and contrasted with the Western heritage addressed by Taylor. In addition, the Russian case is marked by the fact that during the short twentieth century (ca. 1914 to 1991) a form of what Taylor calls "exclusive humanism" achieved hegemonic power and the country became the site of a unique experiment on the part of the ruling authorities to limit, control, and even for a period effectively to attempt the eradication of all public and most private manifestations of religion. Unlike other twentieth century European experiments in France and Turkey, which also aimed at the exclusion of religion from the public sphere, the Soviet campaign of militant atheism targeted all forms of institutional support for religious belief and practice with the intention of achieving their complete elimination.[1] While it varied across time and space in its consistency and virulence and in the religious objects against which it was trained (different confessional practices, religious instruction, church buildings, clergy training, sectarian dissidence, etc.), the campaign can in retrospect be seen to have succeeded in some respects as much as it patently failed in others. Understanding the genealogy and etiology of contemporary secularity across the world should be enhanced by a consideration of the Russian attempt to bring about its birth as if by means of a virtual caesarian procedure. Furthermore, since the experiment occurred in the context of Eastern Orthodox Christianity, the case provides a test for Taylor's claims regarding the unique character of developments in Latin Christianity. And the fact that Russia, alone among all the non-Western cases examined in this volume, has over the last five centuries been an overwhelmingly Christian culture raises the question of whether some contemporary secularities might in fact be the distinctive product of Christianity *tout court* and not just of Latin Christendom.

The chapter first discusses briefly those features of the Russian context which have over time supposedly made it different from that of the West, including those which have particularly marked its religious and ecclesiastical traditions in contrast to those of Latin Christendom. As will be seen, these features do not derive solely from the religious traditions of

---

[1] Aside from local attempts at eradication such as those in parts of Spain during its civil war, the only other national case in Europe was that of Albania between 1967 and 1990.

mainstream Eastern Orthodoxy – there are contextual geopolitical factors which demand attention in addition to those associated with the historic presence of other religious traditions.[2] Having set out the context of Russia's – and Russian Orthodoxy's – supposed "otherness" as it had developed up to the early twentieth century, attention turns to surveying the development over the last hundred years of shifts relevant to Taylor's three Secularities, starting from the tercentenary of the Romanov dynasty in 1913 and the virtual elimination of religion from the public sphere after 1917 (Secularity I). The focus then moves to considering the development of differential levels of religious identity, belief, and practice over time (Secularity II). And finally, evidence for changes in what Taylor calls the conditions of belief (Secularity III), are examined, including those which currently affect the adherents of religious and non-religious traditions other than the country's nominally Orthodox majority. In this context, Taylor's tentative suggestion that the "post-atheist" phenomenon of "minimal religion" in Russia after the demise of the Soviet Union might actually be seen as analogous to the conditions of belief in contemporary Western Europe is evaluated.

THE OTHERNESS OF RUSSIA AND RUSSIAN ORTHODOXY

The origins of Europe's East–West polarity are of long standing. How long depends on whether one goes back to the earliest tensions between Greek and Latin cultures in the ancient world, or to Constantine's division of the Roman Empire and his establishment of Constantinople as its new capital in the fourth century, or just to the Great Schism of 1054 between Latin Roman Catholicism (Western Christianity) and Greek Orthodoxy (Eastern Christianity). Over the course of the twentieth century the Bolshevik Revolution and, after 1945, the Cold War helped to give a renewed prominence to the old polarity and to reinforce some of the ancestral prejudices with which it has long been associated. Nor did all these disappear with the fall of communism; as Samuel Huntington correctly pointed out in 1996, many scholars have traditionally distinguished "a separate Orthodox civilization centered in Russia and separate from Western Christendom as a result of its Byzantine parentage, distinct religion, 200 years of Tatar rule, bureaucratic despotism, and limited exposure to the Renaissance, Reformation, Enlightenment, and other central Western experiences" (Huntington 1996: 45–46). The breadth of

---

[2] As Fagan points out Russia is "the world's only nation-state encompassing sizeable centuries-old communities of Buddhists, Christians, Jews and Muslims" (Fagan 2013: 3).

the range of factors and influences adduced by different scholars in accounting for this purported "otherness," however, raises important issues in the context of Taylor's account of the coming of the secular age in the West. In particular, it raises the questions of which relevant contrasts between Latin and Orthodox Christianity actually subsist, and whether their existence is to be accounted for by intrinsically religious differences or by other – geopolitical, economic, cultural – factors, which might have overridden or over-determined trends in the religious sphere.

Richard Pipes argued that what Huntington calls Russia's "Byzantine parentage" was a key distinguishing factor: "The fact that Russia received its Christianity from Byzantium rather than from the west had the most profound consequences for the entire course of [its] historic development" (Pipes 1995: 223). Tibor Szamuely's survey of the "Russian Tradition," on the other hand, stressed the (more than) "200 years of Tatar rule" (approx. 1240 to 1480) as formative of Russian distinctiveness: the Mongols, he argues, gave Russia "a political and administrative system, a concept of society, quite unlike anything that was to be learned in the West ... The basic Mongol principles of unqualified submission to the State, and of the universal, compulsory and permanent state service of all individuals and classes of society, gradually permeated the Muscovite social structure" (Szamuely 1974: 19, 26). The upholding of these "Mongol principles" throughout most of Russia's last half-millennium, up to and including the twentieth century, has also been held by many observers and commentators to be distinctively Russian. Some of the other ostensible sources of Russian alterity listed by Huntington are reflected in James Billington's interpretive history of Russian culture:

One of the great misfortunes of Russian history is that Russia entered the mainstream of European development at a time of unprecedented division and degradation in Western Christendom. Having missed out on the more positive and creative stages of European culture – the rediscovery of classical logic in the twelfth and thirteenth centuries, of classical beauty in the fourteenth and fifteenth, and the religious reforms of the sixteenth – Russia was suddenly drawn into the destructive final stages of the European religious wars in the early seventeenth. (Billington 1970: 102–103)

Nor, according to Billington, was "missing out" on the Renaissance and Reformation the end of Russia's unfortunate mis-match with Western developments: "As distinct from the pattern developed in the early modern West, secular enlightenment in Russia began late, proceeded fitfully, and was largely the work of monks or foreign technicians – always in response to imperial demands and patronage" (ibid.: 213). And later developments in the nineteenth century failed to compensate for these "deficiencies" as what modest advances the fitful trend of secular enlightenment achieved were soon contested and undermined by official sponsorship of vigorous Anti-Enlightenment tendencies.

In the context of Taylor's implicit thesis about the distinctiveness of the Latin Christian tradition, this conventional listing of factors and influences needs to be supplemented. His tracing of the creative emergence of the modern secular age in the West is resolved into a Reform Master Narrative, the central dynamic of which is a "drive for reform after reform" which he claims is instinctive in, and peculiar to, Latin Christianity: "Probably no other branch of Christendom went through such repeated, far-reaching and global attempts of reform as Latin Christendom has done in this second millennium of our era, and continues to do today" (Taylor 2007: 243–244). The narrative attaches particular significance to the great Hildebrandine Reform of the eleventh century (which occurred *after* the 1054 Great Schism) and the Fourth Lateran Council of 1215, both of which are represented as great reforming moves aimed at raising the standards of religious practice among ordinary Christians. It is clear that the so-called Papal Revolution of the eleventh century found few admirers among the Orthodox, for whom papal pretensions, along with the more theological and liturgical points of contention, had long been a stumbling block. In a manner which agrees with Taylor, Huntington, Billington, and others, the Orthodox scholar Timothy Ware noted the deep roots of a different attitude to religious reform among the Orthodox: he argued that all Western Christians

have been profoundly influenced by the same events: by the Papal centralization and the Scholasticism of the Middle Ages, by the Renaissance, by the Reformation and Counter-Reformation. But behind the members of the Orthodox Church – Greeks, Russians, and the rest – there lies a very different background. They have known no Middle Ages (in the western sense) and have undergone no Reformations or Counter-Reformations. (Ware 1963: 1)

These disparities between East and West might, however, be seen to be just as much a product of contrasting geopolitical contexts as of religious traditions: so far as most of the Slavic territories of Eastern Europe were concerned, the period of the West's High Middle Ages was one of cultural defense and retrenchment, as they were forced to submit to the (formally Muslim) Mongol Yoke. In these constrained circumstances, the Russian Orthodox Church actually enjoyed what many have regarded as something of a "Golden Age" for two centuries, an era which saw great expansion in particular through the establishment of monasteries and the settling and development of large monastic estates (Pipes 1995: 226). While it prospered economically and artistically, however, in the judgment of Pipes, the church was required to immerse itself "so deeply in secular affairs that it ceased to uphold Christianity in any but the most primitive magic-ritualistic sense" (ibid.: 228). On this view, by about 1500, Russian Orthodoxy was ripe for reform, rather like its Western counterpart. And in Russia there was indeed an "inevitable reaction," although despite "its superficial resemblance to the western Reformation," it was, according to Pipes, "*sui generis* with an entirely different outcome" (ibid.). It would appear, then, that it was not so much the absence of episodes of reform as such that distinguished Russia, but the fact that they fell out so differently.

In fact, the historical record shows that Russian Orthodoxy has been far from immune to attempts at religious reform of different kinds over the last half-millennium. Around Taylor's reference date of 1500 various dissident movements of largely foreign inspiration, such as the *Strigol'nik* heresy and the so-called Judaizers, arose, only to be brutally put down by the resurgent Muscovite authorities. Around the same time another – and, in comparative terms, more significant – reform-led controversy erupted within the Church between the so-called Non-Possessors and Possessors, with the former voicing protests against ecclesiastical wealth and monastic landholding, believing that monks and priests should attend entirely to their vows, be poor, work for their living, and otherwise hold themselves truly "dead to the world." The Non-Possessors also maintained that the Church should be independent of the authority of the state, which, since it belonged to a lower order of reality, was seen to have no right to interfere in religious matters. Their opponents, by contrast, spoke for the virtue of a close union between the autocracy and a powerful Church, with the former acting as the natural protector of the latter (Riasanovsky 1993: 123). In 1503, a Church Council finally settled the controversy in favor of the Possessors. Representing as it did distinctive quietist and ascetic traditions within Orthodoxy, the Non-Possessing tradition did not, however, disappear. It continued to manifest itself in different tendencies within the Church and later among the Old Believers (who refused to accept certain liturgical reforms introduced by Patriarch Nikon in the mid-seventeenth century and were subjected to long-lasting persecution as a consequence). Later still, there also emerged a large number of small dissident sects, many of which tended to reject official Orthodoxy altogether. In Taylor's terms, all these movements might be seen as abortive reform initiatives which represented a form of anti-structural resistance to the structural power and culture of the official Church and the secular authorities.

However, some cycles of religious reform in Russia did follow Reformation ideas and successfully implement them, albeit somewhat later than in the West. In the mid-seventeenth century, Patriarch Nikon actually succeeded in introducing the liturgical reforms that resulted in the Old Believer schism. Although he later overreached himself by making theocratic claims vis-à-vis the tsar and was soon sidelined, he probably more than anyone else triggered the most complete reform initiative. Determined that no similar challenges to Tsarist authority should arise in future, Peter the Great (reign: 1682–1725) introduced a series of radical changes in the machinery of church government, which he based on a direct aping of Protestant models. The Russian Orthodox Church had inherited a so-called caesaropapist tradition of church government from Byzantium, meaning that the Church was almost entirely subordinated to imperial authority. Ware concedes that in Tsarist Russia, while the classical Orthodox theory required that state and church should be united in a harmonious (in doctrinal terms, "symphonic") partnership, in practice the civil power exercised virtually complete control over the church. Peter left the patriarchate unoccupied from 1700, and 21 years later introduced the so-called Holy Synod to act as a virtual Ministry of Religion to manage the affairs of the Church, somewhat in the manner of the states of Protestant Germany and Scandinavia. The Petrine reforms extended beyond matters of church government to include a campaign to suppress superstitious traditions and practices, introduce uniformity and order in church services, and raise the education and training of priests so "that they had some knowledge of the scriptures, and could conduct the liturgy consistently, give sermons expounding the faith, and provide elementary religious training ... for their parishioners, at first among elites, then among ordinary people as well" (Hosking 2010: 114). In addition to this attempt at the "confessionalization" of the Orthodox population, in the eighteenth century a campaign was launched to spread Orthodoxy among the non-Christian population groups which the expansion of the Empire had brought under the Tsar's authority. As Geoffrey Hosking points out, however, other aspects of western Protestant culture and organization – the encouragement of literacy among the common population and the existence of strong local congregations, for example – were not introduced, and the Church was required instead "to take on itself the priorities of the 'well-ordered police state'" (ibid.) It was accordingly placed in the classic double-bind of having "the advantages of being the established church, but also the disadvantage of not being able to order its own life according to its own principles" and being required to "fulfil functions delegated to it by the imperial state whose priorities were not its own" (ibid: 117). While this compromised situation was not dissimilar to that of most of the established churches of Protestant Europe, where the civil authorities effectively controlled the churches in their territory (and, for that matter, in much of Catholic Europe where kings typically exerted almost equal control), in Russia it was theologically legitimated by Orthodox teachings of the essential harmony of church and state authority over which the Tsar presided.[3]

In the early nineteenth century, although a significant proportion of the aristocracy had – especially during the reign of another arch-westernizer, Catherine the Great (1762–1796) – fallen under the spell of the Enlightenment, a powerful Anti-Enlightenment movement developed first under the patronage of Tsar Alexander I (1801–1825) and then flourished under his authoritarian successor Nicholas (1825–1855). One product of these cultural shifts was the development among the younger aristocracy of an intelligentsia (note: one of the few Russian words adopted into English) which became deeply disaffected. Amongst these liberal, socialist, and anarchist radicals some Western-imported trends took extreme forms, undeterred by the pressures of church and state censorship, police surveillance, and the frequent use of incarceration in prison camps and exile to Siberia. Their westernizing fashions were opposed by so-called Slavophile opponents who celebrated instead a romantic vision of Russian Orthodoxy. Dostoevsky was unusual, as one who had suffered a mock execution and four years' hard labor in Siberia, in his decisive shift away from Western-influenced radicalism and toward an almost equally radical Russian form of messianic mysticism, which connected with dissident traditions both inside and outside the Orthodox Church. Berdyaev presented him as a prime exemplar of what he called "The Eschatalogical and Prophetic Character of Russian Thought." "The idea of a final perfected condition of mankind, of an earthly paradise, played an immense part in Dostoevsky ... [he] preached a Johannine Christianity, the Christianity of a transfigured earth, and above all a religion of resurrection" (Berdyaev 1992: 217–218). As was the case with Tolstoy, the other great Russian literary prophet of the nineteenth century, Dostoevsky's Orthodoxy was not of the mainstream; they both in their different ways represented, instead, the dissident moral

---

[3] For the effective preponderance of state over church authority in almost all of Western Europe during the early modern period, see Rémond (1999).

and religious traditions associated with the Non-Possessors, the Old Believers, and their various sectarian offshoots. It need hardly be added that these filiations were not looked on with favor by the Chief Procurator of the Holy Synod, K.P. Pobedonostsev, notorious for pursuing hardline reactionary policies throughout his long period of office from 1880 to 1905. The end of Pobedonostsev's term, however, coincided with the onset of what was to be more than a century of momentous shifts in the relationship between Russia's state authorities, its population, and, not least, its diverse religious traditions and organizations. It was at this point that Russia might be seen to have evinced its own radical version of the "drive to Reform" that Taylor identifies in the context of Western Christianity, "the matrix out of which the modern European idea of Revolution emerges" (Taylor 2007: 61).

RELIGION IN RUSSIA'S CHANGING PUBLIC SPHERE

Despite the abolition of serfdom in the 1860s and the onset of major economic changes at the onset of the First World War, which was to bring prior to about its utter ruin, Russia's Tsarist regime remained a largely unreconstructed *ancien régime*. Almost ten years earlier, defeat in war against Japan had precipitated attempts to reform the system and introduce parliamentary institutions, but the promise of those reforms had not been fulfilled and Nicholas II had continued to insist on his prerogatives as Emperor and Autocrat of All the Russias. Just as Charles Taylor cites the pre-revolutionary Bourbons as the paradigm case of the *ancien régime* type in the Western context, the Russian Tsarist regime can stand as its counterpart in the context of the Slavic East. The fact that it survived until 1917, almost 130 years longer than its French counterpart, does not invalidate the comparison. As with the Bourbon regime before the brutal caesura of the 1789 revolution, one feature that survived in Russia into the twentieth century was its claim to be possessed of a divine mission. Early on, the Tsarist regime of the Romanovs had inherited the claim that Moscow represented the Third Rome, which after the 1453 fall of Constantinople was destined to remain the true center of the Christian world until the end of time. After the turbulence of the French Revolutionary and Napoleonic Wars, the regime's motto had again been fixed as "Orthodoxy, Autocracy and Nationality" and the Fundamental Laws of 1832 underlined the triple identification: "Supreme Sovereign power belongs to the Emperor of All the Russias. Obedience to this power, not only out of fear but for the sake of conscience, is ordained by God himself."

Prior to 1917, significant effort continued to be invested in maintaining the representations of divine authority in the public sphere. For example, at the tercentenary of the Romanov dynasty in 1913, two extended series of gala events across the country were used to underline the sacral claims of the regime: "the centrality at each event of the emperor and his family and the almost constant presence at their side of the highest Russian and foreign hierarchs of the Orthodox Church symbolised the unity and sacred mission of the empire under crown and cross" (Dowler 2010: 6). And according to Dowler, the success of these theatrical celebrations was known to have reinforced the Tsar's belief in both the sacred trust that had been committed to him and the popularity of his rule: "the large and enthusiastic crowds that turned out to greet the royal family ... convinced the emperor that his vision of a holy union of tsar and people was shared by ordinary Russians, especially the peasants" (ibid.: 10). What might appear in the light of subsequent events as the delusional musings of the imperial family could of course be considered of little relevance to the brutal realities of the bureaucratic police regime over which the Tsar presided; only four years after the tercentenary celebrations and in the wake of disastrous military defeats, the revolutions of 1917 were to demonstrate how delusional these musings were.

However, secular the Tsarist regime was in terms of its priorities and its modus operandi, it would clearly be wrong to classify Russia at the beginning of the twentieth century as secular in the terms of Taylor's description of Secularity I as a state of affairs where public spaces had been "allegedly emptied of God, or of any reference to ultimate reality" (Taylor 2007: 2). Nicholas Zernov, for example, gives some indication of the profusion of references to God and Orthodox understandings of ultimate reality in both the public and private lives of the Tsar's subjects:

The Orthodox Church permeated every side of Russian life, personal, family, social and national. The majority of Russians identified themselves as members of the Church, and though as individuals they might be sceptics, agnostics and even atheists, few of them broke away entirely from that body which, more than any other, expressed the character of the Russian people and their essential unity. Every Russian home was adorned with holy ikons. These were also displayed at railway stations, public offices, shops and taverns. (Zernov 1963: 35–36)

By contrast with this background, the attempt after the Bolshevik revolution of October 1917 to erase all positive references to religion from the public sphere involved a radical reversal of the predominant pattern of the Tsarist *ancien régime*. After the February 1917 revolution the provisional government of socialists and liberals had committed itself to general measures of religious freedom, which were to include a good measure of organizational freedom for the Orthodox Church – something it had not enjoyed for over 200 years. The promise, which had been made (and later broken) by the Tsar in the aftermath of the 1905 revolution, to convene an All-Russian Church Council to discuss and introduce measures of church reform was finally to be redeemed, and in August 1917 the Church was able to start the process of reintroducing a patriarchal system of church government. The Council finally met just before the Bolshevik takeover and elected the Moscow Metropolitan bishop Tikhon to be Russian Patriarch shortly after. When the Constitutional Assembly was convened in October and summarily dismissed by the Bolsheviks after its first day, however, the old regime's claim of absolute state authority passed directly to the Communist Party leadership. And with the Russian Orthodox Church's identification with the former Tsarist regime in the minds of the revolutionaries, it was among the first casualties of this radical power-shift.

The Soviet campaign for the eradication of religion, which eventually followed, has rightfully been accounted unprecedented in European history (Ware 1963: 145; Greeley 1994: 253; Froese 2008: 1; Lupinin 2010: 20; Marsh 2011: 2). Under Lenin, the Bolsheviks espoused the most radical stream of thought on the future of the Russian Church and religion; according to Ware "the basic attitude of the Communist authorities remained the same: religious belief, in all its manifestations, was an error to be repressed and extirpated," although, as will be seen, the intensity and modalities of the campaign against religion was to vary markedly across the seven decades of the Soviet regime (Ware 1963: 145). Early in December 1917, the revolutionary government announced the confiscation of all church lands and property and appointed an official commission to oversee their liquidation. Shortly after, all religious organizations were ordered to hand over control of their educational institutions to the newly established Commissariat of Enlightenment. Next, the display of "religious images of any description" in any state institution was banned, and two weeks later a requirement for civil marriage was introduced. Finally, in January 1918 the revolutionary government issued a Decree on the Separation of the State from the Church and the Church from the School, which actually deprived the Russian Church of legal personality, thereby rendering it incapable of holding property in its own right. If it had not been clear before, it now became clear that the regime intended to destroy the public role of the

Church and remove it from any influence in the public sphere. On the first day of February 1918, the Church responded to these drastic changes to its status and function when Patriarch Tikhon anathematized the Bolsheviks as "the enemies of Christ, open or disguised," "the godless rulers of the darkness of our time" (Ware 1963: 150). Lenin's government was undeterred and the new constitution promulgated in July 1918 deprived the clergy of the right to elect, or be elected to, any Soviet organs of government or administration (Walters 1993: 6).[4]

Propaganda was to become an important tool in the campaign against the Church and religion generally. The most intensive phase began in 1929, around the time that Stalin finally achieved complete ascendancy in the Communist Party. The League of Atheists, which had been formed in 1925, was renamed the League of Militant Atheists (LMA) and given its head to prosecute the campaign against religion more vigorously. The organization represented the more hardline atheist tendency, which had previously been to the fore in the party's AgitProp department and in *Komsomol* (the ruling party's youth organization). Their assignment to a more prominent role was at the cost of the more pragmatic anti-religious campaigners to be found elsewhere – for example, in the state executive apparatus and the secret police – who were, presumably, no less desirous of the marginalization of religion but maintained that religious believers could be more easily controlled if they were allowed a limited degree of tolerance instead of being driven underground (Marsh 2011). Overriding such pragmatic considerations, at the start of the new decade the LMA announced – in the approved Stalinist manner – an ambitious five-year plan aimed at achieving the total eradication of religion by 1937; "in 1932–1933 all external signs of religion were to be destroyed; during 1933–1934 all religious pictures in books or people's homes were to disappear; during 1934–1935 the whole country (and particularly its youth) were to be subjected to intensive atheistic propaganda; during 1935–1936, any places of worship still standing would be destroyed; and, finally, during 1936–1937, religion was to be rooted out from its most secret hiding places" (Struve, quoted in Knox 2005: 46). A 1929 Law on Religious Associations stepped up the pressure on religious organizations by restricting lawful religious activity to the performance of religious services in registered buildings, and thereby making "almost every other

---

[4] It should be noted, however, that there was no attempt then – or even later, during the bitterest episodes of outright religious persecution – *formally* to ban or abolish the church or other religious organizations as such.

kind of religious witness or activity illegal: conducting evangelistic activity or religious education, producing and distributing religious literature, organizing communal activities for believers, raising money for social or charitable purposes" (Walters 1993: 13). With this law in place and the LMA campaign in full swing, the religious freedom ostensibly guaranteed by the 1936 Constitution meant little or nothing.

Propaganda was not the only means used in the campaign against religion. In the early stages, pressure on leading church officials was attempted, with some success. Thus, in May 1922, Patriarch Tikhon was arrested and, while in prison, persuaded to hand control of the Church over to a group of so-called Renovationist clergy. The new administrators of this "Living Church" then embarked on a reform program not dissimilar to some of those associated with the Protestant Reformation, introducing a vernacular liturgy, promoting married clergy to the episcopate, and reducing the centrality of icons and sacraments in worship. While this attempt to bring about a positive reform of the church failed, another succeeded when, shortly before his release in May 1923, Tikhon was persuaded to issue a "Confession" in which he declared himself and the Church no longer enemies of the Soviet regime. With his death not long after, this seeming reconciliation was confirmed in equally suspect circumstances when, following a four month spell in prison, Metropolitan Sergius (Stragorodsky), who had taken over the leadership of the Church from Tikhon, issued a declaration of loyalty to the Soviet government.

The most violent phase of the anti-religious campaign coincided with what Robert Conquest called the Great Terror, which engulfed and destroyed vast numbers of so-called anti-Soviet elements, including many who came under suspicion because of their religious leanings and activities. The numbers of religious officials and activists that were affected remains unknown, although the identity of many of the most prominent martyrs is now publicly remembered. Froese quotes one former Soviet official who maintained that 85,300 priests, monks, and other religious figures were executed in 1937, 21,000 in 1938, and 3,900 between 1939 and 1941 (Froese 2008: 49–50). And Lupinin references one source to the effect that, between 1917 and 1991, 600 bishops, 40,000 priests, and 120,000 monks and nuns were killed, many of them dying "in the harsh conditions of prison and labor camp; others were shot or buried alive" (Lupinin 2010: 34). Other estimates are less apocalyptic, but hardly less shocking.

In the end, the campaign to destroy religion, or even just to banish it from the public sphere, was not maintained for very long. In 1943, during what

Russians came to call the Great Patriotic War (1941–1945), the Russian Orthodox Church was restored to qualified official favor and many churches and monasteries were reopened. Some twenty years later there was a revival of church closures and anti-religious propaganda under Khrushchev, when the number of Orthodox churches, having grown by 1959 to 22,000, was summarily reduced over a decade to 7,000, and the number of officiating clergy, which had grown to 30,000, was cut back to 6,000, with the number of monasteries in operation similarly cut from 69 to 17. After Khrushchev's fall, however, there was another phase of relaxation, although close control was maintained on the recruitment and appointment of senior religious officials, especially the Orthodox bishops, who were required to involve themselves in international ecumenical organizations and identify themselves with Soviet-sponsored Cold War "peace" initiatives. Finally, in the mid-1980s, Mikhael Gorbachev at last began official moves to dismantle the regime of monitoring and close control of the religious sphere, and in 1988 the Russian Orthodox Church was able publicly to celebrate the millennium of the country's conversion to Christianity with the full cooperation of the Soviet government. This was then followed a year later by the convening of a Church Council at which a large number of new saints were canonized and decisions taken to reform theological training and education. In 1990, the restrictive 1929 Law on Religious Association was at last replaced with a law declaring Freedom of Conscience, which, inter alia, restored to the Church a clear legal and juridical status, so freeing it to receive back many of the church buildings and monasteries which had been seized by the Bolsheviks and to engage once again in charitable and educational activities.

The Russian Orthodox Church was not the only beneficiary of the new regime of religious freedom. Minority traditions, which had in some cases been the target of even harsher means of control or repression, were also able to benefit, as were foreign missionary religious groups who had previously not been legally present in the country at all. The 1993 Constitution of the Russian Federation, written in the aftermath of the 1991 collapse of the Soviet Union, declared Russia to be a secular state, banned the formal establishment of religion, and declared that all religions were to have equal legal standing. It prohibited discrimination on the basis of religious belief, and even went so far as to guarantee the right of conscientious objectors to opt out of military service. In spite of the improvements in its own situation which the new arrangements represented, however, many in the leadership of the Russian Orthodox Church were unhappy that the religious market should be freed up so completely that even groups previously unrepresented in the Russian population could simply enter and engage in often well-funded proselytizing campaigns. The fact that the Church stood ill-prepared to compete in such "market competition" after its long debilitation at the hands of the former Soviet regime was also pleaded. Metropolitan Kirill argued that Russia was "the canonical territory" of the Orthodox Church and should be closed to the missionaries of other faiths (Walters, quoted in Froese 2008: 157). In 1997, these and related viewpoints at last had their intended effect and led to a revision of the 1990 religious freedom law which required that all religious organizations re-apply for registration and introduced a virtual hierarchy of state recognition ranging from the Russian Orthodox Church and the other traditional religions (Judaism, Buddhism, and Islam) at the top all the way down through bodies which were subjected to more onerous official registration requirements and finally, those which were refused recognition and registration. Karrie Koesel has argued that within this new context the Russian Orthodox Church, as the best-placed and most influential insider,

has benefited enormously ... and, with the help of the state, reestablished a religious monopoly. This monopoly is visible from the Kremlin all the way down to local level – Orthodox priests flank politicians at political events, onion-topped cathedrals have been lavishly refurbished, and Orthodox Christianity has become an important cultural marker, defining for the post-Soviet citizen what it means to be Russian. (Koesel 2016: 167)[5]

While neither the constitution nor the 1997 law actually accords explicit privileges or advantages (let alone a monopoly in its strict signification) to the four "traditional" religions, in practice the Orthodox Church can be seen to benefit more from closer relations with the national government than the other religious institutions and/or groups. It has thus, as Koesel documents, entered into a number of formal and informal agreements with various government ministries that give it greater access than other religious groups to public institutions such as schools, hospitals, prisons, police, and the military. For Froese, these developments can be seen as a symptom of a more general regression to the tradition of religious monopoly that had characterized Russia in pre-Soviet times. And Zoe Knox has even argued that "[t]he Moscow Patriarchate's privilege is such that Orthodoxy can be described as a 'pseudo-state church'" (Knox 2005:

---

[5] In addition to these important symbolic advantages, she identifies a large range of more material benefits: "free heating, building subsidies, tax-exempt status to import cigarettes and export vodka, authority over the curriculum of public schools, access to prisons and hospitals, and veto power over where rival churches will be constructed" (ibid.: 167).

191).[6] While the terms in which they are expressed are open to question, these judgments mark and reflect the undoubted reappearance of the Russian Orthodox Church as a major public institution enjoying a de facto privileged connection with the government as well as high levels of esteem among the general public.

THE CHANGING LEVELS OF RELIGIOUS BELIEF AND PRACTICE

For Taylor, the second common meaning of secularity (Secularity II) "consists in the falling off of religious belief and practice, in people turning away from God, and no longer going to Church" (Taylor 2007: 2). While he disputes what he calls the subtraction stories by which orthodox secularization theory attempts to account for these trends, he does not contest the broad "secularization as religious decline" thesis at least as it applies to the countries of Western Europe. He does nonetheless cite "two big grounds for demurral": "you can question whether religion has really receded in our era as much as appears; or while accepting that it doesn't occupy all that much space, you can wonder whether it ever did" (ibid.: 427). Both grounds raise interlinked issues of evidence and interpretation which are relevant to the Russian case, even though the relevant timeline is very different from that of the West. The survival of *ancien régime* patterns into the early twentieth century, their violent inversion during more than seventy years of the Soviet regime, and the alleviation of legal and political restrictions on religion since 1990 each provided very different sets of contexts within which observable levels of religious belief and practice have almost certainly declined or risen. A source of difficulty in judging in what respects and to what extent that might be so is that, while evidence for the changes in the status of religion in Russia's public sphere over the last hundred years has been relatively clear, evidence for levels of religious identification, affiliation, observance, and belief among the population up to and even including the most recent years has been largely absent, heavily contestable, or merely speculative.

Some relatively secure judgments can nonetheless be made. There is little reason to doubt that well into the nineteenth century, Russian culture approximated to Taylor's ideal type of the "ancien régime" matrix: "the understanding of order widespread among the people (as against the

---

[6] Marsh even goes further claiming that the ROC church is "the clearest example of an established Christian church in the world today" (Marsh 2011: 123).

Enlightenment conceptions circulating among the elites) [was] of a pre-modern kind, an order of hierarchical complementarity, which is grounded in the Divine Will, or the Law which holds since time out of mind, or the nature of things" (ibid.: 438). How levels of religious observance and ortho-dox belief might have related to this matrix is on the other hand obscure, not least because it touches on the long-running debates about the state of "the Russian soul" between Slavophiles and westernizers. According to the more romantic Slavophiles, "all the essential differences between Russia and the West were ultimately traceable to religion": while the Western churches had been corrupted by rationalism and hubris, "Orthodoxy had remained con-stant to true Christian ideals. It was a truly communal church which drew its strength from the collective faith and wisdom of the flock" (Pipes 1995: 266–267). They idealized the common folk and "maintained that the Russian was defined by Christian sacrifice and humility. This was the foundation of the spiritual community (*sobornost'*) in which, they imagined, the squire and his serfs were bound together by their patriarchal customs and Orthodox beliefs" (Figes 2002: 133–134). Among the more westernized intelligentsia, on the other hand, there was great skepticism about these claims. In a famous letter to Gogol, the critic Vissarion Belinsky, while acknowledging that the typical Russian peasant appeared full of pious reverence and the fear of God, observed: "But he utters the name of God while scratching his backside. And he says about the icon: 'It's good for praying –and you can cover the pots with it as well.' Look carefully and you will see that the Russians are by nature an atheistic people with many superstitions but not the slightest trace of religi-osity" (ibid.: 318). And Figes himself concludes: "For all the claims of the Slavophiles and the intense devotion of the Old Believers, the Russian peasant had never been more than semi-detached to the Orthodox religion. Only a thin coat of Christianity had been painted over his ancient pagan folk culture" (ibid.: 319). The clear suggestion is that whatever the official appearance of an almost complete adherence to Orthodoxy, at least in European Russia, distinctly unorthodox beliefs and practices were wide-spread among the peasantry, as well as among the other classes of the population.

The picture of Russia prior to 1914 is not monotonic, however. Hosking points out that there was "a broad and varied upsurge of religious life in the late nineteenth and early twentieth centuries" (Hosking 2010: 117). Figes refers to the revival of the medieval hermitic tradition which led to mon-asteries like Optina Pustyn again becoming popular centers of religious spirituality and pilgrimage (Figes 2002: 292). Increasingly, in the monas-teries and hermitages could be found "a form of religious consciousness that was somehow more essential and emotionally charged than the formalistic religion of the official Church" (ibid.: 296). And Zernov goes so far as to claim that in the decades before 1917 there was a "Russian Religious Renaissance," a spiritual awakening and an intensification of Church life and thought, which featured some leaders of exceptional charismatic gifts, as well as "many false prophets, perverted mystics and founders and followers of strange sects and dubious doctrines" (Zernov 1963: 57). Evidence for these claims can be found in the memoirs of many members of the higher social strata (up to and including the royal family), but corresponding evidence for the great mass of the population is almost entirely missing or largely anecdotal.

Outwardly at least, the Russian Orthodox Church appeared on the eve of the First World War well-equipped to serve the religious needs of the population; it "claimed a hundred million adherents, two hundred thousand priests and monks, seventy-five thousand churches and chapels, thirty-seven thousand primary schools, fifty-seven seminaries and four university-level academies, not to speak of thousands of hospitals, old people's homes and orphanages" (Burleigh 2006: 40). This was to change radically after the October revolution, of course, when the assault on the Church had an immediate impact on its ability to perform even its basic liturgical functions. Its peremptory removal from the field of education, the sequestration of all its property in buildings and land, and the requisitioning during the civil war of much of the vestments, icons, and silver which were used in its church services quickly reduced it to virtual institutional impotence, despite any residual loyalty among its surviving adherents. As already noted, around 1925 the anti-religious campaign was broadened to target the minority traditions and denominations as well – for example, the Protestant sects which up to that time had, like Russia's Muslims, generally been regarded as less antagonistic to the revolution (Walters 1993: 12–13). To the extent that Russian Orthodoxy was a public religion, the active presence of which revolved almost entirely around the ritual performance of the liturgy, the virtual suppression of open church services must have had a particularly devastating effect.

Evidence about levels of religious belief in the Russian population is even more scarce than the guestimates which can be made about the decline of church attendance and other public religious practices such as visits or pilgrimages to monasteries. One source does, however, provide some empirical basis for judging levels of belief. In 1937, when, according to the LMA's eradication plan, religion was supposed finally to have been "rooted out from its most secret hiding places," the occasion of the official census was used to measure levels of religious belief and activity. Despite the strong probability that – because of its official provenance – it under-reported actual levels, the preliminary results were extremely unwelcome; to the shock of Yaroslavsky, the president of the LMA, they appeared to show that over half of the population continued to declare a belief in God, with the figure in many rural areas touching two-thirds. Unsurprisingly, the findings were not made public – Froese says analysis of the data was "quickly aborted" – and Yaroslavsky concluded that they indicated the need for the use of yet more draconian measures than those already employed; according to one source, he declared that the results indicated that it would evidently be necessary to liquidate "several hundred reactionary zealots of religion" (Pospielovsky 1987). Froese agrees that this "violent dissatisfaction with the census results" was linked with the decision to move to "a mass liquidation of all religious organizations and leaders" which reached its peak in the late 1930s (Froese 2008: 122). As the suppressed results of the census indicated, however, despite a high level of official disfavor, admitting to the holding of religious beliefs had not disappeared. In addition, there exists much anecdotal evidence that private and/or clandestine acts of religious worship continued in defiance of official persecution (Young 1997). And Ware even went so far as to conclude that "In many places there was an amazing quickening of the spiritual life. Cleansed of worldly elements, freed from the burden of insincere members who had merely conformed outwardly for social reasons, purified as by fire, the true Orthodox believers gathered themselves together and resisted with heroism and humility" (Ware 1963: 148). It also appears clear that among the sects and other marginal groups who had long been used to maintaining themselves in the face of official disfavor and persecution, underground religious services and meetings continued despite the danger of discovery or betrayal.

With the partial restoration to official favor of the Russian Orthodox Church in 1943 and the reopening of many churches and monasteries, there was doubtless a renaissance of church attendance, especially during the immediate period of the war. The last concerted effort to marginalize, if not to eradicate, religion under Khrushchev would presumably have had its effect in making traditional religious practice difficult and even dangerous – to career prospects if not necessarily personal safety and integrity. By the mid-1980s, however, there was evidence of something approaching a resurgence of religious practice and belief, not least among the better educated. Writing in 1986, Jane Ellis was even able to claim that the millions of Orthodox faithful throughout the Soviet Union … make the Russian Orthodox Church one of the largest, most resilient (and well-financed) churches in the world. They have preserved the faith, the traditions and, latterly, the institutional structures which, in the post-Stalin years, have enabled a constantly growing stream of members of the intelligentsia, both young and old, to embrace Orthodox Christianity. (Ellis 1986: 172)

In the immediate aftermath of the collapse of communist rule in Russia, expectations were high that the definitive ending of the anti-religious campaigns and the opening up in 1990 of a free market for religion would presage an even more dramatic resurgence – and early observers of the scene found these expectations confirmed. In 1994, Andrew Greeley published a report on the first major survey of religious belief and behavior. In addition to asking questions about whether or not respondents believed in a life after death, the survey on which he relied asked respondents how close they felt they were to God, whether – if they had once been atheists – they had changed their views or had experienced a "religious turning point experience," and how great or little confidence they had in the Orthodox Church. On this basis he felt able to claim that Russia was experiencing "the greatest religious revival in human history" (Greeley 1994: 254, 272). In the years since, a number of other studies have come to rather more moderate conclusions: in 2000, Michael Bordeaux judged that there had indeed been something of a revival of religious belief and observance "in all its variety," while others referred to an ambiguous mixture of restoration and religious innovation (Bordeaux 2000). The Russian sociologist of religion, Sergei Filatov, on the other hand, dismissed claims of a strong revival of religion as overblown, and even concluded that "Russia is one of the most secularized countries in the world if not the most secularized" (Filatov 2000: 102). Lewis similarly concluded that contemporary Russia was far from being an "Orthodox" or even, for that matter, a "Christian" country (Lewis 2000: 294). In 2006, Borowik, reviewing the accumulating survey and other evidence about a putative "religious revival," concluded that it had been very modest (Borowik 2006). Froese's own 2008 review of the evidence for religious revival across the whole territory of the former Soviet Union found a substantial increase in religious affiliations over the period 1970 to 1995, taking the level in Russia proper from 49 percent to 66 percent of the population (Froese 2008:152). Marsh's more recent review of the evidence qualifies these claims by distinguishing levels of attachment between what he identifies as devout and cultural Orthodox adherents (Marsh 2011).

A problem with assessing these contrasting findings about levels of religious belief and practice after communism is that they typically use different metrics for identifying religiosity, and it is not clear that the ones used are centrally relevant. Miklos Tomka makes a powerful argument that many of the conventional indicators which are regarded as standard in the West are actually ill-suited for assessing religiosity in Eastern Orthodox contexts. He claims, firstly, that "the convergence of socio-economic back- wardness, a socially disengaged religion, and the behavioural remnants of Soviet subservience have resulted in the rough preservation of the tradi- tional socio-cultural pattern" in Russia despite the secularizing impact of urbanization, industrialization, and the development of mass education (Tomka 2006: 256). And, secondly, he argues that the set of criteria which best corresponds to traditional Orthodox patterns of religious obser- vance would need to measure a distinctive style of participation which fits "the mystical nature of the [Orthodox] Christian religion and especially of the liturgy along with the relatively limited freedom of individuals in shap- ing it"; instead of emphasizing correct belief and regular church attendance as in Western Christianity, in Eastern Orthodoxy, "religiosity is less a distinct individual choice than a matter of being part of a social and symbolic universe" (ibid.: 260). David Martin makes a related observation that "[t]o this day religion in Russia remains embedded in gesture, obei- sance and image rather than in discourse, personal faith and intellectual assent," adding the suggestion that perhaps this very fact "helps to account for its survival under prolonged attack and persecution" (Martin 2014: 246). In these terms, Orthodox religiosity should accordingly be under- stood more in terms of identification and ethos than with (lower-case) orthodox belief and regular church attendance.

THE CHANGING CONDITIONS OF BELIEF IN RUSSIA

Over the last century, the conditions of belief (Taylor's Secularity III) in Russia can be reliably assumed to have varied enormously across at least three principal phases. In a manner which bears upon notions of secular- ity, a number of analysts write of the coming of a contemporary "post- secular" era. Alexander Agadjanian, for example, comments that "Russia shared the new condition [of post-secularism] with other post-Soviet states, Turkey, India, Indonesia, Israel, and a few other societies" (Agadjanian 2012: 91). In the Russian case it would appear that – without entering into the complications raised by Jürgen Habermas's use of the term "post-secular" – the country can be seen to have lived through successive pre-secularist, secularist, and post-secularist eras characterized in particular by the nature of the regulatory regimes in the field of religion obtaining during each. In the first decade of the twentieth century, identification with the Orthodox Church was clearly still favored by long tradition and encouraged both by the advantages accruing to that identification and by the restrictive regulations which discriminated against those of other religious affiliations and/or identities. Among the systematically disfavored who belonged to the minority religious communities and traditions, the holding of distinctive religious beliefs and the performance of related observances was doubtless at least as common as – if not more common and regular than – among the Orthodox, with only a relatively small, radicalized minority rejecting religious belief and practice altogether. During the seventy-odd years of the secularist Soviet regime, these conditions were drastically reversed as religious belief and practice – first among members of the Orthodox Church and later among all religious believers – was positively discouraged and penalized, while exclusive humanism of a revolutionary Soviet variety was more or less vigorously promoted. The religious quality (if not the actual content) of the regnant atheist creed should not, however, be passed over; as many authors have pointed out, Soviet communism developed its own form of politicized spirituality connected with underground millennialist traditions while celebrating myths of heroic communist selflessness and dedication to the cause (Froese 2008; Hosking 2010). And as Froese documents, the secularist regime invented and rolled out the provision of strictly secular ceremonies for marking births, marriages, and deaths as part of the campaign to supplant religious rites of passage and so advance its secularist project. Since the complete collapse of Soviet communism ca. 1990, what appears to be a progressively post-secularist regime has presided over a flux of developments including the virtual restoration of the Orthodox Church and a substantial measure of religious freedom for all.[7] It is tempting to represent the three successive eras or phases as describing a virtual Hegelian dialectic between a thesis of religious establishment, an antithesis of the virtual suppression of religion, and a synthesis which combines in a novel pattern new as well as surviving elements of both religiosity and secularity. The ambivalent nature of the

---

[7] This measure of religious freedom has not however been sufficient to prevent the continued harassment of certain marginal sects and groups deemed to be "extremist." Forum 18 regularly monitors these and other derogations from principles of religious freedom. See, for example, Victoria Arnold, Russia: Jehovah's Witnesses Banned, Property Confiscated, *Russia Correspondent*, Forum 18, April 20, 2017: www.forum18.org/archive.php?article_id=2274

emergent post-secularist regime and the setting it provides for the conditions of belief affecting individual religious choice is, however, difficult to ascertain and/or construe.

Taylor discusses Mikhail Epstein's view of the conditions of belief under the current post-secularist regime. Epstein is unusual in believing that during the Soviet Union's seventy-odd years, militant atheism did actually "penetrate into the masses," but that it did so for reasons peculiar to Russia's distinctive religious traditions, in particular the tradition of apophatic or negative theology, which he sees as positively repressive of religious consciousness (Epstein 1999: 379).[8] The religious revival which he observed in 1995 appeared to him to be focused on the "restoration of pre-atheist traditions," although he noted that "the atheist past, the experience of the wilderness, cannot pass without a trace, and this trace of 'the void' will manifest itself in a striving for fullness of spirit, transcending the boundaries of historical denominations" (Epstein quoted in Taylor 2007: 534). The product of this striving is, however, "minimal religion," to use Epstein's descriptive term, which Taylor understands as "a spirituality lived in one's immediate circle, with family and friends, rather than in churches," and he sees in this a parallel with the situation in Western Europe where the decline of traditional beliefs and practices attached to organized religion seems set to continue. It is certainly the case that a large number of treatments of post-Soviet religious developments provide rich (if largely anecdotal) evidence of the emergence or re-emergence of a wide range of different spiritualities, both internal and external to the traditional religious institutions, which, taken together, correspond well to Taylor's notion of a nova effect, "the multiplication of new options around the polemic between belief and unbelief" (Taylor 2007: 391–392).

The Russian Orthodox Church has not been the only beneficiary of the new conditions of relative religious freedom introduced around 1990. Froese argues that by concentrating its anti-religious campaigns on the Orthodox Church, the Communist authorities had "unwittingly introduced new levels of religious pluralism . . . while also intentionally increasing ignorance concerning religious traditions and theology," thereby leading to a situation in which both local and foreign sects and cults could attract "millions of eager converts" (Froese 2008: 143). Similarly, Marat Shterin has argued that in addition to successfully undermining

---

[8] Apophatic or negative theology involves the attempt to clarify religious experience and 'the language of the Divine' by gaining knowledge of what God is *not* (*apophasis*), rather then by attempting to describe what God *is*.

traditional religious cultures, the campaigns effectively contributed to the latter-day proliferation of something like a pervasive "cultic milieu" (Shterin 2012: 2). And in similar vein Lewis argued, as of 2000, that

the religion of most inhabitants of Russia is a folk religion which incorporates into itself many disparate beliefs and practices from a variety of different origins ... on top of the folk religion might be a thin veneer of practices associated with Orthodox Christianity even if in practice their everyday lives have little or nothing to do with this religion. (Lewis 2000: 295)

These parallel observations suggest support for Tomka's argument that the outcome of the turbulent last hundred years has in fact resulted, despite all the surface differences, in a rough preservation of traditional socio-cultural patterns.

Froese's analysis differs from that of Taylor and Epstein. He observes that "by measures of religious participation and belief, Western Europeans today look a lot like the Soviet population under Communism – showing few public displays of religiosity but privately holding onto religious faith" (Froese 2008: 191). The observation is consistent with his argument for the persistence of basic religious beliefs throughout the twentieth century, on the one hand, and the negative effects of religious market regulation on the vitality of religion, on the other. And in this connection it can be argued that the 1997 re-introduction in Russia of a hierarchy of recognition of different religious groups actually makes the country more similar to, rather than more different from, Western European patterns of church–state relations. In 1999, Silvio Ferrari pointed out that an emergent European church–state model, in contrast with the USA's separationist model, involved a significant discrimination in favor of traditional religious bodies and organizations, even if in only a minority of cases did this discrimination involve the survival of actual state churches (Ferrari 1999). Fox's data on degrees of church–state separation across the world can be used to show that in fact, while Russia in 2002 deviated from notionally pure church–state separation with over thirty derogations, it was actually in company with Finland and Greece and only marginally ahead of Spain and the United Kingdom (Fox 2008; Madeley 2009). Norman Doe has provided a useful gloss on the legal underpinning of what amounts to a "common law" relating to religion in Europe (Doe 2010). For Froese (and, more generally, for the largely American rational choice school of sociologists of religion) such deviations from the conditionality of a completely free and open religious market are a principal cause for the low vitality of organized religion in Western Europe. And in this connection he comments wryly in respect of what he regards as the return, particularly since 1997, of a virtual hierarchy of religious privilege in Russia "as religious monopolies flourish, religious fervor will wane – a prospect that would not dishearten Marxist-Leninists" (Froese 2008: 161).

In retrospect, the one seeming success of the Soviet anti-religious project was its breaking of the chain of Russia's collective religious memory or, alternatively put, its effective promotion of religious ignorance and/or anti-religious prejudice. "Whole generations of Soviet citizens would not be baptized or confirmed, have church weddings, sing hymns, attend religious funerals, or celebrate religious holidays. Over time, the memory of religious activity was certainly lost for many Soviet citizens" (Froese 2008:115). While others have claimed that this has not prevented a revival of pre-Soviet patterns of belief and observance, for Filatov, as already noted, the outcome has been that Russia now counts as one of the most secularized countries in the world. Lewis supports a similar claim that "Russia is far from being an 'Orthodox' or even a 'Christian' country," by pointing to the fact that in Moscow only about 150,000 to 200,000 people – i.e. no more than 2 percent of the population – visit the city's Orthodox churches for major festivals such as Easter, and that many who consider themselves to be "Orthodox" profess beliefs which are far from orthodox so that, for example, according to a 1996 survey, 29 percent of "Orthodox" believers were found to believe in astrology and 41 percent in reincarnation (Lewis 2000: 294). This analysis might also, of course, be taken to confirm similarities rather than contrasts with the religious condition of contemporary Western Europe. Taylor refers, for example, to Grace Davie's description of "Christian nominalism," which sits just as loosely to the churches' dogmatic teachings, to Hervieu-Leger's arguments about the rupture of religious memory, and to Paul Heelas's treatment of the wide range of spiritualities, as opposed to religion, on offer in the West (Taylor 2007: 520–521). But this is perhaps to suggest with G.K. Chesterton that as with the Western decline of traditional religion and the belief in God, the dominant option remaining in the Orthodox East as much as in the Latin West is not so much believing in nothing but believing in almost anything.

CONCLUSION

In Charles Taylor's terms, the Soviet campaign to destroy religion and replace it with a utopian atheist alternative can be regarded as an iconic failure to translate the elements of a social theory (*in casu* Marx's dialectical materialism) into what he calls a social imaginary (Taylor 2007: 171–172). For such a project to have succeeded, Marxism–Leninism, as a radical secularist version of exclusive humanism in the possession initially of only a small revolutionary vanguard, would have had to be conjured and inculcated so as to inform "the images, stories, legends" of wide constituencies – if not of the whole – of Russian society. Only by achieving such a feat would it have had a chance of becoming "the common understanding," thereby providing the basis for "a widely shared sense of legitimacy." At certain times, great efforts were expended in attempting this feat, while at others, especially during and after the Second World War, compromises were made as traditional religious sentiments were called in aid of the defense of the Russian fatherland. As noted, the attempt to supplant religion was not decisively abandoned at that time, however, as the Communist party continued to promote an alternative array of symbolic goods of secular-atheist design, intended to "redirect feelings of confidence, commitment, and belonging away from God and religion and toward the Communist Party and Soviet society in general" (Froese 2008: 113). Nor were these efforts entirely fruitless, as some lingering nostalgia for certain aspects of the Soviet way of life continues to attest. Nonetheless, the eventual failure and final abandonment of the campaign to undermine religion by elimination, substitution, or co-optation was probably brought about more by moral exhaustion than by the capacity of organized religion itself to mount a resistance.

The question of whether or how, in religious terms, Soviet or post-Soviet Russia most resembles present-day Western Europe – as, in their different ways, Froese and Epstein both argue – is not easy to determine. Using Taylor's conceptual framework of the three secularities it can perhaps be argued, firstly in terms of Secularity I (the separation of religion from the public sphere) that, while Soviet Russia was marked by its official atheism and its many infringements of religious freedom, post-Soviet Russia is not greatly dissimilar from much of Western Europe, where religious freedom is largely assured in spite of problems which remain at the sectarian margins. And this, because in both East and West simple notions of church–state separation are honored as much in the breach as the observance. In terms of Secularity II (the decline of mainstream religious belief and practice), the contemporary East–West similarities are perhaps more striking than the differences, despite starkly contrasting trajectories of change over the twentieth century – in both currently, levels of conventional belief and practice are respectively modest and low, although, as has been noted, it has been argued that measures of this kind fail to capture other important aspects of Russian Orthodox spirituality. In terms of Secularity III, the "conditions of belief," Taylor's principal focus, these were in Soviet times vastly different from those obtaining in most of Western Europe – instead of being a conventional default option, openly holding to a faith-based identity, maintaining orthodox beliefs, and continuing religious practice in Russia was fraught with difficulty and risk. In the post-Soviet context these options are no longer expensive and/or hazardous; the relative openness of the religious market now allows for choice between many distractions and alterna-tive attractions, including the stubbornly continuing – albeit at a low level – nostalgia for exclusive humanism with its associations with the Soviet past.

David Martin makes the point that following the early Russian tradition of ethnic as opposed to civic nationalism, with the collapse of the Soviet Union "ethno-religion moved into the vacated space," while others have even written of the rebirth of "holy Rus" (Martin 2005: 163; Anderson 2003: 118). As if to symbolize this rebirth, in 1997, on the 850th anniver-sary of the founding of Moscow, the Cathedral of Christ the Redeemer was re-dedicated in the presence of the Patriarch Aleksi and President Yeltsin.[9] The original cathedral had been built to commemorate the victory over Napoleon in 1812, but had been blown up and demolished in 1931 in the most spectacular symbolic act of the anti-religious campaign. The original intention had been to replace it with a grandiose Palace of Soviets topped with a 100-meter-high statue of Lenin, but when this vaunting plan was abandoned the site had instead been used to provide an open-air municipal swimming pool (Garrard and Garrard 2008: 85). For van den Bercken, the 1997 re-dedication provided a symbol of the combination of two post-Soviet trends: "the return of the old national consciousness as a basis for renewed Russian identity" and the increased ideologization of Orthodox Christianity (van den Bercken 1999: 215–216). In 2000 and 2008, under the initiative of Bishop Kirill (who became Moscow Patriarch in 2009), the Church published two major conservative documents on the "Social Concept" of the Church and on human rights, which laid out the contrast between Western and Russian Orthodox approaches (Stoeckl 2012). Whether the overall result of these events should be seen as the sacralization of essentially secular concerns or the secularization and worldly corruption

---

[9] This was of course the same year that the religious freedom law was restrictively modified with the mention of "the special role of Orthodoxy in the history of Russia and in the establishment and development of its spirituality and culture" (Anderson 2003: 124).

of religion, it would appear to fit Taylor's description of "a 'neo-Durkheimian' effect, where the senses of belonging to group and confession are fused, and the moral issues of the group's history tend to be coded in religious categories" (Taylor 2007: 458).

In February 2012, the re-dedicated Cathedral was the scene of an anti-Putin protest stunt by a group of radical feminists going under the name Pussy Riot, whose members were subsequently denied bail, prosecuted for hooliganism, and served with severe prison sentences. David Martin commented that this highly symbolic event

> could be interpreted as a religious protest within an understood Orthodox ritual frame, appealing to the Blessed Virgin for aid in the struggle against tyranny and the collusion of Church and state, or alternatively as a typical Western-style art-protest happening. The reactions to the riot covered the whole range from those who placed the protest within the radical tradition of the Gospels concerning what pertains to Caesar and what to God, to those who invoked the Durkheimian sacred and agitated for condign punishment. (Martin 2014: 259)

And over the following year, as if to symbolize and institutionalize some emergent neo-Durkheimian social-political order, gay pride marches were banned, a blasphemy act was passed into law, and religious education (using a 2002 program called "Fundamentals of Orthodox Culture") was made compulsory in all schools. One hundred years on from the Romanovs' celebration of their tercentenary, all three elements of their *ancien régime* motto "Orthodoxy, Autocracy and Nationality" would seem to be taking on a new reality – albeit in a novel, post-secularist combination – under the aegis of President Vladimir Putin. To adapt the old Russian proverb, Бог дал, Бог и взял ("The Lord giveth and the Lord taketh away"), the current trajectory suggests the addition: "and the Lord now giveth back that which they once tried to take away."

Bibliography

Agadjanian, Alexander. 2012. "Russia's 'Cursed Issues', Post-Soviet Religion, and the Endurance of Secular Modernity," in Massimo Rosati and Kristina Stoeckl (eds.), *Multiple Modernities and Postsecular Societies*. Farnham: Ashgate, 79–96.

Anderson, John. 2003. *Religious Liberty in Transitional Societies. The Politics of Religion*. Cambridge: Cambridge University Press.

Berdyaev, Nikolai. 1992. *The Russian Idea*. Hudson: Lindisfarne Press.

Billington, James. 1970. *The Icon and the Axe: An Interpretative History of Russian Culture*. New York: Vintage Books.

Borowik, Irena. 2006. "Orthodoxy Confronting the Collapse of Communism in Post-Soviet Countries," *Social Compass*, 53: 267–278.

Bourdeaux, Michael. 2000. "Religion Revives in all its Variety: Russia's Regions Today," *Religion, State and Society*, 28: 1: 9–21.

Burleigh, Michael. 2006. *Sacred Causes: Religion and Politics from the European Dictators to Al Qaeda*. London: Harper Collins.

Doe, Norman. 2010. "Towards a 'Common Law' on Religion in the European Union," in Lucian Leustean and John T.S. Madeley (eds.), *Religion, Politics and Law in the European Union*. London: Routledge, 141–160.

Dowler, Wayne. 2010. *Russia in 1913*. DeKalb: Northern Illinois University Press.

Ellis, Jane. 1986. *The Russian Orthodox Church: A Contemporary History*. Bloomington: Indiana University Press.

Epstein, Mikhael. 1999. "'Minimal Religion' and Post-Atheism: From Apophatic Theology to 'Minimal Religion'" in M. Epstein, A. Genis, and S. Vladiv-Glover, *Russian Postmodernism: New Perspectives in Post-Soviet Culture*. New York/Oxford: Berghahn Books.

Fagan, Geraldine. 2013. *Believing in Russia – Religious Policy after Communism*. London: Routledge.

Ferrari, Silvio. 1999. "The New Wine and the Old Cask: Tolerance, Religion, and the Law in Contemporary Europe," in Sajo, Andras and Avineri, Shlomo (eds.), *The Law of Religious Identity: Models for Post-Communism*. The Hague: Kluwer Law International, 1–15.

Figes, Orlando. 2002. *Natasha's Dance: a Cultural History of Russia*. London: Allen Lane.

Filatov, Sergei. 2000. "Protestantism in Postsoviet Russia: An Unacknowledged Triumph," *Religion, State and Society*, 28:1: 93–103.

Fox, Jonathan. 2008. *Religion and the State: A World Survey*. Cambridge: Cambridge University Press.

Froese, Paul. 2008. *The Plot to Kill God: Findings from the Soviet Experiment in Secularization*. Berkeley: University of California Press.

Garrard, John and Garrard, Carol. 2008. *Russian Orthodoxy Resurgent: Faith and Power in the New Russia*. Princeton: Princeton University Press.

Greeley, Andrew 1994 "A Religious Revival in Russia?" *Journal for the Scientific Study of Religion*, 33:3: 253–272.

Headley, S. C. 2010. *Christ after Communism: Spiritual Authority and Its Transmission in Moscow Today*. Rollinsford: Orthodox Research Institute.

Hosking, Geoffrey. 2010. "The Russian Orthodox Church and Secularisation," in Ira Katznelson and Gareth Stedman-Jones (eds.), *Religion and the Political Imagination*. Cambridge University Press 112–131.

Huntington, Samuel. 1996. *The Clash of Civilizations and the Remaking of the World Order*. New York: Simon and Schuster.

Knox, Zoe. 2005. *Russian Society and the Orthodox Church: Religion in Russia after Communism*. New York, London: RoutledgeCurzon.

Koesel, Karrie. 2016. *Religion and Authoritarianism: Cooperation, Conflict and Consequences*. New York: Cambridge University Press.

Lewis, D.C. 2000. *After Atheism: Religion and Ethnicity in Russia and Central Asia*. Surrey: Curzon Press.

Lupinin, Nikolas. 2010. "The Russian Orthodox Church," in Lucian Leustean (ed.), *Eastern Christianity and the Cold War, 1945–91*. London: Routledge, 19–59.

Madeley, John T.S. 2009. "America's Secular State and the Unsecular State of Europe," in Robert Fatton and R. K. Ramazami (eds.), *Thomas Jefferson's Church-State Separation Principle in the Contemporary World*. New York: Palgrave, 109–136.

Marsh, Christopher. 2011. *Religion and the State in Russia and China*. London: Continuum.

Martin, David. 2005. *On Secularization: Towards a Revised General Theory*. Farnham: Ashgate.

2014. *Religion and Power: No Logos without Mythos*. Farnham: Ashgate.

Pipes, Richard. 1995. *Russia Under the Old Regime*, 2nd edn. London: Penguin Books.

Pospielovsky, Dimitry. 1987. *A History of Marxism-Leninist Atheism and Soviet Anti-Religious Policies*. New York: St Martin's Press.

Rémond, Rene. 1999. *Religion and Society in Modern Europe*. Oxford: Blackwell.

Riasanovsky, Nicholas. 1993. *A History of Russia, 5th edn*. New York: Oxford University Press.

Sakwa, Richard. 2011. "The Clash of Post-secular Orders in Contemporary Russia" Paper prepared for the conference "The Postsecular in International Politics," University of Sussex, October 27–28, 2011.

Shterin, Marat. 2012. "Secularisation or De-secularisation? The Challenges of and from the 'Post-Soviet Experience'," in D. Pollack, et al. (eds.), *The Social Significance of Religion in an Enlarged Europe: Secularization, Individualization, and Pluralization*. Farnham: Ashgate.

2012. "New Religious Movements in Changing Russia," in Olav Hammer and Mikael Rothstein (eds.), *Cambridge Companion to New Religious Movements*. Cambridge: Cambridge University Press, 286–302.

Stoeckl, Kristina. 2012. "European Integration and Russian Orthodoxy: Two Multiple Modernities Perspectives," in Massimo Rosati and Kristina Stoeckl (eds.), *Multiple Modernities and Postsecular Societies*. Farnham: Ashgate, 97–114.

Szamuely, Tibor. 1974. *The Russian Tradition 2nd edn*. London: Fontana.

Taylor, Charles. 2007. *A Secular Age*. Cambridge, MA: The Belknap Press of Harvard University Press.

Tomka, Miklos. 2006. "Is Conventional Sociology of Religion Able to Deal with Differences between Eastern and Western European Developments?" *Social Compass*, 53(2): 251–265.

Van der Bercken, Wil. 1999. *Holy Russia and Christian Europe*. London: SCM Press.

Walters, Philip. 1993. "A Survey of Soviet Religious Policy," in Sabrina Ramet (ed.), *Religious Policy in the Soviet Union*. Cambridge: Cambridge University Press, 3–30.

Ware, Timothy. 1963. *The Orthodox Church*. Harmondsworth: Penguin Books.

Young, G. 1997. *Power and the Sacred in Revolutionary Russia: Religious Activists in the Village*. University Park: Pennsylvania State University Press.

Zernov, Nikolas. 1963. *The Russian Religious Renaissance of the Twentieth Century*. London: Darton, Longman and Todd.

12

Piety, Politics, and Identity: Configurations of Secularity in Egypt

Gudrun Krämer

Egypt has not followed the path Charles Taylor described so persuasively in *A Secular Age* for the North Atlantic world, or Latin Christendom at large. In Egypt today, it is not belief (or faith, or religion)[1] that has to defend itself as rational and legitimate. Rather, it is unbelief, religious doubt, critique, and indifference that struggle for space. The public sphere has been subjected to moral norms as defined by conservative Muslims and Christians alike, while skeptics, critics, and agnostics have been largely relegated to virtual space and the private sphere. The Egyptian case ties in with observations that globally speaking, (secularist) accounts of modernity as secular, with religion being either irrelevant or reactive (in the guise of nativism, cultural nationalism, and identity politics), are flawed (Esposito and Azzam 2000; Casanova 2008; Warner 2010; Tezcür 2010). Yet Egypt differs from countries such as Korea, Brazil, and South Africa in that faith is not just prevalent in society, but that specific expressions of religion are imposed by the state, enshrined in the constitution, relevant to law, and widely shared among the population. In order to explore the "conditions of belief" in the North Atlantic world, or Latin Christendom, Taylor scrutinized the philosophical underpinnings of what he called "the secular" and explored the historical constellations enabling these underpinnings to evolve and spread over a period of several centuries. (At the risk of over-simplification, one might speak of internal, "philosophical" and external, "institutional"

General note: All translations from the Arabic are my own.

[1] Whereas Taylor does not seem to systematically distinguish between these terms, the Arabic language does, with *iman* being "faith," *'aqida* "doctrine" and "belief," and *din* "religion" or even "a way of life."

conditions.) This road cannot be taken here for the simple reason that we are at present unable to reconstruct early modern and modern Egyptian intellectual, social, and political history in comparable fashion, allowing for broad generalization and theory-building.

What we can do, however, is examine the dynamics leading to and resulting from the processes of secularization Egypt has been undergoing for nearly two centuries and investigate the configuration of relevant actors and institutions roughly from the 1980s to the present. We can also analyze and contextualize the emergence of secularism as a political doctrine in the country. Even if carried further than is possible here, this exercise does not allow us to test the validity of Taylor's claim that the North Atlantic path to secularity is not just specific but unique, precisely because it is highly contingent. But it sheds light on an important case from the worlds of Islam, which, as Jose Casanova has argued, has replaced Catholicism as the Other of Western secular modernity (Casanova 2008).

Before going into the matter, a few words are in order concerning terminology: "the secular" can either refer to an epistemological position, entailing "neutral," "immanent," "non-religious" standards of reason, or to a "worldly" (non-religious, non-clerical) actor or institution, irrespective of the epistemology, project, and ideology this actor or institution might pursue. I have argued elsewhere (Krämer 2013b) that in the Arab Middle East, functional differentiation between religion, state, and other public domains emerged even prior to the advent of colonialism and the modern territorial state, and that it is not so much the separation of church (or a clerical body more generally) and state that matters to the formation of secularity, but rather the relationship between Islamic law or normativity (*shari'a*), state, and society or community. Modern Arabic usage is uncomfortably unspecific when it comes to the "non-religious standards of reason" at issue here: the term *'almani* can cover anything from non-religious to agnostic to anti-religious, and from secular to secularist.[2] However, Arabic does distinguish between "clerical" and "lay" persons and institutions, although the term *madani*, which is commonly used to describe the layperson, again covers a broad semantic range, from civil to civic to civilized. The call for a "civic state with Islamic references" (*dawla madaniyya bi-marja'iyya islamiyya*), which was raised in the 2000s by non-Salafi Islamists, illustrates the distinction between the (non-clerical) institution and its personnel on the one hand, and

---

[2] Related terms such as *la-dini* (without religion) or *mulhid* (heretic, unbeliever, or atheist) are similarly broad, albeit unmistakably negative.

the (religious) mode of reasoning on the other, that is characteristic of much modern Sunni political thought (Abu ʿAjjur 2012; Krämer 2013a).

In my discussion of Egypt, I will highlight the role of political factors in shaping the function(s) and meaning(s) of secularity in a particular colonial and postcolonial setting (Wohlrab-Sahr and Burchardt 2012). In spite of the current fascination with translocality, migration, and hybridity, the Egyptian nation-state remains a meaningful unit of analysis. There is, however, a tendency in current scholarship on Egypt to over-state the state and, moreover, to collapse diverse state actors into one (see, notably, Agrama 2012). I will argue that regarding secularity, state policies are of critical importance, especially in light of the state's capacity to draw the boundaries of legitimate action and expression, but that state-centered approaches need to be supplemented by a strong emphasis on (1) society and the multiple fields in which the struggle over secularity is fought out, and (2) ideas, norms, and practices coming from the West on the one hand, and certain Arab Gulf states on the other. The lines between state, regime, and society, or civil society, and the contours of the public sphere are notoriously difficult to draw (see, notably, the work of Abaza, Asad, Bayat, Hirschkind, and Salvatore). For lack of space, I cannot go into this discussion here. I will, however, argue that the (authoritarian secular) Egyptian state has shown itself responsive to non-state actors that have called for a stronger role of religion in all spheres of individual and collective life, "private" as well as "public," and that the state is not the only actor involved in boundary drawing and agenda setting. The transnational dimension has no correspondence in Taylor's reading of the North Atlantic experience. With regard to Egypt, external influences may be mutually reinforcing (as concerns capitalist modes of production and consumption) but they may also be conflicting (as regards personal freedom, life style, and self-expression). In either case, they are negotiated locally.

STATE FORMATION, NATION-BUILDING, AND RELIGION

Egypt is often portrayed as a deeply religious society, a feature projected far back into history, predating the advent of Christianity and Islam. This *imaginaire*, or narrative, depicts Egypt as a nation with a well-defined moral and political character (the "Egyptian personality," *al-shakhsiyya al-misriyya*), one formed over the course of millennia and only super-ficially affected by religious and political change, from the pharaohs to Byzantium to the Arabs, Mamluks, and Ottomans to British rule and, finally, the modern nation-state. As an expression of cultural nationalism, serving the aims of identity politics, it is both inclusive (of all *religious* inhabitants of the Nile Valley) and exclusive (of its *non-religious* inhabitants). Significantly, it foregrounds the Egyptian people rather than the Egyptian state. Yet, modern Egyptian discourse is in fact more specific: while it speaks about religion in general it singles out two religions as authentically Egyptian – Sunni Islam and (Orthodox) Coptic Christianity. More specifically still, law and politics heavily privilege Sunni Islam as the religion of the demographic majority. Like any other *imaginaire*, the image of the religious nation is socially constructed. But it is also supported by empirical evidence demonstrating that religion is indeed woven into the texture of everyday life and speech and that most Egyptians declare themselves to be religious (Schielke 2012; Van Nieuwkerk 2013).

Already in the pre-modern period, the state apparatus was overwhelmingly non-"clerical" and guided by political rather than religious maxims, albeit careful not to openly challenge the validity of Islamic norms and values. When Muhammad Ali (Ottoman governor of Egypt, 1805–1848) made a determined effort to carve out an autonomous realm within the empire, and ultimately even independently of it, he created secular institutions (a standing army, a centralized administration, and elements of modern medical, technical, and language training); he rarely referred to religion in order to legitimize his policies; and after eliminating the Mamluks and subduing autonomous socio-political forces such as Bedouin tribes, Sufi brotherhoods, and urban guilds, he also marginalized the religious scholars who had played a leading role in resisting the French invasion of 1798–1801. Like other elite-driven projects of defensive modernization, his was premised on selective borrowing from Europe. Contrary to widespread assumptions, it was not primarily directed against European imperialism but conformed to a pattern of elite assertion within the Ottoman Empire (the "politics of *a'yan*" and, later, the "politics of notables"). As studies of late-Ottoman urban and educational reform have shown, state and provincial elites aimed at creating a specifically Ottoman modernity. While this project entailed secularization of certain fields that had previously been subject to religious norms and authorities (among other things, the Egyptian government introduced European legal codes without, however, abolishing the Muslim, Christian, and Jewish family courts), it did not seek to "produce" *secular* subjects or citizens, but *pious and productive* ones, Muslim as well as non-Muslim.[3] Secularization of law, education, and

---

[3] See e.g., Benjamin Fortna, *Imperial Classroom. Islam, the State, and Education in the Late Ottoman Empire*. Oxford: Oxford University Press, 2001; Jens Hanssen, *Fin de Siècle*

politics was thus not premised on principled secularity, or secularism, as a strategy to secure social and political cohesion in a period of political crisis and transition.

In Egypt, resistance to Ottoman and, from 1882, to British rule rested on both secular and religious references. The Wafd Party, which from 1919 developed into Egypt's first mass-based political movement, employed religious vocabulary to propagate its idea of national self-determination, but famously declared that "religion belonged to God and the fatherland belonged to all" (*al-din li-llah wa-l-watan li-l-jami'*). The "union of crescent and cross" was celebrated as the quintessential expression of Egyptian identity. Many denied the very existence of minorities in a nation so firmly united in character and purpose.[4] Throughout the interwar years and beyond, the relationship between Egyptian nationalism and religion remained supple and ambiguous: whereas non-religious actors used Islamic terms such as *jihad* to describe the national struggle, the Muslim Brothers referred to core notions of territorial nationalism such as the "sacred duty" of Egyptians toward God, country, and community (Gershoni and Jankowski 1987, 1995; Krämer 2010).

In 1923, the constitution of the newly independent kingdom of Egypt declared Islam the state religion, but it did so inconspicuously, in Art. 149, and it did not specify what this entailed.[5] It was only half a century later, after the military coup of the Free Officers in 1952, Egypt's defeat in the 1967 October War against Israel, Nasser's death in 1970, and the succession of Anwar al-Sadat, who was soon to cast himself as the "believing president" (*al-ra'is al-mu'min*), that shari'a was introduced into the constitution as a subsidiary source of legislation. Art. 2 of the new constitution of 1971 named the "principles of Islamic shari'a" as "a main source (*masdar ra'isi*) of legislation"; in 1980, an amendment made them "the chief source (*al-masdar al-ra'isi*) of legislation." In adopting these changes the regime responded to pressure from non-state actors, first and foremost the Islamist opposition and al-Azhar, both of which had been pushing for measures that would make Egypt truly Islamic and identified the Islamic

Beirut. The Making of an Ottoman Provincial Capital. Oxford: Clarendon Press, 2005; for colonial and postcolonial Egypt, see Starrett 1998; Lombardi 2006: 69–73.

[4] The classic reference is al-Bishri 1980; for critical voices, see 'Abd al-Fattah 1984, 1997; Hassan 2003; Scott 2010; Elsaesser 2014.

[5] Research has produced a large body of studies on legal and constitutional thought and practice; see Bernard-Maugiron and Dupret 2002; Asad 2003; Lombardi 2006; Berger and Sonneveld 2010; Gallala 2010; Agrama 2012. The constitutional texts are collected in Hammad 2011; for Art. 2, see also Amin 2012.

character of state and society with the "application of shariʿa." Art. 2 should therefore be seen as a concession rather than the attempt on the part of the modern state to shape public opinion and behavior. This dynamic was changed significantly when, in 2012, a newly elected Islamist majority in parliament drafted a new constitution (see section on "Established Religion II: Law and the Constitutional Order").

ISLAMISTS, SUFIS, AND THE PIETY MOVEMENT

The "Islamic trend" (al-tayyar al-islami) in modern Egypt ranges from the Muslim Brotherhood founded in 1928 to militant groups that emerged in the 1970s and Salafis of various stripes who followed suit in the 1990s, and from the "new Islamic thinkers" and "new Islamic preachers" (al-mufakkirun and al-duʿa al-islamiyyun al-judud) to the piety movement, all with their social, economic, charitable, cultural, and political activities and complex relations with religious as well as non-religious actors at home and abroad.[6] As a result, its articulations range from what has been called "Islam lite" to heavy-duty Salafism. For many years, political activists ("Islamists") overshadowed other expressions of Muslim faith and religiosity, including notably Sufi ones and the piety movement that spread from the early 1990s.[7] In this context, the gender dimension should not be overlooked: whereas political Islam is predominantly male, the piety movement is largely female. The so-called Islamic Awakening (al-sahwa al-islamiyya) is part of an even wider phenomenon of "Islamization" which, albeit dispersed, appears to encompass virtually all aspects of public and private life: everyday speech and conduct, Islamic ethics and aesthetics, charity, business, and commerce, Islamizing landscapes, soundscapes, and mediascapes.

The 1980s and 1990s witnessed the spectacular proliferation of Islamic organizations, institutions, and missionary activities (daʿwa) broadly understood: mosques, prayer rooms, and religious salons; Islamic associations, mosque centers, religious schools, and welfare institutions, from health clinics to literacy classes.[8] The Egyptian state failed in its attempt to

---

[6] Wickham 2002, 2013; al-duʿa al-judud 2010: Krämer 2010; for the Salafis, see Shalata 2011.

[7] For the Sufis, see Hoffman 1995; Hasan 2009; for the piety movement, see notably Hafez 2003, 2011; Mahmood 2005; Hirschkind 2006; Van Nieuwkerk 2013. Research is still mostly focused on Alexandria and Cairo, with large parts of Middle and Upper Egypt, urban as well as rural, neglected.

[8] Zeghal 1996: 165–228; Wippel 1997; Wickham 2002; Clark 2004; Serageldin 2005; Hirschkind 2006; Hafez 2011; Van Nieuwkerk 2013.

control the tens of thousands of mosques or the sermons and lessons given inside and outside of these mosques, and in its attempt to control the Islamic welfare sector (Moustafa 2000; Clark 2004; Hirschkind 2006). By contrast, it managed to rein in the Islamic banking and investment sector, which had been identified as potentially threatening, not least because of its suspected ties to political Islam. Outside the banking and investment sector, "Islamo-business" expanded rapidly, producing not only religious commodities, accessories, and paraphernalia, but also Islamic street wear and fashion. "Islam" clearly "sold."[9] Islamization made a remarkable impact on the media, beginning with publishing and the press, in which Muslim reformers had been involved from the late nineteenth century, moving to radio, TV, and satellite channels to the internet and the social media (Abu-Lughod 2005; Richter 2011; Van Nieuwkerk 2013). In the field of leisure, art, and entertainment, or "edutainment" (Haenni 2005: 21), "pious art" or "art with a mission" (*al-fann al-hadif*) developed at an unprecedented pace. It ranged from "Islamic weddings" to "clean films" and *halal* soaps (a decidedly Western format) which attracted wide audiences, especially during Ramadan. But it was probably in music that "pious taste" was most successful, creating new adaptations of classical religious songs (sing., *nashid*) and adapted Western formats, such as hip-hop and rap, a success that has been interpreted in light of Muslim preferences of aural over visual cultures.[10] The only segments not seriously affected are those having to do with exposing the body in public: dance and sports. Like other kinds of *art engagé*, "pious art" had to balance a variety of principles: not only faith and fun, but also the moral message and market forces, and it was not immune to critical comment from Islamist and secular milieus alike.

Part of the Islamization phenomenon has been classified as youth culture, but it clearly reaches beyond youth and also beyond the urban middle class, with whom pious lifestyles and pious entrepreneurship have been largely identified. In the course of the 1980s and 1990s, the search for piety (*taqwa*, in the sense of love and fear of God) moved socially upwards, from the urban lower-middle and middle classes to the upper-middle and upper classes, "normalizing" religious commitment against

---

[9] Van Nieuwkerk 2013: 230. For the banking and investment firms, see Wippel 1994, 1997; Utvik 2006; for "Islamo-business," see also Haenni 2005; Abaza 2006.

[10] Van Nieuwkerk 2013, esp. 271–272; Haenni 2005: 23–27; Bayat 2007a; for Coptic "hagiopics," see Armanios and Amstutz 2013. The phenomenon is not entirely new: the Muslim Brothers had engaged with "pious art" since the interwar period; see Talayma 2008.

the image of Islamic fundamentalism while projecting gendered messages of individual and communal reform. Popular preachers such as ʿAmr Khalid, who propagated a "pleasant religiosity" (*al-din al-laziz*), quickly attained celebrity status (he was obliged to leave Egypt in 2002). The ostentatious turn to piety by star performers from film, theater, dance, music, and the media provided the public with influential role models, such as "repentant artists," and "veiled actresses" (Van Nieuwkerk 2013; also *al-duʿa al-judud* 2010). Similar processes have affected the Coptic community. Interestingly, analyses of the Coptic piety movement have been more critical than influential readings of the Muslim one, highlighting the repressive potential of conservative gender images rather than their function in strategies of resistance and subversion (Armanios 2002; Armanios and Armstutz 2013).

There are many ambiguities surrounding the piety movement. The Muslim women interviewed by Hafez considered religion a private matter (Hafez 2011: 78). Yet they, too, made their commitment public, and in the 2000s, many joined the ranks of the Salafi movement, parts of which engaged in politics. In light of this development, I consider the concept of "post-Islamism" (Bayat and others) highly problematic. All in all, the piety movement is perhaps less relevant with regard to the state's capacity to regulate the religious field and to shape what I have hesitantly called the "external" conditions of belief. But it matters a great deal to the "internal" conditions of belief studied by Taylor. The fashioning of the pious self through bodily practices has parallels in Protestant understandings of faith as an inner condition, one that needs to be translated into everyday conduct, "sacralizing" everyday life. The parallels are no coincidence. However, the genealogy of modern Muslim practices of pious self-fashioning is complicated, as they draw on Sufism, Christian missionary activities, and late-nineteenth-century Ottoman reform (Krämer 2010). The pietists' search for closeness to God, and their belief in dreams and visions of the prophet Muhammad are of special interest in light of Taylor's thoughts on the transition from the "porous" to the "buffered self" as a major underpinning of "the secular."[11] The women studied by Hafez, Mahmood, and Van Nieuwkerk expressed their yearning for what Taylor called "fullness": spirituality, tranquility, and certainty, a moral equilibrium that could help to root them in a place and time filled with unrest and anxiety, alienating them from God and from

---

[11] See Mahmood 2005; Hafez 2011; Van Nieuwkerk 2013; also Pink 2003a: 74–86; for Coptic experiences, see Armanios 2002; Voile 2004; Armanios and Amstutz 2013.

what according to Islamic tradition is the natural disposition toward Islam, *fitra*.[12]

ESTABLISHED RELIGION I: CLERGY AND STATE

In the present context, I use the term "clergy" in a broad sociological sense, acknowledging the fact that like Jewish scholars, Muslim *'ulama'* do not fulfill the liturgical functions of Christian clergy (Krämer 2013a). Well before the Nasser period, the modernizing state had weakened the ties between the Islamic scholars and influential groups of society, such as merchants, Sufi brotherhoods, and artisans' guilds. As a consequence they no longer filled the role ascribed to religious scholars in many societies – that is, to act as mediators between "the people" and the authorities. True, religious scholars were involved in the 'Urabi revolt of 1879–1882, the "national revolution" of 1919, and resistance to British rule in the interwar period, but they did not stand at the forefront of these struggles. (Incidentally, the same applies to the Arab Spring.) Rather, they were widely perceived as allies of the king and palace, and as subservient to the military rulers of the country, from Nasser to Sadat to Mubarak.

Al-Azhar plays a central role within the "clerical" Sunni establishment in the country, which also includes Dar al-Ifta', the office of grand mufti of the Republic, the ministry of *awqaf* (pious endowments), and Dar al-'Ulum, all of which were either created by the modern state or incorporated into it. State control over al-Azhar culminated in 1961, when it was finally made part of the state bureaucracy.[13] Under Sadat and Mubarak, al-Azhar served the government as an instrument of dual use, against the secular opposition on the one hand and militant Islamists on the other. Incorporation, however, also allowed it to draw on government resources and to regain some of the space it had lost under Nasser. After Mubarak's fall, al-Azhar was able to regain some credibility as a voice of moderation, and after the Islamist electoral victories of 2011–2012, it saw its autonomy and role of advisor on all matters related to shari'a formally endorsed in the new constitution (Dustur 2012, Art. 4).

As a sign of how deeply modern notions of majority and minority have shaped common perceptions, the Sunni and the Coptic clergy are hardly

---

[12] Van Nieuwkerk 2013: 19, 25ff, 35, 237–240. For the tensions and imperfections marking the search for poise and piety, see Hafez 2011; Schielke 2012.

[13] On the following, see Eccel 1984; Zeghal 1996, esp. 229–294; Skovgaard-Petersen 1997; Moustafa 2000; Hatina 2010; Kalmbach 2012.

ever studied in parallel. The Coptic Orthodox Church, with its extensive network of monasteries, schools, and charitable institutions, appears to be less strictly controlled by the state than al-Azhar. This is not only because of its institutional structure and cohesion *as a church* (the Coptic pope is appointed by the president of the republic but elected by internal church bodies), but also because of the successive weakening of non-clerical, secular Coptic elites. In marked contrast to al-Azhar, this weakening has enhanced the role of the Church, and the pope more particularly, as chief representative of the Coptic community, a community whose interests cannot be completely ignored precisely because it is a minority, one closely watched at home and abroad. Like al-Azhar, the Coptic Orthodox Church has served several functions, legitimizing state policies vis-à-vis the Coptic community and broader international audiences while defending communal rights, such as the preservation of separate religious adjudication in personal status matters, the fight against missionaries, and the exclusion of "heretics."[14] In this balancing act, the Church has had to move cautiously, combining advocacy of both citizenship rights *and* special protection with a constant emphasis on the unconditional loyalty of the Coptic community to state and nation.

ESTABLISHED RELIGION II: LAW
AND THE CONSTITUTIONAL ORDER

When in 1971, Islam was finally "established" with the adoption of Art. 2 of the constitution, the lawgiver did not define what the "principles of Islamic shariʿa" consisted of and in which way they should function as sources of legislation, nor did it specify the authorities entrusted with defining these principles and functions. For political as well as for intrinsic reasons having to do with the nature of shariʿa, implementation of Art. 2 proved difficult and controversial. As is well known, shariʿa does not constitute a code, but is accessible through the huge body of literature that makes up Islamic jurisprudence, or *fiqh*; *fiqh* is not unified, but represented in a number of Sunni and Shiʿi law schools of which the Hanafi and Shafiʿi are the most widely followed in Egypt; these law schools are internally plural; the methods of legal reasoning are both variegated and contested; as a result, legal and political authorities have had to elaborate specific rules according to specific methods, and at least since the late nineteenth century, these authorities have not necessarily been "religious"

---

[14] See Hassan 2003; Pink 2003, esp. 164–172; Tadros 2009; Scott 2010; Elsaesser 2014.

in the sense of clerical, involving Islamic legal scholars (*'ulama'* and *fuqaha'*). For this reason, some scholars have considered the implementation of Islamic law (shariʿa and *fiqh*) by the modern state as secularization of Islamic law.[15]

Irrespective of how one assesses a claim that conflates "neutral secular reason" and "non-religious institution," it still remains that up until the late nineteenth century, state authorities did not attempt to translate shariʿa norms into positive law. The "application of shariʿa" is not identical with its codification. Attempts made by the Egyptian parliament and al-Azhar to codify parts of shariʿa, or rather of Sunni *fiqh*, failed or were foiled by the state authorities when, in the late 1970s, Islamist violence escalated, culminating in Sadat's assassination, in 1981.[16] Under the presidency of Husni Mubarak (1981–2011) the state authorities continued to uphold Art. 2 while blocking all attempts to translate them into positive law outside the domain of personal status matters. For a certain period, Art. 2 was even used by private citizens who referred to the principle of *hisba* (based on the Qurʾanic injunction to "enjoin good and prohibit evil," or *al-amr bil-maʿruf wa-l-nahy ʿan al-munkar*) in order to sue other citizens or government bodies for violating Islamic rules. In 1996, the state put a stop to what could have become an uncontrollable challenge and restricted the right to start legal proceedings in personal status matters on the basis of *hisba* to the public prosecutor (Bälz 1997; Thielmann 2003).

With codification stalled, the interpretation and implementation of Art. 2 largely fell to the judiciary. Judges opting for a flexible approach (and these included the Supreme Constitutional Council [SCC]) highlighted the distinction between Qurʾanic references that are classified as "absolutely clear" and "definitive" (sing., *hukm qatʿi*) and others that are considered "speculative" and open to interpretation (*hukm zanni*) – a distinction accepted by most scholars of Islamic law but not necessarily understood in identical fashion and according to the same type of reasoning. The same applies to the differentiation between the "fixed" and the "flexible" parts of shariʿa (*al-thabit wa-l-mutaghayyir*), and notions of a common good (*al-maslaha al-ʿamma*), certain public goods or benefits (*al-masalih al-khams*), and the so-called finality of shariʿa (*maqasid al-shariʿa*), all of which can overlap with "secular" definitions of the public interest. As a result of these

[15] See notably the work of Bälz, Dupret, Lombardi, Asad, and Agrama.

[16] Zeghal 1996, esp. 138–164; Asad 2003; Lombardi 2006; Amin 2012; for the texts of the bills, see ʿAbd al-Fattah 1984: 139–174. In 1977, al-Azhar also submitted a draft constitution, which among other things, would have made shariʿa (and not just its principles) the source of all legislation; see Hammad 2011: 637–646.

ambiguities, the legislator has not been consistent – or, rather, different branches of the judiciary have passed different rulings based on different types of reasoning. Thus, the SCC ruled in the 1990s that in all cases not decided on the basis of "absolutely clear" and "authentic" texts of the Qur'an and Sunna (the Prophetic Traditions), judges should use independent legal reasoning (*ijtihad*).[17]

The space of discretion was considerably narrowed after the overthrow of Husni Mubarak, in 2011, and the election of an Islamist majority into parliament. The new constitution of December 2012 was passed amidst heated debate (Tadros 2013), although for the most part it enacted principles and practices that had already been followed earlier. The constitution retained Art. 2 but went considerably further in spelling out what it implied: Art. 219 provided that the principles of shari'a included "its general proofs or evidences (*adilla kulliyya*), rules of jurisprudence (*qawa'id usuliyya wa-fiqhiyya*), and the sources considered by the Sunni schools of law." This broadened the range beyond Hanafi *fiqh* and excluded Shi'i sources, but given the enormous scope of Sunni jurisprudence, it still left considerable room for manoeuver. Art. 81 stipulated that "rights and freedoms shall be practiced in a manner not conflicting with the principles pertaining to state and society of the constitution." These included the principles of shari'a as defined in Arts. 2 and 219; reference to national unity (Art. 5); and to the moral, cultural, religious, and family values as well as the Arab character of state and society (Arts. 10–12). According to Art. 4, al-Azhar's Association of Senior Scholars (*hay'at kibar al-'ulama'*), had to be consulted on all matters pertaining to shari'a (a practice followed for decades), yet decision on the constitutionality of laws remained with the Supreme Constitutional Court (Art. 175). If applied, the result would have been overlapping competencies and confusion with a high potential for friction.

ISLAM, THE ORDRE PUBLIC, AND RELIGIOUS FREEDOM

The role of the state in setting the parameters of secularity comes out most strongly in the question of religious freedom. Still, the picture is perhaps

---

[17] If the law was silent on a particular issue, the civil code of 1949 instructed judges to apply Islamic law, customary law ('*urf*), and the principle of equity, whereas the personal status law required that they refer to "the most salient opinion" of the Hanafi school of law; see Berger and Sonneveld 2010: 74–78; Gallala 2010: 506–508. For the methodological issues involved, see Lombardi 2006; for the SCC, see also Le Prince et son juge 2000; Amin 2012. For an excellent introduction to Sunni *fiqh*, see Kamali 1991.

less clear than one would expect, for the state is not the only agent involved, and Islamic norms are not the only ones invoked. Since Islam is the state religion, respect for Islam, or for religion at large, is widely identified with the *ordre public* (*al-nizam al-'amm*, a concept with an undisputed European pedigree).[18] Yet the constitution also guarantees the equality of all citizens before the law as well as freedom of thought and conscience and freedom from discrimination. As the constitution leaves the tension between these principles unresolved, dealing with them falls to the courts and other public bodies. Significantly, the term used by the courts is not freedom of religion (*hurriyyat al-din*) but freedom of conviction, or faith (*hurriyyat al-i'tiqad, hurriyyat al-'aqida*) (Pink 2003a: 112–113, 121, 172–182). Egyptian courts have consistently limited freedom of conviction to the *inner forum* – that is to say, a space the authorities would not be able to control anyway. Thus, the Supreme Constitutional Court ruled in 1975 that "freedom of religion is not absolute and that the manifestation of religious beliefs must be subject to and considered in relation to public order, morals and values" (cited in El Fegiery 2013: 6). In accordance with this ruling, the state has restricted *public* expression of faith in a variety of manners: it reserves freedom of public religious practice to monotheists in possession of a book of revelation, that is, Muslims, Jews, and Christians (the "heavenly religions," *al-adyan al-samawiyya*),[19] and it discriminates against non-Sunni Muslims, such as the Shi'a and the Ahmadiyya or Qadyaniyya (the latter are not even recognized as Muslims by the overwhelming majority of Egyptian religious scholars), as well as against post-Qur'anic religious communities that are not recognized as belonging to the family of "heavenly religions," such as the Baha'is, Jehovah's Witnesses, and the Mormons. In the case of the Baha'is, Jehovah's Witnesses, and also the Freemasons, discrimination is not just a matter of belief; in the 1960s they were accused of Zionism and banned. As most of the foreign Christian churches as well as the Baha'is engage in missionary work among local Christians, the Coptic Orthodox Church has consistently endorsed official policies of discrimination and non-toleration.

---

[18] The following relies heavily on Pink 2003. See also El Fegiery 2013.

[19] In accordance with these views and practices, Art. 43 of the constitution of 2012 declared the freedom of belief (*hurriyyat al-i'tiqad*) to be protected but restricted the right to publicly exercise their religious rites and establish their places of worship to the "heavenly religions": Art. 3 recognized the autonomy of Christian and Jewish citizens in personal status and religious matters as well as in the internal affairs of their community.

Citizens are obliged to enter their religious affiliation in all official documents of identification, even if the community concerned has been denied legal recognition (Pink 2003a: 126–129; Pink 2009: 57–59; El Fegiery 2013: 8–18, 22). Religious affiliation is therefore not just a matter of identity but of citizenship, and it is not a private affair unless one classifies access to public functions and services as well as personal status law as "private" (which they are clearly not). Egypt practices what has been called "limited legal pluralism" (Bernard-Maugiron 2011: 373, 384): the courts are unified but follow the personality principle in certain areas of personal status law, while in others they apply Islamic law to Muslims and non-Muslims alike, highlighting the uneasy juxtaposition of toleration, legal recognition, and hierarchy (hegemony) characteristic of pre-modern Muslim polities. Matters are further complicated by the fact that Islamic personal status has not been unified in one code but is found in a number of laws. A few examples must suffice to illustrate the complexity of the subject matter: Islamic law as codified in Egypt is uniformly applied concerning inheritance, testament, custody, and guardianship. By contrast, marriage and divorce are regulated according to the religious laws of (Sunni) Muslims, (Coptic, Greek, Syrian, and Armenian Orthodox, Latin and Eastern Catholic, or Protestant) Christians, or (Rabbanite and Karaite) Jews – provided the parties share the same "denomination" (*ta'ifa*) and "sect" (*milla*). In cases of different affiliation (e.g., Coptic and Armenian Orthodox), Egyptian "general laws" (i.e., Islamic law as codified in Egypt) prevail with the exception of polygamy, which is not permitted to non-Muslims, and divorce, which is restricted in certain cases.[20]

Egyptian law does not recognize non-faith, if made public, as legitimate, and it heavily penalizes all acts considered detrimental to the public order and social peace, including acts ridiculing religion. In an oblique manner, it also denies Muslims the right to change their religious affiliation. The latter occurs especially in the context of marriage and inheritance, and mostly for causes unrelated to religious conviction.[21] Today, apostasy (*irtidad, ridda*) is notoriously difficult to define, especially as it blends easily into heresy and blasphemy.[22] According to Sunni *fiqh*,

---

[20] See Berger 2001, 2003; Bernard-Maugiron and Dupret 2002: 19–36; Pink 2003: 107–109, 117–126; Gallala 2010; Bernard-Maugiron 2011.

[21] The subject has received intensive attention; see notably Pink 2003, 2009; Guirguis 2007; Bernard-Maugiron 2011. Difficulties begin with the fact that conversion of a Muslim to a local Christian church is not always easy to prove as the state sometimes refuses to recognize church documents as valid evidence; El Fegiery 2013: 16–18.

[22] See Saeed and Saeed 2004; Krämer 2006; Guirguis 2007; Schielke 2012.

apostasy and heresy involve the conscious and open denial of religious truth or individual elements of faith and creed. Blasphemy entails not only insult to God but also contempt of the prophets and messengers recognized by Islam, violation of sacred space, disrespectful handling of the Qur'an, and similar acts. All could be used to prosecute religious doubt, critique, and satire as "disrespect for religion," "temptation/disturbance (*fitna*)," or "confusion," and consequently as a threat to public order.[23]

Neither the acts of apostasy, heresy, and blasphemy nor the body authorized to determine their occurrence is clearly defined in Egyptian law. Like in many Muslim countries, apostasy is not explicitly defined as a criminal act but is punishable under civil law. Apostasy literally implies the apostate's civil death: it renders his or her marriage null and void (*batil*); it bars him or her from entering a new marriage; and it excludes him or her from inheritance of Muslims as well as non-Muslims.[24] Judgments are based on case law (Berger 2003; El Fegiery 2013: 6–7), and the most prominent case concerned Nasr Hamid Abu Zayd (1943–2010), a scholar of Arabic and Islamic studies at Cairo University, who was accused of heresy and whose marriage was declared null and void, in 1995/6 (Bälz 1997; Thielmann 2003). However, apostasy and blasphemy can also be subsumed under Par. 98(f) of the Egyptian penal code, which covers a wide range of acts, from extremism and disturbance of the public order, national unity, and social peace to ridiculing the heavenly religions – acts punishable by prison between six months and five years and a fine of 500–1000 Egyptian Pounds. All depends on definition and interpretation, and decisions are again left to ordinary courts and judges, most of them not especially knowledgeable about Muslim or Christian dogma. Thus, the Court of Cassation, referring to Sunni jurisprudence, has treated the conversion of a Muslim as a violation of public order (El Feguiery 2013: 7). This stands in striking contrast to conversions of non-Muslims, be it to another non-Muslim "denomination" or "sect," or to Islam, which the same court considered a private matter, secured by the freedom of belief

[23] Art. 44 of the new constitution of 2012 explicitly banned "contempt" of all messengers and prophets but did not specify the legal sanction.

[24] Gallala 2010: 512. Similar rules apply to non-Muslims, especially Orthodox Copts and Catholics, who leave their denomination or sect; Bernard-Maugiron 2011, esp. 381. Once a marriage has been declared null and void, it no longer needs to be formally dissolved. According to modern Egyptian *fatawa*, sexual intercourse among the (former) spouses is illegal (*zina*), and the children born from the union are considered "null and void" and barred from inheritance; Pink 2003: 98–115. See also Guirguis 2007; Gallala 2010.

(Bernard-Maugiron 2011: 377). Among the scholars, intellectuals, and artists accused of blasphemy, few have actually been convicted. However, the threat is there, and it serves the function of intimidation, especially since the risk of legal prosecution combines with what has been called "street censorship," and self-censorship (La Censure; Van Nieuwkerk 2013: 90, 137–145).

Concerning censorship, the role of al-Azhar and the Coptic Orthodox Church is of special interest, as it highlights the informal exercise of power which need not be laid down in law in order to be effective.[25] Whereas the authority of the Coptic Orthodox Church is limited to its own community, al-Azhar's powers are more wide-ranging. Its role in surveillance and censorship of written materials, exercised in close cooperation with various state security agencies, was formalized in 1994, when al-Azhar's Islamic Research Center (*Majma' al-buhuth al-islamiyya*) was given the right to examine not just publications but also audio and audiovisual materials dealing with Islam and its decisions made binding on the Ministry of Cultural Affairs, which then imposed the ban and confiscated indicted materials. In many instances, control appears to have been exerted still more informally, by getting in touch with the publishers who withdrew the incriminated book, film, video, or play without any involvement on the part of the ministry.

The combination of state control and Islamization at all levels of society has largely silenced voices critical of religion or openly secularist. There is religious doubt, critique, and even satire, but they are usually not directed at Islam and the prophet Muhammad but rather at ordinary Muslims, Islamic scholars, and the state, who and which can more safely be accused of error and "aberration" (see e.g., Schielke 2012). Elements of secular thought have reappeared under the heading of *madaniyya*, which refers to a non-clerical order and which has been used by Islamists and their critics alike. By contrast, the term "secular(ist)" (*'almani*) remains more or less taboo (Krämer 2013a). In spite of a legacy going back to the late nineteenth century and the credibility gained in the national liberation struggle, secularism has not overcome its negative image as a foreign import, unsuited to local culture. The reasons are largely political: secularism is associated with colonial imposition and authoritarian rule and portrayed as both culturally alien and politically intrusive. The advocates of secularism are mostly well-educated members of the urban middle class,

---

[25] On the following, see also Zeghal 1996; Moustafa 2000: 14; Mostyn 2002: 145–151; Pink 2003: 92–93, 140–161; Mehrez 2008; Armanios and Amstutz 2013, esp. 520.

professionals, artists, and intellectuals, whose social impact cannot compare to that of their religious opponents who have been much more successful at playing the identity card (Flores 2012; Krämer 2013b; also Shehata 2010). Faced with Islamism in its various manifestations, secularists and self-declared liberals have tended to side with the (authoritarian) state, both before and after the overthrow of the Islamist government, in the summer of 2013.

CONCLUDING REMARKS

Taylor's reflections on the "conditions of belief" are relevant beyond the North Atlantic world, yet in order for these conditions to be properly addressed, identity politics, market forces, and transregional dynamics under colonial and postcolonial conditions have to be taken into account. These factors are especially relevant to the emergence of Islamic tastes, markets, and media, which have contributed heavily to the current configuration of secularity in Egypt. None of them originated with the Egyptian state. Rather, they reflect global trends, regional influences (mostly from the Arab Gulf countries as their sponsors and consumers), and private interests – factors that did not feature prominently in Taylor's reading of the North Atlantic case. Nor do they figure sufficiently in the state-centered approaches that have been privileged in much recent scholarship on secularism. The frequently asked question of whether the modern Egyptian state is religious or secular is not so difficult to answer: the state is secular (i.e., non-clerical) in structure and composition, but it is not neutral, granting equal access, equal respect, and equal support to all religious communities within its territory. Through its laws and constitution as well as through its support for Sunni Islamic and, to a lesser extent, Coptic religious practices and institutions, the state projects itself as the guardian of Egyptian identity. To the extent that it also uses this position to contain political Islam, even repressive state policies are backed by significant parts of the population, including practicing Muslims, leftists, and self-styled liberals. Given these ambiguities, I suggest to distinguish between (1) faith, belief, and religiosity among the population, which, as in large parts of the globe, have not declined in Egypt despite long-ongoing processes of secularization in the fields of politics, law, education, and economics; (2) the role of shari'a, which serves as a symbol of unity, identity, and authenticity to many and as a major irritant to others, causing conflict at home and abroad; and (3) the Islamic trend in general and the Organization of the Muslim Brothers in particular, whose claims to power and legitimacy have been contested by religious and non-religious forces alike.

Bibliography

Abaza, Mona. 2006. *Changing Consumer Cultures of Modern Egypt. Cairo's Urban Reshaping*. Leiden/Boston: Brill.

'Abd al-Fattah, Nabil. 1984. *Al-mushaf wa-l-sayf. Sira' al-din wa-l-dawla fi misr.* Cairo: Maktabat Madbuli.

1997. *Al-nass wa-l-rasas. Al-islam al-siyasi wa-l-aqbat wa-azmat al-dawla al-haditha fi misr.* Cairo: Dar al-Nahar.

Abu 'Ajjur, Muhammad Muhammad. 2012. *Al-dawla al-madaniyya allati nurid.* Al-Mansura: Dar al-Kalima li-l-Nashr wa-l-Tawzi'.

Abu-Lughod, Lila. 2005. *Dramas of Nationhood. The Politics of Television in Egypt*. Chicago/London: University of Chicago Press.

Agrama, Hussein Ali. 2012. *Questioning Secularism. Islam, Sovereignty, and the Rule of Law in Modern Egypt*. Chicago: University of Chicago Press.

Amin, Ahmad. 2012. *Al-madda al-thaniyya min al-dustur: madluluha … wa-nata'ijuha*. Cairo: Maktabat al-Shuruq al-Dawliyya.

Armanios, Febe. 2002. "The 'Virtuous Woman': Images of Gender in Modern Coptic Society." *Middle Eastern Studies* 38: 110–130.

Armanios, Febe, and Andrew Amstutz. 2013. "Emerging Christian Media in Egypt: Clerical Authority and the Visualization of Women in Coptic Video Films." *International Journal of Middle East Studies* 45(3): 513–533.

Asad, Talal. 2003. *Formations of the Secular. Christianity, Islam, Modernity.* Stanford: Stanford University Press.

Bälz, Kilian. 1997. "Submitting Faith to Judicial Scrutiny Through the Family Trial: The 'Abū Zayd Case'." *Die Welt des Islams* 37(2): 135–155.

Bayat, Asef. 2007a. "Islamism and the Politics of Fun." *Public Culture* 19(3): 433–460.

2007b. *Making Islam Democratic. Social Movements and the Post-Islamist Turn*. Stanford: Stanford University Press.

Berger, Maurits. 2001. "Public Policy and Islamic Law: the Modern Dhimmi in Contemporary Egyptian Family Law." *Islamic Law and Society* 8(1): 88–136.

2003. "Apostasy and Public Policy in Contemporary Egypt: An Evaluation of Recent Cases from Egypt's Highest Courts." *Human Rights Quarterly* 25(3): 720–740.

Berger, Maurits, and Nadia Sonneveld. 2010. "Sharia and National Law in Egypt." *Sharia Incorporated. A Comparative Overview of the Legal Systems of Twelve Muslim Countries in Past and Present*, ed. Jan Michiel Otto. Leiden/Boston: Brill: 51–88.

Bernard-Maugiron, Nathalie, and Baudouin Dupret. (eds.) 2002. *Egypt and Its Laws*. London: Kluwer Law International.

Bernard-Maugiron, Nathalie. 2011. "Divorce and Remarriage of Orthodox Copts in Egypt: The 2008 State Council Ruling and the Amendment of the 1938 Personal Status Regulations." *Islamic Law and Society* 18(3–4): 356–386.

al-Bishri, Tariq. 1980. *Al-muslimun wa-l-aqbat fi itar al-jama'a al-wataniyya.* Cairo: al-Hay'a al-Misriyya al-'Amma li-l-Kitab.

Casanova, José. 2008. "Public Religions Revisited." *Religion: Beyond a Concept,* ed. Hent de Vries. New York: Fordham University Press, 101–119.

La Censure ou comment la contourner. 2001, ed. Dyala Hamzah. Brussels: Éditions Complexe (=*Egypte/Monde arabe* 3.1, 2000), Cairo: CEDEJ.

Clark, Janine A. 2004. *Islam, Charity, and Activism. Middle-Class Networks and Social Welfare in Egypt, Jordan, and Yemen.* Bloomington/Indianapolis: Indiana University Press.

Dustur Jumhuriyyat Misr al-'Arabiyya (Constitution of the Arab Republic of Egypt) 2012. *Official Gazette* 51bis of 25 December 2012.

Al-du'a al-judud bayna "'asrina al-tadayyun" wa-"bay' al-da'wa" 2010. Dubai: al-Misbar.

Eccel, A. Chris. 1984. *Egypt, Islam and Social Change. Al-Azhar in Conflict and Accomodation.* Berlin: Klaus Schwarz Verlag.

El Fegiery, Moataz Ahmed. 2013. "Islamic Law and Freedom of Religion: The Case of Apostasy and Its Legal Implications." *Muslim World Journal of Human Rights* 10(1): 1–26.

Elsaesser, Sebastian. 2014. *The Coptic Question in the Mubarak Era.* Oxford: Oxford University Press.

Esposito, John, and Azzam Tamimi. (eds.) 2000. *Islam and Secularism in the Middle East.* New York: New York University Press.

Flores, Alexander. 2012. *Säkularismus und Islam in Ägypten. Die Debatte der 1980er Jahre.* Berlin: LIT Verlag.

Gallala, Imen. 2010. "Religionsfreiheit und islamisch geprägtes Erbrecht: Gesetzliche Regelungen und Rechtsprechungsauslegungen im heutigen Ägypten und Tunesien." *Beiträge zum Islamischen Recht VII,* ed. Hatem Ellisie. Frankfurt am Main: Peter Lang, 499–521.

Gershoni, Israel, and James P. Jankowski. 1987. *Egypt, Islam, and the Arabs. The Search for Egyptian Nationhood, 1900–1930.* New York/Oxford: Oxford University Press.

   1995. *Redefining the Egyptian Nation, 1930–1945.* Cambridge: Cambridge University Press.

Guirguis, Laure. (ed.) 2007. *Conversions religieuses et mutations politiques en Égypte.* Paris: Non Lieu.

Haenni, Patrick. 2005. *L'islam de marché. L'autre révolution conservatrice.* Paris: Seuil.

Hafez, Sherine. 2003. The Terms of Empowerment. Islamic Women Activist in Egypt. Cairo: Cairo University Press (=Cairo papers in social science 24(4).

   2011. *An Islam of Her Own. Reconsidering Religion and Secularism in Women's Islamic Movements.* New York/London: New York University Press.

Hammad, Muhammad. 2011. *Qissat al-dustur al-misri. Ma'arik wa-watha'iq wa-nusus.* Cairo: Maktabat Jazirat al-Ward.

Hasan, 'Ammar 'Ali. 2009. *Al-tanmiya al-siyasiyya li-l-turuq al-sufiyya fi misr.* Cairo: Dar al-'Ayn.

Hassan, Sanaa S. 2003. *Christians versus Muslims in Modern Egypt. The Century-Long Struggle for Coptic Equality*. New York/Oxford: Oxford University Press.

Hatina, Meir. 2010. *'Ulama', Politics, and the Public Sphere. An Egyptian Perspective*. Salt Lake City: University of Utah Press.

Hirschkind, Charles. 2006. *The Ethical Soundscape. Cassette Sermons and Islamic Counterpublics*. New York: Columbia University Press.

Hoffman, Valerie. 1995. *Sufis, Mystics, and Saints in Modern Egypt*. New York: Columbia University Press.

Kalmbach, Hilary. 2012. "Dar al-ʿUlum." *Encyclopaedia of Islam Three* 2012(3): 109–112.

Kamali, Mohammad Hashim. 1991. *Principles of Islamic Jurisprudence*. Cambridge: Islamic Texts Society.

Krämer, Gudrun. 2006. "Drawing Boundaries. Yūsuf al-Qaraḍāwī on Apostasy." *Speaking for Islam. Religious Authorities in Muslim Societies*, ed. Gudrun Krämer and Sabine Schmidtke. Leiden/Boston: Brill, 181–217.

— 2010. *Hasan al-Banna*. Oxford: Oneworld.

— 2013a. "Gottes-Recht bricht Menschen-Recht. Theokratische Entwürfe im zeitgenössischen Islam." *Theokratie und theokratischer Diskurs*, ed. Kai Trampedach and Andreas Pečar. Tübingen: Mohr Siebeck, 493–515.

— 2013b. "Modern but not Secular: Religion, Identity, and the *Ordre Public* in the Arab Middle East." *International Sociology* 28(6): 629–644.

Lombardi, Clark B. 2006. *State Law as Islamic Law in Modern Egypt. The Incorporation of the* Sharīʿa *into Egyptian Constitutional Law*. Leiden/Boston: Brill.

Mahmood, Saba. 2005. *Politics of Piety. The Islamic Revival and the Feminist Subject*. Princeton: Princeton University Press.

Mehrez, Samira. 2008. *Egypt's Culture Wars: Politics and Practice*. New York: Routledge.

Mostyn, Trevor. 2002. *Censorship in Islamic Societies*. London: Saqi Books.

Moustafa, Tamir. 2000. "Conflict and Cooperation between the State and Religious Institutions in Contemporary Egypt." *International Journal of Middle East Studies* 32(1): 3–22.

Peters, Rudolph. 1988. "Divine Law or Man-Made Law? Egypt and the Application of the Sharia." *Arab Law Quarterly* 3(3): 231–253.

Pink, Johanna. 2003a. *Neue Religionsgemeinschaften in Ägypten. Minderheiten im Spannungsfeld von Glaubensfreiheit, öffentlicher Ordnung und Islam*. Würzburg: Ergon.

— 2003b. "A Post-Qur'ānic Religion between Apostasy and Public Order: Egyptian Muftis and Courts on the Legal Status of the Bahā'ī Faith." *Islamic Law and Society* 10(3): 409–434.

— 2009. "Ägyptische Blogs als Medien zivilgesellschaftlicher Aktivität? Probleme der Analyse und Bewertung am Beispiel der Bahā'ī-Kontroverse." *Vom Chatraum zum Cyberjihad. Muslimische Internetnutzung in lokaler und globaler Perspektive*, ed. Matthias Brückner and Johanna Pink. Würzburg: Ergon, 49–72.

Le Prince et son juge. Droit et politique dans l'Égypte contemporaine. 1999, ed. Nathalie Bernard-Maugiron and Baudouin Dupret (=*Egypte/Monde arabe* 2.2). Cairo: CEDEJ.

Richter, Carola. 2011. *Medienstrategien ägyptischer Islamisten im Kontext von Demokratisierung*. Leipzig: Frank & Timme.

Saeed, Abdullah, and Hassan Saeed. 2004. *Freedom of Religion, Apostasy and Islam*. Aldershot: Ashgate.

Salvatore, Armando, and Mark LeVine. (eds.) 2005. *Religion, Social Practice, and Contested Hegemonies. Reconstructing the Public Sphere in Muslim Majority Societies*. New York/Houndsmills: Palgrave Macmillan.

Scott, Rachel M. 2010. *The Challenge of Political Islam: Non-Muslims and the Egyptian State*. Stanford: Stanford University Press.

Schielke, Samuli. 2012. "Being a Nonbeliever in a Time of Islamic Revival: Trajectories of Doubt and Certainty in Contemporary Egypt." *International Journal of Middle East Studies* 44(2): 301–320.

Serageldin, Samia. 2005. "The Islamic Salon. Elite Women's Religious Networks in Egypt." *Muslim Networks from Hajj to Hip Hop*, ed. Miriam Cooke and Bruce B. Lawrence. Chapel Hill/London: University of North Carolina Press, 155–168.

Shalata, Ahmad Zaghlul. 2011. *Al-hala al-salafiyya fi misr*. Cairo: Maktabat Madbuli.

Shehata, Dina. 2010. *Islamists and Secularists in Egypt. Opposition, Conflict, and Cooperation*. London/New York: Routledge.

Skovgaard-Petersen, Jakob. 1997. *Defining Islam for the Egyptian State. Muftis and Fatwas of the Dar al-Ifta'*. Leiden/Boston: Brill.

Starrett, Gregory. 1998. *Putting Islam to Work. Education, Politics, and Religious Transformation in Egypt*. Berkeley, Los Angeles, London: University of California Press.

Tadros, Mariz. 2009. "Vicissitudes in the Entente between the Coptic Orthodox Church and the State in Egypt (1952–2007)." *International Journal of Middle East Studies* 41(2): 269–287.

Tadroz, Samuel. 2013. "What is a Constitution Anyway?" *Current Trends in Islamist Ideology* 14: 5–26.

Talayma, ʿIsam. 2008. *Hasan al-Banna wa-tajribat al-fann*. Cairo: Maktabat Wahba.

Taylor, Charles. 2007. *A Secular Age*. Cambridge MA/London: Belknap Press.
2009. "The Polysemy of the Secular." *Social Research* 76(4): 1143–1166.

Tezcür, Güneş Murat. 2010. *Muslim Reformers in Iran and Turkey. The Paradox of Moderation*. Austin: University of Texas Press.

Thielmann, Jörn. 2003. *Naṣr Ḥāmid Abū Zaid und die wiedererfundene ḥisba. Šarīʿa und Qānūn im heutigen Ägypten*. Würzburg: Ergon.

Utvik, Bjørn Olav. 2006. *Islamist Economics in Egypt. The Pious Road to Development*. Boulder/London: Lynne Riener.

Van Nieuwkerk, Karin. 2013. *Performing Piety. Singers and Actors in Egypt's Islamic Revival*. Austin: University of Texas Press.

Voile, Brigitte. 2004. *Les Coptes d'Egypte sous Nasser. Sainteté, miracles, apparitions*. Paris: CNRS.

Warner, Michael, Jonathan Vanentwerpen, and Craig Calhoun. (eds.) 2010. *Varieties of Secularism in a Secular Age*. Cambridge MA/London: Cambridge University Press.

Wickham, Carrie Rosefsky. 2002. *Mobilizing Islam. Religion, Activism, and Political Change in Egypt*. New York: Columbia University Press.

2013. *The Muslim Brotherhood. Evolution of an Islamist Movement*. Princeton/Oxford: Princeton University Press.

Wippel, Steffen. 1994. *Gott, Geld und Staat. Aufstieg und Niedergang der islamischen Investmentgesellschaften in Ägypten im Spannungsfeld von Ökonomie, Politik und Religion*. Münster/Hamburg: LIT Verlag.

1997. *Islamische Wirtschafts- und Wohlfahrtseinrichtungen in Ägypten zwischen Markt und Moral*. Münster/Hamburg: LIT Verlag.

Wohlrab-Sahr, Monika, and Marian Burchardt. 2012. "Multiple Secularities. Toward a Cultural Sociology of Secular Modernities." *Comparative Sociology* 11(6): 875–909.

Zeghal, Malika. 1996. *Gardiens de l'Islam. Les oulémas d'Al Azhar dans l'Égypte contemporaine*. Paris: Presses de Sciences Po.

13

The Commander of the Faithful and Moroccan Secularity

Jonathan Wyrtzen

INTRODUCTION

Like the other studies in this volume, this chapter seeks to broaden and challenge the framework Charles Taylor developed to describe processes at work in Latin Christendom in *A Secular Age* (2007) by testing its applicability within very different empirical contexts outside the Western world. This chapter turns to the far Western edge of the Arab–Muslim world to ask how secularity has been understood and expressed in Morocco. At first glance, Morocco appears to be a case in which none of Taylor's three dimensions of secularity apply. Rather than a separation of religious and political structures, a "retreat" of religion from public spaces, expressed by Secularity I (Taylor 2007:1, 15), Islam is the constitutionally recognized official religion of a country in which a four-century-old Islamic dynastic state fuses religious and political authority in the person of the king, who claims the title "Commander of the Faithful." Regarding Secularity II, rather than a decrease in religious belief and practice, empirical evidence would arguably indicate the opposite.[1]

Though a seeming oxymoron, I would argue a "Moroccan secularity," or the potential for one, does exist, however, in reference to Taylor's Secularity III: a shift in the conditions of belief in which religious belief becomes an option among others. While for Taylor this dimension relates

---

[1] A Pew Forum (2012) study of beliefs and practices across the Muslim world which sampled 1474 respondents in Morocco indicates that 98 percent believe in the one God and the Prophet (affirming the *shahada*); 89 percent affirmed religion is very important in their life; 67 percent pray five times a day; 54 percent attend mosque at least once a week; 39 percent read the Qu'ran once a day; 92 percent give alms (*zakat*); and 98 percent fast during Ramadan.

primarily to the conditions of belief for the individual subject, I want to shift the emphasis to the *collective* ramifications of pluralizing processes and their political implications in Moroccan society. In this analysis, I am interested in how Secularity I and Secularity III interact, how Islam's public and political role and various expressions of plurality (political, ethno-linguistic, and religious) have been negotiated in Morocco. This analysis focuses on critical junctures at which the relationship between Islam and the political order were forged, setting up a path dependence impacting the trajectory of the secular settlement, or lack thereof, in the Moroccan context.[2] In Morocco the issue is not so much whether religion, in this case Islam, is to be disassociated from public life (i.e. Secularity I); rather, the rising stakes of a type of Secularity III relate to whether the state, through the king's role as "Commander of the Faithful," continues to monopolize or allows for a pluralization of Islam's political role.

This discussion begins by analyzing the bifurcated modernizing and traditionalizing mode of colonial state-building employed by the French during the protectorate period 1912–1956, which nominally maintained the interlinked religious and political authority of the sultan to legitimate their intervention. Urban anti-colonial nationalists challenged this framework, fusing Islam and Arab identity to reinforce the religious and ethnic unity of the Moroccan *ummah*. Later, the Alawite monarchy skillfully maximized its leverage within both frameworks to consolidate its control over the postcolonial state, aspiring to a state monopoly on the production of Islam in Morocco. The final sections of the chapter turn to recent struggles since the accession of King Mohamed VI in 1999 over this post-independence non-secular settlement. These include challenges from the Amazigh (Berber),[3] women's, and Islamist movements, up to the more recent wave of protests mobilized in the wake of the Tunisian and Egyptian Revolutions in 2011. Through a series of moves culminating in the constitutional reform process initiated immediately after the first "Arab Spring" protests, Mohamed VI has implemented pluralizing and

---

[2] In this case, the historical institutionalist approach (Collier and Collier 1991; Pierson 2004; Mahoney and Thelen 2010) discussed by Gorski in Chapter 2 can also be helpful for analyzing this type of counterfactual where various actors have had vested interests in not reaching a secular settlement.

[3] The term *Amazigh*, or "free person," is used by contemporary activists in place of the word Berber, which is viewed (correctly) as a pejorative label used since the time of the Greeks to mark the uncivilized "barbarians." The word *Tamazight* (one of the three Berber dialects in Morocco) is used to denote the language. For the political genealogy of these usages, see McDougall (2003).

democratizing policies recognizing ethno-cultural and individual rights while still shoring up the monarchy's religio-political monopoly of power. The conclusion considers the stakes of secularity in Morocco, situating these struggles among various parties in the Moroccan political and social field within Gorki's four-fold typology of state–religion settlements and their relationship to the three goods identified by Taylor (2011): religious liberty, civic equality, and political solidarity.

RELIGION AND COLONIAL STATE-BUILDING

To begin, it is important to consider the public and political role religion played within pre-colonial Morocco. What was the historical relationship between religion and the state? Much of Morocco's political history is Islamic dynastic history, stretching back to the founding of the Idrisid state in Fes in the eighth century. Four primary modes of religious legitimation have historically been employed within successive state-building cycles over the past 1,200 years (Kably 1986, Kably 1999). The earliest was *Sharifianism*, claiming physical descent from the Prophet Mohamed, which imbued the political ruler with a form of "hereditary charisma" (Weber 1978: 248). In Morocco, this form of religio-political authority was first invoked by Idriss I, a grandson of Mohamed's daughter Fatima and son-in-law 'Ali, who fled Umayyad persecution in the eighth century and founded a dynastic state in central Morocco. The next mode was *reformist revivalism*, an ideological, puritanical mode of religious legitimation that undergirded the eleventh century Almoravid and twelfth century Almohad empires that extended control over most of Northwest Africa and the Iberian Peninsula. The Almoravids also relied on a third form of religious legitimation, *Malikism*, or state support for the Maliki school of Islamic jurisprudence. The fourth mode, *jihad*, or defense of the Muslim *ummah*, or community, was used to buttress the legitimacy of multiple state-building dynasties, but came to the fore (along with the return of *Sharifianism*) with the Saadian and later Alawite efforts to repel Portuguese and Spanish incursions into Moroccan territory in the sixteenth and seventeenth centuries. Throughout Moroccan history, these modes of religious legitimation have been used, usually in combination, to undergird the political order.

Like corollary examples elsewhere in the Muslim world and in Europe, various expressions of Secularity I – implicit or explicit differentiation between the religious and secular, between two spheres of authority – have also been expressed throughout Moroccan history. This differentiation typically became most clear when political rulers attempted to collapse the two together and were challenged by religious figures or institutions. One of the classic examples of this is the seventeenth century maraboutic Sufi figure, Hassan Al-Yusi, who publicly criticized the great Alawite state-builder, Moulay Ismail, through a series of *nasihat*, or open letters providing "guidance" to the political ruler (Geertz 1971; Munson 1993). This confrontation pitted Al-Yusi's religious authority rooted in his own saintly *baraka*, or charismatic power and authority, against the hierocratic claims to sacred kingship wielded by Moulay Ismail. Al-Yusi invokes a contractual framework of just rule, holding the sultan accountable to implement Islamic law. This episode came at the tail end of the "maraboutic crisis" that emerged with the breakdown of Merenid rule in the fifteenth century, which was typified by a pluralistic topography of political and religious authority (Berque 1982). In addition to charismatic saintly figures such as Al-Yusi, several autonomous religious institutions, including Sufi networks (*tariqat*) and the ulama, particularly in Fes, resisted efforts by the state to unify and monopolize the religious and political spheres. The latter, in particular, used the mechanism of the *ba'ya*, or oath of allegiance, to link political legitimacy to obligations including *jihad* and the implementation of *shari'a*.

This brief overview of pre-colonial Moroccan history clarifies a persistent structural differentiation between temporal and religious authority, representing a latent potential for Secularity I. However, in contrast to Taylor's description of an "emancipation" (2007: 6) of the former from the latter, Morocco's rulers have long attempted to conflate the two, reinforcing monopolies over both. This brings us to the colonial period and the question of how the imposition of external rule impacted the role of religion in the public sphere. This settlement was directly related to the context in which Morocco was colonized and decisions about the formal framework for French intervention.

Morocco was the last (literal) corner of Africa to be colonized in the "scramble for Africa" that transpired among European powers in the late nineteenth century. Because of a diplomatic deadlock related to Morocco's geographic position controlling the Straits of Gibraltar, the Great Powers agreed to refrain from unilateral political or military intervention.[4] In the first decade of the twentieth century, France settled competing colonial

---

[4] Britain, seeking to protect its route to India, was wary of the French, and later the Germans, gaining a position from which to shut down the straits. It therefore had a vested interested in propping up the Moroccan government and providing a diplomatic fire wall against these countries' expansionist aspirations.

claims with Britain and Germany and moved forward with direct military occupation and political incorporation, formally recognized with the signing of the Treaty of Fes by the Moroccan sultan and the French representative in March 1912.

The Treaty of Fes created a formal framework of colonial rule that incorporated a particular symbolic framework of religio-political legitimization that, even though nominally upheld, established important path dependencies for the Moroccan context. The stated purpose of the protectorate (Arabic *himayah*) was to "establish a stable regime founded on internal order and general security that will permit the introduction of reforms and will assure the economic development of the country" while preserving the notional sovereignty of the sultan.[5] According to the logic of this state-building *mission civilisatrice*, the French protector would help develop a modern state apparatus and economy in Morocco. In return, the sultan ceded to the French the responsibilities of maintaining security and order, the right to militarily occupy Moroccan territory, and Morocco's diplomatic representation. The treaty stipulated the French government could institute whatever administrative, judicial, educational, economic, financial, or military reforms it judged necessary within Moroccan territory to facilitate the country's development. The French also pledged to safeguard the traditional religious respect and prestige accorded to the sultan, who continued to control religious institutions (*habous*, or *awqaf*).

In effect, the construction of the colonial state during the French Protectorate introduced a colonial form of Secularity I, dividing between the modern bureaucratic and traditional state but nominally using Islam, via the person of the sultan, to legitimate the entire political sphere. While in France the 1905 law on the separation of churches and states articulated a particular formation of *laïcité*, in the colonies (and particularly within Morocco, where the first Resident General, Hubert Lyautey, was a staunch monarchist), the French typically avoided overt secularization policies (Maghroui 2009: 112), and instead carefully preserved traditional religious structures in order to ensure stability. The result created an ambiguous settlement, with a de facto secularization of parts of the modern state apparatus, which were dominated by French functionaries, but also the state's use of religion to structure public life, for the natives, through the educational and judicial system that differentiated between Muslim and Jewish Moroccans.

[5] The French version of the Treaty of Fes is printed in *L'Afrique française* 22, no. 6 (June 1912), pp. 219–220.

Where the French came closest to explicitly implementing a form of *laicité*, attempting to remove or at least limit the public role of Islam, was in the notorious "Berber Policy" that became a bête noire for the Moroccan Arabo-Islamic nationalist movement in the 1930s. This policy of ethnic differentiation, which evolved from the early pacification operations in the Berber-speaking areas of Morocco in the first decade of the protectorate, entailed the creation of separate administrative, judicial, and educational structures for so-called Berber regions of Morocco. The goal, based on stereotypes informed by the "Berber myth" inherited from Algeria (Lorcin 1995, McDougall 2008, Abi-Mershed 2010), was to ally Morocco's Berbers – who were supposedly more democratic and freedom loving, less Islamized, and more secular (or even residually Christian) – with the French against the Arabs, a task which necessitated preserving their separate ethno-linguistic identity. Administratively, these regions were largely kept under military control through the Direction of Indigenous Affairs. Educationally, the Ministry of Public Instruction established Berber schools in the Atlas ranges and a *college* for Berber chiefs' sons in Azrou. Within this system, the teaching of Islam and Arabic was prohibited, and only Berber and French were taught. A secularizing impulse also informed a decision to maintain and encourage a separate Berber system of customary law courts apart from the *shari'a* judiciary under the purview of the sultan, which, like the Dutch in Indonesia (see Künkler, Chapter 5 in this volume) they hoped would forestall the further consolidation of a unified Muslim political identity (Hoffman 2008, 2010; Wyrtzen 2011).

These divide-and-rule practices vis-à-vis segments of the Berber-speaking population, which were also employed in related ways toward Morocco's Jewish minority, represented a variation of a Luhmann-type of segmentary differentiation, which Gorski describes in Chapter 2. The colonial state aspired to separate three categories of native ethno-religious identity within Moroccan society: Muslim Arab, proto-secular Berber, and Jewish. However, this pluralistic classificatory schema used to impose social divisions in Moroccan society was in direct odds against the legitimacy framework undergirding the protectorate. In the Treaty of Fes, the French had nominally kept the Islamic legitimacy structure of the state in place – namely Sharifianism and Malikism – in their pledge to uphold the religious authority of the sultan. Beginning in the 1930s, Moroccan nationalists began to wage what Bourdieu calls a "classification struggle" from below, contesting the colonial state's segmentation of the politico-religious field in Morocco and calling for linguistic and juridical unification at a national level.

ISLAM, ARABIC, AND MOROCCAN ANTI-COLONIAL NATIONALISM

As Jaffrelot's chapter on Pakistan in this volume emphasizes, processes of colonial state-building politicized religious identity in multiple ways in the non-Western world, often leading to religion being a principal marker and mobilizer of the nation in anti-colonial contention. This was clearly the case in Morocco where, from the 1930s, Moroccan nationalists began to challenge the colonial divisionary logics described above and push for state directed policies of Islamization and Arabization to reinforce the ethno-religious unity of the Moroccan *ummah*. The first wave of urban nationalist protest was catalyzed by a May 1930 decree promulgated by the colonial state that further systematized the separate Berber customary court system and channeled criminal cases into the French system, rather than into the Sharifian Islamic courts (Lafuente 1999). Decrying the "Berber Dahir" as part of a larger French Berber policy intending to separate Morocco's Berbers from Arabs and Christianize them, Moroccan urban activists used a traditional prayer spoken in times of distress or calamity, the *Latif*, to frame the threat and mobilize street demonstrations in Morocco's urban centers, including Rabat, Salé, Fes, Marrakesh, and Casablanca, against the colonial state which continued throughout the summer of 1930 (Wyrtzen 2013). The protests died down that fall in Morocco after the Residency cracked down with mass arrests, but the nationalists, and the Geneva-based Pan-Islamist propagandist, Chakib Arslan, continued to expound on the "Berber Crisis" and its threat against the Muslim *ummah* throughout the early 1930s in journal and newspaper articles published in France and elsewhere in the Muslim world.

This formative episode had a long-term impact on Morocco's anti-colonial nationalist movement. On a tactical level, the Berber *Dahir* protests influenced the evolution of a Moroccan "repertoire of contention" (Tilly 1995) that intertwined Islam and anti-colonial political protest, while forging a popular conception of Moroccan national identity. In mobilizing protest, the nationalists exploited mosques as spaces relatively free of colonial surveillance and the site for the largest public gatherings, particularly for the Friday services. They also relied on informal networks created through Islamic educational institutions, particularly the Qarawiyyin

University where many studied, in the early phases of organization building. Recognizing how the nationalists were using religious symbolic and structural resources, the Residency pressured the sultan to issue an open letter, published on August 11, 1930, condemning the nationalists for politicizing religion in their distortion of the May 16 decree and their use of the *Latif* prayer:

> Some young people, lacking any type of discernment and unaware of the full range of their reprehensible acts, would have one believe that these measures that we have decreed have no goal but the Christianization of the Berbers. They have thus induced the crowds to believe this error and convinced people to gather in the mosques to recite the "*Latif*" prayers after the ritual prayers, transforming prayer by this process into a political demonstration that troubles peoples' minds. Our Majesty absolutely condemns the transforming of mosques, which God made as places of prayer and piety, into halls for political gatherings where hidden political agendas and negative tendencies are given free range. (Quoted in Lafuente 1999: 196)

This letter offers insight into the type of religious/secular settlement the French expected in Morocco: Islam's role in the political field was only for symbolic legitimation of the state, not as a medium of contention. Moroccan nationalists, however, continued to fuse the political and religious in their anti-colonial framing of the threat against the Moroccan *ummah* from the "Christian" French. Countering the pluralistic divisionary logics of the colonial state, Moroccan nationalists conflated the religious community, the *ummah*, with the ethno-religious unity of the *watan*, or nation, introducing what Taylor refers to as a "neo-Durkheimian" expression of religio-political identity (2003: 78). This boundary definition and maintenance around the political community simultaneously recognized and glossed over the separate Berber ethnic identity in Morocco, which had been subsumed by historic assimilationist processes of Islamization and Arabization (which the nationalists expected the protectorate administration to accelerate, rather than forestall with separate "Berber" courts and schools). For the nationalists, Morocco's progress forward was predicated on a continued cultural homogenization, a nation-building process around the "High Culture" of Arabic and Islam.

The nationalist movement included multiple ideological streams, which were strategically deployed in various contexts. One of these was *salafism*, inculcated in the nationalist generation by teachers at the Qarawayn who had been influenced by Islamic *islah*, or reform, movements in the Hejaz and Cairo that prioritized reinterpreting and modernizing *shari'a* in order to rejuvenate Muslim societies (Abun-Nasr 1963; Spadola 2013). The movement also drew on the French liberal tradition, pressing the protectorate administration for more equal distribution of budget appropriations to Moroccans for schools and for economic assistance to farmers and artisans. In addition, they pressed for equal legal and political rights, decrying inequalities maintained by the colonial state. The more "liberal" stream, however, represented by the Paris-educated Hassan El-Ouazzani, within the Moroccan nationalist movement, did not urge any form of a *laicist* political framework but took the fundamental role of Islam as a given (El-Mansour 1996).

This identification of the political and religious community, the de facto conflation of *ummah* and *watan*, had two strategic benefits. First, on a pragmatic level, it helped to mobilize a mass movement by appealing to a shared religious discourse and pre-existing feelings of solidarity. Second, it exploited the protectorate's own formal logic – the French commitment in the Treaty of Fes to modernize and develop the country on behalf of the sultan while respecting his temporal and spiritual authority – to challenge the colonial state's policies. Third, it also appealed to the logic of national self-determination, which by the interwar period had become the normative ideological framework of political legitimacy within the interstate system. Islam played an integral role in defining Moroccan identity and thereby in defining a "legitimate" political order.

Ambiguity about the "civic" and "ethno-religious" boundaries of Moroccan national identity was brought into sharp relief by Morocco's Jewish Question, as this historic minority, though repeatedly assured of their equal position in the nation, was marginalized within the core cultural definition of the national community. However, due to the smaller size of this minority (250,000 out of a total population of 7 million in the 1940s [Gouvernement Chérifien 1946]), the question of minority rights and religious pluralism did not play as large a role in Morocco as in other cases in this volume, such as Indonesia, or elsewhere in the region, such as Egypt, Palestine, or Syria, where larger proportional Christian populations stimulated a sharper distinction between religious and secular framings of national identity (Jankowski and Gershoni 1997). In Morocco, no secular alternative discourse ever emerged to vie with the dominant Arabo-Islamic national identity cultivated in the anti-colonial struggle. In this respect, Morocco exhibits some of the characteristics Jaffrelot defines as Secularity IV in his analysis of Pakistan in this volume, where religion is purposed as an ideology of political identity. However, where ethno-religious national identity was defined in Pakistan in opposition to Hindu-majority India (and similarly in Israel against surrounding Arab countries), in Morocco it was forged in opposition to the colonial power, France, and its attempts to institutionalize and perpetuate internal linguistic and legal differentiation between Arab and Berber Muslims. Beginning in the 1930s, Moroccan nationalists exploited this perceived threat against the *religious* unity of the country to mobilize political activism and no serious secular variant of Moroccan nationalism ever emerged as a viable alternative. In addition, the nationalists themselves put the Alawite monarch, Muhammad V, at the symbolic forefront of this struggle. His emergence in the 1940s–1950s as Morocco's primary nationalist symbol, fusing political and religious capital, established a path dependence that has influenced the postcolonial state ever since (Wyrtzen 2015).

THE RE-ASCENDANT COMMANDER OF THE FAITHFUL: POSTCOLONIAL CONSENSUAL POLITICAL PLURALISM AND THE STATE'S MONOPOLY ON ISLAM

Compared to other cases in the Arab and Muslim world, Morocco's decolonization process was unique on two levels. First, whereas most of the indigenous dynasties maintained by colonial powers to justify indirect rule were delegitimized by this association and ousted before or soon after independence by a charismatic nationalist leader (Habib Bourguiba in Tunisia) or by a military officer coup (Egypt, Iraq, Libya), in Morocco, the sultan-cum-king Mohamed V began to openly counter the French in the late 1940s and emerged in the 1950s as a nationalist martyr and hero after his two year exile in Madagascar (1953–1955). Second, compared to virtually every other mid-century newly independent state in the region, Morocco was one of the few, outside of Jordan and the monarchies in the Arabian Peninsula, where a republican, Arab nationalist ideology was not used to legitimate the postcolonial state. In the Arab East (*Mashriq*), the political order, due to the influential role played by Arab Christian elites in articulating the ideals of Arab nationalism, was legitimated primarily by a discourse of Arab cultural identity, which, while not exclusive of Islam, was more secular in its orientation in the primacy it gave to Arab over Muslim identity. The *Maghrib*, or North Africa, has no corollary Christian minority, and its proportionally much smaller historic Jewish minority did not play an influential role in the nationalist leadership.[6] In

---

[6] In Algeria, Jews had been unilaterally naturalized as French citizens with the 1870 Crémieux Decree, creating tensions with Muslims, who were subjugated to repressive indigenous codes from the 1880s. In Morocco and Tunisia, many Jewish elites were

large part due to the colonial state's own classificatory practices which used Islam as the primary marker of "native" status in North Africa, nationalist elites in Morocco, Algeria, and Tunisia politicized Arab-Islamic identity in defining and mobilizing the nation in anti-colonial struggle. After independence, Bourguiba moved toward a secularist orientation in Tunisia, ousting rivals in the Neo-Dustur party, such as Salah ben Yusuf, with more Arabo-Islamic orientations (Perkins 2004: 126). In Algeria, the FLN referred to Algeria's Islamic identity but primarily reinforced the postcolonial state's legitimacy with reference to the revolutionary struggle in the Algerian War (1954–1962).

In Morocco, the presence of King Mohamed V as a primary actor during the post-independence struggle to define Morocco's political order led to a very different outcome. In the decades following independence, the Alawite monarchy, first under Mohamed V (1956–1961) then, following his death, Hassan II (rule 1961–1999), consolidated a framework of rule in which Islam and Arabic identity remained important pillars legitimating the post-colonial state, but where the monarchy was strategically positioned as the ultimate symbolic referent within the Moroccan political field and ultimate arbiter of national identity. Inheriting the colonial form of Secularity I described in the previous section, the Alawite monarchy combined modernization and traditionalization, explicitly affirming the global expression of Islam within all realms of the public sphere, but implicitly dividing between different spheres within the bureaucratic apparatus of the postcolonial state.

In the political field (Bourdieu 1991: 203–219), this involved the intentional cultivation of a consensus-based multi-party system. Though the king called for the creation of a constitutional monarchy soon after his return from exile in 1955, Mohamed V's democratization rhetoric shifted over the next five years, until his death in 1961. As he deftly consolidated his own power base by establishing firm control over the Royal Armed Forces, cultivating strong support from the rural notables, and neutralizing the potential political threat of the *Istiqlal* party, Mohamed V gradually shifted his discourse toward a *shura*, or consultative, framework of rule. By cultivating a pluralistic political system from the beginning, the

culturally, if not politically, assimilated toward France or were targeted by increasingly aggressive Zionist propaganda and recruitment to immigrate. The North African Jewish community was thus caught between French, Zionist, and the local nationalists' rival appeals to their loyalty. Ultimately, this ambivalent political position, in addition to economic factors, led to the emigration of virtually the entire Jewish population out of North Africa to Israel, France, and North America.

monarchy successfully positioned itself "above," and in ultimate control, of what Waterbury (1970) describes as a "segmentary political system."[7] As arbiter, the king is able to both reward and punish through a pattern of alternance in his nomination of different political actors to positions within the government and the bureaucratic institutions of the state.

This system of rule integrates the religious field at both symbolic and institutional levels, leaving the line between the king, as supreme religious and political figure, and the state intentionally blurred. Harking back to the strategies employed by pre-colonial Moroccan rulers, Mohamed V and later Hassan II relied on a diversified legitimacy portfolio that included their *sharifian* descent from the Prophet Mohamed and the title *amir al-mu'imineen*, or Commander of the Faithful, combining ultimate temporal and spiritual authority as leader of the Moroccan religio-political community. As Combs-Schilling (1989) has described, this fusion is reinforced through performative rituals, including the sacrifice for *Eid al-Adha*, where the king is identified with the nation. This linkage between religion, the monarchy, and the nation has been enshrined since 1962 in Morocco's constitutions, which affirm Morocco is a "constitutional, democratic, and social monarchy" in which Islam is the state religion and Arabic is the official language. The 1962 constitution recognized the country's official motto, the triptych *"Allah, al-Watan, al-Malik"* (God, Nation, King), and affirmed, in Article 19, that

the King, *Amir al-Mu'iminin* (Commander of the Faithful), shall be the Supreme Representative of the Nation and the Symbol of the unity thereof. He shall be the guarantor of the perpetuation and the continuity of the State. As Defender of the Faith, He shall ensure the respect for the Constitution. He shall be the Protector of the rights and liberties of the citizens, social groups and organizations. (Madani, Maghraoui, and Zerhouni 2012: 11)

In the Moroccan case, the state and the king are both separated and conflated.

This ambiguity between sovereign and state is maintained in how the Commander of the Faithful monopolizes the religious field at the institutional level. The king names the head of the Ministry of *Habous* (*Awqaf*) and Islamic Affairs, a bureaucratic apparatus created during the French Protectorate through which the state regulates and supervises the production of Islam in Morocco. This ministry sets the official times for daily prayers and

---

[7] Though this represents a continued dynamic of segmentation, this represents a political differentiation at the elite level, through the cultivation of multiple parties, rather than the broader and deeper type of social differentiation described by Luhmann (1997).

the dates for religious holidays, such as the Ramadan fast, linked to phases of the moon.[8] In this official exercise defining religious practice, the Moroccan state, like other Muslim countries, inserts a national level of sovereignty in the transnational Islamic field, starting Ramadan, for example, on a different day than other countries. The ministry also coordinates the annual *haj*, or pilgrimage to Mecca, designating the number of pilgrims and their selection in a given year and organizing their travel arrangements. The process for getting a permit to build or expand mosques requires the ministry's approval, and the state itself invests significant resources in mosque construction and rehabilitation (which the king also frequently contributes to with his personal funds).[9] Imams, and (since 2006) *murshidat* (female pastoral/spiritual guides), are trained and paid by the state (El-Haitami 2012). Since 1984, the state has provided imams with written *khutba*-s (Friday sermons), and closely monitors what is preached, reprimanding or dismissing those who veer into sensitive topics such as political extremism or excessive criticism of corruption (Laurenson 2012). Since the colonial period, the educational system has been divided into modern and traditional systems, with the Ministry of Education overseeing the former and the Ministry of Islamic Affairs the latter. The schools under the Ministry of Islamic Affairs include the traditional Quranic schools up to the *Dar al-Hadith al-Hassaniya*, the most prestigious school of Islamic studies in Morocco. This division, however, does not designate a total distinction of the secular and religious, as the schools in the normal Moroccan system still teach Islam.

Like the French colonial state, the post-independence monarchy in Morocco has never explicitly drawn lines between the secular and the religious. By symbolically and institutionally blending the political and religious fields, the monarchy attempts to pre-empt any form of viable opposition by identifying itself a priori with Islam and thereby asserting a monopoly on how religion is used within the public sphere. In this respect, the king reinforces the permeation of Islam in the public sphere while simultaneously imposing specific limits on its public and political role. In its effect, this move mimics Secularity I to the extent that, by monopolizing the public use of religion and demarking a political status quo that is

---

[8] Royaume du Maroc, Ministère des habous et des affaires islamique. "Affaires Islamiques," www.habous.net/fr/affaires-islamiques-accueil.html

[9] Royaume du maroc, Ministère des habous et des affaires isalmique. "Construction, réhabilitation et restauration des mosquées," http://habous.net/fr/component/content/article/246-promouvoir-les-mosqu%C3%A9es/498-construction-rehabilitation-et-restauration-des-mosquees.html

labeled "Islamic," the king attempts to strip the public sphere of any potential for oppositional "religious politics" (Casanova 1994).

Since before independence, the Moroccan king, as "Commander of the Faithful," has been able to embody multiple roles ranging from modernizer to reformer to democratizer to religious leader, leaving the line between secular and religious undefined. This marks a distinction of the Moroccan case to others in this volume such as Turkey and Iran, which went through secular, modernizing state-building phases positioned in opposition to the traditional religious establishment, making it more similar to the trajectories in Indonesia and Pakistan. In contrast to military officers like Ataturk or Reza Shah, Mohamed V had, within his own person, a form of religious symbolic capital acknowledged by religious elites. The French, the Moroccan nationalists, and the king all attempted to blend religion and politics, using Islam to legitimize the state from the beginning (Wyrtzen 2015). Though the Alawites have been remarkably successful in maintaining control of this narrative, this does not imply that they have not been challenged.

PLURALISM, RIGHTS, AND OPPOSITION TO THE PALACE'S RELIGIOUS MONOPOLY

Since the 1980s, three grass-roots movements – the Amazigh (Berber), Women's, and Islamist movements – have presented a blend of "center-periphery," "stratificatory," and "functional" conflicts (in Gorski's Luhmann/Bourdieu typology) that challenge different dimensions of the post-independence framework of political legitimacy centered around Arabo-Islamic ethno-religious unity and the Alawite throne. Their trajectories and claims have intersected and overlapped with their respective efforts to renegotiate the ethno-linguistic, gendered, and Islamic dimensions of the public sphere, which are all at least tangentially challenging the religio-political monopoly exercised by the monarchy. The Palace's response to these efforts to pluralize the political order, particularly since Mohamed VI's accession in 1999, has been to pre-empt or to co-opt these movements' goals, subsuming them within the all-encompassing symbolic unity of the monarchy and thereby controlling these "plural streams of Moroccan identity," a phrase repeated in official speeches by the king.

The Amazigh (Berber) movement traces political activism back to the early 1990s, when Berber cultural organizations active since the 1960s began to mobilize (Maddy-Weitzmann 2011: chapter 6; Silverstein and Crawford 2004). In 1991, six Amazigh associations published the Agadir

Charter protesting the official marginalization of Amazigh culture and language and calling for the official recognition of Tamazight as a national language alongside Arabic, the teaching of Tamazight in schools, and the use of the language in public media. In May 1994, several leaders of the Tilelli Amazigh association were arrested after demonstrations in Goulmima and Er-Rachidia in southern Morocco in which they displayed banners, written in the Tifinagh alphabet, that called for the teaching of Tamazight in Morocco.[10] In August that year, however, King Hassan II delivered a speech where he surprisingly affirmed that Tamazight "dialects" should be taught in primary schools, though no actual changes in the curricular policies of Morocco's education ministry were implemented through the rest of his reign up until his death in 1999. Many of these Berber civil society organizations affirmed a secular orientation, defining themselves in opposition and in antagonism against the Arabo-Islamic hegemony that had marginalized Berber identity since before independence. In its place, they affirmed a pluralistic historical narrative that includes North Africa's pre-Islamic "Berber" past in addition to the standard Islamic dynastic history, much of which concerned Berber empires. Leading Amazigh intellectuals, including Mohamed Chafik, used a religious discursive framework to defend a secular demarcation between the religious and political spheres, while a more left-wing pressed for a strong version of *laicité* (Ben-Layashi 2007).

In 2001, the king responded to this segmentary/stratificatory conflict about the unequal ethno-cultural status of Moroccan Berberophones by announcing the creation of the Royal Institute for Amazigh Culture (IRCAM).[11] At the announcement ceremony on the Ajdir plateau near Khenifra in the Middle Atlas Mountains, King Mohamed VI, whose Amazigh mother lived nearby,[12] delivered a speech in which he reaffirmed the trinity of Moroccan national identity, "the tolerant and generous Muslim religion," "defense of the country (*watan*) in its unity and integrity," and "allegiance to the Throne and King," to which a fourth strand, "attachment to a democratic, social, and constitutional monarchy" was

---

[10] They were subsequently released after being amnestied by King Hassan II, following the mobilization of protests by Berber activists in Morocco, Algeria's Kabyle region, and France.

[11] Institut Royal de la Culture Amazigh.

[12] The King's mother, Fatima, was the second wife of Hassan II and the mother of both Mohamed VI and Prince Rachid, as well as Princesses Meryem, Hasna, and Asma. Her cousin, the daughter of the Berber tribal chief, Qaid Amharoq, had born him no heirs (Howe 2005: 5).

added. He then went on to recognize and affirm the historical importance of "Amazighité" for the Moroccan people, signaling a reimagining of national identity that affirmed Berber identity at the highest level.[13] This royal attempt to co-opt the agenda of the Berber movement through the creation of IRCAM has split the movement between those supporting and those rejecting the institute's program, and the state-sponsored patronization of a bi-ethnic, multicultural vision of Moroccan national identity.

In the 1980s, the monarchy faced another challenge from below with the rise of an Islamist movement, which signaled a functional conflict over the public role of Islam. The most prominent oppositional Islamist leader in Morocco was Abdessalam Yassine, who began (in an Al-Yusi mold of ethical-prophetic speaking truth to power) critiquing the Alawite monarchy in the 1970s as an unjust and un-Islamic regime with an open *nasiha* letter addressed to Hassan II. In and out of jail during the 1980s and 1990s, Yassine successfully mobilized what has become the largest Moroccan Islamist organization, *Al-'Adl wa-Ihsan* (Justice and Charity). Though focused on personal spiritual formation and benevolent social programs, the movement remains a formidable potential political player. While Islamist parties such as the PJD (the Justice and Development Party, *Al-'Adl wa al-Tanmiah*) have been brought into the political process, Yassine's movement has rejected overtures from the Palace to "co-opt" the movement and does not yet participate in elections. Yassine's daughter, Nadia, emerged in the past decade as one of the most prominent critics of the Palace, and faced prosecution following remarks in 2005 in which she stated that a democratic republic was more in line with Islamic values than a monarchy. By definition, the type of Islamist reform movement represented by Al-'Adl wa-Ihsan, in calling for an increased Islamization of the personal, social, economic, and political spheres, challenges the predominant position of the Commander of the Faithful in defining what is Islamic. This challenge to the Moroccan form of Secularity I described earlier paradoxically uses Islam itself to gain oppositional leverage against the status quo, attempting to force open the possibility of the type of religious politics Casanova (1994) defines in reference to a secular political settlement. One of the most intense battlegrounds in this confrontation has centered on campaigns to reform the legal status of Moroccan women within the *Mudawanna*, Morocco's family law, or personal status code, which is based on a Maliki interpretation of Islamic law.

---

[13] Text of speech available on the IRCAM website: www.ircam.ma/.

It is here that Islamists come into contention with a third movement within civil society, Morocco's women's movement, seeking to renegotiate the post-independence settlement. This movement traces its origins to the 1980s, when a generation of post-independence, college-educated women began to organize women's rights organizations. The two prominent organizations in this formative stage were the Association Démocratique des Femmes du Maroc (ADFM: Moroccan Women's Democratic Association) and the Union de l'Action Feminine (UAF), both of which targeted Morocco's 1957 personal status code, or *Mudawanna*, which enshrined an Islamic legal interpretation based on the Maliki school of women's rights. This movement, as with the Amazigh movement, reflected different positions with respect to Islam and secular frameworks of feminism (Salime 2011). Two poles can be discerned within the women's movements, with one whose primary referent is a more secular ideological framework of feminism articulated within a universalistic human rights discourse and another, sometimes labeled Islamic feminism, that articulates claims by appealing to an Islamic framework of authority. A third intermediary mode is represented by the approach of one of Morocco's most well-known feminist scholar-activists, Fatima Mernissi (1991), who uses authoritative Islamic texts, including the Qu'ran and Hadith, to attack forms of patriarchy expressed in Morocco and the broader Arab–Muslim world.

Having achieved only a minor revision of the code under Hassan II in 1993, Morocco's women's movement had high hopes following the accession of Mohamed VI in 1999, who had publicly affirmed his support for women's rights. The issue, however, continued to be a flashpoint between rival constructions of the nation proposed by Islamists, who opposed the legislation on the basis that it contradicted "Islam," and women's rights organizations, who stressed a more secular "modernization." A high-profile clash between the two occurred on March 12, 2000 – International Women's Day – when a coalition of women's groups, human rights organizations, leftist political parties, and trade unions gathered for a mass demonstration in support of reforming the *Mudawana*. That same day, Islamist organizations organized a counter-demonstration, with nearly twice the crowd, protesting against the reform of the *Mudawana* as an attack on Islam and the Muslim family. In response to these pressures, the King appointed a royal commission in 2001 to study the potential reform of the Personal Status Code.

This task force made little progress until October 2003, when, partly in response to the May 17 terrorist bombings in Casablanca, which were blamed on extremist Islamist groups, the King himself called for a revision of the code at the opening of the parliamentary session. In his personal sponsorship of the reform, the King moved to undercut the Islamist challenge, beginning the speech with a quote from the Prophet Mohamed, "Women are the equals of men in regards to the law" and "the man who honors them is honorable and he who humiliates them is ignoble," and then stating, "I cannot, in my quality as *Amir Al-Mu'iminin* (Commander of the Faithful), authorize what God had prohibited, nor forbid what the Most High has authorized." Framing the reform initiative as an integral process of *ijtihad* (or active reinterpretation and application of the principles of *shari'a*) consistent with the "homogeneity of the Malikite rite," the King called on Parliament to enact a "modern code of the family, in perfect consistency with the spirit of our tolerant religion."[14] The new legislation was passed by parliament and affixed with the royal seal by the King the following February 2004, and made significant steps toward guaranteeing Moroccan women legal equality, including important provisions granting women the right to initiate divorce proceedings, improving women's inheritance rights, simplifying proof of paternity, granting women the possibility to retain custody of children, and establishing the sharing of property between married couples.[15]

In the post-Casablanca bombing period, however, Moroccan secular-liberal elites, fearing Islamic extremism as a greater evil, relented their pressure on the monarchy for democratic reform and a separation of powers in the political sphere. By the end of Mohamed VI's first decade of rule, the Palace had firmly reconsolidated the "politics of consensus" in which "the position, excessive power and dominance of the monarchy are no longer subject to debate and divergence among the parties regardless of their ideological orientations" (Maghraoui 2011: 683). The King had co-opted the thrust of the Amazigh and women's movements through the recognition of Berber cultural rights and the passage of the 2004 *Mudawana* reform.

---

[14] The text of the speech was included in the dahir instituting the new code published on February 3, 2004 (12 Hija 1424). The official text of the revised Moroccan family code is available online at: http://adala.justice.gov.ma/production/legislation/fr/Nouveautes/Code%20de%20%20la%20Famille.pdf.

[15] In addition, the minimum legal age of marriage for women was raised to eighteen. Also, polygamy was not made illegal, but it was severely restricted, requiring the demonstration before a judge of a clear justifiable motive for it and that the husband can guarantee equality between wives. The woman also retains a right to stipulate in the marriage contract that her husband will not take a second wife. Women without the condition in their marriage contracts have the right of consent to the husband taking a second wife and a right to petition for divorce for harm suffered.

With respect to the Islamist challenge (Willis 2007), a segment had been tamed through incorporation into the parliamentary system (the Justice and Development Party, or PJD), while the state cracked down on a wide swath of the rest, using the 2003 bombings as a reason to incarcerate thousands of suspected Islamic extremists. The king's response to bottom-up pressures incorporated a pluralization on certain levels, a politics of ethnic recognition and positioning on the side of progressive women's rights reform, that did not reconfigure the functional monopoly he maintains over the public, political role of Islam in Morocco.

THE COMMANDER OF THE FAITHFUL
AND THE ARAB SPRING

The situation remained stable until February 2011, when Morocco began to experience unrest in the wake of the Tunisian and Egyptian revolutions. The initial protests were organized by a group called "Freedom and Democracy Now," which represented a loosely networked, intentionally non-hierarchical initiative by young Moroccan activists to challenge the political–religious monopoly of the monarchy. Like counterparts in Tunisia and Egypt, they used social media tools, creating a Facebook page on February 16 to communicate information about the demonstrations.[16] They also posted a YouTube video[17] with thirteen Moroccans articulating, in Arabic, French, and Berber, their reasons for protesting, which included freedom, equality, quality of life, education, and minority rights. The video went viral (Lalami 2011). Beginning on February 20, and on successive Sundays throughout the spring, the movement mobilized thousands of protestors calling for economic, political, and judicial reform, stitching together a broad coalition that included disaffected youth, Morocco's human rights organizations, leftists, and Islamists, including Al-'Adl wa-Ihsan. Instead of the phrase used in Tunisia, Egypt, Yemen, and Syria, "*al-sha'ab yurid isqat al-nidham*" ("the people want the fall of the regime"), in Morocco the chant was more moderate, for "a king who reigns but does not rule" (Maghraoui 2011: 688).

The king responded quickly with a televised speech on March 9 in which he adopted the February 20 movement's own rhetoric in calling for broad constitutional reforms including a regionalization program, recognition of Amazigh identity, consolidation of the rule of law and promotion of human

[16] www.facebook.com/pages/The-20th-of-february-movement/
[17] www.youtube.com/watch?v=Sof6FSB7gxQwhic

rights, judicial independence, separation of powers by strengthening the authority of parliament and the cabinet, a bolstered oppositional political framework, and oversight and accountability on public corruption. He concluded by announcing the creation of an advisory committee charged with drafting the constitution, with consultations with the Moroccan political parties, before a popular referendum in the summer (Mohamed VI 2011). Protests continued in the following weeks, however, as many factions in the February 20 coalition criticized the "consultative" framework of the constitutional reform process, a top-down process that left the monarchy's presuppositional monopoly of control intact.

Part of this critique targeted the post-independence religio-political settlement, challenging the constitutional recognition of Islam as the state religion as well as articles in the penal code criminalizing proselytism (Article 220) and publicly breaking the Ramadan fast (Article 222) by eating during daylight hours. These issues related to personal religious freedom (and freedom to not believe/practice) had already been highlighted in several incidents over the preceding three years, including crackdowns on Shi'a and evangelical Christian missionary activity in Morocco in 2009, which prompted a US congressional hearing on religious freedom and human rights in Morocco (Congressional Hearing 2010). The issue of religious freedom and non-observance was brought to the fore in 2009 with the creation by young Moroccan activists of a group named "le Mouvement alternatif pour les libertés individuelles" (MALI) to defend individual rights in Morocco. This group pushed for a laicist separation of Islam and politics, staging a lunch picnic at the train station in Mohammedia to break the prohibition against public eating in Article 222 of the penal code, after which several members were imprisoned. Though demands from civil society groups for increased personal liberty enjoy support within a portion of the urban elite, particularly in the coastal cities, there is not a critical mass of intense support targeting personal religious freedoms.

The potential for a radical reshaping of the non-secular settlement in Morocco during the constitutional reform process was not realized in 2011. In June, with the support of all of the Moroccan political parties, the new Constitution was unveiled and a public referendum on 1 July received over 98 percent of the vote in favor. The reforms included the recognition of Amazigh (Berber) as an official language and provisions attempting to ensure a more independent government with a popular vote for the prime minister, but the new constitution did little to fundamentally transform the monopoly of control exercised by the monarchy in Morocco's political and religious fields. Though reference to the king's "sacred" character was removed, he is still identified a priori with Islam and the state: Article 41 stipulates his religious role as Commander of the Faithful and Article 42 his political role as king and head of state.

The primary impact of the new constitution came with the success of the Justice and Development (PJD) Islamist party, which won the largest share of parliamentary seats, and whose leader the king appointed as the first Islamist prime minister in Morocco's history. While many Moroccans expressed high hopes for the PJD to change the political dynamics in the country, particularly by cracking down on widespread corruption, most have been disappointed with the resumption of the "politics of consensus," as the parliament and the government seem to have defaulted to what Moroccans refer to as the "*beni oui oui*," or the "yes-men tribe" (Maghraoui 2011: 697) exercising no political will independently of the Palace. The leftist coalition brought together by the February 20 movement, which boycotted the constitutional reform referendum and has attempted to maintain an oppositional voice, initially worried the Islamist victory would entail state-sponsored Islamization policies. Though these fears have proven largely unfounded, the reality remains that the neither the secularists nor the Islamists have yet gained an oppositional position since 2011 from which to truly challenge the monopoly held by the monarchy over the political field in Morocco.

CONCLUSION: THE STAKES OF MOROCCAN SECULARITY

This chapter has traced how the relationship between religion and politics has been negotiated in Morocco at critical junctures related to state and nation formation in the colonial and postcolonial periods. The non-secular settlement that persists in Morocco is exceptional in comparison to many other cases in this volume, including several Muslim-majority countries, where secularization polices were enacted in tandem with modernizing state-building reforms. Within the typological framework of secular settlements and their relative provision of Taylor's three goods – equality, liberty, and fraternity – proposed in Gorski's chapter (consociationalism, religious nationalism, radical secularism, and liberal secularism), Morocco has developed as a case of religious nationalism. It is unique, though, compared to other countries, in the relative homogeneity of its population which, aside from a historic Jewish minority (most of which emigrated to Israel, Europe, or North America after independence), is Sunni Muslim.

While Islam and Arabic were privileged as markers of national solidarity in the anti-colonial struggle, the latter has proven to be negotiable in recent efforts to officially reinscribe Berber identity in the nation. In contrast, Islam remains a seemingly permanent dimension of public and political life, as the Alawite king has maximized his symbolic power as Commander of the Faithful to dominate the political field. The major question as Morocco moves forward relates to the monarchy's hegemony in setting the ground rules of the political game. Within this framework, pressures from above and below to move Morocco toward a liberal secular framework carry high stakes related to the stability of the political system. Thus far, Morocco's "exceptional" proclivity toward a gradualist or "little by little" (*shwiya b'shwiya*) approach, reinforced popularly and by the regime in comparisons to less stable neighbors such as Algeria, Tunisia, and Libya, has indefinitely prolonged this reform process. However, as the collective and individual conditions of belief in the religio-political status quo increasingly pluralize, pressures to renegotiate Morocco's secular settlement will continue to be in play.

References

Abi-Mershed, Osama. 2010. *Apostles of Modernity: Saint-Simonians and the Civilizing Mission in Algeria*. Stanford: Stanford University Press.

Abun-Nasr, Jamil. 1963. "The *Salafiyya* Movement in Morocco: The Religious Bases of the Moroccan Nationalist Movement." In Albert Hourani (ed.), St. Antony's Papers, *Middle Eastern Affairs*, No. 3. (London, 1963): 91–105.

Ben-Layashi, Samir. 2007. "Secularism in the Moroccan Amazigh Discourse." *The Journal of North African Studies* 12(2): 153–171.

Berque, Jacques. 1982. *Ulémas, fondateurs, insurgés du Maghreb: XVIIe siècle*. Paris: Sindbad.

Bourdieu, Pierre. 1991. *Language and Symbolic Power*. Cambridge: Harvard University Press.

Casanova, José. 1994. *Public Religions in the Modern World*. Chicago: University of Chicago Press.

Collier, Ruth Berins, and David Collier. 1991. *Shaping the Political Arena: Critical Junctures, the Labor Movement, and Regime Dynamics in Latin America*. Princeton: Princeton University Press.

Congressional Hearing on Human Rights and Religious Freedom in Morocco, June 17, 2010. Transcript available at: https://humanrightscommission.hou se.gov/sites/tlhrc.house.gov/files/documents/Transcript%20of%20Morocco %20Hearing%20_6-17-2010.pdf

El-Haitami, Meriem. 2012. "Restructuring Female Religious Authority: State-Sponsored Women Religious Guides (Murshidat) and Scholars (`Alimat) in Contemporary Morocco." *Mediterranean Studies* 20(2): 227–240.

El-Mansour, Mohamed. 1996. "Salafis and Modernists in the Moroccan National Movement," in J. Ruedy (ed.), *Islam and Secularism in North Africa*. New York: St. Martin's Press.

Geertz, Clifford. 1971. *Islam Observed: Religious Development in Morocco and Indonesia*. Chicago: University Of Chicago Press.

Gouvernement Chérifien. 1946. *Annuaire statistique de la zone française du Maroc 1945–46*. Rabat: Service centrale des statistiques.

Hoffman, Katherine. 2008. "Purity and Contamination: Language Ideologies in French Colonial Native Policy in Morocco." *Comparative Studies in Society and History* 50(3): 724–752.

2010. "Berber Law by French Means: Customary Courts in the Moroccan Hinterlands, 1930–1956." *Comparative Studies in Society and History* 52(4): 851–880.

Howe, Marvine. 2005. *Morocco: The Islamist Awakening and Other Challenges*. Oxford: Oxford University Press.

Jankowski, James P., and I. Gershoni. 1997. *Rethinking Nationalism in the Arab Middle East*. New York: Columbia University Press.

Kably, Mohamed. 1999. "Legitimacy of state power and socioreligious variations in medieval Morocco." In R. Bourqia and Susan Gilson Miller (eds.), *In the Shadow of the Sultan: Culture, Power, and Politics in Morocco*. Cambridge, MA: Harvard University Press.

1986. *Société, pouvoir et religion au Maroc à la fin du Moyen âge: XIVe-XVe siècle*. Paris: Maisonneuve et Larose.

Lalami, Laila. 2011, February 21. "Morocco's Moderate Revolution." *Foreign Policy*. Retrieved from http://foreignpolicy.com/2011/02/21/moroccos-moderate-revolution/.

Laurenson, John. 2012. "Moroccan imams call for freedom to preach." *Deutsch Welle*, 10/1/2012. Retrieved from www.dw.de/moroccan-imams-call-for-freedom-to-preach/a-15656229

Lafuente, Gilles. 1999. *La politique berbère de la France et le nationalisme marocain*. Paris: Harmattan.

Lorcin, Patricia M. E. 1995. *Imperial Identities: Stereotyping, Prejudice and Race in Colonial Algeria*. London: I.B. Tauris; distributed by St. Martin's Press.

Luhmann, Niklas. 1997. *Die Gesellschaft der Gesellschaft*. Frankfurt am Main: Suhrkamp.

Madani, Mohamed, Driss Maghraoui, and Salwa Zerhouni. 2012. *The 2011 Moroccan Constitution: A Critical Analysis*. Stockholm: International Institute for Democracy and Electoral Assistance.

Maddy-Weitzman, Bruce. 2011. *The Berber Identity Movement and the Challenge to North African States*. 1st edn. Austin: University of Texas Press.

Magharoui, Driss. 2009. "'Ilmaniyya, Laicité, Sécularisme/Secularism." In Carol Gluck and Anna Lowenhaupt Tsing (eds.), *Words in Motion: Toward a Global Lexicon*. Durham: Duke University Press.

2011. "Constitutional Reforms in Morocco: Between Consensus and Subaltern Politics." *The Journal of North African Studies* 16(4): 679–699.

Mahoney, J., and K. A. Thelen. 2010. *Explaining Institutional Change: Ambiguity, Agency, and Power.* Cambridge; New York: Cambridge University Press.

McDougall, James. 2003. "Myth and Counter-Myth: 'The Berber' As National Signifier in Algerian Historiographies." *Radical History Review* 2003(86): 66–88.

2008. *History and the Culture of Nationalism in Algeria.* 1st edn. Cambridge: Cambridge University Press.

Mernissi, Fatima. 1991. *The Veil and the Male Elite: A Feminist Interpretation of Women's Rights in Islam.* Reading: Addison-Wesley Pub. Co.

Mohamed VI. 2011. "Nass al-khitab al-sami aladhi waja-ahu jalalat al-malik ila al-umah." Hukumat al-Mamlakat al-Maghrib. Rabat: Morocco. Retrieved from: www.maroc.ma/ar/%D8%AE%D8%B7%D8%A7%D8%A8%D8%A7%D8%AA-%D9%85%D9%84%D9%83%D9%8A%D8%A9?field_ty pe_discours_royal_value_i18n=All&date_discours[value][year] =2011&page=1

Munson, Henry L. Jr. 1993. *Religion and Power in Morocco.* New Haven: Yale University Press.

Pew Forum on Religion and Public Life. 2012. "The World's Muslims: Unity and Diversity." Available at: www.pewforum.org/Muslim/the-worlds-muslims-unity-and-diversity-executive-summary.aspx.

Pierson, P. (2004). *Politics in Time: History, Institutions, and Social Analysis.* Princeton; Oxford: Princeton University Press.

Ruedy, John. 1996. *Islamism and Secularism in North Africa.* London: Palgrave Macmillan.

Salime, Zakia. 2011. *Between Feminism and Islam: Human Rights and Sharia Law in Morocco.* Minneapolis: University of Minnesota Press.

Schilling, M. E. Combs. 1989. *Sacred Performances: Islam, Sexuality, and Sacrifice.* New York: Columbia University Press.

Silverstein, Paul, and David Crawford. 2004. "Amazigh Activism and the Moroccan State." *Middle East Report* (233): 44–48.

Spadolo, Emilio. 2013. *The Calls of Islam: Sufis, Islamists, and Mass Mediation in Urban Morocco.* Bloomington: Indiana University Press.

Taylor, Charles. 2003. *Varieties of Religion Today: William James Revisited.* Cambridge, MA: Harvard University Press.

2007. *A Secular Age.* Cambridge, MA: Harvard University Press.

Tilly, Charles. 1995. *Popular Contention in Great Britain, 1758–1834.* Cambridge, MA: Harvard University Press.

Waterbury, John. 1970. *The Commander of the Faithful: The Moroccan Political Elite – A Study in Segmented Politics.* London: Weidenfeld & Nicolson.

Weber, Max. 1978. *Economy and Society: An Outline of Interpretive Sociology.* Berkeley: University of California Press.

Willis, Michael. 2007. "Justice and Development or Justice and Spirituality? The Challenge of Morocco's Nonviolent Islamist Movements." In Bruce Maddy-Weitzman and Daniel Zisenwine. *The Maghrib in the New Century.* Gainesville: University of Florida, 150–174.

Wyrtzen, Jonathan. 2011. "Colonial State-Building and the Negotiation of Arab and Berber Identity in Protectorate Morocco." *International Journal of Middle East Studies* 43: 227–249.

2013. "Performing the Nation in Anti-colonial Protest in Interwar Morocco." *Nations and Nationalism* 19(4): 615–634.

2015. *Making Morocco: Colonial Intervention and the Politics of Identity.* Ithaca: Cornell University Press.

14

Conclusions: The Continued Prevalence
of the "Marker State"

Mirjam Künkler and John Madeley

At the outset of *A Secular Age*, Charles Taylor makes the arresting claim
that "the judgment of secularity" applies in particular to the countries of
the North Atlantic world, especially when they are compared with
"almost all other contemporary societies (e.g., Islamic countries, India,
Africa), on the one hand; and with the rest of human history, Atlantic or
otherwise, on the other" (Taylor 2007: 1). It has been the purpose of this
volume to assess the first of these comparative claims by examining the
incidence or absence of secularity in a sample of twentieth-century societies beyond Taylor's North Atlantic World. As Phil Gorski points out in
Chapter 2, Taylor's principal interest was in explicating and interpreting
secularity (particularly Secularity III following the shift in the "conditions
of belief" toward a situation where religion is just one option among
many, "and frequently not the easiest to embrace") as the product of a
series of unique developments in Latin Christendom.[1] Yet Taylor concedes that "secularity extends also partially, and in different ways, beyond
this world" (ibid). The use of the verb "extend" raises the question of
whether what he had in mind was evidence of Western-originated

---

[1] Of Taylor's three notions of secularity, the first two are largely congruent with Casanova's
(1994). Secularity I refers to the emancipation of the spheres of the state, economy,
bureaucracy, law, political authority, and related areas from the influence of religious
norms and authority. Secularity II captures the decline in religious beliefs and practice on
the individual level. While Casanova's third notion referred to the privatization of religion
(a thesis he sought to empirically debunk in his 1994 book), Taylor's notion of Secularity
III captures the phenomenon that belief (and religious practice) has become an option
among many in a given society and that individuals see a need to justify belief more than
unbelief. For further discussion of Taylor's three notions of secularity, see the
Introduction.

secularity that could be observed beyond the margins of the West, or, say, the possible existence of forms and founts of alternative types of secularity traceable to other, non-Western origins. The answer to the question is left tantalizingly open by his subsequent observation that "secularization and secularity are phenomena which exist today well beyond the boundaries of [the West] … Secularity, like other features of 'modernity' – political structures, democratic forms, uses of media, to cite a few other examples – in fact find [sic] rather different expression, and develop [sic] under the pressure of different demands and aspirations in different civilisations" (ibid.: 21).

Each of the case studies in this volume has attempted to identify the extent to which secularity – in one or more of Taylor's three modes or, indeed, some other – has existed or developed in societies shaped by religious traditions other than Western Christianity. All of the cases bear the imprint, some deeper than others, of what Taylor calls Secularity I (the emancipation of law, the state, the economy, and other spheres from the influence of religious norms).[2] Even in the East Asian cases of China and Japan, which evince civilizational patterns established over millennia before their modern encounter with the West, the necessity of responding to the challenge of Western secularity has been unavoidable. Each chapter has also identified features relevant to secularity and religiosity that mark the particularity of the individual cases as well as a shared "non-Western" alterity, evident, for example, in the Russian and Turkish cases despite their strong and sustained connections and involvements with the "North Atlantic World" over long periods. In other words, the case studies suggest that unique combinations of different intensities of Secularities I, II, and III have developed "under the pressure of different demands and aspirations" which generated distinctive patterns of path dependency. As is laid out in more detail in sections 1 and 2 of this chapter, all the cases examined show some marks of Secularity I and most feature low levels of Secularity II (with the possible exception of Japan and China), while few feature

---

[2] Philip Gorski suggests in Chapter 2 that Taylor seems at times to collapse Casanova's first and third notions, that is emancipation and privatization. Thus, Taylor refers in shorthand to Secularity I as the "evacuation of religion from public life," which appears to indicate a movement toward privatization, when what he seems to understand as Secularity I's *core* is emancipation (of the state, etc., from religious influence).

Secularity III, where religious belonging (and belief and practice) is merely optional. That only a few feature Secularity III is to a large extent, the case studies suggest, due to the fact that legal and cultural conditions so often require identification with particular religious traditions and that the option to not believe can therefore hardly arise as an option widely accepted in society. What accounts for the unique combinations of Secularities I, II, and III, the similarities and contrasts across the cases, is the focus of this concluding chapter.

Before delving into the discussion of why Secularity III is rare in the cases studied in this volume, it is worth re-visiting how the approach taken here relates to and differs from Taylor's. Firstly, of course, the focus of this volume has been on societies beyond the West, specifically those where Western Christianity has not been a dominant tradition. Latin American and Sub-Saharan African cases have not been included on the grounds that religious life in many of these is dominated by extensions of Latin Christendom (albeit under very distinctive cultural conditions).[3] Instead the focus has been on societies where Judaism, Islam, Hinduism, Buddhism, Chinese religions, and Eastern Orthodoxy have been dominant. Given the implicit comparison this particular focus involves, Taylor's claim for the unique particularity of Western secularity comes prominently into focus. Secondly, as the conditions for Secularities I, II, and III in the case studies mostly obtained in the nineteenth and twentieth centuries, the chapters in this volume typically encompass a much shorter time frame than Taylor's millennium-long timespan. Thirdly, while the case studies take their starting point from his *A Secular Age* (and are also informed by Taylor's other writings on secularism and sources of the self),[4] the volume focuses on Secularity I (the "emancipation" of law, the administration, the economy, and related spheres from the influence of religious authority and norms) much more closely than does *A Secular Age*. The role of the state in all the cases examined turns out to be central, whether destructively under the

---

[3] There is no doubt however that it would have been important for comparative purposes to include cases of Sub-Saharan Muslim-majority societies. We hope that future endeavors can fill this lacuna.

[4] It is worth reminding readers in this context of Taylor's notion of secularism, which differs sharply from his notion of secularity, as well as from notions of secularism prevalent in other literature. Taylor proposes a reconceptualization of the concept of "secularism," by suggesting that it should be understood as a good-faith attempt on part of the state to address challenges of diversity while maximizing three goods: equality, liberty, and fraternity among its citizens. For further reading, see Taylor 2010 and 2012.

communist regimes in Russia and China, or constructively as in Turkey and Iran where one could speak of a "statist production" of religion. In fact, the first major conclusion of this volume would appear to be that across diverse regime types and varying official labels, ranging from "laic Turkey" to the "Jewish homeland of Israel," from the "Islamic Republic of Iran" to "*pancasila* Indonesia," from "secular India" to "communist China," the one overwhelming factor in qualifying, shaping, and molding conditions of belief has been the modern state. In none of the cases examined (with post-war Japan as a possible limiting case) has it been possible to assess conditions of belief without recognizing how closely the availability of faith and non-faith options are shaped by state policies.

Fourthly, there is the issue of the use of the term "religion" itself. Taylor defines "religion" in terms of "transcendence" (Taylor 2007: 20), which involves belief in a good higher than human flourishing, in a power higher than secular authority, and a view of life as going beyond "this life."[5] As laid out in the Introduction to this volume and in more detail in Künkler and Madeley (2015), his decision to sidestep the debates around rival conceptions of religion, while understandable and defensible in the context of the exclusively Western focus of *A Secular Age*, cannot be finessed in the same way when it comes to identifying and explaining the possible incidence of secularity in non-Western contexts. One ostensible reason why questions of definition could be set aside in the Western context is that the very category "religion" can be seen, as scholars from Cantwell Smith to Talal Asad have long argued, as a distinctively Western concept. Despite the fact that – or perhaps because – the concept was heavily informed by Western perceptions of colonial subjects, it is one which cannot readily be used outside the contexts of Latin Christendom without careful qualification. Gregory Starrett identifies among the first Western students of comparative religion in the nineteenth century the setting of a distinctive "Protestant tendency to see religion primarily as a system of beliefs, doctrines, and dogmas" (Starrett 1999: 149–50). Alternative conceptions which privilege traditional practices as key defining features of religion implicitly challenge such restrictively Latin Christian notions of secularity just as much as of religion itself (Riesebrodt 2003: 95–109; Turner 1991; Asad 2003: 192). By extension they may be

---

[5] For a critique of this choice, see Hans Joas, who argues that it would have served Taylor's arguments better to define religion in reference to the sacred (following Durkheim) and to then differentiate between immanent and transcendent forms of the localization of the sacred (2009: 294/95).

also relativize Taylor's key notions of the different forms of secularity, which are necessarily parasitic on an understanding of religion as defined in Western Christianity.[6] In several cases, the engagement with the Western Christian concept of religion has, in the twentieth century if not before, been necessitated by legal requirements to translate into local languages and legal practice various international obligations – for example, the commitments to respect the terms of the Universal Declaration of Human Rights guaranteeing religious freedom. As Casanova comments, "one of the most important global trends is the globalization of the category of 'religion' itself and the binary classification of 'religious/secular,' that it entails" (Casanova 2010: 62). But as he also points out, "when people around the world use the same category of religion, they actually mean very different things. The actual concrete meaning of whatever people denominate as 'religious' can only be elucidated in the context of their particular discursive practices."[7] A full eventual study of comparative secularity or secularities across the world will require an intensive and extensive exercise in comparative *Begriffsgeschichte* of the concept of religion, something which, alas, cannot be undertaken here.

Finally, while Taylor's rich intellectual history of Latin Christendom from late antiquity to the present day was focused on explicating the meaning of secularity as an emergent broader cultural condition, as social scientists, the authors of this volume have concentrated more on identifying and explaining different patterns of institutional and social change as responses to conflicts around questions of religion. To this effect, the authors complement Taylor's conceptual lexicon that mostly conveys allusive or hermeneutical meaning ("the buffered self," "the age

---

[6] Taylor indicates early on that he is aware of the danger of reducing lived religion to matters of belief (Taylor 2007: 4–5), but from *A Secular Age's* first section, "The Bulwarks of Belief," to the later sustained discussion of the conditions of belief, his study is overwhelmingly concentrated on this aspect of religion, albeit on the basis of an explicitly extended notion of what belief entails. "Belief is less a cognitivist stance than a deep, almost unconscious enmeshment in a thick texture of Christian norms, values and practices." (ibid., 284).

[7] Ibid. This touches on the much-debated question of whether Confucianism as the dominant tradition in China should be thought of as a religion when conventional wisdom suggests that it is an ethic and a philosophy rather than a religion. As Zhe Ji suggests in Chapter 3, in a sociological sense Confucianism should be treated as a religion (with its transcendental discourse, rituals, symbols, sacred matters, and cosmological representations). See in this connection also Billioud and Thoraval (2015), and Goossaert and Palmer (2011).

of authenticity," "the disenchanted world," etc.) with sociological concepts of societal conflict, differentiation, and path dependency.

In seeking to explain the incidence or absence of Secularity III in the societies examined, the present volume provides an opportunity to tease out and test some of the comparative implications of Taylor's treatise, for example, the state of possible causal connections between the three Secularities. Having observed elliptically that Secularity III was "closely related to the second and not without connection to the first," Taylor writes

An age or society would then be secular or not, in virtue of the conditions of experience of and search for the spiritual. Obviously, where it stood in this [third] dimension would have a lot to do with how secular it was in the second sense, which turns on levels of belief and practice, but there is no simple correlation between the two, as the case of the US shows. As for the first sense, which concerns public space, this may be uncorrelated with both the others ... But I will maintain that in fact, in the Western case, the shift to public secularity has been part of what helped to bring on a secular age in my third sense. (Taylor 2007: 3–4)

This third sense, Secularity III, is characterized by the rise of exclusive humanism (which Taylor considers to have been *the* crucial formative move in the emergence of Secularity III (Taylor 2007: 19)), the availability of meaningful options between belief and unbelief (a belief in the self-sufficiency of human agency and a widening of the range of possible options), and the availability of these as meaningful options to a large majority of people, not just the elites. In Taylor's view, then, "the shift to public secularity" (Secularity I) in the West has had a causal influence on the development of Secularity III. At the same time, the *seeds* of what became the immanent frame are sown in the cultural and the spiritual landscape before the onset of Secularity I, institutionally manifested first in the French Revolution (2007: 49), and the bulk of Taylor's narrative concentrates on illustrating how this immanent frame came to be dominant. There were several stages to its construction, starting with the development of the modern theory of society (by scholars like Grotius) as constituted by individuals and based on norms of mutual benefit ("the great disembedding," 2007: 155–158). Next came the construction of providential deism in the 1700s, according to which God designed the world through impersonal laws that can be understood by objective human reason (2007: 221–295). This in turn facilitated the "nova effect" in which subjective narratives dominated in art, science, and politics (2007: 352–353). These complex transformations in how the world, and the individual's place in it, are conceived, in turn paved the way toward accepting the type of political order which the French

Revolution then established: "the disciplined remaking of behaviour and social forms through objectification and an instrumental stance ... in turn helped give force to a conception of society as founded on a covenant, and hence ultimately constituted by the decision of free individuals" (2007: 155). In other words, while the shift to Secularity I (which operates in the political and legal spheres) helped bring on a secular age (which is first and foremost a cultural condition), the seeds for this cultural condition were sown in the philosophical transformation processes of the 1600s and 1700s (which themselves were strongly shaped by the political experience of the confessional wars).

The relevance of the connections between Secularities I and III to the cases treated in this volume is illustrated by Taylor's comment that, by comparison with the USA as an instance of Secularity III, clear contrast cases would be "the majority of Muslim societies, or the milieux in which the vast majority of Indians live." And in that context he ponders, "it seems to me that there are big differences between societies in what it is to believe, stemming in part from the fact that belief is an option and in some sense an embattled option in the Christian (or 'post-Christian') society, and not (or not yet) in the Muslim ones" (Taylor 2007: 3). Here, as elsewhere, the relevance of Taylor's thesis both to comparative analysis and to understanding the nature of causal and other connections is evident. As will be seen in Sections 1 and 2 of this chapter, empirically Secularity I preceded such evidences as exist of Secularities II and III in all our case studies from Morocco to India, Indonesia, and Japan, and in most cases, institutions of a secular public order had been established by elites who were themselves secular in the sense of Secularity II and in many cases also Secularity III. As Nikkie Keddie put it, "there is no doubt but that non-Western modernizing governments greatly preceded their populations in secularist beliefs and practices" (Keddie 1997: 27). Later developments in the 1970s and 1980s in many cases unsettled these secular public orders (most of which had been established in the 1940s and 1950s), and thereby also established new obstacles to a consolidation of Secularity I and the emergence of Secularity III.

The discussion which follows is organized in three sections. In the first section, a brief summary is provided of what evidence of Secularities I and III contributors have observed and the question is broached whether and how Secularities I and III are related. Does one necessitate the other? Does high Secularity I (institutional differentiation) correlate with high Secularity III (the cultural condition where religious belief is but one option among many)? If the construction of the immanent frame is what made Secularities I and III possible in the West, how do the two relate in the cases studied here? In the second section, the question is addressed how the types of conflicts involving religion and the modern state were, at least provisionally, settled in the twentieth century, what critical junctures can be identified, and what path dependencies were created at these junctures. The third section discusses and evaluates three suggestive approaches to accounting for multiple secularities outside the West (derived from the work of Nikkie Keddie, Jay Demerath, Monika Wohlrab-Sahr, and Marian Burchardt respectively) and assesses how they complement or compete with the approach of the present volume. Finally, the general issues thrown up by this particular collection of studies, including questions for further research, are considered.

To foreshadow an overall conclusion, one of the book's key findings is that in all the cases, the state plays a major role in shaping, and in some instances determining, the limits of religious experience, by variably regulating religious belief, practice, property, education, and/or law. What Taylor considers to be the key condition of secularity in the West – namely, the legal permissibility and socio-cultural acceptability of open religious non-belief (Secularity III) – is absent in most of the cases examined. Indeed, in most cases full citizenship is conditional on religious belonging, and even where open unbelief is legally tolerated, as in Japan, it is not socially respectable among most social strata. Post-colonial and post-imperial legacies have made for a strong involvement of the state in matters of religion, although the areas directly affected by state regulation differ greatly between the cases. While in most Muslim countries, India, and Israel questions of religious law have been central to state regulation, in China it first concerned questions of education (later also property rights and political mobilization), while in Soviet Russia church property and public practice were targeted. These differences can best be captured, it is suggested, by the concept of the state's "differential burdening" of religion.

TAYLOR'S THREE SECULARITIES IN THE CASE STUDIES

To formally capture the different dimensions of secularity is notoriously difficult, and even more so across a range of cases with such different religious and cultural backgrounds. In order to provide some comparative overview, the Appendix to this volume presents an attempt to operationalize Taylor's three secularities in terms of available quantitative measures and to compare how various indices relate to levels of Secularities I, II, and III in the cases included in the volume. To summarize here, in terms of Secularity I, Japan is seen to be highly secular, while Iran and Pakistan are judged both by the data and the respective chapter authors to be largely unsecular, with the other countries included falling in between these extremes. Secularity II is viewed as strongly evident in China and quite high in Japan, while the citizens of Morocco, Pakistan and Egypt appear as highly religious. Israel, China and Russia are found to exhibit moderate levels of Secularity III among certain social groups and strata, while Pakistan is shown to offer hardly any space for a socially or culturally acceptable option of not-believing (compare Tables 16.1 and 16.2). The quantitative overview suggests that the phenomena of Secularities I and II are in themselves multidimensional and best represented by not one but multiple indices (Figures 16.1 and 16.2), while the available indices on Secularity III are as of yet still highly unsatisfactory.

A complex picture emerges when attention turns to a comparative assessment of the qualitative evidence of the sort presented in the case studies. In this section the questions are examined a) how Secularities I and III are related, both de jure and de facto, b) what the relationship is between observed levels of Secularities I and III on the one hand and regime type on the other, and c) what accounts for the notably diverse constellations of Secularities I and III that emerge even across cases seemingly similar in terms of religious background.

A first observation is that the relationship between Secularity I and Taylor's particular concern, Secularity III, turns out to be anything but straightforward. For example, the existence of an option not to believe – or, at least, to put one's unbelief on public display without fear of legal or social sanction – seems in part to be a function of the legal environment, specifically of whether official identification as "atheist" or "unbeliever" is an available public option. For Taylor, a central feature of living in the Secular Age of the North Atlantic World is the possibility not to be "religiously marked," that is to live without being identified in public life in terms of one's religious (or expressively non-religious) belonging.[8] In most of the countries studied, however, such a condition of a public sphere

---

[8] Taylor speaks of the "religiously marked" individual, for example, in 2011: 41. He also discusses this term in the 2013 Unseld Lecture on "Religion and Secularism in Modern Democracies," given at the University of Tübingen, June 4, 2013. http://forum-huma num.org/mediathek/sprecher-einzelansicht/sprecher/prof-dr-charles-taylor/. What we suggest with our usage of the term "marker state" is that in many states of Asia, state bureaucracies force citizens to be "religiously marked" – a non-religious identity is from a legal point of view not possible.

blind toward individual religious (or non-religious) identity is not to be found. The state authorities of many countries impose a legal require-ment for citizens to classify themselves in terms of a limited schedule of categories of religious identity. Some do it by requiring the mention of one's religious affiliation on identity cards (e.g. in Egypt, Indonesia, Iran, Israel, Morocco, Pakistan), others through the application of religion-based personal status law (making citizens subject to Hindu, Muslim, Coptic systems of family law, for instance), mandatory religious instruc-tion in public schools, and even differential access to political rights, so that in some cases members of religious minorities are not permitted to run for certain political offices or serve in the military (e.g. in Iran, Israel, Morocco, Pakistan, Turkey). As a consequence of the existence of these rules, attempted deviation from state-recognized categories of religious identity as well as the open expression of unbelief is typically punishable by law, or involves severest disadvantages, such as denied access to education.[9]

Of course, social realities and the meanings attached to them are rarely direct reflections of legal regulations, and it is clear that the requirement to register a religious identity does not mean that those registered are con-scientious believers, adherents, or practitioners. Thus, for example, even though in Turkey citizenship is in fact still dependent on the acceptance of a state-defined religious identity, it is and has for long been *socially* acceptable among certain parts of society to declare oneself agnostic. Secularity III – the option not to believe or be observant – exists in some Turkish milieux, then, even though the current AKP-led government has contributed much to an emergent discourse that equates unbelief with immorality, if not apostasy. There are also counter-cases, such as India and Indonesia, where political rights are not affected by religious affilia-tion, and where religious freedom is a good the government vies to protect, but where – despite this – openly expressed unbelief or professed agnosticism is hardly socially acceptable. A fraction of some elite groups may profess to be agnostic, even atheist, but for the overwhelming major-ity of society such a stance is unheard of.[10] Further, as discussed below, there are cases of the "marker state" such as Morocco and Iran, where the

---

[9] Bahais in Egypt and Iran are a case in point, who are forced to register as Muslim and submit themselves to Islamic family law. Failure to do so can result in charges of apostasy punishable by death.

[10] As Kaviraj reminds us, after all, a religious form of atheism has been part of India's cultural heritage since ancient times (Kaviraj in Bilgrami 2016).

nexus between religion and the state has been so strong ((as per Table A.1 with low scores for Secularity I) that it seems to have triggered over time a trend toward the appreciation of Secularity III in society, that is the conviction among increasing numbers of citizens that how and if they practice religion should not at all be the state's – and perhaps not even the public's – business.

Nor can it be said that the officially secularist states (Soviet Russia from 1917, China from 1949) were religiously "unmarked," since the ruling regimes have on occasion been closely identified with worldviews deeply antagonistic to each country's religious traditions, and open avowal of religious belief and practice was sometimes punished with extremely harsh sanctions. Similarly, if not to the same extent, the Turkish state from 1928 (when its linkage to Islam was constitutionally severed and the "arrow of secularism" proclaimed a guiding principle of the state) until the early 1950s, and Iran under Reza Khan (1925–1941) were officially marked by commitments to values antagonistic to the dominant religious traditions. In all of these cases a clear disconnect can be observed between official policies at the level of the state and the public sphere (where Secularity I operates) and the social and cultural realities in society (where Secularity III operates). So, to summarize a first general observation, while the level of state regulation of the religious field varies considerably between, say, India, Indonesia, Russia, and Turkey (as per Table A.1), none of the states included in this volume – with the possible exception of Japan after 1945 – can be described as "unmarked."

A second general observation that arises from examining the case studies comparatively concerns the relationship between Secularity I and regime type. Because of their formal commitment to religious freedom, one might have expected the democracies among the cases studied to feature relatively high levels of both Secularities I and III, which together provide for freedom to believe or not to believe. Yet, as Table A.1 also indicates, this is not the case. Jonathan Fox, among others, has shown that existing democracies exhibit considerable variance with regard to their levels of Secularity I, and few actually feature a strict separation where, on the one hand, religious authorities and institutions do not interfere with politics, and on the other, the state for its part does not interfere in the religious field (Stepan 2000, Fox 2007, Madeley 2009b). In several of the democracies included here, the state is seen to "interfere" in the religious field quite pervasively (Fox 2012). Thus, for instance, in the case of Israel, the state has since its foundation effectively licensed and conceded establishment status to the Orthodox Rabbinate on issues of deciding who is legally to be classified as Jewish and who is not. In the long-standing democracy of India, Parliament enacted the Hindu Code Bill in 1955/ 1956, which stated that in matters of personal status Jains, Sikhs, and Buddhists should be treated as Hindus in the eyes of the law. And, as a further illustration, the Indian judiciary has often proclaimed judgments that support quasi-theological claims on key religious questions (Sezgin and Künkler 2014), such as in the famous Ayodhya case (2010), where the Uttar Pradesh high court ruled that Lord Ram must indeed have been born in Ayodhya – despite research that is inconclusive even as to his historical existence.

In the two younger democracies included, Indonesia and Turkey, religious and political authority is constitutionally separated, but the state has interfered and continues to interfere heavily in religious life. As Bâli illustrates in the case of Turkey (Chapter 10), the republican national project reconceived the diversity of Muslim life in narrow terms so as to recognize and embrace Sunni Hanafi Islam only, thereby effectively suppressing other Islamic currents, including the large minority of Alevites, estimated at 15–25 percent of the population. Nor is the Indonesian state immune to the charge of having heavily interfered in the religious field, insofar as the practices of Muslim currents other than Sunni Shafi'i Islam are not protected by law, and, where identified, their members (e.g. Shiites, Ahmadis, and others) are routinely persecuted. Further, as Künkler (Chapter 5) shows, after 1945 the state forced the Buddhist and Hindu communities officially to remodel their belief systems along monotheistic lines in order to fit under the pan-religious umbrella of *pancasila*, an ethos of religious diversity, which, for all its seeming inclusiveness, is intolerant of both polytheism and non-theism, as well as, of course, atheism.

What is observed, therefore, across both the long-standing democracies (India, Israel, and Japan) and the newer democracies (Indonesia and, until 2012, Turkey) is great variance in terms of the dimensionality and level of consistency of differentiation between the spheres of state and religion, and, in all cases but Japan, the general *absence* of a strict separation of religion and state.

The way this appears to bear on the absence or presence of Secularity III is also somewhat counterintuitive. While Indonesia and Turkey share the characteristic of being Muslim-majority countries that have democratized more recently, the conditions of belief diverge sharply as between them: in Turkey, as already noted, unbelief is a socially accepted position among certain (mostly metropolitan) elites, whereas in Indonesia it is, as in India, scarcely culturally "available" as an option. A more prevalent trend in both India and Indonesia seems to be toward what Taylor calls neo- and post-Durkheimian social forms of religious experience, either attaching an ethnic marker to religion, or choosing privately to follow practices not strictly associated with the dominant local traditions, but still reminiscent of them.

The relationship between Secularities I and III among the authoritarian cases discussed in this volume appears equally disjointed. One might have expected in this set of cases low levels of Secularity I, and, as a likely consequence, low levels of Secularity III. Yet here too the picture is mixed. The non-democratic Muslim countries included (Egypt, Morocco, Iran, and Pakistan) all have histories of non-secular settlements, and their current governments are not committed to any significant reduction in levels of state interference in the religious field. Traditions of agnosticism – what Taylor calls "exclusive humanism" – can only be cultivated and practiced in the private sphere. China and Russia, on the other hand, offer very different scenarios. In China, while the regime now grants a degree of religious freedom to adherents of the five officially recognized religious associations, the state still tries to limit religion's public influence and to keep control of religious affairs, meantime continuing to use some religious links for diplomatic or economic purposes on the one hand and to repress religious movements which it perceives to be politically threatening, such as the Falun Gong, on the other. In Russia, by contrast, while there is a formal separation of the Russian Orthodox Church and the state, a growing collusion between the Church and senior officials of the regime on issues of common concern (e.g. involving the promotion of Russian national identity and operating a ban on "homosexual propaganda") is evident, while – as in China – newer and more marginal religious groups tend to suffer from many different types of discrimination, including open persecution. In both China and Russia, it should also be noted, atheism continues to subsist among the population despite the shift away from a state commitment to its militant promotion.

A third general observation concerns what can be called multiple secularities involving the range of religion–state arrangements illustrated by the case studies from the Muslim world. Defying essentialist notions of typically "Islamic" religion–state relations often inspired by the view that Islam knows no separation between religion and state, the six Muslim cases could hardly feature greater diversity. Four points in particular stand out. Firstly, independently of each other, three of the contributors – one writing on a case from the Arab world, the other two on cases from the non-Arab world – suggest that Taylor's three notions of secularity need to be complemented by a fourth in order satisfactorily to cover aspects of secularity prevalent in those societies: a notion involving the instrumentalization of religion as political (collective) identity. Thus, Christophe Jaffrelot on Pakistan (Chapter 7), Nader Hashemi on Iran (Chapter 8), and Jonathan Wyrtzen on Morocco (Chapter 13) all note how in order to cope with the growing attraction in society of political Islam, state elites have promoted the notion of Islam as the positive fount of political identity, thereby creating a strong link between nationalism and Islam.[11] The issue is not only relevant to the Muslim-majority countries examined in this volume: a strong nexus between nationalism and religion is also to be found in the contexts of Israel, Russia, and Japan.

Secondly, there is a striking difference between those Muslim-majority case studies where a secular alternative to previously dominant religious discourses emerged at some point, and those where it did not. Because of the nexus between nationalism and religion, Islamization was perceived in Morocco and Pakistan as a way of strengthening the state and its people and buttressing internal cohesion. Jonathan Wyrtzen suggests that it is predominantly for this reason that a secular–nationalist discourse did not establish itself successfully among the Moroccan public (a discourse that would de-couple nationalism from religious identity could easily be criticized as unpatriotic). By contrast, in Iran prior to 1979, Indonesia, and Turkey, modernization policies (in law, the administration and economic development) were more often than not presented in the framework of secular–nationalist campaigns. Sometimes, the modernizing state went so far as to present religion in general as a principal obstacle to progress and development, and Islam in particular as something that "held society back." Wyrtzen relates this difference to the role played by religious minorities. In the Arab East, he argues, "the political order, due to the influential role played by Arab Christian elites in articulating ideals of Arab nationalism, was legitimated primarily by a discourse of Arab cultural identity, which,

---

[11] Jaffrelot identifies this phenomenon as an emergent case of a "Secularity IV." That Taylor would agree with this coinage remains open to question in so far as he refers to tendencies that use religion as political (collective) identity as "neo-Durkheimian" (2007: 455–459), while he describes the North-Atlantic world as having moved into a post-Durkheimian phase "in which the spiritual dimension of existence is quite unhooked from the political" (2007: 455). His analysis would imply that neo-Durkheimianism cannot count as a form of secularity at all.

while not exclusive of Islam, was more secular in its orientation in the primacy it gave to Arab over Muslim identity" (Chapter 13: 326). By contrast, in the *Maghreb*, Wyrtzen suggests, despite the historic presence of Jewish communities, "Arabic and Islamic identities were conflated much more in defining and mobilizing the nation during the anti-colonial struggle" (Chapter 13: 327). The *Mashreq*, by contrast, would show parallels with the Iranian pre-1979, Turkish, and Indonesian contexts, where elite actors had vested interests in reaching non-religious settlements that would facilitate a conception of citizenship as inclusive of religious difference.

Thirdly, the Muslim-majority cases diverge with regard to how aggressively the policies of state-building earlier in the twentieth century worked against religious elites. Some Muslim countries, such as Turkey and Iran pre-1979, underwent secular, modernizing state-building projects often designed in opposition to the traditional religious establishment. In others, such as Morocco and Pakistan, the state never portrayed modernization in necessary opposition to religion. Even New Order Indonesia (1966–1998), in many ways the prototype of a developmentalist regime, tried to co-opt rather than openly antagonize religious authorities. These divergencies led to different patterns of path dependency. In Turkey and Iran, the modern state initially took measures to contain, control, and even in part suppress religion, inter alia by closing religious schools, replacing religious by state courts, and, in Turkey, by going so far as to prohibit religious foundations and replacing all religious with secular law. Religious elites, formerly the principal providers of legal adjudication and education, were robbed of their primary fields of societal influence. In Turkey, they largely failed to resist their gradual marginalization, while in Iran, influential religious authorities were able to countervail the anti-religious policies of the Pahlavi dynasty, and eventually succeeded in toppling the monarchy in 1979 (thanks to the Shiite structure of religious authority around hierarchies and networks, they were much better organized than their Sunni counterparts in Turkey). In Pakistan, state-building and religion were intimately interconnected as the young Pakistani state defined itself against its principal other: the Hindu-majority state of India. The religious establishment profited from the Islamic identity of the state, insofar as madrasa graduation was recognized as a requirement for entry into the state bureaucracy and thereby facilitated access to political positions. In Indonesia, the state also accorded more space to actors in the religious field by tolerating both religious private schools and the continued private training of religious officials (prayer leaders, preachers, etc.). And in Morocco, the state virtually monopolized the "production" of Islam with the Ministry of Religious Affairs paying imams' salaries, training them, and approving *khutbas*.

Finally, while a strong nexus of religious and political authority in Iran and Morocco can be seen to account for the absence of Secularity I, it is interestingly in these two societies (as opposed to Egypt, Turkey, or Indonesia) that a greater societal (as opposed to political) openness to the possibility of exclusive humanism (an important element of Secularity III) seems to have developed. Thus, the authors of the chapters on Iran and Morocco, where political rule is legitimated with reference to religion, note that today's secularizing trends can be identified at the level of society. Given a similar constellation of state and religious identity in Pakistan, this raises the question of what explains the notable weakness of any significant societal secularizing trend there. In spite of the resilience of a secular-minded cosmopolitan elite, and also, as Jaffrelot puts it, of "syncretistic trends" in rural areas, what were once high levels of inter-sectarian and inter-religious tolerance are on the demise, largely due the assault of Islamists and the Islamists' sympathizers in the state, especially those in the army and security services.

In Charles Taylor's *A Secular Age*, the "changing conditions of belief, experience and doubt" (Secularity III) are seen to come about chiefly through theological, social, and intellectual reform. As such, they are fundamentally cultural phenomena that in turn set off new departures which create the original historic possibility for Secularity I's institutional separation of church and state in the West. By contrast, a clear conclusion emanating from this comparison of secularity in the cases studied here is that Secularity III is most unlikely to emerge without minimum levels of Secularity I being in place (religious freedom, a state's blindness as to the citizen's religious belonging). This difference in sequence is largely due to the comparatively later processes of state formation. Beyond this conditionality, various combinations of high Secularity I and low Secularity III or medium Secularity I and low Secularity III appear to be possible and no linear relationship between Secularities I and III can be detected, at least not in the time span observed here. Further, the patterns of evolution respectively of Secularities I and III across the twentieth century have been seen to be highly divergent across the cases studied, with no element, such as regime type, religious background (Muslims vs. Hindu, say), or immediate history (colonized vs. not colonized) emerging as a clear determining factor. An open situation whereby "religion has become one option among many and frequently not the easiest to embrace" has not emerged in most of the cases examined and it is suggested that the types of theological, social, and intellectual reform processes which facilitated the emergence of Secularity III in the North Atlantic World have most often been politically thwarted by the prevailing type of religion–state relations in the cases discussed here. How did these patterns of religion–state relations come about? The next section turns to examine this question.

CONSTITUTIONAL LEGACIES AND SECULAR–RELIGIOUS SETTLEMENTS

While changes in levels of religious belief and practice (Secularity II) or in the conditions of belief, experience, and doubt (Secularity III) have typically occurred unevenly and over extended periods of time, shifts in the relative prominence of religious influences in the realm of political authority (Secularity I) have tended to be precipitated by key political events at what students of historical institutionalism call "critical junctures."[12] In his influential 1978 work *A General Theory of Secularization*, David Martin highlighted the fact that "at certain crucial periods in their history societies acquire a particular frame and subsequent events persistently move within the limits of that frame" (1978: 15). The implicit idea is of course the phenomenon of a "path dependence" – in Martin's metaphor, "a contour of dykes and canals set up at a crucial turning point in history [whereby] the flow of events runs according to that contour" (ibid.); key institutional choices made at critical junctures tend to "stick" because "the costs of reversal are very high. There will be other choice points, but the entrenchments of certain institutional arrangements obstruct easy reversal of the initial choice" (Levi 1997, 28). Martin's 1978 volume illustrated how the working of these and other dynamics across Europe and the Americas set off by a series of revolutionary "crucial events" and subsequent "variable histories" resulted in a series of contrasting patterns of relation affecting religious institutions, beliefs, and ethos – terms which can, incidentally, be seen to reflect distinctions similar to those between Taylor's three secularities.[13]

---

[12] For the notion of critical junctures and path dependencies, see the historical institutionalist literature by Collier and Collier 1991; Pierson 2000; Mahoney and Thelen 2010.

[13] In his later work on contrasting patterns of secularization (and sanctification) in Europe, Latin America, and Sub-Saharan Africa, Martin further expanded on "how the themes of

In almost all the cases surveyed in this volume, the relation between religion, the state, and the public sphere has been profoundly shaped by the setting of state constitutions or other basic laws framed in the aftermath of critical junctures thrown up by episodes of, respectively, decolonization (Egypt, Indonesia, India, Pakistan, Morocco), revolution (Russia, China, Iran), or war (Turkey, Japan, Israel). In seeking to understand the character and development of the resulting patterns, attention has accordingly been paid to the phenomenon of "path dependency" involving both the emergence of challenges to initial frame-setting settlements and the constraints on subsequent developments associated with the heavy costs involved in radical change. Despite the heavy costs, some of the developments studied have involved actual "frame-busting" changes (such as the 1979 Iranian revolution) which themselves set off new path-dependent dynamics.

Attempts to account for the character and variability of the different settlements have necessarily focused attention on the principal actors during critical junctures, especially those with vested interests in particular outcomes for whom those episodes often provided opportunities for entrenchment. In most of the cases studied, such influential actors have included relatively small elite groups whose strength and influence did not depend on their representation within the affected populations. It is to an examination of these initial settlements, contrasting balances (or imbalances) between instances of state and religious authority and the varying degrees of constitutional fixity they exhibited that attention now turns.

Typologies of Secular–Religious Settlements

At first glance, the cases surveyed fall into three contrasting categories. The first is that of explicitly or de facto secular settlements where the resulting constitutions provided no recognition of the claims of religious authorities to special treatment and status, for example, by denying any place for religious sources in public law. This category includes the initial settlements of China in 1912, Russia in 1917, Turkey in 1924, Indonesia in 1945, Japan in 1946, India in 1947, and the status quo agreed upon in Israel in 1948. In addition, later settlements in China in 1949, Indonesia in 2002, and Egypt in 2014 also qualify as secular. To take the Japanese case

the religious repertoire [are] variously inflected" in wider geographical and historical contexts in ways that complement and extend (both geographically and thematically) the coverage of this volume (Martin 2005: 130).

as an illustration, after the 1945 surrender, the process of writing the new constitution was severely constrained by the requirements imposed by the US occupation administration. Unsurprisingly, as Helen Hardacre shows (Chapter 4), the constitution that emerged bore the unmistakable marks of American pressure, despite the retention of the monarchy and the shift to a system of parliamentary government. The removal of the sacred status of the monarch and the disestablishment of what had been the state Shinto cult in particular bore witness to American influence.

The second, much smaller category consists of explicitly unsecular settlements: those where constitutions established a nominally religious state. To this category belong the cases of Morocco in 1958 and Iran in 1979. In Morocco the established position of the king as Commander of the Faithful represented (and continues to represent) a fusion of religious and political authority which fixes the Islamic identity of the state. Jonathan Wyrtzen's chapter shows that the French protectorate of 1912 to 1956, far from imposing *laicité* as in metropolitan France, carefully preserved traditional religious structures in order to ensure stability during the colonial era. After 1956, the ambiguities that characterized the protectorate persisted even with the restoration of the Alawite sultanate (later monarchy), bolstered as it was by its role as a symbol of national identity in contradistinction to French colonial claims. In recent years, the delicate balances involved in this settlement have become difficult to maintain, particularly with rising Islamist radicalism and liberal secular movements of reform in the Maghreb, as the ongoing contestation around constitutional reform illustrates.

In Iran, even though the anti-Shah coalition in the later 1970s included important secular groups, not least among them liberal constitutionalists and human rights lawyers, supporters of Khomeini's leadership were soon able to capitalize on the symbolic power of the clergy, with Khomeini as its figurehead. The first draft of a new constitution, conceived during the last year of Khomeini's exile in France, was based on the 1958 French constitution and was both broadly republican and secular. Khomeini consented to submit this draft to the people in a referendum but revolutionary factions objected. So too – ironically, in hindsight – did the human rights movement, which argued that civil liberties needed to be further strengthened, and that the constitution ought to be the product of an inclusive constitutional process, rather than the work of single legal scholar. Little did they foresee that the process would result in a document according to which civil liberties meant little and the highest political office would be reserved for a religious authority.

The third category of secular–religious settlement includes those with ambiguous formulations which do not establish a nominally religious state but which nonetheless privilege religious authorities in state affairs. Examples would be Iran in 1906/1907, Pakistan in 1956, and, much more recently, Egypt in 2012.

Taking the earliest of these cases first, the 1907 amendment to the 1906 constitution of Iran – the first constitution in the Middle East to be attained through a struggle from below – established an ulama council that would screen the bills of the just-created parliament for their coherence with Islamic law. While executive authority would remain secular (the Shah), in legislative affairs religious scholars would have the last word. The 1907 supplementary law also created what legal scholars refer to as a "repugnancy clause": Art. 2 stipulated that no law shall contradict the teachings of the Qur'an and Sunnah. Interestingly, Iran in 1907 created precedents with two institutions that would later be adopted elsewhere in the Muslim world: the repugnancy clause, and the council of ulama that would participate in the legislative process.

As Christophe Jaffrelot shows, the 1956 constitution of Pakistan was deeply ambiguous in respect of its treatment of religion. While its Art. 18 ostensibly recognized full freedom of religion, the country was declared to be an Islamic Republic, stipulated an Islamic repugnancy clause, and established that the president be Muslim. The repugnancy clause had less power than in 1907 Iran, however, as the Islamic Advisory Board charged with its implementation was constituted for a limited five-year period and could only formulate recommendations to parliament, which was not required to consider these, nor was the repugnancy clause justiciable. In other words, a citizen who felt that legislation was not in line with Islamic law could not plead on this basis in court.

The third example of a highly ambiguous settlement is the most recent one covered in this volume: that of the abortive Egyptian constitution of 2012, which in Art. 2 (like its predecessor) recognized Islamic law as the major source of law and in its new Art. 4 stipulated that scholars of al-Azhar would need to be consulted on matters relating to Islamic law – without, however, clarifying whether these scholars would have veto power over legislation or how frequently and intensively parliament would be required to consult them. As in Iran in 1906 and Pakistan in 1956, political authority was separate from religious authority, but religious scholars were granted a say in the legislative process.

Between State Control of Religion and Religious Control
of the Public Sphere

As important as critical junctures have been in laying down the basis for the three broad types of religion–state settlements just discussed, a glance at subsequent developments makes it clear that the *majority* of cases also feature significant later deviations from the original settlements. These deviations, moreover, emerge as more relevant than the original settlements for assessing the incidence of Secularity I.

Meiji Japan in 1868, China in 1912, Russia in 1917, Turkey in 1924, China in 1949, and Egypt in 2014 all present cases where nominally secular settlements were eventually combined with heavy state control over the religious field. Moves in the opposite direction, by contrast, can be observed in the cases of Indonesia in 1945, India in 1947, Israel in 1948, Pakistan in 1956, and Egypt in 2012, where once formally secular settlements were eventually undermined by state governments ceding important public functions to religious authorities.

In Japan, even though religious and political authority had previously been separate and a number of faiths legally recognized, the 1868 Meiji Restoration embarked upon the elevation of Shinto to a state religion. Efforts were made to separate Shinto from Buddhism and to demote the latter through the destruction of temples, among other measures. Shinto was released from Buddhist administration and its properties restored. An Office of Shinto Worship was established, and the Home Ministry assumed control of all Shinto shrines.

In China, even though some crucial shifts in the relationship between the state, religion, and politics had already begun before the end of the nineteenth century, the foundation of the Republic of China in 1912 marked the beginning of a new epoch. The leadership of the young Republic formally established a degree of religious freedom and declared the equal rights of believers in different religions. With an eye on the example of France, it adopted the principle of attempting to separate politics from religion and relegating matters of religious belief to the private sphere. However, the concept of "religion" which was actually deployed in this new context was anything but neutral. Christianity was taken by political and cultural elites as the model of authentic religion, with its features of scriptures, regular time and place of worship, ecclesiastical establishment, clerical hierarchy, written canon law, and ritual cycles. Chinese traditional religions were accordingly reformed along Christian lines and the leadership of each of them were prevailed upon to create church-like national associations. Popular cults and practices (e.g. fortune-telling and fengshui (geomancy)) that could not be reformed along Christian lines were classified as superstitions, criticized as obstacles to Chinese modernization, and subjected to damaging attacks. After World War II and the years of civil war, the same broad policy of state supervision and control continued under the Chinese Communist Party, with each of the five recognized religions – Buddhism, Taoism, Protestantism, Catholicism, and Islam – maintaining an official Church or association while all non-official religious bodies continued to be regarded with deep suspicion. And after the decade-long aberration of the Cultural Revolution (1966–1976), when an attempt was made to suppress *all* religion as superstition, China returned to the earlier pattern of religious control.

As John Madeley relates (Chapter 11), the 1917 Bolshevik coup in Russia provided an opportunity for the Bolshevik leaders with their dedication to a particularly militant version of exclusive humanism to sideline the Orthodox Church (ROC), degrade its capacity to sustain itself, and in the 1930s subject it to a violent campaign aimed at the total destruction of its remaining influence. Initially, the minority alternative religions of the former Russian Empire fared better, only later to share in a fate similar to that of the ROC. Despite some relaxation of the anti-religious campaign in the 1940s, religious institutions and organizations remained firmly under the control of a state committed to building an entirely secular future, until the radically reforming changes of the 1980s supervened and a modest religious revival occurred. The introduction of a liberal religious freedom reform in the early 1990s was, however, significantly reversed later in that decade, and since then the ROC has regained some of its former precedence, while unrecognized sects, particularly those of foreign origin, continue to suffer discrimination and, occasionally, outright persecution.

Turkey represents another case of what looked at first glance to have been a secular, separationist settlement, but which eventually revealed itself to be one of state domination over religion. As Aslı Bâli analyses, the political settlement of the 1920s and '30s produced a durable regime that institutionalized complete domination of the state in all religious affairs. As reforms emptied public life of open religious references, there was a complete failure to introduce a two-way separationist barrier between religion and the state. The reforms which openly intended to banish religion from public affairs included the abolition of the Caliphate and the closing of shari'a courts in 1924, the abolition of public religious education and the disbanding of religious orders soon after, the removal of Islam from the constitutional order in 1928, and the subsequent elimination of all religious laws from the operative legal codes. All of these reforms could in principle have allowed for a vibrant religious life to flourish in the private sphere and cannot be said to constitute an anti-religious campaign of the sort that was conducted in Russia in the 1930s; they might indeed have produced a type of Secularity I similar to that of the United States during the heyday of Supreme Court separationism. The Turkish reforms, however, also abolished private religious education and placed religious foundations under state control, while setting up a state directorate for religious affairs (*diyanet*) that took exclusive control over the education and training of Islamic scholars (*ulama*) and other regulatory functions in the religious field. In the 1950s, religious public education was reintroduced (while private educational alternatives remained banned), but the content of the teaching was restricted to the Hanafi traditions of Sunni Islam, and had the effect of suppressing other significant Islamic traditions of the country, especially Alevism. This heavy state regulation of religion created a path-dependent pattern that meant that any elected government signaling the possibility of reforming this settlement risked being shut down. Both the 1960 and 1980 military coups and the 1997 soft coup were publicly legitimated with reference to the sense that Turkish *laiklik* was under threat.

After the 2013 military coup in Egypt, the democratically elected government dominated by the Muslim Brothers was arrested and party members most severely persecuted. Religious parties have been outlawed in the 2014 constitution and religious organizations are under close watch of the military. Religious organizations, as civil society organizations in general, can only operate insofar as they are tolerated by the military, which since 2013 has been engaged in transforming Egypt into a police state.

While these five cases illustrate how ostensibly secular and separationist settlements gave way to state control over the religious field, other cases provide examples of the opposite development: secular–separationist settlements that have eventually been undermined by state governments ceding public functions to religious authorities. This pattern can be observed to some extent in Pakistan, Israel, Indonesia, India, and Egypt prior to 2012.

In Pakistan, before the country's first constitution was promulgated in 1956, religion–state relations were organized on the basis of the 1935 Government of India Act, which recognized religious private law but otherwise made no specific provisions regarding religion. In 1956, these relations were fundamentally changed as the constitution defined Pakistan as an Islamic Republic. Despite this declaration, Christophe Jaffrelot maintains that the settlement reached in Pakistan remained fundamentally secular until the mid-1970s, partly because the constitution incorporated important elements also found in the 1950 Indian constitution. Like its Indian counterpart, the 1956 Pakistan constitution secured the freedom to worship and freedom of religion more generally. The judiciary was explicitly tasked with protecting the freedom of religion, and minorities were not excluded from appointment to offices in the bureaucracy or military by virtue of their religious identity – except for the office of prime minister, which was reserved for a Muslim. Until the 1970s, the judiciary defended the rights of religious minorities, including the Ahmadis, but the situation turned in 1974 when, under pressure from the Jamaat-i Islami, Prime Minister Bhutto introduced constitutional amendments regarding which groups were to be considered Muslim, which had the significant effect of excluding the Ahmadis. In 1984, Prime Minister Zia went one step further, and made blasphemy punishable by death, since which time the judiciary has been subject to intimidation by Islamist groups such that it can no longer be considered a neutral force. Hence, in Jaffrelot's eyes, Pakistan counts as a case where an originally largely religiously neutral settlement deteriorated into one clearly advantaging Sunni Muslims over other religious communities and increasingly violating the rights of both Muslim non-Sunni and non-Muslim minorities.

Hanna Lerner's chapter indicates that in the 1948 founding moment Israeli leaders were unable to decide between a secular and a non-secular settlement. On the one hand, in the proclamation of independence, the political elite defined the young state as a Jewish state, though the nature of the state, whether secular or religious, was not specified. The principles to which the leadership committed the country – "complete equality of social and political rights to all its inhabitants irrespective of religion, race or sex … freedom of religion, conscience, language, education and culture" (Chapter 9: 222) – would appear to be incompatible with the privileging in general of one religious identity over others, and, in particular, the Orthodox variant of Judaism in preference to non-Orthodox traditions. Despite this, the young state accorded Judaism, as a religion, special privileges, and within Judaism promoted the Orthodox Rabbinate over other Jewish currents. Crucially, only the Orthodox Rabbinate can determine the criteria of Jewishness, and Orthodox schools (over whose curricula the state has no control) are subsidized by public funds (Künkler and Lerner 2016). The privileges accorded to religious actors appeared at the time relatively insignificant when seen in the context of the country's demography; but over time those benefiting from the privileges have become a potent electoral force, a development which has enabled them to expand their privileges further. The year 1948 created a distinctively ambiguous pattern of path dependency by virtue of the indefinite post-ponement of a decision over the fundamental nature of the state, which protracted the conflict to a point where agreement on a written constitu-tion would now appear to be further from realization than ever.

As Shylashri Shankar demonstrates in her chapter on India (Chapter 6), a major concern for the Constituent Assembly and the dominant Congress party leadership was how to douse the flames of religious strife between Hindus and Muslims resulting from the 1947 partition, while simulta-neously delivering a measure of social justice to the discriminated Hindu castes. The conflicting views in the Assembly debates introduced a stub-born vein of ambiguity into the Constitution, which committed the state on the one hand to ensure social justice by, for example, eliminating the practice of untouchability, while on the other hand promising religious freedom to all groups. Ultimately, the constitution provided no definitions of such key terms as "Hindu," "religion," "secular," and "minorities," and left it to the courts and the crafters of legislative amendments to do so. The path-dependent pattern introduced by these decisions can be seen in the debates around the Uniform Civil Code and the reform of the Hindu Code Bill in 1954–1955, which forced Buddhists, Jains, and Sikhs to follow Hindu law.

Indonesia presents a case of unusual stability in respect of its initial constitutional settlement: what was proposed just six weeks before the country's promulgation of independence on August 16, 1945 (and sig-nificantly altered in a last minute-intervention just one evening prior), proved to establish a constitutional legacy that has stubbornly endured until today. The unique formula of a principle of *pancasila* that identifies Indonesians as a religious citizenry, bound by their faith in the "one God" without specifying a particular religion, has provided the cornerstone of religion–state relations until this day. After the country democratized in 1998, *pancasila* was reaffirmed by constitutional amendment. Although opting for an Islamic alternative has frequently been debated in the country's post-independence history, the argument that Islamic law should become "a" (or even "the") source of public law never prevailed. Despite this constitutional legacy, the status of religious law has drama-tically changed in the realm of family law in the post-independence period. In the 1970s Islamic courts were officially recognized and a marriage law passed that foresaw separate provisions for Muslims and non-Muslims. Until 1989 the decisions of Islamic courts (which adjudicate family law) could be invalidated by civil courts, but this changed when the Islamic courts were elevated to courts of first instance with their own tier for appeals. Expanding the prevalence of Islamic law further, a 2004 decentralization law permitted the smaller administrative units of the country to pass their own laws, in the aftermath of which numerous mandatory zakat provisions, veiling laws, curfew laws, alcohol bans, and limits on press freedom, were introduced, all justified with reference to Islamic provisions. While Indonesia remains constitutionally a quasi-secular state, its legal reality has become significantly more colored by religious provisions in the past twenty years.

Until recently, Egypt also provided a case of relative stability in the field of state–religion relations: the overthrow of the Egyptian monarchy in 1952 by a group of young army officers inaugurated a period of military rule and Arab nationalism which was to last for almost sixty years, until the revolution of 2011 led to the deposition of Husni Mubarak. From the 1970s onward, the earlier designation of the state as Islamic was given more content with the requirement that shariʿa be regarded as "a" and then "the chief" source of legislation. But according to Gudrun Krämer (Chapter 12), the distinctly ambiguous outcome before the crisis, following the election of the Muslim Brothers' Muhammed Mursi as president and his deposition by the military only a year later, has been that in Egypt "the state is secular (i.e., non-clerical) in structure and composition but it is not neutral" (Chapter 12: 296).

The lessons to be drawn from this review of contrasting patterns of state–religion relations over time are two-fold. First, it lends credence to the claim that state constitutions create path dependencies in religion–state relations, at least as far as the constitutional text is concerned. Only very rarely have countries moved from declaring the character of the state to be religious where it was previously secular or vice versa. In fact, as others have shown, the constitutions of the twentieth century tend to maintain similar provisions in religion–state relations to those adopted by their predecessors. Indeed, it would appear that no country since 1990 has disestablished religion as a source of law where it had been recognized as a source of law in the immediately preceding constitution (Künkler, Lerner, and Shankar 2015). In this regard, path dependencies do appear to be created in those foundational moments after the end of colonial rule, civil war, or revolution. What this observation does not capture, however, is that constitutional religion–state relations are often significantly modified in their implementation below the level of state constitutions (Künkler and Sezgin 2016). This introduces a second observation thrown up by these cases: which is that religion–state relations as specified in constitutional texts are often significantly modified by sub-constitutional interventions, such as ordinary legislation (which establishes religion-based family law in the case of Indonesia, for example), bureaucratic provisions (which, as in the case of Israel, require citizens to register in an officially recognized religion or otherwise lose access to state resources – education, health provision, pensions, etc.), or court judgments (as in the case of India, where court rulings have stipulated that someone who eats beef cannot be considered a Hindu).

The Limits of Using Constitutions as Measures of Secularity I

A significant feature of the picture emerging from this comparative discussion of critical junctures and path dependencies is that only three foundational settlements have remained true to their original character: Japan in 1946, Morocco in 1948, and Iran in 1979. Their constitutions qualified these countries as either secular or religious, and the fundamental nature of religion–state relations have remained stable thereafter.

In the eight other cases, formally secular settlements were later undermined. Four moved to adopt measures of more or less heavy state control over religion, while in the remaining four cases political elites conceded state functions to religious authorities. None of these eight, in other words, can be said to safeguard the stipulations of Alfred Stepan's "twin tolerations," according to which religion and state grant space to one another in order to protect human rights.[14]

In all eight of these cases, the nature of religion–state relations changed significantly despite ostensible constitutional continuity, a fact which indicates that constitutions taken alone are not a reliable measure for indices of Secularity I. A constitution may guarantee religious freedom, and create a formally secular executive power, but if religion-based private law prohibits interfaith marriage, if bureaucratic regulations force citizens to identify with state-recognized categories of religion, and if courts deem certain practices of religious believers to be heretical, the formal provision of religious freedom in the constitution carries little weight. The indices of Secularity I discussed in connection with Table A.1 do also take into account a number of indicators aside from

---

[14] Stepan 2000.

constitutions, including ordinary legislation, bureaucratic regulations, and court judgments. Nonetheless, the constitutional status of religion is usually given disproportionate weight as an independent variable, while in eight of eleven cases surveyed here the constitutional status of religion has meant little when compared to the legal reality. The results of this survey would therefore suggest caution against taking constitutional clauses on religion as reliable indicators of the nature of a country's religion–state relations.

ACCOUNTING FOR THE CONTRASTING PATTERNS: ALTERNATIVE APPROACHES

In 1970, Donald E. Smith argued that different paths toward what he called "the secularization of the polity" (for him, "the most fundamental structural and ideological change in the process of political development") could be accounted for by the unique combinations of ideational and structural features found in Muslim, Hindu, Buddhist, and Roman Catholic third-world religions and societies (Smith 1970). He saw each of the four systems as "a distinct complex of belief, ritual, socioreligious institution, and ecclesiastical organization" and argued that "the differences among them produce very different political consequences" (ibid.: 5). Almost fifty years on – and with many of the assumptions of modernization theories now seriously undermined – only a small number of comparativists have attempted to provide explanations for the complex series of contrasting patterns of secularity which have since actually eventuated. Among these, the main focus has been (unlike Taylor's deep engagement with key developments in the world of ideas) more on the role of structural than of ideational factors: in particular, the existence or absence of particular legal traditions; the location, resources, and modus operandi of principal actors; the power of transnational institutional diffusion; and the resulting institutional arrangements intended to address perennial problems of modern polities. The following reviews three such approaches in the light of the case studies.

Keddie: Secularization Harder in the Scriptural Monotheistic Religions

Nikkie Keddie has observed that while secularization has permeated the Muslim world less than Taylor's North Atlantic World, it is actually the societies of non- and poly-theistic religious traditions that in her reading have embraced secularization with least resistance (and, by implication, even more easily than Western Christianity):

Islamic history is different from Western Christian history, partly because modernizing trends began earlier and have been more gradual in the West, and also because Islam has not had a strong secular legal tradition. These are two of the factors that have made secularization more difficult and contentious in recent decades in the Islamic world than in the West, while all the main scriptural monotheistic religions have been more resistant to secularization than have other religious traditions. (Keddie 1997: 27)

The case studies largely confirm the first part of Keddie's thesis – that is that both more abrupt modernizing trends and the absence of a strong secular legal tradition have made secularization more difficult and contentious in the Muslim world than in the West. They tend to corroborate the two reasons she invokes – namely, the abrupt onslaught of modernization starting in the early twentieth century, which provoked significant societal backlash, and the dominant role of religion in legal traditions, which in the modern state has translated into religion being a source of private and often also public law. However, the case studies only partly confirm the second part of her thesis, according to which non- and poly-theistic societies have been less resistant to secularization processes than their monotheist counterparts. Following Keddie's logic, one would expect the societies of Japan, China, and India with their poly-theistic and nontheistic traditions to feature more advanced levels of secularization today. Yet, this general thesis appears to be challenged by the case studies of India and Russia rather than confirmed. While China and Japan are the societies most secularized on the societal level (Secularity II), India fares low on three of four indicators, tending toward the lower end of Secularity II (Table A.2), with Russia in between these poles.[15] In terms of Secularity I, only Japan features high levels with little state interference into the religious field, while China, Russia, and India all regulate religion today with limited protection of religious freedom, and so exhibit moderate to low levels of Secularity I. While according to Keddie's thesis, Russia's Eastern Orthodox tradition as being monotheist and scriptural should have been more resistant to secularization than those of the poly- and nontheistic

---

[15] The observations regarding both Secularities I and II are complicated by the caveats discussed in the appendix: while both should be seen as multi- rather than one-dimensional, the measurement of Secularity II faces the additional challenge of operating on the basis of a concept of religiosity whose universalizability is questionable. If anything, then, Keddie's thesis would require further, more systematic, probing on a higher level of conceptual nuance than extant indices allow for.

traditions of Japan, China, and India, this is not substantiated by the case studies.

The observed levels of secularity in the Japanese case also map onto Keddie's taxonomy only partly. After World War II, separation between the institutions of the state and of religion was mandated by the victorious USA in a manner which has the continuing effect that the state's involvement with religion is uniquely low compared to all the other cases studied (Table A.1). These formal requirements contrast starkly with the pre-war situation when state Shinto was enforced as a national cult. Given the determining role of US constitutional advisors in designing religion–state relations after World War II, and thus laying down the bases for Secularity I, it seems difficult to ascribe the advance of Secularity I to factors associated with the nature of Japanese religious traditions. Similarly problematic for Keddie's thesis, the observed levels of religious belief and practice remain moderately high (thus, moderate Secularity II).

Finally, India, despite its poly-theistic traditions, has features that place it closer to the six Muslim cases than Japan and China. Even though the independent state reformed and secularized much of Hindu law, the law still sees the individual citizen fundamentally through the lens of religious identity (Art. 25,2 (b) of the Indian constitution). The same must be said about monotheist Israel, where the continuation of Ottoman millet-style arrangements in personal law and the maintenance within the majority community of the authority of the Orthodox Rabbinate significantly qualify the country's claims to instantiate Secularity I. As Table A.1 indicates, both India and Israel feature low levels of Secularity I.

Seen in a perspective stretching over several centuries, what appears to be the basic intuition behind Keddie's thesis can be seen to have more substance. Our cases certainly confirm that where a religion has a strong legalistic tradition, it has been difficult to break with this entirely. Levels of Secularity I are generally lower in countries with such traditions, because elements of the legal system often still reflect the influence of religious norms and/or authorities (usually in family law, and sometimes also in constitutional law). Beyond this fundamental linkage, however, it seems difficult to extrapolate from the nature of religious traditions to the likely emergence of particular levels of Secularity I, II, or III outside the West. This is predominantly so because, as far as the twentieth century is concerned, the role of the state has been constitutive in deciding the place and role of religion in public life. With all its regulations on citizenship and laws on societal organizations, on public space, on marriage and inheritance, it has been the dominant player in determining levels of Secularity I, irrespective of whether societies are in their majority mono-, poly-, or nontheistic, and whether these are scriptural or not. Keddie herself acknowledges this predominant role of the state when she writes that modern secularization processes "[have] been more influenced by government action than by autonomous societal changes" (1997: 22). For her, this priority of the political deserves particular recognition because "the very strengthening of a state demanded by modern economies requires considerable state control of public education, civil law, welfare and other spheres that is more secular than anything that existed in the past" (1997: 24). In sum, the case studies confirm her prioritization of state action and policy in determining levels of Secularity I (and, we would add, III), while correlations between the character of particular religious traditions and levels of Secularity II cannot be confirmed.

Demerath: The Key Role of the Actors Driving Secularization

Like Keddie, Jay Demerath has been interested in comparing connections between secularization and diverse religious traditions, partly out of a frustration that the great bulk of secularization studies have focused on religious phenomena in the West. In 2001, he introduced a four-part typology for models of secularization, organized around two axes: whether secularization was driven by external or internal forces, and whether it was directed from above or driven by social forces from below. He identified the four types of secularization that emerge from the cross-cutting combinations as emergent (internal–non-directed), diffuse (external–non-directed), coercive (internal–directed), and imperialist (external–directed).[16] As he conceded, aspects of all four types can be seen at work in each and every case of secularization; nevertheless, one of the four will be dominant in any one particular episode of a society's history. Only one of the authors in this volume has identified the secularization processes of their case study to be overwhelmingly driven by external as opposed to internal forces – namely, Japan. In all the other cases, even though local actors have responded to outside influences, pressures, and interferences, authors have overwhelmingly identified domestic forces

---

[16] Under secularization, he understands "a process of change by which the sacred gives way to the secular, whether in matters of personal faith, institutional practice, or societal power. It involves a transition in which things once revered become ordinary, the sanctified becomes mundane, and things other-worldly may lose their prefix" (Demerath 2007: 65–66).

as the drivers of secularization processes. As such, most chapters are either case studies of emergent (bottom-up) or coercive (top-down) secularization.[17]

In China, Turkey, and the Soviet Russia, secularization was to a large extent coercive, strongly shaped, and, by many means, imposed from above. In all three cases, it was mostly the executive that devised secularizing policies (in law, education, property regimes). They therefore most closely fit Demerath's model of coercive secularization.

In India, Egypt, Israel, and Indonesia, elements of both emergent and coercive secularization can be found. In all four cases, the national movements were intent on transcending either internal religious divides (India, Egypt, and Indonesia) or the secular–religious divide (Israel), and thus did not espouse a vision of the future independent state that would be strongly oriented around religious life. In this regard, they endowed the early republican governments with a secularist bent: the orientation of these nations' founding fathers translated into classic secularist policies. That is, secularization that had been emergent among particular elite milieux fed a later coercive state-driven secularization process. In all four societies, secularizing policies were later complemented and in some areas replaced by policies promoting religious life (state funding for an ever expanding sector of private religious education in Israel or the elevation of shariʿa to the main source of public law in Egypt).

In Iran, Pakistan, and Morocco some secularization pressures have recently arisen within society (cp. Demerath's emergent secularization), partly in response to governmental policies of Islamization. At the same time, it is clear that the Iranian and Pakistani Islamization policies were themselves consequences of earlier societal pressures (pressures among both elites and a larger public) in favor of a greater role for Islam in public life. The two countries therefore feature strong currents of both bottom-up Islamization and bottom-up secularization, the former of which translated into governmental policies, while the latter has remained, until now, largely suppressed.

One weakness of Demerath's approach is that while it sheds light on actors and processes, it has little to say regarding the effects of secularizing policies. Should one assume that coercive secularization leads to high Secularity I and/or II? Few would contest the overall classification of

---

[17] The latter category need not apply to authoritarian environments only. Demerath (2007) gives the example of the First Amendment to the U.S. constitution which can be interpreted as having established a top-down secularization policy.

Atatürk's Turkey as one of coercive secularization, for example, but as Bâli shows, it also involved placing religion in the service of the state: religion was instrumentalized, as well as being banished from public life. Despite decades of coercive secularization, the Turkish case did not develop high levels of Secularity I, nor is Turkish society today characterized by high levels of Secularity II. While Demerath offers a useful typology of the sources and course of secularization processes, how these interact with effects remains unexamined. Further, one may note that since overall the case studies attest to the central place of the state in processes of secularization, and since – globalization, international diffusion, interdependence, and external pressure notwithstanding – state policies are still overwhelmingly determined by internal rather than external actors, coercive (internal–directed) secularization emerges as the dominant category, while the other three fade into the background, a finding which would appear to limit the explanatory potential of the typology.

Wohlrab-Sahr and Burchardt: Secularity as Responses to Reference Problems

A third comparative approach is outlined by Monika Wohlrab-Sahr and Marian Burchardt (2012), who distinguish secularization patterns not by the nature of religious traditions (like Keddie) or the driving forces (like Demerath), but in terms of issue areas. These they identify as arising from four "reference problems": (1) the problem of individual freedom vis-à-vis dominant social units, be they groups or the state; (2) the problem of religious heterogeneity and the resulting potential for actual conflictuality; (3) the problem of social or national integration and development; and (4) the problem of the independent development of institutional domains (2012: 889). As the authors argue, "[i]t is clear that most of these problems are closely associated to the formation of modern societies and states and the ideas on which they are founded, whereas at least the second also arises in pre-modern societies. It is no accident that reflections on premodern sources of modern secularity generally begin here" (2012: 887).

Three of these four reference problems have been of importance in the cases studied. As noted in the introduction to this volume, in all the case studies conflicts around religious questions have intersected with questions of national integration. Sometimes religion has been mobilized for nationalist purposes (post-1979 Iran), while at others it has been perceived as potentially undermining national cohesion (China). Similarly, the negotiation of individual freedom vis-à-vis dominant social units has been a central theme in all chapters, particularly where the state has been highly involved in formulating officially "valid" conceptions of religious belief, practice, and law, thus shaping communitarian identities. And religious heterogeneity is seen to have emerged as a factor in most of the struggles about the proper status of religion in public life.

Based on the identification of the three main "reference problems" of interest here, the authors go on to distinguish the secular solutions aimed at resolving these, each in turn being based on different guiding ideas: secularity for the sake of individual freedom is guided by ideas of freedom and individuality; secularity for dealing with problems arising from religious heterogeneity is guided by ideas of toleration, respect, and non-interference; secularity in the service of national integration is guided by the ideas of progress, enlightenment, and modernity; finally, secularity for the purpose of promoting functional differentiation is guided by ideas of rationality, efficiency, and autonomy. This approach is particularly useful for tracing the *evolution* of secularizing policies over time. For example, in the case of Indonesia, such policies can be seen to be motivated by ideas of progress, enlightenment, and modernity from the 1940s until mid-1950s when ideas of toleration, and respect became more prominent (Künkler and Sezgin 2016). And during the democratization period of the late 1990s, many argued for secularity on the basis of freedom and individuality.

The fourth type of secularizing reference problem is harder to connect to particular policies, precisely because it is not inherently a state-driven process. It is in essence Casanova's first notion of secularization, namely that of differentiation as a macro-historical process. From the viewpoint of this volume, what sets the West apart is its experience of secularization as differentiation, while in all the cases studied here secularization has predominantly been a consequence of particular policies guided variously by type 1, 2, and 3 ideas of the Wohlrab-Sahr and Burchardt schema.

This schema, however, does not easily allow for causal claims to be made about how Secularity I, II, or III typically emerge. Like Demerath's, it elucidates intentionality without assessing outcomes. In this regard, it raises questions without necessarily providing answers: Does secularity dealing with problems arising from religious heterogeneity and driven by ideas of toleration really increase societal acceptance of such values? Does secularity justified with reference to individual freedom really deliver on this good? Further, it is not clear how the reference problems relate to Taylor's distinction between Secularities I, II, and III. For example, it can be argued that reflections on the sources of modern secularity are relevant within a given society with regard to Secularities II and III, while they are largely irrelevant for Secularity I. Again, this might be so because Secularity I in the twentieth and twenty-first centuries has been overwhelmingly determined by state policy, which, as has been shown in several cases, does not need to be sourced from home-grown ideas. Relatedly, one wonders whether ideas perhaps are given too prominent a place. This is not to deny the power of ideas or what Weber calls "ideal interests" in motivating social action, but rather to express caution about the possibility of reading motivating ideas back into the outcomes of social action. The latter connection is not linear; it is nourished by multiple sources, and interests in addition to opportunities may be just as important, if not more so, than ideas in explaining particular outcomes. The case studies of this volume suggest that the study of ideas needs to be better complemented by the study of power relations and contingency to understand why particular secular or non-secular settlements are being reached.

Finally, Wohlrab-Sahr and Burchardt's type 4 secularity is somewhat set apart by virtue of the fact that it is not a process or outcome driven by any particular force. As the authors observe, "[s]ecularity for the sake of the independent development of functional domains is rarely the dominant pattern of an entire society and subordinates other motifs of secularity. It is rather documented in a multiplicity of arenas and developments that, taken as a whole exhibit the same thrust" (2012: 904). There is an asymmetry, in other words, between type 1, 2, and 3 secularity on the one hand and type 4 on the other. Does type 4 represent an option equal to the other three, after the emergence of the modern state with its considerable control of "public education, civil law, welfare and other spheres that is more secular than anything that existed in the past" (Keddie 1997: 24)? It would appear not.

All three approaches (Keddie, Demerath, and Wohlrab-Sahr/Burchardt) can conceivably be employed in complementary fashion for the purpose of identifying different sub-fields of study. One could ask, for example, using Demerath's distinctions, whether responses to Wohlrab-Sahr and Burchardt's "reference problem" type 1 is predominantly driven by external or internal forces, from bottom-up or top-down pressures. Similarly, one can combine such an inquiry with the question of whether certain "reference problems" are more likely to emerge, or easier to solve, in some religious traditions than others (Keddie's approach). In fact, Wohlrab-Sahr and Burchardt do suggest a civilizational perspective themselves when they write that, regarding type 4 secularity, "conflict between religion and science ... was weaker in East Asia [than Europe] because of the diversity of scientific traditions and the greater epistemological openness of religious doctrines" (2012: 904). In addition, one may combine these approaches with that suggested in this volume by Gorski and expanded upon in Künkler and Madeley (2015), which allows for a categorization of religious conflict based on the work of Niklas Luhmann and Pierre Bourdieu. To take a concrete example, Indonesia's *pancasila* could be studied as secularity for the sake of national integration (Wohlrab-Sahr and Burchardt's secularity type 3), driven from above by internal forces (Demerath's coercive secularization) which addresses segmentary conflict (Luhmann) between the religious and non-religious fields (Bourdieu).

CONCLUSIONS

In concluding his introduction to *A Secular Age*, Charles Taylor expressed the hope that it "should be possible some day to undertake a study of the whole phenomenon (of the emergence of secularity) on a global scale." The task would need to take account of crucial ongoing changes associated with "modernity" – changes of political structures, democratic forms, uses of media, etc. – in their different civilizational sites before there could be any question of global generalization (Taylor 2007: 21). This volume can only claim to have started on such a mammoth task by providing some detailed exploration of the complexities involved in eleven significant cases "beyond the West." On the basis of this modest beginning, nonetheless, a few general and a number of particular conclusions emerge.

In general terms, the case studies appear consistent with Taylor's argument that Western secularization was critically contingent upon particular characteristics of Latin Christendom rather than on the ineluctable consequences of some universal multi-stranded process of modernization. While globalizing trends have accelerated the spread of certain technological and economic drivers of some aspects of modernization across the world, the emergence of Secularities I, II, and III – let alone their presence in combination – has not ineluctably followed in their wake. Rather, in the late twentieth/early twenty-first century the trend appears to have been to reverse developments in each respect – including even partially in the West itself, where the renewed political salience of religious (or religion-related) issues is widely in evidence. In the non-Western cases, however, many of the evidences for Secularity I have seen a distinct pegging-back of ostensibly secular settlements achieved earlier in the wake of such critical junctures such as second- and third-world revolutions, decolonizations, and/or wars. The fact of many earlier, ostensibly secular settlements, on the other hand, piques the question of whether those clear evidences found of Secularity I outside the West should be seen as the mere products of international diffusion or imposition from the West or, rather, as responses by local actors to risks of domestic social conflict. The conclusion which emerges is that, while both aspects need to be taken into account in understanding individual cases, domestic political factors with their real legal and regulatory consequences have tended – and tend – in almost all cases to act as the decisive drivers and gatekeepers of change.

A second general conclusion concerns what has been called the differential burdening of religion by the state. Thought of in simple terms, it relates to the observation that religious traditions are not symmetrical in terms of the "contact surface" they offer to state regulation. This is particularly relevant in the field of law: in the Muslim world, India, and Israel, the religious traditions of Islam, Hinduism, and Judaism respectively tend to place greater demands on the nature and content of public law than is the case in those countries where Christianity, Buddhism, and Chinese religions have been historically dominant. Thus, with the expansion of the regulation of private and public spaces on the part of consolidating modern states, religions tend to be *differentially burdened*, depending initially on how many and what type of regulatory practices were historically performed under religious auspices and/or according to religious principles. As Taylor (2007) notes, by the time modern political and legal institutions had achieved full development in the societies of Latin Christendom, religion had already ceased to define the operating principles of the law, in most cases even losing their monopoly hold over family law. By contrast, in all the Muslim-majority countries included in this volume, as well as among the Jewish diaspora, the administration of personal law had remained under the authority of religious elites prior to the emergence of modern state systems. With the introduction of Western-style constitutions and the transplantation of Western legal systems, many of these traditional competencies were stripped rather abruptly from religious authorities. Accordingly, in Islam-state relations it has been in the field of religious law that the most profound interference by the twentieth-century state was experienced, while in China, for example, it was in the field of education. In India, on the other hand, in the context of what the British had come to refer to as Hinduism, such legal monopolies had never existed, any more than they had in Buddhist societies.

Among the more particular comparative conclusions which emerge from the volume's case studies, four stand out. Firstly, undertaking a distinction between Secularities I, II, and III still appears to be pivotal, indeed essential, if one wishes to make causal claims about the place of religion in any modern society, whether in the North Atlantic World or beyond. All three comparative schemata briefly reviewed here (Keddie, Demerath, Wohlrab-Sahr/Burchardt) can most fruitfully be deployed in comparative research if they are used in juxtaposition with Taylor's three-way distinction between the different Secularities. It appears difficult to assess the causal significance of religious traditions (Keddie), actors (Demerath), or guiding ideas (Wohlrab-Sahr/Burchardt) for processes of secularization unless it is specified whether the latter pertain to the place of religion in public life (Secularity I), levels of religious belief and practice (Secularity II), or the open option to profess unbelief (Secularity III).

Secondly, given that Taylor's Secularity III, a situation where believing in God is only one available option among many, relies at least in part on the legal permissibility of open unbelief (negative religious freedom) and its societal acceptance, it would appear all-but impossible of attainment without a significant level of Secularity I being already in place. In many of the cases studied here, citizenship itself is tied to religious identity, and the individual's relationship to state institutions mediated through official religious belonging. It is difficult for social acceptance of unbelief to emerge where one's religious identity determines the type of school one may attend, the person one may marry, the way one may or may not pray, the vocations one may choose, how much one may inherit compared to the opposite sex, etc. Secularity I, in other words, emerges, at least judging from the case studies, as a precondition for Secularity III.

Thirdly, as a number of other recent works also attest, it is positively unhelpful for comparativists to think of Secularity I in terms of a mere binary opposition or even a single continuum between secular and religious states, as Secularity I turns out to be multidimensional. In one dimension its presence or absence can be assessed in terms of state–religion relations which are conceived not only in terms of the constitutional status of religion but also taking account of the various forms of accommodation of or cooperation with religious bodies and officials, and their roles within or vis-à-vis various organs of the state. A second dimension affecting the degrees of (both positive and negative) religious freedom needs also to be included, since these often vary independently of different modes of state regulation and can have important consequences for the shaping of the content and the conduct of affairs in the public sphere.[18]

Fourthly, the case studies indicate the importance for understanding changes in Secularity I in terms of both foundational moments and subsequent path dependencies. Ruptures like the end of colonial rule, civil war, or revolution are typically associated with the writing of new state constitutions that create path dependencies in religion–state relations. These path dependencies are most prominent in terms of the fixity of constitutional texts. Characteristically, no country since 1990 has managed by constitutional change to disestablish religion as a source of law (Künkler, Lerner, and Shankar 2015) despite significant social pressures from below. Religion–state relations in societies studied in this volume whose constitutions were ambiguously worded tended to over time swing toward a greater role of religion in public life, established, variously, by ordinary legislation (which, as in the case of Indonesia, for example, established religion-based family law), by bureaucratic provisions (which, as in the case of Israel, required citizens to register in an officially recognized religions or otherwise lose access to state resources – education, health provision, pensions, etc.), or court judgments (which, as in the case of India, found that someone who eats beef cannot be a Hindu).

What explains how particular sets of arrangements between religion and the state are fixed in the first place is a question that has so far only been answered contextually. What seems clear, in any event, is that guiding ideas (à la Wohlrab-Sahr/Burchardt) are only part of the story, while interests and opportunities associated with variously placed actors (à la Demerath) also appear to be important. Keddie has observed that the "primacy of governments in secularization [in non-Western countries] has been somewhat obscured by the fact that not only Western but also indigenous scholars often prefer to discuss the achievements of intellectuals rather than those of governments. While more intellectuals preceded governments in secularism in the West, even in this field scholarship often overstates the role of intellectuals" (Keddie 1997: 27). Whether a particular idea manages to become sufficiently important to define a constitutional arrangement usually depends on compromises struck and interests that are activated or alternatively re-channeled. Given the prevalence of unintended consequences in policy-making and the multitude of ideational and interest-

---

[18] The concept of religious freedom and how different constructions of it bear upon the public sphere in different civilizational settings is a matter of intense ongoing debate. See Sullivan et al. 2015.

based sources that inform political decision-making, the attempt to trace the place of religion in a given society back to some set of guiding ideas is, it would seem, bound to be quite speculative.

No author in this volume has argued that it was an absence of ideas in favor of Secularity III that accounted for the absence of a widely accepted option to openly profess non-belief (Secularity III) in their case study. Rather, in most cases, highly contextual constellations of interests and institutions precluded the translation of such ideas into a political order that is blind to individual religious belief, practice, and doubt (Secularity I). In those cases where such an order was achieved, later social developments in 10 of 11 cases (the exception being Japan) led to its dismantling. A key step toward understanding when and how Secularity III emerges, then, lies in identifying the conditions under which local ideas in favor of it successfully translate into the institutional constellations of Secularity I that are necessary to sustain it, and which interests, institutions, and (counter-) ideas so often obstruct this act of translation and institutional lock-in.

References

Asad, Talal. 2003. *Formations of the Secular. Christianity, Islam, Modernity.* Bloomington: Stanford University Press.

Berger, Peter L. 2012. *"Further Thoughts on Religion and Modernity." Society,* 49(4): 313–316.

1999. *The Desecularization of the World: Resurgent Religion and World Politics, Grand Rapids*: Wm. B. Eerdmans Publishing.

Bhargava, Rajeev (ed.). 1998. *Secularism and its Critics.* New Delhi: Oxford University Press,

Bilgrami, Akeel (ed.). 2016. *Beyond the Secular West.* New York: Columbia University Press.

Billioud, Sébastien and Joël Thoraval. 2015. *The Sage and the People: The Confucian Revival in China.* Oxford: Oxford University Press,

Casanova, José. 1994. *Public Religions in the Modern World.* Chicago: University of Chicago Press.

2010. "The Secular, Secularizations, Secularisms." In Craig Calhoun, Mark Juergensmeyer, and Jonathan VanAntwerpen (eds.) *Rethinking Secularism.* Oxford: Oxford University Press, 54–74.

Collier, Ruth Berins and David Collier. 1991. *Shaping the Political Arena.* Princeton: Princeton University Press.

Demerath III., N. J. 2007. "Secularization and Sacralization. Deconstructed and Reconstructed." In James A. Beckford and N. J. Demerath III (eds.) *The SAGE Handbook of the Sociology of Religion.* London: Sage.

Eisgruber, Christopher L. and Lawrence G. Sager. 2007. *Religious Freedom and the Constitution.* Cambridge, MA: Harvard University Press.

Eisenstadt, Shmuel N. *The Origins and Diversity of Axial Age Civilizations*. New York: State University of New York Press, 1986.

Ferrari, Silvio and W. Cole Durham (eds.), *Law and Religion in Post-communist Europe*. Leuven: Peeters Publishers, 2003.

Ferrari, Silvio and Rinaldo Cristofori (eds.). 2010. *Law and Religion in the 21st Century: Relations between States and Religious Communities*. Farnham: Ashgate.

2013. *Law and Religion, An Overview*, vol. 1 Farnham: Ashgate.

Fox, Jonathan. 2007. "Do Democracies Have Separation of Religion and State?" *Canadian Journal of Political Science*, 40(1): 1–25.

2012. "Separation of Religion and State in Stable Christian Democracies: Fact or Myth?" *Journal of Law, Religion and State*, 1(1): 60–94.

Gill, Anthony. 2008. *The Political Origins of Religious Liberty* (*Cambridge Studies in Social Theory, Religion and Politics*), New York: Cambridge University of Press.

Goossaert, Vincent and David A. Palmer. 2011. *The Religious Question in Modern China*, Chicago: University of Chicago Press.

Gordon, Peter E. 2008. The Place of the Sacred in the Absence of God: Charles Taylor's A Secular Age. *Journal of the History of Ideas*, 69(4) (October): 647–673.

Joas, Hans. 2009. "Die säkulare Option. Ihr Aufstieg und ihre Folgen." *Deutsche Zeitschrift für Philosophie*, Akademie Verlag, 57(2): 293–300.

Kaviraj, Sudipta. 2016. "Disenchantment deferred." In Akeel Bilgrami (ed.) *Beyond the Secular West*. New York: Columbia University Press, 135–187.

Keddie, Nikki. 1997. "Secularism and the State: Towards Clarity and Global Comparison." *New Left Review*, Vol. 226 (November/ December), 21–40.

Künkler, Mirjam and Hanna Lerner. 2016. "A Private Matter? Religious Education and Democracy in Indonesia and Israel." *British Journal of Religious Education*, September.

Künkler, Mirjam and John Madeley. 2015. "A Secular Age beyond the West: Forms of Differentiation in and around the Religious Field." In *Soft Power*, 1(2): 41–62.

Künkler, Mirjam and Yüksel Sezgin. 2016. "The Unification of Law and the Post-colonial State. Limits of State Monism in India and Indonesia." *American Behavioral Scientist*, July, 60: 987–1012.

Künkler, Mirjam, Hanna Lerner, and Shylashri Shankar. 2015. "From Process to Outcomes: The Place of Religion in post-Cold War Constitutions," working paper, presented at the conference *Inclusiveness, Representation, and Religious Accommodation in Constitutions and Constitutionalism*, July 15–17, Zentrum für interdisziplinäre Forschung (ZiF), Bielefeld.

Levi, Margaret. 1997. "A Model, a Method, and a Map: Rational Choice in Comparative and Historical Analysis." In Mark Irving Lichbach and Alan S. Zuckerman (eds.) *Comparative Politics: Rationality, Culture, and Structure*. Cambridge: Cambridge University Press, 19–41.

Luhmann, Niklas. 2000. *Die Religion der Gesellschaft*. Frankfurt am Main: Suhrkamp Verlag.

Madan, T. N. 1987. "Secularism in its Place." In *The Journal of Asian Studies*, 46(4), (Nov.): 747–759.

Madeley, John T. S. 2009a. "Unequally Yoked: the Antinomies of Church-State Separation in Europe and the USA," *European Political Science*, August 2009.

2009b. "Religion and the State." In J. Haynes (ed.) *Routledge Handbook of Religion and Politics*, London: Routledge, 156–171.

Mahoney, James and Kathleen Thelen. 2010. *Explaining Institutional Change: Ambiguity, Agency, and Power*, Cambridge University Press.

Martin, David. 1978. *A General Theory of Secularization*. Oxford: Blackwell.

2005. *On Secularization: Towards a Revised General Theory*. Routledge.

2014. *Religion and Power. No Mythos without Logos*. Farnham: Ashgate.

Möllers, Christoph. 2014. "Grenzen der Ausdifferenzierung Zur Verfassungstheorie der Religion in der Demokratie." In *Zeitschrift für evangelisches Kirchenrecht*, 59: 115–140.

Norris, Pippa and Ronald Inglehart. 2004. *Sacred and Secular: Religion and Politics Worldwide*. Cambridge: Cambridge University Press.

Pierson, Paul. 2000. "Increasing Returns, Path Dependence, and the Study of Politics." *American Political Science Review*, 94(2): 251–267.

Riesebrodt, Martin. 2003. "Religion in a Global Perspective." In M. Juergensmeyer (ed.) *Global Religions. An Introduction*, Oxford: Oxford University Press, 95–109.

Sezgin, Yüksel and Mirjam Künkler. 2014. "Regulation of Religion and the Religious: The Politics of Judicialization and Bureaucratization in India and Indonesia." *Comparative Studies in Society and History*, 56(2): 448–478.

Smith, Donald E. 1970. *Religion and Political Development*. New York: Little Brown.

Starrett, Gregory. 1999. "Who put the 'Secular' in 'Secular State'?" *The Brown Journal of World Affairs*, 6(1): 147–162.

Stepan, Alfred C. 2000. "Religion, Democracy, and the 'Twin Tolerations,'" *Journal of Democracy*, 11(4): 37–57; reprinted and expanded as chapter 11, "The World's Religious Systems and Democracy: Crafting the Twin Tolerations." In Alfred C. Stepan, *Arguing Comparative Politics*, Oxford University Press, 2001, 213–254.

Sullivan, Winnifred, Elizabeth Shakman Hurd, Saba Mahmood, and Peter Danchin. 2015. *Politics of Religious Freedom* Chicago: Chicago University Press.

Taylor, Charles. 1998. "Modes of Secularism." In Rajeev Bhargava (ed.) *Secularism and its Critics*. New Delhi: Oxford University Press.

2007. *A Secular Age*. Cambridge, MA: Harvard Belknap Press.

2010. "The Meaning of Secularism," *The Hedgehog Review*, Fall, 23–34.

2011. "Why we need a Radical Redefinition of Secularism." In Eduardo Mendieta and Jonathan VanAntwerpen (eds.) *The Power of Religion in the Public Sphere*. New York: Columbia University Press, 34–59.

2012. "How to Define Secularism." In Alfred Stepan and Charles Taylor (eds.) *Boundaries of Toleration*. New York: Columbia University Press, 59–78.

Traunmüller, Richard. 2012. Zur Messung von Staat-Kirche-Beziehungen: Eine vergleichende Analyse neuerer Indizes. *Zeitschrift für Vergleichende Politikwissenschaft* 6: 207–231.

Turner, Bryan S. 1991. *Religion and Social Theory*, 2nd edn, London: Sage.

Warner, Michael, Jonathan Van Antwerpen and Craig Calhoun (eds.). 2010. *Varieties of Secularism in a Secular Age*. Cambridge, MA: Harvard University Press.

Wohlrab-Sahr, Monika and Marian Burchardt. 2012. "Multiple Secularities: Towards a Cultural Sociology of Secular Modernities." *Comparative Sociology*, 11(8): 875–909.

15

Afterword and Corrections

Charles Taylor

This collection of chapters is so interesting, and I have learned so much reading it, that I hardly know where to start, but perhaps a good place would be Philip Gorski's chapter. He's right that one of my main goals in the book was to capture the shift in our culture toward religious/spiritual pluralism; that, and also providing an alternative narrative of the rise of Western secularity to the now discredited thesis that modernization brings on secularization, which basically takes the form of a "subtraction story." On the contrary, the development of our secular age has involved so much innovation in our basic categories of self-understanding – of self, of the social bond, of history – that we should marvel more than we do at the human capacity for cultural change and innovation. Of course, my work has relied heavily on phenomenology and hermeneutics, rather than on mechanisms of historic change, but I don't think it is quite accurate to see it as not concerned with causality at all. An evolving culture opens new possibilities of action and closes others. A fully adequate account has to move between innovative practices – in this case including new disciplines, state action to inculcate these among subordinate classes, new forms of commerce and production, forms of prayer and liturgy (to mention just a few) – and the new institutional forms and modes of self-understanding that they bring in their wake, which in turn make possible a further range of new practices, and so on. The hermeneutical dimension is ineradicable.

I am sure that my account of the conditions of belief today – Secularity III – is still inadequate, but I hope it is moving in the right direction. However, even if it were much better, I would be nervous about the categories I have been using – Secularities I, II, and III, to which we might add my account of secularist regimes – being used as the basis for comparison with other, non-Western societies. In my mind, my decision to try an account of Western secularity meant that the categories I chose seemed useful for this case. I made no assumptions at all about their applicability to other contexts. The idea of fixing on this third category, alongside the familiar ones of the differentiation of spheres, and the decline (where it occurs) of traditional faith and practice, came from the sense that one of the most important features of our contemporary society was getting lost, and that one of the key terms of secularization theory – religion – was taking on new meanings: the phenomenon itself was evolving as the boundary between "religion" and "spirituality" became more porous.

This has led to an unprecedented pluralism of religious/spiritual options, which has become a crucial feature of our culture in the West. But speaking of this as another form of "secularity" is a move which perhaps requires defense. It was possibly a rhetorical move, meant to underline the thesis that the bundle of historical changes we are trying to trace go along with this cultural shift, which is tremendously significant, but at the same time somehow overlooked, once the word "secular" is pronounced.

But perhaps this new culture is so new, and so unprecedented, that comparisons with other epochs and places will be misleading.

Of course, I chose the term "conditions of belief" with the idea of marking a contrast with other times when the issue of adopting or rejecting a faith position (including the rejection of "faith" altogether) had a very different significance. Let's say I am a Huguenot in France in the 1670s. I am pondering whether to convert to the hegemonic Catholic faith. I may be piously weighing which is the orthodox form of Christian faith, or I may be wondering whether it is worthwhile holding out at the price of marginalization and rising persecution. But in either case, weighty questions arise. Similarly, if I am pondering joining an unofficial Christian church in today's China.

But in our society, entering or leaving a certain mode of worship, or direction of spiritual search, has none of the same consequences for my social position (though it may disturb relations with my family), or even for my ultimate commitment to weighty issues of ultimate truth – the step may be much more tentative. A huge proportion of Americans – some say 30 percent – find themselves as adults in another religious setting than the one they were brought up in: another church, or no church, or they break with their childhood experience by joining a church for the first time, or they adopt another religion. There is an immense amount of religious–spiritual exploration.

Again, it is not just that there is an immense variety of religious-metaphysical positions held by people in a contemporary Western society (and some non-Western ones as well). This is not totally new; think of India at almost any time in the last two millennia. It is that the idea of shifting from one to another is now so accepted, so banal, so unsurprising and leaves so many of our relationships unaffected. My being something else is so easily *conceivable*; that is what marks out the contemporary Secularity III. The "conditions of belief" are of a very different order today.

The contrast with the situation of my 1670s Huguenot, or contemporary Chinese worker, could not be more striking. We can speak of these three situations as each generating different "conditions of belief," in the sense that they determine what is at stake in adopting or leaving a faith position. But this seems to understate the differences, because the dynamics are so different in the different cases. We are speaking today of the horizontal spread of a culture of authenticity, which respects, even celebrates, self-determination, even or especially if this involves novelty, whereas in the other two situations, the "conditions" are largely determined by fiat from the apex of political power. (My Huguenot better make up his mind before 1685, when the Edict of Nantes will be repealed; my Shenzen worker would have had an easier time before Xi started his crackdown.)

And there are other dynamics as well. I can refer here to the sophisticated and convincing framework that Philip Gorski lays out in his contribution, involving segmentary relations, center–periphery hierarchies and fields.

What is more daunting is that these dynamics rarely operate alone; they often coexist with and rub against others. Madeley points out, in his very interesting study of Russia, that there are signs of developing spiritual and religious pluralism in that country, in spite of the growing official disapproval of new religions. And pluralism, in other conditions, is gaining ground in the Ukraine.

And then there are contexts in which the "conditions of belief," in the sense used here of the stakes involved in changing faith positions, are much less relevant, because many people already belong, in a sense, to several: as in Japan, where they mix and match *rites de passage* from, say, Shinto and Buddhist traditions, sometimes throwing in a Christian element – and in that case, as Hardacre shows, the mix is quite understandable, since the split between Shinto and Buddhism was engineered quite recently, under the Meiji Restoration.

So the validity of the contrasts between particular dimensions – Secularities I, II, and III, as well as secularism – is very much affected by more holistic features of the civilizational context; for instance, by great differences between what we are tempted to identify as "religion," in the Western, Islamic, Indian, and Confucian contexts, and by the issue of whether one can belong to more than one of these. The beliefs and practices that are classified as "religion" in China exclude Confucianism on one side, and what are described as "dangerous cults," or "super-stitions" (*mixin*), on the other.[1] The congruence with Western categories is very partial.

All this underlines the importance of Shankar's questions about the status of "Hinduism" as a "religion." The non-congruence with the European Deist notion, involving belief in a Supreme Being who demands of us a conformity with morality, is absolutely patent. We are tempted to grasp for another concept, such as "culture," "way of life." But these don't fit well either. And on top of it, this European idea certainly influenced certain movements in Indian, like the Brahmo Samaj. The concepts offering comparison tend to fall apart in our hands.

What to do about this? I confess to perplexity here. Certainly, the chapters in this collection greatly help to see the complexity involved. But the comparisons on the different dimensions of secularity seem to underplay rather than explain the differences. I realize that there is some-thing paradoxical about this stance; I seem to be saying: "forget my book," while I am in fact honored and flattered that you haven't. I confess to being in a muddle.

***

But to return to Secularity III, this is one of the crucial enabling conditions of the form of secularism which is widespread today, and which I try to defend. This involves the hazardous attempt to go "beyond toleration."[2] Toleration is the traditional term under which Westerners have sought to bring people of diverse allegiances and identities – religious, historical, ethnic, linguistic – together under the same political roof. And that means without violence, and without inflicting unnecessary suffering on each other; even, in certain contexts, without the domination of some by others. This last is, of course, one of our major pre-occupations today. But these three goals have recurrently preoccupied people and societies

---

[1] Goossaert and Palmer (2011).   [2] Stepan and Taylor (2014).

throughout history. Even when domination of some by others was considered normal and inevitable (and are we too sanguine today in thinking
it is not?), rulers often tried to avoid its more brutal forms.

The language in which these issues were thought out in earlier centuries
of Western civilization was that of toleration. The milestones in what we
in the West understand as our progress toward a better form of society,
our liberal democracy, were marked by edicts of toleration, by Locke's
Letter on Toleration, by appeals to toleration. This was part of the natural
language of human discourse in the West from the sixteenth century
onwards.

But recently, this term has come under attack. Many people want to
argue, in our multicultural societies today, that we have gone beyond
toleration, and that there is something demeaning to the beneficiaries in
talk of tolerating this or that group. Why?

The logic of toleration is well spelled out in an essay by Ira Katznelson
in the previously cited volume.[3] Proposing to tolerate a group, or a
practice, or a way of life is already to presuppose that there is some
problem with these: they are dangerous, or disturbing to social peace, or
unpleasant, or distasteful; normally we would take measures to counter-
act these negative features, perhaps expelling the group, or isolating it, or
forbidding the practice, or limiting it. But we forbear from applying these
measures, at least to their full extent. That is toleration.

The possible motives are many here. We may think that forbearance
leads to greater social harmony, that it will arouse less conflict, less mutual
hostility than going the whole way in suppressing the objectionable features. Some may argue that a given group is not as dangerous as had been
assumed – see Locke's argument for tolerating Dissenters (although not
atheists and Catholics). Alternatively, we may tolerate out of compassion,
or humanitarian feeling.

But in all these cases, we are admitting that there is something wrong
with the target group or practice, something which would normally call
down on them some negative measures, even though we find reasons to
suspend or mitigate these. We can see why this word can offend today,
since we see ourselves as part of a multicultural, liberal society, where (a)
differences – of culture, of religion, of sexual orientation, etc. – are not
seen as threats to good order or good taste, but on the contrary as
potential enrichment; and thus (b) where immunity to special negative
treatment is secured not by arguments mitigating deserved discrimination,

---

[3] Ibid., 37–58.

but by *rights*. Measures securing individual rights and forbidding discrimination are inscribed in all the Charters, which are an unavoidable
component of contemporary constitution-building. How can anyone say
that I am receiving as a fruit of toleration something that I have a right to?

It is clear that the logic of toleration, and that of multicultural rights
entrenchment, are quite different from each other. We would probably also
agree that the latter is a more satisfactory form of human relations than the
former. It is more in keeping with human dignity where we are insured
against special negative treatment by right, rather than by the wisdom of
governments or majorities who see good reasons to mitigate this treatment
in our case. In that sense, rights take us "beyond toleration."

But we can raise the serious question of whether we have really succeeded in transcending altogether the logic of toleration, and whether
banning the word may not blind us to the case for forbearance in certain
situations which still recur. There is a liberal zealotry which can be as
short-sighted and inhumane as the other modes – religious, national,
ethnic – that we see in history, and many of these older modes can hide
themselves in liberal garb. The present wave of Islamophobia spreading in
the Western world is a good case in point: xenophobic and exclusionary
sentiments which give themselves what seem impeccable liberal and feminist credentials can be unleashed without restraint.

The dangers can be illustrated if we look at the way the culture of
authenticity underpins and supports our present regime of rights. This
culture invites us to accept, even celebrate, difference. It forbids us from
suppressing or restricting certain forms of life which many find objectionable, on the grounds that these forms are central to certain people's
identity and to outlaw them would involve invidious discrimination
between identities. The case of gay rights is a very clear example.
Toleration had been growing in Western society for many decades prior
to the authenticity revolution of the 1960s and beyond. When André Gide
came out of the closet in the 1920s, the values involved were avoiding
cruelty and unnecessary suffering. But since Stonewall the crucial demand
has been ending discrimination. And this has proved much more powerful
and imperious than the earlier humanitarian appeals. Progress has been
steady on this front and, in historical terms, extraordinarily rapid. A
similar point can be made about certain demands of feminism.

But this makes clear where the backlash can come from. One form of
this reaction comes from the fact that today's spiritual pluralism dissolves
the previously dominant mode of religious life, which in Europe took the
form of the confessional state. The tight unity this involves has become

"unbundled" – that is, facets of life which were tied closely together ("bundled") in the past have come apart. There are two facets of this dissolution.

The first is this: many European societies in the last two centuries were confessional societies. The people who belonged to the national church also shared many other forms of belonging: family, parish, and nation. To belong to one was (normally) to belong to all. Belongings were "bundled." But in the last decades this interweaving of belongings has come apart. The people I share citizenship with, or my kin, or the neighbors in my village, are not necessarily those who share my faith option.

Secondly, within churches in our civilization, there was an extraordinary variety of spiritual and other activities: the liturgy, of course, but also the celebration of seasonal feasts; the solemnization of rites of passage, but also special devotions, novenas, pilgrimages, prayers to the Virgin; and then various charitable organizations, and forms of mutual help; and then more private devotions. Different people engaged differentially in these activities, but they were all seen as part of the life of the church.

In contemporary society, these activities often split off into separate, dedicated bodies. I may belong to a church, and then also médecins sans frontières, and then practice some form of meditation, and so on – all in a different context or organization.

The USA was never a highly bundled society in either way, but we can see there too the loosening of ties to the Catholic urban communities which were still very tight in the immediate post-War period.[4] And other societies, like Quebec in one way, and the Netherlands in another, which were highly "pillared," in the recent past have seen a veritable flight from these tighter identities. More and more people want to be more fully part of the bigger society. This, together with the ethic of authenticity, has helped drive unbundling.

What we see emerging from these and other developments is the decline and eventual dissolution of Christendom.[5] By "Christendom," I mean a society and a civilization which has been built with the intention of reflecting the Christian faith in all aspects of life: political, cultural, artistic, and, of course, moral.

Many people have lived the dissolution of this with anguish, either because they feel that the fullness of the Christian faith can only be lived in Christendom or because they believe that such a "bundled"

---

[4] Ehrenhalt (1994) and Wuthnow (1998).
[5] See Emmanuel Mounier's prescient book, *Feu la Chrétienneté*.

religio–political–moral predicament can alone underpin basic understandings of political and ethical order, without which our civilization will decline, or even break up.

This is one form of backlash. But there is another which illustrates the dangers of attempting to move "beyond toleration." This is one with which we are today, alas, only too familiar.

The great migrations of recent decades, combined with the need of many Western societies with declining populations for more workers, frequently create cultural fear and malaise among "old stock" populations. It is tempting to deny entry to populations with unfamiliar religions and customs, or at least to place restrictions on their practice of such customs or faiths. We have lived this in Quebec in recent attempts to deny Muslim women wearing the hijab employment in the public sector (and, of course, this has been done in spades in France).

Under the old regimes of toleration, it might have been possible to say to such migrants: "you make us acutely uncomfortable when you work in government bodies that we all have to deal with, so we shall restrict the practice of your religion there; and please feel grateful that we are tolerating it everywhere else." But in an era of rights, that is just not on. So uncomfortable natives have to up the ante and moralize: "We would never discriminate against legitimate practices, but you are a moral threat, undermining our core moral–political principles (male–female equality is often cited in Quebec), or even our safety (in the light of IS terror)." What would earlier (where toleration was the issue) have been seen as a gentle restriction to make us natives happier is now seen as an imperious demand to fight back against evil and its agents. The result even of announcing restrictive legislation in the new context has been, in Quebec, France, and also the USA (responding to Trump) vicious attacks, verbal and sometimes violent, on visible minorities. The branding of certain people as enemies or subverters of our order has been to liberate xenophobic and illiberal individuals from the inhibitions they previously felt, and unleashing them to poison the atmosphere of society. "Political correctness" can seem very objectionable, until one sees a real wave of political incorrectness. These xenophobes are often a small minority, but their effect can be devastating nevertheless.

I don't back off an inch from my defense of this kind of rights-based secularism of diversity. But I recognize that it is not possible, and can even be dangerous to propose it in societies where it is not backed by a culture of mutual acceptance and respect. For us, an essential role is played by the culture of authenticity, but there are other ethics elsewhere which can play a similar role, such as pancasila in Indonesia, and in India an ethic going back to Ashoka, and more recently renewed by Gandhi. Elsewhere, one often has to fall back on arguments which stress the wisdom of self-limitation by majorities, in the name of humanity, social order, the lowering of conflict, or the introduction of democracy, as for instance, in the Arab world (see Tunisia).

***

These pessimistic considerations, as well as recent unfortunate developments, force our attention onto a phenomenon in Western society which I didn't really see coming: mobilization once more around a religious or denominational marker. The "Age of Mobilization," placed before an "Age of Authenticity," could encourage this blindness. It was not that I thought that political mobilization was a thing of the past; it is the daily bread of the modern world: mobilization for and against certain national or political identities (how could I forget this, I live in Quebec!), or for and against certain party programs. I couldn't forget either the existence of political Islamism. But I did perhaps too easily take for granted that the era of religious mobilizations was over, or at least ending, in the West.

But almost immediately, identities based on historical religion began to gain traction. This was already evident in the wars around the dissolution of Yugoslavia. Atheist communists such as Milošević, successfully instrumentalizing the historic Orthodox identity and invoking the pathos of Kossovo Polye, demonstrated the power of this kind of appeal.

But this historical identity soon began to surface in the already (we thought) stably democratized West, for example in opposition among secular politicians to the accession of Turkey to the EU. ("It would be as though we had lost the siege of Vienna," said one.) And to leap toward the present, Victor Orban erects barbed wire against refugees in the name of "Christian civilization."

Christophe Jaffrelot's very interesting study of Pakistan opens up this whole question. It is clear that political mobilization around religious markers is a complex phenomenon with many variants. The principal variation is between faith- and devotion-inspired mobilization, on the one hand, and largely cultural–historical identity-formation, on the other. But many movements encompass very different motivations within a single movement, and they vary in their proportions and combination.

In some cases, it is largely a question of leaders and followers. The Indian Bharatiya Janata Party (BJP) is a flagrant case in point. The intellectual who inspired it, Savarkar, and, one suspects, many of the existing leadership, were/are largely areligious – that is, uninspired by any form of Hindu devotion. But they certainly use the faith of the masses to mobilize their movement, including unleashing violence against minorities. This seems a clear case of instrumentalizing religion. But in other cases, motives may be mixed throughout the movement, and at all levels.

And in other cases again, the balance of motivation may change over time, as in the case of Pakistan that Jaffrelot examines. In still other cases, the nature of the political identity may be a continuing subject of political conflict, as in the "Culture Wars" in the USA.

What is the dynamic behind this intensification of religious–political mobilization? In some ways, it resembles many forms of nationalist mobilization against an external enemy, colonial power, imperial oppressor, or "neo-colonial" hegemonic civilization (like "the West" or the USA). And indeed, the post-War history of the Arab world shows the similarities between the two, and the contingency involved in the rise or fall of one or the other.

The resentment in the region against the former imperial powers, Britain and France, along with the sense that they were continuing their control through other means, and hampering the development of Arab societies, was articulated first through an "Arab socialism" under Nasser and the Ba'ath Party. Both Nasser and the elder Assad persecuted the Muslim Brotherhood. Fifty years later, the same resentments fuel movements issuing from the Brotherhood. What is behind the shift? Is it the failure of "Arab socialism" to realize the aspirations it helped raise? Is it an independent spread of a "salafist" outlook which can sometimes take apolitical forms?

A similar question arises in relation to Pakistan, which, as Jaffrelot shows, has undergone a similar slide from the cultural Muslim identity of the founder, Jinnah, to a more and more narrow Muslim orthodoxy which has marginalized not only Ahmadis, but also Shi'ites, and some Sufi practices. To what extent is this due to the failures of the original leadership, and to what extent does it reflect a slide toward a narrower, more sharia-centered Islam, partly due to Wahhabi influence?

The increasing vigor of political Islam has consequences not only geopolitically, but also religiously. It brings about a radical narrowing of the permitted forms of Islamic piety, delegitimizing Sufi forms of spirituality and crushing new contemporary forms of ijtihad, all focussing on a narrow notion of sharia. Of course, this narrowing is also being combatted throughout the Muslim umma, but it paradoxically finds an ally in Western Islamophobia, which accredits the notion that this militant persecutory faith is the "real" Islam.

One cannot shut out the possibility that this kind of religio–political mobilization may even bulk larger on the geopolitical scene, nor deny the threat that it poses to regimes everywhere of diversity-oriented secularism and mutual recognition. There is a lot here that needs to be factored into a fuller discussion of our secular age.

I am very grateful for the chance I've had to read these very interesting and insightful chapters. I've learned a great deal, but am probably more perplexed than before. This I consider a gain; we may have to articulate more puzzlement in this field before we get to greater clarity. Yet, I admit my incompetence to judge in many of the domains discussed in this book.

I was inspired to develop these reactions, which I hope may contribute to future discussions.

References

Alfred, Stepan and Charles Taylor. 2014. *Boundaries of Toleration*. New York: Columbia University Press.

Ehrenhalt, Alan. 1994. *The Lost City*. New York: Basic Books.

Goossaert Vincent and David A. Palmer. 2011. *The Religious Question in Modern China*. Chicago: University of Chicago Press.

Mounier, Emmanuel. *Feu la Chrétienneté*

Wuthnow, Robert. 1998. *Loose Connections*. Cambridge, MA: Harvard University Press.

Appendix

A Quantitative Take on the Incidence of Taylor's Three Secularities in the Eleven Country Studies

Mirjam Künkler and John Madeley

The production over the last decade of cross-national indices based on aggregate and survey evidence of a global scale makes it now possible to move beyond reliance on single-case "guesstimates" or small-n comparisons to provide a broader comparative view. Some of the most frequently cited comparative indices include the Religion and State (RAS) dataset, produced by Jonathan Fox, the World Values Survey (WVS), and the International Religion Indexes created by Brian Grim and Roger Finke's team.[1] Tables 16.1 and 16.2, represent an attempt to operationalize Taylor's three secularities in quantitative terms. The exercise comes with unavoidable health warnings: there is no intention of turning a blind eye to the intrinsic shortcomings which critics of such datasets have pointed to, or to the rather narrow limits of quantitative operationalization of phenomena as conceptually complex as Taylor's Secularities I, II, and III (Woodberry 1998, Demerath 2007, Traunmüller 2012).[2] This is one of the reasons why

We thank Arash Pourebrahimi for research assistance and Marian Burchardt, Detlef Pollack, and Kadir Yildirim for valuable comments.

[1] For the RAS dataset and Grim and Finke's data, see The Association of Religion Data Archives at www.thearda.com. For the World Values Survey, see www.worldvaluessurvey.org.

[2] The indicators developed by Grim and Finke (2006), however well-conceptualized they may be, are particularly problematic in the data source they rely on: the annual country reports by the US State Department on International Religious Freedom, which describes the status of religious freedom in every country. The reports cover government policies violating religious belief and practices of groups, religious denominations and individuals, in pursuit of US policies to promote religious freedom around the world. A major point of criticism has been the relatively uncritical reporting on countries with which the United States has good relations, and the obverse on those with which it does not. Under the

TABLE A.1 *Secularity I by country (most recent data available)*

	Demographic Makeup	Secularity I				
		Fox GIR	GFRI	GRRI	RPI	MRPI
China	T+: 30.4 B: 15.4 Non: 40 Ch: 7.9	48	4.5	8.5	9	38–76
Egypt	M: 89.3 Ch: 10.1	62	8.3	8.3	7	64–129
India	H: 72.9 M: 14.2 Ch: 4.7	22	7.0	5.8	9	42–85
Indonesia	M: 79.1 Ch: 12.1 H: 1.6	45	7.6	6.5	10	0.44–2.1
Iran	M: 98.8	67	8.8	9.0	4	1.42–7
Israel	J: 72.5 M: 19.3 Ch: 2.4	37	7.9	4.1		2.95–14
Japan	Sh: 2.1 B: 56.3 Non: 10 Neo: 26	9	1.5	1.0	1	0.01–0.08
Morocco	M: 99.6	51	7.0	6.0	2	0.36–0.65
Pakistan	M: 96.2 Ch: 2.2	48	8.8	8.8	6	6.33–31.6

(continued)

leadership of Brian Grim, the Pew Research Center in 2015 published a new index, the Global Restrictions on Religions Index, which considerably expands the data source and thus provides a better alternative to the International Religion Indexes. It however combines the dimensions of regulation and favoritism in one variable (GHI) and is thus less helpful for our purposes of illustrating the multi-dimensionality of Secularity I.

TABLE A.I *(continued)*

	Demographic Makeup	Secularity I				
		Fox GIR	GFRI	GRRI	RPI	MRPI
Russia	Ch: 81.2 M: 10.4 Non: 8.1	30	5.3	5.2	3	0.15–0.7
Turkey	M: 98.3 (Al: 20+)	47	6.8	5.1	3	0.30–1.45

Notes:

1. Demographic Makeup is based on the World Religion Ratios. B = Buddhist; Ch = Christian; CO: (Russian) Orthodox; H = Hindu; J: = Jewish; M = Muslim; Non = Non-religious/Agnostic; Sh = Shinto; T+ = Taoism and Folk Religions; Neo: Neoreligionists (Japan). Even though the World Religion Ratios are taken from official government statistics, the figures for India, Japan, and Turkey are open to challenge. Note, for instance, the 98.3% Sunni Muslim for the Turkish population when the % of non-Sunni Alevis are estimated to run between 15% and 30% of the population. The fact that the percentages given for Japan sum to well over 100% indicates a further difficulty – the existence particularly in predominantly poly- and non-theistic societies of multiple non-exclusive attachments to different belief systems.

2. The Official Government Involvement in Religion (GIR) is a composite variable from Fox's RAS dataset, round 1. For more information on the methodology of the GIR, see Jonathan Fox, RAS dataset, www.religionandstate.org.

3. The **GFRI**, the **GRRI**, and the **RPI** from Grim and Finke's International Religion Indexes are all based on the coding of information in the US Department of State's annual *International Religious Freedom Reports*. Scores are normalized over a four-year period to control for media spikes.

- **GFRI:** The government favoritism of religion index is a comparative measure of the actions of the state that provide one religion or a small group of religions special privileges, support, or favorable sanctions. A higher GFI score indicates greater religious favoritism. Range: 0–10. The figures given represent the average of scores for 2003, 2005, and 2008.
- **GRRI:** The government regulation of religion index is a comparative measure of the actions of the state that deny religious freedoms, including any actions that impinge on the practice, profession, or selection of religion. A higher GRRI score indicates greater religious regulation. Range: 0–10. The figures given represent the average of scores for 2003, 2005, and 2008.
- **RPI:** Religious Persecution Index; Average number of people physically abused or displaced due to their religion according to US Department of State's 2005 and 2008 International Religious Freedom Reports (as coded by ARDA researchers). 0 = none; 1 = 1–10; 2 = 11–20; 3 = 21–100; 4 = 101–500; 5 = 501–1,000; 6 = 1,001–5,000; 7 = 5,001–10,000; 8 = 10,001–50,000; 9 = 50,001–100,000; 10 = greater than 100,000. We have recalculated the RPI and present here the average number of people *in each million* physically abused or displaced due to their religion, indicated as **MRPI** (Modified RPI).

the contributors to this volume have focused instead on explanatory narratives. But in order to provide an overall perspective, it is nevertheless useful to highlight how the different cases studied fare in terms of key indicators of religiosity, secularity, and religion–state relations in these macro-comparisons, not least in order to evaluate the possibilities and limits of currently available quantitative indicators for global comparison on the topic.

Out of the three indices used here, the International Religion Indexes by Grim and Finke have the largest comparative scope in geographic terms, with 196 countries included at four moments in time (2001, 2003, 2005, and 2008) (Grim and Finke 2006). Fox's RAS Dataset (175 countries) has the best diachronic profile, with annual entries for an 18-year period (1990–2002 in Round 1 and 2003–2008 in Round 2). The WVS in turn has been undertaken since 1981 in seven waves, with different countries participating in different waves. It features responses to questionnaires that are broadly identical across countries, where each country's survey team typically has the right to add some questions of particular relevance to the local context.

The first group of indices in Table A.1 – Secularity I by country – indicates the degree to which states regulate the religious field; it might be thought of as a metric for the "weight" of state regulation of religion. Column 1 provides a simple reminder of the confessional breakdown of populations.

A first general point highlighted by the indicators is that it is clearly unhelpful to think of the religious or secular character of the state in terms of a simple binary. Most states, whether in the West or not, do not adhere to a strict separation of religion and state – indeed, it is impossible for any state to remain free from entanglement in questions of what constitutes a religion and how it should be treated (Fox 2008). In the context of modernity, state regulation of religion is a universal phenomenon, although it takes radically different forms and occurs at widely varying levels of intensity (Madeley 2009a and 2009b). To capture these different levels of intensity of state regulation and interference (which we suggested in Chapter 14 are significantly shaped by the scope of social life regulated by religious authority before the advent of the modern state), we proposed the concept of differential burdening.

Each of the scores in Table A.1 can be interpreted as indications of the differential burdening by public authorities of the practice of religion and the status of religious organizations and institutions. The available indicators permit the measurement of differential burdening along two dimensions: in US jurisprudence parlance, "non-establishment" (separation of religion and state) and "free exercise" (religious freedom). These are operationalized in the table by, on the one hand, indices for state regulation of religion and favoritism (as state "interference" in the religious field which offends against strict separationism; the opposite of non-establishment) and, on the other, limits on individual religious freedom and religious persecution (the subset of regulatory oversight and control affecting issues of religious freedom). The measures corresponding to these two dimensions are Government Involvement in Religion (GIR) and Government Favoritism of Religion Index (GFRI) for state regulation of religion, and Government Regulation of Religion Index (GRRI) and Religious Persecution Index (RPI) for levels of religious freedom.[3]

What emerges clearly from these indices is the empirical non-secularity of the state in most cases. This is in line with Taylor's implication that beyond the North Atlantic world, Secularity I is generally conspicuous by its absence, despite the constitutional commitment of all states included here, except for Iran, to some principle of religious freedom. In other words, constitutional commitments to religious freedom emerge in some cases more as empty signifiers than meaningful justiciable rights. As far as state regulation of religion is concerned, the GIR index from Fox's RAS Dataset (Round 1 for 2002) judges Iran and Egypt to feature the greatest degree of government involvement in religion with a score of 67 and 62 respectively (where 0 is the theoretical minimum and 77 (characterizing Saudi Arabia) the actually existing maximum), while Japan (at 9) occupies the other end of the spectrum. The next two countries on the lower end are India and Russia with 22 and 30 respectively, featuring already quite significant levels of government involvement in religion (by comparison, most Western European countries, not included in the table, have scores in the same range, between 20 and 30).[4] Grim and Finke's GFRI, by contrast,

---

[3] Even though GRRI stands for "Government Regulation of Religion Index," as the notes to Table A.1 make clear, it actually captures state acts of omission and commission that limit citizen's religious freedom.

[4] In his brief initial discussion of Secularity I in the first two pages of *A Secular Age*, Taylor claims that, "with a couple of exceptions," the states of the North Atlantic world are nowadays virtually free of connections to religious organizations (Taylor 2007: 1). This claim of nearly full de facto separation between religion and state in the West has been placed in doubt by the results of several empirical studies, both comparative, using Fox's dataset, and individual country studies. Even US constitutional jurisprudence, which historically has been the most separationist, has turned in recent decades toward a more accommodationist line, leading some to call for the underlying normative principle to be "equal liberty" (Eisgruber and Sager 2007) rather than separation (compare also Johan David Van der Vyver and John F. Witte 1996; Ferrari and Cristofori 2013; Madeley 2009a and b). In addition, Christoph Möllers (2014), among others, has argued that since complete

places Pakistan on a par with Iran, with Japan again toward the secular end of the spectrum, while China and Russia are judged to be more secular than India, in terms of favoring religion less.

As far as religious freedom is concerned, Grim and Finke's GRRI captures actions of the state that undermine religious freedom, while their RPI assesses the intensity of religious persecution. Even though persecution may be perpetrated not only by state but also by societal actors, the measurement can be taken to shed light on state action, as it can be seen to reflect state acts of omission as well as those of commission. To the extent that people fall victim to persecution by social actors, the state can be adjudged insufficiently protective of the victims' right to religious freedom. The RPI index indicates that Indonesia fares worst in this respect. However, given that the RPI is based on absolute numbers of victims rather than numbers relative to the population, this result has very limited meaning. We have therefore recalculated the RPI relative to a country's population, shown as MRPI (Modified RPI) in Table A.1, which indicates that the *reported* number of those physically abused or otherwise persecuted for their religion between 2005 and 2008 was highest (relative to the overall population) in Egypt, followed by India and China. It is also in Egypt and China, as well as Iran and Pakistan, that the government is judged to place the greatest limits on religious freedom (GRRI).

It is the more mixed or ambivalent cases which are perhaps of greatest interest in comparative terms. China's scores indicate a combination of low levels of religious freedom (ranking highest with Iran and Pakistan on the GRRI index) and high levels of societal persecution of minorities, as per the Modified RPI, with a relatively low level of favoritism, reflecting the fact that the few religious organizations that are officially recognized are themselves constrained by strict levels of regulation and oversight.[5] Israel and Russia, meanwhile, score modestly, but in the lower half of the distribution on the regulation measures. Israel presents an unusual combination, evincing a relatively low level of state regulation of religion (GRRI), but combining it with high state favoritism of (one) religion (GFRI). Unsurprisingly, the Islamic Republic of Iran scores

separation is impossible, the yardstick for a secular state should instead be the extent to which positive and negative religious freedom is guaranteed and protected by the state.

[5] It should be noted, however, that even though only official religious organizations are permitted, other religious practices are tolerated and sometimes even encouraged by local authorities in the names of "cultural heritage," "folklore," or "traditional culture." If these were to be taken into account, the assessment of levels of favoritism would likely result in higher scores than the modest GFRI level suggests.

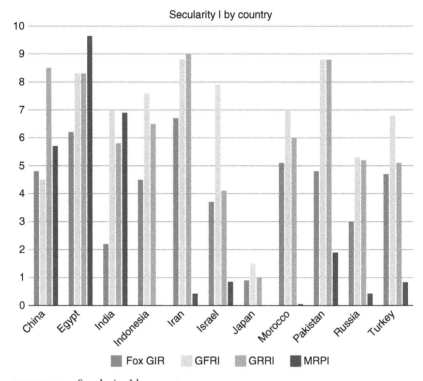

FIGURE A.I Secularity I by country
Note: 1. For the purposes of comparative illustration we have recomputed Fox GIR and MRPI on a 0–10 scale.

highest on three of the four individual indices, indicating high levels of regulation and of favoritism for the dominant religious tradition, and denial of religious freedom to, and religious persecution of, unrecognized religious communities, with Egypt and Pakistan relatively close behind on all indicators, except for religious persecution which in Pakistan is considerably lower, reflecting either real or reported differences. By contrast, Japan scores lowest on all indicators, reflecting assessments of a nearly complete *de jure* separation of religion and state, high levels of religious freedom, a near absence of reported cases of religious persecution, and a very low level of government favoritism of (a particular) religion.

The combination of the different measures highlights the multi-dimensionality of Secularity I: each country appears to present a distinctive profile that cannot be captured by a simple continuum of, say, separation versus official establishment (Figure A.1). Accordingly, the view is taken here that state regulation of religion and the states' (in)ability to protect religious freedom need to be viewed in tandem. For example, the GRRI indicates the raw weight of the burdening of religious practice by state authorities without providing any indication of whether this burdening is associated with a positive favoring of religion, where regulation is presumably aimed at its support and promotion, or with negative oversight aimed at control and even limitation. GFRI, on the other hand, does provide an indicator of the positive (favoring) or negative (disfavoring) bent of regulation, without giving insight into how drastically these affect individual religious freedom. Only a combination of the two dimensions, with each dimension in turn being fed by more than one index, can provide a fuller picture of both the entanglement of state and religion and the effects of this for the level of religious freedom citizens enjoy. To illustrate, China is found to be second lowest after Japan in terms of government favoritism of religion. But China also ranks among the top countries in the persecution of religious minorities, and in this regard ranks among the least secular. A simple combined score (such as Fox's compound GIR alone) would not reveal these significant contrasts.

Moving to measures relevant to Taylor's Secularity II (the decline of religious belief and practice over time), the WVS (1981–2014) provides the only comparative dataset offering data for all the societies included in this volume. The application of measures of Secularity II is undermined by the problems associated with the particularities of non-Western religious traditions where the balance between appropriate behaviors, practices, and patterns of thought vary greatly both internally and as between traditions (compare Künkler and Madeley 2015). The indices reported in Table A.2 represent those that have some cross-cultural validity in a way that conventional Western measures of, for example, "belief in God" or "church attendance" do not. The third column in Table A.2 follows the choice made by Norris and Inglehart (2004) by concentrating on the practice of prayer as one feature which can be found across most religious traditions, although here too problems of the consistency and reliability of survey measures administered in widely contrasting cultural environments are considerable.[6] The

---

[6] A more complex and differentiating combination of measures is provided by the Religion Monitor, constructed under the aegis of the Bertelsmann Foundation, but it only includes 21 countries and has only been conducted twice so far, in 2007 and 2013. The WVS, by contrast, includes dozens of countries across all continents and allows for diachronic comparison: it has been conducted in many countries 3–5 times over a 40-year time span. For an assessment of the WVS, see also Norris and Inglehart 2004: 55–60.

TABLE A.2 *Secularities II and III by country (most recent data available)*

		Secularity II					Secularity III	
	Demographic Makeup	Do you pray?	Rel impt. in life?	Religious person?	Non- rel.l Atheist	MSRI	Pluralism-Index I (WVS)	Pluralism-Index II (RDI)
China	T+: 30.4 B: 15.4 Non: 40 Ch: 7.9	19.6 1990	16.2 2007	21.3 2007	58.9l 17.5 2007	5.2	0.259	0.639
Egypt	M: 89.3 Ch: 10.1	89.7 2008	99.9 2013	92.9 2008	6.8 2008	6	0.120	0.096
India	H: 72.9 M: 14.2 Ch: 4.7	77.9 2006	82.6 2014	78.3 2011	18.2l 2.3 2006	10	0.315	0.350
Indonesia	M: 79.1 Ch: 12.1 H: 1.6	91.7 2006	98.0 2006	75.3 2006	13.5l 0.2 2006	10	0.142	0.228
Iran	M: 98.8	94.6 2007	94.3 2007	80.8 2007	15.7l 0.1 2007	10	0.166	0.009

(continued)

Israel	J: 72.5 M: 19.3 Ch: 2.4	–	62.1 2001	–	–	10	0.260	0.394
Japan	Sh: 2 B: 56.3 Non: 10 Neo: 26	40.5 2005	21.9 2010	25.4 2010	54.3| 12.0 2005	6	0.524	0.543
Morocco	M: 99.6	85.8 2007	98.9 2011	89 2011	8.0 2007	7.3	0.016	0.000
Pakistan	M: 96.2 Ch: 2.2	–	98.2 2012	99.8 2012	8.8 2001	10	0.122	0.070
Russia	Ch: 81.2 M: 10.4 Non: 8.1	36.7 1990	44.2 2011	61.1 2011	3.9 2006	10	0.527	0.429
Turkey	M: 98.3 (Al: 20+)	94.7 2007	93.1 2011	85 2011	0.6	10	0.018	0.035

Notes:

1. Demographic Makeup is based on the World Religion Ratios. B = Buddhist; Ch = Christian; CO: (Russian) Orthodox; H = Hindu; J: = Jewish; M = Muslim; Non = Non-religious/Agnostic; Sh = Shinto; T+ = Taoism and Folk Religions; Neo: Neoreligionists (in Japan).

2. **Secularity II**: Scores shown are taken from the Worlds Values Survey 2005 unless otherwise noted. Data shown is from the most recent year available per country.

The questions were formulated thus:

- V193: "Do you take some moments of prayer, meditation or contemplation or something like that?"
- V9: Indicate how important religion is in your life? Would you say it is: 1. Very important; 2. Rather important; 3. Not very important; 4. Not at all important? The scores given here pool responses 1 and 2.
- V187. Independently of whether you attend religious services or not, would you say you are: 1. A religious person; 2. Not a religious person; 3. An atheist?

3. Secularity III:

MSRI: Modified Social Regulation of Religion Index. The Modified Social Regulation of Religion Index (MSRI) is calculated by (a) transforming a country's value on each of the five variables listed below so that they have ranges from zero to one, (b) taking the sum of the five transformed values, and (c) multiplying the sum by two. Countries may have MSRI values between 0 and 10. The basis of the information is the US Department of State's International Religious Freedom Reports. Last available data referred to 2008.

Variables comprised in the Modified Social Regulation of Religion Index (MSRI) are

- OTHREL08: Societal attitudes toward other or nontraditional religions are reported to be . . .
- PROSE208: According to the Report, do traditional attitudes and/or edicts of the clerical establishment strongly discourage proselytizing, that is, trying to win converts.
- ESTAB08: According to the Report, do established or existing religions try to shut out new religions in any way?
- INTOLE08: According to the Report, are citizens intolerant of "nontraditional" faiths, that is, groups they perceive as new religions?
- NONTRA08: According to the Report, how does the Report characterize citizens' receptivity to proselytizing by nontraditional faiths or faiths other than their own?

See Grim and Finke 2006, for a detailed description of their original Social Regulation of Religion Index (SRI).

Pluralism-Index I is based on WVS data (2010, 2011, or 2012 for all countries except Egypt (2008), Indonesia (2006), Iran (2005), and Israel (2001)). **Pluralism-Index II** is based on the Religious Diversity Index (RDI) of 2010 issued by Pew Research and recalculated to generate a Herfindahl-Index. The Pluralism-Index is the reverse Herfindahl-Index. (Source www.pewforum.org/2014/04/04/methodology-2/, Formula for the re-calculation: RDI*875/10000.)

greatest cross-case variance is seen in responses to the question of whether or not religion was seen as important in a person's life, with over 90 percent of respondents in the Muslim-majority countries replying it was either important or very important (Figure A.2). By contrast, these responses were reported by less than 20 percent of respondents in China and 22 percent in Japan. India with 83 percent and Russia with 44 percent lay at different intermediate points in the distribution. The overall contrast between the East Asian cases and the Muslim-majority cases is reinforced by responses to the question of whether persons counted themselves as either non-religious or atheist, with over 76.4 percent in China and 66.3 percent in Japan reporting one of these.

Notions of religion are notoriously difficult to capture in comparative quantifiable manner. As noted in the respective chapters, in China and Japan it is especially difficult to distinguish the religious from the secular/non-religious (and what the category "Taoism and Folk religions" captures). As Yang 2016 illustrates, a binary category of "belief/unbelief" makes little sense in China and Chinese-influenced areas, and for many Chinese (as well as Japanese), religious identity is not exclusive. Furthermore, the division of the "Three Teachings" is artificial and only operational among religious personnel or elites.[7] As for Japan, the very modern category of religion – *shukyo* – is regarded by the majority of Japanese with some suspicion, so that high indications of non-religiosity may "mask a religious spirit," as Madsen (2011) has suggested.

The figure for unbelief in India (with 18 percent declaring themselves to be non-religious) unsettles the image of India as a country with "high religiosity" and highlights the problem for comparative indices of capturing non-monotheistic options, and more generally: non-religious options, thus further problematizing the religious-secular distinction. As has been argued in depth in Chapter 14, the very question of whether some "spiritual traditions" are at all recognized as religions clearly affects whether people conceptualize their practices as "religious." The figures given for India here appear to indicate a significant degree of polarization among self-images – either religion is rather important in one's life or one does not consider oneself to be a believer at all. Of course, given the fact that some "Hindus"

---

[7] As noted in Chapter 14, this touches on the much-debated question of whether Confucianism should be thought of as a religion. Zhe Yi in chapter 3 suggests that in a sociological sense Confucianism should be treated as a religion, with its transcendental discourse, rituals, symbols, sacred matters, and cosmological representations. On this debate, see also Billioud and Thoraval (2015), and Goossaert and Palmer (2011).

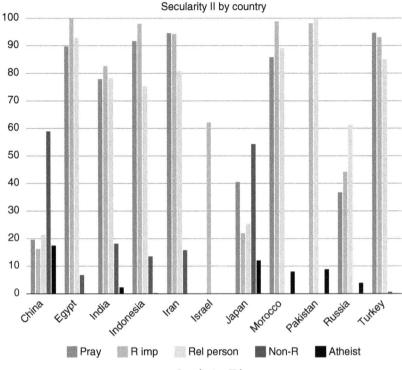

FIGURE A.2 Secularity II by country

consider "Hinduism" a way of life or an ancient order rather than a religion (see Shankar in this volume), the 18 percent could also include those with such more secular convictions, raising doubt as to whether the figure for India's non-believers should be thought to represent non-believers in comparable terms to say, non-believers in Sweden or the former GDR.

In summary, it is not easy to reject the often-made claim that the data emerging from the quantitative indices used here to measure the incidence of Secularity II, capturing individual levels of religious belief and practice, is distorted by their reliance on monotheistic (and usually Christian) understandings of the nature of religion, often combined with a presumption of the virtues of a relatively "free" religious market, when in fact many citizens do not have a free choice to adhere to a particular belief system or rite and governmental policies impact the way citizens conceive of religion/non-religion.

None of the comparative cross-national indices can easily provide a direct measure of Taylor's Secularity III, which relates to changes in "the conditions of belief," consisting as it does in the outcome "of a move from a society where belief in God is unchallenged and indeed, unproblematic, to one in which it is understood to be one option among others, and frequently not the easiest to embrace" (Taylor 2007: 3). Secularity III is a cultural condition, brought about through theological, social and intellectual reform, in which believing may even require some kind of explanation. There are two measures which come closest to capturing this quantitatively, although both fall short of reflecting the complexity of this cultural condition. The first is provided by Grim and Finke's *Modified Social Regulation of Religion Index* (MSRI), which captures notions of societal toleration by combining measures for attitudes "and/or edicts of the religious establishment" relating to nontraditional or minority religions. Insofar as this is based on judgments as to attitudes and the rulings of religious authorities, it can be taken to reflect the degree to which heterodox religious ideas and practices are tolerated.[8] High levels on this index (as in India, Indonesia, Israel, Iran, and Pakistan, which are scored at the maximum) reflect not just extreme intolerance of nontraditional or minority religions but also of secularist positions – something which is confirmed by the very low incidence of atheist responses. This indeed suggests the general absence of Taylor's Secularity III: the public rejection of dominant religious belief systems is scarcely an option, and agnosticism, as well as belief in nontraditional, "new," or minority religions is generally not an easily available option. The overall high level of scores on the MSRI index, with only China, Egypt, Japan, and Morocco scoring less than 8 on a 10-point scale, and Russia, India, Indonesia, Israel, Iran, and Pakistan actually scoring 10, clearly reflects high levels of societal intolerance of nontraditional, "new," or minority religions.

If one looked at MSRI alone, one would conclude that in terms of Secularity III "the majority of Muslim societies, or the milieux in which the vast majority of Indians live" (which Taylor contrasts with the North Atlantic world, 2007: 3) fare not so differently from Israel and Russia. Morocco and Egypt, by contrast, actually indicate higher levels of societal toleration for nontraditional, "new," or minority religions than the other Muslim-majority countries included – even those that were still in the midst of democratization processes at the time data for MSRI was collected (2006–2008): Turkey and Indonesia.

---

[8] The same caveat regarding the source of the data applies as mentioned in footnote 2 above.

The second measure which can be notionally related to Secularity III is a Pluralism-Index based on the Herfindahl quotient; this captures the probability that any two individuals in a given society belong to the same religious group and/or adhere to the same religious beliefs. It can also be taken to convey an idea of how likely it is that a particular belief is so widely shared as to be "taken for granted" (Berger 2012) in a given society. The Pluralism-Index is based on two different data sources.[9] Pluralism I, based on WVS data (recorded confessional breakdown per country), suggests that in Russia and Japan, followed by India, Israel, and China, it is least likely that a particular belief is shared or "taken for granted": citizens in those countries have a greater choice among a variety of faith positions than is the case in the other countries. In Turkey and Morocco, any two citizens are most likely to belong to one faith (with 99 percent likelihood). In Egypt, Pakistan, Indonesia, and Iran, the quotient is slightly, though not much, higher, reflecting the fact that the population is slightly more religiously diverse than in Turkey and Morocco, as recorded by the WVS. Pluralism II is based on the Religious Diversity Index (RDI) issued by the Pew Research Center. Here China, Japan, and Russia feature the lowest likelihood that a particular belief is taken for granted, followed by Israel and India. In Morocco the likelihood is greatest that two individuals adhere to the same religious beliefs, followed by Iran, Egypt, and Turkey. Although the two indices are based on different data sources and apply different criteria to the categorization of religious adherence,[10] they place the same countries at the top (China, Japan, and Russia) and at the bottom (Morocco, Egypt, Turkey, Iran) of the list of the eleven cases included in this volume (Table A.2). This suggests a broad trend of greater societal tolerance toward other faith positions (it is less likely that a particular faith is taken for granted) in China, Japan, and Russia. Comparing the MSRI and the two Herfindahl-based indices, both rank China and Japan at the more secular end of the spectrum but diverge

---

[9] We thank Detlef Pollack and Gergely Rosta for suggesting this alternative way of attempting to operationalize Secularity III and for providing the data for the eleven cases included in the volume.

[10] For example, the methodology for China diverges significantly, where WVS records 85.7 percent "no religion," 9.7 percent Buddhist, and 2.5 percent Protestant, while Pew Research offers an extra category of folk religions, which renders a breakdown of 52.2 percent unaffiliated, 21.9 percent folk religions, and 18.2 percent Buddhist. (For the methodology of the Pew Research regarding China, see www.pewforum.org/files/2011/12/ChristianityAppendixC.pdf.) While Pew thus most likely renders a more nuanced picture regarding China, the opposite is true for Iran and Pakistan, where WVS offers separate identifications for Sunnis and Shiites, while Pew offers only "Muslim/Islam."

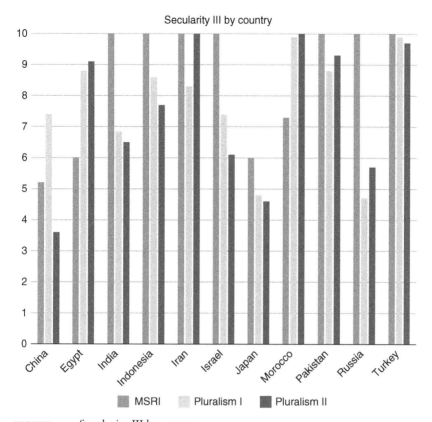

FIGURE A.3 Secularity III by country
Note: 1. For the purposes of comparative illustration we have reversed the scores for Pluralism I and II between 0 and 10.

over Russia, which the MSRI categorizes as rather intolerant of minority faiths (Figure A.3).

A problem with both data sources is that each considers for the most part only those faith categories that are legally recognized within a given jurisdiction. A more accurate index approaching Secularity III would need to take those faith options into account which citizens would like to profess but cannot due to legal restrictions (Jews and agnostics in Egypt, Shiites and agnostics in Indonesia, Alevis in Turkey, Ahmadis in Pakistan, Bahais and agnostics in Iran, to name a few examples). Otherwise, these indices, too, risk reproducing the chimera of relatively "free" and open religious markets, which in the face of looming political or societal sanction hardly exist in any of the included cases except for Japan.

References

Berger, Peter L. 2012. "Further Thoughts on Religion and Modernity." *Society*, July, 49(4): 313–316.

Billioud, Sébastien and Joël Thoraval. 2015. *The Sage and the People: The Confucian Revival in China*. Oxford: Oxford University Press.

Demerath III, N.J. 2007. "Secularization and Sacralization. Deconstructed and Reconstructed." In James A. Beckford and N. J. Demerath III (eds.) *The SAGE Handbook of the Sociology of Religion*. London: Sage, 57–80.

Eisgruber, Christopher L. and Lawrence G. Sager. 2007. *Religious Freedom and the Constitution*. Cambridge, MA: Harvard University Press.

Ferrari, Silvio and Rinaldo Cristofori (eds.). 2013. *Law and Religion, An Overview*, vol. 1. Farnham: Ashgate.

Fox, Jonathan. 2007. "Do Democracies Have Separation of Religion and State?" *Canadian Journal of Political Science*, 40(01): 1–25.

2008. *A World Survey of Religion and the State* (Cambridge Studies in Social Theory, Religion and Politics). New York: Cambridge University Press.

2012. "Separation of Religion and State in Stable Christian Democracies: Fact or Myth?" *Journal of Law, Religion and State*, 1(1): 60–94.

Global Restrictions on Religion Dataset. Pew Research Center. www.pewforum.org/datasets/global-restrictions-on-religion-2007-2014/

Goossaert, Vincent and David A. Palmer. 2011. *The Religious Question in Modern China*, Chicago: University of Chicago Press.

Grim, Brian J. and Roger Finke. 2006. "International Religion Indexes: Government Regulation, Government Favoritism, and Social Regulation of Religion," Interdisciplinary Journal of Research on Religion 2(1): 1–40.

Künkler, Mirjam and John Madeley. 2015. "A Secular Age beyond the West: Forms of Differentiation in and around the Religious Field." In *Soft Power*, 1(2): 41–62.

Madeley, John T.S. 2009a. "Unequally Yoked: the Antinomies of Church-State Separation in Europe and the USA," *European Political Science*, August 2009.

2009b. "Religion and the State." In J. Haynes (ed.) *Routledge Handbook on Religion and Politics*. London: Routledge.

Madsen, Richard. 2011. "Secularism, Religious Change, and Social Conflict in Asia." In Craig Calhoun, Mark Juergensmeyer, and Jonathan VanAntwerpen (eds.). *Rethinking Secularism*. Oxford: Oxford University Press, 248–269.

Möllers, Christoph. 2014. "Grenzen der Ausdifferenzierung Zur Verfassungstheorie der Religion in der Demokratie." In *Zeitschrift für evangelisches Kirchenrecht*, 59: 115–140.

Norris, Pippa and Ronald Inglehart. 2004. *Sacred and Secular: Religion and Politics Worldwide*. Cambridge: Cambridge University Press.

Religion Monitor, Bertelsmann Foundation. www.bertelsmann-stiftung.de/en/our-projects/religion-monitor/

Taylor, Charles. 2007. *A Secular Age*. Cambridge, MA: Harvard Belknap Press.

Traunmüller, Richard. 2012. Zur Messung von Staat-Kirche-Beziehungen: Eine vergleichende Analyse neuerer Indizes. *Zeitschrift für Vergleichende Politikwissenschaft*, 6: 207–231.

Van der Vyver, Johan David, and John F. Witte (eds.). 1996. *Religious Human Rights in Global Perspective: Legal Perspectives*. New Jersey: John Wiley & Sons.

Woodberry, Robert D. 1998. "When Surveys Lie and People Tell the Truth: How Surveys Over-Sample Church Attenders." *American Sociological Review*, 63(1): 119–122.

Yang, Fenggang. 2016. "Exceptionalism or Chinamerica: Measuring Religious Change in the Globalizing World Today." *Journal for the Scientific Study of Religion*, 55(1): 7–22.

Index